Lecture Notes in Computer Science

**Lecture Notes in Artificial Intelligence**     **14381**

Founding Editor

Jörg Siekmann

The series Lecture Notes in Artificial Intelligence (LNAI) was established in 1988 as a topical subseries of LNCS devoted to artificial intelligence.

The series publishes state-of-the-art research results at a high level. As with the LNCS mother series, the mission of the series is to serve the international R & D community by providing an invaluable service, mainly focused on the publication of conference and workshop proceedings and postproceedings.

Max Bramer · Frederic Stahl
Editors

# Artificial Intelligence XL

43rd SGAI International Conference
on Artificial Intelligence, AI 2023
Cambridge, UK, December 12–14, 2023
Proceedings

 Springer

*Editors*
Max Bramer
University of Portsmouth
Portsmouth, UK

Frederic Stahl
DFKI Niedersachsen Germany
Oldenburg, Germany

ISSN 0302-9743            ISSN 1611-3349 (electronic)
Lecture Notes in Artificial Intelligence
ISBN 978-3-031-47993-9       ISBN 978-3-031-47994-6 (eBook)
https://doi.org/10.1007/978-3-031-47994-6

LNCS Sublibrary: SL7 – Artificial Intelligence

This Springer imprint is published by the registered company Springer Nature Switzerland AG
The registered company address is: Gewerbestrasse 11, 6330 Cham, Switzerland

Paper in this product is recyclable.

# Preface

This volume, entitled Artificial Intelligence XL, comprises the refereed papers presented at the forty-third SGAI International Conference on Innovative Techniques and Applications of Artificial Intelligence, held in December 2023. The conference was organised by SGAI, the British Computer Society specialist group on Artificial Intelligence. This year 67 papers were submitted and all were single-blind peer reviewed by either 2 or 3 reviewers plus the expert members of the Executive Program Committee for each stream of the conference.

This year's Donald Michie Memorial Award for the best refereed technical paper was won by a paper entitled 'On Explanations and Hybrid Artificial Intelligence' by Lars Nolle (Jade University of Applied Sciences, Germany and German Research Center for Artificial Intelligence, Oldenburg, Germany) and Frederic Stahl and Tarek El-Mihoub (German Research Center for Artificial Intelligence, Oldenburg, Germany).

This year's Rob Milne Memorial Award for the best refereed application paper was won by a paper entitled 'Explaining a Staff Rostering Problem by Mining Trajectory Variance Structures' by Martin Fyvie, John McCall, Lee A. Christie and Alexandru-Ciprian Zavoianu (Robert Gordon University, Scotland), Alexander Brownlee (University of Stirling, Scotland) and Russell Ainslie (The BT Group, Adastral Park, Ipswich, England).

The other technical stream full papers included are divided into sections on Speech and Natural Language Analysis, Image Analysis, Neural Nets, and Case-Based Reasoning. The other application stream full papers are divided into sections on Machine Learning Applications, Machine Vision Applications, Knowledge Discovery and Data Mining Applications, and Other AI Applications. The volume also includes the text of short papers presented as posters at the conference.

On behalf of the conference Organising Committee, we would like to thank all those who contributed to the organisation of this year's programme, in particular the Program Committee members, the Executive Program Committees and our administrators Mandy Bauer and Bryony Bramer.

September 2023

Max Bramer
Frederic Stahl

# Organisation

## Conference Committee

### Conference Chair

Max Bramer                          University of Portsmouth, UK

### Technical Program Chair

Max Bramer                          University of Portsmouth, UK

### Application Program Chair

Frederic Stahl                      DFKI: German Research Center for Artificial
                                    Intelligence, Germany

### Workshop Organiser

Adrian Hopgood                      University of Portsmouth, UK

### Treasurer

Rosemary Gilligan                   SGAI, UK

### Poster Session Organisers

Juan Augusto                        Middlesex University, UK
Richard Ellis                       RKE Consulting, UK

### AI Open Mic and Panel Session Organiser

Andrew Lea                          PersuasionXP, UK

### FAIRS Organiser

Giovanna Martinez                   University of Nottingham, UK

**Conference Administrator**

Mandy Bauer                        BCS, UK

**Paper Administrator**

Bryony Bramer                      SGAI, UK

## Technical Executive Program Committee

Max Bramer (Chair)                 University of Portsmouth, UK
Frans Coenen                       University of Liverpool, UK
Adrian Hopgood                     University of Portsmouth, UK
John Kingston                      Nottingham Trent University, UK

## Application Executive Program Committee

Frederic Stahl (Chair)             DFKI: German Research Center for Artificial
                                     Intelligence, Germany
Richard Ellis                      RKE Consulting, UK
Rosemary Gilligan                  SGAI, UK
Jixin Ma                           University of Greenwich, UK
Lars Nolle                         Jade University of Applied Sciences, Germany
Richard Wheeler                    University of Edinburgh, UK

## Technical Program Committee

Per-Arne Andersen                  University of Agder, Norway
Juan Augusto                       Middlesex University London, UK
Raed Sabri Hameed Batbooti         Southern Technical University/Basra Engineering
                                     Technical College, Iraq
Lluis Belanche                     Universitat Politècnica de Catalunya, Spain
Soufiane Boulehouache              University of 20 Août 1955-Skikda, Algeria
Max Bramer                         University of Portsmouth, UK
Krysia Broda                       Imperial College London, UK
Ken Brown                          University College Cork, Ireland
Marcos Bueno                       Donders Institute for Brain, Cognition and
                                     Behaviour, Radboud University,
                                     The Netherlands

| | |
|---|---|
| Nikolay Burlutskiy | AstraZeneca, UK |
| Darren Chitty | Aston University, UK |
| Frans Coenen | University of Liverpool, UK |
| Bertrand Cuissart | Université de Caen, France |
| Nicolas Durand | Aix-Marseille University, France |
| Frank Eichinger | DATEV eG, Germany |
| Martin Fyvie | Robert Gordon University, UK |
| Hossein Ghodrati Noushahr | University of Leicester, UK |
| Adrian Hopgood | University of Portsmouth, UK |
| Chris Huyck | Middlesex University London, UK |
| Stelios Kapetanakis | Distributed Analytics, UK |
| John Kingston | Nottingham Trent University, UK |
| Ivan Koychev | University of Sofia, Bulgaria |
| Nicole Lee | University of Hong Kong, China |
| Anne Liret | British Telecom, France |
| Fernando Lopes | LNEG-National Research Institute, Portugal |
| Jixin Ma | University of Greenwich, UK |
| Stewart Massie | Robert Gordon University, UK |
| Ken McGarry | University of Sunderland, UK |
| Silja Meyer-Nieberg | Universität der Bundeswehr München, Germany |
| Roberto Micalizio | Università di Torino, Italy |
| Daniel Neagu | University of Bradford, UK |
| Lars Nolle | Jade University of Applied Sciences, Germany |
| Joanna Isabelle Olszewska | University of the West of Scotland, UK |
| Daniel O'Leary | University of Southern California, USA |
| Filipo S. Perotto | ONERA, France |
| Fernando Saenz-Perez | Universidad Complutense de Madrid, Spain |
| Miguel A. Salido | Universitat Politècnica de València, Spain |
| Sid Shakya | EBTIC, Khalifa University, UAE |
| Simon Thompson | GFT Technology, GFT |
| M. R. C. van Dongen | University College Cork, Ireland |

## Application Program Committee

| | |
|---|---|
| Nadia Abouayoub | SGAI, UK |
| Hatem Ahriz | Robert Gordon University, UK |
| Manal Almutairi | University of Reading, UK |
| Saif Alzubi | University of Exeter, UK |
| Ines Arana | Robert Gordon University, UK |
| Mercedes Arguello Casteleiro | University of Southampton, UK |
| Juan Carlos Augusto | Middlesex University London, UK |

| | |
|---|---|
| Lakshmi Babu Saheer | Anglia Ruskin University, UK |
| Ken Brown | University College Cork, Ireland |
| Nikolay Burlutskiy | ContextVision AB, Sweden |
| Xiaochun Cheng | Swansea University, UK |
| Sarah Jane Delany | Technological University Dublin, Ireland |
| Tarek El-Mihoub | German Research Center for Artificial Intelligence GmbH (DFKI), Germany |
| Richard Ellis | RKE Consulting, UK |
| Andrew Fish | University of Brighton, UK |
| Rosemary Gilligan | University of Hertfordshire, UK |
| Holmer Hemsen | German Research Center for Artificial Intelligence GmbH (DFKI), Germany |
| Carl James-Reynolds | Middlesex University London, UK |
| Colin Johnson | University of Nottingham, UK |
| Mathias Kern | BT, UK |
| Andre Klüner | German Research Center for Artificial Intelligence GmbH (DFKI), Germany |
| Daniel Lukats | German Research Center for Artificial Intelligence GmbH (DFKI), Germany |
| Christoph Manß | German Research Center for Artificial Intelligence GmbH (DFKI), Germany |
| Hung Ngo | Technological University Dublin, Ireland |
| Lars Nolle | Jade University of Applied Sciences, Germany |
| Navya Prakash | German Research Center for Artificial Intelligence GmbH (DFKI), Germany |
| Jing Qi | University of Liverpool, UK |
| Juan Antonio Recio Garcia | Complutense University of Madrid, Spain |
| Sam Richardson | GFT Financial Ltd., UK |
| Georgios Samakovitis | University of Greenwich, UK |
| Janina Schneider | German Research Center for Artificial Intelligence GmbH (DFKI), Germany |
| Frederic Stahl | German Research Center for Artificial Intelligence GmbH (DFKI), Germany |
| Daphne Theodorakopoulos | German Research Center for Artificial Intelligence GmbH (DFKI), Germany |
| Christoph Tholen | German Research Center for Artificial Intelligence GmbH (DFKI), Germany |
| Richard Wheeler | European Sustainable Energy Innovation Alliance, TU Graz, Austria |
| Mattis Wolf | German Research Center for Artificial Intelligence GmbH (DFKI), Germany |

# Contents

## Neural Nets

## Case Based Reasoning

## Short Technical Papers

**Application Papers**

**Machine Learning Applications**

## Machine Vision Applications

## Knowledge Discovery and Data Mining Applications

# Other AI Applications

# Short Application Papers

# Technical Papers

# On Explanations for Hybrid Artificial Intelligence

Lars Nolle[1,2(✉)], Frederic Stahl[2], and Tarek El-Mihoub[2]

[1] Jade University of Applied Sciences, Wilhelmshaven, Germany
lars.nolle@jade-hs.de
[2] German Research Center for Artificial Intelligence, Oldenburg, Germany
{frederic_theodor.stahl,tarek.elmihoub}@dfki.de

**Abstract.** The recent developments of machine learning (ML) approaches within artificial intelligence (AI) systems often require explainability of ML models. In order to establish trust in these systems, for example in safety critical applications, a number of different explainable artificial intelligence (XAI) methods have been proposed, either post-hoc or intrinsic models. These can help to understand why a ML model has made a particular decision. The authors of this paper point out that the abbreviation XAI is commonly used in the literature referring to explainable ML models, although the term AI encompasses many more topics than ML. To improve efficiency and effectiveness of AI, two or more AI subsystems are often combined to solve a common problem. In this case, an overall explanation has to be derived from the subsystems' explanations. In this paper we define the term hybrid AI. This is followed by reviewing the current state of XAI before proposing the use of blackboard systems (BBS) to not only share results but also to integrate and to exchange explanations of different XAI models as well, in order to derive an overall explanation for hybrid AI systems.

**Keywords:** Hybrid Artificial Intelligence · Trust · Blackboard Systems

## 1 Introduction

In recent years, artificial intelligence (AI) has found its way from the research laboratories into many modern-day applications, ranging from personal assistants [1] to autonomous vehicles [2]. To keep up with the technological and social-economic challenges and developments of AI, the European Commission has developed an AI strategy, aiming at boosting excellence in AI and developing trustworthy AI in Europe [3]. State-of-the-art machine learning (ML) models [4], like deep neural networks (DNNs) [5], are often based on extremely complex non-linear functions, which makes it difficult to understand the inner workings of the trained models for humans. Consequently, the outputs of ML models, such as DNNs, are non-interpretable and non-transparent, which limits the trust in the overall system. Especially safety-critical systems [6] and safety critical applications [7, 8] require transparency to be considered reliable and trustworthy. Furthermore, a lack of transparency can have severe consequences in high-stakes domains,

M. Bramer and F. Stahl (Eds.): SGAI 2023, LNAI 14381, pp. 3–15, 2023.
https://doi.org/10.1007/978-3-031-47994-6_1

like medical diagnosis or financial decision-making [9]. This, for example, prompted the European Union Aviation Safety Agency (EASA) to lay out its AI Roadmap in 2020, to ensure that future ML-based systems can be safely integrated into the aviation domain [10].

Despite lack of interpretability, multiple AI methodologies are often combined to form hybrid AI systems for solving a mutual problem more effectively and efficiently. This aims to bring together different and currently separated AI techniques, including low-level perception and high-level reasoning [11]. Many real-world scientific and industrial applications require the results and recommendations derived by AI systems to be trustworthy and explainable. In hybrid AI systems, different types of AI methods collaborate on a mutual problem to arrive at decisions or recommendations for actions.

Blackboard systems (BBS) can be used to integrate and make different types of AI interact and use each other's results [12]. This paper proposes the use of BBS as a possible architecture for hybrid AI Systems where different AI models can exchange/access each other's explanations to derive a global solution.

Section 2 defines and explains the term hybrid AI for the context of this paper and Sect. 3 distinguishes different approaches to explainable and interpretable AI systems. Section 4 poses the research question how to combine explanations produced by different XAI methods in various stages of the hybrid AI system. Section 5 presents the proposed architecture before Sect. 6 summarises the presented work and discusses future work.

## 2  Hybrid Artificial Intelligence

For increased effectiveness and efficiency, two or more AI methods are often combined to solve a common problem. For example, Bielecki and Wojcik [13] recently used such a hybrid AI system based on ART neural networks and Gaussian mixture models for the monitoring of wind turbines. Tachmazidis et al. [14] used a hybrid approach, consisting of a ML model and a knowledge model, which captures the expertise of medical experts through knowledge engineering. The authors in [15] combined artificial neural networks, particle swarm optimisation and K-harmonic means clustering for colour design. Zheng et al. [16] proposed a hybrid AI model for COVID-19 prediction.

In this context, we define hybrid AI as a combination of two or more AI subsystems. There are, in principle, three ways of combining two AIs, in sequence, in parallel, or embedded (Fig. 1). When arranged in sequence, the output of the first AI is used as an input into the second AI, which produces the overall solution.

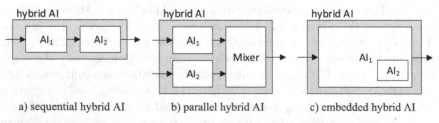

a) sequential hybrid AI        b) parallel hybrid AI        c) embedded hybrid AI

**Fig. 1.**  Three different ways of combining two AI subsystems, $AI_1$ and $AI_2$.

When the AIs are arranged in parallel, they work independently of each other, either on the same data or on different data, and their output needs to be combined in a subsequent mixer stage. For example, a voting system can be used in this stage to produce the final output. Finally, an AI can be embedded into another AI in order to enhance the problem-solving potential of this AI, which would produce the overall output, respectively the solution to the problem [17]. For more than two AI subsystems, any combination of the above are possible.

There is also a need for trust in hybrid AI systems, hence researchers have recently begun to work on making hybrid AI systems explainable. For example, Li, et al. [6], proposed a vision-based object detection and recognition framework for autonomous driving. Here they used an optimized YOLOv4 model for object detection together with CNN models for recognition tasks. For the generation of explanations for the classification results, they used saliency maps-based algorithms. Another example can be found in [18]. Here, a hybrid conceptual/ML model for streamflow predictions was developed, and two model-agnostic techniques were subsequently applied. However, in both examples, the models have been made explainable only partially. Developing a holistic model-agnostic approach for generic hybrid AI models is still an open research question [19].

## 3 Explainable Artificial Intelligence

In the XAI literature, the terms explainability and interpretability are often used interchangeably [20, 21], although explainability has a wider meaning than interpretability [22]. Interpretability is often associated to answering the question of *"why?"*, related to a specific phenomenon and based on a specific opinion. Meanwhile, explainability is the ability to provide a set of related inference rules to answer the questions of *"how?"* and *"why?"* [22]. An explanation relies on facts, which can be described by words or formulas. Explanations can reveal the facts and the rules that are governing the behaviour of a phenomenon. According to [21], an explanation in AI has a different meaning from its traditional meaning and does not require interpretability. They also view causal explanations as the strictest form of scientific explanation. Kim et al. [21] also provided practical guidance for developing XAIs by defining fundamental requirements for such a system. An explanation, according to [23], has a flexible philosophical concept of "satisfying the subjective curiosity for causal information". Explainability in the context of XAI is a concept that enables understanding the overall strengths and weaknesses of AI models, predicting their behaviours and taking corrective actions [24]. However, XAI often shares a common aim of making AI understandable for people. This paper adopts the pragmatic definition of XAI stated in [25], where XAI is considered as broadly encompassing all techniques that service making AI understandable, such as direct interpretability, generating an explanation or justification, providing transparency information, etc.

The main aims of XAI are to establish trust with the stakeholders and to confirm compliance with ethics and regulations. XAI can help in deep understanding of AI models' behaviours and the problems they solve [26]. It is our position that, to achieve these aims, the framework for developing AI models should be adapted so that an AI model produces explanations of the solution in addition to the solution itself. Explaining the solutions introduces changes in the AI model's representation and also adds an explanation interface to the XAI model [24]. Interpretable models and deep explanation approaches can be followed to incorporate explainability within AI models. Interpretable models, also called glass-box or intrinsic models, seek to combine the clarity of the internal behaviour of an AI model with high quality performance. DARPA claims that there is a trade-off between model accuracy and explainability [27], which is a widely accepted view. However, Rudin et al. [20] are of the opinion that there is no such trade-off. Instead, it is possible to have an explainable model with high accuracy. Explainable Boosting Machines (EBMs) [28], for example, support this claim. This technique is a generalised and more efficient version of the Generalised Additive Model (GAM) [29] that produces high-quality explainable models. TabNet [30] combines sequential attention with decision tree-based learning for interpretable and more efficient learning. Deep explanation approaches aim to benefit from the success of deep learning in solving complex problems to resolve the explanation problem. Deep explanations hybridise different deep learning models to produce richer representations of the features utilised during learning to enable extraction of underlying semantic information [31]. For example, a special prototype layer was added to a CNN to utilise case-based reasoning in explaining its predictions [32]. Lei et al. [33] have used extractive reasoning to incorporate interpretation in the framework of a neural network. Generating accurate and suitable explanations of the model behaviour to a user is the main challenge of deep explanation models [24].

However, due to the urgent need for building trust and compliance with regulations and ethics in already existing AI models, induction or post-hoc approaches have been proposed. Figure 2 shows how, in principle, a trained ML (AI) model is post-hoc analysed by a model-agnostic method, which manipulates the input data and measures the changes in output in order to generate an explanation. Commonly, three different types of post-hoc explanations are used: alternative advice, prediction confidence scores, and prediction rationale [34].

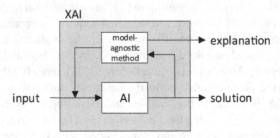

**Fig. 2.** Model-agnostic (post-hoc) explanation method for trained ML model AI.

Jiang et al. [34] have also shown that epistemic uncertainty is most important to users of post-hoc explanations. Meanwhile, the challenges associated with explaining black-box models, i.e. observable models with unknown transfer functions, have motivated researchers to develop different post-hoc interpretation and explanation facilities. Furthermore, the process of incorporating explanations within the framework of AI models sometimes can be more difficult than building a post-hoc tool [21]. Without providing explanations of its explanations, a post-hoc tool can be viewed as a black-box that explains another black-box [20]. It is also possible to generate two conflicting explanations for the same AI model's behaviour using two different post-hoc tools [32].

Various post-hoc tools have been developed. Some of these tools aim to interpret the general behaviour of an AI model, referred to as global post-hoc tools; others focus on a specific behaviour of the model with a specific input or set of inputs, referred to as local post-hoc tools. The surrogate model approach has been used to develop a new simple model that mimics the behaviour of a black-box AI at a global or local level. The new model should be interpretable or explainable. TREPAN [35] and Rule Extraction From Neural network Ensemble (REFNE) [36] are examples of global post-hoc tools that follow this approach. Knowledge distillation [37] can be viewed as a unified method for model extraction. Local Interpretable Model-agnostic Explanations (LIME) [38] builds a linear classifier to mimic the local behaviour of the black-box AI. Another post-hoc approach is to estimate the features' impact on the behaviour of the black-box model. Estimation of the features' importance can be done at a global or a local level. Such estimation can help in ensuring that worthy features are controlling the behaviour of the model. A feature's importance can be presented as a score according to its impact on the model prediction; for example, by generating saliency maps [39] and SHapley Additive exPlanations (SHAP) [40]. The features' importance can be presented as a relation between each feature and the model's global prediction, such as Partial Dependence Profiles (PDP) [41] and Accumulated Local Effects (ALE) [42]. Individual Conditional Expectations (ICE) are used to present such kind of relation at local level [43]. Counterfactual examples [44] can also be used to explain the local behaviour of a black-box model. These examples are used to show how an input can be modified to change the model's prediction. Diverse Counterfactual Explanations (DiCE) [45] uses a set of diverse counterfactual examples to inspect the behaviour of AI models. A generative counterfactual introspection has been used to produce inherently interpretable counterfactual visual explanations in the form of prototypes and criticisms [46]. In addition to model-agnostic post-hoc explanations, there are explanations that make use of some knowledge of a black-box AI model to provide explanations. For example, Grad-CAM [47], uses the inputs and the gradients of a deep neural network to determine the salient pixels to the model prediction. Some of these methods can be applied to AI models with specific properties. For example, Integrated Gradient (IG) [48] can be applied to any differentiable model for different types of input such as images, text, or structured data.

Landscape analysis tools [49] are commonly used to explain the behaviour of population-based metaheuristics, such as evolutionary algorithms. These tools can also help in understanding complex optimisation problems. Furthermore, visualizing the trajectories followed by these algorithms can enhance researchers and developers' comprehension of the behaviours of different search algorithms [50]. Dimension reduction techniques are typically employed to simplify the visualisation of these trajectories [51]. A data-driven, graph-based model, Search Trajectory Network (STNs), has been utilised to illustrate the changes in the algorithm's behaviour throughout the search process [52].

## 4  Explainability for Hybrid Artificial Intelligence

The open research question, which is addressed in this work, is to ascertain how to combine explanations produced by different XAI methods in various stages of the hybrid AI system, so that it provides meaningful explanations to the end-user.

Our approach is, in the case of sequential XAI methods, each of the methods is producing an explanation, which is fed forward to the Explanation Mixer. This produces the overall explanation for the solution for a given input (Fig. 3).

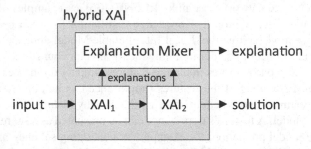

**Fig. 3.** Hybrid XAI consisting of two sequential XAIs and the Explanation Mixer.

In the case of parallel XAI subsystems, each of the methods is producing an explanation, which is forwarded to the Explanation Mixer (Fig. 4). The part solutions generated by each AI must be combined in a subsequent Solution Mixer stage, which produces the overall solution. Likewise, the Explanation Mixer generates the overall explanation for the overall solution.

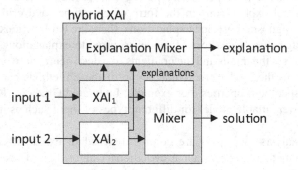

**Fig. 4.** Hybrid XAI consisting of two parallel XAI subsystems, an Explanation Mixer, and a Solution Mixer.

In the case of embedded XAI subsystems, the embedded XAI may be triggered multiple times during the execution of the master AI ($XAI_1$). The embedded AI ($XAI_2$) provides explanations and solutions for specific tasks to the hybrid XAI (Fig. 5). At this stage, it is not clear yet where these explanations can be incorporated in the master AI's explanation. This remains an open research question.

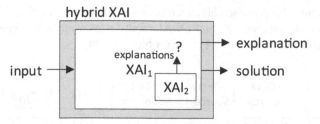

**Fig. 5.** Hybrid XAI consisting of two XAIs one embedded in a master XAI ($XAI_1$).

In the next section, an architecture is proposed for realizing these three types of hybrid AI systems.

## 5   Proposed Architecture

In order to allow for flexible and adaptive systems, the use of the BBS model is envisioned. BBSs facilitate the principles of a group of human experts, solving a common problem [53]. The experts group together around a blackboard. Each of the experts observes the blackboard constantly. If granted access by a moderator, they may add information to or remove information from the blackboard as a reaction to contents changes of the blackboard. By doing so, they contribute towards the global solution, which will evolve eventually on the blackboard. This approach has been proven very successful and is often facilitated in group decision-making processes.

In the BBS model, the human experts are replaced with so-called knowledge sources, i.e. data/information sources and algorithms, the latter often from the field of AI. The analogue to the blackboard is a common database system, and the analogue to the moderator is a scheduler. In such a BBS, the knowledge of the problem domain is distributed over several specialised knowledge sources, also known as agents [54]. The agents are autonomous and communicate with each other only by reading information from and writing information to the common database. Each AI method used in a particular application is implemented as an autonomous knowledge source.

BBSs were successfully employed to a wide range of different problems, ranging from improving classification accuracy in ML [55] or the control of a complex autonomous spacecraft [56], to the automated generation of poetry [57]. He et al. [58] used a BBS for controlling an Earth observation satellite. Stewart et al. [59] used an agent-based BBS for reactor design. Xu and Smith [60] achieved massive data sharing in distributed and heterogeneous environments using a BBS to reduce data sharing delay. However, there are still open research questions related to BBSs. For example, how to allow access to the common data repository [12] or how to maintain the blackboard over a long period of time [61]. There are different types of blackboard architectures available. A distinction can be made between the original monolithic architecture [62], distributed BBSs [12, 63] and fractal BBSs [64]. It is important to choose the appropriate architecture for a problem at hand. However, the BBS model is very flexible, i.e., it can be used to implement both, the sequential hybrid system, and the parallel hybrid system [65]. It is also possible, to change the configuration dynamically during runtime.

Figure 6 shows the proposed architecture based on the BBS design. It consists of application specific data sources and (X)AI modules as well as the generic BBS to produce an overall output (solution) to the problem (input).

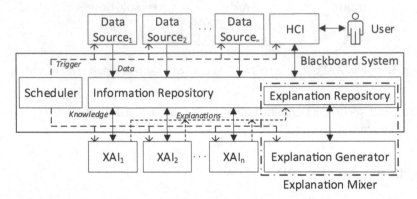

**Fig. 6.** Proposed architecture based on the Blackboard System design.

Here, $m$ data sources receive input data from the environment and put it on the information repository, the shared data base of the Blackboard System. A scheduler is used to synchronise access to the information repository via trigger signals. At the same time, $n$ XAI subsystems observe the data on the information repository in order to generate new knowledge, which is subsequently placed on the information repository. In addition, the XAI subsystems are writing their individual explanations on to the explanation repository, a specialized partition of the blackboard. These explanations are used by the application specific explanation generator to derive the overall explanation for the solutions. The solutions to the input data together with the overall explanations can be accessed via a human computer interface (HCI).

The data sources might supply multimodal data, e.g. images, text and sensor readings. This data might be unstructured, inconsistent, unreliable, and biased. Therefore, different AI algorithms must process the data to enable the detection of an event of interest and for deriving a recommendation for action. For example, there might be an AI algorithm for the identification of event related artefacts in pictures, like harmful algae bloom, or contaminants in bio-waste [66]. Another algorithm has to cluster the data, so that a record is associated with an individual event. Finally, a dedicated AI algorithm must make an expert decision about the positive identification of an event of interest.

If all these different AI algorithms also produce explanations, these explanations must be fused into an overall explanation, suitable for a human user. In order to be able to exchange knowledge in hybrid systems, domain-specific ontologies are often required. In computer science, an ontology is an explicit, formal specification of a shared conceptualisation [67]. An explicit formal representation facilitates sharing of knowledge and human-machine interaction. Utilising the concepts of ontology enables reusing and analysing domain knowledge. Formalising these concepts through logic languages ensures consistency of a domain knowledge, enabling extracting relations and reasoning. For example, a medical-ontology has been used in Doctor XAI [68] to build a model-agnostic explanation to deal with multi-labelled, sequential, ontology-linked data. Doctor XAI shows that utilising medical knowledge can produce a better approximation of the local behaviour of a black-box model. In [69] an explanation ontology is proposed to support user-centred AI system design. When applications span over different domains, their associated ontologies have to be aligned.

## 6 Summary and Future Work

In this work, the term hybrid AI was defined and examples of current applications of such hybrid systems were introduced. A need for trust in hybrid AI systems was identified. Subsequently, a survey of current XAI methods was provided. We presented our proposed architecture for hybrid XAI, which is based on the blackboard architecture. Here, a specialised partition of the information repository is used to collect the individual explanations from the knowledge sources, i.e. the XAI subsystems. In order to derive an overall explanation, an application specific explanation generator was proposed. An application specific ontology has to be followed to facilitate exchanging and sharing knowledge and explanations.

The proposed architecture is currently under development and will be used in subsequent research. For this, a number of research questions are still open: (i) How can multimodal explanations be formulated using an application specific ontology? (ii) How to combine such explanations in order to generate a meaningful explanation to the user? (iii) How to combine explanations in embedded hybrid AI systems? To find answers to these questions, the DFKI is currently conducting a 1.7M€ research project, which builds upon this proposed architecture, and aims at the automated scheduling of weed harvesting campaigns on lakes.

**Acknowledgements.** Partly funded by the Federal Ministry of Education and Research, Germany, grant number 01IW23003, and the Ministry for Science and Culture of Lower Saxony, grant number ZN3683.

## References

1. Maedche, A., et al.: AI-based digital assistants: opportunities, threats, and research perspectives. Bus. Inf. Syst. Eng. **61**, 535–544 (2019). https://doi.org/10.1007/s12599-019-006 00-8
2. Gao, X., Bian, X.: Autonomous driving of vehicles based on artificial intelligence. J. Intell. Fuzzy Syst. **41**, 1–10 (2021). https://doi.org/10.3233/JIFS-189982
3. EC. Artificial Intelligence for Europe, European Commission, COM (2018) 237. European Commission (2018)
4. Jordan, M.I., Mitchell, T.M.: Machine learning: trends, perspectives, and prospects. Science **349**, 255–260 (2015). https://doi.org/10.1126/science.aaa8415
5. Schmidhuber, J.: Deep learning in neural networks: an overview. Neural Net. **61**, 85–117 (2014). https://doi.org/10.1016/j.neunet.2014.09.003
6. Li, Y., et al.: A deep learning-based hybrid framework for object detection and recognition in autonomous driving. IEEE Access **8**, 194228–194239 (2020). https://doi.org/10.1109/ACC ESS.2020.3033289

7. Hernandez, C.S., Ayo, S., Panagiotakopoulos, D.: An explainable artificial intelligence (xAI) framework for improving trust in automated ATM tools. In: 2021 IEEE/AIAA 40th Digital Avionics Systems Conference (DASC), pp. 1–10 (2021). https://doi.org/10.1109/DASC52 595.2021.9594341

8. Wang, Y., Chung, S.: Artificial intelligence in safety-critical systems: a systematic review. Ind. Manag. Data Syst. **122**(2), 442–470 (2021). https://doi.org/10.1108/IMDS-07-2021-0419

9. Zhou, J., Gandomi, A.H., Chen, F., Holzinger, A.: Evaluating the quality of machine learning explanations: a survey on methods and metrics. Electronics **10**, 593 (2021). https://doi.org/10.3390/electronics10050593

10. EASA. Artificial intelligence roadmap: a human-centric approach to AI aviation. European Union Aviation Safety Agency (2020)

11. Kersting, K.: Rethinking computer science through AI. KI - Künstliche Intelligenz **34**(4), 435–437 (2020). https://doi.org/10.1007/s13218-020-00692-5

12. Nolle, L., Wong, K.C.P., Hopgood, A.A.: DARBS: a distributed blackboard system. In: Bramer, M., Coenen, F., Preece, A. (eds.) Research and Development in Intelligent Systems XVIII, pp. 161–170. Springer, London (2002). https://doi.org/10.1007/978-1-4471-0119-2_13

13. Bielecki, A., Wójcik, M.: Hybrid AI system based on ART neural network and Mixture of Gaussians modules with application to intelligent monitoring of the wind turbine. Appl. Soft Comput. **108**, 107400 (2021). https://doi.org/10.1016/j.asoc.2021.107400

14. Tachmazidis, I., Chen, T., Adamou, M., Antoniou, G.: A hybrid AI approach for supporting clinical diagnosis of attention deficit hyperactivity disorder (ADHD) in adults. Health Inf. Sci. Syst. **9**, 1 (2021). https://doi.org/10.1007/s13755-020-00123-7

15. Li, M., et al.: A decision support system using hybrid AI based on multi-image quality model and its application in color design. Future Gener. Comput. Syst. **113**, 70–77 (2020). https://doi.org/10.1016/j.future.2020.06.034

16. Zheng, N., et al.: Predicting COVID-19 in China using hybrid AI model. IEEE Trans. Cybern. **50**, 2891–2904 (2020). https://doi.org/10.1109/TCYB.2020.2990162

17. El-Mihoub, T., Hopgood, A.A., Nolle, L., Battersby, A.: Hybrid genetic algorithms – a review. Eng. Lett. **13**(2), 124–137 (2006). ISSN: 1816-093X

18. Althoff, D., Bazame, H.C., Nascimento, J.G.: Untangling hybrid hydrological models with explainable artificial intelligence. H2Open J. **4**, 13–28 (2021). https://doi.org/10.2166/h2oj.2021.066

19. Akata, Z., et al.: A research agenda for hybrid intelligence: augmenting human intellect with collaborative, adaptive, responsible, and explainable artificial intelligence. Computer **53**, 18–28 (2020). https://doi.org/10.1109/MC.2020.2996587

20. Rudin, C., Chen, C., Chen, Z., Huang, H., Semenova, L., Zhong, C.: Interpretable machine learning: fundamental principles and 10 grand challenges. arXiv (2021). https://doi.org/10.48550/ARXIV.2103.11251

21. Kim, M.-Y., et al.: A multi-component framework for the analysis and design of explainable artificial intelligence. Mach. Learn. Knowl. Extract. **3**, 900–921 (2021). https://doi.org/10.3390/make3040045

22. Buhrmester, V., Münch, D., Arens, M.: Analysis of explainers of black box deep neural networks for computer vision: a survey. Mach. Learn. Knowl. Extract. **3**, 966–989 (2021)

23. Li, X.-H., et al.: A survey of data-driven and knowledge-aware eXplainable AI. IEEE Trans. Knowl. Data Eng. **34**(1), 29–49 (2020)

24. Gunning, D., Vorm, E., Wang, J.Y., Turek, M.: DARPA's explainable AI (XAI) program: a retrospective. Appl. AI Lett. (2021)

25. Liao, Q.V., Varshney, K.R.: Human-centered explainable AI (XAI): from algorithms to user experiences, CoRR, Bd. abs/2110.10790 (2021)

26. El-Mihoub, T.A., Nolle, L., Stahl, F.: Explainable boosting machines for network intrusion detection with features reduction. In: Bramer, M., Stahl, F. (eds.) Artificial Intelligence XXXIX: 42nd SGAI International Conference on Artificial Intelligence, AI 2022, Cambridge, UK, December 13–15, 2022, Proceedings, pp. 280–294. Springer, Cham (2022). https://doi.org/10.1007/978-3-031-21441-7_20

27. Gunning, D., Aha, D.: DARPA's explainable artificial intelligence (XAI) program. AI Mag. **40**(2), 44–58 (2019)

28. Nori, H., Jenkins, S., Koch, P., Caruana, R.: InterpretML: a unified framework for machine learning interpretability. arXiv (2019)

29. Hastie, T., Tibshirani, R.: Generalized additive models: some applications. J. Am. Stat. Assoc. **82**(398), 371–386 (1987)

30. Arik, S.O., Pfister, T.: TabNet: attentive interpretable tabular learning. In: Proceedings of the AAAI Conference on Artificial Intelligence, vol. 35, pp. 6679–6687 (2021). https://ojs.aaai.org/index.php/AAAI/article/view/16826

31. Park, D.H., et al.: Multimodal explanations: justifying decisions and pointing to the evidence. In: 2018 IEEE/CVF Conference on Computer Vision and Pattern Recognition (2018)

32. Li, O., Liu, H., Chen, C., Rudin, C.: Deep learning for case-based reasoning through prototypes: a neural network that explains its predictions. In: The Thirty-Second AAAI Conference, pp. 3530–3537 (2018)

33. Lei, T., Barzilay, R., Jaakkola, T.: Rationalizing neural predictions. arXiv (2016). https://doi.org/10.48550/ARXIV.1606.04155

34. Jiang, J., Kahai, S., Yang, M.: Who needs explanation and when? Juggling explainable AI and user epistemic uncertainty. Int. J. Hum. Comput. Stud. **165**, 102839 (2022)

35. Craven, M.W., Shavlik, J.W.: Extracting tree-structured representations of trained networks. In: Proceedings of the 8th International Conference on Neural Information Processing Systems, Denver, Colorado, pp. 24–30 (1995)

36. Zhou, Z.-H., Jiang, Y., Chen, S.-F.: Extracting symbolic rules from trained neural network ensembles. AI Commun. **16**(1), 3–15 (2003)

37. Hinton, G., Vinyals, O., Dean, J.: Distilling the knowledge in a neural network. arXiv (2015). https://doi.org/10.48550/ARXIV.1503.02531

38. Ribeiro, M.T., Singh, S., Guestrin, C.: Why should i trust you?: Explaining the predictions of any classifier. In: The 22nd ACM SIGKDD International Conference on Knowledge Discovery and Data Mining, San Francisco, California, USA (2016)

39. Fong, R.C., Vedaldi, A.: Interpretable explanations of black boxes by meaningful perturbation. In: 2017 IEEE International Conference on Computer Vision (ICCV), pp. 3449–3457 (2017). https://doi.org/10.1109/ICCV.2017.371

40. Lundberg, S.M., Lee, S.-I.: A unified approach to interpreting model predictions. In: The 31st International Conference on Neural Information Processing Systems, Long Beach, California, USA, pp. 4768–4777 (2017)

41. Friedman, J.F.: Greedy function approximation: a gradient boosting machine. Ann. Stat. **29**, 1189–1232 (2001)

42. Apley, D.W., Zhu, J.: Visualizing the effects of predictor variables in black box supervised learning models. arXiv (2016). https://doi.org/10.48550/ARXIV.1612.08468

43. Goldstein, A., Kapelner, A., Bleich, J., Pitkin, E.: Peeking inside the black box: visualizing statistical learning with plots of individual conditional expectation. J. Comput. Graph. Stat. **24**(1), 44–65 (2015)

44. Karimi, A.-H., Barthe, G., Balle, B., Valera, I.: Model-agnostic counterfactual explanations for consequential decisions. In: Chiappa, S., Calandra, R. (ed.) Proceedings of the Twenty Third International Conference on Artificial Intelligence and Statistics, vol. 108, pp. 895–905. PMLR (2020). https://proceedings.mlr.press/v108/karimi20a.html

45. Mothilal, R.K., Sharma, A., Tan, C.: Explaining machine learning classifiers through diverse counterfactual explanations. In: FAT* 2020, Barcelona, Spain (2020)
46. Liu, S., Kailkhura, B., Loveland, D., Han, Y.: Generative counterfactual introspection for explainable deep learning. In: 2019 IEEE Global Conference on Signal and Information Processing (GlobalSIP) (2019)
47. Selvaraju, R.R., Cogswell, M., Das, A., Vedantam, R., Parikh, D., Batra, D.: Grad-CAM: visual explanations from deep networks via gradient-based localization. In: 2017 IEEE International Conference on Computer Vision (ICCV), pp. 618–626 (2017). https://doi.org/10.1109/ICCV.2017.74
48. Sundararajan, M., Taly, A., Yan, Q.: Axiomatic attribution for deep networks. In: Proceedings of the 34th International Conference on Machine Learning, Sydney, vol. 70, pp. 3319–3328. JMLR.org (2017)
49. Malan, K.M.: A survey of advances in landscape analysis for optimisation. Algorithms **14**(2), 40 (2021)
50. Michalak, K.: Low-dimensional euclidean embedding for visualization of search spaces in combinatorial optimization. In: Proceedings of the Genetic and Evolutionary Computation Conference Companion, New York, NY, USA (2019)
51. De Lorenzo, A., Medvet, E., Tušar, T., Bartoli, A.: An analysis of dimensionality reduction techniques for visualizing evolution. In: Proceedings of the Genetic and Evolutionary Computation Conference Companion, New York, NY, USA (2019)
52. Ochoa, G., Malan, K.M., Blum, C.: Search trajectory networks: a tool for analysing and visualising the behaviour of metaheuristics. Appl. Soft Comput. **109**, 107492 (2021)
53. Serafini, L., et al.: On some foundational aspects of human-centered artificial intelligence. arXiv preprint arXiv:2112.14480 (2021)
54. Weitz, K., Schiller, D., Schlagowski, R., Huber, T., André, E.: "Let me explain!": exploring the potential of virtual agents in explainable AI interaction design. J. Multimodal User Interfaces **15**(2), 87–98 (2021). https://doi.org/10.1007/s12193-020-00332-0
55. Kokorakis, V.M., Petridis, M., Kapetanakis, S.: A blackboard based hybrid multi-agent system for improving classification accuracy using reinforcement learning techniques. In: Bramer, M., Petridis, M. (eds.) SGAI 2017. LNCS (LNAI), vol. 10630, pp. 47–57. Springer, Cham (2017). https://doi.org/10.1007/978-3-319-71078-5_4
56. Golding, D., Chesnokov, A.M.: Features of informational control complex of autonomous spacecraft. In: IFAC Workshop Aerospace Guidance, Navigation and Flight Control Systems. International Federation of Automatic Control, Laxenburg (2011)
57. Misztal-Radecka, J., Indurkhya, B.: A blackboard system for generating poetry. Comput. Sci. **17**(2), 265–294 (2016)
58. He, L., Li, G., Xing, L., Chen, Y.: An autonomous multi-sensor satellite system based on multi-agent blackboard model. Maintenance Reliab. **19**(3), 447–458 (2017)
59. Stewart, R., Palmer, T.S., Bays, S.: Toward an agent-based blackboard system for reactor design optimization. Nucl. Technol. **208**(5), 822–842 (2021). https://doi.org/10.1080/00295450.2021.1960783
60. Xu, J.S., Smith, T.J.: Massive data storage and sharing algorithm in distributed heterogeneous environment. J. Intell. Fuzzy Syst. **35**(4), 4017–4026 (2018)
61. Straub, J.: Automating maintenance for a one-way transmitting blackboard system used for autonomous multi-tier control. Expert. Syst. **33**(6), 518–530 (2016)
62. Engelmore, R.S., Morgan, A.J.: Blackboard Systems. Addison-Wesley (1988)
63. McManus, J.W.: A concurrent distributed system for aircraft tactical decision generation. In: IEEE/AtAA/NASA 9th Digital Avionics Systems Conference, New York, USA, pp. 161–170 (1990)
64. Naaman, M., Zaks, A.: Fractal blackboard systems. In: Proceedings of the 8th Israeli Conference on Computer-Based Systems and Software Engineering, pp 23–29 (1997)

65. Stahl, F., Bramer, M.: Computationally efficient induction of classification rules with the PMCRI and J-PMCRI frameworks. Knowl.-Based Syst. **35**, 49–63 (2012)
66. Stahl, F., Ferdinand, O., Nolle, L., Pehlken, A., Zielinski, O.: AI enabled bio waste contamination-scanner. In: Bramer, M., Ellis, R. (eds.) Artificial Intelligence XXXVIII: 41st SGAI International Conference on Artificial Intelligence, AI 2021, Cambridge, UK, December 14–16, 2021, Proceedings, pp. 357–363. Springer, Cham (2021). https://doi.org/10.1007/978-3-030-91100-3_28
67. Gruber, T.R.: A translation approach to portable ontology specifications. Knowl. Acquis. **5**, 199–220 (1993)
68. Panigutti, C., Perotti, A., Pedreschi, D.: Doctor XAI: an ontology-based approach to black-box sequential data classification explanations, pp. 629–639. Association for Computing Machinery, New York (2020)
69. Chari, S., Seneviratne, O., Gruen, D.M., Foreman, M.A., Das, A.K., McGuinness, D.L.: Explanation ontology: a model of explanations for user-centered AI. In: Pan, J.Z., et al. (eds.) ISWC 2020. LNCS, vol. 12507, pp. 228–243. Springer, Cham (2020). https://doi.org/10.1007/978-3-030-62466-8_15

# Speech and Natural Language Analysis

# Intermediate Task Ensembling for Sarcasm Detection

Jarrad Jinks[✉][iD]

University of Leeds, Leeds, UK
od20jj@leeds.ac.uk

**Abstract.** Navigating nuanced linguistic features through machine learning plays an important role in academic, private, and public sectors as researchers and developers use computational methods to parse, process, and understand an ever-increasing volume of natural language text. While recent advances in natural language processing and large language models have improved access to state-of-the-art performance, partly through the evolution of pre-training and fine-tuning processes, some particularly difficult linguistic tasks, such as sarcasm detection, remain to be solved. Such tasks can be highly disruptive to computational systems that rely on natural language processing. In this paper, we approach sarcasm detection by leveraging the RoBERTa model, a two-step fine-tuning process called Intermediate Fine-Tuning, and ensembling theory. We establish baselines, create ensembles, explore ensemble predictions, and analyze both baseline and ensemble performance. This research shows that intermediate fine-tuning can create sufficiently performant and diverse inducers for ensembles, and that those ensembles may also outperform single-model baselines on sarcasm detection tasks.

**Keywords:** Sarcasm Detection · Fine-Tuning · Transfer Learning · STILTS · Classifier Combination · Ensemble Models · Intermediate-Task Fine-Tuning

## 1 Introduction and Background

The pursuit of state-of-the-art performance in language representation has driven development of increasingly robust, complex approaches known as large language models (LMMs). These approaches rely on specialized development, immense pre-training corpuses, significant computational power, and considerable financial resources. As a result, LMM development and pre-training may often be beyond the means of individuals and small organizations. However, many modern LLMs respond to a process called fine-tuning. Through fine-tuning, a pre-trained model may be adjusted with a modest amount of data to perform linguistic tasks for which it was not specifically pre-trained. The development of fine-tuning and the open availably of many pre-trained models have democratized access to LLMs, placing them into the hands of individuals and organizations for more niche and novel applications. This paper explores a variation of fine-tuning called "Intermediate-Task Transfer Learning" and how developers may use fine-tuning strategies in conjunction with ensembling methods for improved performance, especially

M. Bramer and F. Stahl (Eds.): SGAI 2023, LNAI 14381, pp. 19–32, 2023.
https://doi.org/10.1007/978-3-031-47994-6_2

when quality training data for a particular task is scarce. We consider a ubiquitous form of expression, sarcasm, for its difficulty to detect and disruption to computer systems aiming to model sentiment, mine opinion, and detect harassment [2].

In 2018, Open AI introduced the Generative Pre-trained Transformer (GPT) [21], showing that users may leverage unlabeled data and pre-train a model to effectively learn general linguistic representations. They demonstrated how these representations can then be fine-tuned and leveraged for downstream tasks such as classification, topic modeling, and textual entailment [21]. Their work is predicated on that of Howard and Ruder [8] who leveraged LSTMs to similar ends, though with less practicality. Progressing the state of previous research, Open AI established that general linguistic representations can be reliably extended to downstream natural language processing (NLP) tasks. Fine-tuning may be achieved with significantly smaller fine-tuning corpuses, fewer training steps [4, 20], and are often processes accessible through frameworks such as HuggingFace [27]. These advancements have led to significant performance improvements in NLP, as well as increased adaptation and application of LLMs [3].

Despite access to LLMs, users are still faced with the challenge of acquiring data with which to train downstream tasks, especially if those tasks are novel. Even given sufficient data, a particular linguistic problem may be difficult to model. With advancements in pre-trained model architectures and fine-tuning on downstream tasks [6, 8, 21], recent research has shown promising results for a solution. Phang et al. [17], proposed Supplementary Training on Intermediate Labeled-data Tasks (STILTs). They study Bidirectional Encoder Representations from Transformers (BERT) [6] and GPT in experiments that indicate STILTS improves performance and stabilizes model training, results supported in subsequent research [4, 20]. Similar performance improvements have been echoed and expanded upon by later studies [21, 25, 26]. Sarcasm detection as a downstream task represents both aforementioned difficulties—sarcasm is particularly difficult to discern, and high-quality sarcasm datasets are scarce. This paper seeks to confirm findings in prior related research and further investigate the results of intermediate fine-tuning through ensembling theory.

We explore ensembling as an established methodology to improve predictive performance over individual inducers. Effective ensembles must adhere to two principles—first, participating inducers must be sufficiently diverse with errors in predictions uncorrelated and second, the individual performance of inducers must be as high as possible, at least as good as random guessing [7, 23]. Given related research, we are likely to achieve sufficient individual performance for sarcasm detection through fine-tuning [24] and our selection of intermediate tasks [4, 20, 24]. What remains uncertain is whether we may produce sufficiently diverse inducers through intermediate fine-tuning. We hypothesize that by using different inputs for each model's intermediate fine-tuning step, we can achieve a form of algorithm manipulation allowing the base model to converge upon sufficiently different paths, resulting in diverse inducers [7, 24].

## 2 Related Work

Wang et al. [26] conduct a large-scale study on pre-training tasks in an effort to understand their impact on transfer learning and support of a variety of downstream tasks. They recognize intermediate training as a transfer paradigm, approaching intermediate tasks in terms of a supporting relationship with the pre-training task to improve transfer to a range of target tasks. This perspective contrasted later work that presumed an intermediate-target task relationship. Pruksachatkun et al. [20], for example, explore a matrix of intermediate and target tasks as well as a number of probing tasks designed to reveal what drives transfer, Chang and Lu [4] modify intermediate tasks in an attempt to isolate features that improve performance on a range of target tasks, and Savini and Caragea [24] explore intermediate tasks with pronounced semantic and lexical relationships to the target task. Wang et al. [26] note that a small-data intermediate task tended to outperform large-data intermediate tasks. They suggest that performance improvements driven by intermediate fine-tuning may not rely on additional training alone, but a complementary relationship between pre-training objectives and intermediate tasks. They also note that some intermediate tasks impair BERT's transfer ability but conclude that intermediate training can yield modest performance improvements.

Pruksachatkun et al.'s [20] study further acknowledges that the performance of BERT-based models can be improved by training them on a data-rich intermediate task before fine-tuning on a target task, but when and why the process works is poorly understood. They explored 110 intermediate-target task combinations finding that intermediate tasks requiring complex reasoning and inference show the most consistent improvement over baselines for various target tasks. Pruksachatkun et al. [20] hesitate to speculate on specific skills that enable positive transfer but show a high correlation between probing tasks that are similar to pre-training tasks and subsequent target-task performance, supporting previous work by [26].

Savini and Caragea [24] survey state-of-the-art methods for sarcasm detection and establish baselines revealing that BERT-based models outperform previous models. They improve upon those results by fine-tuning the BERT models on select intermediate tasks, finding more pronounced, positive results when the size of the target-task dataset is small, echoing previous research [4, 17, 20]. While research prior to [24] focused on intermediate tasks that generally inform the performance on various target tasks, [24] considered intermediate tasks with identifiable semantic relationships to the target tasks. Their research concluded that intermediate tasks with sufficient correlation to the target task can improve performance of BERT-based models in both accuracy and F1, finding that sentiment detection as an intermediate task had a higher impact than emotion labeling for sarcasm detection. They also show that sarcastic statements can be identified without additional context such as the prompt that instigated the sarcastic remark.

## 3 Data

We introduce six intermediate tasks and one shared target task—contextless sarcasm detection—for this research. Following the strategies of [24], four of the selected intermediate tasks were appraised and chosen based on their semantic relationships to the target task and/or their previously discovered potential as intermediate tasks that improve sarcasm detection models. We further acknowledge the work of [4] and [20] by selecting two additional datasets which have demonstrated promising results as intermediate tasks on a general range of downstream tasks. All string inputs are unmodified before tokenization and encoding unless otherwise stated.

Train, test, and validation split sizes can be viewed in Table 1. Generally, train splits comprise 80% of the total available samples while validate and test splits represent approximately 10%, each. We deviate from this split strategy where validation and/or test splits already accompanied the source datasets, in which case the splits were used as-is, preserving the intentions of the original researchers during testing. All training splits were perfectly balanced by label and any new validation and test splits retain the original distribution.

When determining intermediate task dataset sizes for our experiments, we consider both the practical implications as well as prior related research. General use-cases for intermediate fine-tuning and ensembling include improving predictive performance where target-task data may be insufficient or difficult to model. We also look at [20] and find that as intermediate task dataset sizes exceed 2000 observations, target-task macro-average performance broadly remains flat. They suggest that using an intermediate task with a training set size of only 2,000 points does not provide RoBERTa with additional linguistic knowledge specific to the target task, but rather offers high-level guidance to connect pre-training and fine-tuning. Similarly, [4] saw potential accuracy improvements between 2,000 and 10,000 samples, with larger datasets showing diminishing returns. Therefore, we use as much available data as possible with respect for training set balance and time.

**Table 1.** Intermediate and target task dataset splits as well as source information; an asterisk marks provided and therefore unmodified splits.

| Name | Train | Validate | Test | Task | Genre/Source |
|------|-------|----------|------|------|--------------|
| Intermediate Tasks | | | | | |
| SARC | 80,000 | 10,000 | 10,000 | Binary Classification | Sarcasm/Reddit |
| XED_fine | 9,496 | 1,200 | 1,200 | Multiclass Classification | Emotion/Film Subtitles |
| XED_coarse | 9,496 | 1,200 | 1,200 | Binary Classification | Sentiment/Film Subtitles |
| IMDb | 40,000 | 5,000 | 5,000 | Binary Classification | Sentiment/IMDb |
| HellaSwag | 34,600 | 10,042* | 4,994 | Sentence Completion | Inference/Video Captions & Wikihow |
| CosmosQA | 22,272 | 2,985* | 2,825 | Question Answering | Inference/Blogs |
| Target Task | | | | | |
| iSarcasmEval | 4,266 | 628 | 1,400* | Binary Classification | Sarcasm/Crowdsourced |

## 3.1 Intermediate Tasks

**SARC.** The Self-Annotated Reddit Corpus (SARC) [11] is derived from Reddit, containing over a million observations of self-annotated sarcastic statements intermixed with non-sarcastic statements. Reddit is a social media platform on which users submit text-based or media-rich posts. Users may then comment and perpetuate discussions on those posts. Given the sometimes-ambiguous nature of intent in textual language and the added difficulty in discerning sarcasm online, Reddit users often self-annotate sarcastic content with the marker "/s". SARC leverages this annotation in its collection and labeling. The non-sarcastic statements contained within the SARC corpus are those collected from Reddit that do not include the "/s" marker.

SARC was selected for this research as an example of a large, weakly-labeled sarcasm dataset that may potentially improve inference capabilities when leveraged in conjunction with a small, strongly-labeled target dataset. Although the dataset is considered self-annotated, false negatives and false positives are possible through various avenues. Those avenues include comments by users who do not know or do not faithfully use the "/s" marker, inappropriate use of the "/s" marker, and the possible collection of automated or bot-contributed content on the platform. The authors address both false-positive and false-negative rates in their paper, though admit that the methodology is only able to consistently account for false positives—comments incorrectly labeled with the "/s" marker. Intermediately fine-tuning with a weakly labeled sarcasm detection task may indicate whether or not weakly-labeled data may support a strongly-labeled sarcasm detection task where only a small dataset is available. This research explores whether SARC can contribute positively to iSarcasmEval both independently and as part of an ensemble.

Given the large size of this corpus, this research uses a randomly-sampled subset of 100,000 observations. Data such as parent comment, topic, and author are not included in training and evaluation.

**Fine-Grain XED.** XED [15] is a multilingual dataset for sentiment Analysis and Emotion Detection. The English-language subset of XED used for this research is composed of 17,528 unique, non-neutral sentences collected from movie subtitles. These 17,530 sentences are human labeled with 24,164 annotations across eight emotions as defined by Plutchik's wheel of core emotions (anger, anticipation, disgust, fear, joy, sadness, surprise, trust) [18].

Sarcasm is often defined in terms of its implied emotional context and subversion of that context. The relationship between emotion and sarcastic intent is not only hypothesized to be a key measure by which to identify sarcasm [5, 19], but has also been explored as a potentially good feature for intermediate-target task pipelines in sarcasm detection [24]. Previous research indicates that models first trained on a dataset called EmoNet, and then fine-tuned on a sarcasm detection task could outperform baseline models fine-tuned solely for sarcasm detection [24]. Similar to XED, the EmoNet dataset is a text analytics corpus labeled according to Plutchik's wheel of core emotions, refined to the same eight labels [1]. However, XED was selected over EmoNet for this research as EmoNet was unavailable. XED is a multilabel dataset including 3,873 instances with more than one annotation. These specific samples were removed for the purposes of this research. The remaining subset frames XED more closely to EmoNet.

**Coarse-Grain XED.** This dataset is the same as the Fine-Grain XED dataset but the emotion labels have been abstracted to a binary representation of sentiment. Emotion labels that imply a negative sentiment (anger, disgust, fear, sadness) have been collated and represented as 0 while those that imply a positive sentiment (anticipation, joy, surprise, trust) have been collated and represented as 1.

Poria et al. [19] likewise describes sarcasm as key to sentiment detection and researchers have further reinforced the correlation between the two by approaching sarcasm detection through sentiment analysis [10, 14, 22]. Poria et al. [19] experiment with ground-truth polarity as a direct feature to inform sarcasm detection but we seek to recreate the success of [24] in their similar treatment of the EmoNet dataset; implemented as an intermediate step to sarcasm detection for better-than-baseline performance.

**IMDb.** The Internet Movie Database (IMDb) dataset [13] is a commonly-used selection of 50,000 movie reviews labeled for binary sentiment analysis. It is noteworthy not only for its size but also due to its diversity—no more than 30 reviews per movie were collected for this dataset. Each movie review is annotated with a classification of negative or positive sentiment derived from the reviewer-provided movie rating. The authors of this dataset did not include neutral reviews, opting to mark polarizing reviews of $\leq 4$ out of 10 as negative and $\geq 7$ out of 10 as positive.

Even though the XED dataset was abstracted into a binary sentiment task, we additionally selected the IMDb dataset as a dedicated sentiment analysis task, given the aforementioned relationship between sentiment and sarcasm. The Coarse-Grain XED dataset, with its original form as an 8-class emotion dataset, is deeply embedded with a wide range of sentiment. Contrarily, researchers behind the IMDb dataset specifically sought polarizing positive and negative content—a comparatively shallow "good" verses "bad" when viewed next to XED's original distinctions.

**HellaSwag.** HellaSwag [29] is a multiple-choice, commonsense natural language inference (NLI) task created to address the quality of negative, or counterfactual, answer choices in its predecessor dataset, SWAG [28]. Both provide a context sequence and four ending choice sequences describing events subsequent to the given context, one of which is correct. The curators of HellaSwag found that models like BERT achieved high accuracy on SWAG without the need for context or structure, likely by detecting distributional stylistic patterns in the counterfactuals. HellaSwag contains 35,905 contextual training samples with refined counterfactuals and factuals which, although trivial for humans, remains challenging for language models. While the counterfactuals in HellaSwag improved upon those in SWAG, artifacting still exists in the machine-generated counterfactuals [25]. Nevertheless, [4, 20] found HellaSwag to be an effective intermediate task for RoBERTa$_{large}$ in their large-scale experiments.

Contrary to the selection of IMDb, SARC, and XED, which exhibit direct semantic and lexical relationships to sarcasm, HellaSwag was chosen for this research as it has proven to be an exceptional intermediate task for a range of target tasks [4, 20].

**CosmosQA.** CosmosQA [9] is a common-sense inference dataset predicated on reading comprehension to correctly select one of four answers to a posed question. Each observation consists of context, a question, and four options, one of which is correct. Selecting the correct option requires reasoning beyond that which is explicitly provided in the context—a contrast to prior reading comprehension datasets. Contextual common-sense reasoning makes CosmosQA a unique and difficult task. In order to construct this dataset, researchers collected context from a blog-based corpus of personal narratives and outsourced human-generated questions and answers derived from those contexts.

CosmosQA was selected for this research for largely the same reasons as Hel-laSwag—it has been shown, in past experiments, to be an exceptional intermediate task for a range of target tasks [4, 20]. The selection of CosmosQA additionally reinforces the range of tasks we have selected for this research.

### 3.2 Target Task

**iSarcasm.** SemEval's iSarcasm 2022 task [2] is a shared task organized as part of the SemEval-2022 workshop. iSarcasm is aimed at evaluating the performance of automatic sarcasm detection systems. The task is designed to encourage the development of models that can accurately identify sarcasm present in various types of texts, such as social media and customer service.

In this research, we take advantage of SemEval 2022's iSarcasmEval English Sub-Task A (hereby known as the "target task"), which is a binary sequence classification task. The provided training dataset is quite small with roughly 3,467 observations and a significant imbalance, favoring the "Not Sarcasm" label. It is a high-quality dataset, as each instance is author-labeled, contrasting similar datasets which are often labeled using weak supervision or manually by a third party, potentially causing bias through annotator perception [2].

Sarcasm detection was chosen as the focus of this research due to its timeliness, value, and difficulty for both humans and automated methods [2]. Given the small size of the iSarcasm 2022 dataset and its quality as a strongly-labeled dataset, it is also an excellent candidate for supplementation through intermediate transfer learning. Through such a task, we may explore not just the diversity of inducers generated by related intermediate tasks, but also the impact of those tasks on a relevant, high-quality sarcasm detection problem.

In order to prepare this dataset, we first sampled a representative distribution of observations for the validation set, and then over-sampled the remaining underrepresented "sarcasm" observations to match the number of samples in the "not sarcasm" class. This results in a balanced training split with 2,113 samples per class. This over-sampling occurred after careful consideration, taking into account size of the dataset as well as the tradeoff between the amount of data and the diversity of observations in the sarcasm class. We use a simple random oversampling method.

## 4 Modeling Overview

Our model selection process for this research considered accessibility, baseline performance on similar text analytics tasks, models used in similar research, and model size. As a result, we selected and studied the pre-trained model RoBERTa$_{base}$ (Robustly Optimized BERT Approach) for all experiments. We implemented these models using

PyTorch [16] and the HuggingFace Transformers library [27]. Training occurred in a PyTorch environment using the Metal Performance Shaders (MPS) backend for GPU training acceleration. Specifically, training was supported by an Apple M1 Pro 14-Core integrated GPU with any unsupported computations set to fall back to the CPU.

We forwent hyperparameter sweeps for all models opting to apply hyperparameters consistent with the limited hyperparameter sweeps performed during the original research team's evaluation of RoBERTa [12]. The selected hyperparameters, defined below, remained consistent for all intermediate and target task fine-tuning sessions. Any unspecified hyperparameters assume a default value and are also kept consistent among all training sessions.

Our models used the *torch.optim.Adam* optimizer with a learning rate of 1e−05, and the optimizer's default weight decay of 0. We additionally set a batch size of 16 for all experiments. We limited input sequence lengths to 256. This was done as the tokenized input length for all training sets, except for the IMDb, do not exceed 256. Although the IMDb dataset has many tokenized sequences that surpass 256, truncating them does not significantly impact performance. Standard cross entropy loss was implemented for both training and validation.

Before fine-tuning each model, a new classification head with randomly initialized weights was applied to the pre-trained RoBERTa$_{base}$ model. The sequence classification head, *transformers.RobertaForSequenceClassification*, used for our SARC, Fine-Grain XED, Coarse-Grain XED, IMDb, and iSarcasm tasks consisted of a linear layer on top of the pooled output, intersected by a dropout layer. The classification head is preceded by an additional dropout layer. We leveraged *transformers.RobertaForMultipleChoice* to intermediately fine-tune on HellaSwag and CosmosQA. This multiple-choice classification head consists of a linear layer on top of the pooled output and a softmax function. The output layer is preceded by a dropout layer.

## 5    Methodology

### 5.1    Control and Target Models

The control models are characterized by the fact that they are fine-tuned solely on our designated target task. These models collectively represent a baseline performance to which we compare our target and ensemble models. Our collection of target models consists of those that have been trained first on one of the six intermediate tasks described in section three, then fine-tuned once more on the target task.

### 5.2    Training Pipeline

Both the control and target models follow a similar training pipeline with several consistent features. The pre-trained RoBERTa$_{base}$ is loaded with the appropriate classification head as defined in our Modeling Overview and is then fine-tuned either on the target or an intermediate task. In order to account for stochastic variation, three individual iterations of each control and target model are trained. We call these sets of iterations "same-model iterations". Given six intermediate tasks and one target task, this results in three control models, six intermediate models, and 18 target models—three per intermediate task. Each control model, intermediate model, and target model are fine-tuned for 10 epochs.

Unlike the control models, target models are the product of fine-tuned intermediate models. Prior to this second fine-tuning, the best intermediate model epoch, as determined by the highest F1 score on the task's associated holdout test set, is selected to be fine-tuned. The selected intermediate model's classification head is discarded and replaced with a new one to generate the three target models from each individual intermediate model. Our training pipelines are represented in Fig. 1.

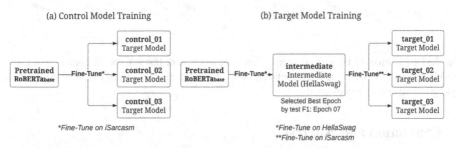

**Fig. 1.** (a) Training procedure for control models, (b) example of training procedure for target models, using HellaSwag as the intermediate task.

## 5.3 Ensembles

We collect and evaluate both three and five-inducer ensembles, none of which include our control models. Although we designate these collections as "three" and "five" inducer ensembles, the naming schema refers to the number of individual intermediate tasks that contribute to the ensemble. Our three-inducer ensembles each consist of nine inducers and each five-inducer ensemble consists of fifteen inducers due to the inclusion of all same-model iterations. This strategy allows us to better consider the contribution of our six intermediate tasks.

Two sets of ensembles are explored. The first set are ensembles created using the best epochs from each target model according to test F1 scores and the second set is created using the best epochs from each target model according to test accuracy scores. All unique unions of three and five target models are considered by leveraging six-choose-three (6C3) and six-choose-five (6C5) combination formulas. We strictly adhere to odd-number inducer combinations as we use a simple majority vote strategy for predictions—eliminating the possibility of a split vote on any given prediction. By forgoing a weighted vote strategy, we also eliminate a dimension that may allow one target model to over-influence the performance of any given ensemble. This enables us to evaluate the outcome of a collective effort rather than resurfacing results overtly similar to those of individual target models. 6C3 evaluates to 20 unique ensembles while 6C5 evaluates to six additional unique ensembles.

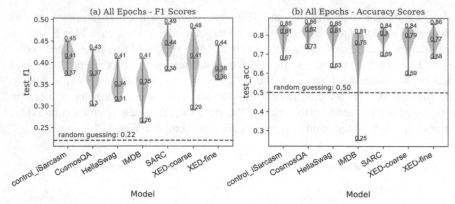

**Fig. 2.** Distribution of F1 and accuracy scores on target task test set for all control and target models epochs. The y-axis denotes control models and target models named for their intermediate task. n = 210 epochs represented

## 6    Evaluation and Analysis

We evaluate all epochs for each control, target, and ensembled model against the target task's holdout test set. We reinforce the findings of [20, 24] that show intermediate fine-tuning may, under certain conditions, improve predictive performance. Referring to Fig. 2a, we see that leveraging SARC and XED_coarse as intermediate tasks improves model performance over our controls when evaluated on our primary metric, F1. Contrarily, we find that both fail to exceed control performance when evaluated on accuracy as shown in Fig. 2b. This performance gap is likely explained by our F1-based fine-tuning selection process, but it is important to address the large discrepancy between reported F1 and accuracy scores overall.

### 6.1    F1 and Accuracy

The discrepancy between F1 and accuracy scores is, in part, driven by the large imbalance in our target task test data. Although trained on a balanced dataset, 87.6% of all models predicted "Not Sarcastic" >70% of the time. With 200 of 1400 test samples labeled "Sarcastic", this closely aligns with the distribution of the iSarcasm dataset and informs the optimistic accuracy scores. We primarily study F1 for this reason. While our models correctly predict the majority of new input, the comparatively low F1 scores indicate that our models positively identify sarcasm at a much lower rate. Our primary goal is to improve F1 in order to identify the underrepresented class, sarcasm, more reliably without sacrificing accuracy.

### 6.2    Ensemble Suitability

As previously noted, the individual performance of participating inducers must be at least as good as random guessing. While Fig. 2b seems to indicate that our pool of inducers significantly outpaces random guessing, this quality is defined in terms of accuracy, our secondary metric. We establish the .22 random guessing baseline for F1, as displayed in Fig. 2a, by evaluating 5,000 uniform random binary arrays against the true labels of our target task test set. By this metric we see additional evidence that our models may be suitable inducers for more performant ensembles.

Although inducer diversity is often cited by researchers outlining the requirements for a successful ensemble, we were unable to identify a generally agreed-upon metric or associated threshold by which to quantify inducer diversity and correlate that diversity to improved performance. Previous research leverages measures of inducer diversity, sometimes incorporating additional metrics such as accuracy, in ensemble pruning and selection [23] but that is beyond the scope of this paper. We note the implication that ensembles outperforming our controls must be sufficiently diverse or that the diversity-performance relationship is likewise sufficient.

We offer supplementary evidence that our inducers exhibit some level of diversity through the Hamming distance—a metric that identifies the proportion of substitutions necessary to transform one vector into another. Hamming distance allows us to assess the similarity of two sets of predictions on a 0–1 scale with consideration for both zero values and position. A distance of 0 indicates that the vectors are the same and 1 indicates that the vectors are absolutely different. We calculate this metric for all two-set combinations of predictions from our target models and aggregate the results of all same-model iterations. We find that due to stochastic variation in training, same-model iterations result in an average distance of .112 from each other. By multiplying the distance by the size of our target task test set we find that a score of .112 translates to ~157 individual predictions that disagree. Same-model iterations have the least diversity in their predictions. The two target models that exhibit the greatest relative diversity are SARC and IMDb with an average distance of .211 or ~296 predictions in disagreement. Excluding comparisons of same-model iterations, our target models' average prediction distance from each other equals .174, or ~244 predictions in disagreement—17.43% of the target task test set.

## 6.3 Ensemble Performance

Figure 3 reveals that while our individual target models, on average, do not outperform the control models, ensembles of our target models outpace the controls on both F1 and accuracy. These averages along with associated deltas, shown in Table 2a, indicate that our best performers, the 5-inducer ensembles, outperform control models in F1 by 5.5 percentage points on average with 3-inducer ensembles outperforming control by 4.1 percentage points on average. Table 2b presents similar, though less pronounced, improvements in accuracy. Assessing data for the models shown in Fig. 3a indicates that 88% of ensembles outperform the dominant control model by F1 and 73% outperform the dominant control model in terms of accuracy. We note that select target models perform comparatively to the ensembles in individual dimensions, but their companion iterations do not imply consistent results—falling behind the outlying performant behavior by as much as .04 points. By comparison, ensemble performance is significantly less variant. Figure 3b and Table 2b show similar results in terms of best control and target model epochs selected by accuracy against ensembles constructed from those most accurate epochs.

Further explorations into the compositions of the top 10 of 26 ensembles reveal that the SARC-based target model appears in all 10 with XED_coarse in seven. XED_fine, HellaSwag, and CosmosQA-based target models appear in six of the 10 top ensembles and IMDB trails with three appearances.

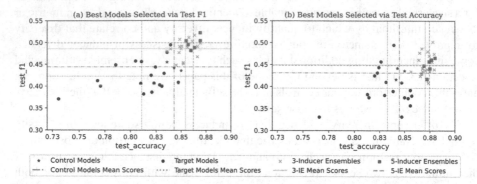

**Fig. 3.** (a) Best control and target model epochs as chosen by test F1 scores compared to ensembles of those select, F1-dominate models and (b) best control and target model epochs as chosen by test accuracy scores compared to ensembles of those select, accuracy-dominate models. n = 47

**Table 2.** Average F1 and accuracy performance across model categories including deltas between control models and experimental models

| Metric | Control | Target Models | 3I-Ensembles | 5I-Ensembles |
|---|---|---|---|---|
| (a) | **Best Models Selected by Test F1** | | | |
| Mean F1 | 0.444 | 0.423 (-0.021) | 0.485 (+0.041) | 0.499 (+0.055) |
| Mean Accuracy | 0.843 | 0.811 (-0.032) | 0.854 (+0.011) | 0.862 (+0.020) |
| (b) | **Best Models Selected by Test Accuracy** | | | |
| Mean F1 | 0.431 | 0.396 (-0.035) | 0.449 (+0.018) | 0.448 (+0.017) |
| Mean Accuracy | 0.845 | 0.833 (-0.012) | 0.87 (+0.026) | 0.875 (+0.03) |

# 7   Conclusion and Future Work

We demonstrate that intermediate fine-tuning may produce sufficient inducers to improve performance on sarcasm detection as a downstream task when due consideration is given to the selection of intermediate datasets for the given target task. Through analysis of experimental ensembles, we find that inducers created with intermediate fine-tuning methodologies are sufficiently diverse and perform above the thresholds necessary to improve both F1 and accuracy over models fine-tuned on sarcasm detection alone. We also establish that weakly-labeled sarcasm datasets may effectively supplement smaller, strongly-labeled sarcasm datasets through intermediate fine-tuning.

This research not only supports progress in sarcasm detection but may hold implications for similar practical applications such as improved analysis of online expression with respect to organizations and products, use in recommendation systems, and customer service. Future work may extend this research to investigate performance on other tasks. We also wish to pursue more performant models through work that incorporates hyperparameter sweeps, more sophisticated ensembling techniques such as weighted voting, and larger language models.

# References

1. Abdul-Mageed, M., Ungar, L.: EmoNet: fine-grained emotion detection with gated recurrent neural networks. In: Proceedings of the 55th Annual Meeting of the Association for Computational Linguistics (Volume 1: Long Papers), 718–28 (2017). https://doi.org/10.18653/v1/P17-1067
2. Abu Farha, I., Silviu, V.O., Steven, W., Walid, M.: SemEval 2022 (2022). https://sites.google.com/view/semeval2022-isarcasmeval
3. Brown, T.B., et al.: Language models are few-shot learners. Adv. Neural. Inf. Process. Syst. **33**, 1877–1901 (2020)
4. Chang, T.-Y., Lu, C.-J.: Rethinking why intermediate-task fine-tuning works. In: Findings of the Association for Computational Linguistics: EMNLP 2021, pp. 706–713 (2021). https://doi.org/10.18653/v1/2021.findings-emnlp.61
5. Chauhan, D.S., Dhanush, S.R., Ekbal, A., Bhattacharyya, P.: Sentiment and emotion help sarcasm? A multi-task learning framework for multi-modal sarcasm, sentiment and emotion analysis. In: Proceedings of the 58th Annual Meeting of the Association for Computational Linguistics, pp. 4351–4360 (2020). https://doi.org/10.18653/v1/2020.acl-main.401
6. Devlin, J., Chang, M.W., Lee, K., Toutanova, K.: BERT: pre-training of deep bidirectional transformers for language understanding. arXiv preprint arXiv:1810.04805 (2018)
7. Dietterich, T.G.: Ensemble methods in machine learning. In: Kittler, J., Roli, F. (eds.) MCS 2000. LNCS, vol. 1857, pp. 1–15. Springer, Heidelberg (2000). https://doi.org/10.1007/3-540-45014-9_1
8. Howard, J., Ruder, S.: Universal language model fine-tuning for text classification. arXiv preprint arXiv:1801.06146 (2018). https://doi.org/10.48550/arXiv.1801.06146
9. Huang, L., Le Bras, R., Bhagavatula, C., Choi, Y.: Cosmos QA: machine reading comprehension with contextual commonsense reasoning. In: Proceedings of the 2019 Conference on Empirical Methods in Natural Language Processing and the 9th International Joint Conference on Natural Language Processing (EMNLP-IJCNLP) (2019)
10. Joshi, A., Bhattacharyya, P., Carman, M.J.: Automatic sarcasm detection. ACM Comput. Surv. **50**, 1–22 (2017). https://doi.org/10.1145/3124420
11. Khodak, M., Saunshi, N., Vodrahalli, K.: A large self-annotated corpus for sarcasm. arXiv preprint arXiv:1704.05579 (2017). https://doi.org/10.48550/arXiv.1704.05579
12. Liu, Y., et al.: RoBERTa: a robustly optimized BERT pretraining approach. arXiv preprint arXiv:1907.11692 (2019). https://doi.org/10.48550/arXiv.1907.11692
13. Maas, A., Daly, R.E., Pham, P.T., Huang, D., Ng, A.Y., Potts, C: Learning word vectors for sentiment analysis. In: Proceedings of the 49th Annual Meeting of the Association for Computational Linguistics: Human Language Technologies, pp. 142–150 (2011)
14. Maynard, D.G., Greenwood, M.A.: Who cares about sarcastic tweets? Investigating the impact of sarcasm on sentiment analysis. In: Lrec 2014 Proceedings. ELRA (2014)
15. Öhman, E., Pàmies, M., Kajava, K., Tiedemann, J.: XED: a multilingual dataset for sentiment analysis and emotion detection. arXiv preprint arXiv:2011.01612 (2020)

16. Paszke, A., et al.: PyTorch: an imperative style, high-performance deep learning library. In: Advances in Neural Information Processing Systems, vol. 32 (2019)
17. Phang, J., Févry, T., Bowman, S.R.: Sentence encoders on stilts: supplementary training on intermediate labeled-data tasks. arXiv preprint arXiv:1811.01088 (2018)
18. Plutchik, R.: Emotion. A Psychoevolutionary Synthesis. Harper and Row, New York (1980)
19. Poria, S., Cambria, E., Hazarika, D., Vij, P.: A deeper look into sarcastic tweets using deep convolutional neural networks. arXiv preprint arXiv:1610.08815 (2016)
20. Pruksachatkun, Y., et al.: Intermediate-task transfer learning with pretrained models for natural language understanding: when and why does it work? arXiv preprint arXiv:2005.00628 (2020). https://doi.org/10.48550/arXiv.2005.00628
21. Radford, A., Narasimhan, K., Salimans, T., Sutskever, I.: Improving language understanding by generative pre-training (2018)
22. Riloff, E., Qadir, A., Surve, P., De Silva, L., Gilbert, N., Huang, R.: Sarcasm as contrast between a positive sentiment and negative situation. In: Proceedings of the 2013 Conference on Empirical Methods in Natural Language Processing, pp. 704–714 (2013)
23. Sagi, O., Rokach, L.: Ensemble learning: a survey. WIREs Data Min. Knowl. Discov. **8** (2018). https://doi.org/10.1002/widm.1249
24. Savini, E., Caragea, C.: Intermediate-task transfer learning with BERT for sarcasm detection. Mathematics. **10**, 844 (2022). https://doi.org/10.3390/math10050844
25. Tamborrino, A., Pellicanò, N., Pannier, B., Voitot, P., Naudin, L.: Pre-training is (almost) all you need: an application to commonsense reasoning. In: Proceedings of the 58th Annual Meeting of the Association for Computational Linguistics (2020)
26. Wang, A., et al.: Can you tell me how to get past sesame street? Sentence-level pretraining beyond language modeling. In: Proceedings of the 57th Annual Meeting of the Association for Computational Linguistics (2019). https://doi.org/10.18653/v1/p19-1439
27. Wolf, T., et al.: HuggingFace's transformers: state-of-the-art natural language processing. arXiv preprint arXiv:1910.03771 (2019)
28. Zellers, R., Bisk, Y., Schwartz, R., Choi, Y.: SWAG: a large-scale adversarial dataset for grounded commonsense inference. arXiv preprint arXiv:1808.05326 (2018)
29. Zellers, R., Holtzman, A., Bisk, Y., Farhadi, A., Choi, Y.: HellaSwag: can a machine really finish your sentence? arXiv preprint arXiv:1905.07830 (2019)

# Clinical Dialogue Transcription Error Correction with Self-supervision

Gayani Nanayakkara$^{(\boxtimes)}$, Nirmalie Wiratunga, David Corsar, Kyle Martin, and Anjana Wijekoon

School of Computing, Robert Gordon University, Aberdeen, Scotland
{g.nanayakkara,n.wiratunga,d.corsar1,k.martin3,a.wijekoon1}@rgu.ac.uk

**Abstract.** A clinical dialogue is a conversation between a clinician and a patient to share medical information, which is critical in clinical decision-making. The reliance on manual note-taking is highly inefficient and leads to transcription errors when digitising notes. Speech-to-text applications designed using Automatic Speech Recognition (ASR) can potentially overcome these errors using post-ASR error correction. Pre-trained language models are increasingly used in this area. However, the performance suffers from the lack of domain-specific vocabulary and the mismatch between error correction and pre-training objectives. This research explores these challenges in gastrointestinal specialism by introducing self-supervision strategies to fine-tune pre-trained language models for clinical dialogue error correction. We show that our mask-filling objective specialised for the medical domain (med-mask-filling) outperforms the best performing commercial ASR system by 10.27%.

**Keywords:** Automatic Speech Recognition · Error Correction · Language Models

## 1 Introduction

In the traditional clinical setting, healthcare providers manually take notes during conversations and patient interactions. This involves physically writing down relevant information, observations, and essential details the patient shares. The process typically entails using pen and paper or a digital device to record the information. This manual note-taking process requires clinicians to quickly process and capture information while focusing on the patient's needs.

The main drawback to this approach is the time burden of record-keeping of clinical communications [14], and it is associated with clinician burnout, increased cognitive load, information loss, and distractions [17]. One of the most promising avenues of automating clinical documentation with digital scribes is to use Automatic Speech Recognition (ASR) [18], where the audio data is converted to textual data.

Given the critical nature of the medical field, ASR systems for clinical applications must demonstrate high performance levels. However, the effectiveness

© The Author(s), under exclusive license to Springer Nature Switzerland AG 2023
M. Bramer and F. Stahl (Eds.): SGAI 2023, LNAI 14381, pp. 33–46, 2023.
https://doi.org/10.1007/978-3-031-47994-6_3

of ASR systems depends on three key factors: speaker variabilities, spoken language variabilities, and other mismatch factors [2]. These factors contribute to the occurrence of errors in the textual outputs. Therefore, it is crucial to explore strategies that can mitigate the likelihood of transcription errors.

In this work, we propose a post-ASR error correction method that uses the advancements in transformer-based pre-trained language models. Our work aims to leverage the strengths of pre-trained language models and adapt them to the clinical domain for error correction. Rather than designing new architectures or fine-tuning models on specialized datasets, we aim to use publicly available clinical domain data to fine-tune these models. For that, we introduce a newly curated PubMed[1] dataset to address the challenge of the lack of clinical dialogue data for fine-tuning language models. The dataset scraped from PubMed alleviates the need for large-scale real-world transcription data for self-supervision. Our method is evaluated using the Gastrointestinal Clinical Dialogue (GCD) Dataset, which is a role-playing dataset collected in partnership with the National Health Service (NHS) Grampian Inflammatory Bowel Disease (IBD) Clinic which emulates a real-world clinical setting. Results from our self-supervision strategy applied to two pre-trained language models, T5-small and BART, demonstrate that it can reduce transcription errors compared to commercial ASR systems. Accordingly, our contributions are:

1. a self-supervision strategy to fine-tune pre-trained language models for clinical dialogue error correction;
2. novel masked and med-masked PubMed datasets to fine-tune pre-trained language models using self-supervision; and
3. an empirical evaluation that compares our method with commercial ASR systems.

The rest of the paper is organised as follows. Section 2 presents related work in the ASR error correction research domain. Our approach is presented in Sect. 3 followed by evaluation and results in Sect. 4. Section 5 concludes the paper with a review of contributions and an outline of future directions.

## 2    Related Work

The performance of an Automatic Speech Recognition (ASR) model is influenced by several factors: speaker variabilities, spoken language variabilities, and other mismatch factors [2]. Speaker variabilities encompass changes in voice due to ageing, illness, emotions, and tiredness. Spoken language variabilities arise from variations in speech patterns, accents, and dialects. Other mismatch factors include variations in communication channels and the devices used during speech recognition. These factors contribute to transcription errors, making it challenging to extract meaningful insights from the generated transcripts [2].

When recognising the importance of error correction, there are two primary approaches to address ASR errors: incorporating an error correction algorithm

---

[1] https://www.ncbi.nlm.nih.gov/pubmed/.

within the ASR model itself or applying post-processing techniques to refine the ASR outputs. In the past, researchers explored the integration of error correction methods within ASR models, utilizing techniques like Hidden Markov Models (HMMs) [4,6] and more recently, deep neural architectures [5]. These approaches aimed to enhance the accuracy of ASR outputs by directly correcting errors during the recognition process.

Alternatively, the post-ASR error correction approach has gained popularity. This method involves applying error correction techniques as a subsequent step to refine the ASR outputs. Initially, unsupervised methods were employed, such as lexical co-occurrence analysis on large ASR transcription corpora [20] and statistical error correction methods [1]. These methods aimed to identify and rectify errors based on linguistic patterns and statistical analysis. More recently, transformer-based [21] language models have emerged as a promising approach for post-ASR error correction. These models, known for their robust contextual understanding, have been leveraged to improve the accuracy of ASR outputs. By fine-tuning transformer-based language models on domain-specific data, they can learn to correct errors present in the ASR transcriptions more effectively.

There are two prominent approaches to leveraging transformer-based language models for post-ASR error correction. One approach is exemplified by FastCorrect [7,8], which introduces modifications to a transformer-based encoder-decoder architecture. This architecture incorporates an error correction module that utilizes the edit distance metric [22] to guide the error correction process [8] FastCorrect models are trained on large-scale datasets and subsequently fine-tuned specifically for error correction using extensive ASR datasets [8,10,24]. In these approach, the models undergo a training process where they learn to correct errors by considering the edit distance between the ASR-generated text and the ground truth text. The models are trained to minimize this edit distance, improving their error correction capabilities.

Alternatively, pre-trained language models can be effectively fine-tuned using self-supervision for error correction, with the self-supervision objective being Machine Translation [12,13,15]. This approach involves training the models to correct errors by treating the ASR output as a source language and the ground truth transcription as a target language for translation. By fine-tuning the models using self-supervised learning, they can learn to align and correct errors in the ASR-generated text. It is worth noting that the fine-tuning process in these methods often relies on a significant portion of the ASR transcription data, typically using it as a training set for self-supervision [13]. Consequently, these approaches are particularly effective when large quantities of ASR transcriptions from the target domain are readily available.

In this paper, our approach is based on post-ASR error correction utilizing transformer-based architectures. However, instead of adopting custom-designed architectures [8,10,24] or fine-tuning specifically for error correction using a large-scale dataset [12,13], we explore how to effectively fine-tune a pre-trained model using publicly available clinical domain data when the domain-specific data is limited.

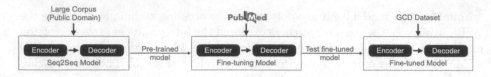

**Fig. 1.** Self-supervision for clinical dialogue error correction

## 3 Methodology

We view error correction as a seq2seq task performed using an Encoder-Decoder (ED) architecture-based language model to perform error correction, treating it as a sequence-to-sequence task. However, before this model can be effectively used for error correction, it needs to undergo a process of fine-tuning. This is necessary to address the following:

**Vocabulary Gap** the pre-trained language models are general-purpose and not initially tailored to handle domain-specific vocabulary (i.e., medical jargon and terms).

**Objective Gap** the general-purpose models are also not initially fine-tuned to perform specific downstream tasks (i.e., error correction).

To resolve these gaps, we introduce self-supervision strategies, which involve fine-tuning the pre-trained model on specific downstream datasets and tasks, specifically in the gastrointestinal domain.

### 3.1 Self-supervision

The approach of using the same unsupervised data to create multiple training objectives is known as self-supervision. When fine-tuning base language models, we need to create self-supervision tasks with the general structure of an input-output text pair (Fig. 1). A self-supervision dataset for fine-tuning a language model consists of input-output text pairs. And in this work, we looked at three approaches to forming a self-supervision strategy best suited for error correction: (i) standard objective approaches, (ii) standard hybrid approaches and (iii) domain-specific approaches.

### 3.2 Standard Objective Approaches

Here we explore three self-supervision objectives from the literature that are best suited to bridge the vocabulary gap and error correction. Examples from the gastrointestinal domain for each objective are presented in Fig. 2, where coloured boxes refer to standard objective approaches: summarization, paraphrasing and mask-filling respectively.

**Summarisation** task generates a summary for given text input. The goal is to capture key points of the input and present them in a concise manner.

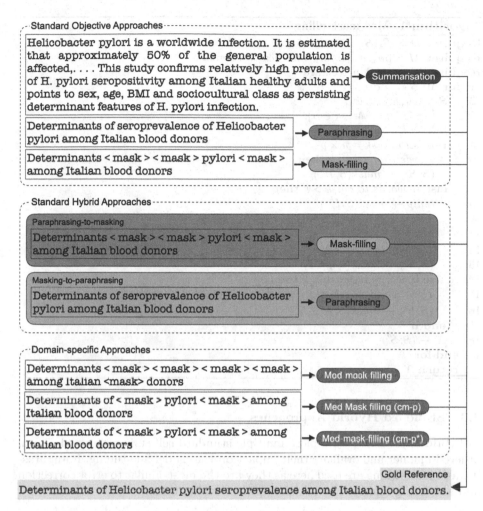

**Fig. 2.** Self-supervision strategies

**Paraphrasing** task generates a rephrased text for a given text input. This aims to rephrase the input text while preserving semantic meaning using synonyms or by re-arranging words.

**Mask-filling** is the task of predicting missing words when indicated by a masked token in the input text. A percentage of the input text is replaced with a $<mask>$ token, and the goal is to predict the masked words based on semantic relations.

**Algorithm 1.** Med-mask-filling

---

**Require:** $D = [S_1, S_2, ..., S_N]$: reference text document
**Require:** $M = [m_1, m_2, ..., m_K]$: medical vocabulary
**Require:** $p$: masking percentage
1: **for all** $S \in D$ **do**
2:     $S = [w_1, w_2, ..., w_n]$
3:     $I^M = \{i \mid w_i \in M, w_i \in S\}$
4:     $|I^M| = k$
5:     $words\_to\_mask = n \times p$
6:     **if** $words\_to\_mask = k$ **then**
7:         $(S, S') \leftarrow mask(S, I^M)$
8:     **else if** $words\_to\_mask > k$ **then**
9:         $temp \leftarrow mask(S, I^M)$
10:         $\hat{I} = \{j \mid w_j \in S, w_j \notin M\}$
11:         $q = p - \frac{k}{n}$
12:         $\hat{I} \leftarrow random\_select(q(n - k), \hat{I})$
13:         $(S, S') \leftarrow mask(temp, \hat{I})$
14:     **else if** $words\_to\_mask < k$ **then**
15:         $I^{\hat{M}} \leftarrow random\_select(n \times p, I^M)$
16:         $(S, S') \leftarrow mask(S, I^{\hat{M}})$
17:     **end if**
18:     $\mathcal{X} \leftarrow (S, S')$
19: **end for**
20: **return** $\mathcal{X}$

---

### 3.3 Standard Hybrid Approaches

In hybrid approaches, we explore multiple standard self-supervision tasks in an ordered manner and evaluate their impact on the model fine-tuning. Paraphrasing and mask-filling are used here as they are the most similar to error correction and also being informed by initial empirical evaluations.

**Paraphrasing-to-masking** is a hybrid approach where we perform paraphrasing followed by mask-filling. As shown in Fig. 2, first, the pre-trained language model is fine-tuned for paraphrasing followed by a second objective of mask-filling. Intuitively, the masking-only approach is limited to the context, but by introducing paraphrasing-to-masking, we focus on expanding the contexts for the words in which they appear.

**Masking-to-paraphrasing** is a hybrid approach where mask-filling is the first fine-tuning objective, followed by paraphrasing.

### 3.4 Domain-Specific Approaches

The goal of domain-specific self-supervision approaches are to further influence the model to reduce the vocabulary gap. Our approach to domain-specific self-supervision using conditional masking is presented in Algorithm 1. Here the inputs to the conditional masking are the reference text document $D$ and the medical vocabulary $M$ which is specific to the medical domain of interest and consists of a list of specialist terms. Dataset compilation is described in Sect. 4.1.

**Med-mask-filling** objective is derived from standard mask-filling where we randomly replaced a percentage ($p$) of the words in each sentence with the token $<mask>$. However, in med-mask-filling, instead of random masking, we are masking all the medical words in the sentence identified using the medical vocabulary (M). This objective ignores masking percentage $p$ but satisfies the condition on Line 6.

**Med-mask-filling (cm-p)** where cm-p stands for conditional masking percentage consider two cases; (1) if the sentence contains at least one medical word ($k > 0$) we ensure they are prioritised before masking non-medical words, this may satisfy one of the three conditions in the Algorithm 1 lines 6, 8 or 14 based on $k$ and $p$; and (2) in the absence of any medical words a random mask is used which satisfies condition in Line 8.

**Med-mask-filling (cm-p\*)** is similar to the previous task; except that sentences with no medical words are not included in the Document $D$. This will enable us to evaluate the impact of including and excluding random masking as part of med-mask-filling.

# 4    Evaluation

In this section, we evaluate self-supervision strategies for clinical dialogue error correction using two pre-trained language models and compare them against commercial ASR systems. The language models are fine-tuned using the PubMed dataset and evaluated using the GCD dataset.

## 4.1    Datasets

**Gastrointestinal Disease Dataset (GCD)** consists of a set of role-playing clinical dialogues that took place at the NHS IBD Clinic. The data collection included clinical dialogues recorded with 7 participants with Scottish accents transcribed using commercial ASR systems. Here, the accent can be viewed as a form of noise in addition to common noise factors such as background noise, interruptions and repetitions. Each audio clip contains around 47 utterances by two persons engaged in a clinical conversation that is about 4–5 min long. Statistics of the GCD dataset can be found in Table 1 and some examples are presented in Table 2.

**PubMed Dataset for Self-supervision** the PubMed dataset consists of abstract and title pairs scraped from articles related to gastrointestinal conditions. Following variants of the PubMed dataset were created for evaluating self-supervision strategies. An example for each self-supervision task is presented in Table 3.

- **Summarisation** considers abstract as the input and title as the expected output.
- **Paraphrasing** considers a paraphrased version of the title as the input and the title as the expected output. The paraphrased title is obtained using the T5 model fine-tuned for paraphrasing using the Google PAWS Dataset [23].
- **Mask-filling** apply $<mask>$ token to 25% of the words in the title to create the input and use the title as the expected output.
- **Hybrid approaches** use the above datasets created for paraphrasing and mask-filling for fine-tuning.
- **Med-mask-filling (cm-p)** strategies use datasets created using Algorithm 1.

The dataset was curated from PubMed articles with the primary goal of introducing domain-specific medical vocabulary to language models pre-trained on public domain data. The lack of availability of a larger spoken corpus in medical conversations has led us to use a written corpus, although we acknowledge the differences between written and spoken language in specialist domains. After pre-processing, we obtain a dataset with title and abstract pairs (see Table 3). This extraction method can be generalised to any medical domain by using domain-specific search queries in the PubMed search engine.

**Medical Vocabulary ($M$)** is a set of domain-specific medical terms extracted from the PubMed articles using the ScispaCy [16] models. This medical dictionary for masking contains 4231 medical terms related to the gastrointestinal area.

### 4.2   Experiment Setup

To compare the different self-supervision strategies we experiment with two pre-trained language models, T5 (T5-small) [19] and BART (BART-base) [9]. Two additional variants of the PubMed dataset were created to support self-supervision strategies: masking and paraphrasing. The hyper-parameters for fine-tuning were kept constant across all strategies as: optimiser is AdamW [11]; loss is cross-entropy; learning rate is $2e-5$; and batch size is 16. The PubMed dataset was split 90/10 as training and validation sets and the fine-tuning was early-stopped between 10–40 epochs based on minimal validation loss. All strategies were evaluated across four commercial ASR transcriptions of the GCD dataset

**Table 1.** Summary of the GCD dataset

| Feature | Value |
| --- | --- |
| No. of audio files | **7** |
| Mean length of an audio file | **4 min 49 s** |
| Mean no. of utterances in a file | **47** |
| Mean no. of words in an utterance | **93** |

**Table 2.** Examples from the GCD dataset

| Gold Reference | Transcription Output |
|---|---|
| So do you have any ideas as to what might be the cause of your symptoms at the moment? | So do you have any ideas as to what might be the cause of your symptoms at the moment? |
| Have you noticed any changes in your weight? | Do you noticed any changes in your *wit*? |
| Okay have you noticed any mucus in your bowel motions? | Okay have you noticed any mucus in your *bible Moshe*? |

**Table 3.** PubMed gastrointestinal dataset pre-processed for self-supervision strategies

| Task | Input | Output |
|---|---|---|
| Summarisation | Helicobacter pylori is a worldwide infection. It is estimated that approximately 50% of the general population is affected, but this percentage varies considerably between countries. ... This study confirms relatively high prevalence of H. pylori seropositivity among Italian healthy adults and points to sex, age, BMI and sociocultural class as persisting determinant features of H. pylori infection. | Determinants of Helicobacter pylori seroprevalence among Italian blood donors. |
| Paraphrasing | Determinants of seroprevalence of Helicobacter pylori among Italian blood donors. | |
| Mask-filling | Determinants *<mask>* *<mask>* pylori *<mask>* among Italian blood donors. | |
| Paraphrasing-to-masking | Determinants *<mask>* *<mask>* pylori *<mask>* among Italian blood donors. | |
| Masking-to-paraphrasing | Determinants of seroprevalence of Helicobacter pylori among Italian blood donors. | |
| Med-mask-filling | Determinants *<mask>* *<mask>* *<mask>* *<mask>* among Italian *<mask>* donors. | |
| Med-mask-filling (cm-25) | Determinants of *<mask>* pylori *<mask>* among Italian blood donors. | |
| Med-mask-filling (cm-25*) | Determinants of *<mask>* pylori *<mask>* among Italian blood donors | |

generated using Amazon Web Services (AWS) Transcribe, Google Speech-to-text, Microsoft Speech-to-text, and IBM Watson. For med-mask-filling masking percentage $(p)$ is considered as 25% denoted by $cm - 25$.

Language models were implemented using Python Hugging Face and PyTorch frameworks while maintaining all default hyper-parameters from the base models. For the summarisation task, the encoder input and decoder output sequence lengths were set to 1024 and 128, respectively; for paraphrasing and mask-filling tasks, both encoder input and decoder sequence lengths were set to 512. Our model implementation and the reproducible code are available in GitHub[2] and the fine-tuned model variants and PubMed datasets are publicly available in Huggingface[3].

### 4.3   Performance Metric

Word Error Rate (WER) was selected to measure the performance of clinical dialogue error correction. WER has been used as a performance metric in ASR systems [2,3] and in post-ASR error correction [8,12]. Given a language model output and a reference text, where $N$ refers to the number of words in the reference text and $SUB$, $DEL$ and $INS$ refer to the number of substitutions, deletions, and insertions operations needed to transform the reference text to the language model output, WER is calculated as in Eq. 1.

$$WER = \frac{SUB + DEL + INS}{N} \tag{1}$$

Lower WER scores are desirable as they indicate higher accuracy in speech recognition systems, reflecting a smaller number of word-level errors in the transcriptions.

### 4.4   Results

Table 4 presents a comparison of WER scores from commercial ASR systems and language models where we applied different self-supervision strategies. The WER of commercial ASR transcription against reference text is considered the baseline against which we want to improve. The best performing self-supervision strategy for each language model is highlighted in bold text. Overall, the best performing strategy is med-mask-filling with the BART model, and it has reduced WER by 10.27% of Microsoft, 12.13 % of IBM and 16.01% of Google transcriptions. In the case of AWS, while both med-mask-filling and mask-filling did lead to improvements, the degree of enhancement was not as substantial when compared to the other ASR systems.

Apart from the missed transcription of clinical terms, different ASR systems introduce different types of errors when generating transcripts from the audio. For example, Google ASR drops many words from the ASR output based on low

---

[2] https://github.com/gayaninan/clinical-error-correction.
[3] https://huggingface.co/gayanin.

**Table 4.** Comparison of self-supervision strategies for clinical dialogue error correction

| Model | Self-supervision Strategy | GCD Dataset WER (%) | | | |
|---|---|---|---|---|---|
| | | AWS Transcribe | Microsoft | IBM Watson | Google |
| Baseline (Commercial ASR) | | 33.02 | 29.03 | 44.28 | 47.78 |
| T5 | Summarisation | 63.39 | 66.89 | 69.44 | 73.80 |
| | Paraphrasing | 48.87 | 47.24 | 54.52 | 57.97 |
| | Mask-filling | 38.83 | 35.86 | 45.16 | 46.87 |
| | Masking-to-paraphrasing | 43.28 | 50.89 | 40.41 | 47.56 |
| | Paraphrasing-to-masking | 39.79 | 46.36 | 34.42 | 45.89 |
| | Med-mask-filling | 56.39 | 51.23 | 58.79 | 61.61 |
| | Med-mask-filling (cm-25) | 48.08 | 47.08 | 55.09 | 57.89 |
| | Med-mask-filling (cm-25*) | 46.10 | 43.03 | 52.23 | 53.06 |
| BART | Summarisation | 76.61 | 77.03 | 78.10 | 75.56 |
| | Paraphrasing | 43.31 | 37.46 | 47.51 | 49.48 |
| | Mask-filling | **32.38** | 26.38 | 38.92 | 40.43 |
| | Masking-to-paraphrasing | 46.43 | 41.45 | 49.24 | 51.15 |
| | Paraphrasing-to-masking | 32.77 | 26.82 | 39.45 | 40.97 |
| | Med-mask-filling | 32.53 | **26.05** | **38.91** | **40.13** |
| | Med-mask-filling (cm-25) | 32.61 | 26.48 | 39.28 | 40.69 |
| | Med-mask-filling (cm-25*) | 32.75 | 26.61 | 39.43 | 40.90 |

transcription confidence. Accordingly, we observe increased deletion operations required to convert the reference to the ASR output (in WER calculation).

We also observed that various ASR systems introduced distinct types of errors while generating transcripts. To investigate this further, in Fig. 3, we analysed the $INS$, $DEL$, and $SUB$ operation counts for the language models that achieved the best performance for each self-supervision strategy. Google ASR tends to drop several words from the ASR output due to low transcription confidence. As a result, we noticed that there is an increased number of deletion operations required to transform the reference text into the ASR output during the calculation of WER.

In addition to that, summarisation resulted in the highest WER scores due to the length difference between generated and reference text, which makes it an unsuitable strategy for error correction. Intuitively, mask filling is more similar to error correction than paraphrasing, which is evidenced in the results. Accordingly, we use mask-filling in a domain-specific approach with additional emphasis given to correcting clinical terms (by masking clinical terms).

Comparing BART and T5, our results showed that BART is more suitable for clinical dialogue error correction. BART and T5 are both language models pretrained for de-noising. To create noise, T5 masked 15% of words in a sequence, each word replaced by a mask [19] whereas BART used text infilling where zero or more consecutive words are replaced by a single mask [9]. Accordingly, BART had learned to predict the number of words masked in addition to predicting

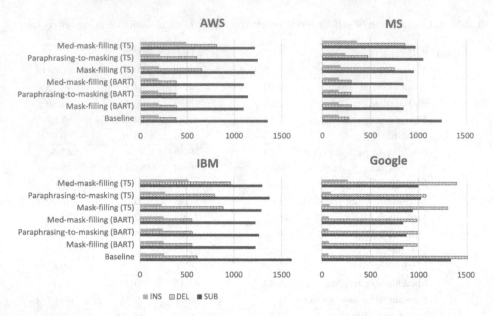

**Fig. 3.** INS, DEL, SUB operation counts for the best performing models for each self-supervision strategy

masked words. This is advantageous when performing clinical dialogue error correction where clinical terms can be erroneously transcribed into one or more commonly occurring words.

## 5   Conclusion

In this paper, we introduce a novel strategy of self-supervision for the task of clinical dialogue error correction utilizing language models. Our method addresses the challenge of sparse real-world clinical dialogue data by incorporating clinical data from the public domain. Our findings reveal that the proposed med-mask-filling strategy effectively reduces transcription errors when benchmarked against prevalent commercial ASR systems. The results underline the criticality of not only choosing the right self-supervision strategy but also understanding the impacts of varying error types generated by ASR systems. Moving forward, our focus will be on refining the GCD dataset and researching ways to continue the reduction of transcription errors. An in-depth analysis of language model outputs indicates an opportunity for further narrowing the domain-specific vocabulary gap, suggesting that the integration of knowledge graph representations is a promising path to explore.

**Acknowledgements.** We would like to thank the NHS Grampian, including Amy Kousha, John Thomson and Jill Ferbrache, who helped to curate the IBD clinic role-playing dialogues.

# References

1. Cucu, H., Buzo, A., Besacier, L., Burileanu, C.: Statistical error correction methods for domain-specific ASR systems. In: Dediu, A.-H., Martín-Vide, C., Mitkov, R., Truthe, B. (eds.) SLSP 2013. LNCS (LNAI), vol. 7978, pp. 83–92. Springer, Heidelberg (2013). https://doi.org/10.1007/978-3-642-39593-2_7
2. Errattahi, R., El Hannani, A., Ouahmane, H.: Automatic speech recognition errors detection and correction: a review. Procedia Comput. Sci. **128**, 32–37 (2018). 1st International Conference on Natural Language and Speech Processing
3. Filippidou, F., Moussiades, L.: A benchmarking of IBM, Google and wit automatic speech recognition systems. In: Maglogiannis, I., Iliadis, L., Pimenidis, E. (eds.) AIAI 2020. IAICT, vol. 583, pp. 73–82. Springer, Cham (2020). https://doi.org/10.1007/978-3-030-49161-1_7
4. Humphries, J.J., Woodland, P.C., Pearce, D.J.B.: Using accent-specific pronunciation modelling for robust speech recognition. Proceeding of Fourth International Conference on Spoken Language Processing, ICSLP 199, vol.6 4, pp. 2324–2327 (1996)
5. Jain, A., Upreti, M., Jyothi, P.: Improved accented speech recognition using accent embeddings and multi-task learning. In: INTERSPEECH (2018)
6. Kamper, H., Niesler, T.: Multi-accent speech recognition of Afrikaans, black and white varieties of south African English. In: Proceedings of the Annual Conference of the International Speech Communication Association, INTERSPEECH, pp. 3189–3192 (2011)
7. Leng, Y., et al.: FastCorrect 2: fast error correction on multiple candidates for automatic speech recognition. In: Findings of the Association for Computational Linguistics: EMNLP 2021, pp. 4328–4337. Association for Computational Linguistics, Punta Cana (2021)
8. Leng, Y., et al.: FastCorrect: fast error correction with edit alignment for automatic speech recognition. In: Ranzato, M., Beygelzimer, A., Dauphin, Y., Liang, P., Vaughan, J.W. (eds.) Advances in Neural Information Processing Systems, vol. 34, pp. 21708–21719. Curran Associates, Inc. (2021)
9. Lewis, M., et al.: BART: Denoising sequence-to-sequence pre-training for natural language generation, translation, and comprehension. In: Proceedings of the 58th Annual Meeting of the Association for Computational Linguistics, pp. 7871–7880. Association for Computational Linguistics, Online (2020)
10. Li, W., Di, H., Wang, L., Ouchi, K., Lu, J.: Boost transformer with BERT and copying mechanism for ASR error correction. In: 2021 International Joint Conference on Neural Networks (IJCNN), pp. 1–6. IEEE (2021)
11. Loshchilov, I., Hutter, F.: Decoupled weight decay regularization. In: International Conference on Learning Representations (2019)
12. Mani, A., Palaskar, S., Konam, S.: Towards understanding ASR error correction for medical conversations. In: NLPMC (2020)
13. Mani, A., Palaskar, S., Meripo, N.V., Konam, S., Metze, F.: ASR error correction and domain adaptation using machine translation. In: ICASSP 2020–2020 IEEE International Conference on Acoustics, Speech and Signal Processing (ICASSP), pp. 6344–6348. IEEE (2020)
14. McDonald, A., Sherlock, J.: A long and winding road - improving communication with patients in the NHS (2016)
15. Nanayakkara, G., Wiratunga, N., Corsar, D., Martin, K., Wijekoon, A.: Clinical dialogue transcription error correction using Seq2Seq models. In: Shaban-Nejad,

A., Michalowski, M., Bianco, S. (eds.) Multimodal AI in Healthcare. Studies in Computational Intelligence, vol. 1060, pp. 41–57. Springer, Cham (2023). https://doi.org/10.1007/978-3-031-14771-5_4D

16. Neumann, M., King, D., Beltagy, I., Ammar, W.: ScispaCy: fast and robust models for biomedical natural language processing. In: Proceedings of the 18th BioNLP Workshop and Shared Task, pp. 319–327. Association for Computational Linguistics, Florence (2019)

17. Quiroz, J., Laranjo, L., Kocaballi, A.B., Berkovsky, S., Rezazadegan, D., Coiera, E.: Challenges of developing a digital scribe to reduce clinical documentation burden. NPJ Digit. Med. **2**, 114 (2019)

18. Radford, A., Wu, J., Child, R., Luan, D., Amodei, D., Sutskever, I.: Language models are unsupervised multitask learners (2019)

19. Raffel, C., et al.: Exploring the limits of transfer learning with a unified text-to-text transformer. J. Mach. Learn. Res. **21**(140), 1–67 (2020)

20. Sarma, A., Palmer, D.D.: Context-based speech recognition error detection and correction. In: Proceedings of HLT-NAACL 2004: Short Papers, pp. 85–88. Association for Computational Linguistics, Boston (2004)

21. Vaswani, A., et al.: Attention is all you need. In: Guyon, I., et al. (eds.) Advances in Neural Information Processing Systems, vol. 30. Curran Associates, Inc. (2017)

22. Wagner, R.A., Fischer, M.J.: The string-to-string correction problem. J. ACM (JACM) **21**(1), 168–173 (1974)

23. Zhang, Y., Baldridge, J., He, L.: PAWS: paraphrase adversaries from word scrambling. In: Proceedings of the 2019 Conference of the North American Chapter of the Association for Computational Linguistics: Human Language Technologies, Volume 1 (Long and Short Papers), pp. 1298–1308. Association for Computational Linguistics, Minneapolis (2019)

24. Zhao, Y., Yang, X., Wang, J., Gao, Y., Yan, C., Zhou, Y.: BART based semantic correction for mandarin automatic speech recognition system. In: Proceedings of the Interspeech 2021, pp. 2017–2021 (2021)

# Exploring Multilingual Word Embedding Alignments in BERT Models: A Case Study of English and Norwegian

Pernille Aaby[1], Daniel Biermann[2], Anis Yazidi[1], Gustavo Borges Moreno e Mello[1], and Fabrizio Palumbo[1(✉)]

[1] Artificial Intelligence Lab (AI Lab), Institutt for informasjonsteknologi,
Oslo Metropolitan University, Oslo, Norway
`fabrizio.palumbo@oslomet.no`
[2] Centre for Artificial Intelligence Research (CAIR), Department of ICT,
University of Agder, Grimstad, Norway

**Abstract.** Contextual language models, such as transformers, can solve a wide range of language tasks ranging from text classification to question answering and machine translation. Like many deep learning models, the performance heavily depends on the quality and amount of data available for training. This poses a problem for low-resource languages, such as Norwegian, that can not provide the necessary amount of training data. In this article, we investigate the use of multilingual models as a step toward overcoming the data sparsity problem for minority languages. In detail, we study how words are represented by multilingual BERT models across two languages of our interest: English and Norwegian. Our analysis shows that multilingual models similarly encode English-Norwegian word pairs. The multilingual model automatically aligns semantics across languages without supervision. Additionally, our analysis also shows that embedding a word encodes information about the language to which it belongs. We, therefore, believe that in pre-trained multilingual models' knowledge from one language can be transferred to another without direct supervision and help solve the data sparsity problem for minor languages.

**Keywords:** Natural Language Processing · Multilingual Bert · Word Alignment · Data Sparsity

## 1 Introduction

Over recent years, the field of AI has made impressive progress regarding the performance of natural language processing tasks such as text classification, question answering, machine translation, or language generation. This progress is mainly driven by purely data-driven models such as transformers. To encode how words relate to their context, transformers are pre-trained on vast, unlabeled and mostly monolingual training corpora. This approach is powerful for languages such as English or Spanish, with an abundance of language resources consisting in raw text, labeled datasets, and benchmarks. However, when it comes to low-resource languages, such as Norwegian, the

M. Bramer and F. Stahl (Eds.): SGAI 2023, LNAI 14381, pp. 47–58, 2023.
https://doi.org/10.1007/978-3-031-47994-6_4

available language datasets are often limited. Unfortunately, the performance in such data-driven models and approaches heavily depends on the quality and amount of training data available. That is, good performance depends on high-quality datasets. At the written time, there are 2181 matches for English datasets and only 67 for Norwegian datasets on huggingface.co[1]. More training data tend to improve the performance of language models [3,17]. Consequently, monolingual Norwegian language models will likely not achieve the same performance as monolingual English language models.

Most existing language models today have been trained on monolingual corpora [7,14], which do not benefit languages with sparse data availability. Isbister et al. [11] proposed an approach that translates the text from a low-resource language to a high-resource language. Then, it uses a state-of-the-art performing model trained on high-resource language to alleviate the data sparsity problem. However, recent work shows that specific multilingual language models manage to align words from different languages without learning from parallel data, which machine translation requires [4,15]. Therefore, we pose the questions:

- Can multilingual models relieve the need for monolingual models?
- Can knowledge from one language be transferred to another without parallel data?

In this article, we explore the similarities and dissimilarities between the word representations in English and Norwegian, using two multilingual language models. To this end, we use different methods from recent literature and combine them in a comprehensive study of the case of the English-Norwegian language pair.

To find similarities we evaluate word retrieval performance, from an English source vocabulary to a Norwegian target vocabulary. To find dissimilarities, we quantify the accuracy of retrieving the original language from the word representation. All methods are non-parametric and rely purely on vector proximity. The model architecture we have used is BERT (Bidirectional Encoder from Transformer) [7] since previous work has shown its capability to align words automatically [4,16].

We believe that this exploration can provide the research community with a better understanding of how the information of different languages manifests inside the word representations of multilingual models and ultimately help improve existing models and applications that suffer from data sparsity.

## 2   Related Work

### 2.1   Multilingual Word Retrieval

Mikolov et al. [22] noticed that the distribution of word embeddings in latent space showed similar characteristics across different languages. Motivated by the similarity of distributions, they hypothesized that they could align two distributions with word embeddings from two different languages to create a bilingual dictionary with word retrieval. Their technique relied on bilingual parallel corpora. Conneau et al. [6] showed that it was possible to align two-word embedding distributions from different languages without any supervision (parallel corpora). They utilized adversarial training to learn a linear mapping from the source to the target language, alleviating the need for parallel corpora.

---

[1] !https://huggingface.co/datasets Visited: 19.01.2023.

## 2.2   Multilingual BERT

BERT is a transformer-based [30] model which improved state-of-the-art results on several NLP tasks at the time of release [7]. It improved on question-answering tasks like SQuAD v1.1 [25] and SQuAD v2.0 [24], and language understanding tasks like GLUE [31] and MutliNLI [33]. The model is trained on vast amounts of text corpora, the original English BERT used the English part of Wikipedia [7], but today it is being trained on bigger collections, even book collections from a whole library [13]. The model has been trained for several languages like French, Swedish, and Norwegian [14,19,20]. BERT can also be trained in several languages simultaneously to obtain multilingual understanding. mBERT is one of these models, and it is trained on Wikipedia corpus for 104 different languages, including English and Norwegian[2].

Notram, Norwegian Transformer Model, is a BERT model initialized from mBERT and further trained on mostly Norwegian book-corpus data [13]. Although the model is mainly trained on Norwegian corpus, after initialization, the authors estimate that a portion of 4% is English. The model scores high on Named Entity Recognition both for the Norwegian language and the English language.

Previous work [4,15] also shows that the semantics of two (and more) languages align automatically in BERT. So the model does not only represent two languages separately, but it is also able to encode connections between two languages through shared semantics of the words, without being trained on parallel data.

## 2.3   From Contextual to Static Embeddings

In order to benefit from previous benchmarks like SimLex999 [10], WordSim353 [1] and SimVerb3500 [9] that evaluate semantics, Bommasani et al. [2] distilled a set of static word embeddings from contextual word embeddings. This way the results could be compared to traditional word embeddings [12,21,23]. To create the static word embeddings from BERT they tried different aggregation and pooling strategies. The best-performing aggregation method was to take the average over several contexts, also referred to as AOC (Average Over Context). They also used *mean pooling*, taking the mean of all token representations over subtokens of a word in case a word consists of more than one token.

## 2.4   Probing BERT

Probing BERT has become a popular area of research to better justify its success and understand the model better so it is easier to improve the architecture [27]. It entails creating a simple classifier and using the features from the pre-trained model. If the simple classifier manages to solve the task, then we can assume that the necessary information is already within the features we extract.

From previous work, we know that BERT represents words with information about syntax and semantics [27]. Tenney et al. [28] discovered that BERT hierarchically learns information that corresponds to the traditional NLP (Natural Language Processing)

---

[2] !https://huggingface.co/bert-base-multilingual-cased.

pipeline. Starting with local syntax structure such as POS tagging and parsing in the lower layers, while finding named entity recognition, semantic roles, and co-reference are information encoded later in the model in the respective order. Similar discoveries can be found in other works as well [16,29].

Naturally, since BERT is a contextual model representing a word based on not only itself but also the surrounding words, the question of whether one could distinguish different meanings of an ambiguous through the representation arose. In previous work [18,32] they find that ambiguous words divide different meanings into clusters from the contextual representation, although it is not always the same clusters as we would have defined from a human perspective.

## 3   Methods

Our analysis examines similarities and differences between word representations in two languages. Similarities are found through static word retrieval and differences through language detection. Our non-parametric method only relies on finding the most similar embedding(s) from a source word to a target collection. We used KNN (K- Nearest Neighbours) with cosine similarity to find the most similar vectors.

### 3.1   Static Word Retrieval

Following the work by Bommasani et al. [2] we created a static set of word embeddings by taking the AOC of several contextual embeddings for a term $t$. The contextual embedding for word $t$ is obtained from a context $c_t \in C_t$, where each $c_t$ is two sentences from the relevant language corpus.

$$s_t = \frac{1}{N_t} \sum_{n=1}^{N} w_{tn} \tag{1}$$

$w_{tn}$ is the $n$th contextual embedding for the number of contexts $N_t = |C_t|$. For words that consist of more than one workpiece, we used mean pooling, taking the mean of all subtokens, to aggregate all token embeddings.

$$w_{tn} = \frac{1}{I_t} \sum_{i=1}^{I} p_{ti} \tag{2}$$

$p_{ti}$ is the $i$th token in the word. We created static embeddings for all 13 intermediate representations from BERT, one after all the 12 stacked layers and the input layer. We aimed to retrieve a Norwegian target word from an English source word. The objective becomes, for each of the English word representations $s_{i-en}$, evaluate the cosine similarity to all the Norwegian word representations $s_{j-no}$, rank the similarities, and return the top(@) match(s). If a translation of the English word is one of the returned words, we achieved a correct word retrieval.

$$k\text{-}neighbours(i) = \underset{j}{\operatorname{argmax}} \ sim(s_{i-en}, s_{j-no}) \tag{3}$$

$$y_i = \begin{cases} 1, & \text{if } k\text{-neighbours}(i) \in \text{translation}(s_{no}) \\ 0, & \text{otherwise} \end{cases} \tag{4}$$

$$\text{accuracy static word retrieval} = \frac{1}{T} \sum_{i=1}^{T} y_i \tag{5}$$

$T$ is the number of terms in the English vocabulary.

Liu et al. [15] test if word retrieval performance increases by doing a *mean shift*. Mean shift entails shifting from an English source word to be closer to a Norwegian target word by first subtracting the mean of all the English word embeddings and then adding the mean of all the Norwegian word embeddings. We define a language vector as the mean of all the static word embeddings in one vocabulary.

$$L_l = \frac{1}{T} \sum_{t=1}^{T} w_t \tag{6}$$

$l \in \{English, Norwegian\}$ and $T$ is the number of words in each vocabulary. Mean shift:

$$s_{t,en->no} = s_{t,en} - L_{en} + L_{no} \tag{7}$$

$L_{en}$ and $L_{no}$ are language vectors for English and Norwegian respectively.

$$y_{i-l} = \begin{cases} 1, & \text{if} \quad sim(s_{i-l}, L_{en}) > sim(s_{i-l}, L_{no}) \quad and \quad l = en \\ 1, & \text{elif} \quad sim(s_{i-l}, L_{en}) < sim(s_{i-l}, L_{no}) \quad and \quad l = no \\ 0, & \text{otherwise} \end{cases} \tag{8}$$

$$\text{accuracy language detection} = \frac{1}{2T} \sum_{i=1}^{T} y_{i-en} + \frac{1}{2T} \sum_{i=1}^{T} y_{i-no} \tag{9}$$

## 3.2 Language Detection

Motivated by the fact that words from the same language could be aggregated to a language vector, we asked the question:
Can we detect the language of a word based on the similarity to the language embeddings?
We detected the language by evaluating which language vector a word representation is most similar to.

## 3.3 Data

The Norwegian News Corpus[3] is used as the raw text corpora for the Norwegian part. We only used the part in Norwegian bokmål (not nynorsk). The articles in the dataset

---

[3] !https://www.nb.no/sprakbanken/ressurskatalog/oai-nb-no-sbr-4/.

are from multiple different newspapers, such as "VG", "Aftenposten" and "Dagens næringsliv" etc., collected from the years 1998 to 2019. We chose a set of contexts from the corpus for each word in our Norwegian vocabulary between 100 and 500. A context is defined as two sentences.

The vocabulary is restricted to only include the 50,000 most common words from the Norwegian News Corpus. In addition, we checked that the word is present in a Norwegian wordlist for Bokmål[4].

To evaluate the word retrieval from English to Norwegian, we have used the English-Norwegian word benchmark from MUSE[5] [6]. We only used the word pairs, where the Norwegian word is in our top 50,000 vocabularies, and the English word is present in the Brown corpus[6] [8]. Some English words have more than one Norwegian word translation. We define a *correct word retrieval* as at least one match.

The Brown corpus gives the context sentences for the English word embedding vocabulary. The number of contexts for a word is the number of times a word stands in the Brown corpus but a maximum of 500 times. We only obtained static word embeddings for the words in the MUSE benchmark. The MUSE-filtered vocabulary ended up with approximately 12,000 English source words.

## 4 Results

### 4.1 Static Word Retrieval

In Fig. 1 we report the results of the English to Norwegian word retrieval using KNN and cosine similarity. We compare the performance of both mBERT (Fig. 1a) and Notram (Fig. 1c) for different numbers of top matches (@1, @3, @10). Notram achieved better accuracy than mBERT in general. The middle layers seem to perform best for both models, with Notram achieving around 50% at @1 match and more than 70% accuracy when using the @10 matches at layer 7. In addition, for the Notram model. we notice a dip in performance for layer 11. Overall, we argue that BERT models are capable of aligning semantics across English and Norwegian without using any supervised datasets with parallel sentences.

### 4.2 Static Word Retrieval with Mean Shift

Figure 1b and Fig. 1d show the static word retrieval performances when adjusted with the mean shift. To illustrate the impact of the mean shift on the word retrieval performance better, the performance increase between the shifted and non-shifted model is depicted by the dashed lines. We can see that the overall influence of the mean shift on performance is relatively low across all layers. When mean shifting, the model retains word retrieval accuracy better from the middle layers to the subsequent layers than without the mean shift. The maximum word retrieval performance increase is reached in layer 11 for the Notram model, improving by 8% for K at @1, @3, and @10. Thus, the mean shift seems to alleviate the cause of the performance dip seen before in later layers.

---

[4] !https://www.nb.no/sprakbanken/en/resource-catalogue/oai-nb-no-sbr-23/.
[5] !https://github.com/facebookresearch/MUSE.
[6] !https://www.nltk.org/nltk_data/.

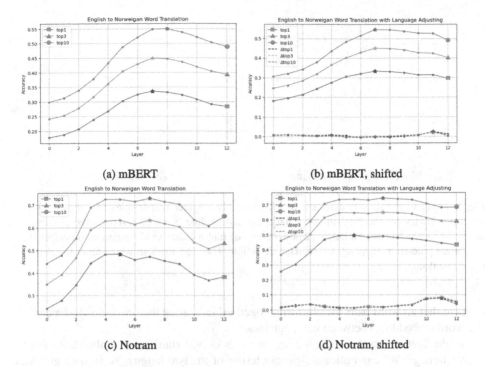

(a) mBERT

(b) mBERT, shifted

(c) Notram

(d) Notram, shifted

**Fig. 1.** Static word retrieval performance from English to Norwegian with layer-wise performance accuracy with and without mean shift. The lower dashed lines depict the performance increase when using the mean shift. The star marker shows at which layer the performance peaked. Both models experience the highest performance increase in layer 11 for all chosen @matches.

### 4.3 Language Detection

Figure 2 reports the results from the language detection experiment. The non-parametric method clearly shows that it is possible to find the language of a word using this method as the performance reaches almost 100% in the top-performing layer. The language detection accuracy reaches values above 95% for both models as soon as layer 1. This strongly indicates that the closest language vector can serve as a strong predictor for the language of the embedding.

### 4.4 Both Semantics and Language Properties Can Cluster

For a more qualitative inspection of the word representations, Fig. 3 illustrates both semantic alignment and language properties between English and Norwegian. The top graph Fig. 3a, inspired by previous work on semantic alignment in BERT [4], shows a plot comparing a set of 5 words in each English and Norwegian, respectively. The words were taken from the parallel corpus with sentences from riksrevisjonen[7] [26]. We can

---

[7] !https://www.elrc-share.eu/repository/browse/bilingual-english-norwegian-parallel-corpus-from-the-office-of-the-auditor-general-riksrevisjonen-website/a5d2470201e311e9b7d40015 5d0267060fffdc9258a741659ce9e52ef15a7c26/.

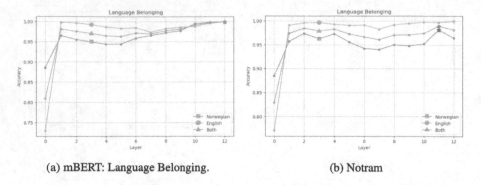

(a) mBERT: Language Belonging.                  (b) Notram

**Fig. 2.** Layer wise language detection performance. The lighter line (circle) describes the prediction accuracy for the English vocabulary, the darkest line (square) describes the prediction accuracy for the Norwegian language and the line of intermediate shade (triangle) describes the combined prediction accuracy of language detection. The stars mark in which layer the performance peaks.

observe that all word pairs are clustering together, indicating the semantic alignment of the word embeddings between the languages.

In the bottom graph Fig. 3b we see two sets of 500 static word embeddings from each language. We can notice a clear clustering of the two languages. In both graphs, we reduce the embedding dimension to two dimensions with the t-SNE method. This further solidifies that BERT models are able to align semantics across English and Norwegian without using any supervised data

## 5   Discussion

Our analysis shows that layers 5–9 (middle layers) have the highest accuracy on static word retrieval. This result is in line with previous work on semantic similarity [5]. We argue that the best-performing layers in semantic similarity will also be the best-performing layers in semantic alignment between two languages. Although we observe a clear separation between languages in the word representation space, the mean shift method did not significantly impact the word retrieval accuracy. In layer 11, the accuracy does increase by around 8% in the Notram model. However, in the best performing layer of the same model, layer 7 (or 5), the increase is only around 1%. We consider this a slight change since the accuracy at @1 is around 50%. Overall, the word retrieval results suggest that the hypothesis that translating one language to another in the word representation space by looking at the closest matched embedding of the other language is a promising approach. Though, the low impact of the mean shift indicates that the translation from one language to another is not as simple as shifting the embedding by a simple mean language vector. This warrants further investigation into better methods to create language vector representations that might improve the impact of such a language vector shift. Nevertheless, the language vectors from the mean shift analysis

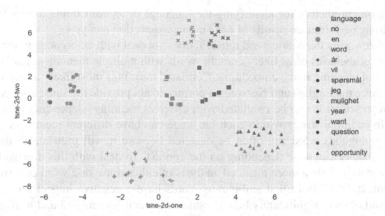

(a) Visualizing contextual word embeddings for word pairs in English and Norwegian. Contextual embeddings taken from layer 8 of the Notram model and the English contextual embeddings have experienced a mean shift. The word embeddings are reduced to 2D with t-SNE. The darker colored markers show contextual word embeddings for Norwegian while the lighter color show contextual embedding for English. Each word pair has its own marker.

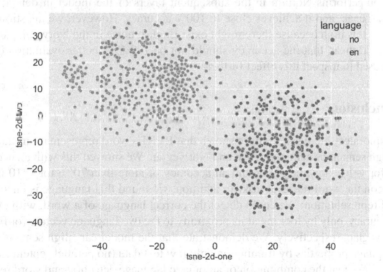

(b) 500 random words from Norwegian and English vocabulary respectively. The static word embeddings are from Notram layer 12. The word embeddings are reduced to 2D with t-SNE. Lighter points correspond to English embeddings and darkest points correspond to Norwegian embeddings.

**Fig. 3.** Visualizing static and contextual word embeddings from BERT

remain strong predictors for identifying the language of an embedding as can be seen by the strong performance results of our language detection analysis.

It is noteworthy that static word retrieval does not deal with ambiguous words. Both language vocabularies most likely contain words with multiple meanings, leading to a conflation of meaning in the embedding. Conflated meanings most likely affected word retrieval since the English and Norwegian corpus do not provide the same contexts, and a word representation can be conflated with different meanings depending on the text corpus. In addition, words within each language can have different meanings. Therefore, an ambiguous word can often be detected because it will translate to different words in another language depending on the context. To deal with this downside, one would have to include a more nuanced analysis of either sense or a word pair from the same context. We believe that ambiguous words have a negative impact on accuracy as we could observe significantly better results when considering @3 and @10 nearest neighbours, with an increase of more than a 20% going from @1 to @10.

Norwegian is a language that borrows many words and phrases from English. It can be single words like "skateboard" or whole phrases like movie titles. Even though we filtered out sentences detected as English from the Norwegian text corpus, single words and smaller phrases may have been hard to remove. The effect could be English *noise* in the Norwegian part of the corpus and hence an effect in language detection. mBERT outperforms Notram in the subsequent layers of the model in detecting the correct language, and it achieves close to 100% accuracy. However, we question if the accuracy is this high because there might exist English noise in the Norwegian corpus, which would mean that the accuracy should not be 100%. A better evaluation dataset could be used to inspect this effect further.

## 6    Conclusion

In this exploratory analysis, we have shown that BERT's word representations automatically align semantics across English and Norwegian. We showed this with an accuracy of 50% for @1 nearest neighbor and an accuracy of more than 70 % for @10 nearest neighbor on the word retrieval task. In addition, we found that language is encoded in the word representation: We could detect the correct language of a word, with close to 100% accuracy, only by looking at its proximity to the two language vectors for English and Norwegian, respectively. We demonstrate that the model can align semantics and learn language properties by training on only raw text data (no parallel sentences).

We believe that the combination of automatic language detection and word retrieval between language embeddings allows for knowledge to be transferred between languages, ultimately helping alleviate the data sparsity problem in low-resource languages, such as Norwegian. While our results show promising tendencies, further investigations into reaching higher word retrieval accuracies and better aligning language vectors are warranted to make this approach reliable. We hope that our findings motivate new ways of using multilingual models and inspire more research in training and investigating multilingual models for low-resource languages.

# References

1. Agirre, E., Alfonseca, E., Hall, K., Kravalova, J., Pasca, M., Soroa, A.: A study on similarity and relatedness using distributional and wordnet-based approaches (2009)
2. Bommasani, R., Davis, K., Cardie, C.: Interpreting pretrained contextualized representations via reductions to static embeddings. In: Proceedings of the 58th Annual Meeting of the Association for Computational Linguistics, pp. 4758–4781 (2020)
3. Brown, T.B., et al.: Language models are few-shot learners. arXiv preprint arXiv:2005.14165 (2020)
4. Cao, S., Kitaev, N., Klein, D.: Multilingual alignment of contextual word representations. arXiv preprint arXiv:2002.03518 (2020)
5. Chronis, G., Erk, K.: When is a bishop not like a rook? When it's like a rabbi! Multi-prototype BERT embeddings for estimating semantic relationships. In: Proceedings of the 24th Conference on Computational Natural Language Learning, pp. 227–244 (2020)
6. Conneau, A., Lample, G., Ranzato, M., Denoyer, L., Jégou, H.: Word translation without parallel data. arXiv preprint arXiv:1710.04087 (2017)
7. Devlin, J., Chang, M.W., Lee, K., Toutanova, K.: BERT: pre-training of deep bidirectional transformers for language understanding. In: NAACL HLT 2019–2019 Conference of the North American Chapter of the Association for Computational Linguistics: Human Language Technologies - Proceedings of the Conference 1(MLM), pp. 4171–4186 (2019)
8. Francis, W.N., Kucera, H.: Brown corpus manual. Lett. Editor **5**(2), 7 (1979)
9. Gerz, D., Vulić, I., Hill, F., Reichart, R., Korhonen, A.: SimVerb-3500: a large-scale evaluation set of verb similarity. arXiv preprint arXiv:1608.00869 (2016)
10. Hill, F., Reichart, R., Korhonen, A.: SimLex-999: evaluating semantic models with (genuine) similarity estimation. Comput. Linguist. **41**(4), 665 695 (2015)
11. Isbister, T., Carlsson, F., Sahlgren, M.: Should we stop training more monolingual models, and simply use machine translation instead? arXiv preprint arXiv:2104.10441 (2021)
12. Joulin, A., Grave, E., Bojanowski, P., Mikolov, T.: Bag of tricks for efficient text classification. In: 15th Conference of the European Chapter of the Association for Computational Linguistics, EACL 2017 - Proceedings of Conference, vol. 2 (2017). https://doi.org/10.18653/v1/e17-2068
13. Kummervold, P.E., la Rosa, J., Wetjen, F., Brygfjeld, S.A.: Operationalizing a national digital library: the case for a Norwegian transformer model. arXiv preprint arXiv:2104.09617 (2021)
14. Kutuzov, A., Barnes, J., Velldal, E., Øvrelid, L., Oepen, S.: Large-scale contextualised language modelling for Norwegian. arXiv preprint arXiv:2104.06546 (2021)
15. Liu, C.L., Hsu, T.Y., Chuang, Y.S., Lee, H.Y.: A study of cross-lingual ability and language-specific information in multilingual BERT. arXiv preprint arXiv:2004.09205 (2020)
16. Liu, N.F., Gardner, M., Belinkov, Y., Peters, M.E., Smith, N.A.: Linguistic knowledge and transferability of contextual representations. arXiv preprint arXiv:1903.08855 (2019)
17. Liu, Y., et al.: RoBERTa: a robustly optimized BERT pretraining approach. CoRR abs/1907.1 (2019). https://arxiv.org/abs/1907.11692
18. Loureiro, D., Rezaee, K., Pilehvar, M.T., Camacho-Collados, J.: Analysis and evaluation of language models for word sense disambiguation. Comput. Linguist. **47**, 387–443 (2021)
19. Malmsten, M., Börjeson, L., Haffenden, C.: Playing with words at the national library of Sweden-making a Swedish BERT. arXiv preprint arXiv:2007.01658 (2020)
20. Martin, L., et al.: CamemBERT: a tasty French language model. arXiv preprint arXiv:1911.03894 (2019)
21. Mikolov, T., Chen, K., Corrado, G., Dean, J.: Efficient estimation of word representations in vector space. In: 1st International Conference on Learning Representations, ICLR 2013 - Workshop Track Proceedings ICLR 2013, pp. 1–12 (2013). https://arxiv.org/abs/1301.3781

22. Mikolov, T., Le, Q.V., Sutskever, I.: Exploiting similarities among languages for machine translation. arXiv preprint arXiv:1309.4168 (2013)
23. Pennington, J., Socher, R., Manning, C.D.: GloVe: global vectors for word representation. In: EMNLP 2014–2014 Conference on Empirical Methods in Natural Language Processing, Proceedings of the Conference (2014). https://doi.org/10.3115/v1/d14-1162
24. Rajpurkar, P., Jia, R., Liang, P.: Know what you don't know: unanswerable questions for SQuAD. arXiv preprint arXiv:1806.03822 (2018)
25. Rajpurkar, P., Zhang, J., Lopyrev, K., Liang, P.: SQuad: 100,000+ questions for machine comprehension of text. In: EMNLP 2016 - Conference on Empirical Methods in Natural Language Processing, Proceedings (II), pp. 2383–2392 (2016). https://doi.org/10.18653/v1/d16-1264
26. Riksrevisjonen: Bilingual English-Norwegian parallel corpus from the Office of the auditor general (Riksrevisjonen) website - ELRC-SHARE (2018). https://www.elrc-share.eu/reposi tory/browse/bilingual-english-norwegian-parallel-corpus-from-the-office-of-the-auditor-gen eral-riksrevisjonen-website/a5d2470201e311e9b7d400155d0267060fffdc9258a741659ce9e 52ef15a7c26/
27. Rogers, A., Kovaleva, O., Rumshisky, A.: A primer in BERTology: what we know about how BERT works. Trans. Assoc. Comput. Linguist. **8**, 842–866 (2020)
28. Tenney, I., Das, D., Pavlick, E.: BERT rediscovers the classical NLP pipeline. arXiv preprint arXiv:1905.05950 (2019)
29. Tenney, I., et al.: What do you learn from context? Probing for sentence structure in contextualized word representations. arXiv preprint arXiv:1905.06316 (2019)
30. Vaswani, A., et al.: Attention is all you need. In: Advances in Neural Information Processing Systems 2017-(NIPS), pp. 5999–6009 (2017)
31. Wang, A., Singh, A., Michael, J., Hill, F., Levy, O., Bowman, S.R.: GLUE: a multitask benchmark and analysis platform for natural language understanding. arXiv preprint arXiv:1804.07461 (2018)
32. Wiedemann, G., Remus, S., Chawla, A., Biemann, C.: Does BERT make any sense? Interpretable word sense disambiguation with contextualized embeddings. arXiv preprint arXiv:1909.10430 (2019)
33. Williams, A., Nangia, N., Bowman, S.R.: A broad-coverage challenge corpus for sentence understanding through inference. arXiv preprint arXiv:1704.05426 (2017)

# Confidence Preservation Property in Knowledge Distillation Abstractions

Dmitry Vengertsev$^{(\boxtimes)}$ and Elena Sherman

Boise State University, Boise, USA
dmitryvengertsev@u.boisestate.edu, elenasherman@boisestate.edu

**Abstract.** Social media platforms prevent malicious activities by detecting harmful content of posts and comments. To that end, they employ large-scale deep neural network language models for sentiment analysis and content understanding. Some models, like BERT, are complex, and have numerous parameters, which makes them expensive to operate and maintain. To overcome these deficiencies, industry experts employ a knowledge distillation compression technique, where a distilled model is trained to reproduce the classification behavior of the original model. The distillation processes terminates when the distillation loss function reaches the stopping criteria. This function is mainly designed to ensure that the original and the distilled models exhibit alike classification behaviors. However, besides classification accuracy, there are additional properties of the original model that the distilled model should preserve to be considered as an appropriate abstraction.

In this work, we explore whether distilled TinyBERT models preserve confidence values of the original BERT models, and investigate how this confidence preservation property could guide tuning hyperparameters of the distillation process.

**Keywords:** Machine Learning Confidence · Knowledge Distillation · Model Property Preservation · Model Abstraction

## 1 Introduction

Deep neural language models such as BERT [2], GPT-3 [1] play a crucial role in screening social media for fake and harmful content [8]. To reliably classify information, those models require high precision, which often comes at the cost of increased the model's size. However, larger size models have high inference latency and are problematic to deploy on mobile devices and embedded systems. A traditional approach by verification community is to reduce large systems while preserving desirable properties through abstraction [18]. There are several examples of constructing explicit abstraction: conversion of neural network to Boolean combinations of linear arithmetic constraints [21], empirical extraction of a deterministic finite automaton using clustering of the hidden states of deep neural networks [27], and leveraged pruning during verification process [6].

M. Bramer and F. Stahl (Eds.): SGAI 2023, LNAI 14381, pp. 59–72, 2023.
https://doi.org/10.1007/978-3-031-47994-6_5

An orthogonal approach to creating smaller models through the knowledge transfer (training) from a larger model without a significant drop in accuracy is known as knowledge distillation. However, the majority of current distillation techniques focuses on the classification correctness while ignoring other properties of the teacher model.

In this work, we investigate whether the knowledge distillation [10] used in TinyBERT behaves as an abstraction of a large BERT model and preserves pairwise confidence property. We call this type of abstraction *implicit* since unlike the previously mentioned clustering and pruning abstraction techniques, it has no direct mappings between BERT and TinyBERT internal architectures.

In this paper, we outline the concept of confidence preservation property and establish a method for assessing it. To uncover the confidence-related distillation disagreements between the teacher and the student models, we introduce a pairwise confidence difference, Fig. 1. We evaluate the preservation of this property on six tasks from the General Language Understanding Evaluation (GLUE) dataset. Our results show that the distilled TinyBERT model maintains the confidence property of the original BERT model in three tasks. For the remaining three tasks, whose models fail to preserve the property, we modify the training hyperparameters so that these models maintain the confidence property without degrading the original accuracy.

Overall, this work has the following contributions: (1) Considering knowledge distillation as an implicit abstraction with anticipated property preservation characteristics. (2) A confidence property preservation criterion based on pair-wise confidence measurements and its empirical evaluations. (3) Identifying and empirically tuning hyperparameters in the distillation process to ensure the confidence property preservation.

## 2  Background and Motivation

### 2.1  Significance of Knowledge Distillation Models

Recent advancements in the area of machine learning for text are driven by transformer-based models. Unfortunately, the size and the efficiency of these models prohibit their use in resource-constrained and time-sensitive applications. For example, a baseline transformer model executes a single query in a few tenths of seconds, which is slow for real time systems. To reduce desirable response latency to milliseconds [15] compressed models that are obtained via knowledge distillation technique [10] are used. The technique essentially trains a compact model, referred to as the student, to reproduce the behavior of a larger model, known as the teacher.

In this paper we focus on distillation of BERT (Bidirectional Encoder Representations from Transformers) model [24], which has significantly advanced the state-of-the-art in natural language processing tasks such as language understanding, text classification, and language translation. Previous work distills BERT into smaller models such as single layer BiLSTM [23], DistilBERT [22], and TinyBERT [13]. In this paper, we examine property preservation of Tiny-BERT models since they outperform other distillation methods and also combine both response and feature-based knowledge transfers. The reason TinyBERT achieves superior accuracy is due to its pre-training feature and a specialized loss function. At the pre-training stage, obtaining a good initialization is crucial for the distillation of transformer-based models. Intermediate loss during feature-based distillation provides a boost of classification accuracy of at least 10% for most of the GLUE tasks [13].

## 2.2 TinyBERT Distillation

TinyBERT distillation consists of two stages: general distillation on general-domain corpus from Wikipedia and task-specific distillation on a specific task focused dataset.

Both the teacher $B$ and the student $S$ models have the same type of the layers, however student model has $m = 1, .., M$ transformer layers and teacher model has $n = 1, .., N > M$ such layers. Embedding layers for the student and the teacher are $m = 0$ and $n = 0$ correspondingly, and the prediction layers are labelled $m = M + 1$ and $n = N + 1$. There are several ways to map the $N$ layers of the teacher model to the $M$ layers of the student model. We use the uniform layer mapping strategy as it provides a superior accuracy for the majority of the tasks [13]. During the training of a student model, TinyBERT uses four loss functions: embedding distillation loss for $m = 0$, attention and hidden distillation losses for transformer layers $0 \leq m \leq M$, and finally, the distillation of the prediction layer. This work focuses on the distillation of the prediction layer, rather than intermediate layers.

At the prediction layer the loss is defined in Eq. 1, where the student cross entropy loss $L_{CE}$ is supplemented with the distillation objective $L_{dist}$ in order to penalize the loss between the student networks logits against the teachers logits, which determines distillation training objectives:

$$L = \alpha \cdot L_{CE} + (1 - \alpha) \cdot L_{distill}$$
$$= -\alpha \sum_i t_i \log y_i^{(S)} + (1 - \alpha) \sum_{x \in X^{train}} \|z^{(B(x))} - z^{(S(x))}\|^2 \qquad (1)$$

where $z^{(B)}$ and $z^{(S)}$ are the logits of the teacher $B$ and the student $S$, correspondingly. The variable $t$ is the one-hot target ground truth label, $\alpha \in [0, 1]$ is a constant, $i$ is the index of the training examples from the augmented dataset.

## 2.3 Distillation as Implicit Abstraction

Abstraction is a powerful technique that is used extensively in software verification. The key to an abstraction is to establish a relationship between a concrete system $P$ and its model $M$ that hides unnecessary details about $P$ while preserving some essential $P$'s properties [18]. Because the relationship is established, we refer to this type of abstraction as an explicit abstraction.

Previous research performs such explicit abstraction on a deep neural network using a clustering approach [27], where a set of nodes in the neural network relates to a single node in the abstracted model. In another approach, researchers eliminate less relevant nodes in a neural network using pruning process [6]. All these techniques indeed reduce the size of the original model to make it more amenable, for example, for verification. However, the drawback of these techniques is that the accuracy of the resulting abstraction suffers. This is because they do not consider accuracy preservation in their abstraction process. Clearly, considering the size of neural networks, identifying such explicit abstraction is a daunting task.

On the contrary, the distillation process ensures that the student model has similar accuracy as the teacher model. Since, by construction, the distilled model is smaller in terms of layers and dimensions, we can essentially consider it as an abstraction of the original model. However, since the student model might have a completely different architecture than its teacher, establishing an explicit mapping between those two systems is challenging. Instead, we say that these models have an *implicit* abstraction, which is created based on correctness preservation. Thus, the question is whether this implicit abstraction preserves properties between two models. One of the properties that we investigate here is confidence, which we discuss in the next section.

## 3   Confidence Property Preservation Criterion

In the real-world classification problems, in addition to a model's accuracy, the level of confidence with which a model performs classification, (i.e., predictive probability) is also considered. Confidence value can be used to determine the model's properties, such as high-confidence and decisiveness [25]. Therefore, preserving these values of the original model should be an important feature of the distilled abstraction.

The literature offers different measurements of the confidence for neural networks. Traditionally, it is defined as the maximum element of the probability vector obtained at the final softmax layer of a model $M$ for an input $x$, i.e.,

$$\mathsf{Cnf}^M(x) = max(\mathsf{softmax}(z^{M(x)})) \tag{2}$$

Recent work has shown that using this definition might be inadequate [19] and general purpose method based on Bayesian interpretation of the neural networks [4], or confidence calibration [7] should be used. Beyond being uncalibrated, the main criticisms of the softmax-based confidence evaluation is its failure to decrease confidence value on inputs far from the training data [19]. Therefore, this work evaluates confidence preservation on the training data set $X^{train}$, and we monitor ECE of both student and teacher models, as well as accuracy and the pairwise confidence on the evaluation dataset.

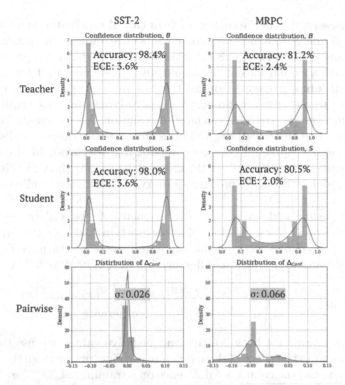

**Fig. 1.** For two linguistic tasks: SST-2 and MRPC, the individual distributions of softmax confidence for the teacher and the student do not show significant difference, under comparable expected calibration error (ECE). However, the distribution of the pairwise confidence does highlight the issue of poor distillation for the MRPC task.

## 3.1   Pairwise Confidence Preservation Property

In order to determine how to define and measure the confidence preservation property, we first examine confidence values for both $S$ and $B$ models. The confidence values $\mathsf{Cnf}(x)$ of a model $M$ over $X^{train}$ represent a distribution in range $[0, 1]$. To better understand the data, we first plotted confidence values for $B$ and $S$ models as density plots. Figure 1 shows these distribution for SST-2 and MRPC benchmarks: in the first top row for $B$ and in the second row for $S$.

From these plots, we can see that the traditional metric of aggregated confidence distributions of $S$ and $B$ models, as well as expected calibrated error (ECE) [7] are not good candidates for identifying differences in confidence. Two plots might have points with the same confidence value for different inputs, which is misleading. That is, such aggregate data loses information on whether confidence is preserved on the same inputs. Likewise, the ECE values of the models can be similar as in the case of MRPC, e.g., 2.4 vs. 2.0, but actually fail to hold the confidence preservation property.

Thus, our main idea is to measure the confidence preservation on the same input example for two models $B$ and $S$. In other words, in this work we focus on confidence preservation in the context of **functional equivalence** where for the same input $B$ and $S$ should have similar confidence values. The notion of functional equivalence is commonly used for verification of traditional programs [11]. Thus, we adapt a similar idea of "input-output" equivalence to define the **property of confidence preservation** for the case of deep neural networks.

Therefore, to measure this property, we introduce a pairwise confidence difference to uncover the confidence-related distillation disagreements between $B$ and $S$ models. The last row in Fig. 1 depicts the pair-wise difference distribution and their difference spread $\sigma$. We use $\sigma$'s value and its threshold of 0.05 as the property preservation criterion. As the data in the graphs show in this example the SST-2 model satisfies the property preservation criterion, while the MRPC fails do so since its $\sigma > 0.05$.

Here we formally describe the measurement of the differences between $\mathsf{Cnf}^B(x)$ and $\mathsf{Cnf}^S(x)$. First, let's define a function $\mathsf{Idx}^M(x)$ that returns an index in the probability vector of the maximum element return by Eq. 2. Then we define the pairwise confidence difference for $\forall x \in X^{train}$ as follows:

$$
\Delta_{Cnf}(x) = \begin{cases} \mathsf{Cnf}^S(x) - \mathsf{Cnf}^B(x) & \text{if } \mathsf{Idx}^B(x) = \mathsf{Idx}^S(x) \\ \bot & \text{otherwise} \end{cases} \tag{3}
$$

Since $\Delta_{Cnf}$ can have both positive and negative values, we use the sum of squares to compute the effect of these differences. Thus, we propose the following formula to compute the confidence difference on a training set $X^{train} \sigma(X^{train}) = \sqrt{\frac{1}{|X^{train}|} \sum_{x \in X^{train}} \Delta_{Cnf}^2(x)}$

**Definition 1 Pairwise Confidence Preservation Property $\varphi_{cnf}$.** We say that the confidence preservation property $\varphi_{cnf}$ holds if for any input $x \in X^{train}$ the spread of the pairwise confidence differences $\sigma$ between distilled $S$ and original $B$ models is small on $X^{train}$:

$$
\sigma(X^{train}) \leq \kappa \tag{4}
$$

where $\kappa > 0$ is a small constant, which is determined by users.

## 3.2   Confidence Preservation Property $\varphi_{cnf}$ Dependencies

Since a traditional distillation process does not take into account the confidence property preservation as in Definition (4), the technique does not guarantee it to hold for all models. In this section, we establish dependencies between $\sigma(X^{train})$ and the distillation parameters that demonstrate the existence of parameters that can be tuned for the property (4) to hold.

To determine such relations, we first define a **distillation quality condition** on student loss $L^{(S)}$ defined in (1)

$$
L^{(S)} \leq \beta \tag{5}
$$

where $\beta$ is a small positive scalar.

Next, from the softmax property [5] (Proposition 4) we obtain the following inequality for any input $x$: $\|\mathsf{softmax}(z^{S(x)}) - \mathsf{softmax}(z^{B(x)})\| < \gamma\|z^{S(x)} - z^{B(x)}\|$, where $\gamma$ is the inverse temperature constant in the softmax function.

Since the norm of a vector is always greater than or equal to any individual value of the vector, we have:

$$\Delta_{Cnf}(x) \leq \|\mathsf{softmax}(z^{S(x)}) - \mathsf{softmax}(z^{B(x)})\| \tag{6}$$

Therefore, from (6) we obtain:

$$\sum_{x \in X^{train}} \Delta^2_{Cnf}(x) < \gamma^2 \sum_{x \in X^{train}} \|z^{S(x)} - z^{B(x)}\|^2 \tag{7}$$

Recall in Eq. 1 the student distillation objective $L^{(S)}$ consists of two positive addends: student's cross entropy loss $L_{CE}$ and the distillation objective $L_{dist}$. If $L_{CE} + L_{dist} \leq \beta$, then $L_{dist} \leq \beta$ holds because the value of $L_{CE}$ is positive as the logarithm of a value that is between zero and one is negative. Therefore, from the distillation quality condition (5) we obtain: $\sum_{x \in X^{train}} \|z^{(S(x))} - z^{(B(x))}\|^2 < \frac{\beta}{(1-\alpha)}$

Finally, using Eq. 7 we produce: $\sigma(X^{train}) < \gamma\sqrt{\frac{\beta}{|X^{train}|(1-\alpha)}}$, which means (4) is satisfied with $\kappa = \gamma\sqrt{\frac{\beta}{|X^{train}|(1-\alpha)}}$. This means that the confidence preservation property depends on several parameters.

However, some of those parameters are predefined for TinyBERT models. Thus, in the TinyBERT model a regular softmax function is used, which sets the inverse temperature constant $\gamma = 1$. Moreover, due to the multi-stage approach in TinyBERT, during the prediction layer distillation only $L_{distill}$ is used, so $\alpha = 0$. As a result, the confidence property preservation mainly depends on the square root of the distillation quality condition $\beta$ and the training set size. That is

$$\sigma(X^{train}) < \sqrt{\frac{\beta}{|X^{train}|}} \tag{8}$$

We assume that the training set is fixed, due to the cost of the data collection, and the main focus is on $\beta$ that depends on the distillation training hyperparameters. We focus on empirical search and fine-tuning to obtain $S$ models for which $\varphi_{cnf}$ holds.

## 4    Experiment Setup

To investigate preservation $\varphi_{cnf}$ as defined in Eq. 4 for TinyBERT models and answer our research questions, we use the training benchmarks for five language tasks with different TinyBERT settings. In this section, we describe datasets, knowledge distillation model settings, and the choice of the threshold parameter $\kappa$. In the next section, we state our two research questions and present evaluation results that answer them.

**GLUE Tasks Benchmarks:** The datasets used for training and evaluation during the knowledge distillation consist of the six benchmarks from the General Language Understanding Evaluation (GLUE) [26]

The selected benchmark tasks are sentiment similarity and the natural language inference for binary classification tasks. Table 1 summarizes each dataset, with the information on both training (Tr) and evaluation (Ev) dataset sizes. For the smaller datasets such as CoLA, RTE, and MRPC we perform data augmentation. Augmentation is only performed for training datasets, we still perform evaluation on non-augmented data.

For the data augmentation we use the same approach as in work by Jiao et al. [13] relying on GLOVE dataset [20]. Specifically, we adopt `glove.6B.300d` that maps text sequences to a 300 dimensional dense vector space. As a result of data augmentation the sizes of the small training datasets - CoLA, RTE and MRPC - have increased to 211,457, 189,277 and 224,132, respectively; the original sizes of these datasets are shown in the parentheses in the table.

**Table 1.** Benchmark datasets GLUE [26]

| Task | Description | Tr | Ev |
|------|-------------|----|----|
| SST-2 | Sentiment analysis | 67,349 | 872 |
| RTE | Natural language inference | 189,277 (2,490) | 277 |
| QQP | Paraphrase similarity | 363,846 | 40,430 |
| QNLI | Natural language inference | 104,743 | 5,463 |
| MRPC | Semantic textual similarity | 224,132 (3,668) | 408 |
| CoLA | Semantic correctness | 211,457 (8,551) | 1,043 |

**Model Settings:** We use a task-specific fine-tuned BERT model $B$ with $N = 12$ transformer layers. Specifically, we use an uncased BERT version, meaning the input text has been changed to lowercase at the input layer. The model $B$ has the dimension of the hidden layer $d' = 768$, with the total number of model parameters at 109 million.

For the students, we use two models $S_{4L}$ and $S_{6L}$. $S_{4L}$ is a smaller distilled model with only four transformer layers $M = 4$ and relatively small dimension of a hidden layer $d' = 312$. In total $S_{4L}$ has 14.5M model parameters. For $S_{6L}$ $M = 6$, $d' = 768$, resulting in 67M model parameters.

For general distillation, we use TinyBERT [13], which is distilled from BERT using domain agnostic corpus from English Wikipedia (2,500M words), sequence length of 128 and feature-based distillation. We do not alter this general distillation model in this work, since the focus is on the task-specific models and prediction-layer distillation.

We perform task-specific distillation for the above six tasks, which produces twelve TinyBERT models. We initialize the student model with the parameters of GeneralTinyBERT, and for the teachers we use BERT that is fine-tuned for the corresponding task. We use the input sequence length of 128 for task specific distillation. As for the learning parameters, we use learning rate of $3e^{-5}$, batch size of 32, the number of epochs for intermediate distillation (embedding layer, attention matrices and hidden layer) is 10 and the number of epochs for prediction layer distillation is 3. The resulting accuracy numbers of the TinyBERT that we distilled from the BERT are comparable to the ones presented in the original paper [13], thus making our reproduction of TinyBERT valid.

We perform the knowledge distillation on GPU NVIDIA V100 computation with 16 GB RAM running on top of Google Cloud Platform (GCP) service.

**Parameters Selection.** As described in Sect. 3, the confidence preservation property $\varphi_{cnf}$ is parameterized by the threshold $\kappa$ in Eq. (4). We select this threshold as $\kappa=0.05$ for our adequacy criterion for $\varphi_{cnf}$ to hold. The final condition we evaluate is:

$$\sigma(X^{train}) \leq 0.05$$

That is, we say that **confidence preservation holds** if the value of $\sigma$ on the training set $X^{train}$ is less or equal to the threshold 0.05.

To avoid negative effect of hyperparameter fine-tuning on $S$'s accuracy, we add a constraint on changes in accuracy value of $S$ that prevents *significant accuracy drop*. We consider a drop of accuracy below 1% to be significant, as according to a Jiao et al. [13] it corresponds to the loss of the "on-par" performance. Thus, the accuracy of the fine-tuned $\tilde{S}$ and the original $S$ cannot be less than 1%.

## 5    Experimental Evaluations and Results

We conduct our empirical evaluations to answer the following research questions:

- **RQ1: Confidence preservation prevalence.** Do the distilled models $S$ from $B$ preserve $\varphi_{cnf}$ property?
- **RQ2: Confidence preservation dependencies.** Can tuning the distillation hyperparameters of a failed model $S$ make the property $\varphi_{cnf}$ hold for its tuned model $\tilde{S}$?

### 5.1    Confidence Preservation Prevalence (RQ1)

In this section, we evaluate whether $\varphi_{cnf}$ holds for the six language tasks. In the Table 2, for each task and the dataset we have two multi-column headers "Models" and "$\varphi_{cnf}$ property". The former describes individual model performance metrics such as accuracy (Acc) and expected calibration error (ECE) for three models $B$, $S_{4L}$, and $S_{6L}$. The $\varphi_{cnf}$ property columns contain data pertaining to evaluations of $\varphi_{cnf}$. Each row corresponds to a task dataset evaluated on the training (Tr) and evaluation (Ev) sets. As we discussed in the beginning of Sect. 3, we examine $\varphi_{cnf}$ on Tr dataset, due to the need to remove the factor that can affect confidence correctness on the inputs that are far from the training dataset. We do present results for Ev dataset as well to demonstrate the

**Table 2.** Confidence Preservation Property $\varphi_{cnf}$ for GLUE language tasks

| Task | Dataset | Models $B$ | | $S_{6L}$ | | $S_{4L}$ | | $\varphi_{cnf}$ property $B$ vs $S_{6L}$ | $B$ vs $S_{4L}$ |
|------|---------|-----|-----|-----|-----|-----|-----|-----|-----|
| | | Acc | ECC | Acc | ECC | Acc | ECC | $\sigma(X)$ | $\sigma(X)$ |
| SST-2 | Tr | 98.4 | 3.6 | 98.0 | 3.6 | 97.0 | 3.5 | 0.026 | 0.055 |
| | Ev | 93.0 | 1.6 | 91.4 | 1.3 | 89.4 | 2.9 | 0.046 | 0.075 |
| RTE | Tr | 94.8 | 22.1 | 84.3 | 14.9 | 86.5 | 21 | 0.062 | 0.109 |
| | Ev | 65.3 | 9.0 | 66.8 | 9.9 | 60.6 | 2.5 | 0.100 | 0.107 |
| QQP | Tr | 96.9 | 7.4 | 95.2 | 7.5 | 92.2 | 6.0 | 0.049 | 0.077 |
| | Ev | 90.7 | 2.7 | 90.9 | 4.2 | 89.1 | 3.5 | 0.055 | 0.079 |
| QNLI | Tr | 97.6 | 9.3 | 96.0 | 9.3 | 91.3 | 4.8 | 0.049 | 0.065 |
| | Ev | 91.4 | 4.8 | 91.1 | 5.8 | 85.8 | 1.8 | 0.079 | 0.094 |
| MRPC | Tr | 81.2 | 2.4 | 80.5 | 2.0 | 79.9 | 3.7 | 0.066 | 0.054 |
| | Ev | 78.7 | 7.5 | 75.5 | 2.3 | 74.2 | 7.2 | 0.070 | 0.075 |
| CoLA | Tr | 98.5 | 5.3 | 96.6 | 5.7 | 94.7 | 6.4 | 0.059 | 0.083 |
| | Ev | 83.2 | 7.6 | 79.6 | 7.4 | 72.6 | 11.5 | 0.098 | 0.129 |

consistency of our experiments, i.e., if $\varphi_{cnf}$ does not hold on Tr, then we expect it to perform the same way on Ev, as well as to observe the same trend in the confidence value change for $\tilde{S}$ models.

The first observation from the table is that for all language tasks, none of $S_{4L}$ models maintain $\varphi_{cnf}$. As a result, we conjecture that distilling BERT to just four transformer layers with the smaller dimension of hidden states (resulting in a 7.5X reduction in parameters) is too aggressive to satisfy $\varphi_{cnf}$.

The second and more important result is that the $S_{6L}$ model satisfies $\varphi_{cnf}$ for the three language tasks (shaded in  light gray ), however it fails to do so for the three other tasks (shaded in  dark gray ).

The answer to RQ1 is that the knowledge distillation does not uniformly preserve $\varphi_{cnf}$ across all six linguistic tasks. This conclusion supports our intuition that a standard distillation process focuses on classification accuracy and does not take into account confidence of predicted classes. Therefore, in the next research question RQ2, we investigate how parameters tuning can help with the tasks for which $\varphi_{cnf}$ fails.

## 5.2    Confidence Preservation Dependencies (RQ2)

We considered several hyperparameters that can improve $\varphi_{cnf}$ adequacy for failed models $S$. In particular, we investigated the tasks that have inadequate values of $\sigma(X^{train})$ that fail $\varphi_{cnf}$ - RTE, MRPC, and CoLA with the original recommended TinyBERT parameters: batch size 32, three epochs, weight decay $1e^{-4}$, intermediate layers distillation learning rate $5e^{-5}$ and prediction layer distillation learning rate $3e^{-5}$. We performed several exploratory studies where we changed the learning parameters of distillation, Table 3.

**Table 3.** Improving $\varphi_{cnf}$ property

| Task | Dataset | Models | | | | | $\varphi_{cnf}$ property | | | |
|------|---------|--------|--------|----------|--------|----------|----------------------|----------------------|----------------------|----------------------|
| | | $B$ Acc | $S_{6L}$ Acc | $\tilde{S}_{6L}$ Acc | $S_{4L}$ Acc | $\tilde{S}_{4L}$ Acc | $B$ vs $S_{6L}$ $\sigma(X)$ | $B$ vs $\tilde{S}_{6L}$ $\sigma(X)$ | $B$ vs $S_{4L}$ $\sigma(X)$ | $B$ vs $\tilde{S}_{4L}$ $\sigma(X)$ |
| RTE | Tr | 94.8 | 84.3 | 84.6 | 86.5 | 88.5 | 0.062 | 0.050 | 0.109 | 0.069 |
| | Ev | 65.3 | 66.8 | 66.4 | 60.6 | 62.5 | 0.100 | 0.084 | 0.107 | 0.119 |
| MRPC | Tr | 81.2 | 80.5 | 80.2 | 79.9 | 79.4 | 0.066 | 0.047 | 0.054 | 0.053 |
| | Ev | 78.7 | 75.5 | 75.9 | 74.2 | 73.7 | 0.070 | 0.060 | 0.075 | 0.074 |
| CoLA | Tr | 98.5 | 96.6 | 98.1 | 94.7 | 95.8 | 0.059 | 0.039 | 0.083 | 0.071 |
| | Ev | 83.2 | 79.6 | 80.8 | 72.6 | 72.1 | 0.098 | 0.093 | 0.129 | 0.120 |

This preliminary investigation show that changing parameters at intermediate layers distillation yields no reductions in $\sigma(X^{train})$ values. To no avail, we varied epochs $\{3, 6, 9\}$, learning rate $\{5e^{-7}, 1e^{-6}, 5e^{-5}, 1e^{-4}, 3e^{-4}, 5e^{-3}\}$, batch size $\{28, 32, 36\}$, and weight decay $\{1e^{-4}, 1e^{-3}, 1e^{-2}\}$.

We experimented with the hyperparameters at prediction layers distillation in the following ranges: epochs $\{2, 3, 4, 5, 6\}$, learning rate $\{3e^{-6}, 1e^{-5}, 3e^{-5}, 7e^{-5}, 4e^{-4}, 5e^{-4}, 8e^{-4}\}$, batch size $\{28, 32, 34, 36, 38, 40\}$, and weight decay $\{1e^{-4}, 1e^{-3}, 5e^{-3}, 1e^{-2}, 5e^{-2}\}$. Changing only the parameters of the prediction layers distillation reduced the values of $\sigma(X^{train})$ so that $\tilde{S}$ models for MRPC and CoLA hold $\varphi_{cnf}$. However, in order for the RTE task to satisfy $\varphi_{cnf}$, it requires the hyperparameter tuning for both prediction and intermediate layer distillations.

The hyperparameters of the original knowledge distillation ($lr_{stg1}$, $lr_{stg2}$, $batch_{stg2}$, $epoch_{stg2}$, $wd_{stg2}$) are equal to ($5e^{-5}, 3e^{-5}, 32, 3, 1e^{-4}$), where "stg1" and "stg2" correspond to intermediate and prediction layer distillation respectively, "lr" and "wd" denote learning rate and weight decay. The resulting property improvement is achieved using the fine-tuning with the following parameters on RTE: ($\mathbf{1e^{-4}}, 3e^{-5}, \mathbf{36}, 4, 1e^{-4}$) for $\tilde{S}_{6L}$ and ($5e^{-5}, 3e^{-5}, 32, 4, 1e^{-4}$) for $\tilde{S}_{4L}$; MRPC: ($5e^{-5}, \mathbf{1e^{-5}}, 32, 4, 1e^{-4}$) for $\tilde{S}_{6L}$ and ($5e^{-5}, 3e^{-5}, 32, \mathbf{2}, 1e^{-4}$) for $\tilde{S}_{4L}$ and CoLA: ($5e^{-5}, \mathbf{1e^{-5}}, 32, 4, 1e^{-4}$) for $\tilde{S}_{6L}$ and ($5e^{-5}, \mathbf{1e^{-5}}, 32, 4, 1e^{-4}$) for $\tilde{S}_{4L}$.

Models $\tilde{S}_{6L}$ were fine-tuned for all three tasks to satisfy $\varphi_{cnf}$ property without any significant drop in the accuracy. We can see that 6L RTE model required the most changes to the original parameters, including the changes on the stage 1 of distillation. This can be attributed to the fact that it is the smallest training dataset. The accuracy of $\tilde{S}_{6L}$ and $B$ on the Ev dataset are comparable, indicating that the fine-tuning did not change the regime of the distillation significantly.

To answer RQ2, we are able to fine-tune all three models to satisfy $\varphi_{cnf}$ property without the changes of the distillation architecture and training sets while avoiding significant drop in accuracy.

## 5.3  Discussion

Based on the information presented, we can conclude that $\varphi_{cnf}$ is a non-trivial property, and satisfying the distillation quality condition guarantees its preservation.

The architecture of the distilled model, such as the number of transformer layers as well as learning hyperparameters at the prediction layer greatly impact $\varphi_{cnf}$, while an early intermediate distillation layer has a much lesser effect on $\sigma(X^{train})$ values.

Monitoring $\varphi_{cnf}$ property therefore guides distillation hyperparameters fine-tuning, so that both accuracy and confidence are preserved. We note that this does not require any architectural modifications to the existing distillation models.

# 6    Related Work

**Black-box Equivalency Checking:** Similar to our work, black-box equivalence checking determines functional equivalence of two programs using concrete inputs. This approach is used in verifying correctness of code compilation by establishing relations between the original and compiled programs [17]. After running tests, the technique discovers possible relationship between variables of two versions of the program. Next, using formal methods, it verifies that the identified equivalence relation indeed holds for all program inputs. Our approach only establishes the relationship between $S$ and $B$ confidence values, and does not generalize it to all possible inputs to those models.

**Abstraction for Large-Scale Deep Models:** The latest research in the area of formal methods for AI does not perform the verification on the state of the art large language models. There are two papers exploring relatively large deep learning models with more than ten million parameters, where one relies on formula-based approach [12] and another on the abstraction via state transition system [3]. The main challenge to make formal methods scalable to the sizes of realistic deep neural networks is the prohibitive size and complexity of a formula in these approaches [14]. Implicit abstraction on the other hand does not require exact formula and state transition representation, hence it is a natural fit for verification of large models. Several papers addressed the verification of deep neural networks by the development of abstractions. Idealized real-valued abstraction was proposed in [9] to verify relatively small visual deep neural networks. The idea is to quantize all the operations in the network to 32-bits, and then feed into SMT solver. In the recent work [6], the authors present verification of feed forward neural network using training pipeline based on the pruning with the goal to make the model amenable to formal analysis. However, the network under verification has only fully connected layers that were reduced using pruning for network reduction and then processing by an SMT solver.

**Distillation and Property Preservation:** There is a substantial research on measuring and calibrating confidence, including techniques such as temperature scaling [7] and on/off manifold regularization [16]. However, to the best of our knowledge, the work on confidence property analysis for the knowledge distillation is limited.

## 7    Conclusion and Future Work

In this work, we study the confidence preservation property under a knowledge distillation abstraction. To the best of our knowledge, this is the first work to view knowledge distillation as an abstraction, as well as to study property preservation under knowledge distillation and defining the pairwise confidence preservation criterion.

We evaluate $\sigma(X^{train})$ using a black-box equivalence approach on six tasks from the linguistic benchmark dataset. For the tasks where the property fails, we modified the hyperparameters of the distillation process to ensure preservation. Our evaluations demonstrate that preservation of this confidence property could aid the distillation process by guiding the selection of hyperparameters.

Our future work will involve using formal methods to study more properties of large deep neural networks. Additionally, due to the complexity of the distillation schema for TinyBERT, not all the learning parameters were examined. Therefore, further research is needed to investigate the impact of pre-trained distillation and the combination of distillation losses.

## References

1. Brown, T., et al.: Language models are few-shot learners. Adv. Neural. Inf. Process. Syst. **33**, 1877–1901 (2020)
2. Devlin, J., Chang, M.W., Lee, K., Toutanova, K.: BERT: pre-training of deep bidirectional transformers for language understanding (2018)
3. Du, X., Xie, X., Li, Y., Ma, L., Liu, Y., Zhao, J.: DeepStellar: model-based quantitative analysis of stateful deep learning systems. In: 27th ACM Joint Meeting on European Software Engineering Conference and Symposium on the Foundations of Software Engineering, pp. 477–487 (2019)
4. Gal, Y., et al.: Uncertainty in deep learning (2016)
5. Gao, B., Pavel, L.: On the properties of the softmax function with application in game theory and reinforcement learning. arXiv e-prints, p. arXiv-1704 (2017)
6. Guidotti, D., Leofante, F., Pulina, L., Tacchella, A.: Verification of neural networks: enhancing scalability through pruning. arXiv preprint arXiv:2003.07636 (2020)
7. Guo, C., Pleiss, G., Sun, Y., Weinberger, K.Q.: On calibration of modern neural networks. In: International Conference on Machine Learning, pp. 1321–1330 (2017)
8. Heidari, M., Jones, J.H.: Using BERT to extract topic-independent sentiment features for social media bot detection. In: 11th IEEE Annual Ubiquitous Computing, Electronics & Mobile Communication Conference (UEMCON), pp. 0542–0547 (2020)
9. Henzinger, T.A., Lechner, M.: Scalable verification of quantized neural networks. In: Proceedings of the AAAI Conference on Artificial Intelligence, vol. 35, pp. 3787–3795 (2021)

10. Hinton, G., Vinyals, O., Dean, J.: Distilling the knowledge in a neural network. arXiv preprint arXiv:1503.02531 (2015)
11. Huang, S.Y., Cheng, K.T.T.: Formal Equivalence Checking and Design Debugging, vol. 12. Springer, Heidelberg (2012)
12. Huang, X., Kwiatkowska, M., Wang, S., Wu, M.: Safety verification of deep neural networks. In: International Conference on Computer Aided Verification, pp. 3–29 (2017)
13. Jiao, X., Yin, Y., Shang, L., Jiang, X., Chen, X., Li, L., Wang, F., Liu, Q.: Tiny-BERT: distilling BERT for natural language understanding. In: Findings of the Association for Computational Linguistics: EMNLP 2020, pp. 4163–4174 (2020)
14. Katz, G., Barrett, C., Dill, D.L., Julian, K., Kochenderfer, M.J.: Reluplex: an efficient SMT solver for verifying deep neural networks. In: Majumdar, R., Kunčak, V. (eds.) CAV 2017. LNCS, vol. 10426, pp. 97–117. Springer, Cham (2017). https://doi.org/10.1007/978-3-319-63387-9_5
15. Kim, Y.J., Awadalla, H.H.: FastFormers: highly efficient transformer models for natural language understanding. arXiv preprint arXiv:2010.13382 (2020)
16. Kong, L., Jiang, H., Zhuang, Y., Lyu, J., Zhao, T., Zhang, C.: Calibrated language model fine-tuning for in-and out-of-distribution data. arXiv preprint arXiv:2010.11506 (2020)
17. Kurhe, V.K., Karia, P., Gupta, S., Rose, A., Bansal, S.: Automatic generation of debug headers through blackbox equivalence checking. In: 2022 IEEE/ACM International Symposium on Code Generation and Optimization (CGO), pp. 144–154 (2022)
18. Loiseaux, C., Graf, S., Sifakis, J., Bouajjani, A., Bensalem, S., Probst, D.: Property preserving abstractions for the verification of concurrent systems. Formal Methods Syst. Design 6(1), 11–44 (1995)
19. Pearce, T., Brintrup, A., Zhu, J.: Understanding softmax confidence and uncertainty. arXiv e-prints, p. arXiv-2106 (2021)
20. Pennington, J., Socher, R., Manning, C.D.: GloVe: global vectors for word representation. In: Proceedings of the 2014 Conference on Empirical Methods in Natural Language Processing (EMNLP), pp. 1532–1543 (2014)
21. Pulina, L., Tacchella, A.: An abstraction-refinement approach to verification of artificial neural networks. In: Touili, T., Cook, B., Jackson, P. (eds.) CAV 2010. LNCS, vol. 6174, pp. 243–257. Springer, Heidelberg (2010). https://doi.org/10.1007/978-3-642-14295-6_24
22. Sanh, V., Debut, L., Chaumond, J., Wolf, T.: DistilBERT, a distilled version of BERT: smaller, faster, cheaper and lighter. arXiv preprint arXiv:1910.01108 (2019)
23. Tang, R., Lu, Y., Liu, L., Mou, L., Vechtomova, O., Lin, J.: Distilling task-specific knowledge from BERT into simple neural networks. arXiv preprint arXiv:1903.12136 (2019)
24. Vaswani, A., et al.: Attention is all you need. Adv. Neural Inf. Process. Syst. 30 (2017)
25. Vengertsev, D., Sherman, E.: Recurrent neural network properties and their verification with Monte Carlo techniques. In: AAAI Conference on Artificial Intelligence, SafeAI@AAAI (2020)
26. Wang, A., Singh, A., Michael, J., Hill, F., Levy, O., Bowman, S.R.: GLUE: a multi-task benchmark and analysis platform for natural language understanding. arXiv preprint arXiv:1804.07461 (2018)
27. Wang, Q., Zhang, K., Liu, X., Giles, C.L.: Verification of recurrent neural networks through rule extraction. arXiv preprint arXiv:1811.06029 (2018)

# Image Analysis

# Exploring Optimal Configurations in Active Learning for Medical Imaging

Alec Parise[✉][iD] and Brian Mac Namee[iD]

School of Computer Science, University College Dublin, Dublin, Ireland
alec.parise@ucdconnect.ie, brian.macnamee@ucd.ie

**Abstract.** Medical imaging is a critical component of clinical decision-making, patient diagnosis, treatment planning, intervention, and therapy. However, due to the shortage of qualified radiologists, there is an increasing burden on healthcare practitioners, which underscores the need to develop reliable automated methods. Despite the development of novel computational techniques, interpreting medical images remains challenging due to noise and varying acquisition conditions. One promising solution to improve the reliability and accuracy of automated medical image analysis is Interactive Machine Learning (IML), which integrates human expertise into the model training process. Active learning (AL) is an important IML technique that can iteratively query for informative samples to be labeled by humans, leading to more data-efficient learning. To fully leverage the potential of active learning, however, it is crucial to understand the optimal setup for different components of an AL system. This paper presents an evaluation of the effectiveness of different combinations of data representation, model capacity, and query strategy for active learning systems designed for medical image classification tasks. The results of this evaluation show that employing raw image representations as input, in conjunction with a ResNet50 model and margin-based queries, yields more reliable and accurate automated methods for medical image analysis.

**Keywords:** Human-in-the-loop (HITL) · Interactive Machine Learning (IML) · Active Learning (AL)

## 1 Introduction

Medical imaging plays a crucial role in clinical decision-making, patient diagnosis, treatment planning, intervention, and therapy. However, the shortage of skilled radiologists poses a significant challenge, placing a growing burden on healthcare practitioners [10]. Consequently, there is an urgent requirement to

This publication has emanated from research conducted with the financial support of Science Foundation Ireland under Grant number 18/CRT/6183. For the purpose of Open Access, the author has applied a CC BY public copyright licence to any Author Accepted Manuscript version arising from this submission.

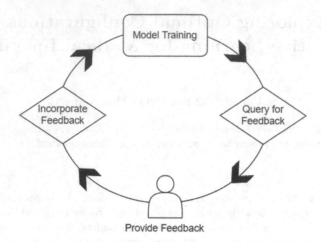

**Fig. 1.** The basic Interactive Machine Learning (IML) framework

devise dependable automated techniques that can alleviate this strain and provide reliable solutions [42]. The field of Interactive Machine Learning (IML) has gained significant attention in the medical field in recent years [2,8,22,25,41]. Training image-based machine learning models typically relies solely on automated processes to learn patterns and make predictions, offering no ability for interaction from clinicians during this process [41]. In contrast, IML incorporates human input and feedback into the modelling process, resulting in more effective models [2,25]. A typical IML workflow is presented in Fig. 1, where the automated model training process is periodically interrupted by user interaction. The user provides feedback to queries posed by the training process, and this feedback is then incorporated into another round of automated model training.

Active learning (AL) is a powerful IML technique for data-efficient model training [38]. By actively selecting informative instances to label, AL reduces the annotation burden while maintaining, or even improving, model performance. In the context of medical imaging, where labeled data is often scarce and costly to obtain, AL holds significant potential to enhance the accuracy and efficiency of diagnostic systems [38]. In this study, we aim to address the challenge of designing optimal AL systems for medical image classification, specifically focusing on three crucial aspects: data representation, model capacity, and query strategies. Our research aims to establish reliable default options for building active learning solutions.

To investigate the impact of model capacity, we consider three distinct models: a high-capacity Resnet50 model, a medium-capacity shallow convolutional neural network (CNN), and a low-capacity random forest model. Through the exploration of these diverse models, we seek to discern the influence of model capacity on the active learning process. Additionally, we examine the utility of image embeddings obtained from pre-trained models as an alternative to raw image inputs for the low-capacity models. This offers potential improvements in computational efficiency but also effectiveness in the presence of limited labeled samples.

Finally, we assess different query strategies to select informative instances during the active learning process: random sampling, margin sampling, and least confidence sampling. Through a comparative analysis of their performance, we aim to identify the sampling strategy that optimally selects informative data points for annotation, maximizing the efficiency of the active learning framework.

The experiments presented in this paper offer valuable insights into the effectiveness of different combinations of AL scenarios for medical image classification problems. This will be particularly useful to practitioners due to the lack of labelled data, where typical hyper-parameter tuning techniques are not suitable. The reminder of the paper proceeds as follows: Section 2 discusses related work; Sect. 3 provides a detailed explanation of the experimental setup; Sect. 4 discusses the experimental results; and finally Sect. 5 concludes the paper.

## 2   Related Work

Unlike typical machine learning algorithms that rely solely on large datasets, Interactive Machine Learning (IML) [2,25] systems enable human interaction, allowing users to provide feedback and guidance to improve the accuracy and relevance of the models. The literature on IML includes algorithm development [23], user interface design [17,18], and applications in diverse fields [1,16,31,47]. Important IML methods include visual pattern mining [32], interactive anomaly detection [12,29], interactive information retrieval [26], and visual topic analysis [27].

Classification problems, in particular, can benefit from two pivotal IML approaches: co-active learning [9] and active learning [13,38]. Co-active learning takes advantage of multiple perspectives and disagreement-based methods to train multiple classifiers on different feature sets, capturing diverse views. The classifiers' disagreements are then identified, and clustering techniques based on proximity to cluster centroids are employed for labeling instances [45]. Active learning (AL) is an interactive approach that focuses on selecting the most informative instances from an unlabeled dataset for labeling. Typically, it involves training a single classifier on a specific feature set. The goal is to minimize labeling effort by selectively querying an oracle for labels on instances that are expected to provide valuable information [38]. AL aims to improve model performance by iteratively incorporating labeled data into the training process. This reduces the "labelling bottleneck" [38] by allowing the model to actively query for the most informative examples. There are three main approaches to active learning [10]: stream-based sampling, membership query synthesis, and pool-based sampling.

Stream-based sampling [5,13,15,35] is employed when data arrives in a continuous stream, necessitating assessment to determine whether annotation is necessary for each incoming data point. The main challenge in designing algorithms for stream-based sampling is that they cannot take into account the overall distribution of the population [10,14]. Alternatively, membership query synthesis [3] (MQS) involves generating synthetic data points rather than obtaining them from a dataset [3,37,38]. Synthetic data can be strategically generated to maximize label informativeness from the oracle. Although MQS can be useful [28] it has been shown to be ineffective for image-based tasks due to the challenges in generating synthetic query images [6,37].

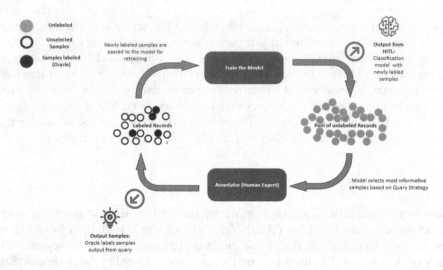

**Fig. 2.** Pool-based active learning framework.

Pool-based sampling [24,30,38] is the most common AL scenario and is the focus of this paper. Figure 2 shows a typical pool-based AL workflow that involves an *initial dataset* of labeled data points and a large collection of unlabeled data points, known as the *pool dataset*. First, the model is trained on the initial dataset, then a selection method ranks the most informative instances from the pool dataset for labeling by a human annotator, often called an *oracle*. The newly labeled samples are re-introduced into the AL model for re-training. This method is especially effective when used with batch-based training in deep learning approaches [11,30,33,38,46]. Pool-based AL can, however, be computationally expensive as it requires repeated re-training of a model and generating new predictions for the instances in the pool dataset at each iteration.

One way to assess the informativeness of instances in Active Learning is by quantifying the uncertainty associated with predictions made for those instance by a trained model. This is based on the assumption that data points with higher uncertainty in their predictions hold more valuable information, making them candidates for labeling and inclusion in the training set. To measure uncertainty in a classification task, the machine learning model assigns confidence scores to the predicted classes. Typically, the uncertainty in active learning is quantified by calculating the sum of probabilities assigned to the classes with the lowest confidence scores. This approach captures the uncertainty of the prediction, as the sum of probabilities for the lowest confidence classes represents the overall uncertainty [38]. When a model assigns high confidence scores to a specific class, the prediction is considered more certain. Conversely, a lower sum of minimum class probabilities indicates higher uncertainty in the prediction [38]. Uncertainty can be summarized as:

$$x^*\text{LC} = \arg\max_x \left(1 - P\theta(\hat{y}|x)\right) \tag{1}$$

where, $\hat{y}$ represents the most probable label determined by $\arg\max_y P\theta(y|x)$.

This formula depicts how uncertainty relates to the prediction made for a specific data point within the context of the data distribution. This method is commonly known as Least Confidence (LC) sampling and provides a way to rank the uncertainty of samples within a distribution [10]. However, LC sampling has a limitation as it solely focuses on the information associated with the most probable label, disregarding information about the remaining label distribution [38].

A margin-based query is a method that addresses the limitations of Least-Confidence queries and is particularly useful for AL for multi-class classification problems [34, 36, 39]. The main idea is that it considers the difference between the first and second most probable labels, resulting in a more accurate measure of the model's confidence in assigning a label. Margin based sampling is defined as:

$$x^*\text{M} = \arg\max_x \left(P\theta(\hat{y}1|x) - P\theta(\hat{y}_2|x)\right) \tag{2}$$

where, $\hat{y}_1$ and $\hat{y}_2$ are the first and second most probable labels predicted by a model. Consequently, the larger the separation between these two labels, the more certain the model is in assigning a label.

Entropy [39] sampling is another query method that selects instances based on the uncertainty of the model's predictions. Entropy sampling can be defined as :

$$x^*\text{EN} = \arg\max_x \left(-\sum y P_0(y|x) \log P_0(y|x)\right) \tag{3}$$

where $y_i$ ranges across all possible annotations. Entropy is a measure of how much uncertainty is present in the predicted class distribution. This means the more uncertain a prediction is, the more information we can gain by including the ground truth for that sample in the training set [10].

Alternatively, query-by-committee is a query strategy used to measure uncertainty of unlabeled data by measuring the agreement between multiple models performing the same task [24, 38]. The premise of this method is that the more disagreement found between predictions on the same data point, the higher the level of uncertainty that data point has and is selected for labeling [24]. This method comes at the cost of computational resources, as multiple models need to be trained and maintained, and each of these needs to be updated in the presence of newly selected training samples [10].

In this study, we focus on pool-based AL and its application to medical images. We explore the effectiveness of different input representations, models of different capacities, and different selection strategies. This comprehensive analysis of AL methods in the context of medical image classification contributes to advancing the field of IML and has the potential to enhance diagnostic and predictive capabilities in healthcare.

# 3 Experimental Setup

This section provides an overview of the experimental design used in this paper, with a particular emphasis on the datasets procured from the MedMNIST collection.

## 3.1 Datasets and Pre-processing

One of the difficulties in studying machine learning applications in medical imaging is obtaining adequately annotated datasets [4]. In the experiments described in this paper we use publicly available, fully labelled datasets from the MedMNIST collection [44]:

- PneumoniaMNIST: 5,856 greyscale pediatric chest X-Ray images each with a size of $28 \times 28$ pixels with two classes (pneumonia: 1 and normal cases: 0). Divided in a training set of 4,708 images and a test set of 624 images.
- BloodMNIST: 17,092 RGB images, each with a size of $28 \times 28$ pixels. The images are categorized into eight classes, representing individual normal cells without any infection, hematologic, or oncologic disease. The dataset includes a training set with 11,959 images and a test set with 3,421 images.
- DermaMNIST: Contains images of common pigmented skin lesions categorized into seven different diseases. The images are represented as RGB and have a size of $28 \times 28$ pixels. The dataset consists of a training set with 7,007 images and a test set with 2,005 images.
- Organ3DMIST: Consists of 185 CT scans categorized into 11 body organ classes. The images are $28 \times 28 \times 28$ pixels and represented in greyscale. The training set contains 971 images, while the test set contains 610 images.
- FractureMNIST3D: Includes 1,267 images obtained from approximately 5,000 rib fractures found in 660 CT scans. The images are organized into four clinical categories and are represented as $28 \times 28 \times 28$ greyscale images. The training set consists of 1,027 images, and the testing set contains 240 images (Fig. 3).

## 3.2 Experimental Design

The experiment aimed to assess the performance of pool-based AL using various combinations of query strategies (random, margin, and Least-Confidence), model representations (raw image and bottleneck features), and model capacities (random forest, 5-layer CNN, and ResNet50). The AL workflow began by selecting an initial subset of labeled images consisting of 20 samples. Instead of relying on human agents for labeling, a simulated approach was used to iteratively label images queried from the AL model (the MedMNIST datasets are annotated, adhering to the standard practice in AL research). Over the course of 240 iterations, we employed the chosen query strategy to identify four unlabeled instances, add labels to them, and then integrated these instances into the labeled pool of data. At each iteration the pool of labeled data was evaluated

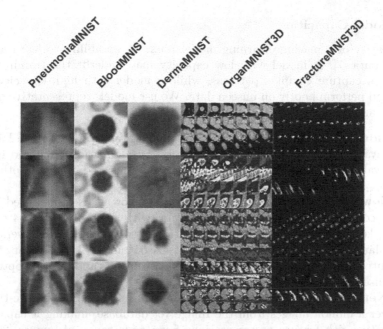

**Fig. 3.** Sample images from each of the five MedMNIST datasets used in these experiments in this paper.

against the MedMNIST-defined test set [44]. Performance evaluation was based on two metrics: the area under the learning curve (AULC) and accuracy (ACC) after 100 iterations. The above process was repeated for each combination of query strategy, model representation, and model capacity.

### 3.3 Image Representations

Image representations refer to the form of input data for machine learning models. In this experiment, two types of image representations were used. The first type, bottleneck feature representation, is a compressed version of intermediate outputs of a neural network. This representation offers a low dimensional representation of the data while preserving the necessary information for classification. In our experiments the bottleneck representations were extracted from the layer immediately prior to the final output layer of a ResNet50 model pre-trained on the Imagenet dataset[1] were used.

The second image representation, raw image representation, simply uses the original images as input to models. This representation contains all the information present in the image, but it may be computationally expensive and require a large amount of memory to process. For the medium and high capacity models the raw images were resized to 224 × 224 pixels.

---

[1] ResNet50 model pre-trained on the Imagenet dataset. Available at: https://pytorch.org/vision/main/models/generated/torchvision.models.resnet50.html.

### 3.4    Model Capacities

The capacity of a machine learning model refers to its ability to learn and fit training data [7]. A model with low capacity may underfit the training data and fail to capture complex patterns, while a model with high capacity may overfit and perform poorly on unseen data. We use models representative of low, medium, and high capacity:

- **Random forest (low capacity):** This model was trained on the labelled data available at each iteration and optimized using a grid search and 10-fold cross-validation. The selected hyperparameters consisted of max depth $= 16$ and $n_{estimators} = 256$.
- **Shallow CNN (medium capacity):** The shallow CNN model used in the study consisted of two convolutional layers (with sizes of 32 and 64 respectively, kernel sizes of 3 and ReLU activations); two max-pooling layers; and, after flattening, a fully connected layer (of size 64 and ReLU activation) before the output layer. To train this model cross-entropy loss and an SGD optimizer were used with a learning rate of 0.01.
- **ResNet50 (high capacity model):** The ResNet50 model was pre-trained on over a million images from the ImageNet database, making it capable of generating rich feature representations for a wide range of images [20]. To fine-tune the ResNet50 model, cross-entropy loss was used [21] with the SGD optimizer [19,40].

To leverage the pre-trained weights of a ResNet50 model it is common practice to freeze some of the layers during training to prevent overfitting when generalizing on a new dataset [43]. Freezing layers prevents the gradients from being computed and backpropagated through the layers [43].

### 3.5    Query Strategies

Query strategies constitute a fundamental aspect of AL, serving the purpose of selecting a subset of the most informative unlabeled data samples to improve the model's accuracy and minimize the number of samples that need to be labeled. In this study three query strategies (random, margin and least-confidence) have been implemented to determine the most suitable combination in the AL framework. The random query method selects data points for labeling without considering their informativeness. In contrast, the margin query method prioritizes labeling data points that the model is most uncertain about, gauging uncertainty by the difference between the two most probable classes [38]. Conversely, the least-confidence method labels data points based on the model's lowest confidence level, determined by assessing the probability of the most probable class [34].

## 4    Results and Discussion

The objective of this study was to investigate which combination of model representation, model capacity, and query strategy is the most effective when using active learning for medical image classification. The experiment involved two types of image representations (bottleneck feature and raw image representations); three model architectures (Random Forrest (low capacity), a 5-layer CNN (medium capacity) and a ResNet50 (high capacity)); and three query strategies (random, margin, and least-confidence). The results of our experiments are shown in Tables 1 and 2.

**Table 1.** Experimental results measured using the Area Under Learning Curve (AULC). The best performing approach for each dataset is highlighted in bold.

| Representation | Model | Query Strategy | Pneumonia MNIST | Blood MNIST | Derma MNIST | Organ MNIST3D | Fracture MNIST3D |
|---|---|---|---|---|---|---|---|
| Bottleneck Features | Random Forest | Random | 0.8270 | 0.6399 | 0.6649 | 0.6529 | 0.4351 |
| | | Margin | 0.8295 | 0.7144 | 0.6783 | 0.6456 | 0.4109 |
| | | Least-Confidence | 0.8284 | 0.6341 | 0.6789 | 0.6531 | 0.4273 |
| Raw Image | ResNet50 | Random | 0.7960 | 0.9194 | 0.6892 | 0.9027 | 0.4329 |
| | | Margin | **0.8614** | **0.9302** | 0.6919 | **0.9211** | 0.4283 |
| | | Least-Confidence | 0.8452 | 0.9262 | **0.7134** | 0.9180 | **0.4542** |
| Raw Image | Shallow CNN | Random | 0.8213 | 0.7421 | 0.6562 | 0.7121 | 0.4098 |
| | | Margin | 0.7879 | 0.6571 | 0.6587 | 0.7558 | 0.3922 |
| | | Least-Confidence | 0.8333 | 0.7488 | 0.6602 | 0.7307 | 0.4073 |

**Table 2.** Experimental results measured using the Accuracy metric (ACC %). The best performing approach for each dataset is highlighted in bold.

| Representation | Model | Query Strategy | Pneumonia MNIST | Blood MNIST | Derma MNIST | Organ MNIST3D | Fracture MNIST3D |
|---|---|---|---|---|---|---|---|
| Bottleneck Features | Random Forest | Random | 83.02 | 62.76 | 65.97 | 68.03 | 40.83 |
| | | Margin | 84.13 | 73.66 | 68.07 | 68.52 | 39.58 |
| | | Least-Confidence | 83.33 | 61.36 | 67.98 | 68.53 | 42.08 |
| Raw Image | ResNet50 | Random | 79.81 | 93.74 | 69.02 | 87.51 | 43.75 |
| | | Margin | **87.82** | **96.66** | 72.15 | **93.12** | 40.41 |
| | | Least-Confidence | 86.70 | 96.14 | **72.76** | 92.89 | **45.00** |
| Raw Image | Shallow CNN | Random | 83.81 | 77.05 | 63.48 | 75.78 | 37.08 |
| | | Margin | 80.81 | 67.52 | 63.91 | 81.76 | 40.83 |
| | | Least-Confidence | 86.86 | 79.63 | 64.66 | 82.13 | 40.41 |
| Benchmark | ResNet50 | | 85.70 | 95.60 | 73.1 | 85.70 | 49.40 |
| | Shallow CNN | | 83.20 | 79.42 | 68.54 | 81.93 | 40.12 |

These results show that the high capacity ResNet50 model using a raw image representation and the margin or least-confidence query strategy achieved the highest accuracy across all experiments. The AL model using bottleneck representation and the low capacity RF model did not exceed the baseline accuracy achieved by Yang et al. [44] (shown in the final rows of Table 2). The convergence of this method is illustrated in Fig. 4.

Figure 5, depicts the high-capacity ResNet50 model using raw image representations alongside three query strategies. The margin query strategy notably converged faster at the $100^{th}$ iteration. However, regardless of the strategy, each

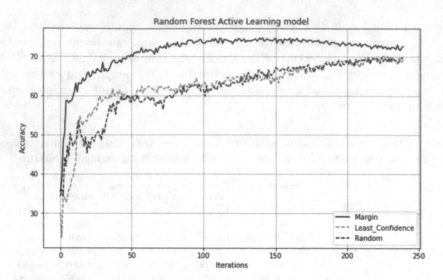

**Fig. 4.** Learning curves using bottleneck features and RF classifier applied to the BloodMNIST dataset.

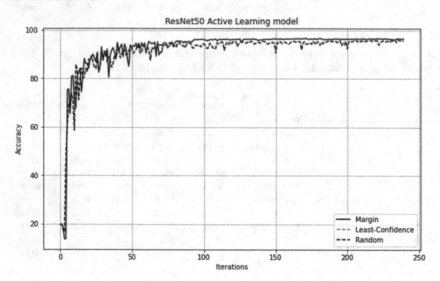

**Fig. 5.** Learning curves using the ResNet50 model and raw image representations for the BloodMNIST dataset.

method performed well including the random query strategy. The results in Fig. 6 depicts the study using a 5-layer CNN with raw images. For this experiment the least-confidence query method proved to be the most robust method. The large discrepancy between each of the methods can be seen at the $100^{th}$ iteration.

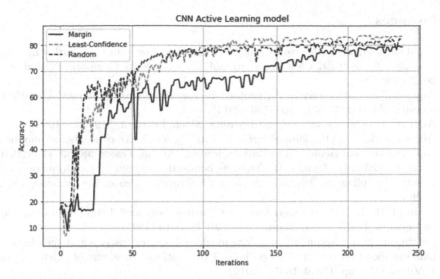

**Fig. 6.** Learning curves using the medium capacity CNN and raw image representations for the BloodMNIST dataset.

## 5 Conclusion

The studies presented in this paper was designed to explore the effectiveness of pool-based AL processes for medical image classification. The investigation considers input representations, model capacities, and selection strategies. The results of the experiments performed using 5 medical imaging datasets demonstrated that using raw image representations with a high capacity ResNet50 model was the most suitable approach across all experiments. Our findings reveal that this combination consistently delivered superior performance when employing the margin query strategy in the cases of PneumoniaMNIST, Blood-MNIST, and OrganMNIST3D datasets. However, it's worth noting that the Least-Confidence query strategy exhibited stronger generalization capabilities on the DermaMNIST and FractureMNIST3D datasets. This suggests that the choice of query strategy should be contingent upon the specific image types and anatomical regions.

Overall, the best AL approach requires significantly fewer labeled samples compared to benchmark models and outperformed both ResNet50 and 5-layer CNN models trained over 200 epochs on the entire training dataset, seen in Table 2. Our findings emphasize the potential for efficient and precise classification tasks, particularly in scenarios where obtaining labeled data is limited or expensive. In future work, we intend to explore alternative query strategies and assess the generalizability across a broader spectrum of medical imaging modalities.

# References

1. Aghdam, H.H., et al.: Active learning for deep detection neural networks. In: Proceedings of the IEEE/CVF International Conference on Computer Vision, pp. 3672–3680 (2019)
2. Amershi, S., et al.: Power to the people: the role of humans in interactive machine learning. AI Mag. **350**(4), 105–120 (2014)
3. Angluin, D.: Queries and concept learning. Mach. Learn. **2**, 319–342 (1988)
4. Arrieta, A.B., et al.: Explainable artificial intelligence (XAI): concepts, taxonomies, opportunities and challenges toward responsible AI. Inf. Fusion **58**, 82–115 (2020)
5. Atlas, L., Cohn, D., Ladner, R.: Training connectionist networks with queries and selective sampling. In: Advances in Neural Information Processing Systems, vol. 2 (1989)
6. Baum, E.B.: Neural net algorithms that learn in polynomial time from examples and queries. IEEE Trans. Neural Netw. **20**(1), 5–19 (1991)
7. Belkin, M., et al.: Reconciling modern machine-learning practice and the classical bias-variance trade-off. In: Proceedings of the National Academy of Sciences, vol. 1160. no. (32), pp. 15849–15854 (2019)
8. Berg, S., et al.: Ilastik: interactive machine learning for (bio) image analysis. Nat. Methods **160**(12), 1226–1232 (2019)
9. Branson, S., Perona, P., Belongie, S.: Strong supervision from weak annotation: Interactive training of deformable part models. In: 2011 International Conference on Computer Vision, pp. 1832–1839. IEEE (2011)
10. Budd, S., Robinson, E.C., Kainz, B.: A survey on active learning and human-in-the-loop deep learning for medical image analysis. Med. Image Anal. **71**, 102062 (2021)
11. Cho, J.W., et al.: MCDAL: maximum classifier discrepancy for active learning. IEEE Trans. Neural Netw. Learn. Syst. (2022)
12. Chung, M.-H., et al.: Interactive machine learning for data exfiltration detection: Active learning with human expertise. In: 2020 IEEE International Conference on Systems, Man, and Cybernetics (SMC), pp. 280–287. IEEE (2020)
13. Cohn, D., Atlas, L., Ladner, R.: Improving generalization with active learning. Mach. Learn. **15**, 201–221 (1994)
14. Dagan, I., Engelson, S.P.: Committee-based sampling for training probabilistic classifiers. In: Machine Learning Proceedings 1995, pp. 150–157. Elsevier (1995)
15. Dasgupta, S., Kalai, A.T., Tauman, A.: Analysis of perceptron-based active learning. J. Mach. Learn. Res. **100**(2) 2009
16. Du, X., Zhong, D., Shao, H.: Building an active palmprint recognition system. In: 2019 IEEE International Conference on Image Processing (ICIP), pp. 1685–1689. IEEE (2019)
17. Dudley, J.J., Kristensson, P.O.: A review of user interface design for interactive machine learning. ACM Trans. Interact. Intell. Syst. (TiiS) **80**(2), 1–37 (2018)
18. Fails, J.A., Olsen Jr, D.R.: Interactive machine learning. In: Proceedings of the 8th International Conference on Intelligent User Interfaces, pp. 39–45 (2003)
19. Goyal, P., et al.: Accurate, large minibatch SGD: training imageNet in 1 hour. arXiv preprint arXiv:1706.02677 (2017)
20. He, K., et al.: Deep residual learning for image recognition. In: Proceedings of the IEEE Conference on Computer Vision and Pattern Recognition, pp. 770–778 (2016)

21. Ho, Y., Wookey, S.: The real-world-weight cross-entropy loss function: modeling the costs of mislabeling. IEEE Access **8**, 4806–4813 (2019)
22. Holzinger, A.: Interactive machine learning for health informatics: when do we need the human-in-the-loop? Brain Inform. **30**(2), 119–131 (2016)
23. Holzinger, A., Plass, M., Holzinger, K., Crişan, G.C., Pintea, C.-M., Palade, V.: Towards interactive machine learning (iML): applying ant colony algorithms to solve the traveling salesman problem with the human-in-the-loop approach. In: Buccafurri, F., Holzinger, A., Kieseberg, P., Tjoa, A.M., Weippl, E. (eds.) CD-ARES 2016. LNCS, vol. 9817, pp. 81–95. Springer, Cham (2016). https://doi.org/10.1007/978-3-319-45507-5_6
24. Hu, R., Namee, B.M., Delany, S.J.: Sweetening the dataset: using active learning to label unlabelled datasets. In: Proceedings of AICS, vol. 8, pp. 53–62 (2008)
25. Jiang, L., Liu, S., Chen, C., Recent research advances on interactive machine learning: Recent research advances on interactive machine learning. J. Vis. **22**, 401–417 (2019)
26. Kelly, D., et al.: Methods for evaluating interactive information retrieval systems with users. Found. Trends® Inf. Retrieval, **30**(1–2), 1–224 (2009)
27. Kim, M., et al.: Topiclens: efficient multi-level visual topic exploration of large-scale document collections. IEEE Trans. Vis. Comput. Graph. **230**(1), 151–160 (2016)
28. King, R.D., et al.: The automation of science. Science **3240**(5923), 85–89 (2009)
29. Kose, I., Gokturk, M., Kilic, K.: An interactive machine-learning-based electronic fraud and abuse detection system in healthcare insurance. Appl. Soft Comput. **36**, 283–299 (2015)
30. Lewis, D.D., Catlett, J.: Heterogeneous uncertainty sampling for supervised learning. In: Machine Learning Proceedings 1994, pp. 148–156. Elsevier (1994)
31. Lin, X., Parikh, D.: Active learning for visual question answering: an empirical study. arXiv preprint arXiv:1711.01732 (2017)
32. Liu, Z., et al.: Patterns and sequences: Interactive exploration of clickstreams to understand common visitor paths. IEEE Trans. Vis. Comput. Graph. **230**(1), 321–330 (2016)
33. McCallum, A., Nigam, K., et al.: Employing EM and pool-based active learning for text classification. In: ICML, vol. 98, pp. 350–358. Citeseer (1998)
34. Rawat, S., et al.: How useful is image-based active learning for plant organ segmentation? Plant Phenomics, 2022 (2022)
35. Sabato, S., Hess, T.: Interactive algorithms: pool, stream and precognitive stream. J. Mach. Learn. Res. **18**, 1–39 (2017)
36. Scheffer, T., Decomain, C., Wrobel, S.: Active hidden Markov models for information extraction. In: Hoffmann, F., Hand, D.J., Adams, N., Fisher, D., Guimaraes, G. (eds.) IDA 2001. LNCS, vol. 2189, pp. 309–318. Springer, Heidelberg (2001). https://doi.org/10.1007/3-540-44816-0_31
37. Schumann, R., Rehbein, I.: Active learning via membership query synthesis for semi-supervised sentence classification. In: Proceedings of the 23rd Conference on Computational Natural Language Learning (CoNLL), pp. 472–481 (2019)
38. Settles, B.: Active learning literature survey (2009)
39. Shannon, C.E.: A mathematical theory of communication. Bell Syst. Tech. J. **270**(3), 379–423 (1948)
40. Smith, S.L., et al.: Don't decay the learning rate, increase the batch size. arXiv preprint arXiv:1711.00489 (2017)
41. Teso, S., Kersting, K.: Explanatory interactive machine learning. In: Proceedings of the 2019 AAAI/ACM Conference on AI, Ethics, and Society, pp. 239–245 (2019)

42. The Royal College of Radiologists. Rcr clinical radiology census report 2021 (2021). https://www.rcr.ac.uk/clinical-radiology/rcr-clinical-radiology-census-report-2021 . Accessed 27 Feb 2023
43. Wang, Y., et al.: Efficient DNN training with knowledge-guided layer freezing. arXiv preprint arXiv:2201.06227 (2022)
44. Yang, J., et al.: MedMNIST v2-a large-scale lightweight benchmark for 2D and 3D biomedical image classification. Sci. Data **100**(1), 41 (2023)
45. Betül Yüce, A., Yaslan, Y.: A disagreement based co-active learning method for sleep stage classification. In: 2016 International Conference on Systems, Signals and Image Processing (IWSSIP), pp. 1–4. IEEE (2016)
46. Zhan, X., et al.: A comparative survey of deep active learning. arXiv preprint arXiv:2203.13450 (2022)
47. Zhang, Y., Lease, M., Wallace, B.: Active discriminative text representation learning. In: Proceedings of the AAAI Conference on Artificial Intelligence, vol. 31 (2017)

# CorrEmbed: Evaluating Pre-trained Model Image Similarity Efficacy with a Novel Metric

Karl Audun Kagnes Borgersen[1]([✉])(ID), Morten Goodwin[1](ID), Jivitesh Sharma[1](ID), Tobias Aasmoe[2], Mari Leonhardsen[2], and Gro Herredsvela Rørvik[3]

[1] University of Agder, Grimstad, Norway
{karl.audun.borgersen,morten.goodwin,jivitest.sharma}@uia.no
[2] Tise, Oslo, Norway
{tobias,mari.leonhardsen}@tise.com
[3] FJONG, Oslo, Norway
gro@fjong.com

**Abstract.** Detecting visually similar images is a particularly useful attribute to look to when calculating product recommendations. Embedding similarity, which utilizes pre-trained computer vision models to extract high-level image features, has demonstrated remarkable efficacy in identifying images with similar compositions. However, there is a lack of methods for evaluating the embeddings generated by these models, as conventional loss and performance metrics do not adequately capture their performance in image similarity search tasks.

In this paper, we evaluate the viability of the image embeddings from numerous pre-trained computer vision models using a novel approach named CorrEmbed. Our approach computes the correlation between distances in image embeddings and distances in human-generated tag vectors. We extensively evaluate numerous pre-trained Torchvision models using this metric, revealing an intuitive relationship of linear scaling between ImageNet1k accuracy scores and tag-correlation scores. Importantly, our method also identifies deviations from this pattern, providing insights into how different models capture high-level image features.

By offering a robust performance evaluation of these pre-trained models, CorrEmbed serves as a valuable tool for researchers and practitioners seeking to develop effective, data-driven approaches to similar item recommendations in fashion retail. All code and experiments are openly available at https://github.com/cair/CorrEmbed_Evaluating_Pre-train ed_Model_Efficacy/tree/main.

**Keywords:** Image Similarity · Content-Based Recommendations · Zero-Shot Learning · Recommender Systems

## 1 Introduction

There are several enticing aspects to using pre-trained computer vision models to recommend similar products. It requires no resources for model training,

© The Author(s), under exclusive license to Springer Nature Switzerland AG 2023
M. Bramer and F. Stahl (Eds.): SGAI 2023, LNAI 14381, pp. 89–102, 2023.
https://doi.org/10.1007/978-3-031-47994-6_7

avoiding the need for labeled data or the computation required to train machine learning models. Neither does it require any product information beyond a product image, lending itself particularly well to relatively small online storefronts or online second-hand sales. Similar item recommendations entail simply recommending items similar to a target item. Fashion, in particular, as a domain has some distinctive properties that make it uniquely suited for recommendations based on image similarity search, namely its emphasis on the visual appearance of the products. Extracting image embeddings from pre-trained models for Recommender Systems(RS) is used in production today. Tise[1], for instance, is a large Norwegian second-hand sales company and the employer of two of our co-authors. The company used embedding comparisons in production as part of an ensemble similar-item recommendation method.

However, existing methods face validation challenges because direct comparisons of image embeddings do not align with the intended use case of pre-trained image models. Consequently, neither their loss nor classification performance metrics effectively indicate a model's performance in this domain. While the efficacy of retrieving similar images based on computer vision model embeddings is apparent to human observers, limited literature exists on evaluating their effectiveness. This paper contributes a more rigorous evaluation of how well each of the models performs as compared to human tag annotation.

This paper introduces CorrEmbed, an evaluation metric based on tag-based similarity within the fashion domain. It takes advantage of human-tagged outfits to evaluate the zero-shot performance of a model's embeddings. The evaluation is performed by calculating the correlation between distances in image-embedding space and in tag-embedding space. These indicator variables, or tag vectors, are augmented by weighting them according to category using statistical entropy. CorrEmbed is used to provide a benchmark for the performance of numerous pre-trained computer-vision models. We discuss the performance of these and which features and model architectures are more conducive to good tag-correlation performance, such as the format of the tensors produced by different pre-trained model versions. In particular, we underline cases in which this performance deviates from the pattern of increased image-classification performance leading to increased CorrEmbed performance. It is our hope that this project will be a source of insight for the already extensively studied field of fashion item recommendations [5,22].

The pre-trained models evaluated for this project are from Torchvision's model set [17].

## 2    Related Work

RS can refer to numerous different approaches, from Collaborative Filtering [13] to Deep Learning [4,21] to (Deep) Reinforcement Learning [1] to Tsetlin Machines [3]. At the core of this paper lies the concept of similar item recommendations. While collaborative filtering models have long been the

---

[1] Tise: htttps://tise.com/.

dominant method for providing recommendations, content-based RSs have often been employed to address problems with linear scaling. These item-based RSs identify relationships between items and recommend items frequently bought together, for which the capability of extracting information from for example text descriptions or images is highly relevant [12]. Image embeddings have also been used in the context of classification for a while. Akata et al. [2] use it to perform zero-shot learning on unsupervised data by detecting clusters of image embeddings. Fu. et al. [6] provide an overview of zero-shot learning in 2019. These papers demonstrate how prevalent the use of image embeddings is in the SotA.

Visual image attributes form the foundation of numerous contemporary RSs, such as [8] and [26]. Evaluating how similar images are is a necessity within Image Retrieval, in this context, Tarasov et al. [24] utilize the embeddings of a trained neural network for this task for which the distance between two images is the Euclidian distances between embeddings. Garcia et al. [7] train a regression NN for this purpose and compare performance to a few other metrics, including cosine distance. Resnick et al. [19] utilize Pearson correlation to measure user similarity. While these previous works parse image (or user) embeddings in a manner comparable to CorrEmbed, none of them quantitatively evaluate how well individual models perform at measuring image similarity.

## 3   Methods

In summary, CorrEmbed entails retrieving image embeddings from pre-trained classification computer vision models and identifying similar items by calculating the distance between them. We evaluate their performance by calculating the correlation of the distances between pairs of image embeddings and the distances between pairs of tag embeddings. The final score represents the mean correlation between image and tag embeddings across $k$ samples.

The datasets used in this paper are generated using data from FJONG, a small clothing rental company with access to approximately $10,000$ human-tagged outfits and around $18,000$ corresponding images. 705 tags constitute the tag-embedding space, each belonging to one out of the 13 tag categories listed in Table 1.

All models and model weights are retrieved from Torchvision's model set[2]. All classification models have trained on the ImageNet [20] dataset with $1k$ classes.

### 3.1   Tag-Based Metric

A one-hot-encoded vector of tags is calculated based on tag presence, resulting in a vector with 705 dimensions. Similarly to the image-embeddings, the clothing items are converted into tag-based representations. We calculate the distances

---

[2] TorchVision's model set is available at https://pytorch.org/vision/stable/models. html.

between an input embedding $i$ and all $n$ other embeddings for both tag and image embeddings. (Eq. 1, 2, 3) in which $T$ and $I$ refer to a set of all image and tag embeddings respectively and $T_i$ or $I_i$ represents the ith element in both of these sets. For a given set of image embeddings, we assess the performance by calculating the correlation between the tag-based metric distance and the distance between image embeddings. This is done using the Pearson correlation coefficient. The final score for a model is obtained by computing the mean correlation across $k$ image samples (Eq. 4). In which $x_i$ and $y_i$ represent a set of $n$ tag and image similarity scores for the vector at index $i$ and $\bar{x}$ and $\bar{y}$ are the mean values of the same sets.

$$\text{cosine\_similarity}(\mathbf{A}, \mathbf{B}) = \frac{\mathbf{A} \cdot \mathbf{B}}{\|\mathbf{A}\|\|\mathbf{B}\|} \tag{1}$$

$$\text{Image\_Similarity}(I_i) = y_i = \{\text{cosine\_similarity}(\mathbf{I}_i, \mathbf{I}_j) : j = 1, 2, \ldots, n\} \tag{2}$$

$$\text{Tag\_Similarity}(T_i) = x_i = \{\text{cosine similarity}(\mathbf{T}_i, \mathbf{T}_j) : j = 1, 2, \ldots, n\} \tag{3}$$

$$CorrEmbed = \frac{1}{k} \sum_{i=1}^{k} \frac{\sum_{j=1}^{n}(x_{ji} - \bar{x})(y_{ji} - \bar{y})}{\sqrt{\sum_{j=1}^{n}(x_{ji} - \bar{x})^2}\sqrt{\sum_{j=1}^{n}(y_{ji} - \bar{y})^2}} \tag{4}$$

In this dataset, tags are grouped into categories, e.g., "Collar" is categorized as "Neckline". All tags present in the dataset, except for brand tags, are shown in Table 1. As the "Size" and "Shoe Size" category isn't necessarily present in the images of the dataset (The same clothing item in different sizes will occasionally share the same product photo), this category is dropped entirely. For the context of recommendation, some tags are more compelling to the average customer than others. We are more interested in representations that appropriately capture the user's interests. A user browsing for a new winter coat will be more interested in other winter coats rather than products with the same color. We evaluate the customers' purchase history and compute the entropy for each tag category. Calculating the entropy was done to capture the likelihood of a customer re-purchasing an item with a similar category, yielding a lower value if the purchased outfits' tag categories exhibit consistent sub-tags. For example, if a user exclusively buys clothing items with "Dots" or "Stripes" patterns, the "Pattern" category will have a low entropy score. Conversely if the user prefers a variety of colors, the "Color" category will have a high entropy score. As shown in Eq. 5, in which $C_i$ refers to a customer's rental history, c is the total number of customers evaluated, $C_i(x_j)$ is the total occurrences of tag $x_j$ in the rental history $C_i$, and $X$ refers to a tag category for which we want to calculate the weights.

$$\text{Entropy(X)} = H(X) = \frac{1}{c} \sum_{i=1}^{c} - \sum_{j=1}^{|X|} \frac{C_i(x_j)}{\|C_i\|} \log \frac{C_i(x_j)}{\|C_i\|} \tag{5}$$

We normalize these entropy values between 0 and 1 based on the maximum possible entropy within this range, and subsequently invert the weights (Eq. 6), $min(H)$ and $max(H)$ refer to the largest and smallest calculated tag category value. Our earlier tag embeddings are then weighted for their respective tag category. This ensures, for example, that the relative tag distance between a blue blazer and a red blazer is shorter than the distance between a blue blazer and a blue jumpsuit.

$$\text{Tag\_Weights}(X) = 1 - \frac{H(X) - \min(H)}{\max(H) - \min(H)} \tag{6}$$

**Table 1.** Tags present in the dataset

| Category | Tags |
|---|---|
| Brand | **552 different fashion brands, omitted for brevity.** |
| Material | Triacetate, Lyocell, Polyester, Cashmere, Linen, Cupro, Velvet, Leather, Spandex, Lace, Beaded, Faux fur, Fur, Rayon, Down, Acrylic, Bamboo, Polyethylene Terephthalate, Acetate, Satin, Chiffon, Silk, Polyamide, Tulle, Wool, Nylon, Denim, Cotton, Vegan Leather, Viscose, Modal, Gold, Elastane, Lurex, Lycra, Lacquer, Silver, Tencel, Polyvinyl Chloride, Polyurethane, Metal |
| Category | Blouses, Accessories, Jewelry, Shirts, Kimonos, Shoes, Bags, Pants, Suits, Coats, Sweaters, Vests, Outerwear, Jumpsuits, Skirts, Blazers, Dresses, Cardigans, Knitwear, Jackets, Shorts, Tops |
| Color | Yellow, Purple, Grey, Blue, Green, Brown, Pink, Multicolor, Beige, Orange, Black, Gold, Red, White, Navy, Silver, Turquoise, Burgundy |
| Size | XXS, Onesize, Large, 4XL, Medium, Extra Small, 3XL-4XL, Extra Large, 3XL, Small, 2XL, XXL-XXXXL |
| No category | Sporty, Winter, Height - 180–190 cm, Dressed-up, Fall, New, Summer, Romantic, Edgy, Spring, Classic |
| Occasion | FJONG Active, Going out, Black-tie, Everyday, FJONG Plus Size, Prom, Wedding, Party, FJONG Bump, Active, Business |
| Sleeve | Mid arms, Spaghetti straps, T-shirt, Cold shoulder, Tube, Straps, Long arms |
| Embellishment | Ruffles, Pearls, Sequins, Feathers, Glitter, Studs, Tassels |
| Neckline | Boat Neck, Deep Neck, Halter Neck, V-neck, Round Neck, Collar, Turtleneck |
| Waist | Empire, High, Normal, Adjustable, Stretchy, Low |
| Shoe Size | 39, 36, 40, 38, 37, 41 |
| Pattern | Floral, Checkers, Dots, Stripes, Animal, Pattern |
| Fit | Loose fit, Wrap, Pregnant-friendly, Slim fit |
| Length | Midi, One, Mini, Maxi |

# 4    Results and Discussions

This section presents the results of our experiments, which benchmark the performance of our pre-trained models. We also employ t-Distributed Stochastic Embedding (t-SNE) plots to visualize the clustering of embeddings in our models.

Model performance on CorrEmbed generally increases by the model size and ImageNet performance, as seen in Fig. 1. While model performance doesn't necessarily directly scale in accordance with its ImageNet score, scaled-up versions of the same model outperform their smaller counterparts. This provides a good sanity check on the veracity of our metric. The correlation between the ImageNet score and the CorrEmbed score holds true for comparisons between the

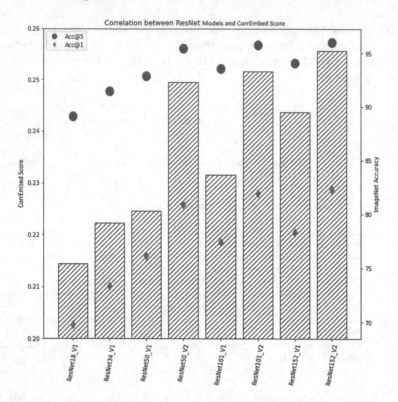

**Fig. 1.** Comparison between ResNet [9] model correlation score and ImageNet1k accuracy across differing ResNet model sizes. CorrEmbed scores have been constrained to the range of 0.2 to 0.26 to emphasize the score differences.

scaled-up versions of the same architecture but isn't necessarily the case when comparing two different model architectures. For instance, EfficientNet models outperform ResNet models with the same accuracy score, e.g., ResNet50 V2 has an Acc@1 score of 80.858 and achieves a CorrEmbed score of 0.249, as compared to EfficientNet B2 which has an Acc@1 score of 80.608 and a CorrEmbed score of 0.273.

Table 2 (and Fig. 2) provides an overview of the performance of various model architectures. We selected the top-performing version of each architecture based on ImageNet1k accuracy. We include two control methods for both tag and image embeddings to establish a baseline for significance. The first random model method generates a random tensor with the same shape as the image embeddings for each image, while the random tag vectors generate a binary vector with the same shape as the tag vector. The two shuffle control methods randomize the association between tag or image embeddings and each outfit.

We observe a significant correlation between ImageNet1k scores and CorrEmbed scores, albeit with some deviations. The top-performing models ViT,

RegNetY [18], and EfficientNet [23] outperform other models by a margin comparable to the performance improvements between AlexNet [14] and ConvNext [15], despite negligible differences in ImageNet1k scores. This observation makes some intuitive sense, as improving a model's accuracy score from, for instance, 87 to 88 likely corresponds to a much greater enhancement of the model's internal representation than an improvement from 56 to 57, in line with the Pareto Principle[3]. However, the observed increase in performance exceeds what we would expect if this were the sole contributing factor.

The embeddings evaluated in this case were all retrieved as the standard output embeddings of the models. This had the added advantage of removing the shape of the embeddings as a factor for the CorrEmbed score since the final output embedding of the classes remains the same 1000-dimensional vector regardless of the model architecture.

**Table 2.** Overview of the performance using the top-performing version of each model architecture, sorted by ImageNet1k score. ImgNet Acc@1 and ImgNet Acc@5 refer to the model's performance on accuracy at ImageNet1k top 1 and top 5, respectively. CorrEmbed is our weighted tag vector scoring, and unweighted refers to the same vectors without the weights. Random and shuffle in both rows and columns are control methods. The CorrEmbed scores of this table are visually represented in Fig. 2

| Model | ImgNet Acc@1 | ImgNet Acc@5 | CorrEmbed | Unweighted | Random | Shuffled |
|---|---|---|---|---|---|---|
| random | 0.0 | 0.0 | 0.0086 | 0.0088 | 0.0229 | 0.008 |
| random shuffle | 0.0 | 0.0 | 0.0016 | −0.0032 | 0.0076 | −0.0058 |
| AlexNet | 56.522 | 79.066 | 0.1463 | 0.1485 | 0.0165 | 0.0008 |
| SqueezeNet1 1 | 58.178 | 80.624 | 0.1508 | 0.137 | 0.012 | 0.0038 |
| GoogLeNet | 69.778 | 89.53 | 0.2103 | 0.1933 | 0.0133 | 0.0036 |
| VGG19 BN | 74.218 | 91.842 | 0.1837 | 0.1733 | 0.0120 | 0.0023 |
| MobileNet V3 Large | 75.274 | 92.566 | 0.2251 | 0.201 | 0.0174 | 0.0048 |
| ShuffleNet V2 X2 | 76.23 | 93.006 | 0.2264 | 0.1977 | 0.0175 | 0.0051 |
| DenseNet201 | 76.896 | 93.37 | 0.2121 | 0.1903 | 0.0146 | 0.0023 |
| MNASNet1 3 | 76.506 | 93.522 | 0.2276 | 0.2083 | 0.0148 | 0.0058 |
| Wide ResNet101 2 | 81.602 | 95.758 | 0.2445 | 0.2182 | 0.0075 | 0.0034 |
| resnet152 V2 | 82.284 | 96.002 | 0.2493 | 0.2243 | 0.0119 | 0.0043 |
| ResNeXt101 64X4D | 83.246 | 96.454 | 0.2393 | 0.2092 | 0.0096 | 0.0048 |
| MaxViT T | 83.7 | 96.722 | 0.1943 | 0.174 | 0.0044 | 0.0039 |
| Swin V2 B | 84.112 | 96.864 | 0.2649 | 0.2417 | 0.0151 | 0.0045 |
| ConvNext Large v1 | 84.414 | 96.976 | 0.2641 | 0.2383 | 0.0157 | 0.0032 |
| EfficientNet V2 L | 85.808 | 97.788 | **0.3680** | **0.3189** | 0.0176 | 0.0051 |
| RegNet Y 32GF | 86.838 | 98.362 | 0.3428 | 0.306 | 0.014 | 0.0038 |
| ViT H 14 E2E | **88.552** | **98.694** | 0.3633 | 0.3184 | 0.0114 | 0.0036 |

The layers preceding the output layer tend to capture a finer representation of the embeddings. Though the degree to which this is the case depends on the model itself. Table 3 details the scores of the models based on the input embeddings to the penultimate layer rather than the output. Working with embeddings

---

[3] https://en.wikipedia.org/wiki/Pareto_principle.

earlier than this is unfortunately too inconsistent to make any direct comparisons. As happened with SqueezeNet [11] in Table 3, any embeddings retrieved before the model pools into the shape $(1, -1)$ tend to reach unworkable sizes.

Table 3 also logs inference time for batches of 90 images, along with the shapes of the evaluated tensors. Unsurprisingly, the best-performing models also clocked in the longest inference time, though in contrast to ImageNet accuracy, some models surpassed expectations significantly based solely on inference time. MaxViT [25] and MobileNet [10] are good examples of these. An explanation for this could be the priorities of the original model developers. As we've only evaluated the top-performing models of each architecture, these are likely the model iterations with the heaviest focus on performance to the detriment of other aspects of the model and are, therefore, subject to a significant degree of diminishing returns. Interestingly, despite the varying tensor shapes, the CorrEmbed score is even more closely associated with the ImageNet1k score in the penultimate model layers (Table 2 when compared to the output layer in Table 3, have a Pearson correlation of 0.767 and 0.941 respectively in relation to ImageNet $accuracy@1$)

**Table 3.** Overview of CorrEmbed performance based on the input to the last layer. Inference time is the time taken to evaluate $\frac{1}{200}th$ of the dataset (90 images). Control values for both image and tag embeddings, along with binary tag vectors have been omitted for brevity. These maintain roughly the same ratio to the CorrEmbed score as seen in Table 2. As the final layer of SqueezeNet is an Average Pooling layer, we were unable to perform our experiment on it due to the size of the tensors it produced. The inference time documented for ViT was run in a separate batch from the rest of the models shown. It is, therefore, possible external factors have influenced it.

| Model | Model Params | CorrEmbed | Inference Time | Embedding Shape |
|---|---|---|---|---|
| AlexNet | 61.1M | 0.1775 | 0.052 | (90, 4096) |
| SqueezeNet1 1 | 1.2M | N/A | 0.094 | (90, 1000, 13, 13) |
| GoogLeNet | 6.6M | 0.2167 | 0.064 | (90, 1024) |
| VGG19 BN | 143.7M | 0.2247 | 0.158 | (90, 4096) |
| MobileNet V3 Large | 5.5M | 0.2299 | 0.054 | (90, 1280) |
| ShuffleNet V2 X2 | 7.4M | 0.2290 | 0.057 | (90, 2048) |
| DenseNet201 | 20.0M | 0.2406 | 0.151 | (90, 1920) |
| MNASNet1 3 | 6.3M | 0.2375 | 0.079 | (90, 1280) |
| Wide ResNet101 2 | 68.9M | 0.2462 | 0.264 | (90, 2048) |
| resnet152 V2 | 60.2M | 0.2491 | 0.202 | (90, 2048) |
| ResNeXt101 64X4D | 83.5M | 0.2469 | 0.608 | (90, 2048) |
| MaxViT T | 30.9M | 0.2516 | 0.197 | (90, 512) |
| Swin V2 B | 87.9M | 0.2659 | 0.404 | (90, 1024) |
| ConvNext Large v1 | 197.8M | 0.2695 | 0.559 | (90, 1536) |
| EfficientNet V2 L | 118.5M | 0.3604 | 1.022 | (90, 1280) |
| RegNet Y 32GF | 145.0M | 0.3824 | 1.137 | (90, 3712) |
| ViT H 14 E2E | 633.5M | **0.4288** | 15.412 | (90, 1280) |

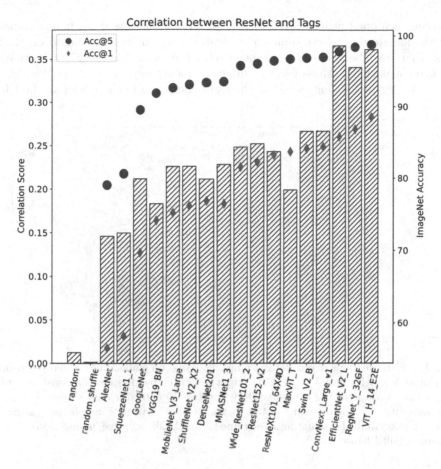

**Fig. 2.** Graph representation of the results from Table 2. Columns display the CorrEmbed score for the different models. The circular and diamond marks show performance on ImageNet

The use of models trained on ImageNet, in particular, could potentially have had the added advantage of the models ignoring any humans appearing in the image. For example, the $4th$ most similar image detected by the upper model in Fig. 4. As none of ImageNet1k's classes involve classifying humans [20], the pre-trained models are incentivized to ignore them. This congrues well with our metrics emphasizing the properties of worn clothing rather than the people wearing them. The ability to overlook the human subjects in images is more pronounced in the stronger models compared to the weaker ones.

### 4.1   Exploring Embedding Space

As shown in Fig. 3, the high-dimensional embeddings of each image can be visualized in low-dimensional space by taking into account the relative distances between each point using t-SNE [16]. Despite the models used not being trained in this domain we observe some clear clustering of embeddings based on their tags. Figure 3 label embeddings tagged with the same "category" (essentially, the type of clothing). Moreover, we notice significant improvements in clustering for the better-performing model on the right compared to the model on the left.

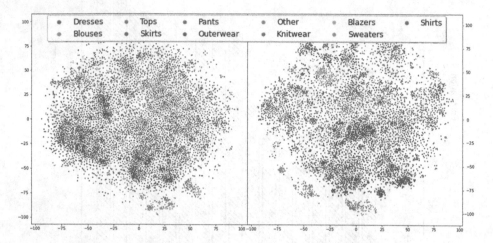

**Fig. 3.** t-SNE diagrams of our dataset's images based on embeddings generated using ResNet50 V1 (left) and ViT H E2E (right). The embeddings are colored according to the "Category" tag category. Only the top 10 categories are shown to maintain legibility. All others are relegated to the "Other" category. See https://github.com/cair/CorrEmbed_Evaluating_Pre-trained_Model_Efficacy/tree/main#figure-3 for a more detailed figure.

An expected flaw with recommending similar items using embeddings is evident in the t-SNE diagrams. Some embeddings are naturally going to end up in isolated positions far away from the larger clusters of embeddings. These isolated items will effectively never be recommended based solely on similar item recommendations. Steps can be taken to increase the recommendation priority of these isolated items, but embeddings placed on the outskirts of clusters will likely rank far too low in the similar item rankings among its neighbors to ever actually be recommended in a natural setting.

## 4.2   Dataset Scale

The dataset used for this paper is relatively small, consisting of around 18000 images in total. This scale ensures that the direct comparison of all image embeddings is feasible even in production when used for similar item recommendations. However, this format also leads to a significant number of outlier compositions. A good example is the input image in Fig. 6. The top-performing model picks up on the worn fleece sweater and finds other warm clothing items to be the most similar, while the lower-performing models are more affected by composition. This makes some intuitive sense. Each image in the ImageNet1k dataset consists of a central subject to be classified and more-or-less irrelevant background information. The better-performing models are the ones able to adequately capture these subjects while avoiding getting hung up on the other details of the images. It is difficult to tell the degree to which the models are affected by the composition, as the majority of the FJONG dataset consists of images with uniform backgrounds and often without a fashion model. A more expansive dataset would better demonstrate how badly composition impacts similarity predictions.

### 4.3 Qualitative Performance Analysis

The main purpose of this paper is to achieve a concrete metric with which the capabilities of embedding evaluation could be measured. Such a metric is of little use, however, if the image similarity does not improve in the eyes of a human as well. This section discusses a few qualitative observations concerning the capabilities of higher-performing methods as compared to lower-performing ones. Figure 5 emphasizes how strong the contrast between the best and worst performing models, ViT_H_14_E2E and AlexNet, can be. The former model can easily pick out a set of similar sweaters, while the latter gets bogged down picking out clothes with similar color schemes. Significant differences exist in the attributes that the models choose to focus on, as illustrated in Fig. 4. Weaker models tend to put too much emphasis on whether a fashion model is present in the image, as well as the model's pose. Stronger models, on the other hand, are more capable of ignoring these factors and, for instance, picking out the original clothing item worn in the input image.

**Fig. 4.** Comparison between a strong and weak model. The original image is displayed to the far left, with the most similar images being displayed in order from left to right. The top row shows the stronger ViT_H_14_E2E model while the row below shows the results from the weaker AlexNet model.See https://github.com/cair/CorrEmbed_Evaluating_Pre-trained_Model_Efficacy/tree/main#figure-4 for a more detailed figure.

The input image in Fig. 6 is among the most challenging images in the dataset. The uncommon composition introduces a degree of visual noise, which causes difficulties with image embedding comparison. The extent to which the visual noise affects the embeddings varies. For example, the products identified by the $vgg16$ model appear close to random, while the outfits found by the $ViT_H$

model focus on the fleece sweater. Note that the actual product sold from the input image is, in reality, the skirt, not the sweater. This highlights another limitation of this method, the inability to specify which component of the image is most relevant.

**Fig. 5.** Comparison between a strong and weak model. The original image is displayed to the far left, with the most similar images being displayed in order from left to right. The top row shows the stronger ViT_H_14_E2E model while the row below shows the results from the weaker AlexNet model. See https://github.com/cair/CorrEmbed_Eval uating_Pre-trained_Model_Efficacy/tree/main#figure-5 for a more detailed figure.

**Fig. 6.** Comparison between ViT_H (top), resnet50_v2 (middle), and vgg16 (bottom) with a difficult image. The ViT performs better than the resnet50 model which perform better than the vgg16 model. See https://github.com/cair/CorrEmbed_Evaluating_Pre-trained_Model_Efficacy/tree/main#figure-6 for a more detailed figure.

## 5   Conclusion

In this paper, we introduce and evaluate the performance of CorrEmbed, a novel method designed to assess the zero-shot image-embedding similarity performance of NNs. We employ this metric to evaluate a myriad of different pre-trained ImageNet1k classification models. Of these models, the vision transformer ViT_H_14_E2E is found to be the most performant, beyond even the performance of Fashion-CLIP, a model tuned to the fashion domain. CorrEmbed score is strongly correlated to ImageNet1k performance. While CorrEmbed performance naturally tends to increase for each successive layer of a model, the final output layer is found to produce consistently worse embeddings than the second to last layer. We note that specific model architectures tend to surpass others with comparable performance on ImageNet. For example, Torchvision's v2 models consistently outperform their v1 counterparts. This study contributes valuable insights into the performance of various models in the context of image-embedding similarity. Though perhaps few surprising conclusions can be drawn from the results, formal evaluation compared to human annotators is an important step to ensure our RSs are as rigorous as possible.

**Acknowledgments.** Funded by the Research Council of Norway through the project "Your green, smart and endless wardrobe", project number 309977. We thank FJONG for providing the data used as a basis for the dataset in this paper.

# References

1. Afsar, M.M., Crump, T., Far, B.: Reinforcement learning based recommender systems: a survey. ACM Comput. Surv. **55**(7), 1–38 (2022). https://doi.org/10.1145/3543846
2. Akata, Z., Reed, S., Walter, D., Lee, H., Schiele, B.: Evaluation of output embeddings for fine-grained image classification. In: Proceedings of the IEEE Conference on Computer Vision and Pattern Recognition (CVPR). IEEE, San Juan, PR, USA (2015)
3. Borgersen, K.A., Goodwin, M., Sharma, J.: A comparison between Tsetlin machines and deep neural networks in the context of recommendation systems. In: Northern Lights Deep Learning Workshop, vol. 4 (2023). https://doi.org/10.7557/18.6807
4. Da'u, A., Salim, N.: Recommendation system based on deep learning methods: a systematic review and new directions. Artif. Intell. Rev. **53**(4), 2709–2748 (2020)
5. Deldjoo, Y., et al.: A review of modern fashion recommender systems. arXiv preprint arXiv:2202.02757 (2022)
6. Fu, Y., Xiang, T., Jiang, Y.G., Xue, X., Sigal, L., Gong, S.: Recent advances in zero-shot recognition: toward data-efficient understanding of visual content. IEEE Signal Process. Mag. **35**(1), 112–125 (2018). https://doi.org/10.1109/MSP.2017.2763441
7. Garcia, N., Vogiatzis, G.: Learning non-metric visual similarity for image retrieval. Image Vis. Comput. **82**, 18–25 (2019). https://doi.org/10.1016/j.imavis.2019.01.001
8. Gomez Bruballa, R., Burnham-King, L., Sala, A.: Learning users' preferred visual styles in an image marketplace. In: Proceedings of the 16th ACM Conference on Recommender Systems, pp. 466–468. ACM, New York, NY, USA (2022)
9. He, K., Zhang, X., Ren, S., Sun, J.: Deep residual learning for image recognition. In: Proceedings of the IEEE Conference on Computer Vision and Pattern Recognition, pp. 770–778. IEEE, New York, NY, USA (2016)
10. Howard, A., et al.: Searching for mobilenetv3. In: Proceedings of the IEEE/CVF international conference on computer vision, pp. 1314–1324. IEEE, New York, NY, USA (2019)
11. Iandola, F.N., Han, S., Moskewicz, M.W., Ashraf, K., Dally, W.J., Keutzer, K.: Squeezenet: Alexnet-level accuracy with 50x fewer parameters and< 0.5 mb model size. arXiv preprint arXiv:1602.07360 1(1) (2016)
12. Karypis, G.: Evaluation of item-based top-n recommendation algorithms. In: Proceedings of the tenth International Conference on Information and Knowledge Management, pp. 247–254. ACM, New York, NY, USA (2001)

13. Koren, Y., Rendle, S., Bell, R.: Advances in collaborative filtering. Recommender Syst. Handb. **1**(1), 91–142 (2021)
14. Krizhevsky, A., Sutskever, I., Hinton, G.E.: Imagenet classification with deep convolutional neural networks. Commun. ACM **60**(6), 84–90 (2017)
15. Liu, Z., Mao, H., Wu, C.Y., Feichtenhofer, C., Darrell, T., Xie, S.: A convnet for the 2020s. In: Proceedings of the IEEE/CVF Conference on Computer Vision and Pattern Recognition, pp. 11976–11986. IEEE, New York, NY, USA (2022)
16. Van der Maaten, L., Hinton, G.: Visualizing data using t-SNE. J. Mach. Learn. Res. **9**(11), 2579–2605 (2008)
17. maintainers, T., contributors: Models and pre-trained weights (2021). http://pytorch.org/vision/stable/models.html. Accessed 17 Jan 2023
18. Radosavovic, I., Kosaraju, R.P., Girshick, R., He, K., Dollár, P.: Designing network design spaces. In: Proceedings of the IEEE/CVF Conference on Computer Vision and Pattern Recognition. pp. 10428–10436. IEEE, Seattle, WA, USA (2020)
19. Resnick, P., Iacovou, N., Suchak, M., Bergstrom, P., Riedl, J.: Grouplens: An open architecture for collaborative filtering of netnews. In: Proceedings of the 1994 ACM Conference on Computer Supported Cooperative Work, pp. 175–186. ACM, New York, NY, USA (1994)
20. Russakovsky, O., et al.: Imagenet large scale visual recognition challenge. Int. J. Comput. Vision **115**, 211–252 (2015)
21. Sarker, I.H.: Deep learning: a comprehensive overview on techniques, taxonomy, applications and research directions. SN Comput. Sci. **2**(6), 1–20 (2021)
22. Strain, N., Olszewska, J.I.: Naive Bayesian network for automated, fashion personal stylist. In: ICAART (2), pp. 814–821 (2020)
23. Tan, M., Le, Q.: Efficientnetv2: Smaller models and faster training. In: International Conference on Machine Learning, pp. 10096–10106. PMLR, Cambridge MA: JMLR, Cambridge Massachusetts, USA (2021)
24. Tarasov, A.S., Tarasova, V.Y., Grinchenko, N.N., Stepanov, M.A.: Development of a search system for similar images. In: 2020 ELEKTRO, pp. 1–6. IEEE (2020)
25. Tu, Z., et al.: Maxvit: Multi-axis vision transformer. In: Avidan, S., Brostow, G., Cisse, M., Farinella, G.M., Hassner, T. (eds.) ECCV 2022. LNCS, vol. 13684, pp. 459–479. Springer, Cham (2022). https://doi.org/10.1007/978-3-031-20053-3_27
26. Zhang, S., Yao, L., Sun, A., Tay, Y.: Deep learning based recommender system: a survey and new perspectives. ACM Comput. Surv. **52**(1), 1–38 (2019). https://doi.org/10.1145/3285029

# A Contrastive Learning Scheme with Transformer Innate Patches

Sander R. Jyhne[1,2(✉)] [iD], Per-Arne Andersen[1] [iD], Morten Goodwin[1] [iD], and Ivar Oveland[2] [iD]

[1] University of Agder, Grimstad, Norway
{sander.jyhne,per.andersen,morten.goodwin}@uia.no
[2] The Norwegian Mapping Authorit, Kristiansand, Norway
{sander.jyhne,ivar.oveland}@kartverket.no

**Abstract.** This paper presents Contrastive Transformer (CT), a contrastive learning scheme using the innate transformer patches. CT enables existing contrastive learning techniques, often used for image classification, to benefit dense downstream prediction tasks such as semantic segmentation. The scheme performs supervised patch-level contrastive learning, selecting the patches based on the ground truth mask, subsequently used for hard-negative and hard-positive sampling. The scheme applies to all patch-based vision-transformer architectures, is easy to implement, and introduces minimal additional memory footprint. Additionally, the scheme removes the need for huge batch sizes, as each patch is treated as an image.

We apply and test CT for the case of aerial image segmentation, known for low-resolution data, large class imbalance, and similar semantic classes. We perform extensive experiments to show the efficacy of the CT scheme on the ISPRS Potsdam aerial image segmentation dataset. Additionally, we show the generalizability of our scheme by applying it to multiple inherently different transformer architectures. Ultimately, the results show a consistent increase in mean Intersection-over-Union (IoU) across all classes.

**Keywords:** Remote Sensing · Contrastive Learning · Deep Learning · Segmentation

## 1 Introduction

Segmentation of buildings from aerial images is a vital task, significantly impacting various sectors such as urban planning, disaster management, and environmental monitoring [10,12,13,18]. The accuracy of this segmentation process is crucial, as it directly influences the estimation of population density, the development of urban planning maps, and more. However, a noticeable gap persists in existing research, especially regarding the precision of building edges. This shortfall primarily stems from challenges such as class imbalances, the high similarity

M. Bramer and F. Stahl (Eds.): SGAI 2023, LNAI 14381, pp. 103–114, 2023.
https://doi.org/10.1007/978-3-031-47994-6_8

between different classes in aerial image datasets, and the inherent complexity of accurately capturing the intricate details of building edges. These issues complicate tasks like fine-grained change detection and map production that rely heavily on accurate building vectorization. Consequently, manual interventions and additional costs become inevitable, underscoring the need for improved automation.

Segmenting buildings from aerial images is challenging due to the wide range of building types, including skyscrapers, residential houses, and industrial buildings. Each category has its unique shape, size, and pattern characteristics. Additional complexities come from elements like shadows, reflections, and changes in lighting that can make it harder to create accurate segmentation masks. Buildings that overlap or are partially hidden by other objects make the task even more difficult. Historically, building segmentation has been directed toward urban planning, disaster damage assessment, and change detection applications. However, the level of precision necessary for these tasks often differs from applications like building vectorization. Even though some studies have focused on the precision of building segmentation [12,13,20], there is still a need for enhancing the accuracy further. This discrepancy underscores the need for continued research and development in segmentation accuracy. Moreover, the models developed must be capable of generalizing across a wide range of building types and environments, spanning urban and rural settings.

In this work, we introduce the Contrastive Transformer (CT), a supervised contrastive learning model that leverages the inherent patch-structure of the general transformer architecture [5]. Our aim with CT is to enhance the precision of existing transformer-based segmentation models through intra- and inter-image contrastive learning facilitated by the intrinsic patch structure of the transformer architecture. Simply put, intra-image contrastive learning identifies patches within a single image, while inter-image contrastive learning gathers them across multiple images. By harnessing these strategies alongside established contrastive loss functions, we aim to boost our model's performance. Depending on the image and patch size, a single image can accommodate over 20,000 patches aggregated over the transformer encoder's four stages. Patch collection is steered by ground truth masks, which enable the selection of anchor and positive samples containing a homogenous class distribution of the target class. Conversely, negative samples can display a varied class distribution, provided they exclude the target class. We implement a straightforward sampling strategy to select challenging samples for contrastive learning. Our central contribution is the Contrastive Transformer learning scheme, which, in preliminary tests, demonstrated adaptability across various vision-transformer backbones and resulted in an improved Intersection over Union (IoU) score across all classes when benchmarked against existing models. We explore these encouraging results in greater detail in the following sections of the paper.

Section 2 provides an overview of prior work, highlighting gaps in the current literature that motivate our contributions. In Sect. 3, we introduce our primary contribution, the CT learning scheme. We evaluate the proposed method and compare it to previous state-of-the-art methods in aerial building segmentation in Sect. 4. Finally, in Sect. 5, we summarize our findings and discuss the implications of our work. We also explore future CT directions in Sect. 6.

## 2 Related Work

Advances in semantic segmentation often depend on developing more powerful deep neural networks. The earliest literature focused on variations of deep convolutional neural networks, such as the U-Net model [19]. Despite the early success of CNN-based models, the focus has shifted to Transformer-based architectures following the release of the Vision Transformer [5]. Transformers have proven effective in semantic segmentation tasks, even though they bring along certain scalability challenges related to the self-attention mechanism [6]. In the preceding years, several works have reduced the computational complexity while maintaining or increasing the accuracy. The authors of [17] introduce a hierarchical transformer model using shifted windows, effectively reducing self-attention computation. Other works, such as [27], replace the attention-based module with a simple spatial pooling operator performing basic token mixing. Furthermore, in [11], the authors propose a more generalizable model that uses convolutions and self-attention for vision tasks.

While advances in architectural design play a crucial role, an equally important aspect is the optimization strategy, which can enhance the network's performance without architectural modifications. One such strategy that has shown promise is contrastive learning. Contrastive learning is a technique aiming to reduce the distance between representations of the same semantic class while increasing the distance between representations for different classes. Contrastive learning uses a similarity metric, such as cosine similarity or Euclidean distance, to evaluate the relation between representations and give feedback to the network. The latest image-based contrastive frameworks determine similarity scores using the global representation of the data, often used in image classification [3,4,7,22]. Contrastive learning can also be applied using dense representations instead of global representations of the image. In this approach, the representation of a specific class derives from a group of pixels, which has shown improved performance in dense prediction tasks such as object detection and semantic segmentation [15]. However, pixel-wise dense representations' computational and memory demands present significant challenges. Our method mitigates these limitations by leveraging the existing representations in the Transformer backbone for contrastive learning, effectively enhancing performance while minimizing computational complexity and memory requirements. This strategy sets our approach apart from other methods in contrastive learning for semantic segmentation, which we will now discuss.

Various strategies have been pursued in contrastive learning for semantic segmentation, each presenting its unique strengths and limitations. One frequently employed technique involves a two-stage training process, where the initial phase focuses on pre-training the backbone with contrastive learning, and the subsequent phase fine-tunes it for segmentation. Examples of this approach can be seen in works like [28] and [29], which generate auxiliary labels in conjunction with ground truth labels for contrastive learning. A drawback to this approach, however, is its substantial memory consumption. In contrast, our work leverages an end-to-end training process, eliminating the need for two-stage training. Other research, including [1,25], has also employed end-to-end training strategies, but these methods typically rely on a memory bank to store features during training, compromising efficiency. Our approach addresses this by selecting features in batches on the fly. Additionally, while the active sampling in [1] uses class-specific attention modules, our method utilizes ground truth labels to choose the patches used for contrastive learning. Lastly, in [15], a contrastive learning framework for regional learning is proposed to support semantic segmentation with end-to-end learning and active sampling. However, they sample key pixels using a class relationship graph, and hard queries are chosen based on the predicted confidence map, a methodology that differs from ours.

In aerial image segmentation, contrastive learning has also been adopted to enhance semantic representations. For instance, [8] explores contrastive learning at the semantic level using the decoder output, which differs significantly from our usage of the encoder representations. Another notable example is [21], which employs a two-stage strategy incorporating a data augmentation policy. They aim to develop a semantically accurate representation in the encoder for aerial scene recognition, showcasing the adaptability and potential of contrastive learning in diverse applications within semantic segmentation.

## 3    Contrastive Transformer

The Contrastive Transformer (CT) is an innovative patch-based contrastive learning paradigm that leverages the inherent patch-structured design of vision transformers to enhance the semantic representation of classes in an image. A high-level overview of the CT mechanism is illustrated in Fig. 1. The input image is sent into the transformer backbone, where we apply contrastive learning at each encoder stage, producing contrastive feedback at multiple levels of abstraction. In each stage of the transformer, CT samples in-batch positive and negative patches, enabling the learning of a wide spectrum of robust signals and semantic representations while still being efficient. In addition to contrastive learning, a conventional segmentation loss is also applied to optimize the model for segmentation collectively. Despite its straightforward design, the CT framework demonstrates remarkable effectiveness, making it versatile and applicable across various transformer models. Its adaptability extends to its compatibility with most image-based contrastive learning methods, enhancing performance for dense prediction tasks. In the subsequent subsections, we will delve into the specifics of the CT learning scheme, the naive sampling strategy, and the contrastive loss functions utilized in our experiments.

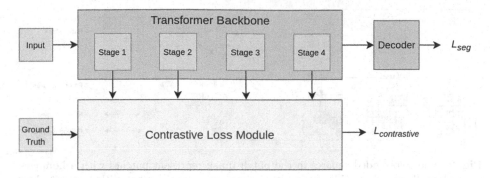

**Fig. 1.** CT uses the innate patch representations from each encoder stage and calculates the contrastive loss between positive and negative samples using the ground truth mask.

## 3.1 Architecture

Let $(X, Y)$ represent the training dataset, where $x \in X$ represents the training images and $y \in Y$ represents the pixel-level classes in the dataset. A segmentation network $g$ is trained to learn the mapping $g_\theta : X \rightarrow Y$, where $\theta$ represents the network's parameters. The segmentation network $g$ consists of two components, the backbone $\phi$, which maps $\phi : X \rightarrow Z$, and the decoder $\omega$, which maps $\omega : Z \rightarrow Y$. To perform patch-level contrastive learning, we attach a projection head $\psi$ in parallel to the decoder network on the $\phi$ mapping, where $\psi : Z \rightarrow F$ and $F$ is an $n$-dimensional representation of $Z$. The projection head only incurs additional computational costs during training and is removed during inference.

CT collects all patch representations at each encoder stage during training and couples them with the corresponding ground truth patch. For each encoder stage $s$, we have feature patches $F_s$ and corresponding ground truth patches $G_s$ constructed with the same patch size as the feature patches. For each unique class $c$ in $G$, we sample positive patches $P_s$ and negative patches $N_s$ from $F_s$. $P_s$ are sampled from $F_s$ where $G_s$ have a homogenous class distribution of class $c$. Similarly, $N_s$ are sampled from $F_s$ where class $c$ is not in $G_s$. Figure 2 visualizes the sampling process for positive and negative samples. The positive and negative samples are then used in a contrastive loss function.

## 3.2 Sampling and Loss Functions

Sampling strategies and loss functions form the cornerstone of contrastive learning. To start, we use a sampling strategy that sifts through and selects positive and negative samples, which are then used in the contrastive loss function. In our experiments, we adopt a simple yet effective 'naive' sampling strategy that randomizes all patches in the batch for both positive and negative samples. For negative contrastive learning, we compute the cosine similarity for a set number of positive and negative pairs, sort these pairs in descending order, and select the top 50%. On the other hand, for positive contrastive learning, we bisect the positive

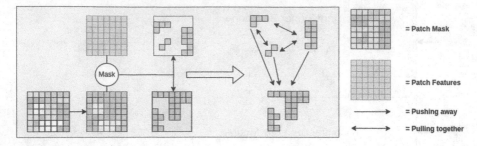

**Fig. 2.** The color-coded squares in the patch mask represent patches with a homogenous class distribution, while the white squares represent patches with a mixed class distribution including the target class. Using the ground truth mask it knows which feature representations to use as positive and negative samples. Positive feature patches consist of a uniform distribution of the target class. In contrast, negative patches may contain a mixture of classes or may be uniform as long as they exclude the target class. Patches with a mixture of classes including the target class are discarded. Ultimately, the selected positive and negative patches contribute to the contrastive loss function, pulling the representations of the positive patches closer together and pushing away the negative patch representations. (Color figure online)

samples, compute the cosine similarity, sort these in ascending order, and again select the top 50%. Following the sampling stage, we calculate the loss via a contrastive loss function. Considering each patch as a separate image lets us use contrastive loss functions from the image classification field, broadening our options scope. Further, as each image comprises numerous patches distributed across multiple stages, there is no necessity for a large batch size to gather enough samples for contrastive learning. We implement the InfoNCE [22] and a custom contrastive loss function for our experiments. This custom Contrastive Loss (CL) function calculates the cosine similarity of the positive and negative samples and normalizes the results between 0 and 1, where 0 denotes dissimilarity, and 1 indicates similarity. We then employ the soft cross-entropy loss function with a smoothing parameter set to 0.1 to compute the loss. The target is set to 0 for negative contrastive learning samples and 1 for positive contrastive learning.

## 4   Experiments

This section provides evidence that CT enhances mean IoU on the ISPRS Potsdam Dataset by applying image-based contrastive loss functions on feature representations from the transformer backbone. Our experimental assessment seeks to address the subsequent key questions:

- How does the performance of a straightforward approach to transformer-based contrastive learning compare to existing state-of-the-art segmentation models?
- Can we deduce conclusions about the model's capability to process semantic classes smaller than the smallest patch in the transformer?

– How does the proposed learning scheme adapt to various transformer backbones?

### 4.1 Experimental Setup

Recognizing the inherent challenges in aerial image datasets, such as large class imbalances and high similarity between different classes, we used such a dataset to test our proposed learning scheme. The capacity to distinguish between similar classes relies on the ability of the network to form robust representations of each class. This challenge is particularly important and present in our chosen dataset, namely the International Society for Photogrammetry and Remote Sensing (ISPRS) Potsdam semantic labeling dataset [9] for our experiments. The dataset consists of 38 tiles, each with dimensions of $6000 \times 6000$. It classifies pixels into six distinct classes: Surface, Building, Vegetation, Tree, Car, and Clutter. Following the methodology of earlier studies [2,14,16], we allocated 24 tiles for training and the remaining 14 for testing, disregarding the 'Clutter' class from the evaluation. We extracted smaller tiles of size $500 \times 500$ from the original tiles and resized them to $512 \times 512$ for training and testing. We excluded the DSMs from our experiments, intending to advance image-based research.

The performance of Contrastive Transformer (CT) was examined using three backbones, namely DCSwin (DS) [23], UnetFormer (UF) [24], and PoolFormer (PF) [27], with the decoder originating from [23]. All experiments used a learning rate of $8e-5$, a batch size of 32, and deployed the AdamW optimizer. Both gradients and contrastive loss were clipped to 1.0 to prevent contrastive learning from overtaking as the primary optimization factor. A joint loss function, constituting soft cross-entropy loss and dice loss, was used across all experiments. Every experiment underwent a training phase of 50 epochs, and the reported results represent the average of three individual runs.

### 4.2 Results

We compare our findings with baseline results for all models, distinguished only by adding the CT learning scheme. We evaluate CT utilizing InfoNCE and CL, both widely used loss functions for image-based contrastive learning. Table 1 enumerates the experimental results, consistently demonstrating advancements over the baselines with at least one of the contrastive loss functions for each model. Figure 3 provides a qualitative comparison across all models, illustrating the enhanced semantic representations achieved via CT.

The results show increased Contrastive Transformer (CT) performance in the car class. Intriguingly, this achievement comes despite the car class often being too small to fill the smallest training patches. Nevertheless, CT outperforms baseline models, suggesting that its capacity to create robust semantic representations does not strictly depend on homogenous class representation within individual patches. The results indicate that the CT model successfully generates superior representations compared to the baseline only using negative samples

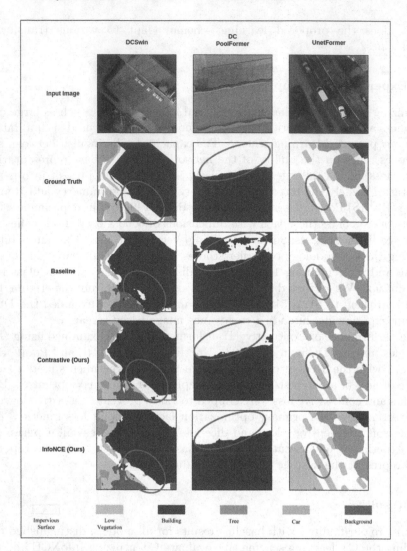

**Fig. 3.** Qualitative comparison for all models depicting the enhanced representations from the CT learning scheme. The areas of interest is highlighted with a red circle, showing examples where the difference between baseline and CT is prominent. All visual samples for the comparison has been gathered from the best run across three distinct runs. (Color figure online)

**Table 1.** These are the results from evaluating the ISPRS Potsdam dataset for all models. Values in the 'Mean IoU' column display the average IoU across all runs and classes with the standard deviation in the row below. The values in the class columns are the average IoU for each class across all runs. The results show that CT achieves comparable or better mean IoU for all model types. The best mean IoU for each model is bolded, while the highest IoU for each class is underlined.

| Model | DS | | | UF | | | PF | | |
|---|---|---|---|---|---|---|---|---|---|
| Backbone | Swin | | | Swin | | | PoolFormer | | |
| Source | [23] | **Ours** | Ours | [23] | Ours | **Ours** | [23,27] | Ours | **Ours** |
| Contrastive | - | **CL** | InfoNCE | - | CL | **InfoNCE** | - | CL | **InfoNCE** |
| Mean IoU | 0.773 | **0.774** | 0.773 | 0.769 | 0.768 | **0.772** | 0.756 | 0.762 | **0.763** |
| Standard deviation | 0.002 | 0.002 | 0.001 | 0.001 | 0.002 | 0.001 | 0.002 | 0.006 | 0.006 |
| Surface | 0.828 | <u>0.830</u> | 0.826 | 0.829 | 0.828 | <u>0.830</u> | 0.811 | <u>0.816</u> | 0.813 |
| Building | 0.885 | <u>0.890</u> | 0.886 | 0.889 | 0.887 | <u>0.890</u> | 0.869 | 0.873 | <u>0.874</u> |
| Vegetation | <u>0.731</u> | 0.728 | 0.726 | 0.722 | 0.720 | <u>0.727</u> | <u>0.708</u> | 0.707 | 0.708 |
| Tree | 0.729 | 0.727 | <u>0.731</u> | 0.719 | 0.715 | <u>0.722</u> | 0.705 | <u>0.711</u> | 0.708 |
| Car | 0.691 | <u>0.695</u> | 0.692 | 0.684 | 0.687 | <u>0.690</u> | 0.685 | <u>0.689</u> | 0.686 |

of that class. This showcases the model's adaptability and capacity to form good class representations.

It is important to highlight the flexibility of CT, as it pairs effectively with two different transformer backbones, notably the Swin Transformer and Pool-Former. Our findings show a larger improvement for CT when paired with the PoolFormer backbone. It indicates that the SwinTransformer is more capable of representation learning than PoolFormer. However, this observation warrants further investigation. In light of these findings, we summarize as follows:

- CT demonstrates compatibility with diverse backbones and outperforms the baseline models in nearly all conducted experiments.
- The model shows an interesting resilience in cases where instances of cars are too small to be considered as positive samples during contrastive learning, suggesting that their inclusion in negative samples is sufficient for CT to enhance the class representation.
- Future work should delve deeper into the exploration of which transformer-based backbones are optimally suited to leverage CT's capabilities.

## 5   Conclusion

In this work, we introduced the Contrastive Transformer (CT), a novel patch-based contrastive learning scheme for transformers, demonstrating its potential in aerial image segmentation. Our experiments show consistent improvements in segmentation results across all models on the ISPRS Potsdam dataset, with an increase in IoU by 0.7%. The simplicity and adaptability of the CT model can easily be added to transformer-based models used for urban planning, disaster management, and other fields that rely on accurate aerial image segmentation.

Additionally, the technique applies to future transformer-based architectures and can increase their performance. There is substantial potential for extending the CT approach to other image segmentation tasks. Additionally, exploring the impacts of different sampling strategies or refining the contrastive learning process could provide additional performance improvements. The CT model lays a robust foundation for future innovations in this field.

## 6 Future Work

The Contrastive Transformer is a novel mechanism that leverages the inherent patch characteristics of vision-based transformers. The results demonstrate the potential to improve the performance and robustness of transformers for dense prediction tasks. Using innate Transformer patches for contrastive learning is simple yet novel and warrants further exploration. This research highlights several avenues for future investigation:

- Investigating the impact of patch size and the number of patches used in contrastive learning on CT's performance for dense prediction tasks.
- Exploring various augmentation techniques on patches to improve the quality of learned representations.
- Developing new architectures that can better leverage the representations learned by contrastive learning.
- Studying the effects of different objective functions on the quality of learned representations.
- Investigating using unsupervised pre-training techniques to initialize the model before fine-tuning it for specific dense prediction tasks.
- Evaluating the generalization capability of learned representations across different datasets and domains.
- Exploring the use of state-of-the-art sampling techniques in CT.
- Preliminary studies indicate that using attention for patch selection could be useful, with work from [26] serving as a key accelerator.
- Examining the use of the heterogenous patches could harvest great potential as hard samples are often present around the edges of two semantic classes.
- Explore the use of CT for other dense prediction tasks such as object detection and instance segmentation.

## References

1. Alonso, I., Sabater, A., Ferstl, D., Montesano, L., Murillo, A.C.: Semi-supervised semantic segmentation with pixel-level contrastive learning from a class-wise memory bank (2021)
2. Audebert, N., Le Saux, B., Lefèvre, S.: Beyond RGB: very high resolution urban remote sensing with multimodal deep networks. ISPRS J. Photogramm. Remote. Sens. **140**, 20–32 (2018)
3. Chen, T., Kornblith, S., Norouzi, M., Hinton, G.E.: A simple framework for contrastive learning of visual representations. ArXiv (2020)

4. Dao, S.D., Zhao, E., Phung, D., Cai, J.: Multi-label image classification with contrastive learning. ArXiv (2021)
5. Dosovitskiy, A., et al.: An image is worth 16x16 words: transformers for image recognition at scale. In: Proceedings of the 9th International Conference on Learning Representations (ICLR), pp. 1–21 (2021)
6. Duman Keles, F., Mahesakya Wijewardena, P., Hegde, C., Agrawal, S., Orabona, F.: On the computational complexity of self-attention (2023)
7. He, K., Fan, H., Wu, Y., Xie, S., Girshick, R.: Momentum contrast for unsupervised visual representation learning (2020)
8. Huang, L., et al.: A two-stage contrastive learning framework for imbalanced aerial scene recognition. In: ICASSP, IEEE International Conference on Acoustics, Speech and Signal Processing May 2022, pp. 3518–3522 (2022)
9. isprs.org. ISPRS Potsdam Dataset
10. Khoshboresh-Masouleh, M., Alidoost, F., Arefi, H.: Multiscale building segmentation based on deep learning for remote sensing RGB images from different sensors. J. Appl. Remote Sens. **14**(03), 1 (2020)
11. Li, K., et al.: UniFormer: unifying convolution and self-attention for visual recognition (2022)
12. Li, Q., et al.: Instance segmentation of buildings using keypoints. In: IGARSS 2020–2020 IEEE International Geoscience and Remote Sensing Symposium, pp. 1452–1455 (2020)
13. Li, W., Zhao, W., Zhong, H., IIe, C., Lin, D.: Joint semantic-geometric learning for polygonal building segmentation. In: 35th AAAI Conference on Artificial Intelligence, AAAI 2021, vol. 3A, pp. 1958–1965 (2021)
14. Liu, Q., Kampffmeyer, M., Jenssen, R., Salberg, A.B.: Dense dilated convolutions merging network for land cover classification. IEEE Trans. Geosci. Remote Sens. **58**(9), 6309–6320 (2020)
15. Liu, S., Zhi, S., Johns, E., Davison, A.J.: Bootstrapping semantic segmentation with regional contrast (2021)
16. Liu, Y., Fan, B., Wang, L., Bai, J., Xiang, S., Pan, C.: Semantic labeling in very high resolution images via a self-cascaded convolutional neural network. ISPRS J. Photogramm. Remote Sens. **145**, 78–95 (2018)
17. Liu, Z., et al.: Swin transformer V2: scaling up capacity and resolution (2022)
18. Matei, B.C., Sawhney, H.S., Samarasekera, S., Kim, J., Kumar, R.: Building segmentation for densely built urban regions using aerial LIDAR data. In: 2008 IEEE Conference on Computer Vision and Pattern Recognition (2008)
19. Ronneberger, O., Fischer, P., Brox, T.: U-Net: convolutional networks for biomedical image segmentation. In: Navab, N., Hornegger, J., Wells, W.M., Frangi, A.F. (eds.) MICCAI 2015. LNCS, vol. 9351, pp. 234–241. Springer, Cham (2015). https://doi.org/10.1007/978-3-319-24574-4_28
20. Shi, Y., Li, Q., Zhu, X.X.: Building segmentation through a gated graph convolutional neural network with deep structured feature embedding. ISPRS J. Photogramm. Remote. Sens. **159**, 184–197 (2019)
21. Tang, M., Georgiou, K., Qi, H., Champion, C., Bosch, M.: Semantic segmentation in aerial imagery using multi-level contrastive learning with local consistency. In: Proceedings - 2023 IEEE Winter Conference on Applications of Computer Vision, WACV 2023, pp. 3787–3796 (2023)
22. Oord, A.V.D., Li, Y., Vinyals, O.: DeepMind representation learning with contrastive predictive coding (2018)

23. Wang, L., Li, R., Duan, C., Zhang, C., Meng, X., Fang, S.: A novel transformer based semantic segmentation scheme for fine-resolution remote sensing images. IEEE Geosci. Remote Sens. Lett. **19** (2022)
24. Wang, L., Li, R., Zhang, C., Fang, S., Duan, C., Meng, X., Atkinson, P.M.: UNet-Former: a UNet-like transformer for efficient semantic segmentation of remote sensing urban scene imagery. ISPRS J. Photogramm. Remote. Sens. **190**, 196–214 (2022)
25. Wang, W., Zhou, T., Yu, F., Dai, J., Konukoglu, E., Van Gool, L.: Exploring cross-image pixel contrast for semantic segmentation (2021)
26. Xia, Z., Pan, X., Song, S., Li, L.E., Huang, G.: Vision transformer with deformable attention (2022)
27. Yu, W., et al.: MctaFormer is actually what you need for vision (2022)
28. Zhang, F., Torr, P., Ranftl, R., Richter, S.R.: Looking beyond single images for contrastive semantic segmentation learning. In: Advances in Neural Information Processing Systems, vol. 34, pp. 3285–3297 (2021)
29. Zhao, X., et al.: Contrastive learning for label efficient semantic segmentation (2021)

# Deep Despeckling of SAR Images to Improve Change Detection Performance

Mohamed Ihmeida$^{(\boxtimes)}$ (ID) and Muhammad Shahzad (ID)

University of Reading, Reading RG6 6DH, UK
m.a.g.ihmeida@pgr.reading.ac.uk, m.shahzad2@reading.ac.uk

**Abstract.** Synthetic aperture radar (SAR) image change detection (CD) focuses on identifying the change between two images at different times for the same geographical region. SAR offers advantages over optical sensors for disaster-related change detection in remote sensing due to its all-weather capability and ability to penetrate clouds and darkness. The performance of change detection methods is affected by several challenges. Deep learning methods, such as convolutional neural networks (CNNs), have shown promising performance in dealing with these challenges. However, CNN methods still suffer from speckle noise, adversely impacting the change detection performance F1 score. To tackle this challenge, we propose a CNN model that despeckles the noise prior to applying change detection methods. We extensively evaluate the performance of our method on three SAR datasets, and the results of our proposed method demonstrate superior performance compared to state-of-the-art methods such as DDNet and LANTNet performance. Our method significantly increased the change detection accuracy from a baseline of 86.65% up to 90.79% for DDNet and from 87.16% to 91.1% for LANTNet in the Yellow River dataset.

**Keywords:** Unsupervised Learning · SAR change detection · Despeckling noise

## 1 Introduction

Remote sensing change detection (CD) is an essential technique for identifying changes in multi-temporal images of the same geographical region [10,16]. It provides valuable information for various applications, including deforestation monitoring, target detection, and agricultural advancement [2,23]. Additionally, CD algorithms support decision-making during natural disasters, enabling timely actions to prevent material losses and save lives [13]. Change detection in remote sensing involves distinguishing changed and unchanged pixels in multi-temporal Earth Observation (EO) images for the same geographical region. These multi-temporal EO images are required to be co-registered. This step is important in aligning EO images to the same coordinate system, which is useful for obtaining consistent radiometric characteristics, such as brightness and contrast. This process enhances the change detection performance [14,19]. Key point extraction

© The Author(s), under exclusive license to Springer Nature Switzerland AG 2023
M. Bramer and F. Stahl (Eds.): SGAI 2023, LNAI 14381, pp. 115–126, 2023.
https://doi.org/10.1007/978-3-031-47994-6_9

techniques like SIFT, SURF, and CNNs are often used for image registration [6]. Classical change detection can be easily obtained by computing the intensity difference between images. The result of this process is called a change map (CM). However, challenges such as co-registration errors, illumination variations, and speckle noise affect the accuracy of change detection algorithms.

Synthetic aperture radar offers advantages over optical sensors for change detection in remote sensing due to its all-weather capability, penetration through clouds and vegetation, and sensitivity to small changes. SAR change detection methods primarily rely on unsupervised learning due to the lack of annotated SAR datasets. Various unsupervised CD methods use clustering algorithms, such as principal component analysis, fuzzy clustering algorithms (FCM) [12] and fuzzy local information C-mean (FLICM) [17]. Researchers make an effort to reduce the impact of speckle noise on CD methods. Qu et al. [22] introduced a dual domain neural network (DDNet) incorporating spatial and frequency domains to reduce speckle noise. Gao et al. [10] proposed a Siamese adaptive fusion network for SAR image change detection, which extracts semantic features from multi-temporal SAR images and suppresses speckle noise. Meng et al. [20] presented a noise-tolerant network called LANTNet that utilises feature correlations among multiple convolutional layers and employs a robust loss function to mitigate the impact of noisy labels. While these deep learning-based approaches show some robustness against speckle noise, they still struggle to eliminate it and reduce its effectiveness in change detection methods. Furthermore, the presence of speckle noise varies between single-look (pre-change) and multi-look (post-change) SAR imaging processes, further degrading the performance of change detection algorithms when considering different instances in time.

To address the issues with degrading CD performance, we propose a robust despeckling model (DM) architecture that effectively suppresses speckle noise in SAR CD datasets. This approach leads to significant improvements in change detection performance. Experimental evaluations on public SAR CD datasets provide compelling evidence of the superiority of our proposed method when compared to existing approaches.

## 2   Related Work

SAR change detection is widely used in various applications, including urban extension [16], agricultural monitoring [23], target detection [21], and disaster assessment [2]. Due to the lack of annotated SAR datasets, most researchers rely on unsupervised methods for SAR change detection. However, the presence of speckle noise poses a significant challenge and reduces the accuracy of change detection. Image pre-processing, including despeckling and image registration, is a crucial step in SAR change detection to enhance image quality and align multi-temporal images [19].

Generating a difference image (DI) is important in SAR change detection. Various methods, such as image differencing, log ratio, and neighbourhood-based ratio, have been proposed to generate the DI [5,30]. The classification of the DI typically involves thresholding and clustering. Some approaches use the pre-classification result to train a classifier model and combine the preclassification and classifier results to generate a change map. These methods aim to improve change detection performance by leveraging preclassification and classifier information [8].

Recent approaches in SAR change detection focus on explicitly suppressing speckle noise to improve accuracy. Methods such as DDNet [22], Siamese adaptive fusion networks [10], and LANTNet [20] have been proposed to mitigate the impact of speckle noise and extract high-level features from multi-temporal SAR images. However, these approaches have limitations in effectively handling different speckle noise characteristics in images prior and after the change, especially when the number of looks varies. To address this challenge, we propose a despeckling model to suppress speckle noise and achieve effective SAR change detection for different numbers of looks in pre- and post-change images.

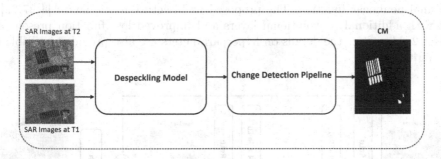

**Fig. 1.** An overview of the proposed modules

# 3   Methodology

The despeckling module applies a sequence of convolutional layers to reduce speckle noise in input SAR images. The resulting image with reduced noise is then passed to the subsequent CD methods. Figure 1 presents the DM and CD methods overview. The following sections explain the proposed despeckling model architecture and the change detection methods.

## 3.1   Despeckling Model Architecture

The proposed despeckling architecture aims to learn a mapping from the input SAR image using convolutional layers to generate a residual image containing only speckle noise. The resulting speckle-only image can be combined with the original image through either subtraction [4] or division [27] operations to produce the despeckled image. The division operation is preferred as it avoids an additional logarithmic transformation step and allows for end-to-end learning. However, training such a network requires reference despeckled images, which

**Table 1.** Proposed Despeckling Model Configuration. Where L1 and L10 refer to a series of Conv-ReLU layers, while the layers between L2 and L9 consist of Conv-BN and ReLU layers as illustrated in Fig. 1.

| –     | layer              | Filter Size | Filters | Output size   |
|-------|--------------------|-------------|---------|---------------|
| L1    | Conv + ReLU        | 3 * 3 * 1   | 64      | 256 * 256 * 64 |
| L2–L9 | Conv + BN + ReLU   | 3 * 3 * 64  | 64      | 256 * 256 * 64 |
| L10   | Conv + ReLU        | 3 * 3 * 64  | 1       | 256 * 256 * 1  |

are typically unavailable for SAR images. To address this, researchers use synthetic reference images generated using multiplicative noise models [4, 27, 29]. This study also employs synthetic SAR reference images to train the proposed despeckling network architecture, consisting of ten convolutional layers with batch normalisation, ReLU activation functions, and a hyperbolic tangent as the final nonlinear function. The proposed architecture is similar to [4, 27, 29], but with additional convolutional layers and improved loss function presented in Fig. 2. Moreover, the details on hyperparameters are also provided in Table 1 for clarity.

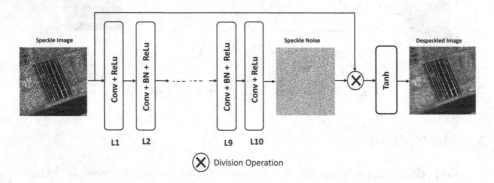

**Fig. 2.** Proposed despeckling model architecture

## 3.2 Proposed Loss Function

A common approach to training the despeckling network is to use the per-pixel Euclidean loss function $LE(\theta)$, computed by comparing the predicted despeckled image with the noise-free SAR image. The $LE(\theta)$ calculates the squared Euclidean distance between corresponding pixels. While effective in various image restoration tasks, such as super-resolution, semantic segmentation, change detection, and style transfer, it often results in artifacts and visual abnormalities in the estimated image. Researchers have incorporated a total variation (TV) loss and an Euclidean loss function $LE(\theta)$ as supplementary measures. The TV loss reduces artifacts but may lead to oversmoothing and information loss, thus impacting change detection performance. To overcome this, we design a loss function which combines the $LE(\theta)$ and a structural similarity index (SSIM), initially proposed for image quality assessment, which offers a better trade-off by removing artifacts while preserving essential information, ultimately enhancing change detection performance.

$$LE(\theta) = \frac{1}{W \cdot H} \sum_{w=1}^{W} \sum_{h=1}^{H} \|X^{(w,h)} - \hat{X}^{(w,h)}\|^2 \tag{1}$$

$$SSIM(x,y) = \frac{(2\mu_x\mu_y + C_1) \cdot (2\sigma_{xy} + C_2)}{(\mu_x^2 + \mu_y^2 + C_1) \cdot (\sigma_x^2 + \sigma_y^2 + C_2)} \tag{2}$$

The total loss is thus calculated as follows:

$$L_T = L_E(\theta) + \lambda_{\text{SSIM}} \cdot SSIM \tag{3}$$

where $X$ and $\hat{X}$ are the reference (noise-free) and despeckled images, respectively, $\mu_X$ and $\mu_{\hat{X}}$ are the mean values of $X$ and $\hat{X}$ respectively. Similarly, $\sigma_X$ and $\sigma_{\hat{X}}$ are the standard deviations of $X$ and $\hat{X}$ respectively. While $\sigma_{X\hat{X}}$ is the covariance between $X$ and $\hat{X}$. Finally, $C_1$ and $C_2$ are constants set to be 0.01 and 0.03 respectively [28].

### 3.3   Change Detection

It is critical to suppress speckle noise in our proposed method to enhance CD performance. To evaluate the performance of the proposed despeckling model, we incorporated state-of-the-art CD methods, including DDNet [22] and LANT-Net [20]. PCA-$k$-means [3] is an unsupervised change detection method that utilises principal component analysis and k-means clustering to identify changes by splitting the feature vector space into two clusters. NR-ELM [9] employs a neighbourhood-based ratio to create a difference image and subsequently utilises an extreme learning machine to model high-probability pixels in the difference image. This information is then combined with the initial change map to produce the final change detection result. DDNet [22] combines spatial and frequency domain techniques to reduce speckle noise, while LANTNet [20] leverages feature correlations across multiple convolutional layers and incorporates a robust loss function to mitigate the impact of noisy labels.

## 4   Experimental Results and Evaluation

In this section, we introduced the datasets and evaluation metrics. Subsequently, we presented and evaluated the results by comparing them with those obtained from state-of-the-art CD methods.

## 4.1 Datasets and Evaluation Metrics

Two types of datasets were used in this paper. The first is the Berkeley Segmentation Dataset 500, widely employed to generate synthetic SAR images for training the despeckling model. Real SAR images were used for testing, specifically for change detection purposes, to assess the model's performance. Detailed descriptions of both datasets can be found in the following subsections:

- **Synthetic SAR Images**
  The Berkeley Segmentation Dataset 500 (BSD-500) was originally developed to evaluate the segmentation of natural edges, including object contours, object interior and background boundaries [1]. It included 500 natural images with carefully manually annotated boundaries and edges of natural objects collected from multiple users. This dataset has been widely used to generate synthetic SAR images for the purpose of despeckling [15,18,25]. Inspired by these studies, we have used it to train our despeckling model.

- **Real SAR Images**
  For the purpose of change detection, we employed three real SAR image datasets that are multi-temporal and have been co-registered and corrected geometrically.
  - *Farmland and Yellow River Datasets:* The images for both datasets were captured by RADARSAT-2 in the region of the Yellow River Estuary in China on 18th June 2008 (pre-change) and 19th June 2009 (post-change). The pre-change images are single-look, whereas the post-change images have been acquired via a multi-look (four) imaging process. The single-look pre-change image is significantly influenced by speckle noise compared to the four-look post-change image [10]. The disparity between the single and four looks in these two SAR datasets poses a significant challenge for change detection methods.
  - *Ottawa Dataset:* The images for this dataset were also captured by RADARSAT-2 in May 1997 (pre-change) and August 1997 (post-change) in the areas affected by floods [11,22,26]. Because of the single imaging process, the pre- and post-change images are less affected by noise in this dataset.

The synthetic SAR images were utilised to train the proposed DM, as depicted in Fig. 1. In contrast, the real SAR images were despeckled for the purpose of change detection (CD datasets). Figure 3 presents the real SAR datasets.

To evaluate the results, we used two common evaluation metrics, including Overall Accuracy and F1 score. The F1 score is usually used to evaluate the change detection accuracy [7,24].

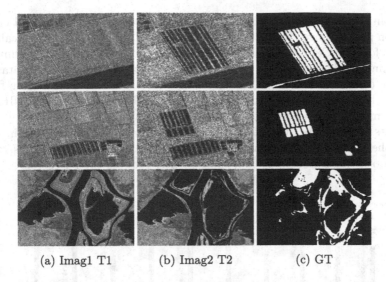

(a) Imag1 T1          (b) Imag2 T2              (c) GT

**Fig. 3.** The real SAR datasets. (a) Image acquired in $T1$. (b) Image acquired in $T2$. (c) Ground truth image(GT).

**Table 2.** Quantitative evaluation on three CD datasets based on despeckling model. Here, w/o means it is the original method without despeckling, and DM is our proposed despeckling model.

| Methods | Metrics | Yellow River | | Farmland | | Ottawa | |
|---|---|---|---|---|---|---|---|
| | | w/o | DM | w/o | DM | w/o | DM |
| PCAK [3] | OA ↑ | 89.80 | 95.82 | 88.22 | 94.44 | 97.55 | 98.31 |
| | F1 Score ↑ | 72.66 | **87.72** | 47.52 | **65.00** | 91.93 | **94.47** |
| NR-ELM [9] | OA ↑ | 94.11 | 95.73 | 97.86 | 98.42 | 98.17 | 95.82 |
| | F1-Score ↑ | 81.59 | **87.04** | 78.28 | **84.96** | 94.15 | 84.84 |
| DDNet [22] | OA ↑ | 95.35 | 96.83 | 98.50 | 98.87 | 98.09 | 98.43 |
| | F1-Score ↑ | 86.65 | **90.79** | 86.67 | **89.70** | 93.90 | **94.87** |
| LANTNet [20] | OA ↑ | 95.61 | 96.91 | 98.77 | 98.84 | 98.3 | 98.44 |
| | F1-Score ↑ | 87.16 | **91.1** | 88.69 | **89.20** | 94.46 | **94.88** |

## 4.2  Experimental Results and Discussion

To evaluate the effectiveness of the despeckling model, we compared the results of change detection methods (namely PCA-$k$-means (PCAK) [3], NR-ELM [9], DDNet [22] and LANTNet [20]) with and without the despeckling model using three real SAR datasets. Figures 5, 6 and 7 demonstrate the proposed despeckling model performance on Yellow River, Farmland and Ottawa datasets. DM has considerably enhanced the F1 score for existing (including state-of-the-art) change detection methods. In all these experiments, we empirically set the $\lambda_{\text{SSIM}}$

to be 5 in the loss objective (3) as a trade-off between despeckling and change detection performance. Table 2 presents the OA and F1 score on three real SAR datasets for four CD methods. However, in Fig. 4, the NR-ELM algorithm with despeckling model achieved a lower F1 score because the Ottawa dataset is less affected by speckle noise. This is why we observe a higher F1 score for all other methods without DM. Additionally, compared to other methods, NR-ELM exhibits more resistance to speckle noise due to its built-in despeckling process within its architecture. Therefore, the decrease in the F1 score when incorporating the DM module is attributed to the extra despeckling process, which over-smooths the input image and subsequently reduces the F1 score.

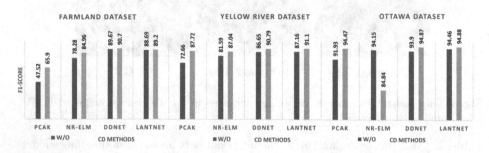

**Fig. 4.** The correlation between DM and the F1 score for SAR CD datasets

It can be observed that in Yellow River and Farmland datasets, the proposed DM achieves a superior F1 score for CD methods compared to without DM (W/O) results due to the ability to efficiently cope with the single-look pre-change and multi-look post-change SAR images via robust loss function. It should be noted that CD methods without the despeckling model perform well on Ottawa dataset because the dataset is slightly affected by speckle noise. Nevertheless, the performance of CD methods was further improved with the proposed DM as presented in Table 2 and Fig. 4.

## 4.3 Hardware and Running Times

The experiments were conducted using three datasets (described in Sect. 4.1) on a Tesla GPU P100 with 16 GB of RAM and 147.15 GB of disk space, resulting in a training duration of approximately 11 h. The framework used to train the proposed despecking model was TensorFlow 2.0.

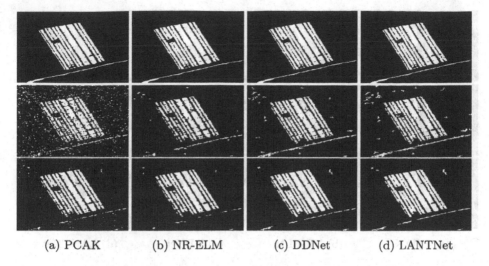

(a) PCAK            (b) NR-ELM            (c) DDNet            (d) LANTNet

**Fig. 5.** Change detection results on Yellow River dataset. Rows: (1st row) Yellow River ground truth(GT), (2nd row) CD methods results without despeckling, (3rd row) the CD methods results with the proposed DM. Columns: (a) PCAk [3], (b) NR-ELM [9], (c) DDNet [22], and (d) LANTNet [20].

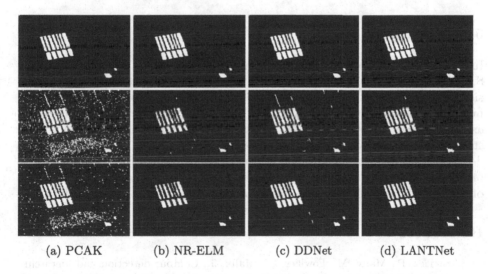

(a) PCAK            (b) NR-ELM            (c) DDNet            (d) LANTNet

**Fig. 6.** Change detection results on Farmland dataset. Rows: (1st row) Yellow River ground truth(GT), (2nd row) CD methods results without despeckling, (3rd row) the CD methods results with the proposed DM. Columns: (a) PCAk [3], (b) NR-ELM [9], (c) DDNet [22], and (d) LANTNet [20].

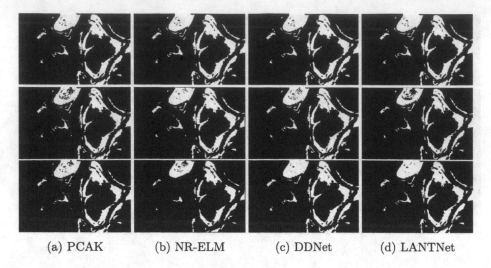

    (a) PCAK        (b) NR-ELM        (c) DDNet        (d) LANTNet

**Fig. 7.** Change detection results on Ottawa dataset. Rows: (1st row) Yellow River ground truth(GT), (2nd row) CD methods results without despeckling, (3rd row) the CD methods results with the proposed DM. Columns: (a) PCAk [3], (b) NR-ELM [9], (c) DDNet [22], and (d) LANTNet [20].

## 5  Conclusion

In recent years, deep-learning architectures have shown promise in improving SAR change detection performance. However, the challenge of speckle noise persists in these methods. To overcome this challenge, we propose a despeckling model that effectively suppresses speckle noise and enhances the performance of existing change detection methods. Extensive evaluations and comparisons with state-of-the-art methods demonstrate the superior performance of our proposed despeckling model. It should be noted that our current approach focuses solely on a single-imaging modality. Future work of this work could explore the domain of multi-modal change detection, incorporating both optical and SAR data.

## References

1. Arbelaez, P., Maire, M., Fowlkes, C., Malik, J.: Contour detection and hierarchical image segmentation. IEEE Trans. Pattern Anal. Mach. Intell. **33**(5), 898–916 (2010)
2. Bai, X., Zhou, F.: Analysis of new top-hat transformation and the application for infrared dim small target detection. Pattern Recogn. **43**(6), 2145–2156 (2010)
3. Celik, T.: Unsupervised change detection in satellite images using principal component analysis and $k$-means clustering. IEEE Geosci. Remote Sens. Lett. **6**(4), 772–776 (2009)
4. Chierchia, G., Cozzolino, D., Poggi, G., Verdoliva, L.: SAR image despeckling through convolutional neural networks. In: 2017 IEEE International Geoscience and Remote Sensing Symposium (IGARSS), pp. 5438–5441. IEEE (2017)

5. Dekker, R.: Speckle filtering in satellite SAR change detection imagery. Int. J. Remote Sens. **19**(6), 1133–1146 (1998)
6. Fan, R., Hou, B., Liu, J., Yang, J., Hong, Z.: Registration of multiresolution remote sensing images based on L2-Siamese model. IEEE J. Sel. Top. Appl. Earth Obs. Remote Sens. **14**, 237–248 (2020)
7. Foody, G.M.: Explaining the unsuitability of the kappa coefficient in the assessment and comparison of the accuracy of thematic maps obtained by image classification. Remote Sens. Environ. **239**, 111630 (2020)
8. Gao, F., Dong, J., Li, B., Xu, Q.: Automatic change detection in synthetic aperture radar images based on PCANet. IEEE Geosci. Remote Sens. Lett. **13**(12), 1792–1796 (2016). https://doi.org/10.1109/LGRS.2016.2611001
9. Gao, F., Dong, J., Li, B., Xu, Q., Xie, C.: Change detection from synthetic aperture radar images based on neighborhood-based ratio and extreme learning machine. J. Appl. Remote Sens. **10**(4), 046019 (2016)
10. Gao, Y., Gao, F., Dong, J., Du, Q., Li, H.C.: Synthetic aperture radar image change detection via Siamese adaptive fusion network. IEEE J. Sel. Top. Appl. Earth Obs. Remote Sens. **14**, 10748–10760 (2021)
11. Gao, Y., Gao, F., Dong, J., Li, H.C.: Sar image change detection based on multiscale capsule network. IEEE Geosci. Remote Sens. Lett. **18**(3), 484–488 (2020)
12. Gong, M., Zhou, Z., Ma, J.: Change detection in synthetic aperture radar images based on image fusion and fuzzy clustering. IEEE Trans. Image Process. **21**(4), 2141–2151 (2012). https://doi.org/10.1109/TIP.2011.2170702
13. Ihmeida, M., Shahzad, M.: Enhanced change detection performance based on deep despeckling of synthetic aperture radar images. IEEE Access (2023)
14. Ihmeida, M., Wei, H.: Image registration techniques and applications: comparative study on remote sensing imagery. In: 2021 14th International Conference on Developments in eSystems Engineering (DeSE), pp. 142–148. IEEE (2021)
15. Intajag, S., Chitwong, S.: Speckle noise estimation with generalized gamma distribution. In: 2006 SICE-ICASE International Joint Conference, pp. 1164–1167. IEEE (2006)
16. Khelifi, L., Mignotte, M.: Deep learning for change detection in remote sensing images: comprehensive review and meta-analysis. IEEE Access **8**, 126385–126400 (2020)
17. Krinidis, S., Chatzis, V.: A robust fuzzy local information C-means clustering algorithm. IEEE Trans. Image Process. **19**(5), 1328–1337 (2010)
18. Li, H.C., Hong, W., Wu, Y.R., Fan, P.Z.: Bayesian wavelet shrinkage with heterogeneity-adaptive threshold for SAR image despeckling based on generalized gamma distribution. IEEE Trans. Geosci. Remote Sens. **51**(4), 2388–2402 (2012)
19. Ma, L., Liu, Y., Zhang, X., Ye, Y., Yin, G., Johnson, B.A.: Deep learning in remote sensing applications: a meta-analysis and review. ISPRS J. Photogramm. Remote. Sens. **152**, 166–177 (2019)
20. Meng, D., Gao, F., Dong, J., Du, Q., Li, H.C.: Synthetic aperture radar image change detection via layer attention-based noise-tolerant network. IEEE Geosci. Remote Sens. Lett. **19**, 1–5 (2022)
21. Moulton, J., Kassam, S., Ahmad, F., Amin, M., Yemelyanov, K.: Target and change detection in synthetic aperture radar sensing of urban structures. In: 2008 IEEE Radar Conference, pp. 1–6. IEEE (2008)
22. Qu, X., Gao, F., Dong, J., Du, Q., Li, H.C.: Change detection in synthetic aperture radar images using a dual-domain network. IEEE Geosci. Remote Sens. Lett. **19**, 1–5 (2021)

23. Radke, R.J., Andra, S., Al-Kofahi, O., Roysam, B.: Image change detection algorithms: a systematic survey. IEEE Trans. Image Process. **14**(3), 294–307 (2005)
24. Tang, X., et al.: An unsupervised remote sensing change detection method based on multiscale graph convolutional network and metric learning. IEEE Trans. Geosci. Remote Sens. **60**, 1–15 (2021)
25. Ulaby, F., Dobson, M.C., Álvarez-Pérez, J.L.: Handbook of Radar Scattering Statistics for Terrain. Artech House (2019)
26. Wang, J., Gao, F., Dong, J., Zhang, S., Du, Q.: Change detection from synthetic aperture radar images via graph-based knowledge supplement network. arXiv preprint arXiv:2201.08954 (2022)
27. Wang, P., Zhang, H., Patel, V.M.: Sar image despeckling using a convolutional neural network. IEEE Signal Process. Lett. **24**(12), 1763–1767 (2017)
28. Wang, Z., Bovik, A.C., Sheikh, H.R., Simoncelli, E.P.: Image quality assessment: from error visibility to structural similarity. IEEE Trans. Image Process. **13**(4), 600–612 (2004)
29. Zhang, K., Zuo, W., Chen, Y., Meng, D., Zhang, L.: Beyond a Gaussian denoiser: residual learning of deep CNN for image denoising. IEEE Trans. Image Process. **26**(7), 3142–3155 (2017)
30. Zhang, W., Jiao, L., Liu, F., Yang, S., Liu, J.: Adaptive contourlet fusion clustering for SAR image change detection. IEEE Trans. Image Process. **31**, 2295–2308 (2022). https://doi.org/10.1109/TIP.2022.3154922

# Neural Nets

# Profiling Power Consumption for Deep Learning on Resource Limited Devices

Aidan Duggan[(✉)] [ID], Ted Scully [ID], Niall Smith [ID], and Alan Giltinan [ID]

Munster Technological University, Cork, Ireland
aidan.j.duggan@mycit.ie

**Abstract.** The introduction of convolutional neural networks (CNN) has had a significant impact on various computer vision tasks. The process of inference, where a CNN takes images as input and produces corresponding predictions, is a complex and resource hungry task that consumes significant power. Originally much of the processing was done on well resourced machines locally or hosted on various cloud platforms but there has been a recent trend towards moving the processing of data closer to where it is produced within resource limited 'edge' devices. It is important to understand the implications and limitations for deployment of a CNN to a device such as an earth observation satellite, which does not have a constant power source. Quantisation is a model optimising technique, where the precision of weights, biases, and activations are reduced, such that they consume less memory and power, and is a common approach to facilitate such deployments. This paper investigates the power consumption behaviour of CNN models from the DenseNet, EfficientNet, MobileNet, ResNet, ConvNeXt & RegNet architecture families, processing imagery on board a Nvidia Jetson Orin Nano platform. It was found that energy consumption varied from 6 mJ to 26 mJ per image for different base (non-quantised) models. Accuracy varied from 69% to 82% and latency varied from 1.3 ms to 7.5 ms per image. The effectiveness of quantisation in reducing the power requirements of CNNs during inference was also investigated, focusing on the use case of deployment to an earth observation satellite. A large difference was found between architectures with some reducing the energy consumption by up to 87% while others achieve less than 10%. The metrics "accuracy-per-joule" and "latency-by-joule" were introduced and used to benchmark and more effectively compare models energy-effectiveness and the impact of quantisation. After quantisation, an improvement in accuracy-per-joule of up to 700% and a latency-by-joule reduction of 99% was achieved.

**Keywords:** Deep learning · Energy optimisation · Satellite data analysis · Edge computing

## 1 Introduction

Technology improvements in the satellite industry have resulted in the miniaturisation of earth observation satellites, driving down development time and launch costs, and opening up the remote sensing market to both commercial and research interests. The quality and quantity of remote sensing imagery being produced, has grown significantly due to higher quality image sensors being deployed on an increasing number of satellites. The suitability of transferring imagery to a ground station on earth for processing is being increasingly challenged, as the increase in communication bandwidth to transfer the imagery has not matched the increase in imagery volume being produced.

A proposed solution [1] to this problem, is to reduce the volume of data that needs to be transferred, by processing the imagery on-board using deep learning. The biggest obstacle to achieving this, is the limited resources (primarily available power) on-board a satellite, making it a challenging environment for digital image processing. Furana et al. [1] outlined several possible benefits of processing imagery on-board including better responsiveness, improved results (including accuracy), bandwidth savings and more flexibility as applications can possibly be changed in situ. They recommend leveraging the advantages (low cost/power/latency) of the latest commercial off-the-shelf (COTS) AI processors, an effective deep learning model selection and design strategy, followed by model optimisation.

There are several ways a CNN model can be optimised including Pruning (removing parameters deemed unnecessary), layer decomposition (reducing the network computational complexity by reducing the size of individual CNN layers) and knowledge distillation (training a smaller student network to mimic the behavior of a larger, well-performing teacher network). The focus of this paper is on Quantisation, an optimisation technique where the bitwidth of values are reduced by encoding full-precision parameters (i.e. weights and activations) with lower-precision ones. During inference a model produces a large amount of intermediate results (activation/feature maps) at each layer which consume a large about of memory e.g. ResNet-50 [2] has 16 million parameters requires around 168 MB memory space, but requires over 3 GB/s memory bandwidth during inference and quantization can alleviate this.

This paper investigates the use case of the deployment of optimised CNN's to a small earth observation (EO) satellite by employing a Nvdia Jetson Orin Nano to carry out classification inference on imagery from the ImageNet validation dataset. The main contribution is to quantify and better understand the impact of different CNN architectures on power consumption and also examine the power saving that can be achieved by employing quantisation as an optimising technique, while also quantifying the corresponding impact on accuracy and latency.

## 2    Related Work

### 2.1    Convolutional Neural Networks

The use of deep learning techniques [3] has revolutionised the area of image analysis, classification and segmentation. Convolutional Neural Networks(CNNs) are now regarded as the most dominant approach for image classification [4].

Early developments such as VGGNets [5], GoogLeNet (Inception v1) [6] and SENets [7] focused on improving the accuracy regardless of size but more recently the focus has been on smaller more efficient models such as MobileNets [8] which can be deployed to low resourced devices such as satellites.

## 2.2 Machine Learning On-Board Small Satellites

Deploying machine learning (ML) algorithms on-board small satellites is relatively new. One of the earliest proof-of-concept efforts to host a computer vision machine learning algorithm on a simulated smallsat environment was in 2017 by Buonaiuto et al. [9] using a Nvidia Tegra X1 (TX1) which is a System on Chip (SoC). George et al. [10] investigated the challenges for onboard computers within small satellites, pointing out the limitations of processing capabilities in CubeSats (satellite built in units of 1 kg and 10 cm$^3$ = 1U), with performance and reliability. The same year Manning et al. [11] explored the same domain. Using a Xilinx Zynq 7020 SoC device, they trained 4 different CNN architectures and compared the accuracy, latency and working memory usage. Around the same time Arechiga et al. [12] proposed a novel approach for ship detection from on-board a smallsat incorporating a slimmed down version of VGGnet using a Nvidia Jetson TX2 (SoC). It was a successful proof-of-concept, that advanced onboard processing applications are possible, with the use of a COTS embedded computer that meets the SWaP (Size, Weight and Power) requirements of a SmallSat. In 2019 Hernandez et al. [13] carried out a feasibility study on the integration of a Jetson TX1 system-on-module (SoM) as the on-board processor for a CubeSat, showing it to be 14 times faster than a typical CubeSat microprocessor (ARM Cortex-A57) with a peak power usage of 8.91 W.

In 2020 a paper was published [14] that represents the first real world deployment of Deep Learning on-board a SmallSat. CloudScout was introduced as a CNN for filtering images to be transmitted to ground operating directly on board a satellite. CloudScout running on an Intel Movidius Myriad 2 Vision Processing Unit (VPU) exceeded the requirements with a model footprint of 2.1 MB, accuracy of 92% and a false positive of 1.03%. performing inference in only 325 ms with an average power consumption of just 1.8 W. The model was installed on a satellite called HyperScout-2 and launched as part of the $\phi$-sat-1 mission, supported by the ESA through a program called PhiSat which is now being replicated across Europe. In September 2020 Reiter et al. [15] proposed an approach to create a real-time, remote-sensed cloud detection solution, using a binarized CNN (called CNV-W1A1) on a FPGA platform (Xilinx Zynq-7000 SoC). The highly compressed network achieved an impressive inference throughput of 358.1 images per second with a maximum power consumption of 2.4 W. While the throughput was approximately 115 times faster than the CloudScout deep neural network, the accuracy of 64% is comparatively low. Spillar et al. [16] investigated the use of CNNs on-board a satellite to detect wildfire using accerators including the Nividia Jetson Nano, Nividia Jetson TX2 and Intel Movidius Myriad 2. All achieved a similar accuracy performance of 0.98 for precision, recall and F1 which was comparable to testing on a high power pc. The Movidius had the lowest power consumption at 1.4 W, the TX2 was the fastest inference time of 3.4 ms but the Jetson Nano was considered the most promising technology for on-board hardware with the best balance of power consumption and speed.

Miralles et al. [17] recently carried a wide ranging review of Machine Learning applied to Earth Observation Operations, concluding that there is a strong argument for further research into optimisation of ML for deployment to on-board earth observation satellites to maximise the satellites potential.

### 2.3   Power Consumption Optimisation

The optimisation of power consumption during model inference can be done at the hardware level by choosing a power efficient device and making power efficient settings, or at the software level by choosing an optimal architecture and optimising it through various techniques (as described earlier).

In 2020 Holly et al. [18] investigated the effects of different CPU and GPU settings on power consumption, latency, and energy for a CNN model as well as for individual layers deployed on board NVIDIA Jetson Nano. They were able to provide insights into how specific hardware configuration settings, as well as network configurations, influence power consumption on the Nano. They also derived optimal settings for inference using the MobileNetV2 model deployed on the NVIDIA Jetson Nano. Hanafy et al. [19] did an evaluation of many popular deep learning models to understand the impact in their accuracy, latency, and energy when running on edge accelerators. It was shown that as models grew in size, any increase in their accuracy came at a much higher energy cost. Courbariaux et al. [20] investigated the impact of the precision of a neural networks parameters on the final error after training. They compared three formats: floating point, fixed point and dynamic fixed point, and trained each on three benchmark datasets. They discovered that very low precision is sufficient not just for running trained networks but also for training them by demonstrating that a model trained with 10-bit precision parameters has very similar error rates to the same model trained with single precision (32-bit) parameters. Han [21] also investigated using a combination of pruning, quantization to 5-bit and Huffman coding to compress the network with no loss in accuracy. Mehlin et al. [22] presented an overview of various approaches to increase the energy efficiency of deep learning categorized by the phases of the learning lifecycle (IT-Infrastructure, Data, Modeling, Training, Deployment and Evaluation). It was noted that previous overviews generally neglected the evaluation phase because this phase tended to be about evaluating the energy efficiency of deep learning models rather than improving it.

To the best of this authors knowledge, there has not been previous publications detailing the impact on power consumption of quantisation, for deployed CNN models. The objective of this paper is to be a reference, to assist in selecting a low energy quantised model that meets the accuracy & latency requirements while meeting the SWaP (Size, Weight and Power) limitations for a resource constrained platform.

# 3   Methodology

In this section, detail is provided about the test environment and how the software is structured.

## 3.1   Test Environment

A NVIDIA Jetson Orin Nano 8 GB was used as the primary test platform for the empirical evaluation. It is capable of facilitating some of the larger deep learning models, while also being a low power device specifically designed for accelerating machine learning applications. In addition it's a relatively inexpensive board and it's physical dimensions are small enough that it can be deployed on board a CubeSat (10 cm$^3$). Nvidia supply the TensorRT SDK which is a high performance deep learning inference framework supporting model quantisation/compilation and the "engine" or run-time for carrying out inference onboard it's devices. They also provide the JetPack which is a full development environment for hardware-accelerated AI applications. It's predecessor, the Jetson Nano, has been used successfully on several other satellite related projects as mentioned in the previous section. As mentioned previously Spiller et al. [16] carried out a feasibility study into deploying a wildfire classification model on board a satellite using several hardware accelerators including the Jetson Nano and showed it performs well and recommended it over the Nividia Jetson TX2 and Intel Movidius Myriad 2 based on a good balance between energy consumption and inference time. Previously Lofqvist et al. [23] explored real-time object detection on constrained devices using a Jetson Nano which was small enough to fit on a CubeSat but capable of running inference for pre-trained models on satellite imagery. Hernandez et al. [13] presented the feasibility of the integration of a Jetson TX1 as the on-board computer for a CubeSat showing inference improvements compared to the typical on-board computer in excess of 14×. It was noted that while the paper was being written the Jetson Nano had been launched and it would offer a more suitable platform as it was lighter smaller and lower electrical requirements.

## 3.2   Quantisated Models Creation

The base (before quantisation) models were generated by instantiating a Keras application object of the chosen architecture with pre-trained weights and saving to file in a SavedModel format. The quantised version was created from the base model using TensorFlow-TensorRT (TF-TRT) which is a deep-learning compiler for TensorFlow that optimizes TensorFlow models for inference on NVIDIA devices. The precision options chosen were FP32 (32-bit precision) and FP16 (32-bit precision). There was also an INT (8-bit) option which was tested but the model accuracy was impacted to an unacceptable degree so it was disregarded.

## 3.3 Inference

Software was developed to monitor important metrics such as energy, latency and accuracy and track relevant timestamps during inference. The main inference process starts a separate power monitoring process which takes voltage (millivolts) and current (milliamperes) readings every 100 ms from a monitor built into the Jetson Nano Orin. The pre-trained model being tested is loaded and inference is run for the ImageNet validation data. Once inference has completed the monitoring process is stopped. The total power consumption during inference is calculated and the power and latency per inference are extrapolated. The entire power consumption profile plot along with results such as accuracy, latency and power measurements are exported for further analysis.

## 4    Results and Analysis

The model architecture families and variants tested are shown in Table 1

**Table 1.** CNN Model Architectures Tested

| Model Architecture | | | | | | |
|---|---|---|---|---|---|---|
| DenseNet | EfficientNet | | MobileNet | ResNet | RegNetX | RegNetY | ConvNeXt |
| DenseNet121 | EfficientNetB0 | EfficientNetV2B0 | MobileNet | ResNet50 | RegNetX002 | RegNetY002 | ConvNeXtBase |
| DenseNet169 | EfficientNetB1 | EfficientNetV2B1 | MobileNetV2 | ResNet50V2 | RegNetX004 | RegNetY004 | ConvNeXtLarge |
| DenseNet201 | EfficientNetB2 | EfficientNetV2B2 | MobileNetV3Large | | RegNetX006 | RegNetY006 | ConvNeXtSmall |
| | EfficientNetB3 | EfficientNetV2B3 | MobileNetV3Small | | RegNetX008 | RegNetY008 | ConvNeXtTiny |
| | EfficientNetB4 | EfficientNetV2S | | | RegNetX016 | RegNetY016 | ConvNeXtXLarge |
| | | | | | RegNetX032 | RegNetY032 | |

Inference was carried on 3000 images from the ImageNet validation dataset, using each of the base (before quantisation) models in Table 1 as well as their FP32 and FP16 quantised versions.

## 4.1    Accuracy

In this section test results are presented for the energy consumed during inference and accuracy achieved by the models in Table 1. The impact that quantisation has on the results is then explored.

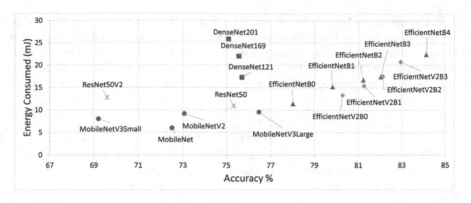

**Fig. 1.** Energy vs Accuracy (Base Models)

Figure 1 shows a plot of the energy consumed by each model during inference against the accuracy achieved for the base models. As one might expect the models that achieve the higher accuracies, generally consume more energy. Within some model families it's broadly a linear relationship (eg EfficientNet, EfficientNet & MobileNet) but there are exceptions. The DenseNet models achieve very similar accuracies (75–76%) but have quite different energy consumption results. Both ResNet models consume similar amounts of energy (11–13 mJ) but differ in accuracy achieved by almost 6%. The Regnet and ConvNeXt families were not shown as all variants have almost identical accuracy (73%) and power consumption (14 mJ) values. (Note: For conciseness the graphs from here on focus on MobileNet and EfficientNet as representative examples of the architectures tested but the tables linked later show data for all models).

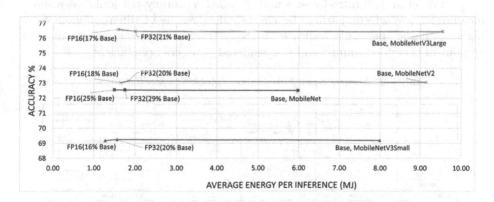

**Fig. 2.** MobileNet - Accuracy vs Energy (Base & Quantized Models)

Figure 2 depicts the accuracy vs average energy consumed for the MobileNet architecture family base models and their respective quantized variants. The text for each quantised measurement includes the percentage value relative to the base (e.g. "FP16(17% Base)" indicates that the FP16 version consumes just

17% of the energy of the base version.) The first point of note is the considerable reduction in energy consumption quantisation achieves. FP32 models average a 77% reduction while the FP16 reduces by an average of 81% which was not such a large difference. Secondly the impact on accuracy is negligible in all cases so it is a very effective way of saving energy consumption based on accuracy alone.

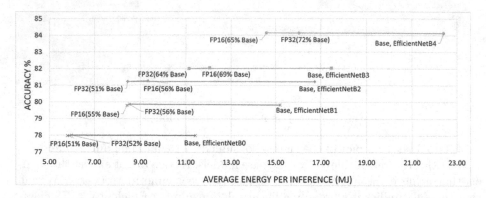

**Fig. 3.** EfficientNet - Accuracy vs Energy (Base & Quantized Models)

Figure 3 depicts a similar plot for the EfficientNet architecture. The impact of quantisation on accuracy is similarly negligible and the energy consumption reduction averages 41% for both FP32 and FP16. This is much less of an improvement compared to the MobileNet architecture. Interestingly for two of the models (EfficentNetB2 & EfficentNetB3) the FP32 variants achieve a slightly larger reduction compared to the FP16 variants which is unexpected and not easily explainable.

Hanafy et al. [19] introduced a metric called "accuracy-per-joule" as a more meaningful way of comparing the energy effectiveness of different models. A higher accuracy-per-joule indicates we're getting a better accuracy for the amount of energy consumed and is considered more energy efficient.

**Table 2.** Accuracy-per-Joule Table - MobleNet & EfficientNet

| Model | Base | | | FP32 | | | | | FP16 | | | | |
|---|---|---|---|---|---|---|---|---|---|---|---|---|---|
| | Energy (mJ) | Accuracy (%) | Accuracy / Energy (%/J) | Energy (mJ) | Energy (% Base) | Accuracy (% Base) | Accuracy / Energy (%/J) | Accuracy / Energy / Base (%) | Energy (mJ) | Energy (% Base) | Accuracy (%) | Accuracy / Energy (%/J) | Accuracy / Energy / Base (%) |
| EfficientNetB0 | 11.41 | 78.01 | 6837 | 5.97 | 52% | 78.01 | 13067 | 191% | 5.78 | 51% | 77.98 | 13491 | 197% |
| EfficientNetB1 | 15.2 | 79.83 | 5252 | 8.53 | 56% | 79.86 | 9362 | 178% | 8.42 | 55% | 79.79 | 9476 | 180% |
| EfficientNetB2 | 16.73 | 81.22 | 4855 | 8.45 | 51% | 81.22 | 9612 | 198% | 9.33 | 56% | 81.25 | 8708 | 179% |
| EfficientNetB3 | 17.46 | 82.03 | 4698 | 11.14 | 64% | 81.99 | 7360 | 157% | 12.05 | 69% | 82.03 | 6807 | 145% |
| EfficientNetB4 | 22.41 | 84.13 | 3754 | 16.04 | 72% | 84.13 | 5245 | 140% | 14.59 | 65% | 84.13 | 5766 | 154% |
| **EfficientNet Av.** | 16.64 | 81.04 | 5079 | 10.03 | 59% | 81.04 | 8929 | 173% | 10.03 | 59% | 81.04 | 8850 | 171% |
| MobileNet | 5.98 | 72.51 | 12125 | 1.76 | 29% | 72.54 | 41216 | 340% | 1.5 | 25% | 72.54 | 48360 | 399% |
| MobileNetV2 | 9.15 | 73.06 | 7985 | 1.84 | 20% | 73.15 | 39755 | 498% | 1.66 | 18% | 73.02 | 43988 | 551% |
| MobileNetV3Large | 9.55 | 76.46 | 8006 | 2.01 | 21% | 76.46 | 38040 | 475% | 1.6 | 17% | 76.59 | 47869 | 598% |
| MobileNetV3Small | 7.99 | 69.2 | 8661 | 1.57 | 20% | 69.24 | 44102 | 509% | 1.28 | 16% | 69.17 | 54039 | 624% |
| **MobileNet Average** | 8.17 | 72.81 | 9194 | 1.80 | 23% | 72.85 | 40778 | 456% | 1.51 | 19% | 72.83 | 48564 | 543% |

Table 2 shows the accuracy-per-joule (Accuracy/Energy column) results for MobileNet and EfficientNet grouped by quantisation type. The "Energy(%

Base)" column shows the energy consumed by the quantised model compared to the base model, which (as mentioned earlier) shows an average reduction of 41% and 77% for EfficientNet and MobileNet families respectively with FP32 quantisation. The accuracies for base models and quantised variants are almost identical. The "Accuracy/Energy/Base (%)" column shows the accuracy-per-joule improvement gained by quantization with an average 73% increase for EfficientNet and a huge 356% for MobileNet families.

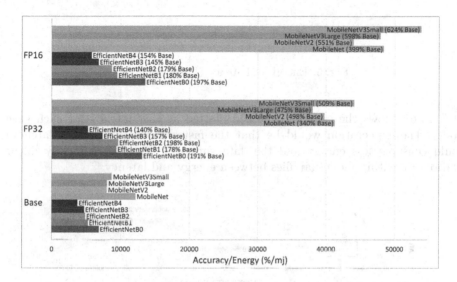

**Fig. 4.** Accuracy-per-Joule Plot - MobleNet & EfficientNet

Figure 4 shows the accuracy-per-Joule results from Table 2 in a bar chart format. The benefits of quantisation is evident in both architectures but the MobileNet benefits (avg 356%) 5 times more than for EfficientNet (avg 73%).

The accuracy/energy results for all models tested are available online at this link [24]. As already observed with MobileNet and EfficientNet, the difference between the accuracies of the base models and their quantised variants is insignificant across all families. The improvement in average accuracy-per-joule varies by model family with the DenseNet, MobileNet and ResNet model families gaining the most. The RegNets and ConvNeXt models gained the least from quantisation with just a 5% average accuracy-per-joule improvement for FP32 and 11% for FP16.

## 4.2  Latency

This section presents the test results focusing on the latency (speed) of each models inference and the impact that quantisation has on it with respect to energy consumed during inference.

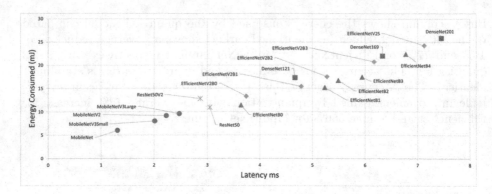

**Fig. 5.** Energy vs Latency (Base Model)

Figure 5 shows the energy consumed plotted against latency for each base model. The expectation would be that the faster models (i.e. lower latency) would consume less energy and the data supports this with a mostly linear relationship within model families between energy and latency.

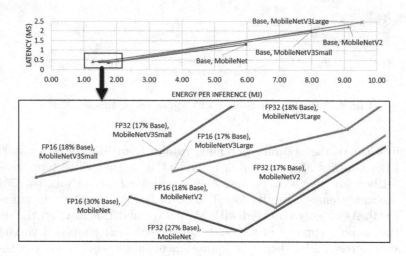

**Fig. 6.** MobileNet - Energy vs Latency (Base & Quantized Models)

Figure 6 depicts the latency plotted against the energy consumed for the MobileNet architecture family and their quantized variants. (A magnified inset is included as it's quiet cluttered). The quantised variants are generally a lot faster (avg. 21%) than their base models. The FP16 energy consumption values are generally slightly lower than the FP32 values. However In a few cases (MobileNet,MobileNetV2) the latency for the FP32 model is very slightly larger than the FP16 model which is unexpected.

**Table 3.** MobileNet - Latency/Energy

| Model | Base Energy (mJ) | Base Latency (ms) | Base Latency * Energy (msJ) | FP32 Energy (mJ) | FP32 Energy (%Base) | FP32 Latency (ms) | FP32 Latency (%Base) | FP32 Latency * Energy (msJ) | FP32 Latency * Energy / Base (%) | FP16 Energy (mJ) | FP16 Energy (%Base) | FP16 Latency (ms) | FP16 Latency (%Base) | FP16 Latency * Energy (msJ) | FP16 Latency * Energy / Base (%) |
|---|---|---|---|---|---|---|---|---|---|---|---|---|---|---|---|
| MobileNet | 5.98 | 1.3121 | 7846 | 1.76 | 29% | 0.357 | 27% | 628 | 8% | 1.5 | 25% | 0.3878 | 30% | 582 | 7% |
| MobileNetV2 | 9.15 | 2.229 | 20395 | 1.84 | 20% | 0.3782 | 17% | 696 | 3% | 1.66 | 18% | 0.4117 | 18% | 683 | 3% |
| MobileNetV3Large | 9.55 | 2.4741 | 23628 | 2.01 | 21% | 0.4492 | 18% | 903 | 4% | 1.6 | 17% | 0.411 | 17% | 658 | 3% |
| MobileNetV3Small | 7.99 | 2.0115 | 16072 | 1.57 | 20% | 0.4282 | 21% | 672 | 4% | 1.28 | 16% | 0.4055 | 20% | 519 | 3% |
| MobileNet Average | 8.17 | 2.01 | 16985 | 1.80 | 23% | 0.40 | 21% | 725 | 5% | 1.51 | 19% | 0.40 | 21% | 610 | 4% |

Table 3 shows the energy consumption along with the latency measurements for the MobileNet family base models along with their quantised variants. A "Latency × Energy" ("latency-by-joule") column was added, similar to how "accuracy-per-joule" was used previously, as a metric (lower is better) for comparing models performance considering both energy and latency. The Latency (% Base) column shows the latency of the quantised model compared to the base model with an average 89% reduction for both FP32 and FP16. The "Latency × Energy/Base (%)" column shows the latency-by-joule improvement gained by the quantization, which is on average over 96% reduced in the quantized models. The improvement in FP16 latency-by-joule is consistently better than FP32 unlike the raw latency value as mentioned previously.

The latency/energy results for all models tested are available online at this link [25]. Quantisation reduces the average latency-by-joule in all cases, being most effective for the DenseNet, ResNet & MobileNet model families (99%, 98%, 96% reductions) and less so for EfficientNet (70%) & EfficientNetV2 (82%) and much less for RegNetX, RegNetY & ConvNeXt (20%).

## 5  Conclusion

In this paper the power consumption behaviour of CNN architecture families DenseNet, EfficientNet, MobileNet, ResNet, ConvNeXt & RegNet were investigated by carrying out inference on the ImageNet validation dataset using a NVidia Jetson Orin Nano. This is a low power SoC edge accelerator that could be deployed to an earth observation satellite by virtue of it's small compact design and low power requirements that meet the strict power budget restrictions for satellite deployment.

It was found that there's a large variance in the average energy consumed per inference between architecture families with an average of 8mJ per inference for MobileNet compared to an average of 22 mJ for DenseNet. Accuracy achieved varied from an average of 73% for MobileNet and ResNet up to 82% for EfficientNetV2. Latency varied from an average of 2ms per inference for MoblieNet to over 6ms for DenseNet. The concepts of accuracy-per-joule (accuracy/energy) and latency-by-joule (accuracy × latency) were introduced and used as "energy effectiveness" metrics to compare models.

The impact of quantisation was evaluated for both 32-bit precision and 16-bit precision by carrying out inference on the same dataset. Accuracy was almost identical after model quantisation, while energy consumption dropped dramatically in most cases which was a positive outcome. There was a large increase in accuracy-per-joule in most models, such as DenseNet which improved from an average of 3574%/mJ for the base model to 16372%/mJ for FP32 quantised variant which is a 4.6× increase. The expected improvement between 32-bit to 16-bit quantisation was not so pronounced in most cases and non-existent in others. The impact of quantisation on latency was very similar to it's impact on energy consumption reducing it by up to 80%. This led to a very large latency-by-joule reduction of up tp 99%. Like the accuracy-per-joule metric the difference between 32-bit and 16-bit precision was marginal. Interestingly there were some model architectures (RegNetX, RegNetY and ConvNeXt) that were almost immune to any quantisation benefits with little or no change to the energy or latency measurements.

In conclusion we have a good picture of the power consumption behaviour of the chosen model families and the effectiveness of quantisation in reducing the consumption, latency and both the chosen metrics. In most cases (with some exceptions) we can say that it is an effective power and latency optimisation technique while most importantly not impacting accuracy for the precisions we tested.

# References

1. Furano, G., et al.: Towards the use of artificial intelligence on the edge in space systems: challenges and opportunities. IEEE Aerosp. Electron. Syst. Mag. **35**, 44–56 (2020)
2. He, K., Zhang, X., Ren, S., Sun, J.: Deep residual learning for image recognition. In: Proceedings of the IEEE Conference on Computer Vision and Pattern Recognition, pp. 770–778 (2015)
3. Krizhevsky, A., Sutskever, I., Hinton, G.E.: ImageNet classification with deep convolutional neural networks. Adv. Neural. Inf. Process. Syst. **25**, 1097–1105 (2012)
4. He, K., Zhang, X., Ren, S., Sun, J.: Deep residual learning for image recognition. In: Proceedings of the IEEE Conference on Computer Vision and Pattern Recognition, pp. 770–778 (2016)
5. Simonyan, K., Zisserman, A.: Very deep convolutional networks for large-scale image recognition. arXiv preprint arXiv:1409.1556 (2014)
6. Szegedy, C., et al.: Going deeper with convolutions. In: Proceedings of the IEEE Conference on Computer Vision and Pattern Recognition, pp. 1–9 (2015)
7. Hu, J., Shen, L., Sun, G.: Squeeze-and-excitation networks. In: Proceedings of the IEEE Conference on Computer Vision and Pattern Recognition, pp. 7132–7141 (2018)
8. Howard, A.G., et al.: MobileNets: efficient convolutional neural networks for mobile vision applications. preprint arXiv:1704.04861 (2017)
9. Buonaiuto, N., et al.: Satellite identification imaging for small satellites using NVIDIA (2017)
10. George, A.D., Wilson, C.M.: Onboard processing with hybrid and reconfigurable computing on small satellites. Proc. IEEE **106**, 458–470 (2018)

11. Manning, J., et al.: Machine-learning space applications on SmallSat platforms with TensorFlow (2018)
12. Arechiga, A.P., Michaels, A.J., Black, J.T.: Onboard image processing for small satellites. In: NAECON 2018-IEEE National Aerospace and Electronics Conference, pp. 234–240 (2018)
13. Hernández-Gómez, J.J., et al.: Conceptual low-cost on-board high performance computing in CubeSat nanosatellites for pattern recognition in Earth's remote sensing. In: iGISc, pp. 114–122 (2019)
14. Giuffrida, G., et al.: CloudScout: a deep neural network for on-board cloud detection on hyperspectral images. Remote Sens. **12**, 2205 (2020)
15. Reiter, P., Karagiannakis, P., Ireland, M., Greenland, S., Crockett, L.: FPGA acceleration of a quantized neural network for remote-sensed cloud detection. In: 7th International Workshop on On-Board Payload Data Compression (2020)
16. Spiller, D., et al.: Wildfire segmentation analysis from edge computing for onboard real-time alerts using hyperspectral imagery. In: 2022 IEEE International Conference on Metrology for Extended Reality, Artificial Intelligence and Neural Engineering (MetroXRAINE), pp. 725–730 (2022)
17. Miralles, P., et al.: A critical review on the state-of-the-art and future prospects of machine learning for earth observation operations. Adv. Space Res. (2023)
18. Holly, S., Wendt, A., Lechner, M.: Profiling energy consumption of deep neural networks on NVIDIA Jetson nano. In: 2020 11th International Green and Sustainable Computing Workshops (IGSC), pp. 1–6 (2020)
19. Hanafy, W.A., Molom-Ochir, T., Shenoy, R.: Design considerations for energy efficient inference on edge devices. In: Proceedings of the Twelfth ACM International Conference on Future Energy Systems, pp. 302–308 (2021)
20. Courbariaux, M., Bengio, Y., David, J.-P.: Training deep neural networks with low precision multiplications. arXiv preprint arXiv:1412.7024 (2014)
21. Han, S., Mao, H., Dally, W.J.: Deep compression: compressing deep neural networks with pruning, trained quantization and Huffman coding. arXiv preprint arXiv:1510.00149 (2015)
22. Mehlin, V., Schacht, S., Lanquillon, C.: Towards energy-efficient deep learning: an overview of energy-efficient approaches along the deep learning lifecycle. arXiv preprint arXiv:2303.01980 (2023)
23. Lofqvist, M., Cano, J.: Accelerating deep learning applications in space. arXiv preprint arXiv:2007.11089 (2020)
24. Duggan, A.: Appendix Table 2 (2023). https://aidanduggancit.github.io/SGAI/SGAI.html#table2
25. Duggan, A.: Appendix Table 3 (2023). https://aidanduggancit.github.io/SGAI/SGAI.html#table3

# Towards Goal-Oriented Agents
# for Evolving Problems Observed
# via Conversation

Michael Free, Andrew Langworthy(✉)(iD), Mary Dimitropoulaki,
and Simon Thompson

BT Applied Research, Ipswich, UK
andrew.langworthy@bt.com

**Abstract.** The objective of this work is to train a chatbot capable of solving evolving problems through conversing with a user about a problem the chatbot cannot directly observe. The system consists of a virtual problem (in this case a simple game), a simulated user capable of answering natural language questions that can observe and perform actions on the problem, and a Deep Q-Network (DQN)-based chatbot architecture. The chatbot is trained with the goal of solving the problem through dialogue with the simulated user using reinforcement learning. The contributions of this paper are as follows: a proposed architecture to apply a conversational DQN-based agent to evolving problems, an exploration of training methods such as curriculum learning on model performance and the effect of modified reward functions in the case of increasing environment complexity.

**Keywords:** Reinforcement Learning · Q-learning · Task-Oriented Chatbot

## 1 Introduction

Task-oriented dialogue systems have found use in a wide variety of tasks. They have been employed successfully in several different applications where the task to be accomplished is well defined. Examples include restaurant booking [12], healthcare [2], and entertainment [13]. These tasks are often 'data collection tasks' where a number of known information points must be collected by the agent to complete an end goal, with the information gathered rarely changing over the course of the conversation.

There are two main drawbacks with this approach, firstly that data-driven task-oriented dialogue systems require large amounts of heavily annotated training data, needing labels for intents, entities, and the flow from one dialogue state to another. This annotated data is often time-consuming to produce, and in some scenarios does not exist. This can severely limit the ability to build and train such systems.

---

M. Free, A. Langworthy and M. Dimitropoulaki—Contributed equally to the paper.

M. Bramer and F. Stahl (Eds.): SGAI 2023, LNAI 14381, pp. 142–155, 2023.
https://doi.org/10.1007/978-3-031-47994-6_11

Secondly, in some tasks, particularly those where the agent is directing the user to perform some action, the changes applied by the user invalidate the information collected by the agent, and so require the beliefs of the agent to be updated. In contrast to many types of conversational problems, these evolving conversations require the agent to properly understand the problem that is being discussed and to be able to produce answers that cannot be the result of memorization. An example of such a task is an IT customer service agent attempting to diagnose and fix a fault (for example, with a router) for an end user. The actions the agent instructs the user to take ("Restart your machine") can change the state of the problem, requiring the agent to update their information ("Is the light still blinking red?").

To study this problem, we introduce a 'gridsworld' navigational game, where the aim is to move a square piece through a 2D maze to a goal. We introduce a simulated user, who can answer questions about the state of the game and, upon instruction, take actions on the gridsworld. Finally, we introduce an agent who can ask questions to the user and instruct the user to take actions on the gridsworld. Crucially, this agent cannot see or interact directly with the gridsworld environment; all interaction goes through the conversational intermediary.

The structure of this paper is as follows. In the next section we describe our goals, the datasets used, and the architectures of the models used during training. Next, we look at related work, in particular task-oriented chatbots, text-based games, and maze-solvers, in order to contextualise our contribution. Finally, we describe our experiments and discuss the results.

## 2    Problem Formulation

The goal of this work is to train a conversational agent to solve an evolving problem that it can only see and interact with via an intermediary.

### 2.1    Overview of Approach

The system we study consists of three components:

1. A gridsworld environment to be navigated by a reinforcement learning (RL) agent.
2. A simulated user, able to answer questions about and take actions in the gridsworld environment.
3. An RL agent to solve a problem in the gridsworld via the simulated user.

These components interact with each other as shown in Fig. 1.

### 2.2    Gridsworld Environment

The gridsworld is a simple 2D environment that the simulated user can interact with at the request of the RL agent. It is a $6 \times 6$ grid containing one circle and one square, between zero and ten impassable spaces ('obstacles'), and between zero

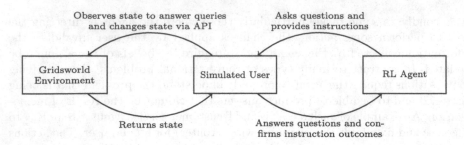

**Fig. 1.** Problem architecture

and ten spaces that prevent the shapes from moving ('traps'). The supplementary material[1] shows an example gridsworld, with black spaces representing traps and light grey spaces representing obstacles.

The goal of the agent is to move the square block through the grid, ignoring the obstacles and traps, to meet with the circle. At each step, the agent has a variety of actions to choose from. These are to move the square (e.g. "Move the square to the right"), to ask a question about where the circle is in relation to the square (e.g. "Is the square above the circle"), or to ask a question about where the nearest trap is (e.g. "Where is the nearest trap?"). A full list of actions can be seen in the supplementary material.

If the agent attempts to move the square onto a space containing an obstacle or outside the grid boundaries, the move fails and the agent is informed. If the agent moves the square onto a space containing a trap, the next two attempts the agent makes to leave the trap fail, with the agent being informed that they are stuck in a trap.

We note that there are in the region of $10^{26}$ possible gridsworld states. While this is far fewer than some other possible problems classically solved using reinforcement learning techniques (the possible board states in a chess game, for example), there is still a considerable amount of complexity in the setup we introduce here. In addition, the problem is made even harder by the fact that the agent cannot observe the entire gridsworld environment; each question the agent asks only returns a small amount of information about the whole space.

**Dataset Generation.** We generated 130,000 gridsworld instances, with the placement of the blocks, traps, and obstacles chosen uniformly at random. For each instance, the number of obstacles and number of traps were also both chosen uniformly at random, with the number of each being between 0 and 10. Any scenes without a path between the circle and the square were discarded to make sure all the instances were solvable. Next, duplicates were removed (approximately 10% of the instances) and the remaining instances were partitioned into an 80/10/10 train/test/validation split. While this meant that the sets were disjoint, there may be some overlap in the conversational data that the agent trains

---

[1] https://github.com/AndrewLangworthy/GoalOrientedAgents.

and is tested on, where the solution is conversationally equivalent or a subset of a training conversation. For instance, the agent may be trained on a scene that involves moving the block 3 spaces to the left, but tested on the same scene with the target moved one space closer to the right. In this case, even though the scenes are different, the agent may be tested on a conversation which is a subset of a conversation seen in training.

## 2.3   Simulated User

The simulated user observes the gridsworld, can answer natural language questions about the environment, and can take actions upon request. This simulated user is based on the MAC network implementation from [9]. The network is a combination of a convolutional neural network (CNN) acting as a feature extractor for the input image and a bidirectional long short-term memory (LSTM) to interpret the input questions. These two representations are then fed into a 'MAC cell' to produce a natural language answer to the proposed questions.

Our MAC network is architecturally identical to that of Hudson and Manning, but we adapt the network to take in images of our gridsworld scenes rather than the CLEVR images of [10] the network was originally designed to interpret.

Given a gridsworld scene we automatically generated questions, actions, and their associated answers in a rules-based fashion. The MAC network was then trained on these in an identical regime to that of [9].

## 2.4   RL Agent

The reinforcement learning agent converses with the simulated user, asking questions about and taking actions in the gridsworld. The simulated user can answer these questions and the RL agent then uses these answers to inform the next action. The RL agent cannot observe the gridsworld directly, it can gain information only through communication with the simulated user.

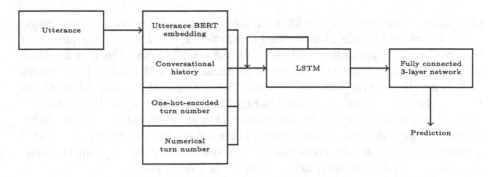

**Fig. 2.** Architecture of the RL agent

The architecture of the agent is shown in Fig. 2. The agent takes as input the most recent utterance from the simulated user and concatenates it to the conversation history (all previous questions/actions/responses), as well as a numerical and one-hot-encoded counter, counting the size of the conversation history.

The conversation utterances are encoded as sentence-level embeddings using a pre-trained BERT model, introduced in [16]. In this work, all utterances from both the agent and user are created from templates and so they follow a fixed pattern, but further work could allow the simulated user to generate natural language without a template, see [14], and therefore an encoding method that could deal with this was chosen.

Once the input has been created, it is fed into an LSTM with 64 hidden units. The output of that is then fed into a 3-layer network that returns a score over the 14 next possible utterances for the agent. The first two layers have 32 hidden units each.

The RL agent is trained using $Q$-learning [18]. This is a reinforcement learning technique where a $Q$ function is learnt to assign a value to state-action pairs of a Markov decision process. The learning process is given by

$$Q^{\text{New}}\left(s_t, a_t\right) \leftarrow r_t + \gamma \max_a Q\left(s_{t+1}, a\right), \tag{1}$$

where $r_t$ is the reward for taking the action $a_t$ at state $s_t$, and $\gamma$ is a discount constant. This function can be approximated by a neural network, as introduced in [15], and that is the architecture our RL agent uses. The specific training regime is that of a double-DQN, where two $Q$-functions are learnt simultaneously, but in the update applied by Eq. 1, the functions are updated on each other. This solves some overestimation problems that Q-learning may have. For details, see [7]. Specific details of the training methods are found in Sect. 4.

The code for our implementation of the RL agent is based on [4], itself an instantiation of the code from [13].

## 3   Related Work

Combining a simulated user with a dialogue manager is a common technique in the literature to train task-oriented chatbots [12,13]. These techniques often involve slot-filling for various tasks such as restaurant or movie theatre booking, and datasets containing these sorts of problems are well known, for example various iterations of the MultiWoZ dataset [5,22]. Our problem space differs from these in that the information gained from asking a question about the gridworld changes over time as the square moves around the environment as its relationship to other objects changes. More recent work in chatbots has experimented with a variety of more complex scenarios, for example negotiation [17], but the same limitations still remain, with information being largely static.

Text-based games and the models built to play them, such as those studied in [1,8,19], offer a richer problem space. In particular, in [20] a DQN-based agent is used to solve a text-based game to navigate a series of rooms. Here the problem evolves over the course of the agent instructions and the agent must remember previous navigation instructions and the results to obtain high performance. However, the agent does not have the ability to query the game or otherwise gain information without taking an action, which renders it different to our approach.

Solving navigational problems similar to the gridsworld we introduce is a natural problem upon which to apply reinforcement learning techniques. Examples include an RL agent designed to navigate a maze built in Minecraft [6]. The RL agent is augmented by a synthetic oracle, that gives one-hot-encoded directional advice to the agent. In related work, Zambaldi et al. [21] require the agent to travel to various locations within a 2D box-world before completing the task. They achieve this by using relational reinforcement learning, where the relations are learned using a self-attention mechanism. This allows the agent to make long term plans about its route. Building from this prior work, the relational grid world is introduced in [11], where an agent should navigate the 2D world to get to an exit point. This world contains various objects including walls and mountains, that affect the movements that the agent can make, and mean that the optimal path may not be the shortest. These all differ from our approach in that the agent trained can all directly act upon and (at least partially) observe the world, whereas our problem formulation requires information to be gained via an intermediary.

## 4    Experiments

The RL agent was trained on the navigation task in a number of scenarios. The neural network was updated using the Bellman equation, Eq. 1, where the states consist of the conversational histories and the actions are the possible actions the agent can take (either ask a question or request the square moved). We set $\gamma = 0.9$. The reward function for the agent was deliberately kept simple, since a future goal of this research is to investigate whether the learning and approaches made in this fairly easy game can be transferred to a more complex domain. The agent was given a reward of $-1$ for each action it took, unless the action completed the gridsworld scenario, i.e. moved the square into the same place as the circle, in which case the reward given was 60. The small negative rewards encourage efficient completion of the scenario. A limit of 30 turns was given to each scenario, and if the agent failed to complete the task within that time, an extra penalty of $-30$ was added.

The agent used an $\varepsilon$-greedy policy with slow annealing. We initialised $\varepsilon = 0.2$, and annealed it so that $\varepsilon = 0.01$ (i.e. there is a 1% chance the action chosen by the agent is random) after 1.15m training episodes. The replay memory size was set to 51200, and the model was updated using a mini-batch size of 512. The optimiser used was Adam with a learning rate of 0.0001.

### 4.1    Curriculum Learning

To speed up training times, we applied a curriculum learning regime [3] to the model. Before training, we partitioned the training data into three sets based on the minimum number of turns required to complete the scenario using an implementation of Dijkstra's algorithm. The three partitions of the training data were given by path lengths of less than 4, path lengths of between 4 and 5 inclusive, and paths of length greater than 5. These numbers include any potential time where the agent is stuck in a trap. The short scenarios made up approximately 40% of the training data, and the medium and long scenarios made up 30% each of the data.

During training, the model learned in a guided way, where at first only the problems with short path lengths are seen. Once the model reached an average reward greater than 10 over 500 scenarios, problems with medium length paths were added in. This is repeated once more, where all scenes were added to the training data. Since the model only got a positive reward upon completion of the scenario, this curriculum learning structure dramatically decreased learning time since it was far easier to get rewards early on in training.

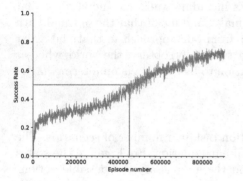 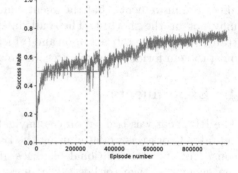

**Fig. 3.** Agent trained without curriculum learning

**Fig. 4.** Agent trained using curriculum learning. The marked spikes in success rate correspond to the addition of more challenging problems into the training data

In Figs. 3 and 4 we see two training runs that highlight the difference between curriculum learning versus no curriculum learning respectively. We can see the hard drops in success rate denoted by the vertical dashed lines in Fig. 4, which correspond to the addition of medium and hard scenes into the training data. The performance graph of Fig. 3 by contrast is comparatively smooth. The agent trained using a curriculum learning regime reached a success rate of 0.5 on the full dataset by 324,000 runs, whereas it took the agent trained on the whole dataset from the beginning 453,000 runs, a 39.8% increase. These spots are marked on the graphs with solid lines.

## 4.2    Alternative Agent Architectures

During testing, we experimented with several architectures for the RL agent. These followed the same structure as in Fig. 2 with the difference that we replaced the LSTM unit with a different one. For the first variant, the DNN-based architecture, we replaced the LSTM module by a fully connected layer with 64 hidden units. For the second variant, the CNN-based architecture, we replaced the LSTM module by two one-dimensional convolutional layers with a pooling layer of pool size 2 after each one. The first CNN layer had 64 filters and the second had 32. Both had a kernel size of 3. Both new architectures were trained in the same way as the LSTM-based architecture, with identical hyperparameter choices.

While an LSTM-based architecture is a classic way to deal with problems such as our conversational traversal of the gridworld due to the nature of the information gathered at earlier timesteps becoming less useful as more utterances are made, we tested the other architectures for comparison's sake.

## 4.3    Modified Rewards

During experiments, we modified the reward function to improve agent performance. We did this by giving the agent a small reward for asking questions to encourage question asking early in training, and for taking a move that moved the square closer to the circle. The introduction of these rewards marginally sped up the training time but did not result in a higher average success rate, implying that even without these extra rewards, the agent was settling on a policy that valued asking questions and moving closer to the target.

# 5    Results

**Table 1.** Success rates of different RL agent architecture

| RL agent architecture | Success rate |
| --- | --- |
| Human Baseline | **0.95**[a] |
| Fully connected layers | 0.49[b] |
| CNN | 0.58[b] |
| LSTM | **0.83** |
| LSTM - modified reward | **0.83** |

[a]Human baseline obtained a lower average reward than the LSTM-based architectures
[b]Agents did not reach a high enough average reward for the threshold to add in the hardest 30% of scenes

Table 1 shows the success rate of various agent architectures when trained to solve the gridsworld problems. The difference in architecture is only in the LSTM layer taking the encoded conversational context and turn numbers as described in Sect. 4.2. All results shown below apart from the human baseline are the average of three different tests on a hold-out dataset. Figures 5 and 6 show the training performance of the DNN and LSTM-based architectures over the three runs, with the solid line denoting the average of the three.

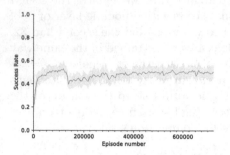

**Fig. 5.** DNN-based architecture. The single drop in success rate corresponds to the first addition of harder training data, but the threshold for even more is never reached

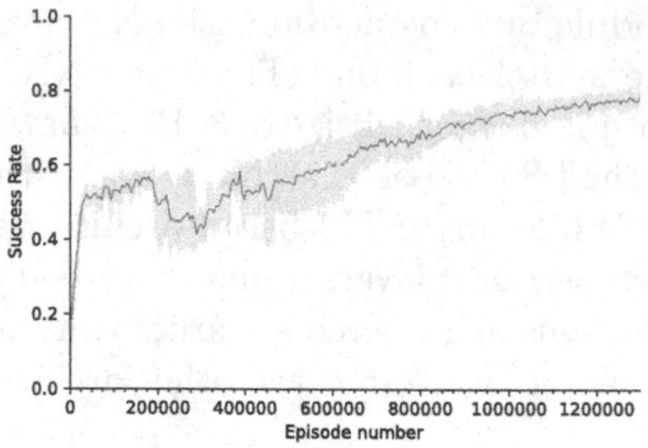

**Fig. 6.** LSTM-based architecture

## 5.1  Human Baseline

As a baseline, we ran human tests on 50 episodes. The success rate was 95%, with an average reward of 43.4. Although this success rate is considerably higher than that of the highest performing agent, we note that the average reward is actually lower. A partial explanation for this result is probably non-optimal questions and movement from the human operator; factors which we would expect the agent to perform better at than a human. However, we conjecture that the main factor is that the agent is optimising based on the reward it is getting, not the successful outcome. This might mean that it makes 'riskier' moves, since this gives a better average reward, rather than playing safe to ensure a success.

## 5.2  DNN Network

Figure 5 shows the results of the fully connected network without an LSTM layer. This model stopped learning quickly. In testing, it achieved a success rate of 49.2%, but it did not achieve a high enough reward to reach the threshold needed to add in the hardest 30% of scenes. This shows the difficulty that the fully connected network has in effectively encoding the long-term history of the conversation. It is possible that better results could have been achieved with a deeper network.

## 5.3    LSTM Network

The trained agent, whose results are in Fig. 6, achieved an episode completion rate of 84%, with an average reward of 44.6 out of a maximum 60. The average reward for successful episodes (considering uncompleted episodes got a total reward of $-60$) was 54. Of the conversational turns taken, 61.6% of them were actions and 39.4% were questions, with 5% of those relating to the whereabouts of the nearest trap.

An interesting point to note about these graphs is the period of slow learning after the initial rapid improvement of the system (see Figs. 3, 4, 6). Since any action taken by the agent carries the same negative reward but only the movement actions have a chance of getting the large reward for completing the task, asking questions is discouraged for a naïve policy. Also, the answer to a question must then be understood in terms of how it relates to the environment. The combination of these factors means that the agent initially learns a suboptimal strategy of exploring without asking questions. Only once the state space is sufficiently explored does the agent's strategy shift to using questions.

This may also explain the behaviour of the agent shown in Fig. 3. After a period of slow improvement success rate the gradient of the performance curve changes and the agents start to improve faster. We hypothesise that this is point where the agent learns how to parse the information given by asking questions, and so the optimal policy rapidly shifts.

## 5.4    Generalisation

To observe the RL agent acting on novel problem spaces, we performed tests of the agent's performance on larger gridsworlds. To do this, we generated 4000 gridsworlds in each $7 \times 7$, $8 \times 8$, and $9 \times 9$ grids. For half of them, all other aspects of the gridsworld (number of traps, obstacles, and objects, as well as their uniformly random placement) remained the same. For the other half, extra traps and obstacles were added to keep the ratio of obstacles and traps to empty spaces approximately equal to those of the original $6 \times 6$ gridsworlds. As before, gridsworlds that were not solvable were discarded. The problems were not split by path length. The agent with the LSTM architecture was used, due to its high performance.

The results are shown in Table 2. Note that performance in larger gridsworlds remains very high, but as expected performance does decrease with increased numbers of traps and obstacles.

It is worth noting that since the RL agent's input is sentence embeddings, this means that the agent can natively solve these unseen problems without any retraining or input-size adjustment. The only retraining that needs to be done in these scenarios is retraining of the user simulator. This is a large advantage of this problem architecture, as it allows direct transfer learning of the agent.

**Table 2.** Success rates of the RL agent on different gridsworlds

| Gridsworld Size | Success rate | |
|---|---|---|
| | Constant obstacles and traps | Proportional obstacles and traps |
| 7 × 7 | 0.83 | 0.77 |
| 8 × 8 | 0.82 | 0.70 |
| 9 × 9 | 0.82 | 0.65 |

# 6   Conclusion

We have shown that the proposed system architecture, a double DQN-based dialogue agent, can be trained to solve evolving problems that it can only observe via conversation with a simulated user. Through this conversation, it can achieve a high degree of success. The simulated user is also demonstrated to be suitable for incorporation into the described framework.

We have demonstrated that by utilising curriculum learning – ordering the training epochs in increasing scene complexity – we need 40% fewer training scenes to reach the same performance, a large gain when considering the resource intensive nature of training RL models.

Exploration of a modified reward function to account for environmental complexity, such as explicit negative reward for traps, showed little performance increase over a reward based solely on task completion metrics such as success and turns taken.

## 6.1   Transferability to Real Problems and Future Work

Whilst we have shown the agent is able to solve problems conversationally in the framework described, there are still shortcomings when it comes to transferring to a real problem. The simulated user is limited to a small number of conversational options, which is not a limitation placed on real users. This in turn means our trained reinforcement learning agent is only trained to deal with those specific utterances. In future work a generative model could be utilised to generate a wider range of conversational responses.

A positive aspect of the system is the non-perfection of the simulated user. As the trained model occasionally makes mistakes, the RL agent learns robustness to individual incorrect answers. The model also exhibits behaviour that is optimal in the context of the reward function given, but may not be suited to real interaction, such as abandoning questions and utilising only movement in a searching pattern as the conversational turn limit is approached. Further exploration of the reward function optimal for customer experience will need to be explored.

To transfer the ideas presented here to a real-world problem, a simulation of that problem, along with a capable simulated user would need to be constructed.

For example, in a diagnostic domain a simulation of a piece of equipment and external visual cues such as coloured lights and error messages could be simulated. A simulated user would then be trained to answer questions and take actions on the simulated equipment.

The relationship between these real-world problems and our gridsworld can be thought of in terms of the numbers of degrees of freedom that we can add to the system. More complex real-world problems can have their complexity mirrored in more complex gridsworld simulations. This means that further experiments on more advanced gridsworld scenarios will provide evidence of the performance of an analogous agent trained on a simulated system of comparable complexity. We have multiple options for increased gridsworld complexity, the grid size or shape could be upgraded or changed; the number of question iterations can be changed; the reward function could be tweaked to better represent the problem; or we could even introduce new elements to the world, taking inspiration from constructions like that in [11].

Section 5.4 shows that the problem architecture naturally lends itself to generalisations of the problem and transfer learning. The transferred element would be the problem solving RL agent itself, which could be fine tuned on the domain from training in simulations such as the one presented in this paper. As we have demonstrated, the transfer from simple to more complex versions of a problem can be achieved relatively easily, in part due to the fact that the language embedding of the conversation gives a complete representation for a conversation of any complexity.

**Acknowledgements.** The authors would like to thank Rob Claxton for his help and guidance, and the anonymous reviewers whose comments and suggestions much improved the paper.

# References

1. Ammanabrolu, P., Riedl, M.O.: Playing text-adventure games with graph-based deep reinforcement learning. ArXiv abs/1812.01628 (2018)
2. Athota, L., Shukla, V.K., Pandey, N., Rana, A.: Chatbot for healthcare system using artificial intelligence. In: 2020 8th International Conference on Reliability, Infocom Technologies and Optimization (Trends and Future Directions) (ICRITO), pp. 619–622 (2020). https://doi.org/10.1109/ICRITO48877.2020.9197833
3. Bengio, Y., Louradour, J., Collobert, R., Weston, J.: Curriculum learning. In: Proceedings of the 26th Annual International Conference on Machine Learning, ICML 2009, pp. 41–48. Association for Computing Machinery, New York (2009). https://doi.org/10.1145/1553374.1553380
4. Brenner, M.: Goal-oriented chatbot trained with deep reinforcement learning (2018). https://github.com/maxbren/GO-Bot-DRL
5. Budzianowski, P., et al.: MultiWOZ - a large-scale multi-domain Wizard-of-Oz dataset for task-oriented dialogue modelling. In: Proceedings of the 2018 Conference on Empirical Methods in Natural Language Processing, pp. 5016–5026. Association for Computational Linguistics, Brussels, Belgium (2018). https://doi.org/10.18653/v1/D18-1547. https://aclanthology.org/D18-1547

6. Frazier, S., Riedl, M.: Improving deep reinforcement learning in minecraft with action advice. In: Proceedings of the Fifteenth AAAI Conference on Artificial Intelligence and Interactive Digital Entertainment, AIIDE 2019. AAAI Press (2019)
7. Hasselt, H.V., Guez, A., Silver, D.: Deep reinforcement learning with double q-learning. In: Proceedings of the Thirtieth AAAI Conference on Artificial Intelligence, AAAI 2016, pp. 2094–2100. AAAI Press (2016)
8. Hausknecht, M.J., Ammanabrolu, P., Côté, M.A., Yuan, X.: Interactive fiction games: a colossal adventure. In: AAAI Conference on Artificial Intelligence (2019)
9. Hudson, D.A., Manning, C.D.: Compositional attention networks for machine reasoning. In: International Conference on Learning Representations (2018). https://openreview.net/forum?id=S1Euwz-Rb
10. Johnson, J., Hariharan, B., van der Maaten, L., Fei-Fei, L., Zitnick, C.L., Girshick, R.: Clevr: a diagnostic dataset for compositional language and elementary visual reasoning. In: CVPR (2017)
11. Küçüksubaşı, F., Surer, E.: Relational-grid-world: a novel relational reasoning environment and an agent model for relational information extraction. Turk. J. Electr. Eng. Comput. Sci. **29**, 1259–1273 (2021). https://doi.org/10.3906/elk-2008-94
12. Lei, W., Jin, X., Kan, M.Y., Ren, Z., He, X., Yin, D.: Sequicity: simplifying task-oriented dialogue systems with single sequence-to-sequence architectures. In: Proceedings of the 56th Annual Meeting of the Association for Computational Linguistics (Volume 1: Long Papers), pp. 1437–1447. Association for Computational Linguistics (2018). https://doi.org/10.18653/v1/P18-1133. https://aclanthology.org/P18-1133
13. Li, X., Chen, Y.N., Li, L., Gao, J., Celikyilmaz, A.: End-to-end task-completion neural dialogue systems. In: Proceedings of the Eighth International Joint Conference on Natural Language Processing (Volume 1: Long Papers), pp. 733–743. Asian Federation of Natural Language Processing, Taipei (2017). https://aclanthology.org/I17-1074
14. Li, X., Lipton, Z., Dhingra, B., Li, L., Gao, J., Chen, Y.N.: A user simulator for task-completion dialogues (2016)
15. Mnih, V., et al.: Playing Atari with deep reinforcement learning (2013)
16. Reimers, N., Gurevych, I.: Sentence-bert: sentence embeddings using siamese bert-networks. In: Proceedings of the 2019 Conference on Empirical Methods in Natural Language Processing. Association for Computational Linguistics (2019). https://arxiv.org/abs/1908.10084
17. Verma, S., Fu, J., Yang, S., Levine, S.: CHAI: a chatbot AI for task-oriented dialogue with offline reinforcement learning. In: Proceedings of the 2022 Conference of the North American Chapter of the Association for Computational Linguistics: Human Language Technologies, pp. 4471–4491. Association for Computational Linguistics, Seattle (2022). https://doi.org/10.18653/v1/2022.naacl-main.332. https://aclanthology.org/2022.naacl-main.332
18. Watkins, C.J.C.H.: Learning from delayed rewards (1989)
19. Yao, S., Rao, R., Hausknecht, M.J., Narasimhan, K.: Keep calm and explore: Language models for action generation in text-based games. ArXiv abs/2010.02903 (2020)
20. Yuan, X., et al.: Counting to explore and generalize in text-based games. ArXiv: abs/1806.11525 (2018)
21. Zambaldi, V.F., et al.: Relational deep reinforcement learning. ArXiv: abs/1806.01830 (2018)

22. Zang, X., Rastogi, A., Sunkara, S., Gupta, R., Zhang, J., Chen, J.: MultiWOZ 2.2 : a dialogue dataset with additional annotation corrections and state tracking baselines. In: Proceedings of the 2nd Workshop on Natural Language Processing for Conversational AI, pp. 109–117. Association for Computational Linguistics (2020). https://doi.org/10.18653/v1/2020.nlp4convai-1.13. https://aclanthology.org/2020.nlp4convai-1.13

# Case Based Reasoning

# Semi-supervised Similarity Learning in Process-Oriented Case-Based Reasoning

Nicolas Schuler[1,3]([✉]) [iD], Maximilian Hoffmann[1,2] [iD], Hans-Peter Beise[3], and Ralph Bergmann[1,2] [iD]

[1] Branch University of Trier, German Research Center of Artificial Intelligence (DFKI), Trier, Germany
{hoffmannm,bergmann}@uni-trier.de
[2] University of Trier, Trier, Germany
[3] Trier University of Applied Sciences, Trier, Germany
{schulern,beise}@hochschule-trier.de

**Abstract.** Supervised learning is typically challenging with insufficient amounts of labeled training data and high costs for label acquisition, creating a demand for unsupervised learning methods. In the research area of *Process-Oriented Case-Based Reasoning (POCBR)*, this demand is created by training data that is manually-modeled and computationally-expensive labeling methods. In this paper, we propose a *semi-supervised transfer learning* method for learning similarities between pairs of semantic graphs in POCBR with *Graph Neural Networks (GNNs)*. The method aims to replace the fully supervised learning procedure from previous work with an unsupervised and a supervised training phase. In the first phase, the GNNs are pretrained with a triplet learning procedure that utilizes *graph augmentation* and random selection to enable unsupervised training. This phase is followed by a supervised one where the pretrained model is trained on the original labeled training data. The experimental evaluation examines the quality of the semi-supervised models compared to the supervised models from previous work for three semantic graph domains with different properties. The results indicate the potential of the proposed approach for improving retrieval quality.

**Keywords:** Semi-Supervised Learning · Transfer Learning · Process-Oriented Case-Based Reasoning · Deep Learning

## 1 Introduction

*Case-Based Reasoning (CBR)* [1] is a research field in artificial intelligence, focusing on experience-based problem-solving. The key components of a CBR application [31] are a case base which contains cases of experiential knowledge, similarity measures for determining which case of the case base is suited to solve a new problem, adaptation knowledge to enable modifications of cases for unseen situations, and a vocabulary that defines the underlying domain of the data and the application. The focus of this work is the *retrieval* phase of a CBR application, in which

M. Bramer and F. Stahl (Eds.): SGAI 2023, LNAI 14381, pp. 159–173, 2023.
https://doi.org/10.1007/978-3-031-47994-6_12

the case base is searched for the most similar, hence most useful, cases w.r.t. a query. Thereby, similarity measures determine the similarity value between the query and the cases, with a higher similarity resulting in a higher problem-solving capability. *Process-Oriented Case-Based Reasoning (POCBR)* [3,24] aims to integrate the CBR principles with process-oriented applications such as cooking assistance [25], manufacturing [23], and argumentation [22]. A retrieval in the context of POCBR typically assesses the similarity between semantically-annotated processes with similarity measures based on graph isomorphism checks [3]. Their inherent computational complexity [28] paired with large case bases can, thus, lead to long retrieval times and a limited practical applicability.

Different approaches tackle these shortcomings by approximating semantic graph similarities with computationally-inexpensive similarity measures that are, for instance, based on graph feature selection [4] or embeddings of entity-relationship triplets [20]. This paper builds upon an approach where whole-graph embeddings are learned by message-passing *Graph Neural Networks (GNNs)* [16,17]. These GNNs embed semantic graphs with three consecutive operations: First, all nodes and edges including semantic annotations and types are embedded to an initial vector representations. The node representations then iteratively share information with each other by merging representations of neighboring nodes according to the edge structure. The whole-graph embedding vector is finally determined by aggregating the representations of all nodes. The resulting embedding in the latent, low-dimensional feature space can then be used to calculate the graph similarity, e.g., by a vector similarity measure such as cosine similarity or other distance-based measures such as normed Euclidean distance. The GNNs are trained with pairs of semantic graphs and ground-truth similarities that stem from a similarity measure based on graph matching [3]. The goal of the approach is to speed up retrieval by using GNNs as (fast) similarity measures to predict graph similarities, rather than computing them with computationally-expensive measures [16,17].

In this paper, we replace the fully supervised training procedure by a semi-supervised transfer learning method [21,34] that uses an unsupervised and a supervised training phase. In the first, unsupervised phase, the GNNs are trained with a triplet learning procedure [33]. Following is a second supervised training phase, where the original supervised training procedure from previous work [17] is employed. The motivation is to reduce the effort for label computation compared to a solely supervised approach, since an unsupervised training phase can be expected to reduce the amount of labeled data for a subsequent supervised training. This strategy has proven to be effective in other domains [35]. To the best of our knowledge, its application to the task of similarity learning between semantic graphs is novel. The remainder of the paper is structured as follows: Sect. 2 describes foundations on the used semantic graph representation format and on embedding semantic graphs with GNNs. Additionally, related work on unsupervised learning is discussed. The proposed approach of semi-supervised transfer learning with semantic graphs is presented in Sect. 3. This approach is experimentally evaluated and compared with previous work in Sect. 4. Finally, Sect. 5 concludes the paper and shows areas of future work.

## 2   Foundations and Related Work

The foundations include the semantic workflow representation and its corresponding similarity measure that is the base for the concept and the experimental evaluation (see Sect. 2.1). In addition, semantic graph embedding with GNNs is examined (see Sect. 2.2) and related work concerning unsupervised learning with graphs (see Sect. 2.3) and unsupervised learning in CBR literature (see Sect. 2.4) is discussed.

### 2.1   Semantic Workflow Representation and Similarity Assessment

The workflow representation format used in the remainder of the paper is the NEST graph format, introduced by Bergmann and Gil [3] and common in POCBR literature (e.g., [17,22,23,37]). A NEST graph is defined as a quadruple $W = (N, E, S, T)$ where $N$ is a set of nodes, $E \subseteq N \times N$ a set of edges, $S : N \cup E \to \Sigma$ a function assigning a semantic description to each node and edge from the semantic metadata language $\Sigma$, and $T : N \cup E \to \Omega$ a function assigning a type from $\Omega$ to each node and edge. $\Sigma$ is usually given by the domain definition in the form of an ontology or some other knowledge model. An exemplary NEST graph representing a sandwich recipe is given in Fig. 1. The sandwich starts by executing the cooking step *coat* (represented as a task node) with the ingredients *mayo* and *baguette* (represented as data nodes). A slice of gouda is then laid on the coated baguette to finish the simple sandwich. All nodes are connected by edges to indicate relations, e.g., *layer* consumes *baguette*. The workflow components, i.e., nodes and edges, are further specified by using semantic annotations (as shown for the example *coat*). The semantic annotation of this example defines a list of auxiliaries and the time to complete the task. In general, semantic annotations can be arbitrarily complex with different data types (e.g., numerics, strings, dates, etc.) and different compositions that form a tree structure, making similarity computation complex [17].

To calculate the similarity between two given NEST graphs, Bergmann and Gil [3] introduce a similarity measure based on the local-global principle [31]. The global similarity of two NEST graphs is determined by a graph matching procedure that takes into account the local similarities of the semantic annotations of mapped nodes and edges. In this process, nodes and edges of the query graph are mapped by an injective function to nodes and edges, respectively, of the case graph. Thereby, the nodes and edges are mapped onto each other in an A* search with the goal of maximizing the global similarity. The matching process is complex and can take a long time for larger graphs, since the number of possible mappings grows exponentially with the number of nodes and edges (see [36] for a quantitative analysis). This emphasizes the need for fast, lightweight similarity measures, such as similarity approximation by GNNs [17], to speed up POCBR applications.

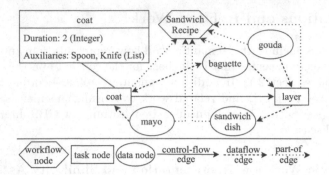

**Fig. 1.** Exemplary Cooking Recipe represented as NEST Graph.

## 2.2  Semantic Graph Embedding

Hoffmann and Bergmann [17] present two Siamese GNNs, i.e., the *Graph Embedding Model (GEM)* and the *Graph Matching Network (GMN)*, for speeding up similarity-based retrieval in POCBR. The GEM and GMN, illustrated in Fig. 2, are trained to predict graph similarities by transforming the graph structure and the semantic annotations and types of all nodes and edges into a whole-graph latent vector representation. These vectors are then combined to calculate a similarity value. Both models follow a shared general architecture composed of four components: First, the *embedder* transforms the features of nodes and edges to initial node and edge embeddings in a vector space. These features comprise semantic annotations and types and are encoded and processed in a very specific way for semantic graphs (see [17] for more information). Second, the *propagation layer* gathers information for each node from its local neighborhood by passing messages [12]. Specifically, the vector representation of a node is updated by merging its vector representation with those of neighboring nodes connected by

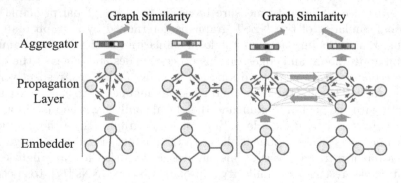

**Fig. 2.** GEM (left branch) and GMN (right branch) (taken from [16]).

incoming edges. This process is iterated multiple times. Subsequently, the *aggregator* combines the node embeddings at that state to form a vector representation of the entire graph. The *graph similarity* between two graphs is eventually computed based on their vector representations in the vector space, for instance, utilizing a vector similarity measure like cosine similarity.

The two models exhibit differences in how they implement the propagation layer and the final graph similarity. These differences result in a trade-off between expressiveness and performance. Specifically, while the GMN provides greater expressiveness than the GEM, it is also associated with a higher computational cost. For a more in-depth exploration of these variances, we refer to Hoffmann and Bergmann [17]. Furthermore, an integral part of the training procedure is to learn the general (implicit) characteristics of semantic graphs without the concrete focus on similarity. This motivates using the GEM and the GMN in an unsupervised or semi-supervised training setup to reduce the needed amount of labeled training data.

## 2.3 Unsupervised Learning with Graphs

A popular model architecture for unsupervised learning with graphs are *Siamese Neural Networks (SNNs)*, originally introduced by Bromley et al. [5] (see [8] for an in-depth review). These neural networks are used by a variety of unsupervised [13], semi-supervised [32], and supervised [17] approaches. At its core, an SNN is a multitude of identical networks sharing trainable parameters [32]. For graph representation learning, specifically, the neural network itself can be any GNN that processes graphs and yields a vector-space representation. To train the shared weights of the networks, different loss functions can be employed, which include, for instance, triplet loss [33].

Another popular model architecture for unsupervised learning with graphs are *Graph Autoencoders (GAEs)* (see [14] for an in-depth review). These models consist of an encoder, reducing the dimensionality of the input data to a (simple) vector representation, and a decoder, increasing the dimensionality of the vector representation. The training procedure has the goal of improving the encoder and decoder to the point where the decoded data closely matches the original input data. In particular, GAEs offer several features that make them suitable models for POCBR applications. First, their flexible nature allows utilizing a variety of architectures [14] for the encoder, which in turn can also be used to pretrain an encoder that might be used later in a different context. In addition, an autoencoder enables the decoding of the embedded graph from the latent space back to its initial representation, enabling generative model architectures. Albeit initially developed for relational graphs such as social networks, Kipf and Welling [19] present variational GAEs as a generative model that is generally also applicable to semantic graphs representing processes.

## 2.4    Unsupervised Learning in CBR

In the present work, unsupervised learning of graph representations is paired with supervised graph embedding and transfer learning. For a more comprehensive discussion of related deep learning and transfer learning applications in the CBR context, see previous work [17,30]. Approaches utilizing unsupervised learning in CBR research are examined in the following: In the field of textual CBR, Naqvi et al. [27] use an unsupervised autoencoder to fine tune a deep language model to adopt it to a specific CBR domain in the context of prognostics and health management. Amin et al. [2] utilize word embeddings for unsupervised text vectorization and word representation learning with SNNs in CBR to perform customer service tasks. Similarly, Lenz et al. [22] apply supervised and unsupervised methods from textual CBR to argument graphs, that is, arguments represented as a graph, in the context of similarity-based retrieval. The work focuses on semantic textual similarity, which is improved by utilizing unsupervised word embeddings and similarity measures beyond simple vector measures. Chourib et al. [9] apply unsupervised k-means clustering to generate representations of medical knowledge from the case base for similarity estimations and quality assessments. For POCBR in particular, Klein et al. [20] use a generic triplet embedding framework for unsupervised triplet representation learning in the context of similarity-based retrieval. However, this work did neither consider the entire graph structure nor the semantic annotations of nodes and edges [20].

These examples show that many of the approaches do not focus on graph-structured data and are thus not suitable to be applied in POCBR applications. To the best of our knowledge, the proposed approach is novel in the sense that it combines unsupervised learning, supervised graph embedding, and transfer learning in a POCBR context.

## 3    Semi-supervised Transfer Learning with Semantic Graphs

In order to reduce the effort for labeling training data for supervised graph similarity learning tasks in POCBR, the approach proposed in this paper aims at using semi-supervised transfer learning with SNNs. An overview of the components and the main steps is given in Fig. 3. The approach uses three separate learning paradigms that are combined and explained in the remainder of this section, i.e., unsupervised triplet learning, supervised graph similarity learning, and a transfer learning scenario.

Transfer learning acts on the highest level of the architecture and combines the other two components. The general idea is that knowledge gained from a source domain in the pretraining phase (see step 2) can be transferred to a target domain in the adaptation[1] phase (see step 3) [21,34]. In our context,

---

[1] Please note that the term "adaptation" refers to its meaning in the context of transfer learning in the remainder of the paper and is not referring to the reuse phase in CBR.

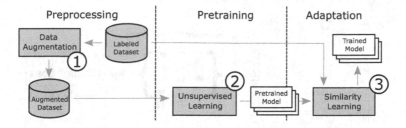

**Fig. 3.** Architecture for Semi-Supervised Transfer Learning With Its Three Main Steps.

a graph embedding model, acting as the knowledge, is transferred from the pretraining phase, an unsupervised learning procedure, to the adaptation phase, a supervised learning procedure. A preprocessing phase for data augmentation (see step 1) precedes the pretraining phase to create a large unlabeled dataset to be used by the unsupervised learning method. The underlying assumption is that unsupervised pretraining with augmented data reduces the need for a large amount of labeled data in a subsequent supervised training, as supported by literature [35]. However, to apply this strategy, all phases of the transfer learning process must be designed to be compatible.

### 3.1   Unsupervised Triplet Learning

The pretraining phase employs an SNN with a triplet loss [33] for learning unsupervised graph embeddings (see Fig. 4). As the concrete models to be used in the SNN configuration, we use the GEM and GMN from previous work [17] (see Sect. 2.2). The idea is to generate similar embeddings for similar graphs and dissimilar embeddings for dissimilar graphs (in terms of vector space similarity). Since we do not compute the ground-truth similarities for graphs in the training data, the loss function operates on graph triplets of an *anchor*, a *negative*, and a *positive*, maximizing the similarity for the pair of the anchor and the positive and minimizing the similarity for the pair of the anchor and the negative. More formally, the triplet loss is defined in Eq. 1: Let $T = (x^a, x^p, x^n)$ be a triplet consisting of one input vector for anchor $x^a$, positive $x^p$, and negative $x^n$. Let $f(x_i) = m_i \in \mathbb{R}^n$ denote the embedding of an input vector $x_i$ as the $n$-dimensional embedding $m_i$. To train a model based on the triplet loss, the loss function $L$ is minimized with $\alpha$ as a margin hyperparameter and $N$ as the cardinality of a batch of triplets [33].

$$L = \sum_{j}^{N} \max\{0, \|m_j^a - m_j^p\|^2 - \|m_j^a - m_j^n\|^2 + \alpha\} \tag{1}$$

The main challenge for this training method in an unsupervised context is to put together triplet training examples of an anchor, a negative, and a positive. There are different solutions in literature, depending on the type of data,

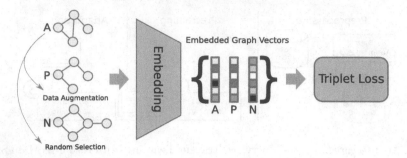

**Fig. 4.** Unsupervised Triplet Graph Embedding using an Anchor (A), a Positive (P), and a Negative (N).

the learning task, and other factors (e.g., [15,29]). We propose to reuse popular methods that originally stem from the domain of computer vision [6]. In this domain, an anchor is commonly selected from the training set and the positive is generated based on the anchor by data augmentation, while the negative is randomly selected from the training set. For instance, Chen et al. [6] use data augmentation like rotation, cropping, color distortion, filtering, and blurring of images. However, while the random selection of a graph from the dataset to generate the negative is trivial, the generation of the positive via data augmentation is challenging due to the complexity of the underlying semantic graphs (see Sect. 2.1).

### 3.2   Semantic Graph Augmentation

In this unsupervised setup, a challenge arises when defining suitable positives $x^p$ using data augmentation methods [11], as it requires configuring the augmentation techniques in a way that ensures the positive samples are actually similar to the anchor. So called hard or semi-hard triplets [15] are needed. In a semi-hard triplet, the negative's embedding has a greater vector-space distance to the anchor's embedding than the positive's embedding, but still within the range of the margin parameter $\alpha$ (see Eq. 1). A hard triplet is stricter, such that the negative's embedding must be closer to the anchor's embedding than the positive's embedding. As there are no similarity labels to ensure this property for generated triplets, the data augmentation methods can only work with heuristics. This is particularly challenging for the domain of semantic graphs due to their characteristics and definition of similarity (see Sect. 2.1) where small changes, for instance on the level of a single semantic annotation, can have large effects on the global similarity. We present two methods of semantic graph augmentation in the following (see [10,26] for a comprehensive overview of graph augmentation techniques) that are simple by design. Their purpose is to demonstrate the aspect of semantic graph augmentation and to be used in the experimental evaluation. A thorough investigation of other, more complex augmentation methods is beyond the scope of this work and, therefore, postponed to future work.

The first method augments processes by randomly changing the order of two subsequent task nodes in the control-flow sequence. Looking at the example in Fig. 1, the method would swap the order of *coat* and *layer*, resulting in *layer* being the first and *coat* being the second task node in the control-flow sequence. In a larger graph, the other parts of the control-flow remain unchanged. The method can be parameterized by the number of swaps and a random seed to ensure reproducibility. The second method randomly deletes edges of a certain type to augment processes. For instance, in Fig. 1, the method could randomly delete two of the shown part-of edges. The connected nodes remain unchanged. The method can be parameterized by the number of deletions, the type of the edges to delete, and a random seed to ensure reproducibility. While both augmentation methods are simple, they are still fundamentally different regarding the resulting augmented processes. The first augmentation method maintains the syntactic correctness of the augmented process in terms of the NEST graph format (see Sect. 2.1). This means that the augmented process could, for instance, be executed in a process execution engine. The second method does not preserve syntactic correctness, making the augmented process unusable for execution or other tasks that require syntactic correctness. Both methods, however, do not preserve semantic correctness that is defined by the POCBR domain and similarity models, e.g., "a baguette cannot be *layered* before *coated*". The method we employ is based on the assumption that neural networks are still able to learn the basic structure and composition of the original processes from the augmented processes, even if the latter do not feature syntactic or semantic correctness.

### 3.3 Graph Embedding with GEM and GMN

The GEM and the GMN (see Sect. 2.2) are used for the task of graph embedding in the *pretraining* phase with triplet learning and in the *adaptation* phase. Their task in the adaptation phase is supervised embedding of graph pairs, which exactly matches their original purpose (see previous work, e.g., [17], and Fig. 2). However, the triplet learning method in the pretraining phase requires adjustments to the models. The GEM is not used, as originally introduced, with pairs but with triplets of graphs in the pretraining phase. These graph triplets are also processed with shared parameters. As the GEM supports processing tuples of graphs independent of their number out of the box, this change is more focused on the implementation. The modifications to the GMN are more substantial due to the cross-graph matching procedure in the propagation layer that is integral to the superior prediction quality of the GMN compared to the GEM. That is, this matching procedure requires pairs of graphs to function properly due to the involved information propagation between the two graphs (see Fig. 2). Since the triplet learning procedure in the pretraining phase works with graph triplets, i.e., anchor, positive, and negative, the GMN must be adjusted. We employ the GMN to compute embeddings for two graph pairs, i.e., a pair of anchor and positive and a pair of anchor and negative. The four resulting graph embedding vectors are then reduced to three for computing the triplet loss. The reduction is done by aggregating the embedding vectors of both anchors in a trainable procedure, which, in this work, is implemented by an MLP. These adjustments to the GEM and the GMN allow the unsupervised pretraining and the supervised adaptation of both models in the transfer learning process.

# 4    Experimental Evaluation

The experimental evaluation compares similarity-based retrieval between the proposed semi-supervised transfer learning approach and the supervised baseline approach (as introduced in Sect. 2.2). We evaluate the quality of the retrieval results in terms of the similarity prediction error and the errors in the order of the retrieval results (see Sect. 4.1 for more details). The evaluation consists of multiple experiments, where the effects of different amounts of labeled training data are investigated. In total, 36 different retrievers with different model configurations are compared in three workflow domains. The aim of the evaluation is to investigate the effect of the proposed approach on the quality of the retrieval results.

## 4.1    Experimental Setup

The experiments involve three different case bases from different domains. These domains are the cooking domain (CB-I), the data mining domain (CB-II), and the manufacturing domain (CB-III). CB-I comprises 40 cooking recipes, manually modeled and then expanded to 800 workflows through the generalization and specialization of ingredients and cooking steps (more details in [17,25]). The case base contains a total of 660 training cases, 60 validation cases, and 80 test cases. In CB-II, the workflows are derived from sample processes provided with RapidMiner. The case base consists of 509 training cases, 40 validation cases, and 60 test cases. Additional information on this domain can be found in [37]. CB-III encompasses workflows originating from a smart manufacturing IoT environment, representing sample production processes. The case base includes 75 training cases, nine validation cases, and nine test cases (more details in [23]).

The workflows of these domains are augmented with the two methods described in Sect. 3.2 to increase the size of the dataset. The augmentation is done in the following set of steps: First, for each workflow of the initial original dataset, one random part-of edge is deleted. In the second step, the set containing the original and the augmented workflows from the first step are augmented again by changing the order of one random pair of subsequent task nodes. Thus, the result is a new, unlabeled dataset containing four times the amount of data of the initial dataset, with parts of the dataset being syntactically and semantically correct and some being not. The augmented datasets are only used for the unsupervised training process in the pretraining phase, while the supervised adaptation phase only uses the original, non-augmented data. To evaluate the effect of the amount of labeled data that is available for training, each supervised training procedure in the adaptation phase is conducted once with 100%, 50%, and 25% of the labeled training data, respectively. Please note, the number of graph pairs used as examples for training, testing, and validation is exactly the square of the respective numbers of graphs given before. For supervised training, there is one ground-truth similarity value calculated for each possible graph pair and for unsupervised training, we select each possible graph pair as anchor and negative and select the positive from the list of augmentations of the anchor. This ultimately results in the following number of supervised/unsupervised training cases: 435600/6494400 for CB-I, 259081/4145296 for CB-II, and 5625/90000 for CB-III. All unsupervised and supervised models are trained until convergence based on the training progress on the validation data (early stopping).

The examined metrics cover the retrieval quality. Quality is measured in terms of *Mean Absolute Error (MAE)* and *correctness* (see [7] for more details). The MAE (lower values are better) measures the average absolute difference between the ground-truth similarity and the predicted similarity of the retrievers. The correctness metric, which ranges between $-1$ and $1$ (higher values are better), evaluates the degree to which the predicted ranking aligns with the ground-truth ranking by penalizing inconsistencies where the predicted ranking contradicts the order of the ground-truth ranking for a given pair of workflows. Consider two arbitrary workflow pairs $p_1 = (W_i, W_j)$ and $p_2 = (W_k, W_l)$. The correctness value is reduced if $p_1$ is ranked before $p_2$ in the predicted ranking, despite $p_2$ being ranked before $p_1$ in the ground-truth ranking, and vice versa.

## 4.2   Experimental Results

Table 1 shows the results of the experimental evaluation for all models in all domains regarding the metrics introduced before. The models are grouped into semi-supervised and supervised and the percentage of total labeled data used in the supervised training step. The values highlighted in bold font mark the best metric values among a domain for a particular model (i.e., GEM or GMN). The median relative distance gives the aggregated difference between the semi-supervised and supervised models of the respective metric, with positive values indicating a better performance of the semi-supervised model and vice versa. The results regarding the MAE show a stronger performance of the semi-supervised over the supervised models. The only exception is the GEM (50%) of CB-I,

**Table 1.** Evaluation Results.

| | | Semi-Supervised | | | | | | Supervised | | | | | | Med. Rel. Diff. | |
| | | GEM | | | GMN | | | GEM | | | GMN | | | GEM | GMN |
| | | 25% | 50% | 100% | 25% | 50% | 100% | 25% | 50% | 100% | 25% | 50% | 100% | | |
| CB-I | Correctness | 0.271 | 0.219 | 0.148 | 0.352 | 0.315 | 0.406 | -0.006 | 0.061 | 0.030 | 0.363 | **0.477** | 0.411 | 260% | -3% |
| | MAE | 0.270 | 0.286 | **0.162** | 0.076 | 0.070 | **0.054** | 0.382 | 0.283 | 0.296 | 0.097 | 0.076 | 0.056 | 29% | 8% |
| CB-II | Correctness | 0.335 | 0.333 | 0.178 | 0.478 | 0.562 | **0.581** | 0.246 | **0.355** | 0.329 | 0.407 | 0.543 | 0.532 | -6% | 9% |
| | MAE | 0.299 | 0.280 | **0.198** | 0.067 | 0.054 | **0.053** | 0.331 | 0.406 | 0.430 | 0.077 | 0.070 | 0.059 | 31% | 13% |
| CB-III | Correctness | **0.414** | 0.349 | 0.358 | 0.670 | 0.747 | **0.781** | 0.258 | 0.301 | 0.195 | 0.464 | 0.479 | 0.583 | 60% | 44% |
| | MAE | 0.153 | 0.145 | **0.111** | 0.051 | 0.046 | **0.032** | 0.399 | 0.386 | 0.402 | 0.078 | 0.081 | 0.064 | 62% | 43% |

where the supervised model outperforms the semi-supervised one. It is particularly notable that the semi-supervised GEMs trained on 25% of the data consistently outperform their supervised counterparts trained on 100% of the data. The results w.r.t. the correctness show no clear dominant training method. In the smallest domain CB-III, the semi-supervised models show a stronger performance than the supervised models. The results in CB-I and CB-II, however, are mixed and give no clear indication on the superiority of either the semi-supervised or the supervised models w.r.t. correctness. The median relative differences indicate two aspects: First, the simpler GEM model profits more from the semi-supervised training than the already stronger performing GMN model, though both models show an increased performance w.r.t. their MAEs. Second, the smallest domain CB-III profits much more from semi-supervised training than the two larger domains CB-I and CB-II, with improvements of up to 83%.

We want to further discuss the correctness values and the influence of smaller amounts of labeled data. The correctness values can generally not be improved as much as the MAE values throughout the experiment. We suppose the focus on minimizing the similarity prediction error in training to be the main reason for this. The results might be different when training directly to improve the correctness, as done in previous work [18]. Furthermore, it can be observed that the median relative differences of CB-III show the strongest results in this comparison. The reason for this might be that it is by far the smallest dataset and, thus, benefits more from additional unlabeled training data. However, the effect of smaller amounts leading to a higher relative difference of the semi-supervised compared to the supervised model is not consistent within the domains. For instance, the MAE values of the GEMs of CB-II show a relative difference of 9.7% for 25%, 31% for 50%, and 54% for 100% of the dataset.

In summary, the quality results show a consistent improvement of the MAE metric and mixed effects w.r.t. the correctness when comparing semi-supervised and supervised learning.

## 5    Conclusion and Future Work

The proposed approach presents a semi-supervised transfer learning method for similarity learning in POCBR applications. Thereby, previous work on supervised graph similarity prediction is combined with an unsupervised pretraining phase that uses a large, unlabeled and augmented dataset. The goal is to reduce the amount of labeled training data needed in this procedure, with the underlying assumption that unsupervised pretraining with augmented data enables this. The experiments compare the proposed semi-supervised models with baseline supervised models in retrieval scenarios w.r.t. retrieval quality. Overall, the experimental results indicate that the semi-supervised models predict similarities more accurately.

In future work, it is planned to increase the efficacy of the introduced SNN architecture by improving the data augmentation process with other augmentation methods. These methods should deal with the specific properties of semantic workflows, which complicates the use of standard augmentation methods, as described in [10, 26]. Furthermore, future work should aim at implementing the proposed unsupervised training method with GAEs, which are briefly discussed in Sect. 2.3. A major benefit of using GAEs is the ability to extend the decoding process for enabling the generation of new graphs (so-called Variational GAEs [19]). Graph generation might be an important topic for many active research areas of CBR and POCBR such as case reuse (e.g., [23,37]).

# References

1. Aamodt, A., Plaza, E.: Case-based reasoning: foundational issues, methodological variations, and system approaches. AI Commun. **7**(1), 39–59 (1994)
2. Amin, K., Lancaster, G., Kapetanakis, S., Althoff, K.-D., Dengel, A., Petridis, M.: Advanced similarity measures using word embeddings and Siamese networks in CBR. In: Bi, Y., Bhatia, R., Kapoor, S. (eds.) IntelliSys 2019. AISC, vol. 1038, pp. 449–462. Springer, Cham (2020). https://doi.org/10.1007/978-3-030-29513-4_32
3. Bergmann, R., Gil, Y.: Similarity assessment and efficient retrieval of semantic workflows. Inf. Syst. **40**, 115–127 (2014)
4. Bergmann, R., Stromer, A.: MAC/FAC retrieval of semantic workflows. In: Proceedings of the 26th International Florida Artificial Intelligence Research Society Conference. AAAI Press (2013)
5. Bromley, J., et al.: Signature verification using a "Siamese" time delay neural network. IJPRAI **7**(4), 669–688 (1993)
6. Chen, T., Kornblith, S., Norouzi, M., Hinton, G.E.: A simple framework for contrastive learning of visual representations. In: Proceedings of the 37th ICML, Virtual Event, vol. 119, pp. 1597–1607. PMLR (2020)
7. Cheng, W., Rademaker, M., De Baets, B., Hüllermeier, E.: Predicting partial orders: ranking with abstention. In: Balcázar, J.L., Bonchi, F., Gionis, A., Sebag, M. (eds.) ECML PKDD 2010. LNCS (LNAI), vol. 6321, pp. 215–230. Springer, Heidelberg (2010). https://doi.org/10.1007/978-3-642-15880-3_20
8. Chicco, D.: Siamese neural networks: an overview. In: Cartwright, H. (ed.) Artificial Neural Networks. MMB, vol. 2190, pp. 73–94. Springer, New York (2021). https://doi.org/10.1007/978-1-0716-0826-5_3
9. Chourib, I., Guillard, G., Farah, I.R., Solaiman, B.: Structured case base knowledge using unsupervised learning. In: 2022 6th International Conference on Advanced Technologies for Signal and Image Processing (ATSIP). IEEE (2022)
10. Ding, K., Xu, Z., Tong, H., Liu, H.: Data augmentation for deep graph learning. ACM SIGKDD Explorations Newsl. **24**(2), 61–77 (2022)
11. van Dyk, D.A., Meng, X.L.: The art of data augmentation. J. Comput. Graph. Stat. **10**(1), 1–50 (2001)
12. Gilmer, J., et al.: Neural message passing for quantum chemistry. In: Proceedings of the 34th ICML, Australia, vol. 70, pp. 1263–1272. PMLR (2017)
13. Gong, Y., Yue, Y., Ji, W., Zhou, G.: Cross-domain few-shot learning based on pseudo-Siamese neural network. Sci. Rep. **13**(1) (2023)
14. Hamilton, W.L.: Graph Representation Learning. Springer, Cham (2020)

15. Hermans, A., Beyer, L., Leibe, B.: In defense of the triplet loss for person re-identification. CoRR abs/1703.07737 (2017)

16. Hoffmann, M., Malburg, L., Klein, P., Bergmann, R.: Using Siamese graph neural networks for similarity-based retrieval in process-oriented case-based reasoning. In: Watson, I., Weber, R. (eds.) ICCBR 2020. LNCS (LNAI), vol. 12311, pp. 229–244. Springer, Cham (2020). https://doi.org/10.1007/978-3-030-58342-2_15

17. Hoffmann, M., Bergmann, R.: Using graph embedding techniques in process-oriented case-based reasoning. Algorithms 15(2), 27 (2022)

18. Hoffmann, M., Bergmann, R.: Ranking-based case retrieval with graph neural networks in process-oriented case-based reasoning. In: The International FLAIRS Conference Proceedings, vol. 36 (2023)

19. Kipf, T.N., Welling, M.: Variational graph auto-encoders. CoRR abs/1611.07308 (2016)

20. Klein, P., Malburg, L., Bergmann, R.: Learning workflow embeddings to improve the performance of similarity-based retrieval for process-oriented case-based reasoning. In: Bach, K., Marling, C. (eds.) ICCBR 2019. LNCS (LNAI), vol. 11680, pp. 188–203. Springer, Cham (2019). https://doi.org/10.1007/978-3-030-29249-2_13

21. Kudenko, D.: Special issue on transfer learning. Künstliche Intell. 28(1), 5–6 (2014)

22. Lenz, M., Ollinger, S., Sahitaj, P., Bergmann, R.: Semantic textual similarity measures for case-based retrieval of argument graphs. In: Bach, K., Marling, C. (eds.) ICCBR 2019. LNCS (LNAI), vol. 11680, pp. 219–234. Springer, Cham (2019). https://doi.org/10.1007/978-3-030-29249-2_15

23. Malburg, L., Hoffmann, M., Bergmann, R.: Applying MAPE-K control loops for adaptive workflow management in smart factories. J. Int. Inf. Syst. 61, 83–111 (2023)

24. Minor, M., Montani, S., Recio-García, J.A.: Process-oriented case-based reasoning. Inf. Syst. 40, 103–105 (2014)

25. Müller, G.: Workflow Modeling Assistance by Case-Based Reasoning. Springer, Cham (2018)

26. Mumuni, A., Mumuni, F.: Data augmentation: a comprehensive survey of modern approaches. Array 16, 100258 (2022)

27. Naqvi, S.M.R., et al.: CBR-based decision support system for maintenance text using NLP for an aviation case study. In: 2022 Prognostics and Health Management Conference (PHM), London. IEEE (2022)

28. Ontañón, S.: An overview of distance and similarity functions for structured data. Artif. Intell. Rev. 53(7), 5309–5351 (2020)

29. Ott, F., et al.: Cross-modal common representation learning with triplet loss functions. CoRR abs/2202.07901 (2022)

30. Pauli, J., Hoffmann, M., Bergmann, R.: Similarity-based retrieval in process-oriented case-based reasoning using graph neural networks and transfer learning. In: The International FLAIRS Conference Proceedings, vol. 36 (2023)

31. Richter, M.M.: Foundations of similarity and utility. In: Proceedings of the Twentieth International Florida Artificial Intelligence Research Society Conference (2007)

32. Sahito, A., Frank, E., Pfahringer, B.: Semi-supervised learning using Siamese networks. In: Liu, J., Bailey, J. (eds.) AI 2019. LNCS (LNAI), vol. 11919, pp. 586–597. Springer, Cham (2019). https://doi.org/10.1007/978-3-030-35288-2_47

33. Schroff, F., Kalenichenko, D., Philbin, J.: FaceNet: a unified embedding for face recognition and clustering. In: CVPR, USA, pp. 815–823. IEEE (2015)

34. Tan, C., Sun, F., Kong, T., Zhang, W., Yang, C., Liu, C.: A survey on deep transfer learning. In: Kůrková, V., Manolopoulos, Y., Hammer, B., Iliadis, L., Maglogiannis,

I. (eds.) ICANN 2018. LNCS, vol. 11141, pp. 270–279. Springer, Cham (2018). https://doi.org/10.1007/978-3-030-01424-7_27

35. Weiss, K., Khoshgoftaar, T.M., Wang, D.: A survey of transfer learning. J. Big Data **3**(1), 1–40 (2016)

36. Zeyen, C., Bergmann, R.: A*-based similarity assessment of semantic graphs. In: Watson, I., Weber, R. (eds.) ICCBR 2020. LNCS (LNAI), vol. 12311, pp. 17–32. Springer, Cham (2020). https://doi.org/10.1007/978-3-030-58342-2_2

37. Zeyen, C., Malburg, L., Bergmann, R.: Adaptation of scientific workflows by means of process-oriented case-based reasoning. In: Bach, K., Marling, C. (eds.) ICCBR 2019. LNCS (LNAI), vol. 11680, pp. 388–403. Springer, Cham (2019). https://doi.org/10.1007/978-3-030-29249-2_26

# PertCF: A Perturbation-Based Counterfactual Generation Approach

Betül Bayrak[✉][iD] and Kerstin Bach[iD]

Norwegian University of Science and Technology, Høgskoleringen 1,
7034 Trondheim, Norway
{betul.bayrak,kerstin.bach}@ntnu.no

**Abstract.** Post-hoc explanation systems offer valuable insights to increase understanding of the predictions made by black-box models. Counterfactual explanations, an instance-based post-hoc explanation method, aim to demonstrate how a model's prediction can be changed with minimal effort by presenting a hypothetical example. In addition to counterfactual explanation methods, feature attribution techniques such as SHAP (SHapley Additive exPlanations) have also been shown to be effective in providing insights into black-box models. In this paper, we propose PertCF, a perturbation-based counterfactual generation method that benefits from the feature attributions. Our approach combines the strengths of perturbation-based counterfactual generation and feature attribution to generate high-quality, stable, and interpretable counterfactuals. We evaluate PertCF on two open datasets and show that it has promising results over state-of-the-art methods regarding various evaluation metrics like stability, proximity, and dissimilarity.

**Keywords:** Explainable artificial intelligence (XAI) · Counterfactual generation · Counterfactual explanations · Post-hoc explanation

## 1 Introduction

With the increasing use of artificial intelligence and machine learning models in our daily lives, understanding how these models make decisions has become increasingly important. Also, the increasing complexity of machine learning models has created understanding of how they make their predictions challenging. For example, two individuals with similar backgrounds submitted applications for a loan to purchase a home to the bank, which uses a black-box model to decide loan application assessments. But one applicant, Leo, was declined while the other, Maya, was approved as in Fig. 1. Leo wants to learn the reasons for the rejection of his loan application and what he needs to do to make an acceptable application. Counterfactual Explanations, a popular research field recently, can generate highly satisfactory explanations in such situations. [3,12]

Counterfactual explanations, a type of post-hoc explanation, provide valuable insights that help users understand the predictions made by black-box models, especially when the factors influencing the model's decision are not immediately

ⓒ The Author(s), under exclusive license to Springer Nature Switzerland AG 2023
M. Bramer and F. Stahl (Eds.): SGAI 2023, LNAI 14381, pp. 174–187, 2023.
https://doi.org/10.1007/978-3-031-47994-6_13

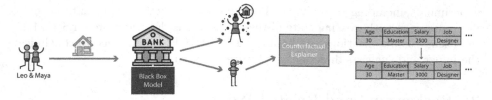

**Fig. 1.** Illustration of how a counterfactual explainer can provide insight into a loan application decision.

clear [4]. They also aim to demonstrate how a model's prediction can be changed with minimal effort by presenting hypothetical examples that answer the "what if?" question. For instance, "What if Leo earns $500 more, would his application be accepted?" is an example of a counterfactual explanation. Section 2.2 provides a more technical definition of counterfactual explanations.

Feature attribution based explanations are another method for post-hoc explanations. Those methods identify the contribution of each feature to a model's prediction and help to explain how changes in the input data can affect the output. One popular feature attribution technique is SHAP (SHapley Additive cxPlanations), proposed by Ludberg and Lee [9] and uses game theory to assign values to each feature based on its contribution to the model's output. Another technique is LIME (Local Interpretable Model-Agnostic Explanations) [11], proposed by Ribeiro et al., and generates explanations by approximating the black-box model with a local linear model.

In this research paper, we introduce PertCF, an innovative approach to generating counterfactual explanations using perturbations, leveraging the feature attributions. Our method combines the advantages of perturbation based counterfactual generation and feature attributions to produce counterfactuals that are of high quality, reliable, and easy to interpret.

This work presents several contributions, which are summarized as follows:

- PertCF combines the strengths of counterfactual explanation and feature attribution explanation methods.
- PertCF employs custom distance metrics tailored to the specific problem, offering two key benefits: (I) It utilizes SHAP values calculated individually for each class, enabling distinct class-based feature attribution. (II) It facilitates the incorporation of domain expertise and semantic data representation.
- Provided reproducible benchmarking experiments using open datasets and open-source implementation of the PertCF method and compared its performance with state-of-the-art methods (https://github.com/b-bayrak/PertCF-Explainer).

The structure of this paper is as follows. Section 2 provides an overview of the theoretical foundations of SHAP and counterfactual generation for counterfactual explanation with the state-of-the-art method. Section 3 presents the details of our proposed PertCF method. Section 4 reports the details and results of our experiments, including an analysis of PertCF's performance on open datasets and its comparison with existing state-of-the-art methods. Furthermore, in Sect. 4.5, we discuss the implications and limitations of PertCF. Finally, Sect. 5 concludes the paper and suggests directions for future research.

## 2    Background and Related Work

This work focuses on counterfactual-based explanation systems and in this section, we provide fundamental information about SHAP, which is used as a feature attribution method and counterfactual explanation systems and how popular methods work.

### 2.1    SHAP

SHAP (SHapley Additive exPlanations) is introduced by Ludberg and Lee [9] and it is a popular feature attribution explanation method. SHAP is based on Shapley values which is a game theory concept and aims to assign a value to each feature in a prediction based on how much it contributed to the prediction compared to all other possible combinations of features.

Basically, Shapley values simulate the absence of a feature using the marginal expectation over a background distribution and SHAP values apply this concept to machine learning models by determining the contribution of each feature in the prediction of the model, while accounting for interactions between features.

### 2.2    Counterfactual Generation Methods

In philosophy, a counterfactual is a conditional statement that expresses what would have happened if circumstances were different from what actually occurred. In machine learning, counterfactuals are used to explain the decision-making process of a model by providing alternative hypothetical scenarios for a given prediction [13,14]. These systems are named counterfactual explainers and a simple example of counterfactual explainer usage can be seen in Fig. 1.

$S$ is the set of samples and $x \in S$ and given an observed sample $x =< x_1, x_2, ..., x_m >$ with corresponding class label $A$, m is the number of features. $x'$ represents a counterfactual of $x$ (i.e. Fig. 2b), $x' =< x'_1, x'_2, ..., x'_m >$. $x'$ belongs to class label $B$, where $B \neq A$.

NLN (Nearest Like Neighbour) refers to the nearest neighbor of a given sample that belongs to the same class. On the other hand, NUN (Nearest Unlike Neighbour) refers to the nearest neighbor of a given sample that belongs to a different class (See Fig. 2a). In other words NUN is the closest dissimilar observed point to sample $x$. Basically, NUN is one of the counterfactuals of sample $x$. However, the important thing is generating a good/feasible counterfactual to give hypothetical examples and generate higher quality explanations.

To generate high-quality explanations, several requirements need to be fulfilled. While some of these requirements highly dependent on the problem and domain, others are common across various applications. Ideally, a counterfactual should be realistic, relevant, insightful, and trustworthy. In other words, it should allow for the interpretation of the explanation and the implementation of the changes required to achieve it in the real world. Another crucial requirement is diversity. Generating diverse counterfactuals does not mean generating more than one counterfactual but generating the counterfactuals by considering different characteristics of the data, covering a wide range of possibilities, providing a comprehensive understanding of the decision-making process of the model, and enhancing the explanatory power. While some requirements may not be objectively measurable without user reviews, others can be assessed using qualitative metrics to determine whether they have been met by the generated counterfactuals (See Sect. 4.3).

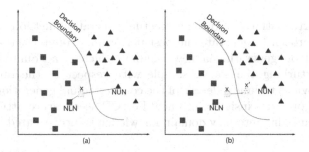

**Fig. 2.** (a) NLN and NUN of x, (b) NLN and NUN of x together with x': one of the possible counterfactuals of x.

In the past few years, several methods for generating counterfactuals have been proposed. We describe two of these methods and their details, which we use for comparison with our proposed approach.

The DiCE (Diverse Counterfactual Explanations) method [10], emphasizes the significance of diversity in producing actionable counterfactual explanations. It presents a comprehensive optimization framework that highlights the need to balance trade-offs, considers causal implications, and addresses optimization challenges when generating counterfactual explanations. In the publication, the authors provide a quantitative evaluation framework for counterfactuals that evaluates validity, proximity, and diversity. The iterative nature of DiCE allows for generating more than one counterfactual for an instance. Instead of using customized distance measures, it uses the mean of feature-wise $l_1$ distances between the counterfactual and the sample for continuous features. For categorical features, it uses a simple metric that assigns one if the counterfactual's value for any categorical feature differs from the sample input; otherwise, it assigns zero.

CF-SHAP[1], which is a feature attribution based counterfactual generation method, calculates Shapley values of each feature, and for each individual prediction, the method generates a set of counterfactual examples that show how changing the input features would affect the predicted outcome. The counter-factual examples are generated by iterative adjusting the input features using a greedy optimization algorithm until a desired outcome is achieved. In the publication, the authors provide a quantitative evaluation framework for coun-terfactuals that evaluates plausibility and counterfactual-ability. Instead of using customized distance measures, it uses the Manhattan distance over the quantile space.

Both, the DiCE and CF-SHAP approaches may not fully capture the rele-vance between the categories as they do not use customized distance measures. Also, they only work with binary classification models which decreases the com-patibility of the methods.

## 3   PertCF Method

PertCF is a perturbation-based counterfactual generation method that proposes a recursive approach to generate the best-performing counterfactual. The app-roach is based on generating a new sample, which is a counterfactual can-didate, by perturbing the source sample with respect to the target sample. Section 3.2 provides technical details of the counterfactual generation procedure, while Sect. 3.1 provides insights into how PertCF uses feature attribution, and Sect. 3.3 gives insights into how domain knowledge is incorporated into PertCF.

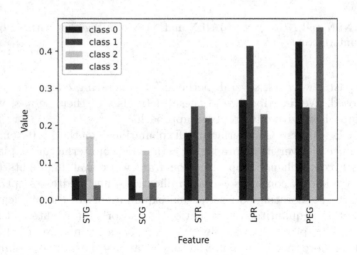

**Fig. 3.** Average SHAP values calculated for User Knowledge Modeling Dataset.

### 3.1   Feature Attribution

The PertCF method benefits from feature attribution for similarity and distance functions. For each class, the average SHAP values are calculated, and they are used for setting similarity and distance functions. In this way, we project the different attribution levels of the features as characteristics of the classes. For example in Fig. 3, there are 4 classes and 5 features and for $class0$ the most important feature is 'PEG' but for $class1$ it is 'LPR'.

In the counterfactual generation process, the counterfactual candidates are generated by perturbation (details in Sect. 3.2), and the amount of perturbation is calculated using $shap\_target$ which is the average SHAP values of the target class for the counterfactual to be generated. Also, the average SHAP values are used as weights of the similarity functions for each class. In this way, when the distance between two instances is measured, a feature with higher attribution will affect the result more than others. In PertCF, similarity measures are used in 3 different aims: (I) detecting the NUNs and (II) measuring the distance between the last two generated candidates (Sect. 3.2), and (III) evaluation metrics to measure the quality of the generated counterfactuals (Sect. 4.3).

## 3.2   Counterfactual Generation Procedure

To generate counterfactuals for given instances, the input is $x$ and its correspond-ing class label. The output will be the generated counterfactual $x'$ of instance $x$.

Initially, we detect the $NUN$ of $x$ which is the nearest observed counterfac-tual (Fig. 4a), and assign $target\_label$ as the class of $NUN$. To generate $x'$, we generate counterfactual candidates $c_i$ by perturbing $s$ (*source*) with respect to $t$ (*target*). For the first iteration, $x$ is assigned as $s$ and $nun$ is assigned as $t$, and the first counterfactual candidate ($c_1$) is generated by perturbing $x$ with respect to $NUN$ (Fig. 4b). This process is repeated by selecting new $s$ and $t$ to generate better candidates until the termination criteria are met. There are two termination criteria, (1) the number of iterations $num\_iter$ for generating $c_i$ and (2) the distance between the last two generated candidates. In each iteration, before setting $s$ and $t$, we check if the current situation satisfies the termination criteria. If one of the criteria is met, the last generated candidate is selected and assigned as $x'$, and then the process ends.

If the iteration limit is not reached and $c_i$ does not belong to $target\_label$, we need to approach $t$ in the next iteration and we perturb $c_i$ with respect to $s$ to generate $c_{i+1}$. For example, in Fig. 4b, after generating $c_1$ that does not satisfy termination criteria and does not belong to $target\_label$, we perturb $c_1$ and $c_2$ is generated as shown in Fig. 4c.

If the iteration limit is not reached and $c_i$ belongs to $target\_label$, we add $c_i$ to the candidate list. Then, we check the distance between $c_i$ and $c_{i-1}$. If the distance is smaller than the threshold $\mu$, which is calculated based on the distance between $s$ and $t$ with a provided coefficient, it means that the generated candidates are getting closer to each other, and we need to stop at an optimal point to improve efficiency. Thus, the process ends, and $c_i$ is selected as $x'$. Otherwise, in the next iteration, we perturb $c_i$ with respect to $t$ to generate $c_{i+1}$. For example, in Fig. 4c, after generating $c_2$, which belongs to $target\_label$ but does not satisfy the termination criteria, we perturb $c_2$ with respect to $c_1$, and $c_3$ is generated as shown in Fig. 4d.

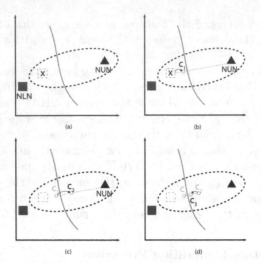

**Fig. 4.** Steps for generating counterfactual examples using PertCF. (a) Starting scenario that shows instance $x$ and its $NUN$. (b) Generation of the first candidate $c_1$ by perturbing $x$ with respect to $NUN$. (c) Generation of the second candidate $c_2$ by perturbing $c_1$ with respect to $NUN$. (d) Generation of the next candidate $c_3$ by perturbing $c_2$ with respect to $c_1$.

If the iteration limit is reached, the last generated candidate is selected and assigned as $x'$, and the process ends. However, if the candidate list is empty, it means no candidates from the expected class could be generated during the iterations, and the process starts over with the second closest NUN of $x$.

The perturbation process is designed differently for numeric and categoric features. For numeric features, a calculated perturbation value is added to the feature value. The same procedure applies to ordinal features. For nominal features, the feature value changes if the similarity value ($w$) of the categories is lower than threshold $\alpha$.

To perturb $s$ with respect to $t$ and generate the perturbed instance $p$, for each feature $f$ if $f$ is numeric,

$$p_f = s_f + shap\_target_f * (t_f - s_f) \tag{1}$$

however, if $f$ is nominal,

$$p_f = \begin{cases} t_f & \text{if } w_f < \alpha \\ s_f & \text{otherwise} \end{cases} \tag{2}$$

## 3.3 Incorporation of Domain Knowledge

In explanation systems, incorporating domain knowledge is crucial for improving the accuracy and interpretability of machine learning models. Domain knowledge helps to generate meaningful explanations and mitigate the risk of unintended consequences or bias. The PertCF method facilitates the incorporation of expert knowledge by modeling the distance and similarity measures. For instance, it allows projecting the relationship among values of nominal features. By utilizing these measures, the challenges can be addressed in the field and ensure compliance with GDPR regulations. This approach streamlines the process of incorporating domain knowledge, enabling to the generation of more accurate and interpretable results.

## 4  Experiments

To understand how PertCF performs on different datasets and setups. We compare it with state-of-the-art methods and conduct a series of experiments. This section provides details on the experimental setup, results, and discussion.

### 4.1  Experimental Setup/Design

Instance-based post-hoc explanation systems use the instance and its corresponding predicted class label. In our experiments, we required well-performed decision-making models to obtain accurate predictions. Therefore, we utilized the Gradient Boosting Classifier for the User Knowledge Modeling and South German Credit datasets, achieving accuracy scores of approximately 0.98 and 0.81, respectively.

To model distance and similarity measures and to retrieve most similar samples using the customized similarity measures, we use myCBR [2], an open-source tool providing a framework for similarity-based retrieval.

### 4.2  Datasets

In the experiments, the User Knowledge Modeling Dataset [7] and the South German Credit Dataset [6] are used (See Table 1). The User Knowledge Modeling dataset pertains to students' knowledge levels regarding Electrical DC Machines. It comprises five numeric features and one categorical (label) feature, constituting a multi-class classification task. The South German Credit Dataset encompasses 21 columns detailing attributes of credit applicants and their creditworthiness categorized as either good or bad. It encompasses three numeric and 18 categorical features, suitable for binary-class classification.

Our motivation is testing PertCF on open datasets to ensure that our work is reproducible and does not depend on a certain kind of data collection. Further, by providing our source code we aim at increasing the transparency of the experiments, providing a benchmark for evaluating the performance of future methods, and covering different domains and problems, addressing a diverse set of challenges.

**Table 1.** Characteristics of the Datasets

|  | Size | Feature | Numeric | Categoric | Class |
|---|---|---|---|---|---|
| $Credit^a$ | 1000 | 21 | 3 | 18 | 2 |
| $Knowledge^b$ | 403 | 6 | 5 | 1 | 4 |

[a]South German Credit Dataset
[b]User Knowledge Modeling Dataset

### 4.3 Evaluation Metrics

There are various methods in the literature to measure the quality of generated counterfactuals 2. In our experiments for PertCF we selected applicable metrics, namely dissimilarity, sparsity, instability, and run-timeto compare its results with state-of-the-art methods[1,10]. Additionally, we discuss important considerations in Sect. 4.5.

- **Dissimilarity:** Measures how dissimilar $x$ and $x'$ and it is calculated as mean of the distances between $x$ and each elements of $C$. The lower, the better.

$$dissimilarity = \frac{1}{\|C\|} \sum_{x' \in C} dist(x, x') \quad (3)$$

- **Sparsity:** Measures how many features of $x$ should be changed to achieve $x'$.

$$f(x_i, x_i') = \begin{cases} 1 & \text{if } x_i = x_i' \\ 0 & \text{otherwise} \end{cases} \quad (4)$$

$$sparsity = \frac{1}{\|C\|} \sum_{x' \in C} \frac{1}{m} \sum_{i=1}^{m} f(x_i, x_i') \quad (5)$$

- **Instability:** Measures the stability of generated counterfactuals. If $x$ and $y$ are very similar samples, a stable counterfactual generation system should generate very similar counterfactuals $x'$ and $y'$. To measure the stability, $x$ is perturbed to generate a very close sample ($y$) to $x$ and measure the distance between $x'$ and $y'$. The lower, the better.

$$instability = dist(x', y') \quad (6)$$

- **Runtime:** Refers to the time taken to generate a counterfactual for a given input instance. The lower, the better.

### 4.4 Experimental Results

As stated in Sect. 3, PertCF employs two termination criteria, both of which rely on pre-defined variables. Therefore, in the experiments, we demonstrate the performance of the PertCF method using different parameters and datasets. Additionally, we compared PertCF with state-of-the-art methods using the selected parameters.

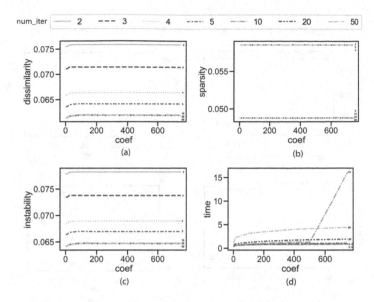

**Fig. 5.** The results of the parameter experiments for the User Knowledge Modeling dataset.

**Performance of the PertCF.** The first termination criterion is the maximum number of iterations to generate a counterfactual, and it is represented as *num_iter*. The other criterion is the distance between the last two generated candidates $d$, and it relies on the *coef* variable, $d = dist(x, NUN)/coef$. Therefore, *num_iter* and *coef* parameters affect the performance of PertCF and the outperforming parameters differ according to the dataset characteristics. Thereby, we ran a series of experiments with various different values *num_iter* and *coef*.

Figure 5 illustrates the results of the User Knowledge Modeling dataset. The performance of higher *num_iter* is better in terms of dissimilarity, instability, and sparsity, and in general, when *coef* is higher than 10, the results are almost stabilized. Therefore, choosing *coef* between 1 and 10 and *num_iter* as 5 or 10 might be optimal when considering runtime complexity. Figure 6 illustrates the results of the South German Credit dataset. When *num_iter* is set to 3 or 5, there is a boost in performance in terms of dissimilarity, instability, and sparsity. However, the effect of *coef* is not clearly observable in the experiments. Therefore, considering the runtime complexity, which is directly proportional to *num_iter* and *coef*, it might be optimal to choose *coef* between 5 and 10 and *num_iter* as 3 or 5.

The choice of parameters mainly depends on the characteristics of the datasets, but we can observe that there is a trade-off between computation time and the value of *coef*.

**Comparison with the State-of-the-Art Methods.** To evaluate the performance of our proposed method, we compared it with several state-of-the-

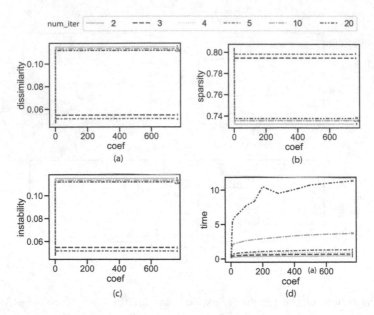

**Fig. 6.** The results of the parameter experiments for the South German Credit dataset.

art methods on the same datasets (See Table 2). The results indicate that our method outperforms the others in terms of dissimilarity and instability, which means that the PertCF method generates more stable and consistent counterfactuals than the compared methods. However, when considering the sparsity measure, the DICE method outperforms our method. It is important to note that in the South German Credit dataset, the majority of the features are nominal, which makes the comparison between DICE and PertCF results closer than in an all-numeric dataset.

Our findings suggest that PertCF can effectively address the challenges of the counterfactual generation process. However, there are still several limitations and open questions that need to be addressed to improve its performance further. Some of these limitations and open points are discussed in detail in Sect. 4.5.

## 4.5   Discussion

The experiments conducted in this work aimed to evaluate the effectiveness of the proposed PertCF method compared to state-of-the-art methods for generating counterfactual explanations using two open datasets to demonstrate the performance of PertCF under different conditions. The results showed that PertCF outperformed other state-of-the-art methods in terms of dissimilarity and instability. However, if we consider the higher sparsity is better, our method does not outperform others. In the literature, sparsity is implemented as $L_0$ norm between $x$ and $x'$ [5] or as a pre-defined threshold [8]. We implemented it as in

**Table 2.** Performance of Counterfactual Generation Methods

| | Dissim. | Sparsity | Instability | Time |
|---|---|---|---|---|
| South German Credit | | | | |
| DICE | 0.0557 | **0.9111** | 0.0560 | 0.0736 |
| CFshap | 0.2555 | 0.5842 | 0.2555 | **0.0058** |
| $PertCF^c$ | **0.0517** | 0.7983 | **0.0518** | 0.4069 |
| User Knowledge Modeling | | | | |
| DICE | 0.1727 | **0.6423** | 0.1769 | 0.1180 |
| CFshap | 0.1792 | 0.0293 | 0.1806 | **0.0011** |
| $PertCF^d$ | **0.0636** | 0.0585 | **0.0664** | 0.2827 |

$^c num\_iter = 5$ and $coef = 5$
$^d num\_iter = 5$ and $coef = 3$

the first definition, which basically measures how many features were changed to go from the original data point ($x$) to the counterfactual ($x'$). However, sparsity strongly depends on the topic or field being studied. For example, in a medical diagnosis explanation that mainly consists of numeric features, the possibility of having dependencies between features is high, and the target to change the diagnosis might include a set of changes in the features, and this explanation has low sparsity. In contrast, in the bank loan example, if the application owner has many changes that could result in changing the application result in the explanation, having a higher sparsity makes the explanation more reasonable and applicable. Therefore, the discriminative power of the sparsity metric is related to the concept being studied.

While our proposed method may not outperform others in terms of runtime, there are several underlying reasons like the used tools, implementation, and the number of generated candidates to reach the final counterfactual. The PertCF method generates multiple candidate counterfactuals before selecting the final one, which requires additional computational resources. This process ensures that we consider various possibilities and choose the most effective counterfactual. Nevertheless, the increased computational cost of generating multiple candidate counterfactuals may affect the run-time of our method compared to other methods. However, we believe that the advantages of generating these candidates outweigh the potential cost in terms of run-time, especially for complex datasets or critical applications where dissimilarity and stability are crucial for effective counterfactual generation. With further research and improvements in the algorithms and tools used, it may be possible to optimize the run-time of our method while maintaining its advantages.

Another issue that should be taken into consideration is whether the number of generated counterfactuals can be used as a metric to evaluate the performance of the method. Some methods generate multiple counterfactuals, and depending on the application field, it might be useful to provide multiple counterfactuals. However, the important thing is not the number of counterfactuals but their diversity of them. However, the PertCF method provides only one counterfactual for an instance, and we believe that it can be applied as a multiple counterfactual generator. With the current setup, this can be done in two ways. First, several of the generated candidates with high diversity can be selected and provided as counterfactuals. Second, in multi-class classification, a counterfactual can be generated to provide insights into how to switch the model's prediction from the current situation to all other classes.

One of the key limitations of the proposed method is that it is only applicable to tabular data. Counterfactual generation methods are highly compatible with tabular data because they rely on manipulating individual feature values to generate counterfactual instances that are close to the original instance but result in a different predicted outcome. However, recent research has shown that counterfactual explanation methods can also be applied to other types of data, such as text and image data. Another limitation of counterfactual generation methods is that it is typically used with classification models, as the method requires discrete prediction output. However, researchers are actively exploring ways to extend counterfactual explanation methods to other types of models, such as regression models, to make them more widely applicable.

## 5   Conclusion and Future Work

The experimental results demonstrate that the proposed PertCF method is a promising approach as a perturbation-based counterfactual generator for counterfactual explanations. Using SHAP values that are calculated for each class helps to project the different levels of feature attributions for every class. By combining the strengths of perturbation-based counterfactual generation and feature attributions, PertCF outperforms existing state-of-the-art methods on evaluation metrics such as proximity and dissimilarity. Moreover, it offers valuable insights into black-box models and helps improve their interpretability. We believe that PertCF can be applied in various domains, including healthcare, finance, and e-commerce, where interpretability and transparency are essential. Future research can explore the application of PertCF in these domains and further evaluate its effectiveness.

**Acknowledgements.** This work has been supported by the Research Council of Norway through the EXAIGON project (ID 304843).

## References

1. Albini, E., Long, J., Dervovic, D., Magazzeni, D.: Counterfactual shapley additive explanations. In: 2022 ACM Conference on Fairness, Accountability, and Transparency, pp. 1054–1070 (2022)
2. Bach, K., Althoff, K.-D.: Developing case-based reasoning applications using myCBR 3. In: Agudo, B.D., Watson, I. (eds.) ICCBR 2012. LNCS (LNAI), vol. 7466, pp. 17–31. Springer, Heidelberg (2012). https://doi.org/10.1007/978-3-642-32986-9_4

3. Celar, L., Byrne, R.M.: How people reason with counterfactual and causal explanations for artificial intelligence decisions in familiar and unfamiliar domains. Mem. Cogn., 1–16 (2023)
4. Dai, X., Keane, M.T., Shalloo, L., Ruelle, E., Byrne, R.M.: Counterfactual explanations for prediction and diagnosis in XAI. In: Proceedings of the 2022 AAAI/ACM Conference on AI, Ethics, and Society, pp. 215–226 (2022)
5. Dandl, S., Molnar, C., Binder, M., Bischl, B.: Multi-objective counterfactual explanations. In: Bäck, T., et al. (eds.) PPSN 2020. LNCS, vol. 12269, pp. 448–469. Springer, Cham (2020). https://doi.org/10.1007/978-3-030-58112-1_31
6. Groemping, U.: South German credit data: correcting a widely used data set. Rep. Math. Phys. Chem. Berlin, Germany, Tech. Rep. **4**, 2019 (2019)
7. Kahraman, H., Colak, I., Sagiroglu, S.: Developing intuitive knowledge classifier and modeling of users' domain dependent data in web, knowledge based systems (2013)
8. Keane, M.T., Smyth, B.: Good counterfactuals and where to find them: a case-based technique for generating counterfactuals for explainable AI (XAI). In: Watson, I., Weber, R. (eds.) ICCBR 2020. LNCS (LNAI), vol. 12311, pp. 163–178. Springer, Cham (2020). https://doi.org/10.1007/978-3-030-58342-2_11
9. Lundberg, S.M., Lee, S.I.: A unified approach to interpreting model predictions. In: Advances in Neural Information Processing Systems, vol. 30 (2017)
10. Mothilal, R.K., Sharma, A., Tan, C.: Explaining machine learning classifiers through diverse counterfactual explanations. In: Proceedings of the 2020 Conference on Fairness, Accountability, and Transparency, pp. 607–617 (2020)
11. Ribeiro, M.T., Singh, S., Guestrin, C.: "Why should I trust you?" explaining the predictions of any classifier. In: Proceedings of the 22nd ACM SIGKDD International Conference on Knowledge Discovery and Data Mining, pp. 1135–1144 (2016)
12. Shang, R., Feng, K.J.K., Shah, C.: Why am I not seeing it? understanding users' needs for counterfactual explanations in everyday recommendations. In: Proceedings of the 2022 ACM Conference on Fairness, Accountability, and Transparency, FAccT 2022, pp. 1330–1340. Association for Computing Machinery, New York (2022). https://doi.org/10.1145/3531146.3533189
13. Wachter, S., Mittelstadt, B., Russell, C.: Counterfactual explanations without opening the black box: Automated decisions and the GDPR. Harv. JL Tech. **31**, 841 (2017)
14. Yacoby, Y., Green, B., Griffin Jr, C.L., Doshi-Velez, F.: "If it didn't happen, why would I change my decision?": how judges respond to counterfactual explanations for the public safety assessment. In: Proceedings of the AAAI Conference on Human Computation and Crowdsourcing, vol. 10, pp. 219–230 (2022)

# Short Technical Papers

# Speech Emotion Recognition Using Deep Learning

Waqar Ahmed, Sana Riaz, Khunsa Iftikhar, and Savas Konur[✉]

Department of Computer Science, University of Bradford, Bradford, UK
{wahmed22,s.riaz23,k.iftikhar3,s.konur}@bradford.ac.uk

**Abstract.** Speech Emotion Recognition (SER) systems use machine learning to detect emotions from audio speech irrespective of the semantic context of the audio. Current research has limitations due to the complexity posed by language, accent, gender, age and intensity present in the speech and developing accurate SER systems remain an open challenge. This study focuses on a novel approach for developing a deep learning system which unifies four datasets, i.e., RAVDESS, TESS, CREMA-D and SAVEE to detect emotions from speech. This combination of datasets is used along with the most relevant features, i.e., Zero Crossing Rate (ZCR), Chroma Feature, MFCC, Root Mean Square (RMS) and Mel Spectrum. A 4-layer Convolutional Neural Network (CNN) is used on the training data achieving an accuracy of 76%. The results show that the proposed approach increases the reliability and makes the model less variant to new data compared to models trained on single datasets. The shortcomings of the current approach and their respective solutions are also discussed.

**Keywords:** Speech Emotion Recognition · Deep Learning · Classification

## 1 Introduction

Emotions play an important part in our daily interactions. Machine learning is being researched and used to develop accurate emotion recognition systems in which audio and visual data is used. However, due to the complexity posed by language, accent, gender, age and intensity present in the speech, only a small number of applications have been developed which are not sufficient to provide a generic solution to speech emotion recognition [1]. The detection of emotions with the help of machine learning is of great significance due to its application in marketing, user experience and health care. Some of the previous work in this domain has achieved significant results such as [2] and [3] achieved noticeable results. However, most of these experiments are based on single datasets which are limited in terms of actors, genders, and class distribution which may lead to overfitting and hindering the accuracy. Here, we propose a CNN based solution which unifies multiple datasets and their most relevant features with the aim to increase the generalization capability. This combination of datasets and features is not mentioned in the previous papers and our results signify that this approach increases the overall classifying capability of the model when tested on new data.

M. Bramer and F. Stahl (Eds.): SGAI 2023, LNAI 14381, pp. 191–197, 2023.
https://doi.org/10.1007/978-3-031-47994-6_14

## 2   Related Work

The system proposed by [2] used the Berlin EmoDB, IITKGPSEHC and the RAVDESS and extracted spectral features to a desired feature set and applied Support Vector Machines (SVM) achieving an accuracy of 86.90% for EmoDB and 72.91% for RAVDESS dataset. The work done by [4] uses MFCC, discriminant analysis and Neural Structured Learning (NSL). This study used EmoDB, RAVDESS and SAVEE individually producing accuracy rates of over 90%. The system proposed by [5] used FEC-CNN combined to characterize emotional state using a transfer learning strategy on PDC images from MAHNOB-HCI, DEAP, and DREAMER databases and the model's accuracy was 92.5%, 94.27%, and 96%, respectively. A feed-forward and RNN experiment conducted by [3] proposed an SER system based on IEMOCAP database. It used processing formulation based on frames which employs filter banks based on Fourier transform voice using multi-layered neural network with spectrograms achieving an accuracy of 64.78%. The above mentioned studies are limited to one dataset per experiment and it is not known how these models perform on data with noise or variation. In this experiment four different datasets are unified into one large dataset and then a CNN is trained and tested on features from this dataset. The results suggest that this method increases the overall generalization capability of a CNN model. This approach has not been mentioned in the previous works.

## 3   Methodology

### 3.1   Data Collection and Pre-processing

The datasets used in this project are Ryderson-Audio-Visual Database of Emotional Speech and Song (RAVDESS) [6], Toronto Emotional Speech Set (TESS) [7], Crowd-Sourced Emotional Multimodal Actors Dataset (CREMA-D) [8]and Surrey Audio-Visual Expressed Emotion (SAVEE) Database [9]. Five main emotions, i.e., happy, sad, fear, angry, neutral are selected for this experiment. Table 1 shows the details of the datasets used.

**Table 1.** Dataset details

| Dataset | Instances | Actors | Emotion Intensity | Total Emotions |
|---------|-----------|--------|-------------------|----------------|
| RAVDESS | 1440 | 12-Male, 12- Female | Normal, Strong | 8 |
| TESS | 2800 | 2-Female | Normal | 7 |
| SAVEE | 480 | 4 Male | Normal | 6 |
| CREMA-D | 7442 | 48-Male, 43-Female | Low, Medium, High | 6 |

Each dataset is processed separately and labels are tokenized and saved in a label file path in a pandas data frame to create a data frame for each dataset. All processed data frames are merged to create a final CSV which stores the emotion associated with the files and assigns strings to each emotion, e.g. (1 = neutral, 3 = happy). Data augmentation is applied to the dataset with the methods of stretch, noise injection, pitch and shift in order to make the distribution similar across all emotion classes and for robustness and performance of the algorithm in the presence of known amounts of noise. The final dataset consists of 37120 instances in which each emotion category counts for 20% of the dataset.

## 3.2  Feature Selection and Extraction

The selected features for this experiment are, i.e., Zero Crossing Rate (ZCR), Mel Spectrogram, Chroma Shift, Mel Frequency Cepstral Coefficients (MFCC) and Root Mean Square (RMS). ZCR is the rate of change of signal from positive value to negative value and vice versa [10]. It is significant because it differentiates noise from silence.

It is mathematically represented as in Eq. 1.

$$ZCR = \frac{1}{T-1} + \sum_{T=0}^{T-1} 1R_{<0}(S_t S_{t-1}) \tag{1}$$

where $S_t$ is the signal of length t.

Mel Spectrum visually depicts the signal's frequency over a period of time. The Mel spectrogram provides our model the sound data similar to what humans would perceive. The raw audio waveforms are passed through filter banks to create a Mel spectrogram [4]. Mathematically this is represented as in Eq. 2.

$$m = 2595 \, log_{10}(1 + \frac{f}{700}) \tag{2}$$

where $f$ represent the frequency in hertz.

Chroma Features of an audio represent the intensity of the twelve distinctive pitch classes that represent tonal content of a sound in a condensed form. Mel Frequency Cepstral Coefficients is calculated when passing the Fourier transformed signal through the set of band-pass filters known as Mel-filter bank. Its correspondence is not related linearly to the physical frequency of the tone because the human auditory system apparently does not perceive pitch linearly. Root Mean Square is an averaging process in which audio waveform is analyzed and all peaks are summed and divided to create an average peak reference which then acts as the standard for normalizing value [10].

The feature selection in this experiment is based on two factors. Firstly, a thorough review has been done and the features suggested in [1] are selected against the databases used in this paper since reliable results have been achieved by using these features in previous papers. Secondly, the time domain and frequency domain features are selected since these features are the most important features for audio processing and classification.

## 3.3  CNN Model Workflow

The categorical data of the target variable contains strings which are converted to numerical form using One Hot Encoder. The training and testing datasets are scaled using a standard scaler in which each input variable is scaled separately by subtracting the mean and dividing by the standard deviation in order to shift the distribution and to have a mean of zero and a standard deviation of one. Each dataset is initially used in a baseline CNN model separately in order to evaluate the results produced by using one dataset. No data augmentation or model optimization is applied at this point. All the datasets are then combined in a single dataset and given as input to a four convolution layer network. A split of 80% and 20% and dropout of 0.2 applied to the dataset. Table 2 presents the CNN model architecture.

**Table 2.** CNN Model Architecture

| Layer Type | Filters | Output Shape | Kernel | Activation Function | Learning Parameters |
|---|---|---|---|---|---|
| Conv1D | 256 | 162 × 256 | 5 × 5 | ReLU | 1536 |
| Conv1D | 256 | 81 × 256 | 5 × 5 | ReLU | 327936 |
| Conv1D | 128 | 41 × 128 | 5 × 5 | ReLU | 163968 |
| Dropout | Rate = 0.2 | 21 × 128 | | | 0 |
| Conv1D | 64 | 21 × 64 | 5 × 5 | ReLU | 41024 |
| Flatten | | Vector = 704 | | | 0 |
| Dense | | 32 | | | 22560 |
| Dropout | | 32 | | | 0 |
| Output | | Categories = 5 | | Softmax | 264 |

### 3.4   Performance Evaluation and Optimization

The loss function used with the CNN is the "categorical crossentropy" with the following optimizers, i.e., Adam, Adelta and Adagrad. The performance of the model is tested on each optimizer, the evaluation is based on training and testing loss and the accuracy produced by the model with the given optimizer. The model is run for a specific number of epochs in various tests and the results are recorded. The proposed CNN is tested with a different number of layers and four layers provided optimum results, therefore, a CNN with four layers is selected for the further experimentation.

## 4   Results and Discussions

The individual datasets are tested on baseline models initially and the results suggest that the models start overfitting after 50 epochs and the testing loss starts to increase. The accuracy of baseline models is around 70% while the model based on TESS dataset achieved an accuracy of 99%. All datasets are then combined into a single dataset and tested on the CNN model with a split 80% and 20% respectively. The CNN model is trained for 50, 250 and 500 epochs in each experiment. It is observed that the model starts overfitting on epochs above 50 and the testing loss starts to increase as shown in Fig. 1. The CNN model is tested with different optimizers in which Adam optimizer produced the highest accuracy of 76%. The proposed model is tested on unseen data from each dataset and the classification results show consistency and reliability on all test data, suggesting that combined data model has more generalization capability compared to the baseline models and the models suggested in previous studies. Table 3 shows the results comparison to previous works.

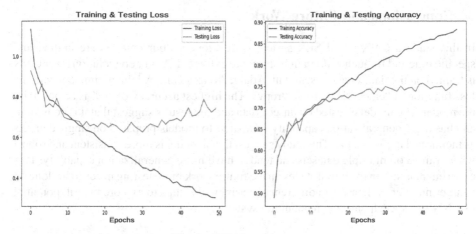

**Fig. 1.** CNN learning curve

**Table 3.** Results comparison to previous works

| Author | Datasets | Methodology | Merging Data | Accuracy |
|---|---|---|---|---|
| Proposed by [2] | 1 | SVM | NO | 72% |
| | 1 | SVM | NO | 86% |
| Proposed by [4] | 1 | NSL | NO | 90% |
| | 1 | NSL | NO | 90% |
| Proposed by [3] | 1 | CNN | NO | 65% |
| **Proposed methodology** | **4** | **CNN** | **YES** | **76%** |

Results obtained by [2] and [4] are based on single datasets, despite achieving a high accuracy rate these experiments cannot be compared directly to our work since the number of datasets and the features are different. The baseline models created for this experiment have provided less accurate classification results when tested on samples from a different dataset. Therefore, suggesting that a model trained on one type of dataset has less generalization capability compared to a model which is trained on multiple types of datasets. The results obtained from the current approach suggest that a model based on multiple datasets provide consistent results and a greater generalization capability. The work done in [3] is also limited to a single dataset and therefore cannot be directly compared to the current approach. The key difference is our approach and previous studies is that we have unified the dataset and then extracted the features from the unified dataset. Therefore the model trained on this combination of datasets is performing better on new data compared to models which are only trained and tested on one type of dataset. The results suggest that the proposed model is less variant to noise and perturbations in the new data.

## 5  Conclusions and Future Work

In this study a CNN based SER system is developed. Four datasets are unified and specific time and frequency domain features are extracted. A four convolution layer CNN is trained on the dataset and tested with Adam, Adagrad and Adelta optimizers with the loss function of "categorical crossentropy". The highest accuracy of 76% is achieved by the model. The model is tested on unseen data and the results suggest that it is consistent and has more generalization capability compared to models prepared on single datasets as mentioned in [3] and [4]. This study suggest that a model is more consistent and robust when trained on multiple datasets and tend to have more generalization capability. This experiment is still in the initial stages, in the future work more testing needs to be done on a larger number of datasets in different experimental setups to explore the full potential of CNN's in speech emotion recognition systems.

## References

1. Abbaschian, B.J., Sierra-Sosa, D., Elmaghraby, A.: Deep learning techniques for speech emotion recognition, from databases to models. Sensors **21**(4), 1249 (2021). https://doi.org/10.3390/s21041249
2. Bhavan, A., Chauhan, P., Hitkul, Shah, R.R.: Bagged support vector machines for emotion recognition from speech. Knowl.-Based Syst. **184**, 104886 (2019). https://doi.org/10.1016/j.knosys.2019.104886
3. Fayek, H.M., Lech, M., Cavedon, L.: Evaluating deep learning architectures for speech emotion recognition. Neural Netw. **92**, 60–68 (2017). https://doi.org/10.1016/j.neunet.2017.02.013
4. Uddin, M., Nilsson, E.G.: Emotion recognition using speech and neural structured learning to facilitate edge intelligence. Eng. Appl. Artif. Intell. **94**, 103775 (2020). https://doi.org/10.1016/j.engappai.2020.103775
5. Bagherzadeh, S., Maghooli, K., Shalbaf, A., Maghsoudi, A.: Recognition of emotional states using frequency effective connectivity maps through transfer learning approach from electroencephalogram signals. Biomed. Signal Process. Control **75**, 103544 (2022). https://doi.org/10.1016/j.bspc.2022.103544
6. Livingstone, S.R., Russo, F.A.: The Ryerson audio-visual database of emotional speech and song (RAVDESS): a dynamic, multimodal set of facial and vocal expressions in North American English. PLoS ONE **13**(5), e0196391 (2018). https://doi.org/10.1371/journal.pone.0196391
7. Pichora-Fuller, M.K., Dupuis, K.: Toronto emotional speech set (TESS). Borealis (2020). https://doi.org/10.5683/SP2/E8H2MF

8. Cao, H., Cooper, D.G., Keutmann, M.K., Gur, R.C., Nenkova, A., Verma, R.: CREMA-D: crowd-sourced emotional multimodal actors dataset. IEEE Trans. Affect. Comput. 5(4), 377–390 (2014). https://doi.org/10.1109/TAFFC.2014.2336244

9. Jackson, P., Ul Haq, S.: Surrey audio-visual expressed emotion (SAVEE) database (2011)

10. Panagiotakis, C., Tziritas, G.: A speech/music discriminator based on RMS and zero-crossings. IEEE Trans. Multimed. 7(1), 155–166 (2005). https://doi.org/10.1109/TMM.2004.840604

# Distinct Sequential Models for Inference Boosting

Rune Alexander Laursen[✉][iD], Peshang Alo[iD], Morten Goodwin[iD],
and Per-Arne Andersen[iD]

Department of Information and Communication Technology, University of Agder,
Jon Lilletuns Vei 9, 4879 Grimstad, Norway
{runeal17,peshaa18}@uia.no

**Abstract.** Type 1 Diabetes (T1D) is a chronic disease where the
body is unable to regulate the Blood Glucose Level (BGL), leading
to severe health consequences if not regulated. Accurate BGL predictions can enable better disease management and improve treatment
decisions. However, predicting future BGLs is a complex problem due
to the inherent complexity and variability of the human body. This
paper investigates using a new technique to outperform a State-of-the-
Art (SotA) Convolutional Recurrent Neural Network (CRNN) model
by forecasting BGLs on the same dataset. The problem is structured,
and the data is preprocessed as a multivariate multi-step time series.
The Distinct Sequential Models for Inference Boosting (DSMIB) technique is used, which manages missing data and counters potential issues
from other techniques by employing both a Long Short-Term Memory
(LSTM) model and a Transformer-based model together. The experimental results show that this technique reduces the Root Mean Squared Error
(RMSE) by approximately 14.28% when predicting the BGL 30 min in
the future compared to the SotA model. This improvement highlights
the potential of this approach to assist diabetes patients with effective
disease management.

**Keywords:** Transformer · Diabetes · Multivariate Multi-step Time
series

## 1 Introduction

Diabetes, especially T1D, is a pressing global health challenge. T1D is marked
by the body's inability to produce insulin, which is vital for regulating BGL.
Miss-management of BGL for individuals with T1D can lead to grave health
issues. Given the rising global prevalence of diabetes, accurate BGL prediction becomes central to improving the quality of life for patients, mitigating
healthcare burdens, and averting severe complications. In this context, Artificial
Intelligence (AI) and Machine Learning (ML) have emerged as significant contributors, enhancing the precision of BGL predictions using historical and other
pertinent data.

© The Author(s), under exclusive license to Springer Nature Switzerland AG 2023
M. Bramer and F. Stahl (Eds.): SGAI 2023, LNAI 14381, pp. 198–203, 2023.
https://doi.org/10.1007/978-3-031-47994-6_15

The primary focus of this paper is to predict BGL in T1D patient data employing both a LSTM [1] and Transformer-based model [2] sequentially in the method DSMIB. Accurate prediction is indispensable for determining the suitable insulin dosage, thereby effectively managing the condition [3]. Our study leverages the OhioT1DM dataset, introduced specifically for a blood glucose prediction challenge [4]. The findings of this paper are benchmarked against the top-performing model from the challenge, henceforth referred to as "SotA".

To better understand the effectiveness of our proposed approach, we put forward two main hypotheses:

**Hypothesis 1:** A Transformer model has the potential to surpass the state-of-the-art CRNN model suggested by J Freiburghaus et al. [5] in predicting BGLs 30 min ahead with a reduced RMSE using the same dataset.

**Hypothesis 2:** Rather than merely filling in missing BGL values with zeros, an intelligent approach could further enhance model accuracy.

The subsequent sections provide a deeper understanding. Section 2 shines a light on the current state of the field and identifies areas ripe for further investigation. Section 3 delineates our chosen methodology, followed by Sect. 4, which unpacks the experimental design and results. Section 5 wraps up with conclusions and possible avenues for future research.

## 2  Related Work

Various traditional and advanced ML methods, along with preprocessing techniques, are utilized in the domain to enhance prediction results in time series forecasting. A notable instance is the Informer model introduced by Haoyi Zhou et al. [6]. This is a transformer model designed to address issues such as slow quadratic dot-product calculations, memory bottlenecks, and sluggish inference when predicting lengthy inputs and outputs. The model was assessed using four extensive datasets and consistently outperformed other models by at least 10%, underscoring the potential of the Transformer model in time-series prediction tasks like BGL prediction.

Daniels et al. [7] adopt a CRNN Multitask Learning (MTL) approach to devise individualized models. Their transfer learning approach generates precise models for each individual in the OhioT1DM dataset, even when processing all data concurrently with patients batched together. Their findings suggest that it's challenging to train a generalized model using patient data, paving the way for the exploration of models that can accommodate inter-individual variability.

Nemat et al. [8] employ three distinct models: linear regression, Vanilla LSTM (VLSTM), and Bidirectional LSTM (BiLSTM) in an ensemble fashion to outdo previous models on the OhioT1DM dataset. This multi-model strategy can be further investigated using more robust models, such as the transformer model.

J. Freiburghaus et al. [5] introduce a CRNN model for forecasting future BGL using the OhioT1DM dataset. An examination of their code reveals that they address missing values using forward-filling. Furthermore, the basal insulin feature values are allocated to a single timestamp. This approach is flawed because, in reality, this value signifies the hourly rate. This inconsistency could compromise the model's predictive accuracy by overlooking data during prolonged periods when the insulin dosage remains unchanged. Incorporating supplementary temporal features and refining data preprocessing could filter out irrelevant data, thereby boosting prediction precision and overall applicability, which is crucial for enhancing patient care in T1D management.

Lastly, missing values in time series data can potentially result in imprecise forecasts and issues during model training. Solutions to these problems, as discussed in [9–12], encompass imputation techniques like linear interpolation or model-based extrapolation. The outcomes from these referenced papers are detailed in Table 1. Collectively, this body of research indicates numerous avenues for further exploration aimed at refining BGL prediction.

## 3    Method

The first step is to obtain a dataset and identify sufficient preprocessing mechanisms. We use the OhioT1DM dataset [13], which contains eight weeks of 5-minute data from 12 diabetes patients across 20 features. For preprocessing, each patient's training and testing files are treated as follows: a time series is constructed using initial to final BGL timestamps, aligning all timestamps to 5-minute intervals. **BGL** values are incorporated, **Finger stick** values are added where Continuous Glucose Monitor (CGM) readings are missing, and features like **Meal, Basis heart rate, Basis Galvanic Skin Response (GSR)**, and **Basis steps** are slotted into their timestamps. **Bolus** data, including Normal Bolus and Dual Bolus, are directly integrated, while Square types are spread across intervals. **Basal** values are distributed between start times, **Exercise** values are adjusted and spread by intensity, and **Basis sleep** values are populated between start and end times.

The proposed algorithms synergize two prediction models sequentially: an LSTM model followed by the previously mentioned Informer model. The dataset is divided horizontally into subsets a and b (shown in Fig. 1). Subset a (20% of data) trains and evaluates the LSTM Model using only one feature, this model subsequently imputes missing values in subset b for the Informer Model's training, validation, and testing. The DSMIB addresses challenges in time series: imputing missing values effectively and mitigating data leakage during interpolation in test data. Evaluation relies on RMSE and Mean Absolute Error (MAE) metrics.

## 4    Experiments and Results

This section presents the experiments designed to test the formulated hypotheses. Results are quantified using the RMSE and MAE metrics for predicting BGL value 30 min into the future, averaged over all patients, and compared in Table 1.

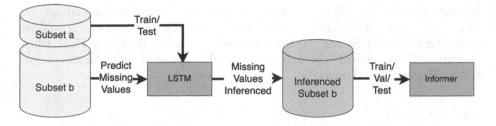

**Fig. 1.** Distinct Sequential Models for Inference Boosting

## 4.1  Baseline: Validation of Previous Results

The SotA model by J Freiburghaus et al. [5] was first validated to set a baseline for comparison. A data leakage issue was identified in their preprocessing, which potentially invalidated their published result of RMSE 17.45 and MAE 11.22. Upon rectifying this, the retrained model yielded an RMSE of 18.49 and a MAE of 12.11.

## 4.2  Handling Missing Values: Zero-Filling Vs. Interpolation

Two approaches were compared to test **Hypothesis 2**: zero-filling and linear interpolation. Two separate models were trained using these data handling strategies, with the validation RMSE being 21.4 for zero-filled data and 14.76 for interpolated data. This outcome indicates that intelligent handling of missing values, such as interpolation, can significantly improve a model's accuracy, thus confirming Hypothesis 2.

## 4.3  Performance of Transformer Model: Informer

**Hypothesis 1** postulates that a Transformer model can outperform the SotA model. As mentioned in the previous section, the Informer model was tested with both zero-filled and interpolated data. Results indicated that the model performed better with interpolated data compared to zero-filled data. However, even if the model surpassed the corrected SotA model, confirming **Hypothesis 1**, the interpolation method exhibited a data leakage problem, which means this method cannot be used in real-life scenarios.

## 4.4  Distinct Sequential Models for Inference Boosting

Unsatisfied with results from prior experiments that couldn't be utilized in real-life scenarios, the authors devised a novel approach: Distinct Sequential Models for Inference Boosting (DSMIB). This method employs two sequential models for improved inference. Initially, an LSTM model leverages the BGL feature to predict and fill missing values in subset 'a' of the data, achieving an RMSE of 4.5. The filled data from subset 'a' is then used to fill missing values in subset 'b'. Subsequently, the Informer model is trained using the now filled subset 'b', with the aim to enhance the performance further. This sequential application of the LSTM and Informer models led to a remarkable RMSE of 15.85 when forecasting 30 min ahead. The outcome not only surpassed the SotA model but also reaffirmed **Hypothesis 1**.

### 4.5   Summary

Table 1 provides a concise summary of the results from various experiments, alongside the original and corrected results from the SotA model, as well as the papers mentioned in Sect. 2. The table shows that both the Informer model using interpolated data and the DSMIB method outperformed the SotA model at the time of writing.

**Table 1.** Comparison of Results (30 min)

| Method | RMSE | MAE |
| --- | --- | --- |
| Informer (interpolated data) | **14.76** | 11 |
| DSMIB | **15.85** | 9 |
| SotA (J. Freiburghaus et al.) | 17.45 | 11.22 |
| SotA (corrected) (J. Freiburghaus et al.) | 18.49 | 12.11 |
| Daniels et al. | 18.8 | 13.2 |
| Nemat et al. | 19.63 | 13.88 |
| Informer (zero-filled data) | 21.4 | 11.2 |

## 5   Conclusion

This work introduces the DSMIB technique, which harnesses the capabilities of both LSTM and Transformer models for predicting BGLs in T1D patients using the OhioT1DM dataset. Three overarching goals drove this research: (1) validating the SotA CRNN model, (2) preprocessing the OhioT1DM dataset tailored for the model, and (3) crafting a model with superior prediction accuracy. The validation of the SotA uncovered issues leading to data leakage and subsequent inaccuracies. Throughout our investigation, we tested various models with the aim of enhancing prediction precision. Among these, the Informer using interpolated data emerged as the most effective; however, it is impractical in real-life scenarios due to the challenge of interpolating between a current value and a future one. On the other hand, while the DSMIB technique slightly underperforms compared to the Informer model using interpolated data, it holds a practical advantage for real-world applications. Furthermore, the DSMIB technique reduced the RMSE by 14.28% compared to the SotA model.

The limited quantity and quality of data in the dataset may have influenced our results, highlighting the need for more comprehensive diabetes datasets.

Despite constraints related to length and features in the dataset, our DSMIB approach outperformed prior methods while avoiding data leakage, underscoring its promise for further research.

# References

1. Hochreiter, S., Schmidhuber, J.: Long short-term memory. Neural Comput. **9**(8), 1735–1780 (1997)
2. Vaswani, A., et al.: Attention is all you need. In: Advances in Neural Information Processing Systems, vol. 30 (2017)
3. DiMeglio, L.A., Evans-Molina, C., Oram, R.A.: Type 1 diabetes. Lancet **391**(10138), 2449–2462 (2018)
4. KDH 2020 - BGLP Challenge
5. Freiburghaus, J., Rizzotti, A., Albertetti, F.: A deep learning approach for blood glucose prediction of type 1 diabetes. In: ECAI 2020 (2020). https://ceur-ws.org/
6. Zhou, H., et al.: Informer: beyond efficient transformer for long sequence time-series forecasting (2021). arXiv:2012.07436 [cs]
7. Daniels, J., Herrero, P., Georgiou, P.: A multitask learning approach to personalized blood glucose prediction. IEEE J. Biomed. Health Inform. **26**(1), 436–445 (2021)
8. Nemat, H., Khadem, H., Eissa, M.R., Elliott, J., Benaissa, M.: Blood glucose level prediction: advanced deep-ensemble learning approach. IEEE J. Biomed. Health Inform. **26**(6), 2758–2769 (2022)
9. Enders, C.K., Du, H., Keller, B.T.: A model-based imputation procedure for multi-level regression models with random coefficients, interaction effects, and nonlinear terms. Psychol. Methods **25**(1), 88 (2020)
10. Lin, W.-C., Tsai, C.-F.: Missing value imputation: a review and analysis of the literature (2006–2017). Artif. Intell. Rev. **53**(2), 1487–1509 (2019). https://doi.org/10.1007/s10462-019-09709-4
11. Park, J., et al.: Long-term missing value imputation for time series data using deep neural networks. Neural Comput. Appl. **35**(12), 9071–9091 (2023)
12. Salgado, C.M., Azevedo, C., Proença, H., Vieira, S.M.: Missing data (2019)
13. Marling, C., Bunescu, R.: The OhioT1DM dataset for blood glucose level prediction: update 2020. In: CEUR Workshop Proceedings, vol. 2675, p. 71. NIH Public Access (2020)

# On Reproducible Implementations in Unsupervised Concept Drift Detection Algorithms Research

Daniel Lukats[1,2](✉) and Frederic Stahl[1]

[1] German Research Center for Artificial Intelligence, Marie-Curie-Straße 1,
26129 Oldenburg, Germany
{Daniel.Lukats,Frederic_Theodor.Stahl}@dfki.de
[2] Carl-von-Ossietzky-Universität Oldenburg, Ammerländer Heerstraße 114-118,
26129 Oldenburg, Germany

**Abstract.** In order to create reproducible experimentation and algorithms in machine learning and data mining research, reproducible descriptions of the algorithms are needed. These can be in the form of source code, pseudo code and prose. Efforts in academia commonly focus on accessibility of source code. Based on an internal study reproducing unsupervised concept drift detectors, this work argues that a publication's content is equally important and highlights common issues affecting attempts at implementing unsupervised concept drift detectors. These include major issues prohibiting implementation entirely, as well as minor issues, which demand increased effort from the developer. The paper proposes the use of a checklist as a consistent tool to ensure better quality and reproducible publications of algorithms. The issues highlighted in this work could mark a starting point, although future work is required to ensure representation of more diverse areas of research in artificial intelligence.

**Keywords:** Reproducibility · Pseudo code · Data mining

## 1 Introduction

Reproducible research is a core tenet of the scientific method. In contrast with natural sciences, computer science offers a unique benefit in this regard, as source code and data sets can be published on platforms such as GitHub or GitLab to provide access to the experiment. Accordingly, there is a lot of effort in academia to encourage researchers to publish their code alongside their papers and to ensure certain quality standards [8,11,14]. Furthermore, publishers and conference organisers address reproducibility more generally, addressing issues affecting reproducibility such as pseudo-randomness [11] or discussing the topic of reproducibility in machine learning itself [9,12]. Various publications deal with reproducibility in their respective domain of machine learning, e.g. [3,7].

However, there is little discussion about pseudo code in the literature, with the exception of the research area of pseudo code generation and an analysis

M. Bramer and F. Stahl (Eds.): SGAI 2023, LNAI 14381, pp. 204–209, 2023.
https://doi.org/10.1007/978-3-031-47994-6_16

about the psychological effects of pseudo code [1]. Most online resources are similarly one-sided, explaining possible syntax for pseudo code in brief tutorials—various blog posts and documents provided by university lecturers are available online.

This work argues that publishing source code alone is not sufficient for the reproducibility of machine learning and data mining algorithms. In various cases, access to good quality pseudo code might be more beneficial even when source code is available, as one might need to re-implement the algorithm. The reasons therefor may include:

- There are contradictions in the source code and the algorithm's description.
- The source code is not available in the desired programming language.
- The poor quality of the source code.
- The implementation is no longer maintained, causing errors due to version mismatches or use of deprecated functions for example.
- There is no license or the license does not match the intended use-case.

This paper is based on experiences made during an internal scientific study on unsupervised concept drift detectors for analysis of data streams, for which 23 publications were considered for implementation. In the following, the issues encountered are described—in both source code and algorithm descriptions—and how they affected the implementations. Finally, possible solutions to these issues are discussed.

## 2   Observed Issues

The issues detailed in the following and the analysis of the 23 publications were observed and conducted by the authors of this paper. It is acknowledged here that there may be bias in this work, since of some of the perceived issues may be subject to the background of the authors. Yet, these issues are present in publications related to artificial intelligence in general to varying degrees from the experience of the authors, although the extent of reproducibility issues may differ between various areas of research.

### 2.1   Issues with Source Code

In the aforementioned case study it was observed that only 8 papers out of 23 provided source code. First, the source of the 8 publications was examined. Although not all of the observed issues make reproduction impossible, they negatively affect the usability and may diminish the publication's impact preventing researchers reproducing its result. The occurrences of the following issues are summarised in Table 1:

1. Only three repositories contained a license detailing the terms of use. If no license is included, the work cannot be used by others as default copyright laws apply [5,6].

2. All but one repository contained incomplete instructions for installation or no information on required dependencies at all, thus making this step of reproducing the authors' experiments error-prone.
3. Merely two repositories contained documented source code, again increasing the risk of erroneous use of the provided repository.
4. Five out of eight implementations did not match the algorithm description in the corresponding publication. In most instances the implementation included normalisation steps, which were not mentioned in the paper. This can prove problematic in two different scenarios. On the one hand, if one attempts to reproduce a publication's result by implementing the algorithm ourselves, one may leave out a crucial component of the algorithm and therefore may not be able to achieve the desired results. On the other hand, if one decides to include the algorithm as a third-party library, one will not know that our data may be pre-processed by the algorithm already, e.g. data may accidentally be normalised twice, which can introduce errors.
5. Three publications provided incomplete access to the data sets used for evaluation. Hence, the results of these publications cannot be reproduced.
6. Seeds were given in 2 out of 4 publications, which used algorithms depending on pseudo-randomness. Without seeds reproducing exact results is impossible, although similar results should be achievable.

**Table 1.** 8 out of 23 publications published source code. The publications are number-coded. A ✗ indicates an issue in the respective column, e.g. a missing license or declarations of dependencies. A ~ indicates that information is given but incomplete, as install instructions may be missing. Not all detectors include pseudo-random components; seeds were only considered for those which do.

| Publication | License | Dependencies | Documentation | Consistency | Data streams | Seed |
|---|---|---|---|---|---|---|
| 7 | ✗ | ✗ | ✗ | ✗ | ✓ | — |
| 8 | ✗ | ✗ | ✗ | ✗ | ✓ | ✗ |
| 12 | ✓ | ✗ | ✗ | ✓ | ~ | ✗ |
| 15 | ✗ | ~ | ✗ | ✗ | ✗ | — |
| 16 | ✓ | ✓ | ✓ | ✓ | ✗ | ✓ |
| 19 | ✗ | ✗ | ✗ | ✗ | ✓ | ✓ |
| 20 | ✓ | ✓ | ✓ | ✓ | ✓ | — |
| 22 | ✗ | ~ | ✗ | ✗ | ✓ | — |
| % ✗ | 63% | 50% | 75% | 63% | 25% | 50% |

If one would like to use an algorithm that was published without a license, it must be implemented from scratch for legal reasons [5,6]. The other issues need to be weighed by the developers and users of said algorithm. Missing dependencies and a poor documentation may be on a subjective level irritating. However, if the code quality is sufficient otherwise, using the published repository may be reasonable. Similarly, undocumented implementation choices, seeds and incomplete data streams may not matter depending on the intended use case.

## 2.2   Issues with Publication Texts

When one decides to implement a published AI or data mining algorithm, from a scientific perspective the publication must provide all information required. Various issues can affect attempts, as missing information might make an authentic implementation impossible whereas other issues merely make these attempts more demanding. In the aforementioned internal study, the following issues were observed (see Table 2 for occurrences):

1. Only 15 publications provided pseudo code providing a higher level view of the algorithm's design. The remaining 8 papers are described in prose only, which can cause the implementation process to be cumbersome and error-prone, as the interplay of different components of the algorithm may not be obvious without a singular abstract overview. None of these 8 provided source code either.
2. Most crucially, 11 publications are incomplete and miss details. Some include undefined symbols and others lack information on some components of the algorithm, e.g. how to update data windows. In either case a faithful implementation of the algorithm is impossible, as one simply cannot know the intended behavior of undefined components.
3. Many concept drift detectors model data by estimating probability distributions. In 6 publications the required approximations are foregone; the publications describe only the ideal theoretical distributions. Often properties of probability distributions can be approximated with multiple methods, e.g. when estimating a variance [15]. Likewise, models such as Gaussian mixture models often feature different initialisation techniques [13]. Consequently, when implementing an algorithm one may need to make assumptions about the chosen estimators, thus introducing at least slight deviations from the original publication.
4. 3 publications provide no intra-document references in the form of equation numbers or otherwise. Admittedly this is a minor issue, although it demands further effort during implementation, since the correct definition needs to be searched for.
5. 7 publications included definitions in prose without any noteworthy highlight through typesetting or formatting like in-line code listings or equations formatted as in the LaTeX math mode. This is another minor issue that demands more effort by the developer implementing the algorithm.
6. Finally, in 4 publications the pseudo code and the publication text contradict each other. Out of experience, this ambiguity can only be resolved by testing all options.

**Table 2.** Different issues affected attempts at implementing 23 unsupervised concept drift detectors. The publications are number-coded. A ✗ indicates an issue in the respective column. Empty cells indicate no issue.

| Publication | Pseudo Code | Complete Definitions | Approximations | References | Prose Definitions | Consistency |
|---|---|---|---|---|---|---|
| 1 | ✗ | | | | | |
| 2 | | ✗ | | | | |
| 3 | | ✗ | ✗ | ✗ | ✗ | ✗ |
| 4 | ✗ | | | | | |
| 5 | ✗ | ✗ | | ✗ | | |
| 6 | | ✗ | | | ✗ | ✗ |
| 7 | | ✗ | | | | |
| 8 | | ✗ | | | | |
| 9 | ✗ | | ✗ | | ✗ | |
| 10 | ✗ | | | | ✗ | |
| 11 | ✗ | | | | | |
| 12 | | | | | ✗ | |
| 13 | | ✗ | ✗ | | | |
| 14 | ✗ | | | | | |
| 15 | | ✗ | | | | ✗ |
| 16 | | ✗ | | | | |
| 17 | | ✗ | | | | |
| 18 | ✗ | | ✗ | | ✗ | |
| 19 | | ✗ | | | | |
| 20 | | | | | | |
| 21 | | ✗ | | | | |
| 22 | | ✗ | | | | |
| 23 | | | | ✗ | ✗ | ✗ |
| % ✗ | 35% | 48% | 26% | 13% | 30% | 17% |

# 3  Discussion

The issues discussed in Sect. 2 were spotted neither by the authors nor by reviewers of the respective papers. A checklist would be the easiest solution; it can be consulted by both authors and reviewers. The issues highlighted in Sect. 2.2 could mark a starting point, although they are limited in two regards: Firstly, the perception of some of these issues is subjective, so more diverse perspectives are desired. Secondly, these issues are based on a small sample of 23 unsupervised concept drift detectors only. Though many of these issues will apply to machine learning and data mining publications in general, the list may be missing important issues from other areas of research. Since pseudo code is not formalized like programming languages, tools like linters would be difficult to establish. Other solutions to improve the understanding of algorithms involve literate programming [4], or more recently literate computing [10]. But these solutions depend on the availability of source code. Checklists can be powerful tools improving efficiency and consistency [2]. They are easier to develop and implement than complex tools, a checklist might be a suitable start to discuss reproducible pseudo code. However, more work is required to ensure diverse backgrounds and areas of research in artificial intelligence are represented. Therefore, experiences from other research groups in the areas of machine learning and data mining will be incorporated into a more comprehensive study in the future.

**Acknowledgements.** This paper has received partial funding from the European Union's Horizon 2020 research and innovation programme under grant agreement No 101000825 (NAUTILOS).This work also received partial funding from Niedersächsisches Vorab under grant number *ZN3683* (ChESS).

# References

1. Bellamy, R.K.: What does pseudo-code do? A psychological analysis of the use of pseudo-code by experienced programmers. Hum. Comput. Interact. **9**(2), 225–246 (1994)
2. Gawande, A.: The Checklist Manifesto. Metropolitan Books, New Delhi (2009)
3. Heil, B.J., Hoffman, M.M., Markowetz, F., Lee, S.I., Greene, C.S., Hicks, S.C.: Reproducibility standards for machine learning in the life sciences. Nat. Meth. **18**(10), 1132–1135 (2021). https://doi.org/10.1038/s41592-021-01256-7
4. Knuth, D.E.: Literate programming. Comput. J. **27**(2), 97–111 (1984). https://doi.org/10.1093/comjnl/27.2.97
5. Licensing a Repository. https://docs.github.com/en/repositories/managing-your-repositorys-settings-and-features/customizing-your-repository/licensing-a-repository. Accessed 26 June 2023
6. No License | Choose a License. https://choosealicense.com/no-permission. Accessed 26 June 2023
7. Olorisade, B.K., Brereton, P., Andras, P.: Reproducibility of studies on text mining for citation screening in systematic reviews: evaluation and checklist. J. Biomed. Inform. **73**, 1–13 (2017). https://doi.org/10.1016/j.jbi.2017.07.010
8. Papers with Code. https://paperswithcode.com. Accessed 26 June 2023
9. Pineau, J., et al.: Improving reproducibility in machine learning research (a report from the NeurIPS 2019 reproducibility program). J. Mach. Learn. Res. **22**, 7459–7478 (2021)
10. Pérez, Fernando, K.J.M.: Developing open-source scientific practice. In: Implementing Reproducible Research. Chapman and Hall/CRC (2014)
11. Reproducibility Checklist | AAAI 2023 Conference. https://aaai-23.aaai.org/reproducibility-checklist. Accessed 26 June 2023
12. Reproducibility in Machine Learning. https://sites.google.com/view/icml-reproducibility-workshop/home. Accessed 26 June 2023
13. Shireman, E., Steinley, D., Brusco, M.J.: Examining the effect of initialization strategies on the performance of Gaussian mixture modeling. Behav. Res. Meth. **49**(1), 282–293 (2016). https://doi.org/10.3758/s13428-015-0697-6
14. Tips for Publishing Research Code. https://github.com/paperswithcode/releasing-research-code. Accessed 26 June 2023
15. Wolter, K.M.: Introduction to Variance Estimation. Statistics for Social and Behavioral Sciences, Springer, New York, NY (2007). https://doi.org/10.1007/978-0-387-35099-8

# Unveiling the Relationship Between News Recommendation Algorithms and Media Bias: A Simulation-Based Analysis of the Evolution of Bias Prevalence

Qin Ruan[1,3]($\boxtimes$)(iD), Brian Mac Namee[1,2,3](iD), and Ruihai Dong[1,2,3](iD)

[1] School of Computer Science, University College Dublin, Dublin, Ireland
{brian.macnamee,ruihai.dong}@ucd.ie
[2] Insight Centre for Data Analytics, Dublin, Ireland
[3] Science Foundation Ireland Centre for Research Training in Machine Learning, Dublin, Ireland
qin.ruan@ucdconnect.ie

**Abstract.** Media bias has significant negative effects, such as influencing elections and shaping people's perceptions. However, the relationship between media bias and personalised news recommendation algorithms (widely adopted by many news platforms) remains unclear. In this study, we describe a novel framework that simulates user interactions with recommendation algorithms, allowing us to explore how the degree of bias in the news articles presented to users by personalized recommendation systems changes over time. Our experiments show that leading personalized news recommendation algorithms are sensitive to media bias, causing shifts in the proportion of biased news articles they recommend over time. These findings emphasize the importance of recognizing the influence of media bias on personalized news recommendation algorithms and the need to raise user awareness about media bias to encourage more diverse and balanced news consumption. The source code is available at https://github.com/ruanqin0706/UserRecSimulation.git.

**Keywords:** Media bias · News recommendations · Bias prevalence evolution · Filter bubble · Simulation

## 1 Introduction

News recommendation algorithms are ubiquitous in today's online landscape, offering personalized content to users by analyzing their reading history [12]. While these algorithms help combat information overload, they can inadvertently contribute to the "filter bubble" phenomenon [5], narrowing users' exposure to

This publication has emanated from research conducted with the financial support of Science Foundation Ireland under Grant number 18/CRT/6183. For the purpose of Open Access, the author has applied a CC BY public copyright licence to any Author Accepted Manuscript version arising from this submission.

diverse viewpoints. Media bias [3], which manifests in various forms, can further limit users' access to balanced news coverage. This can lead to confirmation bias, where users seek information that aligns with their beliefs.

Despite their individual impacts, limited research [14] explores the combined effects of news recommendation algorithms and media bias. In this study, we address this gap by investigating how biased news articles in a user's reading history influence personalized news recommendation algorithms, and how these algorithms affect the prevalence of biased media in recommended news articles over time.

We have developed a novel news recommendation simulation framework with an embedded media-bias detector [6] to simulate interactions between users and recommendation algorithms. This simulation framework is capable of generating synthetic users' data based on different reading interest distributions and different appetites for biased media; supports various models for how users choose which articles to read; and integrates state-of-the-art news recommendation algorithms. This study contributes to providing a nuanced understanding of the relationship between news recommendation algorithms and media bias.

The remainder of the paper is organized as follows. We first review related work on media bias, news recommendation algorithms and simulated experiments (Sect. 2). Then, we present the details of our news recommendation simulation framework focusing on media bias evaluation (Sect. 3). Next, we describe experiments that study the relationship between media bias and news recommendation algorithms (Sect. 4). Finally, we discuss the results and implications of our findings (Sect. 5) and conclude the paper (Sect. 6).

## 2 Related Work

Media bias has adverse effects, including confirmation bias, societal polarization, trust erosion, and potential impacts on politics and voting behaviour, all of which contribute to a polarized society and hinder critical information exchange [1]. Recently, there has been growing interest in developing sequential news recommendation algorithms that use neural network models to analyze users' reading history and recommend articles based on their interests [12]. To assess the impact of news recommendation algorithms, researchers consider simulation experiments a valuable choice [2]. Simulation experiments replicate real-world scenarios and allow researchers to manipulate variables to study their effects [2]. For instance, Szl'avik et al. [7] examined the influence of recommendation algorithms on recommendation diversity by creating various user choice models with distinct preferences for accepting recommended items.

## 3 Simulation Framework

To investigate the relationship between news recommendation algorithms and media bias, we have developed a news recommendation simulation framework. Our framework simulates a recommendation feedback loop where the algorithm

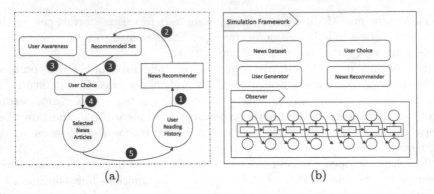

**Fig. 1.** (a) An illustration of the recommendation feedback loop under the news recommendation simulation framework. (b) An illustration of the news recommendation simulation framework.

suggests a set of $n$ news articles from a candidate set based on the user's reading history, which is then passed into the user choice model. The user choice model simulates the user's decision-making process using a given user choice strategy, resulting in the selection of $k$ articles. Finally, these $k$ articles are added to the user's reading history to complete the recommendation process. The process is illustrated in Fig. 1(a). The simulation framework executes the recommendation feedback loop $s$ times to analyze the evolution of bias prevalence in recommended news. The news recommendation simulation framework is illustrated in Fig. 1(b). The components of the simulation framework include a **news dataset**, a **user generator**, a **user choice model**, and a **news recommender**.

The simulation framework can utilise any news article dataset as long as the articles in that dataset are ordered by date; the articles contain a title and summary text; each article has a theme label; and each article is labelled as biased or non-biased. The titles and summaries are used by the News Recommender, the bias labels and theme labels are used in our experiments (in the User Generator and in the User Choice Model).

To generate synthetic users, we consider two aspects: their *News Theme Preference* and their *Media Bias Preference*. News Theme Preference represents a user's interest in predefined themes and is represented as a probability distribution. In the simulation, news articles have specific themes, and each user's preference for these themes is determined by sampling from a truncated standard normal distribution. These preferences are normalized to create a theme distribution. Media Bias Preference reflects a user's inclination for biased media and ranges from 0% to 100%. At the beginning of a simulation, the User Generator creates an initial reading history for each user, which serves as training data for recommender systems. These initial reading histories are assumed to have been read before the user started using the recommender system. For each day in the initial reading history, the framework determines how many news articles a user will read, denoted as $r$. This is determined by sampling from a truncated discrete log-normal distribution, with a mean of 1.5, a standard deviation of 1, and values truncated between 0 and 100. The themes for these articles are then chosen by sampling from the News Theme Preference probability distribution for that user. Articles from each theme are randomly selected from that day's articles. The user's Media Bias Preference determines whether each selected article is biased or non-biased. After the initial reading history is generated, the simulation uses the Media Bias Preference for each user in the User Choice Model, and the News Theme Preference is no longer considered.

The user choice model is designed to simulate user decision-making when presented with the results of recommendation algorithms. We designed the "Equal-Rec" strategy based on the assumption that users have an equal preference for all recommended items.

The task of a news recommender is to select $n$ items from a candidate news set to maximize a user's engagement based on their reading history. The performance of recommender systems is evaluated using accuracy-based metrics: area under the curve $(AUC)$, mean reciprocal rank $(MRR)$, and normalized discounted cumulative gain $(NDCG)$.

## 4   Experiments

This section describes the setup and results of experiments that have been designed to address the research questions posed in Sect. 1 using the simulation framework (see Sect. 3). We created eight user groups with varying proportions of biased news articles in their reading histories, from 10% to 80%, each comprising 250 simulated users with 50 reading records per user. We trained one random recommender and five state-of-the-art personalized news recommendation algorithms (NPA [10], NAML [9], NRMS [11], FIM [8], and PLM-empowered [13]). These algorithms use different input features, such as news titles, summaries, and themes. We built a total of 65 rounds of the algorithm recommendation feedback loop. In experiments, we used the Equal-Rec user choice strategy to examine the impact of biased articles on news recommendation algorithms. We tracked the evolution of bias prevalence by calculating the proportion of biased articles in users' reading histories over multiple recommendations. The results of the experiments are presented in Fig. 2.

## 5   Discussion and Findings

Referring to Figs. 2(b), 2(c), 2(d), 2(e), and 2(f), we observed that FIM, NRMS and PLM-empowered news recommendation algorithms are influenced by users' bias preferences in their reading history. Biased content preference (70% and 80% groups) results in more biased recommendations, while those favouring non-biased articles (10%, 20%, and 30% groups) receive more non-biased suggestions. Users evenly consuming both biased and non-biased articles (40%, 50%, and 60% groups) tend to receive more non-biased recommendations. These algorithms rely solely on news titles as input, indicating titles often carry significant bias,

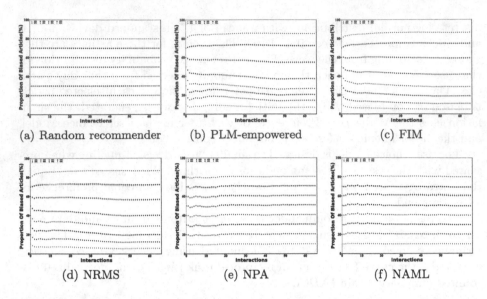

(a) Random recommender    (b) PLM-empowered    (c) FIM

(d) NRMS    (e) NPA    (f) NAML

**Fig. 2.** (a)-(f) show the relationship between recommendation iterations (horizontal axis) and the proportion of biased articles (vertical axis) in different bias proportion user groups under random recommender, PLM-empowered, FIM, NRMS, NPA, NAML. The figures suggest that PLM-empowered, FIM, and NRMS are sensitive to media bias in users' reading history and have a significant effect on the evolution of bias prevalence of recommending news articles. NPA and NAML are barely affected.

aligning with Lee et al.'s findings [4] suggesting titles indicate framing bias. This sensitivity to bias is significant as it may reinforce users' preferences, potentially creating a cycle of biased news consumption and altering habits. Interestingly, we observed a saturation effect where the proportion of biased media read by users levels off at a maximum or minimum level after a period of increase or decrease, indicating a potential limit to users' tolerance for biased content.

## 6    Conclusion

In this work, we describe a news recommendation simulation framework designed to analyze the relationship between news recommendation algorithms and media bias. We use this framework to address the lack of research in the literature on the direct evaluation of the relationship between media bias and news recommendation algorithms. The experiments using the simulation framework reveal that certain recommendation algorithms are sensitive to biased news articles in a user's reading history and tend to recommend more biased articles to users who prefer such articles and fewer biased articles to those who do not. In the future, we plan to optimize the simulation framework and develop more advanced recommendation algorithms that help to mitigate the impact of media bias. We will also explore the impact of news recommendation algorithms on user attitudes and opinions, and the potential social impact of biased news recommendations.

# References

1. Hamborg, F., Donnay, K., Gipp, B.: Automated identification of media bias in news articles: an interdisciplinary literature review. Int. J. Digit. Libr. **20**(4), 391–415 (2019)
2. Hazrati, N., Ricci, F.: Recommender systems effect on the evolution of users' choices distribution. Inf. Process. Manag. **59**(1), 102766 (2022)
3. Kiesel, J., et al.: Semeval-2019 task 4: hyperpartisan news detection. In: Proceedings of the 13th International Workshop on Semantic Evaluation, pp. 829–839 (2019)
4. Lee, N., Bang, Y., Yu, T., Madotto, A., Fung, P.: NeuS: neutral multi-news summarization for mitigating framing bias. In: Proceedings of the 2022 Conference of the North American Chapter of the Association for Computational Linguistics: Human Language Technologies, pp. 3131–3148 (2022)
5. Pariser, E.: The Filter Bubble: What the Internet is Hiding from You. Penguin, London (2011)
6. Ruan, Q., Mac Namee, B., Dong, R.: Bias bubbles: using semi-supervised learning to measure how many biased news articles are around us. In: AICS, pp. 153–164 (2021)
7. Szlávik, Z., Kowalczyk, W., Schut, M.: Diversity measurement of recommender systems under different user choice models. In: Proceedings of the International AAAI Conference on Web and Social Media, vol. 5, pp. 369–376 (2011)
8. Wang, H., Wu, F., Liu, Z., Xie, X.: Fine-grained interest matching for neural news recommendation. In: Proceedings of the 58th Annual Meeting of the Association for Computational Linguistics, pp. 836–845 (2020)
9. Wu, C., Wu, F., An, M., Huang, J., Huang, Y., Xie, X.: Neural news recommendation with attentive multi-view learning. In: IJCAI (2019)
10. Wu, C., Wu, F., An, M., Huang, J., Huang, Y., Xie, X.: NPA: neural news recommendation with personalized attention. In: Proceedings of the 25th ACM SIGKDD International Conference on Knowledge Discovery & Data Mining, pp. 2576–2684 (2019)
11. Wu, C., Wu, F., Ge, S., Qi, T., Huang, Y., Xie, X.: Neural news recommendation with multi-head self-attention. In: Proceedings of the 2019 Conference on Empirical Methods in Natural Language Processing and the 9th International Joint Conference on Natural Language Processing (EMNLP-IJCNLP), pp. 6389–6394 (2019)
12. Wu, C., Wu, F., Huang, Y., Xie, X.: Personalized news recommendation: methods and challenges. ACM Trans. Inf. Syst. **41**(1), 1–50 (2023)
13. Wu, C., Wu, F., Qi, T., Huang, Y.: Empowering news recommendation with pre-trained language models. In: Proceedings of the 44th International ACM SIGIR Conference on Research and Development in Information Retrieval, pp. 1652–1656 (2021)
14. Zhang, H., Zhu, Z., Caverlee, J.: Evolution of filter bubbles and polarization in news recommendation. In: Kamps, J., et al. (eds.) Advances in Information Retrieval. ECIR 2023. LNCS, vol. 13981, pp. 685–693. Springer, Cham (2023). https://doi.org/10.1007/978-3-031-28238-6_60

# A Novel State Space Exploration Method for the Sparse-Reward Reinforcement Learning Environment

Xi Liu[1] , Long Ma[1] , Zhen Chen[1] , Changgang Zheng[2] , Ren Chen[3] ,
Yong Liao[1] , and Shufan Yang[4(✉)]

[1] University of Science and Technology of China, Hefei, China
yliao@ustc.edu.cn
[2] University of Oxford, Oxford, UK
[3] Anhui Medical University, Hefei, China
[4] Edinburgh Napier University, Edinburgh, UK
S.Yang@napier.ac.uk

**Abstract.** Sparse-reward reinforcement learning environments pose a particular challenge because the agent receives infrequent rewards, making it difficult to learn an optimal policy. In this paper, we propose NSSE, a novel approach that combines that stratified state space exploration with prioritised sweeping to enhance the informativeness of learning, thus enabling fast learning convergence. We evaluate NSSE on three typical Atari sparse reward environments. The results demonstrate that our state space exploration method exhibits strong performance compared to two baseline algorithms: Deep Q-Network (DQN) and noisy Deep Q-Network (Noisy DQN).

**Keywords:** Sparse-reward · Replay Sub-buffers · DQN · Exploration · Reinforcement Learning

## 1 Introduction

Reinforcement learning (RL) conducts agent learning by interacting with the environment and trial errors. Specifically, by sensing rewards from the environment, the RL policy will be updated regularly over time in order to maximise cumulative rewards. Not all environment provides informative rewards, which is known as the sparse reward problem. Under the sparse reward environment, agents mainly receive rewards with the same value, barely gaining feedback with valid values [1]. The lack of informative feedback leads to inefficient agent exploration and diffused policy optimisation, ultimately hindering RL convergence. Addressing the challenge of sparse rewards is an active research area in the reinforcement learning paradigm. The most widely used methods, mainly based on experience replay buffers [8,13,17], can mitigate the effect but are resources

Dr Yang is supported by Royal Academy Engineering SHE project RAEng (IF2223-172) and Royal Society of Edinburgh (961_Yang).

consuming, especially in terms of storage and computational. In this paper, we propose Novel State Space Exploration (NSSE), a new experience replay method with prioritised sweeping on multi-buffer for the sparse reward environment. This method reduces computational and storage requirements compared to approaches with prioritised storage and improves the sample efficiency of reinforcement learning algorithms.

## 2    Background

**Sparse Reward Problem.** The sparse reward challenge in reinforcement learning arises from the sparsely distributed rewards in the environment, posing a training difficulty for deep RL [1]. A classic approach to address this issue involves the integration of intrinsic rewards, which augment exploration by introducing dense rewards. Typically, these intrinsic rewards are generated based on training experiences, encompassing factors like novelty [4,9], curiosity [10,15], or information theory [14,16]. While these methods enhance exploration, they may introduce training challenges such as derailment and detachment [5].

**Prioritised Sweeping.** Prioritised sweeping is a common technique used for addressing Markov Decision Problems, which assigns update priorities based on temporal difference errors (TD-error) magnitudes. Saglam et al. [12] applied this approach to actor-critic algorithms. Prioritised sweeping in replay memory selects experiences by prioritising those with higher anticipated learning potential on future iterations. Schaul et al. [13] implemented this prioritisation mechanism within the replay buffer to increase the replay frequency of more critical experiences. Horgan et al. [8] expanded prioritised experience replay to distributed architectures for large-scale training, yielding effective learning with high-dimensional data. Nonetheless, prioritised experience replay shares limitations with its reliance on historical experiences. While it proves especially beneficial in scenarios featuring sparse reward signals, it necessitates frequent priority calculations and updates, slowing down the training process and consuming more memory.

## 3    Problem Formulation

We consider a Markov Decision Process (MDP) [11] formulated as $(\mathcal{S}, \mathcal{A}, \mathcal{P}, \mathcal{R}, \gamma)$, where $\mathcal{S}$ is the set of state, $\mathcal{A}$ is the set of actions, $\mathcal{P}(s'|s,a)$ is the state-transition probability function, $\mathcal{R}(s,a)$ is the immediate reward from state $s$ to state $s'$ given an action, and $\gamma \in [0,1]$ is the discount factor. At time $t$, the agent observes the state $s_t$, takes an action $a_t$; and then obtains an immediate reward $r(s_t, a_t)$ and a new state $s_t'$, determined from the probability distribution $\mathcal{P}$. A stochastic policy $\pi$ indicates the action taken by the agent in the case of given $s$. The objective of the agent is to find the policy $\pi$ mapping from states to actions that maximise the discounted cumulative sum of random rewards formulated as $Z^{\pi}(s,a) = \sum_{i=t}^{\infty} \gamma^{i-t} r(s_i, a_i)$. The expected value is $Q^{\pi}(s,a) = E[Z^{\pi}(s,a)]$ where

$E$ is the expectation over the distribution of the trajectory $(s_0, a_0, s_1, a_1, \cdots)$. $Q^\pi$ can be determined by solving the Bellman equation [3]:

$$Q^\pi(s, a) = E^\pi[r(s, a) + \gamma Q^\pi(s', a')] \tag{1}$$

Experience replay Buffer $\mathcal{B}$ is a collection of agent store experiences, which is used to update the neural network. In our work, each experience $\langle s, a, r, s' \rangle$ is stored in the corresponding buffer according to the reward classification when storing, and then we obtained some sub-buffers $(\mathcal{B}_1, \mathcal{B}_2, \mathcal{B}_3, \cdots)$. We propose a new sampling method to get the ratio of samples from each sub-buffer $\mathcal{B}_i, i = 1, 2, 3, \cdots$, and then obtain the corresponding number of samples.

## 4   Methods

In the sparse reward environment, agent obtains few useful rewards, so it is very important to make the best use of these rewards. Using an experience replay buffer leads to two design problems: how to store experience, and how to replay experiences. In this paper, we propose a Novel State Space Exploration (NSSE) method, where multi-buffer stores experience separately and priority is used to represent the learning situation of each buffer to determine the sampling ratio from each buffer. The following are the details of how we solve the above two problems.

### 4.1   Multiple Replay Buffer

Generally, the experiences obtained by the agent over a period of time are stored in the replay buffer. We use multiple buffers to store experiences, and priorities to clear the sampling ratio from each buffer. This has a great advantage: the agent can learn better by increasing the replay probability of the sparse rewards.

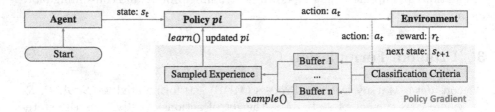

**Fig. 1.** The overview of the method of grouping reply buffers.

The schematic view of our algorithm is shown in Fig. 1. There are four important components including (1) Policy $\pi$ which takes as input the state $s_t$, then produces action $a_t$ to interact with the (2) Environment. The environment returns a new state $s_{t+1}$ and the reward $r_t$ to the agent. The state $s_t$, action $a_t$, reward $r_t$, and new state $s_{t+1}$ are respectively stored into the corresponding sub-buffer according to (3) Classification Criteria. When learning, our new method is adapted to sample from all sub-buffers, and then we obtained (4) sampled experience to update our neural network.

## 4.2 Asynchronous Priority Method

Inspired by the prioritised sweeping method, the experiences sampled from each sub-buffer are determined by a sampling ratio based on the temporal difference (TD) error. The TD-error reflects the difference between the predicted reward and the actual reward, serving as an indicator of the agent's learning progress for each sub-buffer. If the TD-error calculated from the sampling data in a particular sub-buffer is larger, it indicates that the experience within that sub-buffer is more valuable for the agent's learning. Therefore, it is necessary to use more experience in this sub-buffer during the training of the neural network. Due to the large amount of calculation of the experience priorities in each sub-buffer, we utilise the sample mean to estimate the population mean, and this is statistically rational. The specific sampling method is as follows.

For every sub-buffer $\mathcal{B}_i, i = 1, 2, \cdots, n$, where $n$ is the number of sub-buffers, we sample a batch of data $\{(s_{ij}, a_{ij}, r_{ij}, s_{ij}')\}, j = 1, 2, \cdots, m$ from $\mathcal{B}_i$, where $m$ is the size of the batch. For every data, according to the Eq. 1, we use the target network $Q^{\pi^*}$ to calculate

$$y_{ij} = r_{ij} + \gamma max_{a_i} Q^{\pi^*}(s_{ij}', a_i) \tag{2}$$

We define the sampling ratio $ratio_i$ of the batch $\mathcal{B}_i$ as $ratio_i = \delta_i / \sum_{k=1}^{n} \delta_k$, where $\delta_k$ is the TD error calculated by the average of $|Q^\pi(s_{kj}, a_{kj}) - y_{kj}|, j = 1, 2, \cdots, m$. Thus, we obtain $num_i = \lfloor ratio_i \times m + 1/2 \rfloor$ as the number of samples in sub-buffer $\mathcal{B}_i$. Due to the accuracy problem, the above calculation method can be used for the number of the first $n - 1$ sub-buffers, and the number of the last buffer, we can obtain from $m - \sum_{k=1}^{n-1} num_k$. Then we obtain a minibatch by sampling the corresponding number of samples from every sub-buffer by uniform sampling. It should be noted that it is unnecessary to update $ratio_i$ frequently, we can update it once in a while. After that, we use the newly sampled data to update the policy $\pi$.

## 5    Experiment

We selected three typical discrete sparse reward environments in Atari 2600 [2], RiverRaid-v5, Centipede-v5, and AirRaid-v5. In our experiment, every experiment contains three algorithms (three curves), and We test the performance of the agent every 10 episodes. We considered two baseline algorithms that use uniform experience replay buffers. One is the DQN algorithm [7], and the other is the Noisy DQN algorithm [6]. The neural network contains three Convolutional layers and two Linear layers. For Noisy DQN, we add factorised Gaussian noise in the Linear layers.

In this paper, the most relevant component of these baseline algorithms is the experience replay buffer. The replay buffer is uniformly set to a queue with a size of 1000. The baseline algorithms process a minibatch of size 16 sampled uniformly from the replay buffer. We can divide the experience into 2 sub-buffers. The first sub-buffer store experience with rewards greater than 0, and the second one is equal to 0. The initial sampling ratio is both $\frac{1}{2}$.

We compared our novel state space exploration with two baselines (DQN and Noisy DQN) on the three Atari Environments (RiverRaid, Centipede, and AirRaid). The applied evaluation metric is the total reward for interacting with the environment in each episode. As shown in Fig. 2, our algorithm performed better than the two baselines. While in Fig. 2(a) RiverRaid and Fig. 2(b) Centipede, part of the reward curves become a line and no longer change. The main reason is that the policy gradient update is too slow, causing the gradient to disappear. Some oscillations are observed in our experiment, especially in Fig. 2(c) AirRaid, the likely cause is q value overestimation, which results in significant errors in neural network parameters. These errors, in turn, have an adverse effect on policy learning.

Additionally, we also provide a system performance analysis. Compared with the method of applying Priority Experience Replay (PER) buffer [13], since no storage prioritisation is required, our method NSSE saves storage requirements by around 50%.

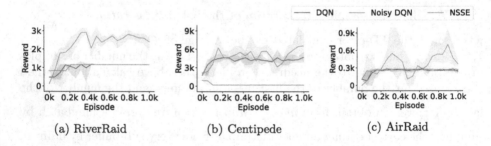

**Fig. 2.** Experimental Test Results in Atari.

## 6   Conclusion

This paper presents NSSE, a new state space exploration method for the discrete sparse-reward environment. By dividing the discrete rewards into sub-buffers based on their sparsity and calculating the sampling ratios of these sub-buffers using TD-error, the proposed method enables better learning efficiency and system performance. We evaluate our method on three classical Atari environments.

The results show that our method has superior learning efficiency compared to DQN and NoisyDQN, with lower memory consumption compared to PER. In the future, we will extend our work to more practical environments.

# References

1. Aubret, A., Matignon, L., Hassas, S.: An information-theoretic perspective on intrinsic motivation in reinforcement learning: a survey. Entropy **25**(2), 327 (2023)
2. Bellemare, M.G., Naddaf, Y., Veness, J., Bowling, M.: The arcade learning environment: an evaluation platform for general agents. J. Artif. Intell. Res. **47**, 253–279 (2013)
3. Bellman, R.: A Markovian decision process. J. Math. Mech. 679–684 (1957)
4. Burda, Y., Edwards, H., Storkey, A., Klimov, O.: Exploration by random network distillation. arXiv preprint arXiv:1810.12894 (2018)
5. Ecoffet, A., Huizinga, J., Lehman, J., Stanley, K.O., Clune, J.: First return, then explore. Nature **590**(7847), 580–586 (2021)
6. Fortunato, M., et al.: Noisy networks for exploration. arXiv preprint arXiv:1706.10295 (2017)
7. Hester, T., et al.: Deep Q-learning from demonstrations. In: Proceedings of the AAAI Conference on Artificial Intelligence, vol. 32 (2018)
8. Horgan, D., et al.: Distributed prioritized experience replay. arXiv preprint arXiv:1803.00933 (2018)
9. Jo, D., et al.: LECO: learnable episodic count for task-specific intrinsic reward. Adv. Neural. Inf. Process. Syst. **35**, 30432–30445 (2022)
10. Pathak, D., Agrawal, P., Efros, A.A., Darrell, T.: Curiosity-driven exploration by self-supervised prediction. In: International Conference on Machine Learning, pp. 2778–2787. PMLR (2017)
11. Puterman, M.L.: Markov decision processes: discrete stochastic dynamic programming. In: Wiley Series in Probability and Statistics (1994)
12. Saglam, B., Mutlu, F.B., Cicek, D.C., Kozat, S.S.: Actor prioritized experience replay. arXiv preprint arXiv:2209.00532 (2022)
13. Schaul, T., Quan, J., Antonoglou, I., Silver, D.: Prioritized experience replay. arXiv preprint arXiv:1511.05952 (2015)
14. Seo, Y., Chen, L., Shin, J., Lee, H., Abbeel, P., Lee, K.: State entropy maximization with random encoders for efficient exploration. In: International Conference on Machine Learning, pp. 9443–9454. PMLR (2021)
15. Yu, X., Lyu, Y., Tsang, I.: Intrinsic reward driven imitation learning via generative model. In: International Conference on Machine Learning, pp. 10925–10935. PMLR (2020)
16. Yuan, M., Pun, M.O., Wang, D.: Rényi state entropy maximization for exploration acceleration in reinforcement learning. IEEE Trans. Artif. Intell. (2022)
17. Zheng, C., Yang, S., Parra-Ullauri, J.M., Garcia-Dominguez, A., Bencomo, N.: Reward-reinforced generative adversarial networks for multi-agent systems. IEEE Trans. Emerg. Top. Comput. Intell. **6**, 479–488 (2021)

# Optimal Manufacturing Controller Synthesis Using Situation Calculus

Omar Adalat, Daniele Scrimieri(✉), and Savas Konur

Department of Computer Science, University of Bradford, Bradford, UK
{o.adalat,d.scrimieri,s.konur}@bradford.ac.uk

**Abstract.** In this paper, we discuss a framework for synthesising manufacturing process controllers using situation calculus, a well-known second-order logic for reasoning about actions in AI. Using a library of high-level ConGolog programs and logical action theories for production resources, we demonstrate how to efficiently synthesise an 'optimal' plan, i.e. the plan that minimises the number of actions for a target high-level program of a process recipe.

**Keywords:** Situation calculus · Controller synthesis · ConGolog · Planning · Manufacturing

## 1  Introduction

Traditional planning formalisms and languages are often difficult to work with for automated synthesis within the manufacturing domain in a practical sense. While many other formalisms have been proposed and developed for manufacturing controller synthesis [1,9], many of these formalisms only allow expressing and representing states propositionally instead of a data-aware first-order state representation of objects [6] and their intertwined relationships. As a direct consequence almost all approaches in prior literature yield lower expressive power. The approach presented in this paper uses situation calculus and builds upon [6,12]. Briefly, we consider the problem of synthesising a high-level controller that orchestrates a number of manufacturing resources composed of logical action theories and high-level programs. Such a controller implements a 'recipe', i.e. a manufacturing process specification for making a product, modelled as a high-level program. We provide an easily controllable progression-based search algorithm instead of relying on computationally intensive fixpoint calculations.

## 2  Preliminaries

### 2.1  Situation Calculus

Situation calculus is a many-sorted second-order logic with equality for reasoning about actions to represent dynamically changing worlds [11]. The three disjoint

M. Bramer and F. Stahl (Eds.): SGAI 2023, LNAI 14381, pp. 222–227, 2023.
https://doi.org/10.1007/978-3-031-47994-6_19

sorts are: *situations*, *actions*, and *objects* ($\Delta$). Situations are terms derived by action histories with $S_0$ representing the initial situation constant.

*Fluents* are dynamic properties that can change across situations, where relational fluents operate on objects and return a proposition of $\{\top, \bot\}$, such as *equipped(effector, s)*. Functional fluents instead return against a range of objects. We also use the standard closed-world and domain-closure assumptions.

Additionally, we track two situation-independent static predicates, specifically for the manufacturing domain, following from [6]. The first is *routable(i, j)*, stating that there exists a valid route between resource $i$ with resource $j$ (usable with In and Out actions that model transferring parts). The second is *coopMatrix(i, j)*, stating that resource $i$ can cooperate with resource $j$.

*Actions* are n-arity terms. The binary function $do(a, s)$ signifies that action $a$ is performing in situation $s$, such that do : action × situation → situation. To determine whether an action $a$ is possible or executable within a situation $s$, we use the following binary predicate Poss : action × situation, which is determined by a situation-suppressed formula of the form $\text{Poss}(a(\boldsymbol{x}), s) \equiv \varphi(a(\boldsymbol{x}), s)$ where $\varphi$ is a situation-suppressed formula with $\boldsymbol{x}$ denoting the vector of arguments. *Compound actions* (denoted by **a**) [6] refer to joint or simultaneous actions, such as $\{\text{LiftAndHold}(\mathbf{p}), \text{Drill}(\mathbf{p})\}$.

*Successor state axioms* encode the causal laws of the system. A successor state axiom is of the form $F(\boldsymbol{x}, do(a, s)) \equiv \varphi_F(\boldsymbol{x}, a, s)$, one for each fluent. The update of a fluent is given by $F(\boldsymbol{x}, do(a, s)) \equiv \varphi_F^+(\boldsymbol{x}, a, s) \vee F(\boldsymbol{x}, s) \wedge \neg \varphi_F^-(\boldsymbol{x}, a, s)$ where $F$ is a fluent, $\varphi_F^+(\boldsymbol{x}, a, s)$ and $\varphi_F^-(\boldsymbol{x}, a, s)$ are formulae that make $F$ true or false respectively.

Each manufacturing production resource that we model comes with its own *basic action theory* (BAT), which is a set of sentences $\mathcal{D}$, formed from

$$\mathcal{D} = \mathcal{D}_{S_0} \cup \mathcal{D}_{ap} \cup \mathcal{D}_{ss} \cup \mathcal{D}_{una} \cup \Sigma$$

where $\mathcal{D}_{S_0}$ initial situation description, $\Sigma$ is the set of domain-independent foundational axioms [11], $\mathcal{D}_{ss}$ is the set of successor state axioms, $\mathcal{D}_{ap}$ represents the set of action precondition axioms, and $\mathcal{D}_{una}$ provides the unique name axioms for actions. $\phi[s]$ denotes substituting situation term $s$ in the situation-uniform formula $\phi$.

## 2.2 ConGolog

*ConGolog* is a high-level programming language for situation calculus that supports a rich notion of concurrency and non-determinism [8]. ConGolog uses transition-step semantics, with two predicates, $Trans(\delta, s, \delta', s')$ denoting that a program transition exists from $\delta$ to $\delta'$ starting from situation $s$ and resulting in situation $s'$, and $Final(\delta, s)$ denoting whether a program configuration is final in situation $s$. The constructs available within a ConGolog program $\delta$ are given by:

$$\delta ::= \mathbf{a}(\boldsymbol{x}) \mid \delta_1; \delta_2 \mid \phi? \mid (\delta_1 \mid \delta_2) \mid \pi x.\delta \mid \delta^* \mid (\delta_1 \parallel \delta_2) \mid (\delta_1 \parallel\parallel \delta_2)$$

The full semantics is presented in [8], with ||| being introduced solely to represent simultaneous/joint execution (true concurrency) between two programs [6]. We use the standard abbreviations **if** $\phi$ **then** $\delta_1$ **else** $\delta_2$ **endIf** $\overset{def}{=}$ $\phi?; \delta_1 | \neg\phi?; \delta_2$, **while** $\phi$ **do** $\delta$ **endWhile** $\overset{def}{=}$ $(\phi?; \delta)^*; \neg\phi?$ and **loop** : $\delta$ $\overset{def}{=}$ **while** $\top$ **do** $\delta$.

Putting this together with the situation calculus, each manufacturing production resource is thereby modelled by a pair of $\langle \delta, \mathcal{D} \rangle$. An example resource production program $\delta$ is given by:

$$\textbf{loop: } \mathsf{Nop} | (\mathsf{In}(part, 2); (\mathsf{Nop} | \mathsf{Hold}(part, force, 2)))^*; \mathsf{Out}(part, 2)$$

This program states that it can either hold in no-operation, Nop, or it can take a part in, afterward performing either no-operation or holding it in place with a given force, possibly indefinitely, and then afterward it must transfer the part back out.

## 2.3  Characteristic Graphs

*Characteristic graphs* [5] allow a succinct representation of all subprogram configurations of a program $\delta$. A characteristic graph $\mathcal{G}$ consists of the triple $\langle V, E, v_0 \rangle$, defined as follows:

- The set of vertices $V$ correspond to reachable subprograms, formed of a pair $\langle \delta', \varphi \rangle$, where $\delta'$ is the remaining executable program and $\varphi$ provides the conditions under which the current execution is final.
- $v_0$ is the symbol for the distinguished initial program vertex, $v_0 = \langle \delta^0, \varphi^0 \rangle$.
- Edges in $E$ are labelled with tuples $\pi x : t/\psi$, stating a transition can occur for action $t$ with a choice ($\pi$) of instantiations for the variable list $x$ (omitted if not required), as long as the condition specified in formula $\psi$ holds.
- Edges in $E$, restricted to recipes, can have actions that are compound.

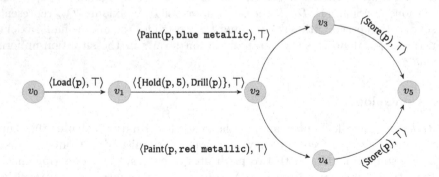

**Fig. 1.** Characteristic graph for a process recipe $G_\sigma$. For brevity we omit vertex labels, however, note that $v_5$ is a final configuration $\langle nil, \top \rangle$.

An example characteristic graph of a recipe is represented in Fig. 1. This corresponds to: $\mathsf{Load}(\mathsf{p}); (\mathsf{Hold}(\mathsf{p}, 5) ||| \mathsf{Drill}(\mathsf{p})); (\mathsf{Paint}(\mathsf{p}, \texttt{metallic blue}) | \mathsf{Paint}(\mathsf{p}, \texttt{metallic red})); \mathsf{Store}(\mathsf{p})$

## 3 Controller Synthesis

A *controller* is composed of executions of compound actions, partially ordered, that realise all recipe transitions of a target ConGolog recipe program (note that, unlike resources, the recipe does not have a basic action theory $\mathcal{D}$). We assume recipes are terminating processes, allowing us to consider final configurations and not infinite runs. Also, observe that, since the action Nop (no-operation) for any resource $i$ has no effect, it is given that $\text{Poss}(\mathbf{a} \cup \text{Nop}, s) \equiv \text{Poss}(\mathbf{a}, s)$.

---

**Algorithm 1:** Synthesise

**Data:** Recipe characteristic graph $\mathcal{G}_\sigma$, resources' characteristic graphs $\mathcal{G}_{i=1}^n$, $\mathcal{D}_{global}$, $S_0^F$, plan length limit $N$, fairness limit $F$, object domain $\Delta$

**Result:** Controller $\chi$ if realisable

$\chi_{initial}.\mathcal{Q}.\text{push}(\text{AddStages}(S_0^F, v_0 \text{ of } \mathcal{G}_\sigma, F))$;

$\chi_{best}.length \leftarrow \infty$; $frontier.\text{push}(\chi_{initial})$;

**while** $\neg empty(frontier) \wedge \chi_{best}.length \geq frontier.top().length$ **do**

    $\chi_c, \mathcal{P}_c \leftarrow frontier.\text{pop}(), \chi_c.\mathcal{Q}.\text{pop}()$;

    **if** *compound actions in* $\chi_c \geq N$ **then**

        ⌊ **continue**;

    **forall** *compound actions ca of trace* $\in GatherTransitions(\mathcal{G}_{i=1}^n, \Delta)$ **do**

        **if** $Poss(ca, \mathcal{P}_c.S) = \bot \vee \bigwedge_{i=1}^n transition \, \psi_i[\mathcal{P}_c.S] = \bot$ **then**

            ⌊ **continue**;

        **Form** $\chi'$, $\mathcal{P}'$ with $\text{Do}(\mathbf{ca}, \mathcal{P}_c.S)$ and *trace*;

        $\chi'.length \leftarrow 1 + (1 * \text{simple actions (non-Nop) of } \mathbf{ca})$

        **if** *ca from recipe transition* $\mathcal{P}_c$ *is executed* **then**

            AddStages($\mathcal{P}'.S, \mathcal{P}'.to, F$);

            **if** $\mathcal{P}_c.to$'s *transitions in* $\mathcal{G}_\sigma = \emptyset \wedge \neg \bigwedge_{i=1}^n \mathcal{G}_i's \, Final \, \varphi[\mathcal{P}'.S] = \bot$ **then**

                ⌊ **continue**;

            **if** $empty(\chi'.\mathcal{Q})$ **then**

                Potentially **update** $\chi_{best}$;

                **continue**;

            **else**

                ⌊ Enqueue $\chi'$ into *frontier*;

        **else**

            Enqueue $\mathcal{P}'$ into $\chi'.\mathcal{Q}$;

            Enqueue $\chi'$ into *frontier*;

⌊ **return** either $\chi_{best}$ or **unrealisable** if $\chi_{best}.length = \infty$

---

Controller synthesis resorts to a two-player game between the proponent *controller*, and the antagonist *environment*, due to the non-determinism possibly involved in recipes that allow runtime choices such as $\pi x.\delta$. That is, no matter what 'devillish' non-determinism move the recipe program $\delta_\sigma$ makes, the controller can respond, where the resources' ConGolog programs operate under 'angelic' non-determinism (that is, non-determinism we can control) [7,12].

We start by defining $\mathcal{D}_{global} \overset{def}{=} \bigcup_{i=1}^{n} \mathcal{D}_i$ which is the result of combining the individual basic action theories. The initial facility situation constant is then represented by $S_0^F$. While the state space involved may appear to be finite, given a finite number of subprogram configurations, finite number of actions types, and finite object domain $\Delta$, this is not the case. In particular, the construct $\delta^*$ is considered 'unsafe' [3, 10] since it allows infinite computations, and by proxy, the same extends to higher-level constructs **while** and **loop**. The way we deal with this is through a *fairness assumption*, i.e. placing a limit on the number of folds a $\delta^*$ execution can reoccur.

**Proposition 1.** *There is a finite number of transitions that can be considered under a fairness assumption as each explored cycle is only allowed k unfoldings, or a finite number of considerations by imposing a plan upper limit of N at any stage (per recipe transition or globally)*

Reasoning about preconditions (Poss) formulas for compound actions typically decomposes into $\bigwedge_{n=1}^{i} \text{Poss}(\mathbf{a}_n, s)$. However, we also allow special mappings for certain actions, such as for the In and Out actions:

$\text{Poss}(\text{In}(part, i), s) \equiv part(part, s) \wedge \neg \exists p. \, at(p, i, s)$

$\text{Poss}(\text{Out}(part, i, s)) \equiv part(part, s) \wedge at(part, i, s)$

$\text{Poss}(\{\text{In}(part, i), \text{Out}(part, j)\}, s) \equiv \text{Poss}(\text{In}(part, i), s) \wedge \text{Poss}(\text{Out}(part, j), s) \wedge routable(i, j)$

$withinReach(part, i, s) \equiv at(part, i, s) \vee (\exists j. \, j \neq i \wedge at(part, j, s) \wedge coopMatrix(i, j))$

Successor state axioms are aware of compound actions and can reason about containment for simple actions within compound actions, for example:

$equipped(e, i, do(\mathbf{a}, s)) \equiv \text{Equip}(e, i) \in \mathbf{a} \vee (equipped(e, i, s) \wedge \text{Unequip}(i) \notin \mathbf{a})$

Algorithm 1 outlines the synthesis strategy we consider. The priority queue *frontier* contains the controller candidates that have been generated sorted by number of actions, where the candidate with the lowest number of actions is at the top of the queue. The inner queue of each controller, $\mathcal{Q}$, considers the recipe transitions/'phases' that are yet to be completed from (AddStages, which holds responsibility for the fairness limit). Function GatherTransitions operates on the object domain and resource characteristic graphs. It picks all potential transitions, keeping in mind the current characteristic graph states $\mathcal{G}_{i=1}^n$, and action permutations with variable substitution from $\Delta$. The *cost* (*length* in the algorithm) ascribed to each controller can be viewed as the sum of the number of all simple actions (non-Nop) and the number of compound actions.

One possible controller execution (as controllers involve runtime execution choices), once flattened out, would appear like this, assuming three arbitrary resources including our previously defined example resource and example recipe:

$\{\text{Load}(\text{p}), \text{Nop}, \text{Nop}\} \rightarrow \{\text{Out}(\text{p}, 1), \text{In}(\text{p}, 2), \text{Nop}\} \rightarrow$

$\rightarrow \{\text{Hold}(\text{p}, 5), \text{Paint}(\text{p}, \texttt{blue metallic}), \text{Nop}\} \rightarrow \{\text{Nop}, \text{Out}(\text{p}, 2), \text{In}(\text{p}, 3)\} \rightarrow$

$\rightarrow \{\text{Nop}, \text{Nop}, \text{Store}(\text{p})\}$

In this execution, part p is first loaded by the first resource, then transferred to the second resource, which holds it and paints it in blue metallic. Finally, the part is transferred to the third resource and stored.

# 4 Conclusion

In summary, we present an *optimal progression search* approach for synthesising manufacturing controllers using the situation calculus. The next step is to carry out experimental evaluation using our prototype (https://github.com/nightly/scs). In the future, our tool could be easily extended to provide an explicit treatment of time, further exploration of heuristics and abstraction techniques, non-Markovian actions and effects, exogenous events, as well as noisy [2] and fallible [4] sensing.

**Acknowledgements.** This work was supported by the SURE Research Projects Fund and Research Development Fund of the University of Bradford and Innovate UK grant no: 10028947 (Made Smarter Innovation: Sustainable Smart Factory).

# References

1. Adalat, O., Talal, M., Ali Cherif, M.A., Scrimieri, D.: Model-based generation of manufacturing process plans through incremental topology formation. In: Panoutsos, G., Mahfouf, M., Mihaylova, L. (eds.) Advances in Computational Intelligence Systems - Contributions Presented at the 21st UK Workshop on Computational Intelligence, Sheffield, UK, 7–9 September 2022. Advances in Intelligent Systems and Computing. Springer, Cham (2023, in press)
2. Bacchus, F., Halpern, J.Y., Levesque, H.J.: Reasoning about noisy sensors and effectors in the situation calculus. Artif. Intell. **111**(1–2), 171–208 (1999)
3. Beck, D., Lakemeyer, G.: Reinforcement learning for Golog programs with first-order state-abstraction. Log. J. IGPL **20**(5), 909–942 (2012)
4. Claßen, J., Delgrande, J.P.: An account of intensional and extensional actions, and its application to belief, nondeterministic actions and fallible sensors. In: Proceedings of the International Conference on Principles of Knowledge Representation and Reasoning, vol. 18, pp. 194–204 (2021)
5. Claßen, J., Lakemeyer, G.: A logic for non-terminating Golog programs. In: KR, pp. 589–599 (2008)
6. De Giacomo, G., Felli, P., Logan, B., Patrizi, F., Sardina, S.: Situation calculus for controller synthesis in manufacturing systems with first-order state representation. Artif. Intell. **302**, 103598 (2022)
7. De Giacomo, G., Lespérance, Y.: The nondeterministic situation calculus. In: Proceedings of the International Conference on Principles of Knowledge Representation and Reasoning, vol. 18, pp. 216–226 (2021)
8. De Giacomo, G., Lespérance, Y., Levesque, H.J.: ConGolog, a concurrent programming language based on the situation calculus. Artif. Intell. **121**(1–2), 109–169 (2000)
9. De Giacomo, G., Vardi, M., Felli, P., Alechina, N., Logan, B.: Synthesis of orchestrations of transducers for manufacturing. In: Proceedings of the AAAI Conference on Artificial Intelligence, vol. 32 (2018)
10. Kalantari, L., Ternovska, E.: A model checker for verifying ConGolog programs. In: AAAI/IAAI, pp. 953–954 (2002)
11. Reiter, R.: Knowledge in Action: Logical Foundations for Specifying and Implementing Dynamical Systems. MIT Press, Cambridge (2001)
12. Sardina, S., De Giacomo, G.: Composition of ConGolog programs. In: Twenty-First International Joint Conference on Artificial Intelligence (2009)

# Predicting Social Trust from Implicit Feedback

Eseosa Oshodin(⊠) ⓘD

University of the West of England, Coldharbour Lane, Bristol BS16 1QY, UK
eseosa.oshodin@uwe.ac.uk

**Abstract.** Element of trust exists in every network structure of diverse fields, but suitable computational methods for evaluating the trust remain a problem since there are different definitions of trust in diverse fields where several entities interact with each other. As there might be some social entities (e.g. social actors) who could be deceived by others behaving maliciously in a social network, there is the need to compute the trustworthiness of entities in determining which entity will be more reliable to other entities for future interaction. This paper will reveal how the reciprocity from analysed social activities could be used in predicting the trustworthiness of entities based on their activeness in a social network. An example will be used to demonstrate the effectiveness of the proposed framework's application.

**Keywords:** Trust · Social network · Graph/network Theory · Interpersonal behaviour

## 1 Introduction

In every dialogue or engagement between entities, there is the element of trust, which can be used to predict the decision to be made by entities to either continue with a dialogue or disengage from the dialogue. Experience of humans with other humans or items in the real world has assisted them to decide if they should trust these other humans/items or not. We can also ask: "Can trust be measured/predicted from observed behaviour"?

Even though there are diverse definitions of trust, we will be focusing mainly on interpersonal trust [1], which can be defined as the probability that an entity will behave in a similar and expected manner without any fault. Insight from the observation of past situations could be used towards supporting decision-making for efficient operations [2].

The rest of this paper is organized as follows: Sect. 2 will discuss the importance of behavioural patterns, and some motivational ideas for analysing social data, which could facilitate our work. Section 3 will present the strength of our proposed framework for computing the trustworthiness of entities, which was introduced in previous research [2]. An example will be presented to demonstrate the application of the framework.

M. Bramer and F. Stahl (Eds.): SGAI 2023, LNAI 14381, pp. 228–233, 2023.
https://doi.org/10.1007/978-3-031-47994-6_20

## 2    Related Works

Exploring social network graphs reveals several network concepts that are essential in understanding the pattern of entities' behaviour. Social data is often viewed as a **one-mode network**, where all vertices are members of the same class (i.e. a social actor's class). However, previous research [3,4] revealed that these vertices are connected based on their initial shared association with another set of entities (context class). This type of network was referred to as a **two-mode network** [4], as it consists of two different vertex sets. Newman [3] considered this type of network to be useful as it enables easy analysis to be carried out to determine relevant context vertices (e.g. written research papers) that could be suggested for active entities (e.g. human researchers).

**Definition 1 (Two-Mode Network).** *A two-mode network is represented as a graph $G^t = (V_X, V_P, E^t)$ that consists of a set of active vertices $V_X$ associated with a set of context vertices $V_P$ using a set of edges $E^t$. That is, entities from the same set do not have direct ties to each other; they are only reachable if an entity from another set connects them. An example of this type of network can be seen in Fig. 1, which will be described later in Sect. 3.2.*

Previous research [4] suggested two methods of conversion for the two-mode network: **Sum and Newman projection method**. 'Sum' projection method on a two-mode network involves the addition of all weights from a vertex $i \in X$ that shares ties towards vertex $t \in P$ with another vertex $j \in X$. The output in a directed edge network[1] from these summed-up weights are represented as the vertex $i$'s in-degree weight [4] from the other vertex $j$.

$$w_{i,j \in X} = \sum_{t \in P} w_{i,t} \tag{1}$$

**where:** $w_{i,t}$ is the weight on edges that active vertex $i$ had towards context vertex $t$ which is also linked with active vertex $j$.

In the case of Newman's projection method, normalizing Eq. 1 provides the strength of ties $w_{ij}$ (See Eq. 2 below), which are considered to be affected by the number of other vertices that were also active towards context vertices $t$. This was based on Newman's argument [3] that social scientists in a collaborative network will have stronger bonds if there are fewer or no other scientists collaborating with them on a paper.

$$w_{i,j \in X} = \sum_{t \in P} \frac{w_{i,t}}{N_t - 1} \tag{2}$$

**where:** $N_t$ is the number of vertices (i.e. $i, j \in X$) that had connection with the context vertex $t$.

The next section will discuss the outputs from the use of the Sum projection method on a two-mode network, which could assist in our proposed framework for measuring the trustworthiness of an entity from set $X$.

---

[1] Directed edges between a vertex $i$ and vertex $j$ in a network are distinct from each other.

# 3   Computing Trust from Social Activeness

The proposed framework for computing the trustworthiness of an entity (social actor) introduced in [2] can be represented in a pseudo-code, which considers the input data as a two-mode network of a certain number of entities.

---

**Algorithm 1.** Trust Algorithm

1: **procedure** GIVEN:  a two-mode network of $n$ entities with each entity $v \in V1$ that interacted at frequency $f \in V3$ with $e \in V2$.

2:    Analyse the network data to retrieve activity information of entities (i.e. using either the Sum method or Newman method).

3:    **for** Each entity $i \in V1$ **do**

4:    Evaluate trust between a entity $i \in V1$ and each entity $j \in V1$ using a probabilistic measure to form elements in activeness matrix $M_{n \times n}$

5:    **return** $M_{n \times n}$ as the activeness matrix revealing trust between $i$ and $j$.

---

## 3.1   Dataset with Social Activeness

The dataset (Two-mode dataset) used in demonstrating how to predict an entity's trustworthiness was a **Facebook-like forum dataset** which is similar to that used in previous work [2], extracted from original data used by Tore Opsahl [4]. The data reveals interaction amongst a Set of users $V1$ that share ties with a Set of items $V2$. Each $v \in V1$ represents an active user interacting at a particular frequency $f \in V3$ with an item $e \in V2$.

This type of dataset is required for analysis of social engagement to determine a trustworthy entity that could share knowledge of particular items with less active users who have never encountered these items in the past.

## 3.2   Predicting Trustworthiness

The following example will describe the application of the algorithm to a two-mode network example where similar social actors could be identified to assist in predicting the trustworthiness of a target social actor.

*Example 1.* A two-mode network data with vertices of different sets (i.e. $V_u$ and $V_s$) as shown in Table 1 represents a collaboration amongst a set of film producers (i.e. $V_1 \in V_u$ and $V_2 \in V_s$) on a certain number of movies $V_3$.

**Table 1.** Example of a Two-mode Network Data

| $V_1$ | 1 | 2 | 2 | 2 | 2 | 4 | 8 | 9 | 9 | 14 | 21 | 21 | 22 | 22 | 23 |
|---|---|---|---|---|---|---|---|---|---|---|---|---|---|---|---|
| $V_2$ | 63 | 63 | 80 | 95 | 97 | 63 | 95 | 63 | 81 | 66 | 67 | 68 | 63 | 80 | 97 |
| $V_3$ | 3 | 2 | 1 | 2 | 1 | 1 | 2 | 1 | 5 | 1 | 2 | 1 | 1 | 1 | 1 |

This type of network data can be represented in a network graph, which clearly shows each film producer's relationship and their number of collaborations is indicated as their weight on the edges.

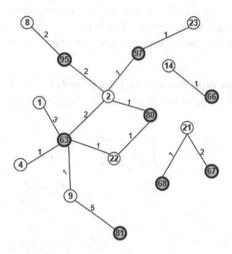

**Fig. 1.** Two-mode network graph from the given Data Example (Table 1)

Applying our proposed Trust Algorithm to this two-mode network example considers the measure of reciprocity to enable accurate comprehension of the mutual exchange of implicit ratings amongst producers based on their interaction with a set of movies from the two-mode network data. This comprehension can only be possible after the two-mode network has been transformed into a one-mode network.[2]

Considering the projection of the two-mode network using the Sum method will generate the following output:

**Table 2.** Data for a projected Two-mode Network using Sum method

| $i$ | 1 | 1 | 1 | 1 | 2 | 2 | 2 | 2 | 2 | 2 | 4 | 4 | 4 | 4 | 8 | 9 | 9 | 9 | 9 | 22 | 22 | 22 | 22 | 23 |
|---|---|---|---|---|---|---|---|---|---|---|---|---|---|---|---|---|---|---|---|---|---|---|---|---|
| $j$ | 2 | 4 | 9 | 22 | 1 | 4 | 8 | 9 | 22 | 23 | 1 | 2 | 9 | 22 | 2 | 1 | 2 | 4 | 22 | 1 | 2 | 4 | 9 | 2 |
| $w$ | 3 | 3 | 3 | 3 | 2 | 2 | 2 | 2 | 3 | 1 | 1 | 1 | 1 | 1 | 2 | 1 | 1 | 1 | 1 | 1 | 2 | 1 | 1 | 1 |

The generated one-mode network data using the Sum method (See Table 2) reveals only a network amongst the producers, where $i$ represents a producer vertex that has ties with another producer vertex $j$. Both vertices reward weights $w$ to each other based on the frequency of their collaboration on producing

---

[2] To enable the application of our proposed Trust Algorithm, R software along with **tnet** package was required to load the extracted two-mode network dataset from Tore Opsahl's original data [4].

movies; Equation 1 was used to evaluate the weights. It can be observed from the one-mode network data output that vertex 2 is more active amongst other vertices, as this vertex collaborated with every other vertex.

Based on a real-world scenario where two or more persons trust themselves, we will then consider a probabilistic approach to determine the level of trust an entity will have towards another entity. The trust level of an entity was previously modelled in [2], where it was estimated based on the probability expectation of future outcomes [5].

**Definition 2.** *The probability that a target vertex* $i \in V_u$ *will interact with another vertex* $j \in V_u$ *based on past actions towards common subject* $c \in V_s$ *is:*

$$
P^c_{i,j \in V_u} = \begin{cases} \dfrac{N^c_{ij}}{N^c_{ij} + N^c_{ji}}, & N_{ij} \neq 0 \\ 0, & N_{ij} = 0 \end{cases}
\tag{3}
$$

$$i \neq j$$
$$P_{i,j} \in [0,1] \quad \forall i,j$$
$$P_{i,j} + P_{j,i} = 1$$

**where:** $N^c_{ij}$ *is the sum of node* $i$*'s actions towards all subject* $c$ *which node* $j$ *has also acted upon.* $N^c_{ji}$ *is the sum of node* $j$*'s actions towards all subject* $c$ *which node* $i$ *has also acted upon.*

Considering only the sum-based one-mode generated network, we can easily estimate this probability as the sum of an entity's actions towards all common subjects shared with another entity, which was initially observed from a two-mode network data. Applying Eq. 3 on the sum-based one-mode generated network (See Table 2) will generate the activeness matrix of dimension $9 \times 9$ (See Fig. 2) to reveal the trust value awarded amongst the producer vertices; this indicates if a particular producer will trust to collaborate with another producer vertex in the future.

|      | [1]  | [2]  | [4]  | [8]  | [9]  | [14] | [21] | [22] | [23] |
|------|------|------|------|------|------|------|------|------|------|
| [1]  | 1.00 | 0.40 | 0.25 | 0.00 | 0.25 | 0.00 | 0.00 | 0.25 | 0.00 |
| [2]  | 0.60 | 1.00 | 0.33 | 0.50 | 0.33 | 0.00 | 0.00 | 0.40 | 0.50 |
| [4]  | 0.75 | 0.67 | 1.00 | 0.00 | 0.50 | 0.00 | 0.00 | 0.50 | 0.00 |
| [8]  | 0.00 | 0.50 | 0.00 | 1.00 | 0.00 | 0.00 | 0.00 | 0.00 | 0.00 |
| [9]  | 0.75 | 0.67 | 0.50 | 0.00 | 1.00 | 0.00 | 0.00 | 0.50 | 0.00 |
| [14] | 0.00 | 0.00 | 0.00 | 0.00 | 0.00 | 1.00 | 0.00 | 0.00 | 0.00 |
| [21] | 0.00 | 0.00 | 0.00 | 0.00 | 0.00 | 0.00 | 1.00 | 0.00 | 0.00 |
| [22] | 0.75 | 0.60 | 0.50 | 0.00 | 0.50 | 0.00 | 0.00 | 1.00 | 0.00 |
| [23] | 0.00 | 0.50 | 0.00 | 0.00 | 0.00 | 0.00 | 0.00 | 0.00 | 1.00 |

**Fig. 2.** Activeness matrix from one-mode dataset (See Table 2) Example

## 3.3   Algorithm Performance

The activeness matrix solely relies on the one-mode network, which can be generated using the Sum method. The generated matrix consists of elements derived from a probabilistic measure, which requires information on entities' frequency of interaction with subjects. Comparing the one-mode network structure with the details from the activeness matrix, it could be observed that vertex 2 has ties with all active vertices, and it had the majority of its ratings amongst these vertices greater than 0.50, which was described in previous research [2] to be the threshold for predicting that an entity will be active in the future. This output could also imply that the entity will be trustworthy to continue to be active with other social actors/items in the network. Based on the two-mode network, vertices 14 and 21 were predicted to be non-active/less trustworthy for future interaction as they did not share interactions with any other vertices in their previous activities.

## 4   Discussion and Conclusion

The study of network structure is an attractive topic, which is a useful tool for retrieving relevant information for future decision-making. This paper revealed how we could consider using the information retrieved from both a two-mode network and a one-mode network in predicting if entities will remain active to interact with other entities in the future.

In future work, a longitudinal network which considers how ties evolve over a period will further be explored in the computation of trust for an entity. Also, there will be a need to explore the possible ways of identifying if a tie between entities will strengthen or weaken. As this framework applies to a social playground of individuals, there is also the need to consider identifying the manipulative behaviour of particular individuals in future works. This will be necessary as we have these malicious actors on the internet who might manipulate stories, information or their behaviour to influence others [6].

## References

1. Bhuiyan, T.: Trust for Intelligent Recommendation. Springer, Heidelberg (2013). https://doi.org/10.1007/978-1-4614-6895-0
2. Oshodin, E.: Encouraging inactive users towards effective recommendation. Ph.D. thesis, De Montfort University, Leicester (2019)
3. Newman, M.E.: Scientific collaboration networks. II. Shortest paths, weighted networks, and centrality. Phys. Rev. E **64**(1), 016132 (2001)
4. Opsahl, T.: Triadic closure in two-mode networks: redefining the global and local clustering coefficients. Soc. Netw. **35**(2), 159–167 (2013)
5. Josang, A., Ismail, R.: The beta reputation system. In: Proceedings of the 15th Bled Electronic Commerce Conference, pp. 41–55. Citeseer (2002)
6. Carley, K.M.: Social cybersecurity: an emerging science. Comput. Math. Organ. Theory **26**(4), 365–381 (2020). https://doi.org/10.1007/s10588-020-09322-9

# A Neural Network Approach to Dragon Boat Partition Problem(Abstract)

Brett Regnier and John Z. Zhang$^{(\boxtimes)}$

University of Lethbridge, Lethbridge, AB, Canada
{brett.regnier,john.zhang}@uleth.ca

**Abstract.** We investigate approximating the Dragon Boat Partition problem, a practical real-world variant of the Integer Partition problem, using convolutional neural networks and reinforcement learning. A team of dragon boat rowers must be partitioned with an approximately balanced arrangements. We first present one variant of our approach and then demonstrate its effectiveness through experiments. We omit many technical details in this abstract.

**Keywords:** Neural Networks · Convolutional Neural Networks · Reinforcement Learning

## 1 Introduction

In this work, we present our recent progress to make use of *Convolutioal Neural Networks* (CNN) [1] to tackle a variant of the Integer Partition problem [5], the so-called *Dragon Boat Partition* (DBP). Splitting a group of items into two or more numerically equal unique groups is a prominent problem. For a list of $n$ positive integers, the problem asks for a partition such that the set is evenly split [4]. Formally, given a set $S \subset \mathbb{Z}^+$, find a partition $S_1 \subset S$, and $S_2 \subset S$ where $S_1 \cup S_2 = S$ and $S_1 \cap S_2 = \emptyset$, such that the difference, known as the *discrepancy*, $E(A) = \sum_{s \in S_1} s - \sum_{s \in S_2} s$ is minimized [4].

The original DBP problem is defined as follows. As shown in Fig. 1, a dragon boat is filled with a team of 22 members with 20 rowers sitting side by side down the boat, a steersman at the back directing the boat, and a drummer at the front facing the rest of the team [3]. Before rowers are put into the boat, in practice, the first step is to find an approximate partitioning of the rowers in desirable positions. Having a balanced dragon boat ensures that the boat is parallel with the water, allowing maximum surface area and water flow around the boat and therefore increasing boating efficiency and speed [8]. Multiple constraints must be considered. For instance, there are certain positions in the boat that each rower prefers to be in, such as the second seat on the left. After the rowers are placed in their preferred positions, the next step is to put them according to their dominant hand, such that the weight difference between the left and right sides is minimized. Then, the front and back are staffed such that the weight

© The Author(s), under exclusive license to Springer Nature Switzerland AG 2023
M. Bramer and F. Stahl (Eds.): SGAI 2023, LNAI 14381, pp. 234–240, 2023.
https://doi.org/10.1007/978-3-031-47994-6_21

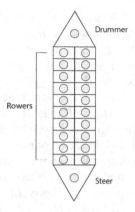

**Fig. 1.** Top down view of a dragon boat.

difference between them is close to 30 lbs, with the front-half being heavier. Lastly, the heaviest rowers should be put in the center of the boat and the weights are gradient outwards towards the front and back [8]. It is obvious that the DBP problem is a variant of the partition problem. Our primary goal is to design and implement a practical solution to investigate the DBP problem using a CNN-based approach, in conjunction with the *reinforcement learning* [1].

## 2  Problem Statement

While the Dragon Boat Partition problem (DBP) problem is not proposed by us, to our knowledge, our work is the first that attempts to handle it using convolutional neural networks. The objective of the DBP problem is to partition the rowers when staffing a dragon boat under four requirements. (1) Handed Rule (there cannot be any left-rowers on the right-side, nor any right-rowers on the left-side), (2) Left-Right Weight Rulethe left-right discrepancy must be close to the left-right optimal weight within the range of the left-right relaxation), (3) Front-Back Weight Rule (the front-back discrepancy must be as close to the front-back optimal weight, with the front heavier, within the range of the front-back relaxation), and (4) Weight Gradient Rule (the rowing participants should be graded by heaviest to lightest from the center of the board outward).

We define the left-handedness as a rower's ability to row effectively with their left hand and call them as *left-rowers*, and similarly, *right-rowers*. A rower may also have the ability to row both left-handed and right-handed, called *ambidextrous-rowers*. The left-handedness of rower is denoted as $p_l \in \{0,1\}$ and similarly the right-handedness, $p_r \in \{0,1\}$. A rower's weight, $p_w \in \mathbb{Z}^+$, is a positive integer number in pounds (lbs). Let $P$ represent the set of rowers, where rower $p \in P$ is a tuple $(p_w, p_l, p_r)$. We assume that $|P|$ is even. Let $L \subset P$ where $|L| = |P|/2$ and $\forall p \in L, p_l = 1$ denote the left group, and let $R \subset P$ where $|R| = |P|/2$ and $\forall p \in R, p_r = 1$ denote the right group. An ambidextrous rower can be in both $L$ and $R$. $F \subset P$, where $|F| = |P|/2$, denotes the front group, and $B \subset P$, where $|B| = |P|/2$, denotes the back group.

Let $L_w = \sum p_w \; \forall p_w \in L$ be the total weight of the rowers in the left-group, $R_w = \sum p_w \; \forall p_w \in R$ of the rowers in the right-group, $F_w = \sum p_w \; \forall p \in F$ of the rowers the front-group, and $B_w = \sum p_w \; \forall p_w \in B$ of the rowers in the back-group. Let $V_{lr}$ and $V_{fb}$ represent the left-right and front-back discrepancy *relaxations*, respectively. $W_{lr} = |L_w - R_w|$ is the left-right weight discrepancy while $W_{fb} = F_w - B_w$ is the front-back weight discrepancy. We use $W_{lr}^*$ to denote the left-right optimal weight discrepancy and $W_{fb}^*$ the optimal front-back weight discrepancy. It is desirable that $W_{lr}$ and $W_{fb}$ be as close to $W_{lr}^*$ and $W_{fb}^*$, respectively, as possible, under the condition of $V_{lr}$ and $V_{fb}$.

The DBP problem seeks a partition, where $|L| = |R|$, $|F| = |B|$, $L \cap R = \emptyset$, $F \cap B = \emptyset$, $L \cap (F \cup B) = L$, $R \cap (F \cup B) = R$, $(F \cap L) \cup (F \cap R) = F$, and $(B \cap L) + (B \cap R) = B$, such that $|W_{lr} - W_{lr}^*| \leq V_{lr}$ and such that $B_w < F_w$ and $|W_{fb} - W_{fb}^*| \leq V_{fb}$, where typically $W_{lr}^* = 0$ and $W_{fb}^* = 30$.

## 3    A CNN-based Approach to DBP

In our proposed approach, we make use of the *Convolutional Neural Networks* (CNN) by converting our *Dragon Boat Partition* (DBP) problem into a set of characteristics of rowers. Our approach houses three variants. But we only report the first variant in this abstract. We call it *SL-model*, which uses supervised learning in CNN. Whenever we need to find two rowers on the opposite sides of the boat to reduce the weight discrepancy, the SL-model will predict a swap operation to do so. In our discussions, we use $n$ to represent the number of rowers. We emphasize that the DBP problem does not become more difficult in our approach even if more rowers are involved, But the training time becomes exponentially longer. It would be desirable that we can deal with the DBP instances with more rowers. But our current computer hardware environment is limited. Therefore we decide to simulate and experiment our approach with small problem sizes, i.e. $n = 8$. The general process is to partition equally the rowers into the left side and right and then into the front side and back side, to meet the requirements in Sect. 2.

For the input into our CNN, from a top-down view, as shown in Fig. 1, it is clear that a dragon boat can be represented as an image, where there is a width of 2 for the columns of positions, and the height is equal to $n/2$, which $n$ is the number of rows. Each rower has 4 channels that describe their characteristics, corresponding to their weight, handedness, etc., This effectively converts a DBP instance into an image. Given $n$ rowers, we have $n/2$ rows and 2 columns with each grid (for each rower) having 4 channels. So the dimensions of a DBP instance would be $n/2 \times 2 \times 4$.

We use separate CNN architectures for our approach, as shown in Fig. 2, which contains four layers: one convolutional layer and three fully connected layers. Unlike most CNNs, we do not include a pooling layer, solely due to that our input image is small spatially and each position is vital. Pooling would

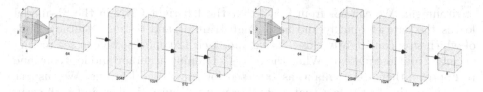

**Fig. 2.** CNN architectures used for the Left-Right phase and Front-Back phase during pretraining in supervised learning.

destroy the spatial data significantly. Also we use the *sigmoid* function [2] as the activation function. The training time on our network does suffer from the use of it, but the trade-off is worthwhile. In our attempts, no other activation functions appear to improve the final performance. To our advantage, we do not encounter the vanishing gradient problem [1]. For the reinforcement learning in our model, the most important component in reinforcement learning is the action space and rewarding functions. We propose two reward functions to fit the situation in our approach. The first reward function involves shaping the reward based on how closely the current state matches a perfect partition and a terminal state receives a reward of 10. This proves very difficult when estimating the weights, positions, and the handedness of each rower in a meaningful manner. Our second reward function is a significantly more productive, albeit far simpler, sparse reward function. A sparse reward function is where each state is given a reward of 0, except a reward of 10 on approximately optimal partition terminal states. Our reinforcement learning will converge towards finding an approximately optimal partition as only terminal states receive a positive reward. The learning strategy in our approach is the *Double Deep Q Learning* [9]. We omit the details of our CNN and learning in this abstract.

For the outputs, since they are considered as actions, we treat each action as a class label in the supervised training. For the hyperparameters [6] in our CNN, the number of layers and neurons is one of the starting points for our neural networks. The left-right CNN has 3,420,240 learnable weights and the front-back CNN has 3,416,136 learnable weights. For the learning rate in our approach, in our SL-model, we set it between 0.0004 and 0.001, with 0.001 being the best. We use *Adam* as our optimizer [1] for adjusting weights. For the training data of our experiment, unfortunately, as we are researching a niche problem, there are no large datasets available for our DBP problem. We have used a similar approach as the one in [7] to generate a dataset for our experiment. After generating state-action classes, there are 600,000 data points in our dataset and we use 70% of them for training and 30% for testing.

## 4    Results and Discussions

During our training process, the CNNs in our model are trained separately, one solely trained using a left-right boat environment, and the other front-back boat environment. We can see from Fig. 3 that the left-right CNN in the SL-model learns the dataset quickly and has a high training and testing accuracy, both of which stay consistently close. As we approach 120 epochs, we can see testing accuracy and loss plateau. While the model's training accuracy and loss continue to improve, they are stagnant, as expected for supervised learning. We suspect that this is due to the fact that each data point is quite similar, and each swap has some related consequences to others. We conduct the same training and testing for the front-back CNN, as shown in Fig. 4. However, we have a different result in this training instance. While we do allow training to continue further, resulting in the testing accuracy and loss to deteriorate, we can see the front-back phase is significantly quicker to learn, but the testing never has a second spike. We can see that after 60 epochs, the model overfits. While we see some impressive training occurring from our SL-model, it appears to perform slightly worse than the heuristic approach in [7]. Although our intuition tells that the supervised model would perform better, since it is trained on perfect partition training data only, we can see that there is still some missing context in the input. We believe the supervised learning model fails to be comparable to the heuristic approach because the latter is provided with some explicit calculations such as $W_{lr}^*$, $V_{lr}$, $W_{fb}^*$, and $V_{fb}$. In addition, the heuristic model calculates the $W_{lr}$, and $W_{fb}$ while our SL-model must implicitly discover these requirements itself, which is the advantage of our CNN-based model.

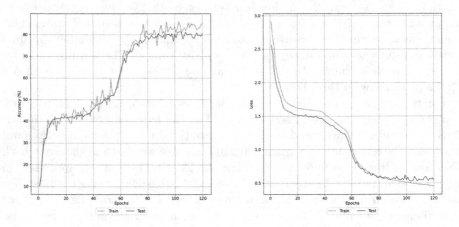

**Fig. 3.** The SL-model: left-right policy training and testing. Left: training and testing accuracy. Right: training and testing loss.

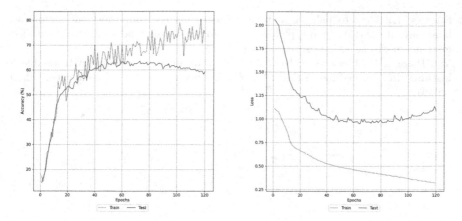

**Fig. 4.** The SL-model: front-back policy training and testing. Left: training and testing accuracy. Right: training and testing loss.

## 5   Conclusion

The Dragon Boat Partition problem, a variant of the partition problem, seeks to partition rowers such that certain constraints are met. Finding a perfect partition is a hard problem. As has been shown, our CNN-based approach successfully tackles the problem. We believe that our approach could be helpful in other incarnations of the partition problem, such as cargo configurations in freight ships. Due to the limited space, we are only able to report a portion of our work.

## References

1. Aggarwal, C.C.: Neural Networks and Deep Learning. Springer, Heidelberg (2018). https://doi.org/10.1007/978-3-319-94463-0
2. Goodfellow, I., Bengio, Y., Courville, A.: Deep Learning. MIT Press, Cambridge (2016). http://www.deeplearningbook.org
3. Health, S.: What is dragon boat racing. https://www.mountsinai.on.ca/staff/sinai-lightning/what-is-dragon-boat-racing
4. Mertens, S.: The easiest hard problem: number partitioning. Comput. Complexity Stat. Phys. **125**(2), 125–139 (2006)
5. Pedregal, P.: Introduction to Optimization, vol. 46. Springer, Heidelberg (2006)
6. Radhakrishnan, P.: What are hyperparameters and how to tune the hyperparameters in a deep neural network? (2017). https://towardsdatascience.com/what-are-hyperparameters-and-how-to-tune-the-hyperparameters-in-a-deep-neural-network-d0604917584a
7. Regnier, B., Zhang, J.: Where to put a rower: a novel and practical solution to dragon boat partition problem. In: Proceedings The 32nd Conference of Open Innovations Association (FRUCT), pp. 238–245 (2022)

8. Stickels, K.: How to balance a dragon boat: tips for your most successful race boat layout (2015). http://paddlechica.com/how-to-balance-a-dragon-boat-tips-for-your-most-successful-race-boat-layout
9. Van Hasselt, H., Guez, A., Silver, D.: Deep reinforcement learning with double q-learning. In: Proceedings of the AAAI Conference on Artificial Intelligence, vol. 30 (2016)

# Auditing AI Systems: A Metadata Approach

Carl Adams[1,2(✉)], Mohsen Eslamnejad[1,3], Anita Khadka[4], Andrew M'manga[5],
Heather Shaw[6], and Yuchen Zhao[7]

[1] Mobi Publishing, Chichester, UK
ca.mobipublishing@gmail.com
[2] Cosmopolitan University Abuja, Abuja, Nigeria
[3] University of Portsmouth, Portsmouth, UK
mohsen.eslamnejad@myport.ac.uk
[4] Northeastern University London, London, UK
anita.khadka@nulondon.ac.uk
[5] Bournemouth University, Poole, UK
ammanga@bournemouth.ac.uk
[6] Lancaster University, Bailrigg, UK
h.shaw5@lancaster.ac.uk
[7] University of York, York, UK
yuchen.zhao@york.ac.uk

**Abstract.** The EU AI regulatory framework and corresponding AI Act, call for stronger 'product safety regime' for AI development and set out requirements for more testing, transparency, and impact evaluation in AI based systems, along with significant penalties for corporations that do not follow these requirements. Similar rhetoric is emerging from the UK and USA governments. There is an immediate emerging theme within AI looking at how to test and how to audit compliance within these evolving requirements. This paper presents a metadata model to support auditing compliance and capturing key attributes of bounding of applicability of AI elements to support compliant reuse within AI systems development. The metadata model builds on the IEEE Learning Object Metadata (LOM) model standard to develop the AI-LOM, which provides a base for compliance within the ISTQB' AI Development Framework' covering testing of AI.

**Keywords:** Testing AI · Auditing AI · Metadata

## 1 Introduction

The testing and auditing of AI based technology is becoming a prominent topic within the AI field. This has been driven internally striving to achieve better and more robust AI systems as well as externally with concerns about and demand for more transparent and testable AI systems (Goa et al. 2019).

This work-in-progress paper focuses on auditability of AI systems, sub-systems and elements, and of providing a base for identifying bounds of applicability of such elements. It is hoped that this will support auditable reuse of AI elements by providing

M. Bramer and F. Stahl (Eds.): SGAI 2023, LNAI 14381, pp. 241–246, 2023.
https://doi.org/10.1007/978-3-031-47994-6_22

a verifiable mechanism to show provenance and suitability on the key attributes of an AI's component elements.

The EU legal framework on AI (EU 2023) takes a proportionate risk assessment approach to AI, that will develop human-centric, sustainable, secure, inclusive, and trustworthy AI systems. Similarities towards responsible AI development have emerged in the USA with the introduction of the AI Bill of Rights (Whitehouse 2022). Within the EU's risk-based approach they identify four categories based on level of risk: Unacceptable risk (AI systems considered a clear threat to the safety, livelihoods & rights of people will be banned), High-risk (AI within safety-critical systems or that would significantly impact people's lives), Limited risk (AI systems with specific transparency obligations, such as chatbots where people can make informed decision to use or not) and, Minimal risk (such as AI-enabled video games and spam filters). They envisage that the vast majority of current AI systems would be classed as minimal risk.

The evolution and applications of AI are evolving and expanding with expectation that more AI based systems will move into the limited and high-risk categories in the future. The high-risk AI systems will be subject to strict obligations before they can be put on the market which would include:

- "Adequate risk assessment and mitigation systems;
- High quality of the datasets feeding the system to minimise risks and discriminatory outcomes;
- Logging of activity to ensure traceability of results;
- Detailed documentation providing all information necessary on the system and its purpose for authorities to assess its compliance;
- Clear and adequate information to the user;
- Appropriate human oversight measures to minimise risk;
- High level of robustness, security and accuracy." (EU 2023)

Of note, high level risk classification includes all remote biometric identification systems, critical infrastructures (e.g. transport), safety components of products (e.g. robot-assisted surgery), systems that may determine the access to education and professional courses or employment (e.g. scoring of exams or CVs), essential private and public services, law enforcement that may interfere with people's fundamental rights and, migration, asylum and border control management systems.

For AI systems that fall into high-risk classifications, they will need to be auditable systems to show compliance within the EU guidelines. One approach to achieve this is to use metadata, effectively a standard set of data about the AI elements that quantify the relevant validation, testing, and other attributes (Gao et al 2019; Adams 2023). The ISTQB (2021) AI development framework gives some guidance on what the range of AI element attributes would consist of. Having standard metadata would provide a base to show the provenance of each of the elements used to make the AI system and show that they are appropriate and suitable for a particular application. Effectively they would capture the key elements showing the bounds of applicability for that AI system (e.g. context of training data).

The rest of this paper explores options for suitable metadata systems, then focuses on the LOM metadata standard, then explores the extra AI elements that would need to be included, and finishes with a presentation of the developed AI-LOM, the discussion and limitations.

## 2  Metadata Options

There are two main options to develop metadata to support AI auditing: One is to develop a set of metadata from scratch and the other is to take an existing metadata standard and evolve it to accommodate the distinct attributes of AI systems and elements.

There are advantages to taking an existing standard, particularly in that we would be starting with a tried and tested base, and it would already capture important elements such as application, creation, ownership, and sub elements. There will also be existing software and systems that would support an existing standard.

The approach taken in this research is to adopt an existing metadata standard and expand it for application to AI systems and elements. There are several existing metadata specifications and standards. A prominent one is the Dublin Core Metadata Set, particularly the Simple Dublin Core (the ANSI Z39.85 - 2001 standard), aimed at the education community. A similar standard, which is also used at the education domain, is the Learning Object Metadata (LOM) standard IEEE 1484.12.1 - 2002.

Of particular interest with the LOM is the power to capture a wide range of attributes covering learning objects that would make up a course or learning system, and the ability to combine the metadata for sub-components and retain those in developing the metadata for the whole course or programme of study. For instance, it can capture items such as who created the learning object(s), licensing and reuse elements, technical aspects, format aspects, data aspects, time stamp and relevance aspects, and application area aspects. So a case study involving the set of learning activities for developing a simple computer program to book in patients in a dentist, might have multiple metadata items covering the application domain (e.g. dentistry system requirements within a particular content - country, city, public/private; number of people, number of users), covering the technology used (e.g. programming language - and attributes of the language being explored, the development environment/platform), testing requirements (test specifications) and, datasets to use (e.g. patient records templates, sample dataset; booking system structures).

For this research, the LOM standard is chosen as the base metadata standard to adapt to the AI development content for the reasons above and the flexibility afforded in enhancing and extending the structure to accommodate changes (such as being able to accommodate new technologies). Also of particular interest with the LOM standard is the ability to stack or combine the metadata for learning objects together, which allows reuse of the elements and building up of multiple learning objects into bigger learning objects (e.g. a whole lesson), and even into a whole system of objects (e.g. a whole course). The schematic representation of the LOM is given in Fig. 1.

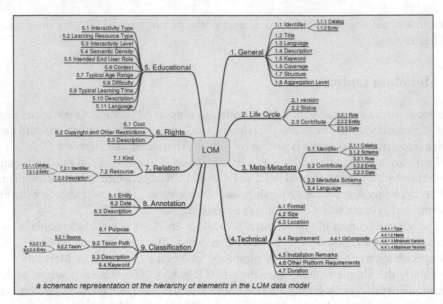

Fig. 1. LOM Schematic, from IEEE LOM standards brief (Barker 2002)

## 3 LOM to AI-LOM: Extra Elements for AI

The LOM standard is aimed at objects that would contribute to a learning system, such as a whole course, a set of learning activities, tutorials, lectures, or an exam, test or coursework. There is likely an overlap on metadata items with AI elements and systems, however there will also be extra attributes that would need to be incorporated. This section examines those extra AI elements to be incorporated. These would mostly fit within an extra set of classifications in the LOM schematic branching off under "10.x AI Elements". Extra AI metadata elements would include attributes related to the technology and development frameworks used, testing activities (including testing datasets and results), bounds of applicability and limitations, datasets used and application details. These would include AI development framework attributes, AI technologies attributes, application attributes, and provenance, testing, and limitations.

The above suggested AI-LOM provides a base to capture AI relevant metadata to support appropriate reuse, auditability, and general compliance to EU legal framework on AI (EU 2023). There is a growing and imminent need for approaches to show compliance towards the EU legal framework and emerging legislation, originally expected to come into force in September 2023, since the penalties for non-compliance could be significant with bigger fines than non-compliance to GDPR (Wright 2023).

## 4 Discussion and Limitations

The AI classification at a high-level needs further discussion. The vast majority of AI systems have been and will likely be the Narrow/Weak AI varieties based on very specific sets of tasks. These would include the voice interface apps and assistants (e.g. Google

Assistant, Siri, Alexa), customer-service chatbots, pattern or image recognition software, facial recognition software, game-playing systems, spam filters, test case generators, complex data analytics of machines performance, or a range of very specific well defined AI applications.

The General AI or Strong AI would have more general or wide-ranging 'cognitive' abilities closer to human cognition. These would imply some level of reasoning and 'understanding' of their environment, much as humans do. It is often described as an AI system that is equal in intelligence to a human. However, this gross yes/no approach to classifying Strong AI is perhaps not very useful, especially when one considers the aggregation of multiple attributes that make up the very complex embodiment of human cognition. The works on (human) consciousness (Chambers 2010, 2013; Varela and Engel 1997, Shear and Varela 1999; Adams 2013a, and others - see Blackmore 2005) point to the need for more granulated attributes of AI intelligence and consciousness. For instance, in recognising 'self', in recognising 'others' and different types of 'others', in context assessment, and in self-awareness within a context, similarly with different attributes of sensory inputs, and varieties in these, and different approaches to sensory transductions (Fain 2003). Different combinations of these different attributes would produce a mix of Strong AI cognitive systems, and would probably result in much scientific and philosophical debate on whether a level of Strong AI has been reached. Similarly, there is a lack of granularity when considering the classification of 'Super AI systems' that would have capabilities exceeding those of humans, the point at which AI-based systems transition from general AI to super AI which has been referred to as the technological singularity (Bostrom 2016, Adams 2013b). The singularity is not likely to be one event but a series of several singularities where different aspects of intelligence, cognition, and human capability are surpassed by AI systems. For instance, in spatial awareness, in extended sensory capability and awareness, in language and context awareness, in emotions awareness, in temporal awareness, in empathy and wider human perception. Again, the combination of these different attributes of Super AI elements would result in different types of Super AI singularities. Consequently, the proposed AI-LOM will likely require further consideration and extension as AI moves more into the Strong AI and Super AI categories.

There are several further areas of limitations in this work. There are clearly areas for refinement. For instance, some of the original education object related items may in the fullness of time be removed as not relevant to AI. Similarly, the evolution of AI technologies, application and sciences would require further metadata elements to be included. The AI-LOM will evolve as it is applied to more AI elements and systems. As discussed in the paper, there are multiple existing metadata schemas and standards, with the IEEE LOM being just one example that seems to fit many aspects of AI elements and systems. However, other metadata models may prove to be more appropriate to AI, or indeed it may evolve to generate a distinct model.

AI is a very dynamic field. It is in a state of hyper competition with large commercial and technology companies and governments vying for supremacy. This will ensure that the nature of AI will continually evolve, and what was the forefront of AI will become the norm in the use of AI based systems. This is known as the AI Effect (Geist 2016) and will have consequences for any metadata we may want to attach to AI elements and systems. Just as we have tried to include 'use by' details of data in the elements, perhaps whole segments of the AI-LOM will have its own 'use-by' attributes to reflect this dynamism. The next stage of this research is to retrofit existing examples of AI systems to the AI-LOM metadata, and to apply the AI-LOM during the development of a complex AI system (the use of AI to support processing of migrant data). Hopefully the application of AI-LOM to these and other AI systems will evolve the metadata model to provide a good fit of metadata for AI systems and to fulfil some of the requirements of the emerging EU legal framework on AI. Further aspects of the work will explore how AI metadata can be applied to the concepts of Strong AI and Super AI systems.

**Acknowledgements.** This research was supported by UKRI Transformative Tech. Grant No.10074452.

# References

Adams, C.: Unpicking consciousness: Break away from human-only view. In: The 12th Conference on Towards the Science of Consciousness Conference, Dayalbagh, Agra, India (2013a)

Adams, C.: Rethinking the consciousness and intelligence singularity. In: The 12th Conference on Towards the Science of Consciousness Conference, Dayalbagh, Agra, India (2013b)

Barker, J.: What is IEEE Learning Object Metadata. CETIS. (2002). http://publications.cetis.org.uk/wp-content/uploads/2011/02/WhatIsIEEELOM.pdf

Bostrom, N.: Superintelligence: Paths, Dangers, Strategie. OUP (2016)

Chalmers, D.J.: The character of consciousness. OUP (2010)

Chalmers, D.J.: How can we construct a science of consciousness? In: Michael, G (Ed.) The Cog. Neurosciences III, pp.1111–1120 (2013). https://doi.org/10.1111/nyas.12166

EU AI (2023). AI regulatory Framework. From https://digital-strategy.ec.europa.eu/en/policies/regulatory-framework-ai

EU AI Act EU Artificial Intelligence Act: The European Approach to AI (2023). https://futurium.ec.europa.eu/

Gao, J., Tao, C., Jie, D., Lu, S.: Invited paper: what is AI SOFTWARE testing? and why. In: 2019 IEEE International Conference on Service-Oriented System Engineering (SOSE), San Francisco, CA, USA, pp. 27–2709 (2019). https://doi.org/10.1109/SOSE.2019.00015

Geist, E.M.: It's already too late to stop the AI arms race—we must manage it instead. Bull. At. Scientists **72**(5), 318–321 (2016)

ISTQB Certified Tester AI Testing (CT-AI) Syllabus Version 1.0 (2021). https://astqb.org/assets/documents/ISTQB_CT-AI_Syllabus_v1.0.pdf

Shear, J., Varela, F.J.: The View from Within: First-person Approaches to the Study consciousness. Imprint Academic (1999)

Varela, F.J., Engel, J.: Sleeping, Dreaming, and Dying: An Exploration of Consciousness. Wisdom Publications (1997)

Wright, J.: AI testing. BCS Software Testing Interest Group Conference. London (2023)

Whitehouse (2022). https://www.whitehouse.gov/ostp/ai-bill-of-rights/

# Prospective Responsibility for Multi-agent Systems

Joe Collenette[(✉)][iD], Louise Dennis[iD], and Michael Fisher[iD]

Department of Computer Science, University of Manchester, Manchester, UK
joe.collenette@manchester.ac.uk

**Abstract.** The notion of 'responsibility' as a higher-level construct that dynamically impacts each agent's goals, priorities and actions is very appealing, especially since humans regularly use such concepts in everyday reasoning. In this paper we describe a new model of responsibilities that is philosophically-grounded. We identify traits from the philosophical literature to model, focusing on *prospective* responsibility and task responsibility. These responsibilities comprise heterogeneous entities, including tasks to be completed, properties that need to be maintained, and sub-responsibilities that need to be fulfilled.

**Keywords:** Multi-agent Systems · Responsibility · Decision Making

## 1 Introduction

Responsibilities represent an appealing way of reasoning about who should be doing what at a high level and what actions we want to take to fulfil our responsibilities. In addition they can decentralise group decision-making and have the ability to contextualise actions without dictating exactly which action should be done. In this paper we consider whether we can construct a model of responsibility that encompasses features of this concept, as identified in Philosophy. To identify these features we analysed the philosophical literature concerning responsibilities, focusing will be on *prospective* responsibility and, specifically, *task responsibility. Prospective responsibility* deals with how responsibility affects future choices, while *task responsibility* concerns what needs to be done and who is responsible for doing it.

We provide a model of agent responsibilities including sub-responsibilities that need to be fulfilled, and new responsibilities generated when a particular responsibility fails. A responsibility is associated with a task, as well as the sub-responsibilities. A task consists of a number (possibly zero) of actions that need to be achieved, as well a number (possibly zero) of desired states of the world to be brought about. The agents are able to reason about which responsibility they 'care' about most in order to decide what actions they wish to do (or not do). The agents can also decide to delegate some responsibility to other agents.

A key contribution of the paper is the identification of a number of traits that should be included in computational models of responsibility in order for the model to be an accurate reflection of current philosophical understanding.

M. Bramer and F. Stahl (Eds.): SGAI 2023, LNAI 14381, pp. 247–252, 2023.
https://doi.org/10.1007/978-3-031-47994-6_23

## 2    Background

Generally responsibilities can be split into *prospective* and *retrospective* responsibilities. Retrospective responsibilities focus on who was responsible and/or accountable, after a particular outcome [12]. Prospective responsibilities focus on who is currently responsible for achieving an outcome that has not already happened. Informally, a prospective 'responsibility' captures the answer to "who is to do what someone needs to do?" [3], or more formally, "A ought to see to it that X" [7,10,12]. Responsibilities do not define *what* actions need to be taken; the agent is free to decide what actions should be utilised to fulfil a responsibility; 'duties' and 'obligations' are similar but they ascribe specific or possible actions that can be taken [3,10]. A basic formalisation of prospective responsibility is a structure comprising: the agent that is responsible; the activity or condition the agent is responsible for; a representation of who the agent is responsible to; and from what grounds the responsibility has arisen [13].

Key features of prospective responsibility include that there are a number of different ways of focusing responsibilities, such as task [10], legal [7,11], and moral [2,9,16] responsibilities. The outcome of a given responsibility is not always binary; they can be partially fulfilled. *Fixed-target responsibilities* have clear binary outcomes, *Receding-target responsibilities* may be able to approximately, or partially, fulfil some outcome(s) [10]. Taking on a responsibility can lead to further responsibilities being adopted [3]. If a responsibility fails, then a new responsibility can arise which the agent takes on [1]. Multiple agents can work on the same responsibility [15]. When an agent has a responsibility they may be able to delegate the responsibility to another agent [3,10,12]. The agent is considered to have fulfilled the responsibility if the agent they delegated a responsibility to has fulfilled the responsibility in their place. Agents can delegate parts of a responsibility, or other responsibilities that arise from taking on the initial responsibility [3].

Crucially, an agent can choose to take on a responsibility [6], reason about how much it cares about fulfilling it, its priority [1,7], and if it is capable of fulfilling it [1,11].

### 2.1    Related Work

There are a number of areas of Computer Science which focus on similar themes of organising tasks among a group of agents, in particular extensive work on norms, obligations, and organisations [5,12] looks at how we can scaffold frameworks within which multiple agents can co-operate. As responsibilities are distinct from obligations and norms [1,3,4,11], a key distinguishing feature of responsibilities being the non-centralised decision making process. Approaches to modelling responsibilities in agents often focus on retrospective responsibility and aim to say who is responsible for what has already happened [8,14]. Responsibilities have also been integrated with norms and roles in normative agent systems [4], in this work responsibilities allow agents to chose to do or not do some action. Our contribution is to provide a model of responsibility that can be justified by a more holistic view of the concept of prospective responsibility as derivable from Philosophy.

## 3   Prospective Responsibility Model

We have identified the features from the philosophical literature that we wish to model: responsibilities can be decomposed into sub-responsibilities [3]; responsibilities can apply to multiple agents or individual agents [1], and responsibilities can be shared [13] among the agents; responsibilities can be compared based on which is most important to the agent [7]; agents should be able to reason about whether they do (or do not) 'care' about a given responsibility as well as the degree to which they 'care' [1]; whether a responsibility is fulfilled can be non-binary [10], and responsibilities can be partially fulfilled; agents should be able to delegate their responsibilities to other agents [12]; agents should know whether a responsibility is internal to itself, or external and affects other agents [15]; an agent should be able to decide whether they take on a responsibility [3,7]; an agent should reason about whether it has the capacity to fulfil that responsibility [12]; how a responsibility is fulfilled is up to the agent, and not obligated by the responsibility [3,10].

Responsibilities can arise from a variety of sources, including: an agent's role; an agent's liability [11]; tasks [12]; agreements; and the environment itself [1].

We assume a standard first-order logical language, $\mathcal{L}$, built from constants, variables, terms, and formulae, with the standard connectives and quantifiers: $\wedge, \vee, \neg, =, \implies, \forall, \exists$. We are working with a system $\Gamma$ which contains a set of agents $Agr_\Gamma$ and a set of responsibilities, $Res_\Gamma$ (to be defined). Since we focus on *task responsibility* we begin with the definition of a task.

**Definition 1.** *A task is a tuple $\langle Actions, States \rangle$ where Actions is a set of actions that need to be completed and States are a set of Linear Temporal Logic (LTL) statements which must hold in the environment for the task to be completed.*

Here an action describes things that need to be done. The actions described are at a higher level than the actions available to the agent.

Either *Actions* or *States* may be empty. For example, throwing of a ball: $task = \langle \{throwball\}, \emptyset \rangle$. The use of LTL allows us to describe more abstract tasks.

**Definition 2.** *A responsibility $res \in Res_\Gamma$ is a tuple $\langle RSub, task, RFail, length \rangle$, Where RSub is a set of sub responsibilities, task is a task per Definition 1, RFail is a set of responsibilities that arise when the responsibility fails, and length is a constant in the set $\{repeat, oneshot\}$.*

The length of responsibility relates to what happens when the responsibility is fulfilled: *oneshot* responsibilities when fulfilled can be discarded, *repeat* responsibilities are reset when fulfilled, and will need to be repeatedly fulfilled. The responsibilities modelled here are task responsibilities, other representations for other kinds of responsibilities such moral/legal can be included.

**Definition 3.** *An* assignee *is an element of* $\mathcal{P}(Ag_\Gamma) \cup Res_\Gamma \cup \{env, initial\}$, *where* $\mathcal{P}$ *represents the power set construction, and* $env, initial$ *are symbols representing the environment and the initial assignment of a responsibility respectively.*

**Definition 4.** *For some system* $\Gamma$, *some agent,* $ag \in Ag_\Gamma$, *and responsibility* $res \in Res_\Gamma$ *we write* $\Gamma \models accepts(ag, res)$ *if ag has accepted res*

**Definition 5.** $\Gamma \models assigment(assignee, res, Ag)$ *when assignee has assigned the responsibility res to the set of agents Ag and* $\Gamma \models \forall ag \in Ag.\ accepts(ag, res)$ **if** $\Gamma \models delegated(ag, res, Ag')$ **then** $\Gamma \models assignment(Ag, res, Ag')$ **where** $ag \in Ag$

Here, *assignment* represents the fact that a responsibility *res* has been assigned to an agent or group of agents *Ag* by the (group of) *assignee*(s). Furthermore, *assignment* only holds when the agent has (or, agents have) accepted the responsibility. An agent is free to reject an assignment in which case *assignment* does not hold. Delegation is a special case of the assignment function. An agent has delegated a responsibility if there is an assignment where that agent is in the group of assignees and the agent or group of agents the responsibility has been assigned to have accepted it.

Responsibility functions available to the agent are: a 'care' function, a capacity function, a failed responsibility function, and partially fulfilled responsibility function.

**Definition 6.** *The function* $care : (Ag_\Gamma, Res_\Gamma) \to \mathbb{R}$ *captures how strongly an agent cares about a responsibility. Thus* $care(ag, res)$ *represents the degree to which ag cares about res.*

**Definition 7.** $\Gamma \models ach(ag, action)$ *if* $ag \in Ag_\Gamma$ *can perform action action and* $\Gamma \models ach(ag, state)$ *if* $ag \in Ag_\Gamma$ *is capable of bringing about state, state.*

**Definition 8.**
$\Gamma \models capacity(Ag, \langle RSub, task, RFail, l \rangle) = \Gamma \models capacity(Ag, task)$ *where* $task \equiv \langle Actions, States \rangle$ *when the set of agents* $Ag \subseteq Ag_\Gamma$ *can achieve all the actions and states in the task.*

$$capacity(Ag, task) = \begin{cases} \forall ac \in Actions.\ \exists ag \in Ag.ach(ag, ac) \text{ \textbf{and}} \\ \forall st \in States.\ \exists ag \in Ag.ach(ag, st) \end{cases}$$

The care function allows an agent to reason about how much they care about a responsibility in terms of a real number. The agent is free to chose how they calculate this. Agents are capable of achieving a responsibility when they can achieve the task.

A responsibility is fulfilled if its associated task and sub-responsibilities have been fulfilled. A task is fulfilled when all actions have been achieved and all states are true. A failed task means there is no agent or group of agents that have the capacity to fulfil the responsibility.

**Definition 9.** $\Gamma \models failed(task)$ if, $\Gamma \models \neg\exists Ag \subseteq Ag_\Gamma.capacity(Ag, task)$

**Definition 10.** $\Gamma \models ach(action)$ if action has been successfully performed. $\Gamma \models ach(state)$ if $env_\Gamma \models state$ (recall that state is an LTL formula).

**Definition 11.** $\Gamma \models partial\_fulfill(task)$ if $task = \langle Actions, States \rangle$ and for all action $\in$ Actions either the action has been performed or there is no $ag \in Ag_\Gamma$ such that $\Gamma \models ach(ag, action)$ and for all state $\in$ States either the state has been achieved for there is no $ag \in Ag_\Gamma$ such that $\Gamma \models ach(ag, state)$. The function partial : task $\rightarrow \mathbb{Z}$ measures the extent to which a task has been fulfilled.

$$partial(task) = \frac{ach\_count(Actions) + ach\_count(States)}{|Actions| + |States|}$$

Where for some set $S$ of actions or states $ach\_count(S) = |\{s \in S | \Gamma \models ach(s)\}|$. Note that if task has succeeded then $partial(task) = 1$

A task is partially fulfilled when some actions and states have been achieved and all others have failed. A responsibility has been fulfilled when the task and all sub-responsibilities have been fulfilled A responsibility has failed when the task and all sub-responsibilities have failed, defined as:

**Definition 12.** $\Gamma \models failed(res)$ where $res = \langle RSub, task, RFail, l \rangle$ when $\forall rsub \in RSub. \Gamma \models failed(rsub) \wedge \Gamma \models failed(task)$

A partial fulfilment of a responsibility relates to the proportion of subresponsibilities that have failed or been fulfilled and whether the task has been fulfilled, partially fulfilled, or failed.

**Definition 13.** $\Gamma \models partial(res)$ where $res = \langle RSub, task, RFail, l \rangle$.

$$partial(res) = \begin{cases} \frac{\frac{\Sigma_{r \in RSub} partial(r)}{|RSub|} + partial(task)}{2} & if |RSub| > 0 \\ partial(task) \ otherwise \end{cases}$$

A full JAVA implementation of this model, an experimental environment involving a cleaning scenario together with raw results of the model's performance within the environment are available at https://github.com/JoeCol/ResponsibilitySimulation.

## 4   Conclusion

We have described a new model of responsibility which focuses on *prospective* responsibility and *task* responsibility. To ground the model of responsibility in the philosophy literature, we identified a number of features which the model should exhibit. What actions an agent takes in order to fulfil its responsibilities is up to that individual agent a responsibility does not dictate what actions must be taken.

**Acknowledgements.** For the purpose of open access, the author has applied a Creative Commons Attribution (CC BY) licence to any Author Accepted Manuscript version arising. All data supporting this study is provided in Sect. 3, and at the GitHub repository https://github.com/JoeCol/ResponsibilitySimulation This work is supported in the UK both by EPSRC, through the "Computational Agent Responsibility" project, and by the Royal Academy of Engineering, through its "Chair in Emerging Technologies" scheme.

# References

1. Björnsson, G., Brülde, B.: Normative responsibilities: structure and sources. In: Hens, K., Cutas, D., Horstkötter, D. (eds.) Parental Responsibility in the Context of Neuroscience and Genetics. ILELNM, vol. 69, pp. 13–33. Springer, Cham (2017). https://doi.org/10.1007/978-3-319-42834-5_2
2. Braham, M., Van Hees, M.: An anatomy of moral responsibility. Mind **121**(483), 601–634 (2012). https://doi.org/10.1093/mind/fzs081
3. Calhoun, C.: XI-Responsibilities and Taking on Responsibility. In: Proceedings of the Aristotelian Society, vol. 119(3), pp. 231–251. Oxford University Press (2019). https://doi.org/10.1093/arisoc/aoz017
4. Derakhshan, F., Bench-Capon, T., McBurney, P.: Dynamic assignment of roles, rights and responsibilities in normative multi-agent systems. J. Log. Comput. **23**(2), 355–372 (2013). https://doi.org/10.1093/logcom/exr027
5. Dignum, V., Dignum, F.: A logic of agent organizations. Logic J. IGPL **20**(1), 283–316 (2012). https://doi.org/10.1093/jigpal/jzr041
6. Enoch, D.: Being Responsible, Taking Responsibility, and Penumbral Agency. Oxford University Press, Oxford (2012)
7. Feinberg, J.: Responsibility for the future. Philos. Res. Arch. **14**, 93–113 (1988). https://doi.org/10.5840/pra1988/19891427
8. Glavaničová, D., Pascucci, M.: Alternative semantics for normative reasoning with an application to regret and responsibility. Logic Logical Philos. **30**(4), 653–679 (2021). https://doi.org/10.12775/LLP.2021.023
9. Glavaničová, D., Pascucci, M.: Making sense of vicarious responsibility: moral philosophy meets legal theory. Erkenntnis, pp. 1–22 (2022). https://doi.org/10.1007/s10670-022-00525-x
10. Goodin, R.E.: Utilitarianism as a Public Philosophy. Cambridge Studies in Philosophy and Public Policy, Cambridge University Press, Cambridge (1995). https://doi.org/10.1017/CBO9780511625053
11. Hart, H.L.A.: Punishment and Responsibility?: Essays in the Philosophy of Law, 2nd edn. Oxford University Press, Oxford (2008)
12. Van der Hoek, W., Wooldridge, M.: Cooperation, knowledge, and time: alternating-time temporal epistemic logic and its applications. Stud. Logica. **75**(1), 125–157 (2003). https://doi.org/10.1023/A:1026185103185
13. Neuhäuser, C.: Structural injustice and the distribution of forward-looking responsibility. Midwest Studies Philos. **38**, 232–251 (2014). https://doi.org/10.1111/misp.12026
14. Oddie, G., Tichy̌, P.: The logic of ability, freedom and responsibility. Stud. Logica. **41**(2), 227–248 (1982). https://doi.org/10.1007/BF00370346
15. Schmidtz, D., Goodin, R.E., Goodin, R.E., et al.: Social Welfare and Individual Responsibility. Cambridge University Press, Cambridge (1998)
16. Talbert, M.: Moral Responsibility: An Introduction. Polity Press, Cambridge (2016)

# Fighting Lies with Intelligence: Using Large Language Models and Chain of Thoughts Technique to Combat Fake News

Waleed Kareem[✉] and Noorhan Abbas

University of Leeds, Leeds, UK
od21wk@leeds.ac.uk

**Abstract.** The proliferation of fake news in the digital age presents a substantial challenge, outpacing the capabilities of conventional fact-checking methods. To address this, we introduce a pioneering strategy that utilizes fine-tuned Large Language Models (LLMs) for discerning fake news through the generation of logical reasoning that validates or critiques news headlines. This strategy seamlessly merges the predictive prowess of LLMs with the requisite for coherent explanations, facilitating not only the detection of fake news but also offering transparent, reasoned justifications for each classification. Leveraging the inherent "Chain of Thought" (CoT) reasoning and model distillation processes of pre-trained LLMs, our approach enhances detection accuracy while rendering the models' complex decisions accessible to human understanding. This research signifies a groundbreaking contribution, extending beyond mere methodological progress by presenting an open-source dataset fortified with CoT annotations, establishing a new benchmark for fake news detection. This dataset, consisting of a diverse mixture of human-annotated news and those generated under human-guided contexts using the OpenAI GPT 3.5 model, promises to be a valuable resource for future scholarly endeavours in the field. By optimizing two distinct LLMs (FLAN-T5 and Llama-2), our methodology demonstrates unprecedented efficacy, surpassing the existing state-of-the-art results by 11.9% and elevating the overall performance of LLMs in fake news detection.

**Keywords:** Fake News Detection · LLM · COT

## 1 Introduction and Background

In the digital age, the rapid spread of fake news seriously threatens democracy, public health, and societal trust, potentially altering electoral outcomes and impeding crisis responses, including during the COVID-19 pandemic [3, 4]. This research endeavors to mitigate the far-reaching impacts of misinformation by harnessing the latest advances in Natural Language Processing (NLP) for more effective fake news detection. Utilizing LLMs such as FLAN-t5 and Llama-2, trained extensively on substantial text datasets, this study seeks to discern linguistic patterns and nuances integral to detecting misleading narratives. Incorporating the CoT framework, we aim to foster transparency and

© The Author(s), under exclusive license to Springer Nature Switzerland AG 2023
M. Bramer and F. Stahl (Eds.): SGAI 2023, LNAI 14381, pp. 253–258, 2023.
https://doi.org/10.1007/978-3-031-47994-6_24

user trust in fake news detection by mimicking structured human reasoning processes, thus addressing vital issues in AI interpretability [1]. While initial mitigation efforts had limitations, modern techniques employing sentiment analysis and deep learning models promise superior accuracy in combatting evolving fake news narratives. Notably, a deeper understanding of linguistic nuances and visual cues has been highlighted as pivotal in enhancing detection mechanisms, despite the persistent challenges posed by sophisticated misinformation generators [5, 6, 8, 9]. This study underscores a continual need for innovation in the sector to keep pace with the changing tactics of fake news creators.

## 2   Methodology

This study adopted a rigorous data collection and processing methodology, involving data gathering from online sources, data generation using a pre-trained LLM, and then the refinement of these data using supplementary datasets. We detail the various stages of this process in the sections below.

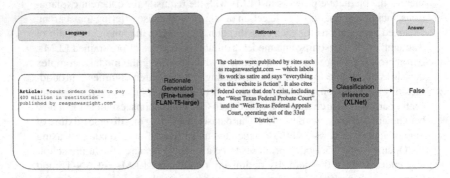

**Fig. 1.** An overview of the fact checking process

The flowchart in Fig. 1 maps out the fact checking process. First, we generate the rationale using the news headlines as an input to the fine-tuned LLM, then the generated text is used as an input to the final classification stage. The figure illustrates the intricate processes of data augmentation, model distillation, and text classification, which assist in visually grasping the complexity and coherence of our methodology. The initial dataset was procured from the PolitiFact.com website. This dataset encapsulates a variety of political news, including the headline, the source of the headline, and an accompanying article that provides a substantiation for the veracity of the news—categorised as true, mostly true, half true, or false.

### 2.1   Data Augmentation Using a LLM

The raw data collected from Politifact was augmented utilizing the OpenAI GPT-3.5 LLM, generating CoT justifications which are grounded in the headlines and details of each article. The following carefully crafted query was utilised for this purpose:

```
query = f"""
You are a political fact checking auditor, your job is to provide
logical reasoning for why a certain news article is either true,
half-true, false, flip-flop, pants-fire or partially true. Your
reasoning should be a paragraph of a minimum of 70 words and a
maximum of 150 words
Statement: {claim}
Conclusion: {label}
Background: {context}
Task: Write a step-by-step logical summary in a paragraph to jus-
tify the conclusion based on the statement ONLY. The background
section is only provided to help with the conclusion, ignore any
irrelevant information in this section. Do NOT refer to anything
in the context when building the summary. Start the justifica-
tion right away without quoting the statement or conclusion again
logical summary paragraph (no bullet points):
"""
```

The query has three variables: the claim, which represents the news headline; the label determined by the human auditor, which is one of 6 labels (true, false, mostly-true, barely-true, half-true and pants-on-fire) and the context, which represents the article that explains the label in detail. This process is akin to a form of 'model distillation', where we generate new data (the CoT justifications) that are highly informative and provide additional layers of depth to the dataset. It also helps to minimise the reliance on data types that could introduce unwanted noise or bias into the subsequent analysis.

In essence, model distillation is a form of transfer learning that, in our case, aims to compress the knowledge from a larger, more complex model (the teacher model - GPT-3) into a smaller, more manageable model (the student model). The distillation process occurs during the generation of the CoT information. Here, the LLM processes the contextual information from the news articles, and then provides detailed, logically coherent justification for the veracity of the news, thus creating a distilled knowledge representation. Through this distillation process, we created an enriched dataset consisting of 8597 CoT justifications [7]. These effectively serve as distilled knowledge representations that capture the complex reasoning process of the LLM, offering a deeper, more nuanced understanding of the news articles. We elaborate further on this process and its implications in the next section. The dataset was then supplemented by scientific misconception and facts to achieve a balance between the true and fake records.

## 2.2 Fine-Tuning LLM and Developing the Classification Model

Once the dataset was refined and balanced, we employed it to fine-tune smaller LLMs. We selected two distinct LLM architectures: FLAN-T5 LLM by Google and Llama-2 LLM by Meta, owing to their high performance in language tasks, noted by Llama-2's top rank on the Hugging Face Open LLM Leaderboard at the time of this study[1]. FLAN-T5 stands out for its adaptable architecture, facilitating ease in tuning across various NLP tasks, while Llama-2 excels in reasoning and handling extended contexts,

---

[1] https://huggingface.co/spaces/HuggingFaceH4/open_llm_leaderboard.

essential for generating news headline justifications. Additionally, FLAN-T5's previous fine-tuning on the CoT dataset [10] augments its ability to craft logical justifications. For each architecture, we experimented with different model sizes in terms number of parameters. Initially, we fine-tuned T5-large (738M), x-large (3B), and T5-xxl (11B) using the Hugging Face 'Transformer' library and PyTorch framework. This was followed by fine-tuning Llama-2-7b (7B) and Llama-2-13b (13B). A pivotal aspect of our experimentation was tasking these student models with generating CoT (provide definition or context) justifications based on news titles and headlines. The objective was to endow the language model with the capability to reason about and justify the veracity of a news headline, enhancing the sophistication of our approach. By leveraging model distillation, we transferred the reasoning and justification abilities of the GPT-3 model (176B) to a simpler classification model. This procedure enables the capture of essential features learned by the language model for detecting fake news. Consequently, our distilled model serves as a practical, deployable tool that can swiftly and accurately classify news headlines based on their veracity.

The last stage of our process involved refining a model to classify the outputs derived from the LLM in the previous stage. For this task, we utilised the RoBERTa model, a variant of the BERT model, but also incorporated the XLNet model to test its efficacy.

## 3  LLM Model Evaluation

**Table 1.** Evaluation of fine-tuning different open source LLMs

| Model Name | CE loss | GPUs | Training time |
| --- | --- | --- | --- |
| Llama-2-13b | 5.37 | 4 Nvidia A100 | ~ 2.25 h |
| **Llama-2-7b** | **5.74** | **4 Nvidia A100** | **~ 1.12 h** |
| FLAN-T5-large | 7.93 | 4 Nvidia V100 | ~ 1 h |
| FLAN-T5-xlarge | 6.23 | 8 Nvidia V100 | ~ 2 h |
| FLAN-T5-xxlarge | 6.01 | 8 Nvidia V100 | ~ 5 h |

The evaluation of the fine-tuned text generation models focused on accuracy and loss metrics to gauge correct predictions and error degree in justifications, respectively. Initially utilising the Cohere language model, we achieved a 60% accuracy, a 6% increment from the default setup, and decreased the loss to 1.9%. Enhancements, including adding news source and date as a context in the prompt, further increased accuracy marginally to 62.7% and reduced loss to 1.6%. Exploring the performance across various sizes of FLAN-T5 and Llama-2 models revealed diminishing returns in benefits beyond certain model sizes, as evident from stagnant performance between larger versions of both models. The experiment, constrained by GPU capacity, highlighted a plateau in performance enhancement despite increasing the model size, with a notable reduction in generation loss and hallucinations and improved knowledge retrieval in certain stages of fine-tuning. The cross-entropy (CE) loss is detailed in Table 1.

When fine-tuning Llama-2 models, we used an efficient technique for fine-tuning quantized LLMs called Quantized Low Rank Adapters (QLoRA) [11]. Using QLoRA, it was possible to fine-tune Llama-2 models on 4 GPUs for a maximum of 2.5 h. Below is an example FLAN-T5 and Llama-2 models responses compared to the same base model before fine-tuning. The highlighted part shows the model's conclusion, knowledge recollection and CoT ability:

**Statement:** It will only cost one million dollars to build the wall between US and Mexico.- a statement by Facebook posts on April 22, 2020.

**Llama-2 fine-tuned model:** The statement that it will only cost one million dollars to build the wall between the US and Mexico is false. This is because the cost of the wall proposed by President Donald Trump was estimated to be between $21.6 billion and $70 billion, depending on the design and materials used. Trump himself asked for $5.7 billion for a 200-mile segment of the wall...

**Llama-2 base model response:** The statement is false. The cost of building the wall between US and Mexico is estimated to be around $21.6 billion

**FLAN-T5 fine-tuned model response:** The statement that it will only cost one million dollars to build the wall between US and Mexico is false. According to the U.S. Department of Homeland Security, the estimated cost of building the wall is $1.6 billion.

**Analysis:** the Llama-2 fine-tuned model's adeptness in forming coherent and credible narratives by recollecting external factual knowledge, particularly in assessing the underestimated cost of building a US-Mexico wall. In comparison, the FLAN-T5 model, although reaching a correct conclusion, displays a tendency towards speculative reasoning and offers less logical consistency

## 4 Classification Model Evaluation

We evaluated our classification model on the well-known LIAR dataset. The LIAR dataset comprises news headlines, which we harnessed to generate justification using the fine-tuned LLM. The model was then tested using the LIAR test dataset2. Our evaluation results 39.25%, 77.17%, 39.25% and 21.38% for the test accuracy, precision, recall and F1 score respectively. It is worth mentioning that our model surpassed the performance of the current top-ranked model on paperswithcode.com, which held a test accuracy of 27.4% on LIAR dataset[2]. The initial model's accuracy of 39.25% improved to 84.26% when classifications were reduced to true or false, also boosting precision to 85.33% and the F1 score to 77.41%. However, further optimization is needed to enhance recall and the F1 score.

---

[2] https://paperswithcode.com/sota/fake-news-detection-on-liar.

## 5  Conclusion

This study ventures into the scarcely explored domain of combining NLP, machine learning, LLMs, and cognitive psychology to enhance fake news detection, particularly emphasizing the nuanced integration of fine-tuned LLMs with a CoT approach to foster transparency and improve human intelligibility in AI predictions. The introduced method is innovative in its dual focus on precise detection and transparent reasoning, aiding not only in identifying fake news but also in logically justifying or refuting headlines, thus proposing a comprehensive solution to tackle misinformation. This significant advancement paves the way for future research to potentially revolutionize society's approach to combating fake news, nurturing a more informed and discerning global populace.

## References

1. Wei, J., et al.: Chain of thought prompting elicit reasoning in large language models. (2022). arXiv:2201.11903
2. Hinton, G., Vinyals, O., Dean, J.: Distilling the knowledge in a neural network. In: Proceedings of the NIPS 2014 Deep Learning and Representation Learning Workshop, (2014). Accessed 09 July 09 2023. https://arxiv.org/abs/1503.02531
3. Cantarella, M., Fraccaroli, N., Volpe, R.: Does fake news affect voting behaviour?, Research Policy. North-Holland. (2022). Accessed 17 July 2023). https://www.sciencedirect.com/science/article/pii/S0048733322001494
4. Kim, H.K., Tandoc, E.C.J.: Consequences of online misinformation on covid-19: Two potential pathways and disparity by eHealth Literacy, Frontiers. Frontiers. (2022). Accessed: 17 July 2023. https://www.frontiersin.org/articles/10.3389/fpsyg.2022.783909/full
5. Shu, K., Sliva, A., Wang, S., Tang, J., Liu, H.: Fake news detection on social media: a data mining perspective. ACM SIGKDD Explor. Newsl **19**(1), 22–36 (2017)
6. Conroy, N.J., Rubin, V.L., Chen, Y.: Automatic deception detection: methods for finding fake news. Proc. Assoc. Inf. Sci. Technol. **52**(1), 1–4 (2015)
7. Dataset. https://huggingface.co/datasets/od21wk/political_news_justifications
8. Wang, Y., et al.: EANN: Event adversarial neural networks for multi-modal fake news detection. In: Proceedings of the 24th ACM SIGKDD International Conference on Knowledge Discovery, pp. 849–857 (2018)
9. Gupta, A., Lamba, H., Kumaraguru, P., Joshi, A.: Faking sandy: characterizing and identifying fake images on Twitter during hurricane sandy. In: Proceedings of the 22nd International Conference on World Wide Web Companion, pp. 729–736 (2013)
10. Chung, H. W., et. al.: Google Scaling Instruction-Finetuned Language Models (2022)
11. Dettmers, T., Pagnoni, A., Holtzman, A., Zettlemoyer, L.: QLORA: Efficient Finetuning of Quantized LLMs. University of Washington. Email: {dettmers, artidoro, ahai, lsz}@cs.washington.edu (2023)

# A Knowledge Rich Task Planning Framework for Human-Robot Collaboration

Shashank Shekhar[1](✉), Anthony Favier[1,2], Rachid Alami[1,2], and Madalina Croitoru[3]

[1] LAAS-CNRS, Universite de Toulouse, CNRS, INSA, Toulouse, France
{shashank.shekhar,anthony.favier,rachid.alami}@laas.fr
[2] Artificial and Natural Intelligence Toulouse Institute (ANITI), Toulouse, France
[3] LIRMM, University of Montpellier, Montpellier, France
madalina.croitoru@lirmm.fr

**Abstract.** In this paper, we position ourselves within the context of collaborative planning. Drawing upon our recent research, we introduce a novel, knowledge rich task planning framework that represents and reasons and effectively addresses agents' *first-order* false beliefs to solving a task planning problem with a shared goal. Our contributions to this work are as follows: First, to enhance the reasoning abilities of an existing framework, an intuitive observability model for situation assessment is addressed, and for that, an improved knowledge modeling is considered. This effectively captures agents' predictable false beliefs and motivates us to exploit the power of off-the-shelf knowledge reasoners. Second, a new planning approach that incorporates this improved encoding. And, to show the effectiveness of our planner and present our initial findings and proof of concept, we conduct a thorough use case analysis.

**Keywords:** Collaborative planning · Knowledge reasoning ·
Inference · Theory of Mind (ToM) · Human-aware task planning

## 1 Introduction

Human-robot collaboration/interaction (HRC/I) is a current research focus due to the growing number of robot-assisted applications [13]. Collaborative robots add clear value to real-world domains like household [17], workshops [15], or medical facilities [12].

In this work, we address a task planning problem where humans and robots jointly achieve a shared goal. For seamless human-robot collaboration, we believe that it is essential not to restrict human behaviors and, hence, consider humans as uncontrollable agents [7]. Our focus is on developing a planning framework that generates collaborative behaviors for an autonomous robot while anticipating the possible human behaviors and being congruent to humans'

© The Author(s), under exclusive license to Springer Nature Switzerland AG 2023
M. Bramer and F. Stahl (Eds.): SGAI 2023, LNAI 14381, pp. 259–265, 2023.
https://doi.org/10.1007/978-3-031-47994-6_25

choices. Frameworks that support such requirements, in general, include HAT-P/EHDA [6], ADACORL [16] and CommPlan [17], to cite but a few.

Restricted observability available in the environment often leads agents to form false beliefs about the progress of the task and other agents' beliefs. For instance, an agent may rely on "only believing what they see or can infer" to update or form new beliefs. For the robot to anticipate such situations while planning its behavior to collaborate, it should consider Theory of Mind (ToM) to maintain and manage agents' distinct beliefs.

Our recently proposed planner extends the HATP/EHDA framework and considers the first-order ToM, that is, managing (false) beliefs about the physical world [10]. Roughly, its main idea works as follows: First, the existing problem encoding is enhanced. To be specific, we categorize each environmental property as either *observable* – meaning its real value can be assessed directly from the environment – or *indirectly inferable*. In the latter case, the changes in the property's status persist in the environment when an action is executed, but cannot be observed directly. However, an agent can assess this knowledge either as an observer or as an actor, or when they are communicated. Second, to consider restricted observability, we introduce the concept of *co-presence* and *co-location*. We formulate the environment such that a collection of discrete places where action manipulation can take place, permitting the enhanced encoding to enable precise action executions, or an agent assessing the value of an environmental property when they are physically situated within a specified place.

The encoding is used in HATP/EHDA as input, modifying the planner to use improved knowledge modeling to handle better the evolution of agents' first-order (false) beliefs and estimate the actions humans are likely to perform. (Due to space restrictions, we will provide only a high-level description of it.)

However, some limitations to the above line of work are: First, the context under which the reasoning works is limited. For example, associating an observable state property directly to a discrete place in the environment is not always intuitive and straightforward and enables sound reasoning. To understand this, consider the following scenario: A robot holding a coffee mug can be assessed from where the robot is currently situated. Moreover, if the robot moves from one place to another, then the *condition* under which the robot holding the coffee mug can be assessed, also changes implicitly. Or, if a table is moved, then the condition to assess the orientation of blocks on top of it would change implicitly, too. Second, the system's ability to *refute* a false belief is limited.

In this regard, our contributions to this paper are the following.

1. We first extend and generalize the concepts introduced earlier for observing the value of an environmental property. We provide a new encoding that is much cleaner and intuitive and achieves a sound resolution and refutation.
2. Second, the planning algorithm is improved by incorporating the new encoding for better managing the evolution of agents' predictable (false) beliefs. To show the efficacy of our planning approach and present our preliminary findings and proof of concept, we conduct a use case analysis.

## 2    The Illustrative Example

Consider an adapted version of the scenario appearing in [10]. The scenario includes a pot of water on the stove, while the pasta packet is in the adjacent room. One sub-task is to pour the pasta into the pot, which can only be done after turning on the stove (results in holding StoveOn) and adding salt to the water (results in SaltIn). Suppose, the robot is responsible for turning on the stove (turn-stove-on), while the human is tasked with fetching the pasta (grab-pasta, however, for that, they need to move to the other room where the *pasta* packet is kept) and pouring it into the pot (pour-pasta). Both the robot and the human have the capability to add salt (add-salt) to the pot. Humans can be *uncontrollable* but assumed to be *rational*, so they can choose to either first add salt, or first fetch the pasta. Next, the robot's actions depend on the human's decision, resulting in the generation of different false beliefs. Such variability in beliefs observed can be precisely attributed to the restricted observability and available human choices within the system.

Suppose, when the human is temporarily absent to bring pasta, the robot can act in *kitchen*. When they return, they can *"assess"* whether the robot turned on the stove, which is observable. However, the presence of salt (*SaltIn*) is not directly observable to her. To prevent misunderstandings, a proactive robot needs to anticipate false beliefs held by humans. Here, humans may mistakenly believe that salt is not added to the pasta or be uncertain about it.

## 3    The Basic Architecture and Recent Advancements

We provide a brief overview of the HATP/EHDA (*human-aware task planning by emulating human decisions and actions*) architecture [6], building upon previous research, e.g. [1,2,5,8]. We also discuss recent advancements that have been made based on its planning framework. (For a better understanding of the basic terminologies, definitions, and planning models, we refer readers to [11].)

The HATP/EHDA architecture considers: (1.) distinct capabilities and characteristics of humans and robots, (2.) utilization of human task and/or action models by the robot to inform decision-making, considering human capabilities and environmental dynamics, and (3.) flexibility for humans to choose an action from the available choices, which is congruent to the shared goal.

The HATP/EHDA planning scheme utilizes a two-agent model consisting of a *human* and a *robot*, represented as two-agent-HTN (*hierarchical task networks*) [11], adapted as per the requirements. Roughly speaking, each agent has their own initial belief state, action model & methods, and task network. Our focus is on a sequential task to be solved, where both agents have a shared initial task network that needs to be decomposed. Considering perfectly aligned agents' beliefs with the real world to begin with, the classical scheme assumes that the belief state of an agent consists of properties that are either *true* or *false*. Assuming the environment is fully observable, the planning scheme uses agents' task/action models and beliefs to decompose their task network into valid primitive components, resulting in an implicitly coordinated plan for the robot within a joint solution policy [6]. This policy encompasses both the robot's actions and an estimated policy for the human. For more details, see [10].

A new formalism is proposed to enhance the planning scheme's robustness for estimating human initiatives when dealing with restricted observability. It considers the first-order Theory of Mind for managing agents' (false) belief updates, resulting in improved management of their mental state and enhanced collaboration [9]. As we pointed earlier, this scheme addresses the need for a less abstract problem formulation, and conceptualizes place-based *situation-assessment* models, and hence capturing collaboration nuances more accurately.

An offline planning approach is proposed to detect predictable false beliefs of humans and address them through explicit communication actions if mandatory w.r.t. the goal. It promotes more accurate understanding and alignment between the robot and humans, allowing for minimal communication. Another way, as mentioned in [10], is to delay critical actions, enabling humans to reach a state s.t. the robot's actions become perceivable.

## 4  Improved Problem Encoding

We consider two types of agents. First is *GT*, which stands for *ground truth*, an omnipresent (virtual) agent that cannot achieve any task, however, it immediately knows all the effects when an action is applied. The second type refers to real agents, e.g., a robot. Real agents can have false beliefs, which means their beliefs about the world may diverge from the *GT*'s beliefs. Moreover, no real-world uncertainty is considered w.r.t. agents' beliefs.

An environmental property is Boolean type, and is augmented by an argument, ?a - agent (e.g., *Human/Robot*), which is also its first argument. It represents that the agent believes that this property holds true given it is contained in the agent's beliefs. In this work, we restrict ourselves to those properties that are directly observable in the environment, while relying on the existing concepts with some minor updates required, for managing beliefs w.r.t. the facts that are indirectly inferable. To manage appropriate dynamics of the world, we augment the parameter list of *relevant* state properties which are observable with an argument ?p - Places (at the end of its parameter list). However, for those that are observable but associating them directly to a place is not intuitive to the domain modeler, e.g., *StoveOn* is a property of a stove and can be assessed from where it is currently situated, we use a different strategy to cater to them.

With a lifted (primitive) action schema, we specify how it is only modeled to affect the beliefs of the GT agent, in principle, focusing on observable state properties.

```
:action turn-stove-on (?a - agent ?st - stove ?k - kitchen)
  :precondition (and (not(= GT ?a))(at ?a ?a ?k)(stoveAt ?a ?st ?k) ...)
  :effect (and (stoveOn GT ?st) ...)
```

Real agents assess available information systematically from the environment, and for that, we include the following in our problem specification:

**Language and Interpretation:** Informally, to assess the value of a property, an agent needs to respect certain *condition(s)*. Of course, a condition could be that the agent is co-located, as supported by the existing system. However, inspired by the work in [4], we generalize this idea and specify *rules* for knowledge reasoning to capture more complex contexts. For one observable property (representing the *consequent*), conditions for assessing its value are "formulated" in the *antecedent* of a knowledge rule. Formally, a rule is of the form $p(a_1, x, y), q(x) \rightarrow s(y, b_1)$, which also means that $\forall x \forall y (p(a_1, x, y), q(x) \rightarrow s(y, b_1))$, where $x$ and $y$ are free variables, and $p$, $q$ and $s$ are names. $a_1$ and $b_1$ are constants.

For example, when an agent is situated at the stove's location, it will acknowledge the current status of *StoveOn*. A corresponding rule to it is, R1: $\forall s \forall k \forall a (stoveAt(a, s, k), stoveon(GT, s), at(a, a, k) \rightarrow stoveon(a, s)$. Note that the GT's beliefs play a key role here. Similarly, we can write other important rules for our example domain: R2: $\forall a_1 \forall k (at(GT, a_1, k) \rightarrow at(a_1, a_1, k))$, R3: $\forall a_1 \forall a_2 \forall k (at(GT, a_1, k), at(a_2, a_2, k) \rightarrow at(a_2, a_1, k))$, and R4: $\forall a \forall s (\neg stoveat(GT, s, kitchen), at(a, a, kitchen) \rightarrow \neg stoveat(a, s, kitchen))$. It treats the stove as a mobile object, which alters the context to also evaluate the status of *StoveOn* along with determining its current location.

Page restrictions allow us to offer a concise overview only, reserving detailed semantics for future research. In rules, it is important to note that the implications must not be contraposed. Anything that cannot be evaluated as true is considered false for agents. Our focus on *stratified* rule sets avoids potential issues related to unsafe negation usage and ambiguity in interpretation [3,14].

## 5    Incorporating New Encoding for Planning

We adapt our planning mechanism presented in [10], to assess new encoding's effectiveness. It assumes that the robot's beliefs never deviate from GT's beliefs, and hence essentially two distinct belief states are handled by the scheme.

Two questions arise at this point: First, how does the state transition occur during planning and how are the agents' (*false*) beliefs updated? Second, how are the relevant false beliefs detected and addressed? We rely on the existing mechanism to address the second question and how beliefs are updated when agents do indirect inference. Our main focus will be to address how the new observability model is incorporated into the planning workflow.

Once an action is executed, such as the human moving to the kitchen, the process of situation assessment is initiated to evaluate the environment from the perspectives of individual agents. Here, our approach diverges from current methods. Instead of directly matching the *co-location* of agents with state properties and assessing the latter's values, we invoke an external reasoner to deduce such knowledge. Using the agent's beliefs, the reasoner verifies the formula that captures the context specified (in the rules) to deduce new knowledge or to refute a fact that humans believe but is no longer true in the robot's beliefs. This departure from the existing encoding allows us to remove the hardcoded context within an action. For instance, if the human moves from one room to another, carrying the pasta packet that was initially in the room, the new location for assessing the packet switches to the kitchen. Moreover, we needed to hardcode it within each action that updates the place of an agent in the environment. However, with the new encoding, if the robot sees the human in the kitchen, then given the domain rules, it can assess whether the human is holding the pasta packet, by their presence in the kitchen.

**Acknowledgments.** This work has been partially financed by Défi Clé "Robotique Centrée sur l'Humain" supported by Région Occitanie and the Artificial and Natural Intelligence Toulouse Institute (ANITI).

# References

1. Alami, R., Clodic, A., Montreuil, V., Sisbot, E.A., Chatila, R.: Toward human-aware robot task planning. In: AAAI Spring Symposium 2006: to Boldly go Where no Human-robot Team has Gone Before (2006)
2. Alili, S., Warnier, M., Ali, M., Alami, R.: Planning and plan-execution for human-robot cooperative task achievement. In: Proceedings of ICAPS (2009)
3. Apt, K.R., Blair, H.A., Walker, A.: Towards a theory of declarative knowledge. In: Minker J. (ed.) Foundations of Deductive Databases and Logic Programming, pp. 89–148, Morgan Kaufmann (1988)
4. Baget, J.-F., Leclère, M., Mugnier, M.-L., Rocher, S., Sipieter, C.: Graal: a toolkit for query answering with existential rules. In: Bassiliades, N., Gottlob, G., Sadri, F., Paschke, A., Roman, D. (eds.) RuleML 2015. LNCS, vol. 9202, pp. 328–344. Springer, Cham (2015). https://doi.org/10.1007/978-3-319-21542-6_21
5. Buisan G., Alami, R.: A human-aware task planner explicitly reasoning about human and robot decision, action and reaction. In: Proceedings of HRI (2021)
6. Buisan G., Favier, A., Mayima, A., Alami, R.: HATP/EHDA: a robot task planner anticipating and eliciting human decisions and actions. In: Proceedings of ICRA (2022)
7. Cirillo, M., Karlsson, L., Saffiotti, A.: A human-aware robot task planner. In: Proceedings of ICAPS (2009)
8. De Silva, L., Lallement, R., Alami, R.: The HATP hierarchical planner: Formalisation and an initial study of its usability and practicality. In: Proceedings of IROS (2015)
9. Favier, A., Shekhar, S., Alami, R.: Robust planning for human-robot joint tasks with explicit reasoning on human mental state. In: AI-HRI, AAAI Symposium (2022)
10. Favier, A., Shekhar, S., Alami, R.: Anticipating false beliefs and planning pertinent reactions in human-aware task planning with models of theory of mind. In: PlanRob 2023, the ICAPS Workshop (2023)
11. Ghallab, M., Nau, D.S., Traverso, P.: Automated Planning - Theory and Practice. Elsevier, Amsterdam (2004)
12. Jacob, M.G., Li, Y.T., Akingba, G.A., Wachs, J.P.: Collaboration with a robotic scrub nurse. Commun. ACM **56**(5), 68–75 (2013)
13. Selvaggio, M., Cognetti, M., Nikolaidis, S., Ivaldi, S., Siciliano, B.: Autonomy in physical human-robot interaction: a brief survey. IEEE Rob. Autom. Lett. **6**, 7989–7996 (2021)

14. Thiébaux, S., Hoffmann, J., Nebel, B.. In defense of PDDL axioms. In: Proceedings of IJCAI (2003)
15. Unhelkar, V.V., et al.: Human-aware robotic assistant for collaborative assembly: integrating human motion prediction with planning in time. IEEE Rob. Autom. Lett. **3**(3), 2394–2401 (2018)
16. Unhelkar, V.V., Li, S., Shah, J.A.: Semi-supervised learning of decision-making models for human-robot collaboration. In: Proceedings of CoRL (2019)
17. Unhelkar, V.V., Li, S., Shah, J.A.: Decision-making for bidirectional communication in sequential human-robot collaborative tasks. In: Proceedings of HRI (2020)

# Q-Learning: Solutions for Grid World Problem with Forward and Backward Reward Propagations

Snobin Antony[✉], Raghi Roy, and Yaxin Bi

School of Computing, Ulster University, Belfast, Northern Ireland
`{antony-s1,roy-r1,y.bi}@ulster.ac.uk`

**Abstract.** In the area of adaptive and responsive problems, Reinforcement Learning algorithms have made significant progress. This paper presents solutions to the grid world problem using the model-free reinforcement learning method known as the Q-Learning algorithm. The solutions are developed with forward and backward reward propagations under the assumption of a Markov decision process for the grid world problem. This study detail the implementation and comparison of these two reward calculation methods. The paper also illustrates how an agent interact with the gird environment during both forward and backward propagations and compare their benefits followed by hyperparameter tuning for better understanding of the model's convergence.

**Keywords:** Reinforcement Learning · q-Learning · Markov Processes · Rewards · Grid World

## 1 Introduction

Machine learning includes supervised, unsupervised, and reinforcement learning, with the latter involving trial and error to discover optimal policies for sequential decision-making. The Markov Decision Process (MDP) is a reframing of Markov chains which uses the decision-making process in the stochastic setting. A Markov Decision Process (MDP) is typically used solve the challenges in Reinforcement Learning (RL). MDP aims to offer a mapping of the best course of action for each environmental state via only considering the present and ignoring past knowledge, future state prediction is totally independent from the state in the previous step [5].

### 1.1 Exploration and Exploitation

The trade-off among exploration and exploitation is an issue frequently occurring in reinforcement learning [5]. Agents must balance between choosing known successful actions to maximize immediate rewards and exploring new actions to potentially discover better strategies. Striking this balance is crucial because relying solely on exploitation can lead to missed opportunities, while pure exploration is inefficient. In dynamic environments,

M. Bramer and F. Stahl (Eds.): SGAI 2023, LNAI 14381, pp. 266–271, 2023.
https://doi.org/10.1007/978-3-031-47994-6_26

the effectiveness of exploited strategies can change, making the decision even more complex [9]. Exploration is valuable as it helps the agent gain a deeper understanding of all available actions, leading to potential long-term benefits. Conversely, exploitation involves choosing actions primarily based on current estimated values, potentially missing out on higher rewards due to its reliance on these estimates.

To address this dilemma, various action selection strategies exist. Greedy selection involves always choosing the action with the highest estimated value, which is a pure exploitation approach. Alternatively, an Epsilon-Greedy policy introduces randomness by selecting actions randomly with a small probability epsilon ($\epsilon$) and otherwise choosing the best-known option. This approach helps strike a balance between exploration and exploitation, allowing the agent to adapt to changing environments while still maximizing rewards [3].

## 2 Methodology

In a grid world environment, an agent learns to accomplish a mission through movements and several unique tasks. The grid world environment consists of $5 \times 5$ grids, the agent is initially positioned on the (2, 1) start cell at the beginning of episode, and the terminal position is on the cell (5, 5). The agent state inputs $u_t$ at each step, and produces an output vectors of action values, $z_t = [Q1_t, Q2_t, Q3_t, Q4_t]$ whose elements are corresponding to" four actions: "go north", "go east", "go south" and "go west", respectively [4]. In addition, there is a special action "jumps" from (2, 4) to (4, 4) with a $+$ 5 bonus reward. The agent will receive a $+$ 10 reward when it reaches the end location (5, 5) or the win state. Any movements over other grids, the agent will receive a -1 penalty. The agent will move over the grid board and encounter some barriers in the environment. We can apply a Q-learning approach to solve this grid world problem.

### 2.1 Q-Learning

Q-learning is a type of reinforcement learning algorithms. The Q-value represents the expected cumulative reward the agent will receive by interacting an environment in given states, which can be updated by Eq. (1) below:

$$Q_{t+1}(s, a) \leftarrow Q_t(s, a) + \alpha \left[ r + \gamma max_a Q_t\left(s', a\right) - Q_t(s, a) \right] \qquad (1)$$

For any actions to be taken, the agent will receive either a reward or penalty, then accumulate it together using Eq. (1), and generate an output $z_t = [Q1_t, Q2_t, Q3_t, Q4_t]$. To solve the grid world problem using Q-learning, an agent takes actions, receives rewards, and updates Q-values. Two reward accumulation strategies affect convergence time in finding an optimal path.

### 2.2 Deterministic and Non-Deterministic

Deterministic algorithms yield consistent outcomes, while non-deterministic one's display variability across executions. Balancing exploration and exploitation are essential in Q-learning, involving the choice of actions in each state to identify the optimal policy [6]. This choice between the best-known action and exploration is critical. We used the widely adopted "$\epsilon$-greedy" exploration technique for a non-deterministic agent navigating a grid to find goals. This technique employs an exploration parameter, $0 \leq \epsilon \leq 1$ to determine which action to take $Q_t(s_t, a)$. In the current condition, the agent with probability $1 - \epsilon$ chooses the action with the greatest Q-value, while in all other cases, it selects a random action. A higher $\epsilon$ value encourages more exploration, which is essential for an agent navigating a stochastic grid to discover the optimal path [8].

In this implementation, the action based on the epsilon greedy value ($\epsilon$) with lower epsilon values, or a random action is returned by the action selection function in the loop which is a stochastic method. The best action is chosen based on maximum next reward. The position update function is used when taking actions, and, as the "determine" flag is set to False for non-deterministic behaviour, actions are selected with probabilities using epsilon-greedy. Higher probabilities allow for the same action but also encourage exploration of alternative actions.

## 3   Implementation

Deterministic and non-deterministic methods tackle the grid world challenge. This paper employed Bellman's equation and epsilon-greedy exploration for the latter. Bellman's equation, pivotal in MDP and RL problems since 1953, calculates utility recursively for future expected rewards [7].

$$U(s) = R(s) + \gamma \, max_a \Sigma T \, (s, \, a, \, s')U(s') \tag{2}$$

The Bellman equation explains that the sum of the agent's benefit for reaching the current state $s$ and the maximum possible reward for state $s'$ equals the maximum future reward. The basic idea behind Q-learning is that by applying the abovementioned Bellman equation, we can iteratively estimate $Q^*$. The Q-learning formula is given below, where learning rate $\alpha$ is determines how much of the difference between the old and new Q-values are considered [1].

$$Q_{t+1}(s_t, a_t) = Q_t(s_t, a_t) + \alpha(r_{t+1} + \gamma \, max_a Q_t(s_{t+1}, a) - Q_t(s_t, a_t)) \tag{3}$$

The algorithm in this study has distinct features, involving four actions: South, North, West, and East. Q-values are stored in a dictionary, initially set to '-1'. The learning rate, ranging from 0 to 1, controls learning speed, higher values accelerate initial learning [2]. The algorithm operates non-deterministically using epsilon-greedy strategy for action selection. Training iterates until the maximum episode limit, or a early stopping condition is met (1,000 episodes for learning). Actions are chosen via epsilon-greedy or random selection, with the best action based on maximum expected reward. Reward calculation differs between backward and forward propagation. Back propagation computes rewards and next Q-values only at the episode's end, while forward propagation calculates them after each action. A special jump path offers + 5 bonus and + 10 win reward. Equation (3) calculates next Q-values. In back propagation, actions follow a greedy approach, calculating rewards only at episode's end. In contrast, forward propagation computes rewards after each action. Cumulative rewards are determined by summing all rewards within a given episode, and average cumulative rewards divide cumulative reward by total action states. Additionally, SARSA is implemented for forward propagation, similar to Q-Learning but using on-policy techniques and current policy action values for Q-Values learning.

$$Q_{t+1}(s_t, a_t) = Q_t(s_t, a_t) + \alpha(r_{t+1} + \gamma Q_t(s_{t+1}, a_{t+1}) - Q_t(s_t, a_t)) \tag{4}$$

Since the Temporal Difference method is implemented in SARSA, it keeps updating the Q-table after every step till it reaches the maximum iteration or converges to an optimal solution.

## 4 Result and Evaluation

To find the optimum path based on the reward function, the Q-learning stochastic method was examined in this study. Using the non-deterministic Q-learning method, the agent achieves the win state in a variety of ways, but eventually determines the most effective route. In the stochastic method, agents utilise exploration technique with an epsilon greedy approach and make decisions based on the long-term rewards or policy method, as opposed to the deterministic Q-learning algorithm where agents only choose those actions that offer larger immediate rewards. This algorithm enables the agent to investigate various potential paths and discover the best route in a smaller number of episodes.

### 4.1 Comparison Between Forward, Backward Propagation and SARSA

This section will provide comparative discussions about both forward and backward propagation, and a comparison with SARSA later.

Figure 1a shows the state values of each grid cell, which are the highest Q-values an agent may attain in a specific grid cell if it chooses one of the four actions. The board layout and state data for each grid cell are generated for the backward propagation. The agent's travel path or converging direction to the end state is assumed to be represented by the maximum Q-value of a given state. It is clear from the figure that the agent travelled across every grid cell and discovered the best route, which is the incremental q-values starting from the start cell $(1, 0)$. The agent uses several actions and a jump in the optimum path to get the win state with the fewest number of movements.

Figure 1b shows the board layout and state data for each grid cell generated for the forward propagation. But in this method agent receives a maximum of 12 reward and it has travelled through different path even if it is finding the optimum path because of the algorithm did not converge within 1000 episodes.

Figure 1c depicts the board layout and state data for each grid cell generated using the forward propagation for SARSA. The key difference here is the how they update the Q-values during the learning process. In SARSA, the Q-values are updated based on the observed state-action-reward-state-action transitions. The important characteristic of SARSA is that it uses the current policy to select the next action and estimates the Q-value accordingly. In SARSA, the update considers the Q-value of the next state-action pair $(s_{t+1}, a_{t+1})$ based on the action actually taken using the current policy. The update depends on the learning rate $\alpha$, the observed reward $r_{t+1}$, the discount factor $\gamma$, and the current and next Q-values.

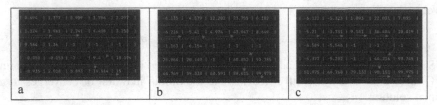

a            b            c

**Fig. 1.** Board layout of grid world state values (a. Backward, b. Forward, c. SARSA)

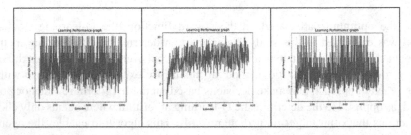

**Fig. 2.** Performance graph of Forward Propagation, Backward Propagation, and SARSA

### 4.2 Performance Comparison

Overall, forward propagation updates rewards with Q-values more frequently, considering rewards after each action. On the other hand, backward propagation updates rewards with Q-values only when the agent successfully reaches the win state per episode. However, SARSA specifically employs an on-policy learning approach and uses a different update equation to calculate the next Q-value. The choice between these approaches depends on the specific requirements and dynamics of the grid world problem being addressed. Performance graphs are shown in Fig. 2.

## 5   Conclusion

This study applies non-deterministic Q-learning to solve the grid world problem, with the agent predicting its next actions based on experience. It uses a grid layout and Q-table to display performance, navigating obstacles, and accumulating rewards to find the optimal path to the win state. This paper introduced Bellman's equation and explored the backpropagation approach in stochastic Q-learning. Epsilon-greedy exploration is persistent, causing fluctuations in average cumulative reward even at maximum episodes. Our analysis compares exploration and exploitation strategies in backward, forward propagation and SARSA. Backward propagation achieves higher cumulative average rewards than forward propagation and SARSA.

# References

1. Campbell, J.S., Givigi, S.N., Schwartz, H.M.: Multiple-model Q-learning for stochastic reinforcement delays. In: Conference Proceedings - IEEE International Conference on Systems, Man and Cybernetics. Institute of Electrical and Electronics Engineers Inc, pp. 1611–1617 (2014)
2. Chen, Y., Schomaker, L., Wiering, M.: An investigation into the effect of the learning rate on overestimation bias of connectionist q-learning. In: ICAART 2021 - Proceedings of the 13th International Conference on Agents and Artificial Intelligence. SciTePress, pp. 107–118 (2021)
3. Coggan, M.: Exploration and Exploitation in Reinforcement Learning
4. IEEE Computational Intelligence Society, International Neural Network Society, Institute of Electrical and Electronics Engineers, IEEE World Congress on Computational Intelligence (2020 : Online) 2020 International Joint Conference on Neural Networks (IJCNN) : 2020 conference proceedings
5. Macready, W.G., Wolpert, D.H.: Bandit problems and the exploration/exploitation tradeoff. IEEE Trans. Evol. Comput. **2**, 2–22 (1998). https://doi.org/10.1109/4235.728210
6. Manju, M.S., Punithavalli, M.M.: An Analysis of Q-Learning Algorithms with Strategies of Reward Function
7. Naeem, M., Rizvi, S.T.H., Coronato, A.: A Gentle introduction to reinforcement learning and its application in different fields. IEEE Access **8**, 209320–209344 (2020). https://doi.org/10.1109/ACCESS.2020.3038605
8. Tijsma, A.D., Drugan, M.M., Wiering, M.A.: Comparing exploration strategies for Q-learning in random stochastic mazes. In: 2016 IEEE Symposium Series on Computational Intelligence, SSCI 2016. Institute of Electrical and Electronics Engineers Inc. (2017)
9. Yen, G., Yang, F., Hickey, T., Goldstein, M.: Coordination of exploration and exploitation in a dynamic environment. In: Proceedings of the International Joint Conference on Neural Networks, pp. 1014–1018 (2001)

# Application Papers

# Explaining a Staff Rostering Problem by Mining Trajectory Variance Structures

Martin Fyvie[1]([✉])(iD), John A. W. McCall[1](iD), Lee A. Christie[1](iD),
Alexandru-Ciprian Zăvoianu[1](iD), Alexander E. I. Brownlee[2](iD),
and Russell Ainslie[3](iD)

[1] The Robert Gordon University, Garthdee Road, Aberdeen, UK
{m.fyvie,j.mccall,l.a.christie,c.zavoianu}@rgu.ac.uk
[2] University of Stirling, Stirling, UK
alexander.brownlee@stir.ac.uk
[3] The BT Group, Adastral Park, Ipswich, UK
russell.ainslie@bt.com

**Abstract.** The use of Artificial Intelligence-driven solutions in domains involving end-user interaction and cooperation has been continually growing. This has also lead to an increasing need to communicate crucial information to end-users about algorithm behaviour and the quality of solutions. In this paper, we apply our method of search trajectory mining through decomposition to the solutions created by a Genetic Algorithm— a non-deterministic, population based metaheuristic. We complement this method with the use of One-Way ANOVA statistical testing to help identify explanatory features found in the search trajectories—subsets of the set of optimization variables having both high and low influence on the search behaviour of the GA and solution quality. This allows us to highlight these to an end-user to allow for greater flexibility in solution selection. We demonstrate the techniques on a real-world staff rostering problem and show how, together, they identify the personnel who are critical to the optimality of the rosters being created.

**Keywords:** Evolutionary Algorithms · PCA · Explainability · Population Diversity

## 1 Introduction

Artificial Intelligence (AI) including non-deterministic meta-heuristics such as Genetic Algorithms (GA) have seen a considerable increase in their application in domains involving end-user interaction and cooperation. These domains typically include Transport and Logistics [1] and Engineering [2]. An important aspect of this interaction is the need for some level of trust to be maintained between the end-users and the results generated. It is often recommended that such AI-powered systems follow a design philosophy that highly emphasises the interpretability of the results or the operations of these systems. This can include

© The Author(s), under exclusive license to Springer Nature Switzerland AG 2023
M. Bramer and F. Stahl (Eds.): SGAI 2023, LNAI 14381, pp. 275–290, 2023.
https://doi.org/10.1007/978-3-031-47994-6_27

the development of methods capable of explaining these processes post-hoc, such as the recommendations of PHG [3]. More recently, this has become one of the core considerations of AI, as seen in its inclusion in the European Commission on Trustworthy AI publications [4]. Explainable AI (XAI) techniques have, in recent years, also seen an increase in attention, most likely driven by this growth in the adoption in these key domains.

This growth in XAI methods can be seen in XAI survey papers [5,6] of these techniques and approaches which aim to help key stakeholders determine which AI system and XAI techniques are right for their application. The growing interest in the intersection of XAI with genetic and evolutionary algorithms can be seen in the newly created Genetic and Evolutionary Computation Conference (GECCO) XAI workshop in 2022 and follow-up in 2023.

There is a wide array of approaches to generating explanations regarding AI-generated solutions and their decision-making processes. These approaches include the extraction of some level of understanding from the sensitivities of the fitness function to specific variables. Sensitivity Analysis (SA), applications of which can be seen in [7,8], is used to calculate solution fitness sensitivity to changes in variable values. Feature importance can also be mined from the fitness function through the use of Surrogate Modelling [9–11]. GAs, however, are often utilized as tools to enhance XAI techniques such in fuzzy logic systems [12] and counterfactual creation [13] and are rarely the focus of such analyses.

In this paper, we test our hypothesis that GA-generated search trajectories can be mined for features capable of adding a level of explanation to the resulting solutions. These explanations have the capacity to aid an end-user in understanding and interpreting the results and how they reflect the algorithm's search behaviour. This, in turn, may help build trust that the solutions provided are of high quality and relevant to the end users' goals. We then complement these results with those generated by an Analysis of Variance (ANOVA) technique to highlight any overlap between the two approaches.

The remainder of this paper is structured as follows: Sect. 2 contains an overview of the experimental setup used to generate the search trajectories. This section includes our definition of a search trajectory, the optimisation problem definition and any algorithm-specific setup used. Shown in Sect. 3 are the methods used to extract the explanatory features from the search trajectories. This section covers the implementation of Multiple Correspondence Analysis, Analysis of Variance implementation and the method by which we compare and merge the results - Weighted Ranked Biased Overlap. Section 4 presents the results of our analysis and finally, Sect. 5 contains our conclusions and plans for further work to extend this research.

# 2    Definitions and Target Algorithm

## 2.1    Search Trajectory Definition

During its run, a population-based algorithm visits a collection of solutions $X$. These are ordered by generation $g$ and gathered into a search trajectory $T$ as shown in Eq. (1).

$$T = [X_1, \ldots, X_g]$$
$$X = \{x^1, \ldots, x^N\} \tag{1}$$
$$x = [x_1, \ldots, x_n] \text{ in } \mathbb{Z}^n$$

Here, $N$ is the population size and $n$ is the problem size. Thus, we define a *trajectory* as a list of $\mathbb{Z}^{gN}$ solutions of size $n$, drawn from the discreet integer space $\mathbb{Z}$ as outlined fully in Sect. 2.2. It is important to note that this definition of a trajectory is not limited to the integer domain. The approach has also be applied to problems in which the solutions lie in real-valued space $\mathbb{R}$ as shown in [14].

## 2.2    Problem Definition

The search trajectories we analyse in this paper were generated by solving a modified version of the staff rostering problem detailed in [15,16]. This problem aims to minimize the variance in the number of workers assigned to work on each day of the week, over a 3-month period. A pre-generated set of 100 roster patterns, varying in length from 2 to 13 weeks, details what days a worker will be required. Each of these rosters ensures two consecutive days off per week. Workers are assigned a sub-pool of between one and five potential rosters from the initial pool. All optimization runs are initialised with the same, pre-determined "starting state" which represents the initial configuration of rosters and the currently worked week of that roster. This allows for secondary goals aiming to minimize disruption to the workforce. In this problem, all workers may change from their currently assigned week to a different week within their initial roster however only a fraction of the workforce are allowed to change to a new roster in their sub-pool.

**Table 1.** Solution Representation

| $x_1$ | $x_2$ | $x_3$ | ... | $x_{n-1}$ | $x_n$ | Index | ... | 32 | **33** | 34 |
|---|---|---|---|---|---|---|---|---|---|---|
| 12 | **33** | 15 | ... | 9 | 45 | Rota,Week | ... | 7,2 | **7,3** | 7,4 |
| | (a) Sol. Extract | | | | | | (b) $x_2$ Roster-Week | | | |

An example solution representation can be seen in Tables 1a and 1b. Here, each worker is represented by the variable $x_i, 1 \leq i \leq n$ in 1a. The value each variable can take refers to the index of a variable-specific table containing all possible combinations of their roster sub-pool and starting weeks. 1b shows an example of this index table for variable $x_2$. The solution shown indicates that variable $x_2$ – with a value of 33 – represents Roster 7, starting week 3. This in turn would be understood by the user as Worker $x_2$ beginning the 3-month period using the working hours determined by that selection and would repeat roster 7 from week 1 if the roster is completed before the end of the three-month period.

We use an "attendance matrix" $A_{kd}$ which, in our 3-month problem, is a $12 \times 7$ matrix of the sum of the workers assigned to work on week $k$, day $d$. These totals are determined by the variable values in solution $X$ which will in turn determine the total number of workers scheduled for each day $d$, in all 12 weeks of $k$. This maps the original problem definition to our trajectory definition.

The range between total workers assigned for each day is calculated by taking the minimum and maximum of matrix $\mathbf{A}$ for each column $d$, to calculate the normalized range of column $d$ as shown in Eq. (2). This in turn us used to calculate the fitness value of a solution, shown in Eq. (3) subject to the constraint detailed in Eq. (4).

$$R_d = \frac{\max_{d}(a_{kd}) - \min_{d}(a_{kd})}{\max_{d}(a_{kd})} \tag{2}$$

$$\text{minimize: } \sum_{1 \leq d \leq 7} w_d R_d^2 + \left(\sum_{n \in x} P_n\right) S \tag{3}$$

$$\text{subject to: } \sum_{i=1}^{n} \mathrm{CV}_i \leq 0.2 \cdot \mathrm{len}(x) \tag{4}$$

The cost function shown in Eq. (3) aims to minimise the overall range between the number of workers assigned to work on each of the week days. This calculation has a set of weights, $w$, applied to each day of the week to reduce the impact of the lower availability of workers during the weekend. These are applied to each day $d$, with the values being set at $w = (1,1,1,1,1,10,10)$. This was done as "... a range of 10 on Saturday should not be considered the same as a range of 10 on any other day of the week due to the smaller number of attending resources" [15]. The function contains constraints designed to minimize the disruption to the workforce. The hard constraint, shown in Eq. (4), defines $CV$ as the total number of workers who have been assigned to a new roster from their sub-pool. This constraint aims to limit the total number of workers from being assigned new rosters to 20% of the total workforce. The cost function contains a soft constraint linked to the second summand of $x$, the set of all variables in a solution, and $P = (p_n)$, a binary array in which $p_n = 1$ if the value of variable $n$ results in two consecutive Saturdays being scheduled or 0 otherwise, due to changing from the initial Roster pattern and week to those outlined in a solution. This soft constraint adds a small penalty of $S = 0.01$ for each violation of this constraint in each solution to help reduce the total occurrences of this. As the aim is to reduce the total range to 0, a minimum value of 0 would be achieved should all ranges be reduced to 0 and no consecutive Saturdays be worked. The source data files used for rosters and allocations can be found here [17].

## 2.3   Algorithm Runs

The trajectories representing runs of a GA with a population $\mu$ form the target of the explanation techniques presented in this paper. Here, $\mu$ is the starting population of solutions and the resulting next generation of solutions is created through the application of the internal operators of the GA. The operators are Selection, Crossover and Mutation which are applied to the parent population to generate the child population of solutions. Shown in Table 2 are the run settings used to create the datasets for this paper.

**Table 2.** Algorithm Run Settings

| n | N | g | Runs | Sel. | Mut. | eta | Cross. |
|---|---|---|---|---|---|---|---|
| 141 | 20 | 100 | 100 | Tournament | Polynomial | 3.0 | SBX |

Here, $n$ is the size of the solution string, $N$ is the number of solutions in each generation and $g$ is the number of generations allowed in each run. The GA was run for a total of 100 optimization runs.

The Python Multi-Objective Optimisation (PYMOO) library [18] was used to implement the GA with the required parameters. After some initial testing, the values in Table 2 were selected to allow for reasonable solution convergence however it is important to note that refining the algorithm's performance was not a consideration in this study. Provided that higher quality solutions were being generated, we are able to continue with our analysis. As this was the case, where possible the default values and operators outlined in the PYMOO documentation were used.

As the mutation used was a polynomial mutation [19] function, details of which can be found in [20], the setting **eta** was set to 3. The higher the value is set the more similar and less mutated the child solution will be. The solutions were encoded as discrete variable strings, in which each value in the string represented the value given to a specific worker. These values represented the index of a worker-specific table that contained all possible combinations of Rota and Starting Weeks. This representation required an implementation of the GA that could account for possible disruptions to a solution introduced by the internal operators.

# 3    Feature Extraction

## 3.1    Multiple Correspondence Analysis

The method to extract explanatory features outlined in this paper utilizes the process of trajectory decomposition into a set of derived variables or dimensions. There are many decomposition techniques available, and previous work has included the use of Principal Component Analysis [21] to that end. In this paper, we apply a variation of correspondence analysis called Multiple Correspondence Analysis (MCA) to allow for the decomposition of the dataset in which the variables, while taking integer values, are in practice nominal which would reduce the applicability of PCA directly. As shown in [22], it is possible to link MCA to PCA such that the application of an un-standardized PCA to an indicator matrix such as a Transformed Complete Disjunctive Table (TCDT), can lead to the same results as MCA. This process involves the creation of the Complete Disjunctive Table (CDT) by replacing the categorical variables with one-hot encoded dummy variables. This must be transformed as seen in Eq. (5) in which the value of the CDT table, $x_i k$ is transformed using $y_{ik}$, the proportion of solutions containing that value.

$$x_{ik} = y_{ik}/P_k - 1 \tag{5}$$

The application of PCA to the resulting TCDT provides us with the necessary directional vectors from our dataset as both approaches project the values to a lower-dimensional Euclidean space for the purpose of data analysis. Shown in Eq. (6), this creates a set of $m$, $n \times 1$ orthonormal eigenvectors in $\mathbb{R}^n$. The elements of the $p^i$ vectors represent the weighting of each variable, $[p_1^i, \ldots, p_n^i]$. These coefficients help describe the contribution of each variable to the corresponding principal component in terms of maximizing the variance in the dataset through a best-fit hyperplane.

$$P = [p^1, \ldots, p^m], m \leq n$$
$$p^i = [p_1^i, \ldots, p_n^i] \tag{6}$$

With these, we can calculate the Mean Squared Cosine (MSC) value associated with each variable in the problem. Equations (7), (8), (9) outline this process.

$$PC_{x_n c} = \sqrt{\lambda_m} \cdot \text{Factor Loadings}(x_n, p^m) \tag{7}$$

$$PC_{x_n} = \sqrt{\sum_{c=1}^{num_c} \lambda_m \cdot \text{Factor Loadings}(x_n, p^m)} \tag{8}$$

$$\text{MSC}(x_n) = \frac{1}{num_c} \sum_{c=1}^{num_c} \left( \frac{PC_{x_n c}}{PC_{x_n}} \right)^2 \tag{9}$$

The principal coordinate of variable $x_n$ in category $c$ is denoted as $PC_{x_n c}$, while $PC_{x_n}$ represents the same variable's principal coordinate across all categories, whose count is $num_c$. The eigenvalue of component $p^m$ is $\lambda_m$, and the

associated loadings are the Factor Loadings($x_n, m$). The Mean Squared Cosine
(MSC) value, a measure of the proportion of variance captured by each category
in each variable, is the squared cosine of the angle between a variable and its categories in the Multiple Correspondence Analysis (MCA) space. A higher MSC
value indicates a stronger relationship between the categories and the variable
in the MCA space, implying greater importance of those categories in capturing
the structure and variability in the MCA analysis. We decompose the search trajectories from each optimization run, resulting in subspaces each characterizing
the algorithm's search trajectory in terms of the variance of one variable and its
categories. This reveals which variables are crucial to the algorithm's position
on the fitness gradient. The output of this process is a collection of datasets
representing each variable's influence, ranked in ascending order from 1 to $n$
(141), where 1 is the least influential and $n$ is the most, across a subset of the
$m$ eigenvectors created.

## 3.2   Analysis of Variance

To gain a better understanding of the trajectory analysis results, we employ
Analysis of Variance (ANOVA), which is a statistical method for the comparison of means across multiple groups. This is used to generate a comparative
set of variable rankings. In our datasets, we can use ANOVA to compare the
means of each variable in our solutions to the dependent variable - solution fitness. This analysis technique is used to detect whether there is a relationship
between each variable and the fitness of a solution. This is done by using the
sum of squares between value groups and the sum of squares within groups. The
resulting *p-value* can be used to indicate whether any detected relationship is
statistically significant. For the purpose of this paper, we consider all variables
to be independent. This decision means that we can apply the ANOVA test
to each variable-fitness pair separately and calculate the "partial eta squared"
value for each pair. Partial eta squared is a measure of effect size in ANOVA that
represents the proportion of total variance that is explained by an effect while
controlling for other effects. To calculate the partial eta squared values, we use
the Python "statsmodel" package [23] implementation of ANOVA. Equations
(10), (11), (12) show how we calculate the partial eta value ($\eta_p^2$). Here, $k$ is the
number of solutions in our trajectory ($gN$), $n$ is the number of variables, $x_{ij}$ is
the $j$th variable in the solution $i$ of the whole trajectory. The mean value of all
variables in solution $i$ is shown as $\bar{x}_i$.

$$SS_{\text{within}} = \sum_{i=1}^{k} \sum_{j=1}^{n_i} (x_{ij} - \bar{x}_i)^2 \tag{10}$$

$$SS_{\text{between}} = \sum_{i=1}^{k} n_i (\bar{x}_i - \bar{x})^2 \tag{11}$$

$$\eta_p^2 = \frac{SS_{\text{between}}}{SS_{\text{between}} + SS_{\text{within}}} \tag{12}$$

We use the value $\bar{x}_i$, in conjunction with the resulting $p$-$value$ generated for each variable, to determine the influence that the variable $x_i$ has on Fitness and whether that influence is statistically significant. For this paper, if $p < 0.05$, we reject the null hypothesis that $x_i$ has no measurable influence on fitness across all trajectories. Once complete, we use the partial eta to rank each variable in terms of the size of their effect on the fitness measured. It is important to note that as all 100 optimization runs were performed separately, the ANOVA analysis must be performed a total of 100 times, each resulting in a set of partial eta values and $p$-$values$. There are several methods of accommodating this approach that would allow us to use the $p$-$values$ from across multiple runs to determine the significance of our findings.

One process is Bonferroni [24] however, as we are using 100 total runs, this would require us to adjust to $p$-$value$ threshold to a prohibitively small value due to how the Bonferroni correction is calculated. We opted to use the less conservative Benjamini-Hochberg [25] process to instead account for the false discovery rate (FDR) that using 100 runs may introduce. This method, as shown in Algorithm 1 involves the ranking of all calculated $p$-$values$ before calculating the "Benjamini-Hochberg critical value".

---

**Algorithm 1.** Benjamini-Hochberg Procedure

---

**Require:** p-values $P[1..m]$, false discovery rate $Q$
**Ensure:** List of rejected hypotheses $R$
  1: Arrange the p-values in ascending order: $P[1] \leq P[2] \leq ... \leq P[m]$
  2: Initialize an empty list of rejected hypotheses: $R = []$
  3: **for** $i = m$ to 1 **do**
  4:     Calculate the Benjamini-Hochberg critical value: $BH = \frac{i}{m}Q$
  5:     **if** $P[i] \leq BH$ **then**
  6:         Add $i$ to the list of rejected hypotheses: $R = R + [i]$
  7:         Break the loop
  8:     **end if**
  9: **end for**
10: **return** $R$

---

This is then used to determine, for each variable, what the relevant adjusted $p$-$value$ should be to keep the FDR below 0.05 and results that are higher are rejected and removed from the dataset.

### 3.3  Weighted Ranked Biased Overlap

To facilitate the comparison of the variable rankings produced by both MCA and ANOVA, we use a method known as Weighted Rank Biased Overlap (WRBO) [26], which has been used in the past to increase the interpretability of machine learning results [27]. This method allows the comparison of ranked-lists with the added benefit that both lists can be of varying length and do not need to contain all of the same elements. It is this ability that led us to use WRBO over more classical rank-comparison methods such as Spearman Rank Correlation or the Kendall Tau method. A further benefit of this method is that it can place a higher weighing to elements at the top of a list which can be customised. The output of this method is a similarity score representing the proximity between both lists. This score takes a value of $[0, 1]$, with 1 showing a complete overlap and 0 no similarity between the order of the list elements and the number of shared elements. This process also takes into account any weightings given to the top elements. This process can be seen in Algorithm 2 which was created from a Python implementation of the WRBO function outlined in [28].

---

**Algorithm 2.** Rank Biased Overlap (RBO) Python

---

**Require:** Two lists $S$ and $T$, weight parameter $WP$ (default: 0.9)
1: Determine the maximum length $k \leftarrow \max(\text{len}(S), \text{len}(T))$
2: Calculate the intersection at depth k: $x_k \leftarrow |\text{set}(S) \cap \text{set}(T)|$
3: Initialize summation term: summ_term $\leftarrow 0$
4: **for** $d = 1$ to $k$ **do**
5:     Create sets from the lists:
6:     set1 $\leftarrow$ set($S[: d]$) if $d < \text{len}(S)$ else set($S$)
7:     set2 $\leftarrow$ set($T[: d]$) if $d < \text{len}(T)$ else set($T$)
8:     Calculate intersection at depth d: $x_d \leftarrow |\text{set1} \cap \text{set2}|$
9:     Compute agreement at depth d: $a_d \leftarrow \frac{x_d}{d}$
10:    Update: summ_term $\leftarrow$ summ_term $+ WP^d \cdot a_d$
11: **end for**
12: Calculate Rank Biased Overlap (extrapolated):
13: $rbo\_ext \leftarrow \frac{x_k}{k} \cdot WP^k + \frac{(1-WP)}{WP} \cdot$ summ_term

---

As the results of our analysis are sets of ranked variables, from most to least influential, the ability of WRBO to set a higher weight in its similarity calculation to the top members of a list was of great benefit. The method has a parameter that can increase the weighting of a top subset of variables. This $WP$ value is dependent on the presumed size of the lists. For our purposes, setting this value at 0.9 results in the top 10 variables being responsible for 85.56% to the total scoring. This is done to allow for the most influential variables found in both methods to influence the scoring more than the other, lower influence variables. It is also possible to set the $WP$ to 0.98. This will result in requiring the first 100 items in the list to result in a similar weighting of $\sim$85%.

With this rank-comparison method, we are able to generate a measure of similarity between the findings of the MCA and ANOVA analyses. As ANOVA measures the impact that varying a variable has on the variance in fitness, we can use this measure to show any overlap. This overlap may represent some level of shared findings, highlighting that our trajectory mining method may also be able to detect some level of structure that the ANOVA approach is discovering.

## 4    Results

In this section, we analyse and interpret the results of the optimization of the rostering problem and the features we are able to mine from the search.

## 4.1  Rostering Results

The results of running the optimization a total of 100 times can be seen in Figs. 1a and 1b. These show the mean results for fitness and usage of both the hard and soft constraints in the problem. Figures 1a shows the results between solution fitness and the number of variables that were assigned a value resulting in a change of rosters (CV). We see that averaging over 100 runs, the GA was able to find considerably better solutions than the initial starting state of the problem – from a mean fitness of 14 to approximately 0.7. Within the first 100 generations, the value of CV increases from 0 to 6.

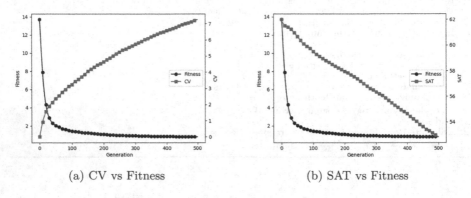

(a) CV vs Fitness                    (b) SAT vs Fitness

**Fig. 1.** Constraints vs. Mean Fitness

Over the course of the remaining 400 generations, this value continues to increase but at a lower rate. This shows that within the first 100 generations, a significant improvement in solution quality is achieved with approximately 6 roster reassignments. As the rate of fitness change slows, we see that the GA makes small, incremental improvements to solutions at the expense of adding new roster assignments. Figure 1b shows the results of fitness and the soft constraint SAT - the number of consecutive Saturdays assigned. The results show a slow, steady reduction in this value over all 500 generations from an initial value of 62 to approximately 52.

The changes in daily range values can be seen in Fig. 2. Here, we show the distribution of range values for each day of the week over all 100 runs. Figure 2 shows the range values at 3 different generations - 5, 100 and 500. Between generation 5 and 100 we see a clear reduction in the mean range values across all runs for all days of the week except Saturday, with this day showing a small increase from 0.075 to 0.078. We also see a reduction in the upper limit of ranges seen on Mon, Tue and Wed. Between generations 100 and 500 we see an increase in the mean range on Mon and Sat while the other days show either a reduction or little change. As the fitness value continues to reduce over this period, solutions with a higher range value on some days are being found that achieve a higher quality solution with a more balanced overall range across the week.

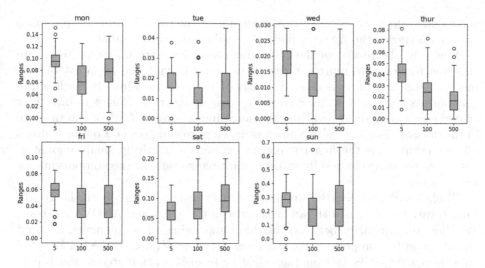

**Fig. 2.** Range Results - Unweighted

## 4.2   MCA and ANOVA Feature Results

After the results of the ANOVA testing were gathered, we performed the Benjamini-Hochberg *p-value* adjustment method to allow for the comparison of all 100 runs. Shown in Fig. 3a and 3b is the explained variance by component for MCA and the distribution of $p - values$ resulting from the adjustment respectively. The ANOVA results show that all included values in the analysis are below the set threshold of 0.05, with nearly all being below 0.003.

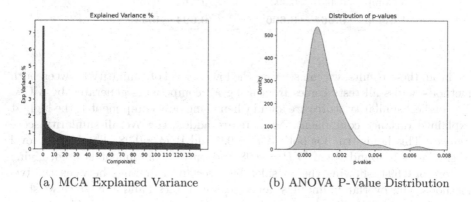

(a) MCA Explained Variance          (b) ANOVA P-Value Distribution

**Fig. 3.** MCA and ANOVA Results

This process resulted in roughly 30% of the variable partial eta values being removed from the dataset as the associated *p-value* for those results did not meet the required threshold of 0.05. This ensured that the variable rankings produced via the ranking of the ANOVA partial eta values remained viable.

Similarly, the results of the MCA decomposition were inspected to ensure that the results were representative of the level of variance captured by this method. Seen in Fig. 3a is the percentage of variance explained by each of the components generated when averaged across all 100 runs. These results show that the first component explains a mean value of around 7.4% of the variance in the dataset. The level of explained variance from component 2 onwards drops off significantly. As the first component explains a relatively small amount of variation, we show the results of using multiple subsets of the components for comparison.

Table 3 shows the WRBO similarity scores when comparing both the Top-10 ranked variables and all 141 variables between the MCA and ANOVA methods. We show the similarity between variable ranks using all components, the first 50, 10, 5 and 1st component. We also show the effect of altering the WRBO $WP$ value from 0.0 to 0.98, shifting the weighting from 85% attributed to the Top-10 to 100 for the same effect. The highest similarity score for each test is shown in bold.

**Table 3.** WRBO Similarity Scores - MCA to ANOVA

| Dataset | WP = 0.9 | | WP = 0.98 | |
|---|---|---|---|---|
| | WRBO | WRBO-Top 10 | WRBO | WRBO-Top 10 |
| All Comp | 0.234 | 0.166 | 0.495 | 0.194 |
| 50 Comp | 0.301 | 0.232 | 0.524 | 0.293 |
| 10 Comp | 0.363 | 0.322 | 0.568 | 0.311 |
| 5 Comp | 0.449 | 0.394 | 0.607 | 0.327 |
| 1 Comp | **0.664** | **0.606** | **0.694** | **0.449** |

From these results, we can see that the lowest level of similarity between both methods across all tests comes from using all components generated by MCA. The highest similarity scores are found when using only component 1, the highest explained variance component. As more are added, the overall similarity score reduces. This holds true for both $WP = 0.9$ and $WP = 0.98$. The highest level of similarity is found when $WP = 0.98$ and only 1 component is used, giving a score of 0.694, showing the considerable overlap in findings between the two methods. This overlap in findings can be seen in Tables 4 and 5 in which we show the variables identified as being both high and low importance. Tables 4 shows the variables identified as most influential for both MCA and ANOVA. Also shown are the results for the top 1, 5, 10, 50 and all components for comparison. Highlighted in bold and brackets are any variables found in both the ANOVA and any components' Top-10 list. Here, we show that variables of both high MCA-cosine squared ranking and high ANOVA partial-eta ranking in common are [121, 65, 1 and 60]. As these are ranked highly by both methods, these would be considered highly influential in both algorithm search direction and impact on fitness, based on the MCA and ANOVA results respectively. The results in this table also reflect the higher WRBO similarity scores, as the 1 component results show 4 overlapping variables. The remainder shows only 3 except when using all components, where the overlap drops to one, mirroring the decreasing WRBO scores. This would indicate that when viewing these results from the perspective of an end-user, workers [121, 65, 1, 60] would be of particularly high interest due to their high influence. Further explanations may be gained from a closer assessment of their working pattern preferences as those assigned to these workers are consistently required for high-quality solutions to the scheduling problem.

**Table 4.** Most Influential Variables by Dataset

| Rank | ANOVA | 1 Comp | 5 Comp | 10 Comp | 50 Comp | All Comp |
| --- | --- | --- | --- | --- | --- | --- |
|     | Var | Var | Var | Var | Var | Var |
| 141 | (121) | (121) | (1) | 96 | (1) | (1) |
| 140 | (65) | (65) | (65) | (1) | 96 | 70 |
| 139 | 51 | (1) | (121) | (65) | (65) | 135 |
| 138 | (1) | 96 | 96 | (121) | 135 | 67 |
| 137 | 33 | 135 | 135 | 135 | 48 | 76 |
| 136 | (60) | (60) | 128 | 119 | 91 | 65 |
| 135 | 129 | 72 | 72 | 128 | 67 | 68 |
| 134 | 126 | 128 | 119 | 67 | 119 | 96 |
| 133 | 110 | 48 | 48 | 72 | 72 | 91 |
| 132 | 66 | 119 | 68 | 48 | (121) | 72 |

The results in Table 5 show the overlap in rankings between the MCA and ANOVA methods for the lowest-ranking variables. These variables would be considered to have a low impact on fitness due to their low partial eta value, and of low influence on the overall search path due to their low cosine squared ranking. The overlap between the two methods identifies variables [21, 137 and 69]. These results also show a similar pattern to the highly ranked variable such that, as more components are used in the calculation, the lower the overlap and similarity between ANOVA and MCA becomes. To an end-user, these results could help highlight that workers [21, 137 and 69] have a lower impact on solution quality and algorithm direction. The results would suggest that these workers have a higher capacity for roster allocation with minimal impact on the overall quality of the schedule, allowing for more customization to accommodate any additional goals.

Table 5. Least Influential Variables by Dataset

| Rank | ANOVA Var | 1 Comp Var | 5 Comp Var | 10 Comp Var | 50 Comp Var | All Comp Var |
|------|-----------|------------|------------|-------------|-------------|--------------|
| 10 | 118 | 97 | 97 | 97 | 97 | 97 |
| 9 | (21) | 15 | 15 | 4 | 4 | 15 |
| 8 | 88 | (21) | 4 | 15 | 15 | 4 |
| 7 | (137) | 4 | (21) | (21) | (21) | (21) |
| 6 | 38 | 77 | 9 | 9 | 9 | 77 |
| 5 | 25 | 9 | 77 | 77 | 77 | 9 |
| 4 | 83 | (69) | 93 | 93 | (69) | 36 |
| 3 | 84 | 79 | 79 | 79 | 93 | 93 |
| 2 | (69) | 93 | (69) | (69) | 79 | 105 |
| 1 | 37 | (137) | 105 | 105 | 105 | (69) |

# 5    Conclusions and Future Work

In this paper, we used Multiple Correspondence Analysis to analyze the search trajectories generated by a Genetic Algorithm for a staff rostering problem. We calculated the squared cosine value for each variable from the subspace, which was derived from decomposing the trajectories. These results were then compared with the outcomes of one-way ANOVA testing on the same datasets, leading to a set of statistically significant measurements of the partial-eta value. This value measures the relative impact a variable has on fitness variance in the data. We ranked both sets of results and used the Weighted Rank-Biased Overlap similarity metric to measure the overlap in findings. Our results show a significant overlap (0.69) when only the first component is used, averaged across all 100 runs. However, the addition of more components showed diminishing returns, possibly because the first component captures key structures in a widely spread dataset. The significant level of residual variance might contain a lot of noise, which could disrupt the process as more components are added. Further study would be needed to identify any missed structure in the residual variance.

Our experiments identified key variable subsets, corresponding to individual workers, using both methods together. The overlap between the two methods in the top and bottom rankings provides a subset of variables that have either a high or low influence on the search path and fitness impact. This gives end-users a way to identify key individuals and those who, due to their lower impact, could be moved to another observed rota schedule with minimal disruption. This tool is valuable to end-users, helping to explain key drivers towards high-quality solutions and the capacity for minimal impact change.

# References

1. Abduljabbar, R., Dia, H., Liyanage, S., Bagloee, S.A.: Applications of artificial intelligence in transport: an overview. Sustainability **11**(1), 189 (2019)
2. Brownlee, A.E., Wright, J.A., He, M., Lee, T., McMenemy, P.: A Novel encoding for separable large-scale multi-objective problems and its application to the optimisation of housing stock improvements. Appl. Soft Comput. **96**, 106650 (2020)
3. Hall, A., Ordish, J., Mitchell, C., Richardson (nee Murfet), H.: Black box medicine and transparency - interpretability by design framework. Technical report MSR-TR-2020-53, PHG Foundation (2020). https://www.microsoft.com/en-us/research/publication/black-box-medicine-and-transparency-interpretability-by-design-framework/
4. European Commission: Ethics Guidelines for Trustworthy AI (2021). https://digital-strategy.ec.europa.eu/en/library/ethics-guidelines-trustworthy-ai
5. Barredo Arrieta, A., et al.: Explainable artificial intelligence (XAI): concepts, taxonomies, opportunities and challenges toward responsible AI. Inf. Fusion **58**, 82–115 (2020). https://www.sciencedirect.com/science/article/pii/S1566253519308103
6. Dwivedi, R., et al.: Explainable AI (XAI): core ideas, techniques, and solutions. ACM Comput. Surv. **55**(9) (2023). https://doi.org/10.1145/3561048
7. Wright, J., Wang, M., Brownlee, A., Buswell, R.: Variable convergence in evolutionary optimization and its relationship to sensitivity analysis. In: Building Simulation and Optimization 2012, Loughborough, UK, pp. 102–109 (2012). https://repository.lboro.ac.uk/articles/conference_contribution/Variable_convergence_in_evolutionary_optimization_and_its_relationship_to_sensitivity_analysis/9438080
8. Cortez, P., Embrechts, M.J.: Using sensitivity analysis and visualization techniques to open black box data mining models. Inf. Sci. **225**, 1–17 (2013)
9. Jin, Y.: Surrogate-assisted evolutionary computation: recent advances and future challenges. Swarm Evol. Comput. **1**(2), 61–70 (2011)
10. Wallace, A., Brownlee, A.E.I., Cairns, D.: Towards explaining metaheuristic solution quality by data mining surrogate fitness models for importance of variables. In: Bramer, M., Ellis, R. (eds.) SGAI-AI 2021. LNCS (LNAI), vol. 13101, pp. 58–72. Springer, Cham (2021). https://doi.org/10.1007/978-3-030-91100-3_5
11. Singh, M., Brownlee, A.E.I., Cairns, D.: Towards explainable metaheuristic: mining surrogate fitness models for importance of variables. In: Proceedings of the Genetic and Evolutionary Computation Conference Companion, GECCO 2022, pp. 1785–1793. Association for Computing Machinery, New York (2022)
12. Duygu Arbatli, A., Levent Akin, H.: Rule extraction from trained neural networks using genetic algorithms. Nonlinear Anal.: Theory Methods Appl. **30**(3), 1639–1648 (1997)
13. Sharma, S., Henderson, J., Ghosh, J.: CERTIFAI: counterfactual explanations for robustness, transparency, interpretability, and fairness of artificial intelligence models. In: Proceedings of the AAAI/ACM Conference on AI, Ethics, and Society (2020)
14. Fyvie, M., McCall, J.A.W., Christie, L.A., Brownlee, A.E.: Explaining a staff rostering genetic algorithm using sensitivity analysis and trajectory analysis. In: Genetic and Evolutionary Computation Conference Companion (GECCO 2023 Companion), 15–19 July 2023, Lisbon, Portugal (2023)
15. Dimitropoulaki, M., Kern, M., Owusu, G., McCormick, A.: Workforce rostering via metaheuristics. In: Bramer, M., Petridis, M. (eds.) SGAI 2018. LNCS (LNAI),

vol. 11311, pp. 277–290. Springer, Cham (2018). https://doi.org/10.1007/978-3-030-04191-5_25

16. Reid, K.N., et al.: A hybrid metaheuristic approach to a real world employee scheduling problem. In: Proceedings of the Genetic and Evolutionary Computation Conference, GECCO 2019, pp. 1311–1318. Association for Computing Machinery, New York (2019)

17. Fyvie, M., McCall, J.A., Christie, L.A., Zăvoianu, A.C., Brownlee, A.E., Ainslie, R.: Explaining a staff rostering problem by mining trajectory variance structures definition (2023). https://github.com/rgu-subsea/mfyvie_sgai2023_varstruct.git

18. Blank, J., Deb, K.: Pymoo: multi-objective optimization in python. IEEE Access **8**, 89497–89509 (2020)

19. Deb, K., Deb, D.: Analysing mutation schemes for real-parameter genetic algorithms. Int. J. Artif. Intell. Soft Comput. **4**, 1–28 (2014)

20. Deb, K., Sindhya, K., Okabe, T.: Self-adaptive simulated binary crossover for real-parameter optimization. In: Proceedings of the 9th Annual Conference on Genetic and Evolutionary Computation, GECCO 2007, pp. 1187–1194. Association for Computing Machinery, New York (2007)

21. Fyvie, M., McCall, J.A.W., Christie, L.A.: Towards explainable metaheuristics: PCA for trajectory mining in evolutionary algorithms. In: Bramer, M., Ellis, R. (eds.) SGAI-AI 2021. LNCS (LNAI), vol. 13101, pp. 89–102. Springer, Cham (2021). https://doi.org/10.1007/978-3-030-91100-3_7

22. Pagés, J.: Multiple Factor Analysis by Example Using R, 1 edn. Chapman and Hall/CRC (2014)

23. Seabold, S., Perktold, J.: Statsmodels: econometric and statistical modeling with python. In: Proceedings of the 9th Python in Science Conference 2010 (2010)

24. Dunn, O.J.: Multiple comparisons among means. J. Am. Stat. Assoc. **56**(293), 52–64 (1961)

25. Benjamini, Y., Hochberg, Y.: Controlling the false discovery rate: a practical and powerful approach to multiple testing. J. Roy. Stat. Soc.: Ser. B (Methodol.) **57**(1), 289–300 (1995)

26. Webber, W., Moffat, A., Zobel, J.: A similarity measure for indefinite rankings. ACM Trans. Inf. Syst. (TOIS) **28**(4), 1–38 (2010)

27. Sarica, A., Quattrone, A., Quattrone, A.: Introducing the rank-biased overlap as similarity measure for feature importance in explainable machine learning: a case study on Parkinson's disease. In: Mahmud, M., He, J., Vassanelli, S., van Zundert, A., Zhong, N. (eds.) BI 2022. LNCS, vol. 13406, pp. 129–139. Springer, Heidelberg (2022). https://doi.org/10.1007/978-3-031-15037-1_11

28. Raikar, K.: How to objectively compare two ranked lists in python (2023). https://towardsdatascience.com/how-to-objectively-compare-two-ranked-lists-in-python-b3d74e236f6a

# Machine Learning Applications

# Quantitative Approach of Geospatial Sentiment Analysis to Reveal Opinions on the War in Ukraine

Chris Prusakiewicz and Ken McGarry(✉)

School of Computer Science, Faculty of Technology, University of Sunderland,
Sunderland, UK
ken.mcgarry@sunderland.ac.uk

**Abstract.** The escalation of the full-scale military conflict between Russian and Ukrainian forces in February 2022 initiated a worldwide conversation. The manifestation of diverse opinions about the war on Twitter demonstrates a social phenomenon that reveals peoples' perceptions, thoughts, and interactions with war-related information in a digitalised world. Whereas the majority of media outlets in the UK have been following the events in Ukraine, little is known about people's sentiment toward sending military, financial, or medical aid at the regional level. Therefore, this work aims to develop a broader understanding of the UK public opinions through Sentiment Analysis (SA) where we collected 2,893 English-language tweets from Twitter API and additional geolocation data is integrated from external sources. The acquired dataset is preprocessed and prepared for textual analysis. In addition to SA, this work compares and contrasts different approaches and four selected ML models. Finally, this work uses data visualisation techniques to demonstrate the results from three perspectives: quantitative, temporal, and geospatial. The results reveal that in the UK, people express on Twitter more negative sentiments towards the conflict, with a large number of positive tweets towards military and financial issues.

**Keywords:** Sentiment Analysis · Twitter · Geospatial · Machine Learning

## 1 Introduction

In this work, we analyse Twitter as a means of revealing public opinion and beliefs regarding military, financial, and medical aid in the Russo-Ukrainian conflict (RUC). According to NATO [24], this conflict is the biggest threat to the security of the Euro-Atlantic area since the end of the Cold War. The military training and equipment, medical supplies, and financial support to Ukraine instigated a worldwide conversation in cyberspace. We use the Twitter API to collect tweets and prepare a dataset for Geospatial Sentiment Analysis (GSA). Our objective compare different approaches and evaluate their effectiveness. Although we collect tweets expressing opinions about military, financial, and

M. Bramer and F. Stahl (Eds.): SGAI 2023, LNAI 14381, pp. 293–306, 2023.
https://doi.org/10.1007/978-3-031-47994-6_28

medical aid, the analysis is more about sentiment towards the conflict in general, rather than a breakdown between sentiment towards military, medical, or financial aid to Ukraine. Nevertheless, the main objective is to answer three research questions:

(i) How is the opinion about sending military, medical, and financial aid to Ukraine reflected on the map of the UK?
(ii) How can Machine Learning methods identify the key issues of public concern?
(iii) Can Geospatial Sentiment Analysis provide further information regarding any differences of opinion between the UK regions?

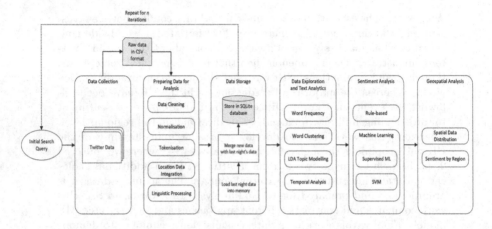

**Fig. 1.** System overview of data flow and processing

In Fig. 1, we present an overview of our approach to analysing Twitter data related to the Russo-Ukrainian conflict. We retrieve tweets via Twitter API and store them in a CSV file. We prepare the raw data for analysis, merge data with the previous night's data, and store processed data in an SQLite database. We repeat this process until we collect enough tweets that match our keywords and topics of interest. Ideally, our baseline would be 5,000 tweets, however, due to the limitations, i.e., short timeframe, rigorous selection of search keywords, limited processing capabilities, as well as the lack of access to the academic Twitter API, we were only able to collect a total of 2,893 tweets. We conduct data exploration and text analytics, followed by sentiment analysis and geospatial analysis.

We apply a quantitative analysis approach to achieve objective and precise measurement of sentiment within tweets in order to understand people's thoughts, feelings, perceptions, behaviours, or emotions expressed in online discussion [20]. Therefore, in the context of this work, a positive sentiment refers to tweets expressing warm feelings towards sending aid to Ukraine, whereas a negative sentiment refers to tweets expressing cold feelings. The approach implemented in this work involves statistical analysis and the identification of relationships between variables. This work is carried out in Python and NLP libraries.

The search keywords are identified using Twitter, Google Trends, and relevant news articles. This project uses the Tweepy library to acquire a dataset of tweets that are preprocessed, cleaned, and normalised to minimise noise and made suitable for Machine Learning (ML) algorithms. The SA process is experimental and the results are evaluated based on the number of positive and negative tweets, and also evaluation metrics, e.g., precision and accuracy.

The work carried out conforms with legislations and guidelines that govern the collection and use of personal information such as the Data Protection Act and the UK General Data Protection Regulation [14]. Moreover, in terms of Twitter API, we also consider the End User Licence Agreement (EULA) that defines the relationship between the user and the service provider Terms of Service that describe permissive use of the platform and associated services [39].

## 2   Related Work

Over the past 10 years or so, sentiment analysis has seen a massive expansion both in research and practical applications [13,30,44]. For good review articles see Wang [41], Singh [35] and Birjali [5]. The process of sentiment mining involves the preprocessing of text using either simple text analytics or the more complex NLP such as the Stanford system [28]. The text data can be organised by individual words or at the sentence and paragraph level by the positive or negative words it is comprised of [15]. Words are deemed to be either neutral, negative or positive based on the assessment of a lexicon [10,36].

Sentiment analysis is employed in many different areas from finance [9,22] to mining student feedback in educational domains [16,32]. Sentiment analysis in conjunction with named entity recognition has also been used to automatically create ontologies from text by identifying terms and their relationships using keywords [23]. However, it is mining customer emails/reviews for improving satisfaction with products or services that has experienced huge growth [6,34]. For example, computer gaming forums can provide information on bugs from mining user posts to highlight issues [21]. Natural Language Processing and speech recognition provide many insights into modelling the sequence of information, especially when dealing with strings, letters and word occurrences [31,42]. For example, a part-of-speech-tagging (POS) allows the sequence of words to be represented to resolve ambiguity [33]. The recent expansion of chatbots for online help, employs a mixture of Deep Learning, NLP and sentiment analysis to provide context and the emotion of the users [7].

Previous studies demonstrated that Twitter played an important role in studying the dynamics of public opinion about war-afflicted areas otherwise impossible with traditional research methods. Such as opinions towards the Syrian refugee crisis in European and Middle Eastern countries [4] investigated public opinion toward the Syrian Chemical Attack, whereas Lee et al. carried out a sentiment analysis of a political situation in Afghanistan after the withdrawal of US troops [18]. However, only a few studies have focused on the analysis of public opinion expressed on Twitter toward the RUC, and to the best of our knowledge, none have been done in the UK. Therefore, this work is motivated by the premise that the RUC offers the opportunity to analyse public discourse in cyberspace about military conflicts and their impact on humankind in a digitally connected world.

There are existing datasets such as "Russia-Ukraine war - Tweets Dataset" [29] and "Twitter Dataset for 2022 Russo-Ukrainian Crisis" [12]. However, these datasets would have to be filtered to extract tweets that originated in the UK, and it is possible that the use of existing datasets would not benefit the learning outcomes such as data collection, and also raise ethical and social concerns regarding authors' data collection methods and handling of sensitive information.

## 3   Methods

We search Twitter with various keywords, download these tweets, and preprocess the tweet data to remove stopwords, perform stemming, and remove non-ASCII characters. We also discuss our methods for sentiment analysis and topic map modelling, and the ML methods used on the data. We write Python code in Jupyter Notebook and make the source code available on GitHub: https://github.com/Chrisu892/sentiment_analysis.

Furthermore, whilst the research involves user-generated content, we employ an ethical framework proposed by Taylor and Pagliari [37]. The framework provides ten considerations when dealing with social media data, such as privacy, ethical theory, and geographical information. Other personally identifiable information, e.g., usernames, will not be collected to ensure anonymity and privacy.

### 3.1   Data

The dataset contains 2,893 English-language tweets related to the Russo-Ukrainian conflict and people's opinions about military, financial, and medical aid sent to Ukraine. To collect this dataset, the initial search terms applied to Twitter included "military aid to Ukraine", "medical aid to Ukraine", and financial aid to Ukraine". Other keywords were determined using Twitter, Google Trends, and news articles [1,3]. The tweets were acquired through Twitter API (Application Programming Interface provided by Twitter Developer Platform), in conjunction with search-tweets, and search-30-days methods available in the Tweepy library, which enabled us to find tweets relevant to our criteria shown in Table 1. To avoid duplication of content, all retweets were removed. Tweets originated outside the UK were also removed. Furthermore, we extract location data from geotagged tweets, otherwise, we use tweet author's location. Since Twitter provides tweet' longitude and latitude, further data about tweets' location, such as country and region, was extracted from Postcodes.io, an open-source API for geocoding UK postcodes.

**Table 1.** Keywords and main topics of interest

| Topics | Keywords |
|---|---|
| Military | military, war, unprovoked, border, escalation, conflict invasion, attack, tension, force, battalion, invade power, offensive, weapon, javelin, tank, aircraft, armour munition, arms, jet, lethal, equipment, fuel, rocket, stringer rifle, vest, grenade, gun, nuclear, missile, #ukraine, @ukraine |
| Financial | financial, money, economy, economic, package, aid relief, donation, subsidy, loan, budget, sanction, commit, dollars, euros, pounds, billion, million, grant, fund, pledge, figure, deficit, cost, finance, bank, investment, worth, donor, #ukraine, @ukraine |
| Medical | medical, supply, supplies, food, emergency, energy, humanitarian, medicine, wounded, victim, hospital, 'red cross', food, hygiene, healthcare, zeolite, oxygen, patient, shipment, doctor, nurse, #ukraine, @ukraine |
| UK | united kingdom, uk, england, wales, scotland, northern ireland, boris johnson, liz truss, ben wallace, parliament, #ukraine, @ukraine |

Although Twitter API returns a dictionary of tweet objects each represented by a list of attributes, only attributes such as tweet id, created-at, text, user-location, place-id, place-name, place-full-name, and hashtags are used. In preparing Tweets for Analysis, we retained all hashtags for analysis to provide early insights about the dataset such as discussed topics. However, although additional white spaces between words were trimmed, an extra space was added between words adjacent to emoji characters, and also words adjacent to the left of punctuation marks. Nevertheless, special characters were removed, whereas HTML entities, hyphenated words, quotation marks, country names, etc. were normalised as shown in Table 2.

We implemented tokenisation to split the text into unigrams and bigrams. Whereas unigrams were generated using the NLTK's casual-tokenize function, bigrams were created with the spaCy's pattern-based phrase extraction. Not all bigrams are useful in text analytics, therefore as shown in Table 2, this work used PoS tagging and the Textacy library to extract bigrams of nouns and adjectives.

**Table 2.** Example of text tokenised into unigrams and bigrams

| Tokenisation type | Tweet | Tokenised tweet |
|---|---|---|
| Unigrams | america's realise far away war merely pond war problem think narrow minded | america \|'s \| realise \| far \| away \| war \| merely \| pond \| war \| problem \| think \| narrow \| minded |
| Bigrams | novel idea peace talk wouldnt needed putin chosen invade putins negotiation require giving territory withdrawal | idea-peace \| idea-peace-talk \| peace-talk territory-withdrawal |

## 3.2 Sentiment Analysis and Machine Learning Models

The rule-based approach was implemented with VADER, this approach is regarded as one of the most reliable and computationally efficient sentiment intensity analysers. However, this work used VADER's compound rather than individual scores [2]. Then, a new feature "rulebased-sent" was added to the pre-processed data structures to save VADER's classification results in a binary format, whereas all other scores were discarded. Consequently, these results become a baseline for all other approaches.

We used Multinominal Naive Bayes (MNB) [43], Support Vector Machines (SVM) [11], and Bidirectional Encoder Representations from Transformers (BERT) [19]. NB is a probabilistic classifier based on Bayesian Theorem (that relies on Bag of Words features BoW). A MNB is a text classification technique that can calculate the probability of a term in a corpus based on the term frequencies but the classification accuracy decreases with the number of n-grams. SVMs are a non-probabilistic classifiers that use a hyperplane as a dimensional space to separate vectors either linearly or non-linearly into two classes. Whereas NB relies on vectors of term frequencies, SVM uses numerical matrices as an input, i.e., vectors of numbers, each within a range between 1 and 0. Additionally, SVM classifiers use matrices to calculate similarities between terms in a corpus including distances and statistics about the language. Although SVM exhibits higher computational costs [40], some studies show that SVM increases accuracy and reduces overfitting problems [38]. Finally, we use a derivation of BERT called BERTweet, a deep learning model engineered and pretrained on 850 million English tweets that can handle the challenges of shorter in length and grammatically irregular social media text [26].

Therefore, this work generated a BoW with the NLTK's casual-tokenizer because it can process complex language used in social media text [17]. Moreover, all empty values were filled with 0, and the occurrences of words were counted to create a BoW that was used to perform binary MNB classification. In terms of SVM and BERTweet models, this work reused the results of VADER's classification because ML requires a sample of labelled datasets. Firstly, the dataset was split into 80% training and 20% testing, and the data was vectorised with Scikit-learn's TfidfVectorizer to be used by SVM. In terms of BERTweet, we tokenise the dataset with AutoTokenizer module provided in the HuggingFace's Transformers library. We then use TensorFlow to encode and transform the dataset into tensors and use it to fine-tune the model. We trained all our models on CPU, and the models were evaluated and utilised to predict sentiment on the full dataset. The results of VADER, MNB, SVM and BERTweet classifiers were saved into DataFrame for geospatial analysis.

## 3.3    Geospatial Analysis

To implement geospatial analysis we used QGIS software and GeoPandas library in the geovisualisation of tweets. Firstly, the dataset was saved as a CSV file to be later imported into the QGIS software. The imported data was plotted onto an ESRI world map, and portion of the map showing the distribution of tweets over the UK was cropped and saved for analysis. GeoPandas was employed to generate geographic heat maps. A shapefile containing vector boundaries for the nomenclature of territorial units in the UK was downloaded from the ONS website [27]. The file was imported into the program using GeoPandas but the region names were renamed to match the one returned by Postcodes.io, for instance, "North East (England)" was changed to "North East". Then, the number of positive and negative tweets per region classified by VADER, MNB, SVM, and BERTweet were visualised on the map of the UK.

# 4 Results

The text analysis revealed that the terms used in the dataset relate to the research topics. Based on the word frequencies shown in Fig. 2a and Fig. 2b, tokens such as "war", "missile", and "invasion" could be related to the military aspect, "money", "support", and "cost" to the financial, whereas "need", "support", and "covid" to the medical aid. However, words such as NATO, EU, or US do not appear as frequently. Moreover, a high frequency of tokens such as "breaking", "news", and "exclude" could be an indicator that a large number of tweets was published by media outlets rather than real users. This does seem to depend on the number of keywords used during data collection, therefore this work used a number of carefully curated keywords shown in Table 2 to acquire a more specific and robust dataset albeit much smaller.

The trained BERTweet in Fig. 3b model exhibits an accuracy of 88% and the SVM in Fig. 3a exhibits 82%, the performance of the two models can be improved by adjusting the hyper-parameters or by applying different preprocessing techniques on the acquired dataset. The confusion matrices demonstrate

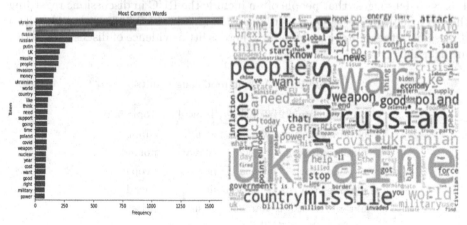

(a) Frequency of most common words          (b) Word cloud of top 300 words

**Fig. 2.** Word analysis

that SVM classified only 55.09% of tweets as true-negative and 6.38% as true-positive. Although BERTweet's accuracy is 88%, the confusion matrix does not reveal false-negative or false-positive predictions.

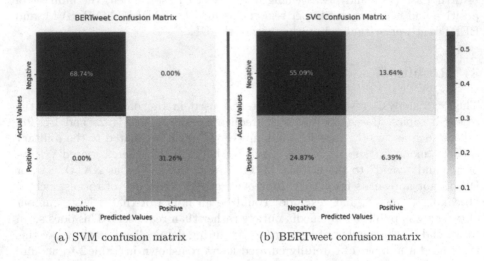

(a) SVM confusion matrix          (b) BERTweet confusion matrix

**Fig. 3.** Model accuracy

The Latent Dirichlet Allocation (LDA) modelling revealed a number of topics regarding sending aid to Ukraine. In Table 3, terms such as "Ukraine", "Russia" and "war" are the most frequent. However, topics 5 and 7 reveal that people are more concerned about financial costs associated with the RUC, whereas topics 4, 6, 8, and 9 suggest that people often include the RUC in discussions regarding the UK's politics and economy. Although the standard LDA algorithm identified topics about the military and finance, there is little evidence of discussions about medical aid.

**Table 3.** LDA topic modelling results

| Topic 1 | Topic 2 | Topic 3 | Topic 4 | Topic 5 |
|---------|---------|---------|---------|---------|
| ukraine | russian | war | attack | supply |
| ukraine | missile | russian | russia | poland |
| ukraine | war | russia | news | people |
| ukraine | war | inflation | uk | friend |
| ukraine | cost | war | crisis | price |
| Topic 6 | Topic 7 | Topic 8 | Topic 9 | Topic 10 |
| ukraine | eu | uk | pandemic | brexit |
| ukraine | putin | money | support | war |
| ukraine | war | uk | russia | right |
| ukraine | war | tory | minister | party |
| ukraine | war | russia | invasion | putin |

This work quantified and aggregated tweets into four groups, one for each classifier. The first set of analyses examined the number of tweets and the sentiments expressed in England, Scotland, Wales, and Northern Ireland, whereas the second set examined the evolutional trends in the number of tweets published on Twitter between 8th October and 17th November 2022. The most interesting observation was that in comparison to other techniques, VADER classified nearly as many tweets as positive and negative as MNB and BERTweet. In comparison to previous work, Chen et al. used RoBERTa-wwm model on 5,000 micro-blogs related to the RUC, out of which 69.79% were classified as positive and 30.21% as negative [8]. Our system classified BERTweet 75.73% of tweets as negative and 24.27% as positive. The results shown in Table 4 illustrate that SVM classified more tweets as negative than any other technique however the SVM's accuracy is 82%.

The temporal sentiment analysis examined tweets by date due to the small dataset. As shown in Fig. 4, VADER, MNB, and BERTweet classified a similar number of tweets as positive, whereas SVM classified more tweets as negative. Moreover, the results show that all models classified a comparable number as negative which could be due to the unbalanced dataset.

**Table 4.** Distribution of positive and negative tweets in the UK

|  | VADER | | Multinominal NB | | SVM | | BERTweet | |
|---|---|---|---|---|---|---|---|---|
|  | Pos | Neg | Pos | Neg | Pos | Neg | Pos | Neg |
| England | 721 | 1579 | 640 | 1660 | 419 | 1881 | 553 | 1747 |
| Scotland | 130 | 290 | 112 | 308 | 66 | 354 | 113 | 307 |
| Wales | 39 | 85 | 30 | 94 | 18 | 106 | 30 | 94 |
| Northern Ireland | 12 | 37 | 10 | 39 | 10 | 39 | 6 | 43 |
| Total | 902 | 1991 | 792 | 2101 | 513 | 2380 | 702 | 2191 |
| % | **31.18** | **68.82** | **27.38** | **72.62** | **17.73** | **82.27** | **24.27** | **75.73** |

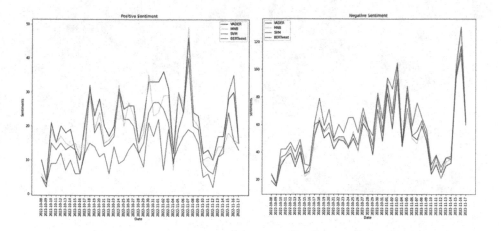

**Fig. 4.** Temporal analysis of sentiments

The geospatial work relied on clustering and geospatial mapping techniques to understand the geospatial distribution of tweets and their sentiments. Therefore, this work focused on binary classification due to smaller dataset compared with a similar study [25]. As shown in Fig. 5a and 5b, the visual examination reveals that the majority of tweets originate in large urban areas, e.g., London, North West, Yorkshire and the Humber, whereas Wales and Northern Ireland were less likely to share opinions about the conflict due to smaller population density or active Twitter users. However, unbalanced geospatial distribution was expected because the majority of the UK's population resides in England. This work implemented a point pattern analysis proposed by Anselin (2021) to determine whether tweets were published randomly or clustered. As shown in Fig. 5a and 5b, the analysis shows that the distribution of tweets is largely correlated with the distribution of the UK population.

In this work we employed geospatial mapping at the regional instead of county level due to smaller dataset. The results reveal that people in London, South East, and Scotland were more likely to post positive tweets than people in other regions. Moreover, contrary to VADER, MNB, and BERTweet, the SVC model classified more tweets as positive in North West, and Yorkshire and the Humber. Hence, the results demonstrate two things. First, the outcome of VADER classifier is comparable to MNB, SVC, and BERTweet likely because VADER's results were used to assign positive and negative label to each tweet, later used to train other models. Second, the time and computational resources required by BERTweet outweigh the benefits of DL model because smaller and computationally more efficient models return similar results.

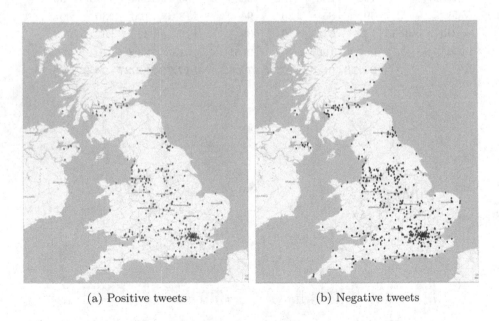

(a) Positive tweets                    (b) Negative tweets

**Fig. 5.** Spatial distribution of tweets

# 5   Conclusions

In conclusion, the public opinion regarding sending aid to Ukraine was largely positive, and negative towards the conflict in general. It is based on the number of negative tweets regarding the RUC published between 8th October and 17th November 2022, the number of topics discussing the conflict, and the frequency of positive and negative words within the acquired dataset. In terms of patterns and correlations, this work shows that urban areas experience a higher number of positive and negative tweets.

The temporal analysis demonstrates that the polarity of sentiment expressed within tweets fluctuates in correlation with news stories regarding the RUC published by media outlets. This suggests that conventional media remain a significant driver of public opinion. However, this study was limited in several ways. Firstly, it is difficult to arrive at conclusions with regard to a comprehensive understanding of public opinion because this analysis was limited to 2,893 tweets. Secondly, not all words in the LDA topic modelling were necessarily relevant to the analysis.

Therefore, this work shows that GSA requires significantly more geotagged tweets, which could allow to implement under-sampling techniques to reduce imbalance and consequently train more accurate models. Nevertheless, this work demonstrates a robust data preprocessing techniques, including geolocation data integration. The overall success of this research is the acquired knowledge and development of skills that could be useful in NLP tasks. Moreover, this research can be a starting point for the further analysis of public opinion in the UK regarding the RUC, something that to the best of the authors' knowledge, has not been done before with the demonstrated tools and techniques.

Future research could focus on acquiring a larger dataset, possibly since the start of the RUC. The analysis of larger dataset could result with a better understanding of public opinion towards different types of aid to Ukraine. From a geospatial perspective, the researchers could analyse sentiment also at county or city level. As shown in this research, small dataset produced sparsely populated point analysis that could be improved. However, future studies should carefully scrutinise existing datasets to determine whether the data consist of relevant and non-sensitive information, or whether the data collection practices were ethical and socially responsible. Future studies should consider the presence of personally identifiable information such as user handles, mentions, and also geolocation data. The latter could be an issue because although Twitter users can stop sharing their geolocation, the location data can be integrated from secondary sources based on the metadata available in each tweet object.

Finally, from a technical perspective, future studies could investigate and evaluate the effectiveness of deep learning models on shorter, social media text, whereas from a social science perspective, future studies could analyse and investigate implications of sending different types of support to Ukraine on British citizens and compare the results with studies focused on domestic issues.

**Acknowledgements.** We would like to thank the two anonymous reviewers for their helpful comments for improving the quality of this paper.

# References

1. Ainsworth, D.: Funding tracker: who's sending aid to Ukraine? (2022). https://www.devex.com/news/funding-tracker-who-s-sending-aid-to-ukraine-102887
2. Albrecht, J., Ramachandran, S., Winkler, C.: Blueprints for Text Analytics Using Python. O'Reilly Media, Inc. (2021)
3. Aljazeera: which countries are sending military aid to Ukraine (2022). https://www.aljazeera.com/news/2022/2/28/which-countries-are-sending-military-aid-to-ukraine
4. Bashir, S., et al.: Twitter chirps for Syrian people: sentiment analysis of tweets related to Syria chemical attack. Int. J. Disaster Risk Reduct. **62**, 102–397 (2021). https://doi.org/10.1016/j.ijdrr.2021.102397
5. Birjali, M., Kasri, M., Beni-Hssane, A.: A comprehensive survey on sentiment analysis: approaches, challenges and trends. Knowl.-Based Syst. **226**, 107134 (2021). https://doi.org/10.1016/j.knosys.2021.107134
6. Bose, S., Saha, U., Kar, D., Goswami, S., Nayak, A.K., Chakrabarti, S.: RSentiment: a tool to extract meaningful insights from textual reviews. In: Satapathy, S.C., Bhateja, V., Udgata, S.K., Pattnaik, P.K. (eds.) Proceedings of the 5th International Conference on Frontiers in Intelligent Computing: Theory and Applications. AISC, vol. 516, pp. 259–268. Springer, Singapore (2017). https://doi.org/10.1007/978-981-10-3156-4_26
7. Caldarini, G., Jaf, S., McGarry, K.: A literature survey of recent advances in chatbots. Information **13**, 41 (2022). https://doi.org/10.3390/info13010041
8. Chen, B., et al.: Public opinion dynamics in cyberspace on Russia-Ukraine war: a case analysis with Chinese Weibo. IEEE Trans. Comput. Soc. Syst. **9**, 948–958 (2022). https://doi.org/10.1109/TCSS.2022.3169332
9. Crone, S.F., Koeppel, C.: Predicting exchange rates with sentiment indicators: an empirical evaluation using text mining and multilayer perceptrons. In: 2014 IEEE Conference on Computational Intelligence for Financial Engineering and Economics (CIFEr), pp. 114–121 (2014). https://doi.org/10.1109/CIFEr.2014.6924062
10. Ding, Y., Li, B., Zhao, Y., Cheng, C.: Scoring tourist attractions based on sentiment lexicon. In: 2017 IEEE 2nd Advanced Information Technology, Electronic and Automation Control Conference (IAEAC), pp. 1990–1993 (2017). https://doi.org/10.1109/IAEAC.2017.8054363
11. Gupta, A., Tyagi, P., Choudhury, T., Shamoon, M.: Sentiment analysis using support vector machine. In: 2019 International Conference on Contemporary Computing and Informatics (IC3I), pp. 49–53 (2019). https://doi.org/10.1109/IC3I46837.2019.9055645
12. Haq, E., Tyson, G., Lee, L., Braud, T., Hui, P.: Twitter dataset for 2022 Russo-Ukrainian crisis (2022). https://arxiv.org/abs/2203.02955. Accessed 25 June 2022
13. Hemmatian, F., Sohrabi, M.: A survey on classification techniques for opinion mining and sentiment analysis. Artif. Intell. Rev. **52**, 1495–1545 (2017). https://doi.org/10.1007/s10462-017-9599-6
14. ico.org.uk: Guide to the UK General Data Protection Regulation (UK GDPR) (2022). https://ico.org.uk/for-organisations/guide-to-data-protection/guide-to-the-general-data-protection-regulation-gdpr/. Accessed 28 Oct 2022

15. Kim, R.Y.: Using online reviews for customer sentiment analysis. IEEE Eng. Manag. Rev. **49**(4), 162–168 (2021). https://doi.org/10.1109/EMR.2021.3103835
16. Kumar, A., Jai, R.: Sentiment analysis and feedback evaluation. In: 2015 IEEE 3rd International Conference on MOOCs, Innovation and Technology in Education (MITE), pp. 433–436 (2015)
17. Lane, H., Howard, C., Hapke, H.M.: Natural Language Processing in Action: Understanding, Analyzing, and Generating Text with Python. Manning Publications (2019)
18. Lee, E., Rustam, F., Ashraf, I., Washington, P.B., Narra, M., Shafique, R.: Inquest of current situation in Afghanistan under Taliban rule using sentiment analysis and volume analysis. IEEE Access **10**, 10333–10348 (2022). https://doi.org/10.1109/ACCESS.2022.3144659
19. Liu, Y., et al.: RoBERTa: a robustly optimized BERT pretraining approach (2019). http://arxiv.org/abs/1907.11692. Cite arxiv:1907.11692
20. Mandloi, L., Patel, R.: Twitter sentiments analysis using machine learning methods. In: 2020 International Conference for Emerging Technology (INCET), pp. 1–5 (2020). https://doi.org/10.1109/INCET49848.2020.9154183
21. McGarry, K., McDonald, S.: Computational methods for text mining user posts on a popular gaming forum for identifying user experience issues. In: British HCI 2017 Conference Digital Make Believe. University of Sunderland, UK (2017). https://doi.org/10.14236/ewic/HCI2017.100
22. Mishev, K., Gjorgjevikj, A., Vodenska, I., Chitkushev, L.T., Trajanov, D.: Evaluation of sentiment analysis in finance: from lexicons to transformers. IEEE Access **8**, 131662–131682 (2020). https://doi.org/10.1109/ACCESS.2020.3009626
23. Missikoff, M., Velardi, P., Fabriani, P,: Text mining techniques to automatically enrich a domain ontology. Appl. Intell. **18**, 323–340 (2003). https://doi.org/10.1023/A:1023254205945
24. NATO: NATO-Russia: setting the record straight (2022). https://www.nato.int/cps/en/natohq/115204.htm. Accessed 25 June 2022
25. Neppalli, V., Caragea, C., Squicciarini, A., Tapia, A., Stehle, S.: Sentiment analysis during hurricane sandy in emergency response. Int. J. Disaster Risk Reduct. **21**, 213–222 (2017). https://doi.org/10.1016/j.ijdrr.2016.12.011
26. Nguyen, D.Q., Vu, T., Nguyen, A.T.: BERTweet: a pre-trained language model for English Tweets (2020)
27. Office for National Statistics: Overview of the UK population (2021). https://www.ons.gov.uk/peoplepopulationandcommunity. Accessed 25 June 2022
28. Phand, S.A., Phand, J.A.: Twitter sentiment classification using stanford NLP. In: 2017 1st International Conference on Intelligent Systems and Information Management (ICISIM), pp. 1–5 (2017). https://doi.org/10.1109/ICISIM.2017.8122138
29. Putrova, D.: Russia-Ukraine war - tweets dataset (65 days) (2022). https://www.kaggle.com/datasets/foklacu/ukraine-war-tweets-dataset-65-days?select=Ukraine_war.csv. Accessed 27 Nov 2022
30. Ravi, K., Ravi, V.: A survey on opinion mining and sentiment analysis: tasks, approaches and applications. Knowl.-Based Syst. **89**, 14–46 (2015). https://doi.org/10.1016/j.knosys.2015.06.015. https://www.sciencedirect.com/science/article/pii/S0950705115002336
31. Rieck, K., Laskov, P.: Linear-time computation of similarity measures for sequential data. J. Mach. Learn. Res. **9**, 23–48 (2008)
32. Romero, C., Ventura, S.: Educational data mining: a review of the state of the art. IEEE Trans. Syst. Man Cybern. Part C Appl. Rev. **40**(6), 601–618 (2010)

33. Rouhani, S., Mozaffari, F.: Sentiment analysis researches story narrated by topic modeling approach. Soc. Sci. Human. Open **6**(1), 100309 (2022). https://doi.org/10.1016/j.ssaho.2022.100309. https://www.sciencedirect.com/science/article/pii/S2590291122000638

34. Seetharamulu, B., Reddy, B.N.K., Naidu, K.B.: Deep learning for sentiment analysis based on customer reviews. In: 2020 11th International Conference on Computing, Communication and Networking Technologies (ICCCNT), pp. 1–5 (2020). https://doi.org/10.1109/ICCCNT49239.2020.9225665

35. Singh, N., Tomar, D., Sangaiah, A.: Sentiment analysis: a review and comparative analysis over social media. J. Ambient. Intell. Humaniz. Comput. **11**, 97–117 (2020). https://doi.org/10.1007/s12652-018-0862-8

36. Taboada, M., Brooke, J., Tofiloski, M., Voll, K., Stede, M.: Lexicon-based methods for sentiment analysis. Comput. Linguist. **37**(2), 267–307 (2011). https://doi.org/10.1162/COLI_a_00049

37. Taylor, J., Pagliari, C.: Mining social media data: how are research sponsors and researchers addressing the ethical challenges? Res. Ethics **14**, 1–39 (2017). https://doi.org/10.1177/1747016117738559

38. Tripathy, A., Agrawal, A., Rath, S.K.: Classification of sentiment reviews using n-gram machine learning approach. Expert Syst. Appl. **57**, 117–126 (2016). https://doi.org/10.1016/j.eswa.2016.03.028. https://www.sciencedirect.com/science/article/pii/S095741741630118X

39. Twiter: Developer Policy - Twitter Developers (2022). https://developer.twitter.com/en/developer-terms/policy. Accessed 31 May 2022

40. Wang, H., Hu, D.: Comparison of SVM and LS-SVM for regression. In: 2005 International Conference on Neural Networks and Brain, vol. 1, pp. 279–283 (2005). https://doi.org/10.1109/ICNNB.2005.1614615

41. Wang, R., Zhou, D., Jiang, M., Si, J., Yang, Y.: A survey on opinion mining: from stance to product aspect. IEEE Access **7**, 41101–41124 (2019). https://doi.org/10.1109/ACCESS.2019.2906754

42. Wilson, W., Birkin, P., Aickelin, U.: The motif tracking algorithm. Int. J. Autom. Comput. **5**(1), 32–44 (2007). https://doi.org/10.1007/s10453-004-5872-7

43. Wongkar, M., Angdresey, A.: Sentiment analysis using Naive Bayes Algorithm of the data crawler: Twitter. In: 2019 Fourth International Conference on Informatics and Computing (ICIC). pp. 1–5 (2019). https://doi.org/10.1109/ICIC47613.2019.8985884

44. Yue, C., Chen, W., Li, X.: A survey of sentiment analysis in social media. Knowl. Inf. Syst. **60**, 617–663 (2018). https://doi.org/10.1007/s10115-018-1236-4

# Solar Flare Forecasting Using Individual and Ensemble RNN Models

Mangaliso Mngomezulu🅞, Mandlenkosi Gwetu$^{(\boxtimes)}$🅞,
and Jean Vincent Fonou-Dombeu🅞

School of Mathematics, Statistics and Computer Science,
University of KwaZulu-Natal, Pietermaritzburg 3021, South Africa
{mngomezulum,gwetum,fonoudombeuj}@ukzn.ac.za

**Abstract.** Solar flares release radioactive energy rapidly and have lethal effects on Space and Earth. Forecasting solar flares remains a challenging task as their occurrence is stochastic and multi-variable dependent. In this study, Recurrent Neural Network (RNN) models, namely Long Short Term Memory (LSTM), Gated Recurrent Units (GRU), and Simple Recurrent Neural Network (Simple RNN); and their Homogeneous and Heterogenous ensembles are compared for solar flare forecasting. This study adopts a dataset from the Space-weather Helioseismic and Magnetic Imager (HMI) Active Region Patches, in correspondence with Geostationary Operational Environmental Satellite (GOES) X-ray flare data catalogs, which are made available by National Centers for Environmental Information (NCEI). Solar flares emit X-rays when they occur. The focus of this study is on solar flares that are associated with an X-ray peak flux of at least $10^{-6}$ Watts per square meter $(W/m^2)$. The forecast period is 24 h prior to solar flare occurrence. Despite very comparable results from models, the Simple RNN surpassed the performance of other models. The LSTM model's performance was most closely comparable to that of the Simple RNN. Comparison based on the True Skill Statistic (TSS), precision, and balanced accuracy (BACC), shows that this study produced better results than related studies that used LSTM models. This study improves the TSS by a margin of $9\% \pm 0.009$ when compared to the benchmark study.

**Keywords:** Solar flares · Recurrent Neural Networks · Long Short Term Memory Networks · Simple RNNs · Gated Recurrent Units · $\geq C$ class solar flares

## 1 Introduction

Solar flares are rapid electromagnetic radiation energy outbursts that take place on the solar surface [27,28]. Extreme ultraviolet (EUV) radiation, gamma rays,

---

Supported by the University Of KwaZulu-Natal, National Research Foundation and Barclays Endowment.

M. Bramer and F. Stahl (Eds.): SGAI 2023, LNAI 14381, pp. 307–320, 2023.
https://doi.org/10.1007/978-3-031-47994-6_29

and X-rays are produced in the process. While some flares are of less significance, some are cataclysmic. Their lifespan is within the range of milliseconds
to multiple hours, over which they release energy of approximately $10^{17}$ to $10^{25}$
Joules. The key factors that determine if a solar flare will take place or not and
if it does take place how intense will it be, have not been fully comprehended
yet [1,17,24,28,30]. The occurrence of solar flares is mainly stochastic [5].

Powerful solar flares can deform some of the sun's coronal surface, thus causing a Coronal Mass Ejection (CME), which has a direct terrestrial impact [17].
Large CMEs can result in human extinction. Solar flares disturb the orbiting of
satellites and disrupt radio wave propagation which can lead to inaccurate information from satellites like the Global Positioning Systems (GPS) [28]. Based on
approximations, a major flare can result in a loss of US \$163 billion in North
America alone [12]. When a solar flare takes place, X-rays are emitted. The X-
ray peak flux is measured in Watts per square meter $(W/m^2)$. Solar flare classes
namely A, B, C, M, and X are each associated with a range of the X-ray peak
flux values. Within each flare class, there are numerical divisions that aid with
the precision of intensity description within each class i.e. $M.5$ class flares are in
a midpoint of $M$ & $X$ class flares. Flare classes along with their X-ray peak flux
range can be enumerated as follows: $X- \geq 10^{-4}$, $M- \geq 10^{-5}$ up to $< 10^{-4}$,
$C- \geq 10^{-6}$ up to $< 10^{-5}$, $B- \geq 10^{-7}$ up to $< 10^{-6}$, and $A- < 10^{-7}$ [25]. This
study focuses on $\geq C$ class flares, which are $C$, $M$, $M.5$ and $X$; this is motivated
by poor classification results achieved in these categories of solar flares by related
studies [17,19,28].

The National Aeronautics and Space Administration (NASA) initiated a
space weather-dedicated mission in 2010 [21]. The Solar Dynamics Observatory
(SDO) was the main tool used. The SDO's instruments are namely Atmospheric
Imaging Assembly (AIA) [15], the Extreme Ultraviolet Variability Experiment
(EVE), and the Helioseismic and Magnetic Imager (HMI) [21]. The HMI and
AIA made it possible to record magnetographs and ribbon imaging simultane-
ously [13], which is an advantage. This data is publicly available and has been
reported to be about 19 petabytes in size [2].

Solar flare forecasting is challenging since the theorized cause of solar flares
(active regions) is not a deterministic indicator of an upcoming flare. Not only is
the process stochastic, but it also has cycles with variances in the occurrence of
solar flares [28]. The uniqueness of this study is the overall combination of the
mentioned RNN models and the ensembles used. The remainder of the paper
is structured as follows: Sect. 2 provides a review of related previous studies.
Section 3 describes the RNNs and their ensembles, Sect. 4 discusses results and
Sect. 5 concludes the paper.

## 2   Literature Review

Recurrent Neural Networks (RNNs) have become more common in predicting
solar flares [1,17,22,27,28]. The most common version of the RNNs is the Long

Short-Term Memory (LSTM). The LSTM in most cases is preferred for its ability to handle long-term dependencies in contrast to the standard RNNs.

LSTM and a Random Forest(RF) were utilized to forecast solar flares in [17]. The classes used were $\geq M.5$, $\geq M$ and $\geq C$. Each class had a dedicated binary classification model. The X-ray flare data was from the GOES satellite. Features used were from the SHARP data. Feature ranking reduced an initial set of 40 parameters to at most 22 and at least 14, with improvement in the predictions. This showed how significantly noisy data can affect a model's performance. As similarly observed in [3], $C$ class flares were associated with a higher dependency on historical information. The results obtained were better than those from [7,10], SVM [3,7,23,31] and Deep Flare Net [19]. The final results showed that LSTMs and RFs are very comparable in solar flare forecasting. Feature ranking proved to be a critical effort in performance improvement.

RNNs have also been used in [22] to forecast solar flares within the next 24 h. The study used the Helioseismic and Magnetic Imager's (HMI's) SHARP, with 20 parameters of interest. The LSTM, GRU, and Simple RNN models were used for binary and multi-class classification of solar flares. The former outperformed the latter. The minimum performance of the RNN models was 60% on the accuracy metric. The GRU was better than the Simple RNN and the LSTM model. Data were down-sampled to achieve the smallest balanced dataset. While that seems to be a good and fair way to train the models, the results show that models struggled to classify the negative classes well. Using an unbalanced dataset with the right metrics would possibly alleviate this issue, as done in this study.

Another study [28] used the LSTM on twenty HMI's data features to forecast the occurrence of solar flares in the next 24 h. Probing solar cycle relationships with solar flares was the main aim of the study. The data used spanned the years 2010–2018 and it was used along with the related flares realized through GOES X-ray data. Classes were namely strong flare ($\geq M$), medium flare ($\geq C$), and any flare ($\geq A$). It was found that medium-class flares ($\geq C$) are more predictable in the periods of 2015 to 2018 than in 2011 to 2014. This conclusion was made based on metrics, namely True Skill Statistic (TSS) and Heidke skill score. This study achieves better results compared to [17] and [28] without considering solar cycle dependence on the data. This proves that the areas of improvement are both in the data and models.

## 3   Methodology

The data used was adapted from a solar flare forecasting study [17] - the benchmark study. After partitioning, the training set had 66311 and 18266 negative and positive samples (spanning 2010–2013), respectively. For validation, 19418 and 7055 negative and positive instances (spanning 2014) were used, respectively. Lastly, 35957 and 8732 negative and positive samples were partitioned for testing, respectively (spanning 2015–2018). The data was split based on years of observation, in the original dataset [17]. In this study, the same partitions were used. Using data from some range of years for training, validation, and testing can improve the performance of the model in contrast to randomly stratified

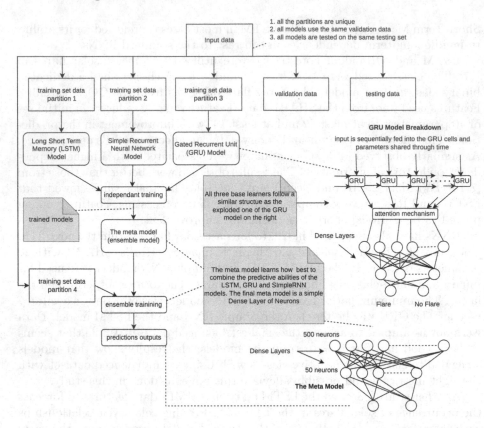

**Fig. 1.** A Setup of the Heterogeneous Stacking Ensemble (HtrSE)

samples with a similar class proportionality. This is due to the solar cycle dependence nature of the solar flare data [28]. To preserve the seasonality in the data and ensure equally proportional class distribution, some samples in each partition were dropped. Finally, in each partition, the ratio of positive to negative samples was 1: 2.75, e.g. $18266 \geq C$ positive samples and 50274 negative samples for (2010–2013). This study forecasts the occurrence of a solar flare within the next 24 h. The main models used are the GRU, Simple RNN, and LSTM. All models were implemented with an attention mechanism as it helps with learning the sequential data [20]. There is no difference in the attention mechanism used in [28] and the one used in this study.

Ensemble models were implemented by combining the LSTM, GRU, and Simple RNN. The choice of 3 models helps the majority voting ensemble to always have a majority preference in class choice. The ensembles used are a hard voting ensemble (uses majority voting), a soft voting ensemble, and stacking ensembles. For the stacking ensembles, there is a heterogeneous stacking ensemble of the three models, then homogeneous stacking ensembles, one for each model, each with three base learners trained on 25% of the training set. Each base learner was trained on a stratified sample from the training set. These base learners were all trained on data that spans (2010–2013) since individual models performed better when trained on this data. The use of different data partitions in training helps improve diversity in the base learners, which is critical for the ensemble's success [26]. As the RNNs use data that is in the form of sequences, the sequence length used was 10, which is the same as in [17]. The cadence between the elements of each sequence is 1 h. In this study, the loss functions, optimizers, data, and model structure were the main deliberate means of making the models diverse.

Figure 1 shows an example of the setup for the ensemble models. Base learners are all trained on different partitions of the original dataset. Due to limited positive instances in the data, models share validation data. For comparable results, the models are all tested on the same testing set. The meta-learner uses the outputs of the base learner outputs as inputs to learn the best combination.

## 3.1 The Simple Recurrent Neural Network

[30] mathematically define the standard recurrent cell as:

$$h_t = \sigma(W_h h_{t-1} + W_x x_t + b),$$
$$y_t = h_t,$$

where $x_t$, $h_t$, and $y_t$ at time $t$ of the cell, are the input, recurrent information, and output, respectively. $W_x$, $W_h$, $b$ are the input weight, recurrent information weight, and bias, respectively. This architecture has demonstrated success in some studies [16].

## 3.2 The Long Short-Term Memory (LSTM)

The LSTM extends the Simple RNN architecture to improve long-term dependency learning [30]. [11] came up with the idea of the LSTM in Fig. 2. The LSTM has been modified numerous times starting from its initial proposal. The most commonly used variation is the LSTM with a forget gate, which is a result of work by [8], and can be mathematically expressed as:

$$f_t = \sigma(W_{fh} h_{t-1} + W_{fx} x_t + b_f),$$
$$i_t = \sigma(W_{ih} h_{t-1} + W_{ix} x_t + b_i),$$
$$\tilde{c}_t = tanh(W_{\tilde{c}h} h_{t-1} + W_{\tilde{c}x} x_t + b_{\tilde{c}}),$$
$$c_t = f_t \cdot c_{t-1} + i_t \cdot \tilde{c}_t,$$
$$o_t = \sigma(W_{oh} h_{t-1} + W_{ox} x_t + b_o),$$
$$h_t = o_t \cdot tanh(c_t),$$

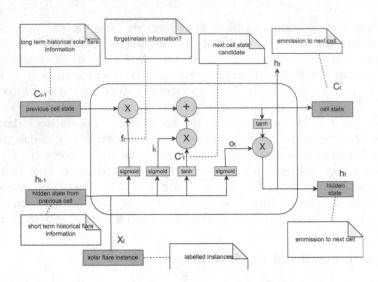

**Fig. 2.** LSTM Diagrammatic Overview As Used In this Experiment

where the $W$s are weights and the $b$s are biases. Both the weights and biases are learned during the training. $x_t$ denotes the input. $h_{t-1}$ is the resulting vector from time step $t-1$. $\tilde{c}_t$ is the candidate cell state. $h_t$ is the resulting vector at time step $t$, which is dependent on the new cell state $c_t$. $i_t$ regulates the amount of new information going into the cell. The key feature of this model is the ability to learn what to forget [30], through $f_t$, the forget gate. $f_t \in (0,1)$ and $f_t \in \mathbf{R}$ with 0 for forget and 1 for retain.

LSTMs perform better than the standard RNN in practice [30]. The price for better performance is computational load due to extra operations. As a means to balance the trade-off between computational load and performance, [6] introduced the Gated Recurrent Unit (GRU).

### 3.3   The Gated Recurrent Unit (GRU)

The GRU combines the forget $f_t$ and input $i_t$ gates as an update gate making it to have one less gate compared to the LSTM. Sacrificing that one gate from the LSTM to form the GRU comes with limitations of the GRU in contrast to the LSTM [4,29]. Both the LSTM and GRU are better than the standard recurrent cell [6].

Table 1 shows the details for each model's configurations. The variation of the configurations are means for inducing or increasing diversity in the performance of the RNNs. Diverse base learners are more likely to form a superior ensemble [26]. Some of the models make use of the following methods/techniques: Dense Layers Activation (DLA) function, Binary Cross Entropy (BCE), Kullback Leibler Divergence (KLD) and Stochastic Gradient Descent (SGD). The activation function used in output layers is the softmax for all models. The dropout rate is 0.5. The LSTM, GRU, and Simple RNN models have common configurations. Each sequence of length 10 where each element contains 14 features goes into a layer with 10 RNN (LSTM, GRU, or SimpleRNN) cells. The hidden states are then passed to the attention mechanism [17]. The outputs of the attention mechanism are then passed to a dense layer of a neural network. All the models have 3 dense layers. In all models, the second dense layer has 500 neurons and 2 for the output layer. The input (first) dense layers of the Simple RNN and LSTM have 200 neurons whereas the GRU first dense layer has 300 neurons.

**Table 1.** Configurations for LSTM, GRU and Simple RNN Models

| Model | Loss Function | Optimizer | DLA |
|---|---|---|---|
| LSTM | KLD | SGD | Relu |
| GRU | BCE | Adam | LeakyReLU |
| Simple RNN | BCE | Adamax | Relu |

The key metrics used in this study are TSS, BACC, f1-score, precision, and recall. The receiver operating characteristic curve, confusion matrices, and reliability diagrams are also used as means to increase the interoperability of the RNN models. The Q-statistic helps with quantifying the diversity of two RNN models. Since diversity increases the likelihood of ensemble success [26], it is critical to measure the base learner's Q-statistic to give a stronger intuition of the likelihood of the ensemble's success with the given base learners. Due to class imbalance, BACC is used since it gives a better impression of the model's performance when taking into consideration the class distribution. The accuracy metric is not reliable in this context of imbalanced data e.g., if a model gets 90% accuracy by correctly forecasting 100% of negative solar flare samples which make 90% of the solar flare test data, where the remaining 10% are positive samples. Other metrics like the Heidke Skill Score and accuracy were also considered for comparison with other works. [24] outlines the mathematical definitions of the terms used in some of the metrics as seen in [17].

The TSS is used because the data is imbalanced. The class imbalance does not make the TSS by the majority or minority class weight in the data [3]. The possible values of the TSS range from $-1$ to 1. A score of 1 means perfect forecasting, whereas $-1$ means all forecasts are wrong. Random guessing scores a 0. Basically, the TSS gives an idea of how better than random the model forecasts. The ROC curve is also used in this study along with precision-recall curves. It is normally presented as a line graph where the Area Under the Curve (AUC) shows the model's degree of separability amongst classes and the best possible value is 1 [18]. Since the TSS does not consider the probabilities used in the forecasting, its values do not give an idea about how well the models are calibrated (how the predicted solar flare probabilities are related to the observed frequency of the solar flare events). Hence this study uses the calibration curves (see Fig. 4) to address this shortcoming. The meaning of the calibrations is explained here Table 3.

The experiment employed some parameter optimization techniques. Training epochs are optimized as follows, if the validation loss does not improve in 6 consecutive epochs then the training stops. The best weights are restored and used. The learning rate is decreased by 15% if the validation loss does not decrease in 4 consecutive epochs. This helps the RNNs find more desirable solutions and avoid getting stuck in local minima. In consideration of the possibility of very low (close to zero) learning rates, a boundary is placed to stop the learning rate from decreasing any further once it reaches $1 \times 10^{-7}$. The described parameter optimization process applies to all models that require direct training in the experiment. The choice of the values used in the optimization was subjective and based on observations when models were trained.

The experiment was run through Google Colab on an Intel(R) Xeon(R) CPU @ 2.20 GHz machine with 2 CPU cores. The Graphics Processing Unit (GPU) feature helped with speeding up the training at most 17 min per model. Base learners of ensembles' training time was almost directly proportional to the size of data allocated.

## 4   Results and Discussion

Figure 3 shows from the left to the right, the precision vs. recall, receiver operating characteristics, and confusion matrices for LSTM, GRU, SimpleRNN, and select Ensemble models. The ROC curves show how the RNN models compare in terms of their degree of separability of positive and negative instances of $\geq C$ class flares. The AUC measures the area under the ROC curve. A lower AUC value means that the associated model has a lower ability to distinguish between sequences that lead to $\geq C$ class flares and those that do not. A higher AUC is usually associated with higher precision scores as the trend can be seen in the corresponding confusion matrices. A good example is the Soft Voting Ensemble (SVE) with an AUC = 0.87 (the maximum is 1) and the most correct positive forecasts for sequences that result in $\geq C$ solar flares, with a precision of 0.9 (the maximum is 1). The general trend of the precision vs. recall curves shows that the models tend to trade off precision for recall as the recall increases. This means that the RNNs are more focused on correctly forecasting sequences that result in a positive solar flare as positive. The downside of this is that the false positive rate increases. In a real application, the models are likely to predict that a sequence of observations will result in a flare when this is actually not the case. The advantage of this trade-off is the models will be less likely to miss a strong solar flare.

Table 2 shows the Q-statistic for the models LSTM, GRU, and Simple RNN which were trained on the entire dataset. A Qstatistic value $q$ is such that $q \in \mathbb{R}$, $q \in [-1, 1]$. A $-1$ shows that the two models are highly disagreeable, a 1 indicates that models are highly agreeable, and a 0 shows that the models are making worse than random [14]. All the models LSTM, GRU, and Simple RNN demonstrated

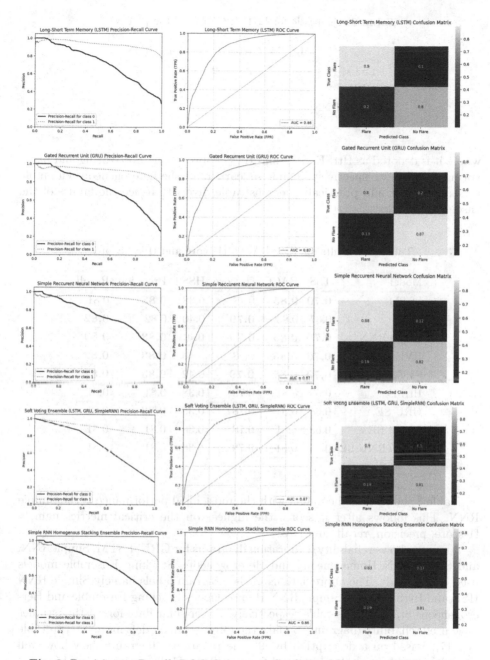

**Fig. 3.** Precision vs Recall, ROC Curve and Confusion Matrix for RNN models

to be highly agreeable in the experiment. The high agree-ability is part of the reason for the heterogeneous stacking ensemble's failure to surpass the individual models. The results of the heterogeneous stacking ensemble can be seen in Table 3

**Table 2.** Qstatistic for LSTM, GRU and SimpleRNN

|           | LSTM | GRU                     | SimpleRNN               |
|-----------|------|-------------------------|-------------------------|
| LSTM      | –    | $9.98 \times 10^{-1}$   | $9.95 \times 10^{-1}$   |
| GRU       | –    | –                       | $9.98 \times 10^{-1}$   |
| SimpleRNN | –    | –                       | –                       |

where it is denoted as HtrSE. SVE and HVE abbreviating Soft-voting and hard-voting ensembles respectively. The base learners of the heterogeneous ensemble lacked sufficient and practically demonstrable diversity hence the failure of the ensemble [26].

**Table 3.** Results on TSS, BACC, f1-score and HSS2 Scores

| Model         | TSS  | BACC | f1-score | HSS2 | Precision | Recall |
|---------------|------|------|----------|------|-----------|--------|
| LSTM          | **0.70** | **0.85** | 0.77     | 0.38 | **0.83**  | 0.81   |
| GRU           | 0.67 | 0.83 | **0.79** | 0.40 | 0.82      | **0.82** |
| SimpleRNN     | **0.70** | **0.85** | **0.79** | **0.43** | **0.83** | **0.82** |
| HVE           | **0.70** | **0.85** | 0.78     | 0.40 | **0.83**  | **0.82** |
| SVE           | **0.70** | **0.85** | **0.79** | 0.42 | **0.83**  | **0.82** |
| HtrSE         | 0.63 | 0.81 | 0.78     | 0.38 | 0.81      | 0.81   |
| GRU SE        | 0.68 | 0.84 | 0.78     | 0.39 | **0.83**  | 0.81   |
| LSTM SE       | 0.63 | 0.81 | 0.78     | 0.38 | 0.81      | 0.81   |
| SimpleRNN SE  | 0.63 | 0.81 | 0.78     | 0.38 | 0.81      | 0.81   |

Table 3 shows that the model with the most ideal performance is the Simple RNN. This follows after it scores the highest on the critical metrics namely f1-score, precision, recall, and BACC.

Figure 4 shows reliability/calibration diagrams for GRU, LSTM, SimpleRNN, and SimpleRNN Homogeneous and Heterogeneous Stacking Ensemble models used in the study. The abbreviations in the diagram labels namely Simple RNN HSE and HtrSE are for Simple RNN Homogeneous Stacking Ensemble and Heterogeneous Stacking Ensemble respectively. Other solar flare forecasting studies have used reliability diagrams to make the forecasting models more interpretable i.e. [17]. Based on a description by [9], the reliability diagrams show how well a model is calibrated. The diagonal from $(0, 0)$ to $(1, 1)$ represents perfect calibration. That is a case when the model gives the best possible forecasting of the event of interest. The mean predicted value for the range marked in blue is plotted against the fraction of positive instances in the data (the actual flares belonging to $\geq C$). The ideal case is when the model's calibration graph is a straight line from

$(0, 0)$ to $(1, 1)$. While that is rarely achievable for complex problems, an ideal graph is one that is as close as possible to the diagonal line. A high prediction probability means the model was more confident. Besides the inferior performance of the ensemble models, the calibration curves show that the ensemble models are well-calibrated in comparison to individual models. Part of the reason is that the meta model's objective was to find the best way to combine the predictive ability of its base learners. The different predictions for the same input from each base learner allowed the ensembles to generalize better. The curves show that the ensembles had higher confidence when making predictions.

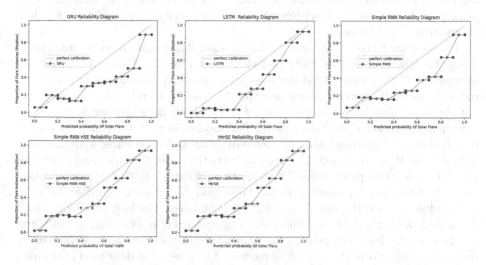

**Fig. 4.** Reliability Diagrams for RNN models (Color figure online)

## 4.1   Comparison with Previous Works

Some of the previous studies results can be seen in Table 4. Studies that share some of the data and type of method(s) used are [17] and [28]. The study in [22] used a different dataset and implemented the individual RNNs. The study in [19] used a method specialized for solar flare forecasting. Models from this study can be seen in bold. This study obtained a higher TSS, f1-score, balanced accuracy, precision, and recall. There are other studies on solar flares that may obtain better results in different contexts, i.e. using other models or a different dataset. The relationship between TSS and HSS2 shows that the RNNs obtain a better TSS score sacrificing the HSS2 metric, in comparison to [17]'s work. The TSS is more important than the HSS2 in this context. That is because the RNN models perform better than random forecasting in all tests. So the concern was how better than random forecasting are they. The TSS metric addresses that concern. Some studies have been completely dedicated to increasing the TSS [19].

**Table 4.** Previous solar flare forecasting studies for C or $\geq C$-class flares

| Author and Year | TSS | BACC | f1-score | HSS2 | Precision | Recall |
|---|---|---|---|---|---|---|
| Liu et al., 2019 | 0.61 | 0.80 | – | 0.54 | 0.54 | 0.76 |
| **LSTM** | 0.70 | 0.85 | 0.77 | 0.38 | 0.83 | 0.81 |
| **SimpleRNN** | 0.70 | 0.85 | 0.79 | 0.43 | 0.83 | 0.82 |

Based on Table 3, the Simple RNN model emerges as best for the task of solar flare forecasting when using the data used in the study. By Occam's razor principle, the Simple RNN is preferred for its simplicity, in contrast to the most comparable LSTM model.

It can be noted that $\geq M$ and $\geq M.5$ are solar flares that are more predictable using the dataset from this study as demonstrated in [17]. Recall that this study forecasts $\geq C$ class flares. That includes $M$, $M.5$ and $X$ class flares. One possible room for difficulty for the models was that $C$ class flares rely more on historical data to be predictable as stated in [3]. $M$ & $M.5$ class flares are not so reliant on historical information as $C$ class flares. The models in this study may have tried to use historical information on instances of $M$ & $M.5$ class flares with the same weights (i.e. $W_{fh}$) as in instances that fall strictly under $C$ class flares. This can result in erroneous predictions. To alleviate this issue, multi-class classification seems to be a possible solution in the hope that there is enough data to allow the models to learn the feature ranking for each class. The individual classes $C$, $M$ & $M.5$ were available in almost equal proportions in training, testing, and validation data. Based on existing literature, the ensemble models are more likely to strictly outperform the individual models. The size of the data used in training standalone individual models is bigger than that used to train base learners for stacking ensembles. This is because the data partitions used to train each base learner are distinct from those used to train the meta-model. Although in some cases this might not be a problem, it may at times decrease the generalization ability of the base learners since they are trained on less data. Ultimately, the ensemble model is not guaranteed to outperform the individual models. This explains why in some metrics the standalone models do better.

## 5    Conclusion

This study presented and motivated the use of RNN models and RNN ensembles in solar flare forecasting by practically demonstrating their better performance compared to results from previous studies. The models compared for forecasting $\geq C$ class flares were namely LSTM, GRU, SimpleRNN, Heterogenous Stacking Ensemble (LSTM, Simple RNN, GRU), and Homogeneous Stacking Ensembles (for GRU, LSTM, SimpleRNN). The data used in this study was from Space-weather Helioseismic and Magnetic Imager (HMI) Active Region Patches were used in correspondence with Geostationary Operational Environmental Satellite

(GOES) X-ray flare data catalogs made available by National Centers for Environmental Information (NCEI). The data was adopted as is from a study by [17] which is used as a benchmark study. The Simple RNN & LSTM both obtained a TSS value of 0.7. The best model from this study demonstrated superiority over previous studies forecasting $\geq C$ flares. The contribution of this study is that it proposed the use of the Simple RNN model and further validated the need to explore ensembles in solar flare forecasting by showing that the Simple RNN Stacking Ensemble obtained very promising results.

Future research will explore the use of RNNs learning directly from image data with the help of CNNs for feature extraction. This is motivated by the possibility of realizing sub-optimal feature selection from the dataset used.

# References

1. Aktukmak, M., et al.: Incorporating polar field data for improved solar flare prediction. arXiv preprint arXiv:2212.01730 (2022)
2. Bobra, M.G., et al.: Science platforms for heliophysics data analysis. arXiv preprint arXiv:2301.00878 (2023)
3. Bobra, M.G., Couvidat, S.: Solar flare prediction using SDO/HMI vector magnetic field data with a machine-learning algorithm. Astrophys. J. **798**(2), 135 (2015)
4. Britz, D., Goldie, A., Luong, M.T., Le, Q.: Massive exploration of neural machine translation architectures. arXiv preprint arXiv:1703.03906 (2017)
5. Campi, C., Benvenuto, F., Massone, A.M., Bloomfield, D.S., Georgoulis, M.K., Piana, M.: Feature ranking of active region source properties in solar flare forecasting and the uncompromised stochasticity of flare occurrence. Astrophys. J. **883**(2), 150 (2019)
6. Chung, J., Gulcehre, C., Cho, K., Bengio, Y.: Empirical evaluation of gated recurrent neural networks on sequence modeling. arXiv preprint arXiv:1412.3555 (2014)
7. Florios, K., et al.: Forecasting solar flares using magnetogram-based predictors and machine learning. Sol. Phys. **293**(2), 28 (2018). https://doi.org/10.1007/s11207-018-1250-4
8. Gers, F.A., Schmidhuber, J., Cummins, F.: Learning to forget: continual prediction with LSTM. Neural Comput. **12**(10), 2451–2471 (2000)
9. Guo, C., Pleiss, G., Sun, Y., Weinberger, K.Q.: On calibration of modern neural networks. In: International Conference on Machine Learning, pp. 1321–1330. PMLR (2017)
10. Haykin, S., Chen, Z., Becker, S.: Stochastic correlative learning algorithms. IEEE Trans. Sig. Process. **52**(8), 2200–2209 (2004)
11. Hochreiter, S., Schmidhuber, J.: Long short-term memory. Neural Comput. **9**(8), 1735–1780 (1997)
12. Kaneda, K., Wada, Y., Iida, T., Nishizuka, N., Kubo, Y., Sugiura, K.: Flare transformer: solar flare prediction using magnetograms and sunspot physical features. In: Proceedings of the Asian Conference on Computer Vision, pp. 1488–1503 (2022)
13. Kazachenko, M.D., Lynch, B.J., Savcheva, A., Sun, X., Welsch, B.T.: Toward improved understanding of magnetic fields participating in solar flares: statistical analysis of magnetic fields within flare ribbons. Astrophys. J. **926**(1), 56 (2022)
14. Kuncheva, L.I., Whitaker, C.J.: Measures of diversity in classifier ensembles and their relationship with the ensemble accuracy. Mach. Learn. **51**(2), 181 (2003). https://doi.org/10.1023/A:1022859003006

15. Lemen, J.R., et al.: The *Atmospheric Imaging Assembly* (AIA) on the *Solar Dynamics Observatory* (SDO). Sol. Phys. **275**, 17–40 (2012). https://doi.org/10.1007/s11207-011-9776-8

16. Li, S., Li, W., Cook, C., Zhu, C., Gao, Y.: Independently recurrent neural network (IndRNN): building a longer and deeper RNN. In: Proceedings of the IEEE Conference on Computer Vision and Pattern Recognition, pp. 5457–5466 (2018)

17. Liu, H., Liu, C., Wang, J.T., Wang, H.: Predicting solar flares using a long short-term memory network. Astrophys. J. **877**(2), 121 (2019)

18. Marzban, C.: The ROC curve and the area under it as performance measures. Weather Forecast. **19**(6), 1106–1114 (2004)

19. Nishizuka, N., Sugiura, K., Kubo, Y., Den, M., Ishii, M.: Deep flare net (DeFN) model for solar flare prediction. Astrophys. J. **858**(2), 113 (2018)

20. Niu, Z., Zhong, G., Yu, H.: A review on the attention mechanism of deep learning. Neurocomputing **452**, 48–62 (2021)

21. Pesnell, W.D., Thompson, B.J., Chamberlin, P.: The solar dynamics observatory (SDO). In: Chamberlin, P., Pesnell, W.D., Thompson, B. (eds.) The Solar Dynamics Observatory, pp. 3–15. Springer, New York (2012). https://doi.org/10.1007/978-1-4614-3673-7_2

22. Platts, J., Reale, M., Marsh, J., Urban, C.: Solar flare prediction with recurrent neural networks. J. Astronaut. Sci. **69**(5), 1421–1440 (2022). https://doi.org/10.1007/s40295-022-00340-0

23. Qahwaji, R., Colak, T.: Automatic short-term solar flare prediction using machine learning and sunspot associations. Sol. Phys. **241**, 195–211 (2007). https://doi.org/10.1007/s11207-006-0272-5

24. Raboonik, A., Safari, H., Alipour, N., Wheatland, M.S.: Prediction of solar flares using unique signatures of magnetic field images. Astrophys. J. **834**(1), 11 (2016)

25. Ribeiro, F., Gradvohl, A.L.S.: Machine learning techniques applied to solar flares forecasting. Astron. Comput. **35**, 100468 (2021)

26. Sagi, O., Rokach, L.: Ensemble learning: a survey. Wiley Interdisc. Rev. Data Min. Knowl. Discov. **8**(4), e1249 (2018)

27. Sun, Z., et al.: Predicting solar flares using CNN and LSTM on two solar cycles of active region data. Astrophys. J. **931**(2), 163 (2022)

28. Wang, X., et al.: Predicting solar flares with machine learning: investigating solar cycle dependence. Astrophys. J. **895**(1), 3 (2020)

29. Weiss, G., Goldberg, Y., Yahav, E.: On the practical computational power of finite precision RNNs for language recognition. arXiv preprint arXiv:1805.04908 (2018)

30. Yu, Y., Si, X., Hu, C., Zhang, J.: A review of recurrent neural networks: LSTM cells and network architectures. Neural Comput. **31**(7), 1235–1270 (2019)

31. Yuan, Y., Shih, F.Y., Jing, J., Wang, H.M.: Automated flare forecasting using a statistical learning technique. Res. Astron. Astrophys. **10**(8), 785 (2010)

# Deep Reinforcement Learning for Continuous Control of Material Thickness

Oliver Dippel[1,2](✉) ⓘ, Alexei Lisitsa[1] ⓘ, and Bei Peng[1] ⓘ

[1] University of Liverpool, Liverpool, UK
{oliver.dippel,lisitsa,bei.peng}@liverpool.ac.uk
[2] Centre for Doctoral Training in Distributed Algorithms, Liverpool, UK

**Abstract.** To achieve the desired quality standards of certain manufactured materials, the involved parameters are still adjusted by knowledge-based procedures according to human expertise, which can be costly and time-consuming. To optimize operational efficiency and provide decision support for human experts, we develop a general continuous control framework that utilizes deep reinforcement learning (DRL) to automatically determine the main control parameters, in situations where simulation environments are unavailable and traditional PID controllers are not viable options. In our work, we aim to automatically learn the key control parameters to achieve the desired outlet thickness of the manufactured material. We first construct a surrogate environment based on real-world expert trajectories obtained from the true underlining manufacturing process to achieve this. Subsequently, we train a DRL agent within the surrogate environment. Our results suggest a Proximal Policy Optimization (PPO) algorithm combined with a Multi-Layer Perceptron (MLP) surrogate environment to successfully learn a policy that continuously changes parameter configurations optimally, achieving the desired target material thickness within an acceptable range.

**Keywords:** Reinforcement Leaning · Deep Learning · Real World Manufacturing · Intelligent Decision Support

## 1 Introduction

In recent years reinforcement learning (RL) has achieved groundbreaking success in sequential decision-making problems by utilizing function approximation in deep learning [10]. The resulting deep reinforcement learning (DRL) methods have achieved superhuman performance in domains ranging from Atari [19] to Go [23] to chip floorplanning [17]. DRL has also been successful in industrial applications such as robotics [11,12] and the sanitary area [20]. These works demonstrate the potential of DRL to solve complex control tasks with high-dimensional state and/or action spaces and provide valuable contributions to modern engineering.

ⓒ The Author(s), under exclusive license to Springer Nature Switzerland AG 2023
M. Bramer and F. Stahl (Eds.): SGAI 2023, LNAI 14381, pp. 321–334, 2023.
https://doi.org/10.1007/978-3-031-47994-6_30

In current manufacturing processes, the traditional Proportional Integral Derivative (PID) controller [3] is commonly used in combination with the expertise of human operators to optimize the process. The PID controller's simplicity in implementation and tuning [24] makes it well-suited for most control problems without much mathematical modelling and analysis [2]. However, PID controllers face the challenge of planning ahead to avoid driving either the control effort or the process variable outside their acceptable ranges, which constrains control and does not handle dynamic environments well. Furthermore, in environments with multi-variable control issues and conflicting requirements, PID controllers suffer a multi-objective problem [15]. In this work, we investigate dynamic environments in which PID controllers are not used due to their aforementioned shortcomings. We deal with complex industrial manufacturing processes where the main challenge is finding a (semi-) automatic continuous control policy, primarily due to non-existing simulation environments, non-existing PID controllers, and major barriers to online testing such as high implementation costs. However, expert empirical data is usually collected in these industrial manufacturing processes. Hence, we aim to develop a general control framework that enables us to train a DRL agent to deal with dynamic, uncertain, and (soft-) constrained environments by utilizing expert empirical data.

Inspired by [16], our control framework can be summarized as follows. First, to overcome the difficulty of building a precise simulator, we train a surrogate model using authentic real-world data to forecast the thickness of the manufactured material given the input parameter configuration. Second, we use this trained surrogate model as an environment for training a DRL agent, with the ultimate goal of learning a policy that continuously "finds" the optimal key control parameter configuration to achieve the desired outlet thickness of the manufactured material.

While numerous parameters may be pertinent to an industrial manufacturing process, our focus is on managing the thermal profile at distinct stages of the procedure, which is crucial for determining certain properties of the material and for eliminating significant defects. Managing the thermal profile demands continuous control due to fluctuations caused by unobserved or not controllable exogenous factors, which can cause the material thickness to vary even when all controllable parameters remain constant. The need for continuous control arises from the constant changes in the material target thickness, requiring continuous parameter adjustments.

In order to find the optimal setting for our framework, we test various established DRL algorithms, namely PPO [22], DDPG [13] and DQN [18], in diverse surrogates, including Random Forest (RF) and Multilayer Perceptron (MLP) environments. We compare their respective performances and determine the most effective combination. Our experimental results show that the combination of PPO with the MLP surrogate is the most effective one. It can rapidly and accurately identify the optimal material thickness-inducing parameters to meet the desired thickness needs and reduce the loss incurred during the process, even under uncertain environmental conditions. Our approach is capable of

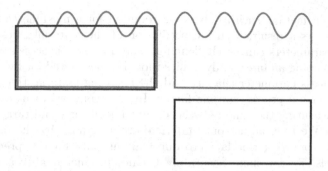

**Fig. 1.** Material Profile: The black rectangle denotes the optimal product, while the grey rectangle represents the actual fabrication. Any excess material above the black line signifies potential material savings, whereas falling below the black threshold indicates an unsellable product.

incorporating these uncertainties, encoded in the state, into the decision-making process. Furthermore, our experiments demonstrate that, interestingly, although both RF and MLP surrogate models achieve equally good accuracy in predicting the material thickness, the MLP surrogate model proves to be a superior simulation environment for training the DRL agent to develop an effective policy for addressing the underlying control problem. In addition, to validate if our trained surrogate model can provide a good approximation to an existing simulation environment for training a DRL agent, we utilize the widely recognized Mountain Car simulation environment [4]. We show that the PPO agent trained in the MLP surrogate environment achieves similar final performance to the PPO agent trained in the Mountain Car environment, demonstrating the ability of our MLP surrogate model to serve as a reliable approximation of a simulation environment.

In this work, we successfully use a DRL agent trained solely on empirical data to control the material thickness in unknown environmental conditions. Our control framework offers a practical solution to comparable industrial control problems where simulation environments are unavailable and traditional PID controllers are not viable options.

## 2  Background

### 2.1  Material Thickness Control

The parameters determining the material thickness of certain industrial processes are often still adjusted by human experts. However, unconsidered factors can cause material thickness to vary, even when all controllable parameters are held constant. Moreover, in many industrial processes, a time delay between the change of a process parameter and the resulting material thickness adaptation is common and impedes the control process even more. This delay can be caused by a variety of factors, such as the time required for a machine to respond to new changes. As a result, accurate prediction of the material thickness based on process parameters can be challenging. The unknown process-specific delay can be learnt using an internal dynamics model or accounted for by shifting the match of process parameter changes and the resulting material thickness adaptation by a certain process-specific factor. In this work, we focus on the latter approach, measuring the time between parameter changes and target thickness convergence. We then adjust our empirical training data by the observed lag time. By incorporating this lag into our training data for our predictive surrogate models, we can more accurately predict product quality and optimize manufacturing processes for improved efficiency and quality control.

In accordance with the requirements of the customer, various material thicknesses are manufactured, while the surface exhibits inherent roughness that we aim to enhance. Figure 1 shows the material profile, where the black rectangle signifies the ideal material thickness, and the grey rectangle represents the actual underlying profile. The objective is to ensure that the material thickness is at least as thick as the optimal black rectangle at every point, while being as close as possible to the optimum.

Various parameters in different zones of the manufacturing process are considered to determine the material thickness and can affect the material properties. In this work, we focus on controlling the heating-related parameters only, which are key parameters that contribute to most of the material thickness variability and can be influenced by external factors.

## 2.2  Data

For our experiments, we use empirical data collected by the material manufacturer. The data originates from different thickness runs over the course of different years, and is selected based on the quality of the data, e.g., no sensor failures. Measurements are acquired in a short time interval during the entire manufacturing process and cover a wide range of material thicknesses, resulting in a set of multiple distinct target thickness values.

When adjusting the heat parameters, a natural lag occurs which causes the material thickness to change only after a certain time. As a result, observed heat and measured material thickness do not align at the same time. To account for this difference, we train a machine learning model to predict the material thickness given the heating parameter at several time shifts. In this case, the heat measurements are equated with thickness measurements, which are measured $8 * k$, with $k = \{0, 1, ..., 20\}$ min later. To evaluate the predictive power, we use 10-fold cross-validation for each time shift between 0 and 160 min. We do not test for possible transitions longer than 160 min due to data preservation. Our results show that a lag of 72 min results in the lowest mean absolute error (MAE) and is therefore considered consequently. It is important to note that this is an empirical finding based on our data sample and may not generalize to other datasets.

## 2.3   Reinforcement Learning

**Markov Decision Process.** Reinforcement learning considers the problem of a goal-directed agent interacting with an uncertain environment and trying to maximize its long-term expected cumulative reward. The underlying decision-making problem can be modelled as a Markov Decision Process (MDP), which can be represented by a tuple $<S, A, P, R, \gamma>$. At each discrete timestep $t$, the agent is in an environment state $s_t \in S$, which is a momentary representation of the world the agent finds itself in. The agent then selects an action $a_t \in A$ to take to influence the environment. After executing action $a_t$, the agent moves to the next state $s_{t+1}$ with some probability defined by the state transition function $P(s_{t+1}|s_t, a_t)$, and receives a numeric reward $r_t$ specified by the reward function $R(s_t, a_t)$. $\gamma \in [0, 1]$ is a discount factor specifying how much immediate rewards are preferred to future rewards.

Through the training process, the agent can learn a stochastic policy $\pi(a_t|s_t) : S \times A \rightarrow [0, 1]$, which is a per-state action probability distribution that fully defines an agent's behavior. The goal of the agent is to find the optimal policy $\pi^*$, which maximizes the expected cumulative discounted reward, denoted as follows:

$$G_t = \sum_{k=0}^{\infty} \gamma^k r_{t+k}, \tag{1}$$

where $r_t$ is the reward received at timestep $t$. When the agent follows some policy $\pi$, a so-called trajectory $\tau$ is generated, forming a sequence of states, actions, and rewards. In DRL, the policy $\pi$ is represented by a neural network, which can be seen as a universal function approximator [9]. With the use of neural networks, reinforcement learning can become more unstable, as high correlations between actions and states may cause network weights to oscillate. To overcome this problem, we can use the experience replay mechanism to store the agent's experiences at each timestep and randomly sample a small batch of experiences to facilitate learning [14].

**State-Value Function and Action-Value Function.** The state-value function and action-value function are two important concepts in MDPs, which can be used to predict future rewards. The state-value function $V^\pi(s)$ of an MDP can be defined as: $V^\pi(s) = \mathbb{E}_\pi[G_t|s_t = s]$, which estimates the expected total discounted reward the agent will receive starting from state $s$ and following some policy $\pi$ thereafter. The action-value function $Q^\pi(s, a)$ of an MDP can be defined as $Q^\pi(s, a) = \mathbb{E}_\pi[G_t|s_t = s, a_t = a]$, which estimates the expected total discounted reward the agent will receive after taking action $a$ in state $s$ and following some policy $\pi$ thereafter. These equations can be recursively defined using the Bellman equation [25]:

$$V^\pi(s) = \sum_a \pi(a|s) \sum_{s'} P(s'|s, a) \Big[R(s, a) + \gamma V^\pi(s')\Big]. \tag{2}$$

$$Q^\pi(s, a) = \sum_{s'} P(s'|s, a) \Big[R(s, a) + \gamma \sum_{a'} \pi(a'|s') Q^\pi(s', a')\Big]. \tag{3}$$

# 3    Related Work

While DRL has shown impressive performance in a large variety of complex sequential decision-making problems, in the literature, there have only been a few attempts at applying DRL to real-world manufacturing to control material thickness.

Process control has been addressed in several works. [6, 8, 26, 29] use a DQN, [28] use PPO and [7, 27] use a DDPG approach. Of existing work, the approach proposed by [16] and [5] is closest to the control framework presented in this paper. To control the flatness of steel [5] combines PPO with ensemble learning to reduce the risk of falling into local optima. In [16], the aim is to control heating and speed process parameters, called "recipe", in an industrial electric furnace with the goal of reaching a specific desired outlet temperature. Typically, the recipe is discovered by a trial-and-error procedure of human experts, leaving room for improvement in terms of time and cost invested to discover a recipe. To solve the problem of parameter identification, [16] train a DQN [18] agent, whose policy decisions yield such a recipe. A classic environment in the context of RL is provided by a "self-prediction" model. This model is a RF which predicts the outlet temperature of a material given the heat and speed parameters. The data used to train the "self-prediction" model is acquired by simulation.

In contrast to the work of [16], we focus on tackling the problem of controlling material thickness. Furthermore, we compare the performance of three different DRL algorithms instead of only using DQN. DQN aims to learn a good estimate of the optimal action-value function in order to find the greedy deterministic policy. Standard DQN only works for discrete action tasks since maximizing a complex nonlinear action-value function at each update becomes difficult in continuous action tasks. However, using a discrete action space for temperature adjustments is questionable since it can lead to discretization errors or sparse rewards. By the introduction of an unnecessary discretization hyperparameter, we are running the risk of overshooting if the step size is too large. At the same time, a step size too small can result in sparse rewards, making it more difficult for the agent to learn. To overcome this problem, we use a continuous action space. We choose DDPG [13] and PPO [22] due to their competitive performance in continuous control tasks and compare them against the performance of DQN in a discrete action setting. In addition, [16] rely on simulated data to train their self-prediction model, whereas we utilize an authentic real-world dataset to acquire knowledge of the intrinsic dynamics of a manufacturing process. Their self-prediction model is based on a RF approach, but we demonstrate that its capacity for generalization to unobserved instances can be inadequate compared to an MLP approach. This inadequacy can hinder the training of the RL agent and lead to unnecessary complex policies. Our experimental results demonstrate that, interestingly, although both RF and MLP surrogate models achieve equally good accuracy in predicting the material thickness, the MLP surrogate model acts as a better simulation environment for training the DRL agent to learn a more effective policy for solving our problem.

# 4  Methodology

In this section, we present our control framework that utilizes DRL to automatically determine the main control parameters to achieve the desired outlet thickness of the material. We start by describing the self-prediction model and refer to it as a surrogate model. To train the surrogate model, we use real-world data to predict the thickness value of the material. We then discuss how this learned surrogate model is used as a simulation environment for training the DRL agent and how the material thickness control problem is formulated as an RL problem in our framework.

## 4.1  Surrogate Model

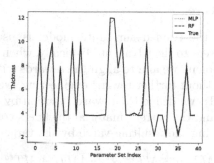

**Fig. 2.** Predicted thicknesses from either the RF or MLP surrogate model versus the true thickness values. Test data is randomly drawn and consists of 40 different parameter constellations from the empirical dataset.

An RL agent learns how to solve a sequential decision-making problem through real-time interaction with an uncertain environment. The agent learns what actions to take based on a scalar reward signal provided by the environment. In most RL works, (simulation) environments are pre-given with well-defined reward functions. However, we entirely lack a simulation environment for the real-world material process due to its complexity and variability. Hence, real-world data collected from an industrial process is extremely valuable, providing a good representation of the internal dynamics. In our work, we utilize available real-world process data from a production site to build our own simulation environment by learning a good representation of the data itself.

We explore two surrogate models: a Random Forest (RF) with 128 decision trees and a MLP with one hidden layer containing 128 units. These surrogates are trained end-to-end in a supervised manner on the full dataset, using L2 loss to predict material thickness from input parameters. We assess surrogate model performance through 10-fold cross-validation (80/20 split) using L1 loss. To ensure comparability, both RF and MLP matching an L1 loss of approximately 0.02.

These trained surrogate models serve as the simulation environment for training the subsequent DRL agent. They provide state updates and scalar rewards after agent actions. Figure 2 showcases the surrogate models' predictive accuracy for material thickness based on input parameters.

In our experiments, we find that, even though both RF and MLP surrogate models achieve equally good accuracy in predicting the material thickness, the MLP surrogate model demonstrates superior generalization performance over the RF surrogate model, acting as a better simulation environment for training the DRL agent. Specifically, the RF surrogate model, when presented with previously unseen parameter configurations, has a tendency to predict the most frequently observed material thickness value. This results in a significant degree of volatility in the predicted material thickness, even when input parameters exhibit only minor changes.

## 4.2   Reward Structure

We now explain how the trained surrogate model is used to determine the numeric reward signal sent to the RL agent. Typically, when designing the reward function for an RL problem, we aim to align the rewards with the long-term goal as best as possible. Without further reward engineering, we follow the approach used in [16]. Specifically, we define the reward function by taking the difference between the previous and the current material thickness compared to the target thickness and normalizing the resulting value by the target thickness:

$$r_t = \frac{|MT_{t-1} - MT^{target}| - |MT_t - MT^{target}|}{MT^{target}}. \tag{4}$$

With $MT_{t-1}$ being the previous and $MT_t$ the currently observed material thickness. If the agent's action choice results in a material thickness within a certain acceptance interval, an additional reward of +1 is provided to the agent and the current episode is terminated early. Noticeably, the acceptance interval might differ between different target material thickness runs. Mostly, the acceptance interval is set to be $[MT^{target} - 0.2, MT^{target} - 0.1]$, with the lower bound determined by the customer's minimum tolerance. A target thickness of 2 mm constitutes an exception, as empirically we never observe thicknesses below 2 mm and the exact reason is unknown to us. Consequently, the maximum cumulative reward the agent can earn within one episode, assuming an initial random state with a material thickness of 2 mm, is approximately 1.75 for a target thickness of 8 mm. Further experiment results refer to a target thickness of 8 mm.

## 4.3   State and Action Spaces

The state space consists of the current measured heat of several different zones and the actual material thickness observed, denoted as follows:

$$s_t = (FH_t^1, FH_t^2, ..., FH_t^J, MT_t) \in S, \tag{5}$$

where $FH_t^j$ is the heat of the $j$th zone and $MT_t$ is the material thickness currently observed based on the trained surrogate model. At each timestep $t$ of an episode, the RL agent takes an action $a_t$ in environment state $s_t$, moves to the next state $s_{t+1}$ and receives a scalar reward $r_t$. Such a sequence describes a trajectory $\tau_t$ by which the agent uses to learn to maximize the expected cumulative reward.

We consider both continuous and discrete action spaces by modelling the temperature of each zone as a continuous action or as a set of discrete actions. For the continuous action setting, the action space is defined as:

$$a_t = \{\alpha_t^1, \alpha_t^2, ..., \alpha_t^J\} \in A, \tag{6}$$

where $\alpha_t^j$ implies the increase or decrease in temperature of the $j$th zone. Hence, the agent is able to change each zone temperature at every timestep $t$. The natural limitation in the actions is the maximum or minimum observed temperature of the respective zone with an action range of $[-10, 10]$.

In the discrete action setting, the state representation stays the same. However, the action space doubles and we insert an action-step size $\zeta$, which defines a hyperparameter in our setting. The action space in the discrete setting is then defined as:

$$a_t = \{\alpha_t^1, \alpha_t^2, ..., \alpha_t^J, \alpha_t^{J+1}, ..., \alpha_t^{J+J}\} \in A, \tag{7}$$

where $\alpha_t^1, ..., \alpha_t^J$ implies an increase in temperature of the $j$th zone by $\zeta = 10\,°C$ and $\alpha_t^{J+1}, ..., \alpha_t^{J+J}$ implies a decrease in temperature of the $j$th zone by $\zeta = -10\,°C$.

### 4.4 Agent Description

This work compares the performance of three different DRL algorithms in various surrogate model environments. We now give a brief summary of the DRL methods used.

The first is PPO [22], a policy gradient method that aims to optimize a stochastic policy in a stable and sample-efficient manner similar to Trust Region Policy Optimization (TRPO) [21]. Different to TRPO, PPO uses a clipped surrogate objective function that constrains the update to a small region around the current policy, preventing large policy updates while ensuring policy sustainability. Secondly, we use DDPG [13], an actor-critic algorithm that learns a deterministic policy, meaning it directly outputs the optimal action for a given state. It combines deep neural networks with the traditional actor-critic algorithm to handle high-dimensional continuous action spaces. And thirdly DQN [18], a Q-learning algorithm that uses a deep neural network to estimate the action-value function. It employs an experience replay buffer and a separate target network to stabilize the learning process and prevent overfitting.

## 5 Experiments

We train the DRL agent by interacting with the surrogate model. All experiments use the same hyperparameters, run for 1000 episodes with 10 random seeds and limit episodes to 2000 timesteps. If the agent reaches the target thickness within an acceptable range, it receives +1 reward, ending the episode early. Initial states are randomly sampled from empirical data, excluding those already within the acceptable range. Action limits are based on observed data. We use $\gamma = 0.999$ for all experiments. Surrogate models include Random Forest (RF) and Multi-Layer Perceptron (MLP), while DRL agents encompass DQN, DDPG, and PPO. We evaluate their performance combinations for solving the continuous control problem. Experimental results are reported for a target thickness of 8 mm.

As we do not have a simulation environment or access to online testing for our control problem, it is intriguing to determine whether the surrogate model can accurately depict the dynamics of the actual underlying environment. We validate our approach by comparing the performance of a PPO agent either trained in the Mountain Car Gym environment (continuous) [4] or trained in the MLP surrogate environment. The training of the MLP surrogate is based on expert trajectories generated from an optimal policy for the Mountain Car Gym environment. In this environment, the agent receives a negative reward of $-0.1 * action^2$ for each step in which the car fails to reach the final position on the hill and a positive reward of +100 upon reaching the final position.

**PPO.** We use 8 parallel environments and approximate policy and value functions using neural networks with a 2-layer, 64-unit fully-connected MLP architecture. The policy network outputs adjustments for each of the six zones as mean and standard deviation from a normal distribution. We train these networks using stochastic gradient ascent and descent, both using Adam optimizer at a learning rate of 0.004. Advantages are computed with Generalized Advantage Estimation (GAE) as suggested [1] and minibatch normalization with a size of 68 and a lambda of 0.95 during training.

**DDPG.** We maintain two networks: a policy network mapping states to actions and a critic network assessing expected cumulative rewards. Both networks have MLP architectures with 2 hidden layers of 64 units each and ReLU non-linearities. We train the actor and critic networks using Adam optimizer with a learning rate of 0.004. We employ soft updates for the target networks and an exploration strategy based on the Ornstein-Uhlenbeck process.

**DQN.** We use a Q-network and a target network as twin initialization. Both networks consist of 2 hidden layers with 64 units and ReLU non-linearities. The parameters of the Q-network are updated via Adam optimizer with a learning rate of 0.004. The target network parameters are soft updates of the Q-network parameters. Exploration is performed during training using $\epsilon$ greedy. The output of the network is of size *number of zones* $* 2$ and the index of the maximum value indicates which zone temperature is to be increased or decreased.

The left pane of Fig. 3 shows the mean cumulative reward attained by the agent during training for a fixed target thickness, using various surrogate models and DRL algorithm combinations in our framework. The maximum cumulative reward achievable ranges between approximately $[1.1, 1.75]$, depending on the difference between the initial material thickness and the target thickness. We can

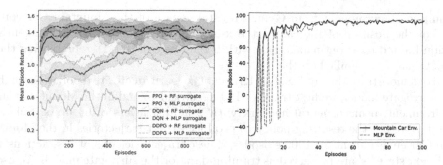

**Fig. 3.** Left: Mean episode return achieved during training when using various surrogate model and DRL algorithm combinations in our framework. The mean across 10 random seeds is plotted and the ± standard deviation is shown shaded. Right: Mean episode return achieved during training for a PPO agent either trained in the Mountain Car simulation environment or trained in our MLP surrogate environment.

see that the combination of PPO and the MLP surrogate model performs the best among the tested algorithms and surrogate models. It quickly and successfully converges to the maximum attainable reward and learns policies to accurately identify the optimal parameter configuration for the target material thickness within an acceptance interval.

Moreover, when trained in the MLP surrogate environment, all three DRL algorithms demonstrate superior performance compared to their performance in the RF surrogate environment. Compared to PPO, DQN and DDPG are more sensitive to the choice of the surrogate model. Specifically, when trained in the RF surrogate environment, both DQN and DDPG exhibit significantly worse performance in terms of both absolute performance and learning speed, compared to when they are trained in the MLP surrogate environment. The RF surrogate model tends to revert to the most commonly observed target thickness for unseen parameter configurations, thereby introducing noise in the reward signal. Additionally, the DQN algorithm's discrete and fixed step size of $10\,°C$ seems to cause the predicted target thickness of the RF surrogate model to vary significantly, further increasing the noise in the reward signal and prolonging the training process. Whereas the discrete step size does not appear to pose any issues for the combination of DQN and MLP surrogate. In our setting, DPPG fails to converge to a good policy completely in the RF surrogate environment and exhibits highly volatile training performance in the MLP surrogate environment.

**Surrogate Validation.** In this work, we consider industrial manufacturing processes where online evaluation is unfeasible due to significant financial costs and the absence of compatible simulations. Consequently, the question arises as to whether our trained surrogate model can provide a good approximation to a simulation environment for training the DRL agent to learn (sub-) optimal performance. To assess this, we utilize the well-known continuous Mountain Car simulation environment from Gym. The state space of the Mountain Car consists of the position of the car on the x-axis and its velocity, with the agent's action limited to a continuous scale within the range of $[-1, 1]$, representing the directional force applied on the car.

To demonstrate the ability of an RL agent to learn an effective policy through our surrogate model, we first train a PPO agent end-to-end in the Mountain Car environment, using a neural network with 2 hidden layers of 64 units. Subsequently, we use the resulting policy to produce expert trajectories in the Mountain Car environment for 1000 episodes. These trajectories of states $s$, actions $a$ and next states $s'$ are preserved as training data for the surrogate model. We use the MLP surrogate model, with the states $s$ and actions $a$ as input parameters to predict the next state $s'$. We employ the same MLP architecture as mentioned above and train it for 5000 episodes with a batch size of 32, resulting in an L2 loss of $<0.01$. Upon successful training of the surrogate model, we train another PPO agent using the surrogate predictions (to provide reward signal and state updates) instead of using the Gym environment.

Our argument posits that a few predictions emulate the true dynamics with a high degree of accuracy, and thus, each 50th state update is undertaken by the dynamics of the true environment to stabilize the training procedure. Subsequently, we compare the policy trained with the MLP surrogate model to the policy trained exclusively in the Mountain Car environment. The right pane of Fig. 3 shows the training curves of both PPO agents in either the true Mountain Car environment or in the MLP surrogate environment. We can observe that the PPO agent trained in the MLP surrogate environment requires more training iterations to converge compared to the PPO agent trained in the Mountain Car environment, but ultimately achieves similar performance levels. This demonstrates that our MLP surrogate model serves as a reliable approximation of the Mountain Car simulation environment.

## 6   Conclusion and Future Work

In this paper, we proposed a new framework in which we successfully train a DRL agent in a surrogate environment based on real-world data. Our aim is to continuously control the optimal input parameters to achieve a desired pre-specified material thickness in a manufacturing process while reducing the loss incurred during the process. To achieve this, we first established an RL environment by training a surrogate model (i.e., an MLP model) on real-world data to predict the material thickness given the input parameters. We then trained a PPO agent by interacting with the established RL environment, to automatically find the main control parameters that lead to the desired target material thickness. To the best of our knowledge, this is the first time a DRL approach has been successfully used to control material thickness in a manufacturing process using real-world data. We validate our approach by showing that a DRL agent trained in our MLP surrogate environment can achieve similar final performance to the one trained in the Mountain Car simulation environment.

Our framework is general and can be applied to similar control problems where no simulations and online testing are available but access to empirical data is given. Our results identified the optimal pairing of a DRL algorithm with a surrogate environment to be the PPO algorithm when coupled with the MLP surrogate. This is a general recommendation, although a solution tailored to the problem should achieve equal or better results. We argue that rising environmental complexity should be encountered with a fine-tuned surrogate model to minimize the reality gap. In future work, a human-in-the-loop is considered. While other methods are not applicable such as real-world testing due to enormous costs.

# References

1. Andrychowicz, M., et al.: What matters for on-policy deep actor-critic methods? A large-scale study. In: International Conference on Learning Representations (2021)
2. Araki, M.: PID control. In: Control Systems, Robotics and Automation: System Analysis and Control: Classical Approaches II, 58–79 (2009)
3. Bennett, S.: Development of the PID controller. IEEE Control Syst. Mag. **13**(6), 58–62 (1993)
4. Brockman, G., et al.: OpenAI Gym (2016)
5. Deng, J., Sierla, S., Sun, J., Vyatkin, V.: Reinforcement learning for industrial process control: a case study in flatness control in steel industry. Comput. Ind. **143**, 103748 (2022)
6. Dornheim, J., Link, N., Gumbsch, P.: Model-free adaptive optimal control of episodic fixed-horizon manufacturing processes using reinforcement learning. Int. J. Control Autom. Syst. **18**, 1593–1604 (2020)
7. Gamal, O., Mohamed, M.I.P., Patel, C.G., Roth, H.: Data-driven model-free intelligent roll gap control of bar and wire hot rolling process using reinforcement learning. Int. J. Mech. Eng. Robot. Res. **10**(7), 349–356 (2021)
8. Guo, F., Zhou, X., Liu, J., Zhang, Y., Li, D., Zhou, H.: A reinforcement learning decision model for online process parameters optimization from offline data in injection molding. Appl. Soft Comput. **85**, 105828 (2019)
9. Hornik, K., Stinchcombe, M., White, H.: Multilayer feedforward networks are universal approximators. Neural Netw. **2**(5), 359–366 (1989)
10. LeCun, Y., Bengio, Y., Hinton, G.: Deep learning. Nature **521**(7553), 436–444 (2015)
11. Levine, S., Finn, C., Darrell, T., Abbeel, P.: End-to-end training of deep visuomotor policies. J. Mach. Learn. Res. **17**(1), 1334–1373 (2016)
12. Levine, S., Pastor, P., Krizhevsky, A., Ibarz, J., Quillen, D.: Learning hand-eye coordination for robotic grasping with deep learning and large-scale data collection. Int. J. Robot. Res. **37**(4–5), 421–436 (2018)
13. Lillicrap, T.P., et al.: Continuous control with deep reinforcement learning. arXiv preprint arXiv:1509.02971 (2015)
14. Lin, L.J.: Reinforcement Learning for Robots Using Neural Networks. Carnegie Mellon University (1992)
15. Martínez, M.A., Sanchis, J., Blasco, X.: Multiobjective controller design handling human preferences. Eng. Appl. Artif. Intell. **19**(8), 927–938 (2006)

16. Mazgualdi, C.E., Masrour, T., Hassani, I.E., Khdoudi, A.: A deep reinforcement learning (DRL) decision model for heating process parameters identification in automotive glass manufacturing. In: Masrour, T., Cherrafi, A., El Hassani, I. (eds.) A2IA 2020. AISC, vol. 1193, pp. 77–87. Springer, Cham (2021). https://doi.org/10.1007/978-3-030-51186-9_6
17. Mirhoseini, A., et al.: A graph placement methodology for fast chip design. Nature **594**(7862), 207–212 (2021)
18. Mnih, V., et al.: Playing Atari with deep reinforcement learning. arXiv preprint arXiv:1312.5602 (2013)
19. Mnih, V., et al.: Human-level control through deep reinforcement learning. Nature **518**(7540), 529–533 (2015)
20. Ruelens, F., Claessens, B.J., Quaiyum, S., De Schutter, B., Babuška, R., Belmans, R.: Reinforcement learning applied to an electric water heater: from theory to practice. IEEE Trans. Smart Grid **9**(4), 3792–3800 (2016)
21. Schulman, J., Levine, S., Abbeel, P., Jordan, M., Moritz, P.: Trust region policy optimization. In: International Conference on Machine Learning, pp. 1889–1897. PMLR (2015)
22. Schulman, J., Wolski, F., Dhariwal, P., Radford, A., Klimov, O.: Proximal policy optimization algorithms (2017)
23. Silver, D., et al.: Mastering the game of go with deep neural networks and tree search. Nature **529**(7587), 484–489 (2016)
24. Stewart, G., Samad, T.: Cross-application perspectives: application and market requirements. Impact Control Technol. 95–100 (2011)
25. Sutton, R.S., Barto, A.G.: Reinforcement Learning: An Introduction. MIT Press, Cambridge (2018)
26. Wu, T., Zhao, H., Gao, B., Meng, F.: Energy-saving for a velocity control system of a pipe isolation tool based on a reinforcement learning method. Int. J. Precis. Eng. Manuf.-Green Technol. **9**(1), 225–240 (2021). https://doi.org/10.1007/s40684-021-00309-8
27. Yu, J., Guo, P.: Run-to-run control of chemical mechanical polishing process based on deep reinforcement learning. IEEE Trans. Semicond. Manuf. **33**(3), 454–465 (2020)
28. Zinn, J., Vogel-Heuser, B., Gruber, M.: Fault-tolerant control of programmable logic controller-based production systems with deep reinforcement learning. J. Mech. Des. **143**(7), 072004 (2021)
29. Zirngibl, C., Dworschak, F., Schleich, B., Wartzack, S.: Application of reinforcement learning for the optimization of clinch joint characteristics. Prod. Eng. Res. Devel. **16**(2–3), 315–325 (2022)

# SANTA: Semi-supervised Adversarial Network Threat and Anomaly Detection System

Muhammad Fahad Zia$^{(\boxtimes)}$ (iD), Sri Harish Kalidass(iD), and Jonathan Francis Roscoe(iD)

Future Cyber Defence, BT Plc, Ipswich, UK
{muhammadfahad.zia,sriharish.kalidass,jonathan.roscoe}@bt.com

**Abstract.** With the exponential increase in devices connected to the Internet, the risk of security breaches has in turn led to an increase in traction for machine learning based intrusion detection systems. These systems involve either supervised classifiers to detect known threats or unsupervised techniques to separate anomalies from normal data. Supervised learning enables accurate detection of known attack behaviours but requiring quality ground-truth data, it is ineffective against new emerging threats. Unsupervised learning-based systems address this issue due to their generalizable approach; however, they can result in a high false detection rate and are generally unable to detect specific types of each threat. We propose an ensemble technique that addresses the shortcomings of both approaches through a semi-supervised approach which detects both known and unknown threats in the network by analysing traffic metadata. The robust approach integrates A) an adversarial regularisation based autoencoder for unsupervised representation learning and B) supervised gradient boosted trees to detect the type of detected threats. The adversarial regularisation enables a reduced false positive rate and the combination of the autoencoder with the supervised stage enables resiliency against class imbalance and caters to the ever-evolving threat landscape by detecting previously unseen threats and anomalies. SANTA's ability to detect never-before-seen threats also indicates its potential to address the concept drift, a phenomenon where the known threat changes its behaviour/attack sequence over time. The system is evaluated on the CSE-CIC-IDS2018 dataset, and the results confirm the resilience and adaptability of the SANTA system against known shortcomings of both supervised and unsupervised approaches.

**Keywords:** Anomaly detection · Semi-supervised learning · Adversarial regularization · concept drift

## 1 Introduction

Forecasts suggest that by 2025, there would be more than 75 billion devices connected to the internet – an approximate of 300% increase from the 2019 baseline [1]. This sharp increase in devices connected to the network has increased the network intrusion and cyberattack incidents across the globe. According to the report published by AAG [2]

---

M. F. Zia and S. H. Kalidass—Equal Contribution.

© The Author(s), under exclusive license to Springer Nature Switzerland AG 2023
M. Bramer and F. Stahl (Eds.): SGAI 2023, LNAI 14381, pp. 335–349, 2023.
https://doi.org/10.1007/978-3-031-47994-6_31

in 2023, there has been 125% increase in cyber-attacks in 2021. Undetected threats on a network can have severe impact on essential services and facilities for businesses; this includes loss of data, revenue, and reputation and threat to national security in the case of governments. The development of efficient intrusion detection systems has, therefore, become more important than ever in the face of evolving threat techniques.

The challenges in the domain of intrusion detection can be broadly classified into two categories; sufficient accuracy in detection of known attack patterns and the generalization ability to cater to the evolution of attacks. Signature-based intrusion detection systems address the first challenge through the use of supervised learning-based models. These models are trained on large historical datasets [3] to establish signatures or patterns of these attacks thereby enabling detection of future attacks conforming to these patterns. The problem with these models, however, is there inability to cope with new attack patterns and types as there are no available signatures to match to for these attacks. This second challenge is addressed by anomaly-based intrusion detection systems which cater to this using unsupervised learning. These systems use models that are trained to cluster data based on different criteria including similarity measures. This enables the system to separate normal and anomalous data by assigning different clusters to each. These systems are subsequently able to deal with new attacks, which would still be tagged as abnormal or anomalous since they differ from the normal behaviour or pattern. Further classification to detect specific type of attacks, however, is limited in these unsupervised learning-based systems as is their accuracy in comparison to supervised approaches. In addition to this, these systems also suffer from the known generalization problem where models misclassify malicious attacks as normal if their pattern deviates only slightly from normal behaviour.

Machine Learning (ML)-based Network threat detection systems have proven to perform better than traditional intelligence tool to protect networks against cyberattacks. The supervised tree-based classifiers and results on publicly available re-search Network dataset is discussed here (Thaseen, S.; Kumar) [5]. The unsupervised network threat and anomaly detection results are not reliable as the accuracy seems to vary from 57% to 80% and with very high false positive rate of 20% and over. (Syarif, I.; Prugel-Bennett) [6]. The promising unsupervised work identified is ARCADE (Adversarially Regularized Convolutional Autoencoder for Anomaly Detection) (Lunardi, W.T., Lopez, 2022) [4] approach. The ARCADE uses the raw packets instead of aggregated NetFlow features to train the network. In the detection stage, ARCADE uses both the encoder and decoder networks. A semi supervised approach (J. Ran, Y. Ji and B. Tang, 2019) [7] carried on Aegean Wi-Fi Intrusion Dataset (AWID) public dataset, the results outperformed other ML approaches. One of the interesting semi-supervised algorithms that was identified is XGBOD (Zhao, Y. & Hryniewicki, M. K., 2018) [8] which is an ensemble semi-supervised algorithm that was experimented on non-security datasets.

In this paper, we propose a unique combination of the aforementioned intrusion detection approaches that deals with the known challenges in intrusion detection. SANTA is a robust semi-supervised threat and anomaly detection system that enables the classification of both known and unknown attack patterns using limited labelled data and adversarial training to reduce the false detections or misses during inference.

The contributions of the paper are: (a) the combination of adversarially regularised autoencoder to enrich data for supervised learning. (b) Evaluation of the pro-posed model in terms of accuracy on known and unknown attack types. (c) Evaluation of the proposed model in terms of resiliency when less labelled data is available for training. (d) Comparison against other known methods of anomaly detection.

The remainder of the paper is organized as follows; Sect. 2 depicts the architecture of the proposed model and the methodology behind each component; Sect. 3 outlines the dataset used in experimentation and its specifications; Sect. 4 details the experimentation and model evaluation results; conclusions are presented in Sect. 5.

## 2   SANTA

Our semi-supervised adversarial network threat and anomaly detection (SANTA) system comprises of two modules in a meta-learning pipeline where the output of first is used to enrich the input of the second. The simplified flowchart is presented in Fig. 1 showing the processing pipeline and individual components. The NetFlow data is passed through the autoencoder to output the embeddings, also referred to as the newly learnt enriched features (through unsupervised representation learning). The original NetFlow is then concatenated with the enriched features to produce the enriched data. The supervised classifier is provided with the enriched data and learns to detect and identify threats and anomalies. Each of these steps are detailed in the corresponding sections below – unsupervised learning module and training strategy, supervised learning module, data enrichment and finally the inference strategy.

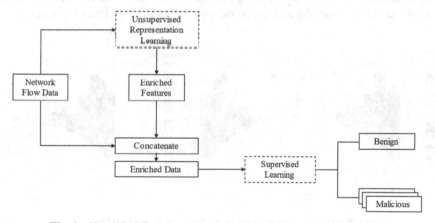

**Fig. 1.** Simplified flowchart showing the key components of SANTA

### 2.1   Unsupervised Representation Learning

We implement unsupervised representation learning using an adversarially trained autoencoder based on work published by Lunardi [4].

The autoencoder involves the use of 3 deep neural networks – **Encoder, Decoder** and **Critic**. The Encoder is 4-layer deep convolutional autoencoder that "encodes" the input data by learning latent features at each layer to output an encoding of the original data. This encoding captures a rich summary of the data and is used to reproduce the original data by the Decoder. The Decoder has an architecture similar to the encoder network but uses transpose-convolutions to expand the encoding in each step to accurately reproduce the original data.

These two networks are trained in tandem on solely normal (benign) traffic flows with the objective of minimizing the reconstruction error, which is the difference between the original and reconstructed data. This ensures that the network only learns to reconstruct normal traffic and not anomalies thus ensuring that the reconstruction error for anomalous flows will be high and can be used to distinguish between real and anomalous flows.

A known problem is that of generalisation; the network can be generic enough to be able to reconstruct anomalous data to sufficient quality, despite being trained on solely normal data flows thus reducing the ability of the algorithm to distinguish between anomalous and normal input data. **Adversarial regularisation-based training** using the Critic network in SANTA addresses this issue. The Critic network has a similar architecture to the encoder network with a difference in the output layer to output a single value as a score (instead of an encoding). It is trained to discriminate between reconstructed and original data by output high scores for original data and low for reconstructed data. The objective for this network is thus to maximize the difference between the scores it gives to original and reconstructed data. This strategy of training is called adversarial regularisation owing to the Encoder-Decoder and Critic network being trained with opposing objectives. This ensures that the trained network is more tightly bound to the data it is trained on (normal traffic in this case) and reduces the generic nature of the network thereby addressing the generalization problem to an extent.

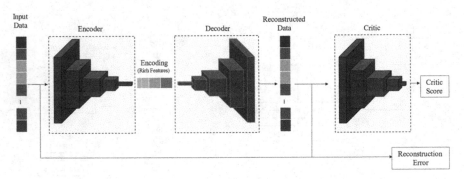

**Fig. 2.** Architecture diagram of SANTA's unsupervised module.

The complete architecture of the unsupervised learning module is shown in Fig. 2 with further details into the precise architecture of each separate network summarized in Table 1.

Once the autoencoder is trained using the adversarial regularisation strategy, the encoder is used to encode the input data and output rich encodings that are concatenated

**Table 1.** Encoder, Decoder and Critic Architecture.

| Layer | Kernel, Stride | Output | Parameters |
|---|---|---|---|
| **Encoder** | | | |
| Input | – | $1 \times 41$ | |
| Convolution | 4, 2 | $16 \times 21$ | 80 |
| Leaky ReLU | – | – | – |
| Batch Normalization | – | – | 64 |
| Convolution | 4, 2 | $32 \times 11$ | 2,080 |
| Leaky ReLU | – | – | – |
| Batch Normalization | – | – | 128 |
| Convolution | 4, 2 | $64 \times 6$ | 8,265 |
| Leaky ReLU | – | – | – |
| Batch Normalization | – | – | 256 |
| Linear | – | 6 | 2,310 |
| **Total** | | | **13,174** |
| **Decoder** | | | |
| Layer | Kernel, Stride | Output | Parameters |
| Input | – | 6 | |
| Linear | – | $64 \times 6$ | 2,688 |
| Transpose Convolution | 4, 2 | $32 \times 11$ | 8,224 |
| ReLU | – | – | – |
| Batch Normalization | – | – | 128 |
| Transpose Convolution | 4, 2 | $16 \times 21$ | 2,064 |
| ReLU | – | – | – |
| Batch Normalization | – | – | 64 |
| Transpose Convolution | 4, 2 | $1 \times 41$ | 65 |
| Sigmoid | – | – | – |
| **Total** | | | **13,233** |
| **Critic** | | | |
| Layer | Kernel, Stride | Output | Parameters |
| Input | – | $1 \times 41$ | |
| Convolution | 4, 2 | $16 \times 21$ | 80 |
| Leaky ReLU | – | – | – |
| Batch Normalization | – | – | 64 |

(*continued*)

**Table 1.** (*continued*)

| Layer | Kernel, Stride | Output | Parameters |
|---|---|---|---|
| Convolution | 4, 2 | 32 × 11 | 2,080 |
| Leaky ReLU | – | – | – |
| Batch Normalization | – | – | 128 |
| Convolution | 4, 2 | 64 × 6 | 8,265 |
| Leaky ReLU | – | – | – |
| Batch Normalization | – | – | 256 |
| Linear | – | 6 | 4,230 |
| Leaky ReLU | – | – | – |
| Layer Normalization | – | – | 12 |
| Linear | – | 1 | 7 |
| **Total** | | | **15,113** |

to the original data to provide a more enriched feature space for the next stage of the SANTA pipeline. The details of the training strategy are presented below.

## 2.2 Training

During training, the unsupervised module is trained based on two objectives.

The first objective ($\mathscr{L}_A$) is to reduce the reconstruction error which is the $\mathscr{L}_2$ loss between the reconstructed ($\bar{x}$) and original data (x). The $\mathscr{L}_2$ loss can be expressed as:

$$\mathcal{L}_2(x, \bar{x}) = \sum_{i=0}^{F} (x_i - \bar{x}_i)^2 \tag{1}$$

where F is the total number of features in the dataset. The first objective is additionally regularized to reduce the critic score on the reconstructed data as is expressed below:

$$\mathcal{L}_A = \mathbb{E}_{x \sim \mathbb{P}_r}[\mathcal{L}_2(x, \bar{x}) + \lambda_A C(\bar{x})] \tag{2}$$

where $\mathbb{P}_r$ is the data distribution and $\lambda_A$ is a regularization coefficient. The second objective ($\mathscr{L}_B$) is to increase the squared difference between the critic score ($C$) on original and reconstructed data which is the adversarial regularization previously discussed. This is shown below:

$$\mathcal{L}_B = \mathbb{E}_{x \sim \mathbb{P}_r}\left[(C(x) - C(\bar{x}))^2\right] \tag{3}$$

The three networks are thus trained in tandem with the decoder and critic essentially training the encoder which is then extracted apart and used to generate encodings on the original data to concatenate to the same and pass to the supervised module for training.

Training in the supervised module is encompassed by trees being trained to optimize the multinomial deviance and the module learning to output the correct classification for each data instance.

## 2.3  Data Enrichment

As mentioned above, the output from the unsupervised module, in the form of embeddings generated by the adversarially trained encoder, is used to enrich the original data; the details of which are as follows.

The data enrichment process involves exploiting the input data to a great extent to harness its potential to unprecedented levels to benefit the model development. This section describes the parameters, factors, and the process of the data enrichment stage.

The enrichment process produces newly learned representations of the original raw input data. Two forms of data that are concatenated to produce the enriched data, A) the encoded data from unsupervised stage and B) raw input data. The data enrichment is an output of meta learning process where the encoded data is produced by the encoding component of the autoencoder which was trained using a critic network through the aforementioned adversarial training strategy. Since the autoencoder is trained using solely benign data, the model's learning is limited to only effectively encode benign data, this limits the model's ability to encode malicious or anomalous flows. Since the encodings represents the raw data in a new latent space the encodings of malicious or anomalous data have a unique signature which distinguishes them from normal or benign data and thus helps the subsequent supervised model to detect and identify known threats, unknown threats and to some extent address the concept drift as is evident in the results from experiments documented in Sect. 4; the specific evaluation of the data enrichment process is discussed in the Sect. 4.2.

Delving deeper into the enrichment process it involves generating the embeddings ($e$) for input data ($d_{input}$) and transforming the embeddings by normalizing and adding weights to form the transformed embeddings ($e_T$) as represented in Eq. 4.

$$e_T = N(e) * U \tag{4}$$

where $N(e)$ represents the normalized embeddings and $U$ represents the weights; is a real number chosen through an empirical process. There is ongoing research to find an optimal way to produce fine-tuned weights for the embeddings.

This is followed by normalising the input data, and finally concatenating the transformed embeddings with the normalised input data to form the final enriched data ($d_E$) which is represented in Eq. 5.

$$d_E = e_T + N(d_{input}) \tag{5}$$

where $N(d_{input})$ represents the normalized input data.

In the IDS-2018-V2 dataset with originally 43 features, the label and the description of labels was removed, and the total number of features used was down to 41 dependent variables. The length of embeddings extracted from the unsupervised stage is 6 based on the architecture of the autoencoder finalised by an empirical process of hyperparameter tuning. The 6 real-valued embeddings, multiplying weight value (U) to the normalised embeddings and further concatenating with normalised input data containing 41 dependent variable produces 47 real-valued features, which is the size of the enriched data ($d_E$). This enriched data is used to train the supervised gradient boosted tree classifier.

## 2.4 Supervised Learning

The supervised learning algorithm used is a gradient boosted tree which offers generalisation of boosting to arbitrary differentiable loss functions, based on work by Friedman [9]. The encodings from the previous stage are concatenated to the original data to form the input for this stage of processing which takes in labelled training data and learns to output a classification on each flow of data.

The complete architecture for this supervised stage of processing is shown in Fig. 3.

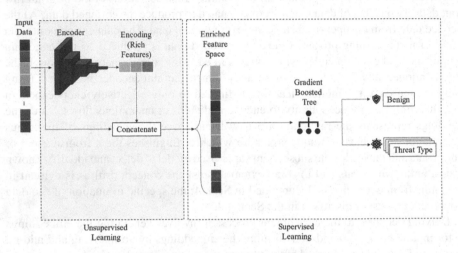

**Fig. 3.** SANTA complete architecture (Inference)

## 2.5 Inference

In the inference stage, the trained encoder is used to generate encodings to enrich the data before passing it on to the supervised module for threat classification. SANTA is thus able to identify each individual class that it was previously trained on.

In the case of previously unseen data, we introduce a post processing step where the confidence scores on each class are used to determine how confident the model is in its predictions. Ideally, for previously unseen classes the model confidence scores on each known class will be low. Hence thresholding measures on the scores for each class are used to ascertain whether the input data belongs to the known classes or should be classified as a new but generic anomaly class.

For example, a data instance with a confidence score of less than 50% for all the known classes (including the *normal* class) can be considered as a new anomaly or attack pattern. The threshold is currently intuitively set at 50% using manual inspection of the results. The inference on new data is explained in further detail in Sect. 4.2.

# 3   Dataset

The SANTA model was experimented using two datasets, A) an internally generated synthetic carrier data from the preconfigured network infrastructure and B) CSE-CIC-IDS2018-V2 dataset [10]. Both the datasets comprise of a form of network metadata known as NetFlow data. NetFlow Is a Network Protocol Developed by Cisco for Collecting IP Traffic Information and Monitoring Network Flow. The details of the two datasets used for experimentation are as follows.

## 3.1   Synthetic Carrier Dataset

The initial analysis and testing of the SANTA model was carried using the synthetic carrier data. The synthetic carrier data refers to the aggregated NetFlow generated from a custom experimental setup. The data itself is confidential and therefore we have limited the discussions and the results to appropriate levels and focusing more on the CSC-IDS-2018-V2 dataset-based results.

The synthetic carrier data is a small dataset that comprises of benign and port-scan activity type flows. Port scan activity consists of a variety of techniques that aim to discover information about networks and hosts. The discovered vulnerabilities could be exploited in a future attack which could have severe consequences. Port scans may be indicative of reconnaissance by threat actors, but they are a common activity for security teams to assess and monitor networks.

The dataset consists of raw NetFlow containing predefined set of features and a time windowed pre-processing technique is applied to extraction 17 dependent variables. Depending on the value set for time (t, (mins)) in time windowing the volume of extracted flows are generated. The lower the time(t) value, higher number of extracted flows and vice versa, however at any instance time(t) can only be positive and the total number of extracted flows can't exceed the volume of original raw NetFlow. In our experiment, a time(t) value of 30(mins) is applied on the raw NetFlow data. The timestamp is used for each observation in the dataset to partition group the data by specified time intervals, which can be assumed as time frequency-based aggregation of the data. This aggregated data is used to extract some features based on pre-defined empirical relations, which results in the final processed dataset. Table 2 illustrates the pre-processing description.

**Table 2.** Synthetic carrier dataset description

| Data Type | Raw NetFlow | Time windowed (Mins) | Extracted Flows | Data Ratio |
|---|---|---|---|---|
| Benign | 430,437 | 30 | 9962 | 89% |
| Port Scan attack | 313,770 | 30 | 1167 | 11% |

A snapshot of the list of extracted flow variables are furnished below.
{ 'ip_addresses',   'syn_flag_count',   'dst_port_count',   'dst_srv_port_count',
'dst_ip_count',        'proto_count',        'tcp_proto_count',        'udp_proto_count',

'icmp_proto_count',
'tcp_proto_ratio', 'udp_proto_ratio', 'icmp_proto_ratio', 'reply_count', 'reply_ratio',
'mean_packets', 'max_packets', 'mean_bytes', 'max_bytes', 'n_flows', 'duration'}.

### 3.2  CSE-IDS-2018-V2 Dataset

Further experimentation was carried out with the CSE-CIC-IDS2018 dataset [10]. The creators evaluated the shortcomings of the eleven publicly available datasets since 1998 and came up with a dataset to address those. It conforms to each of the eleven criteria of the last intrusion detection dataset evaluation framework [11] which none of the other datasets could completely meet. More details on the dataset creation are available in [12]. The version used for evaluation takes the original.pcap files from this dataset to generate NetFlow-based data and is called NF-CSE-CIC-IDS2018.

The NF-CSE-CIC-IDS2018 consists of, in addition to a benign or normal class, six different common update-to-date attacks which conform to real world criteria; we trained and validated our model on a subset of four commonly occurring attack scenarios out of the six – botnet, brute force attacks, DDoS (Distributed Denial of Service) and infiltration attacks. We included a fifth web attacks category in the test set to evaluate model performance on previously unseen data. Each row of data contains aggregated statistics on each flow of packets in the network in the form of 41 features. The number of flows or occurrences for each type of attack used in our experiments is given in Table 3.

**Table 3.** Dataset classes and corresponding number of occurrences

|   | Class | # of occurrences |
|---|-------|------------------|
| 1 | Normal | 998,135 (62.63%) |
| 2 | Botnet | 143,097 (8.98%) |
| 3 | Brute Force | 120,912 (7.59%) |
| 4 | DDoS | 211,607 (13.28%) |
| 5 | Infiltration | 116,361 (7.30%) |
| 6 | Web Attacks | 3,502 (0.22%) |

## 4  Evaluation

The NF-CSE-CIC-IDS2018 dataset was split into two sets with 70% of data used for cross-fold validation and 30% used as a separate evaluation set containing an additional class of web attacks that is not included in the first set in order to evaluate the model on new and evolving threats.

For evaluation purposes, we use the three common information retrieval metrics:

- **Precision (Pr)** – ratio of correctly classified attack flows (true positives - TP) and total classifications (sum of true positives and false positives - FP).

- **Recall (Re)** – ratio of correctly classified attack flows (TP) and all flow instances (sum of true positives and false negatives - FN).
- **F-Measure (F1)** – the harmonic combination of precision and recall values.

The three measures are calculated as shown in Eq. 6.

$$Pr = \frac{TP}{TP + FP}, Re = \frac{TP}{TP + FN}, F1 = \frac{2}{\frac{1}{Pr} + \frac{1}{Re}} \tag{6}$$

### 4.1  Comparison with Other Models

SANTA was then trained and evaluated using the first set of data using 5-fold cross validation technique. This technique involves splitting of the dataset into 5 folds with a different combination of 4 sets to train and 1 to validate at each run. The results are then averaged across each combination to ensure a report with less bias. The technique is visualized in Fig. 4 showing the data split into 5 folds and each of the 5 runs with different combination of train and test set.

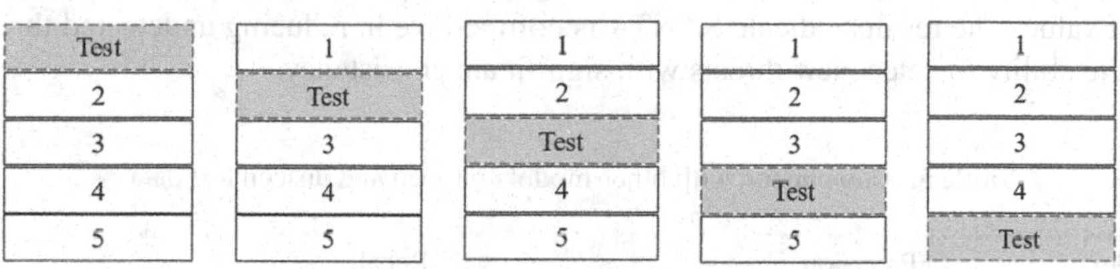

**Fig. 4.**  Cross validation technique with 5 folds.

The results are compared to those from known supervised models and the results are shown in Table 4.

**Table 4.**  Results on NF-CIC-IDS2018 dataset

| Model | Precision | Recall | F1-Score |
|---|---|---|---|
| **SANTA** | **0.98** | **0.84** | **0.86** |
| **Gradient Boosting Classifier** | **0.98** | **0.84** | **0.86** |
| **Random Forest Classifier** | **0.95** | **0.87** | **0.89** |
| Linear SVC | 0.73 | 0.44 | 0.43 |
| Logistic Regression | 0.68 | 0.43 | 0.43 |

The initial results demonstrate that the SANTA model performs competitively with Random Forest and Gradient Boosted Trees on the dataset in terms of classifying known attacks.

## 4.2 New Attack Scenarios

The separated test set with the additional unseen class of web attacks was then used to evaluate the SANTA model against the top contenders from the cross-validation stage – Gradient Boosting Classifier and Random Forest Classifier. Table 3 also shows the attack classes present in the set and the results in Table 5 show the precision and recall values on each class.

The results are calculated based on confidence thresholds on the output of each model. If a predicted class has a confidence (or probability) of less than 0.5, it is classified as an anomaly or a previously unseen attack pattern. The threshold of 0.5 as mentioned previously is currently set intuitively after manual inspection of results. All the predicted web attacks also form part of this category. In the cyber security scenario and with the detection logic that is in place for this experiment, the two values of note for each model are the precision on the $1^{st}$ class (normal instances) and the recall on the $6^{th}$ class (anomalies or unseen attacks). This is because of our two objectives. Firstly, we want to reduce the instances that are falsely classified as normal as this can lead to threats going through to a system undetected; these false positives are captured by the precision value on the first class. Secondly, we want to ensure that there are no unseen threats that are missed by the model; these $6^{th}$ class false negatives are reflected in the corresponding recall value. The results indicate SANTA is competitive in reducing undetected threats and the ability to detect new threats with significant consistency.

**Table 5.** Comparison with other models on seen and unseen test data

| Model | Precision | | | | | | Recall | | | | | |
|---|---|---|---|---|---|---|---|---|---|---|---|---|
| | 1 | 2 | 3 | 4 | 5 | 6 | 1 | 2 | 3 | 4 | 5 | 6 |
| SANTA | **0.91** | 1.00 | 0.69 | 1.00 | 0.84 | 0.10 | 0.94 | 0.94 | 1.00 | 0.40 | 0.00 | **0.85** |
| Random Forest Classifier | **0.93** | 1.00 | 1.00 | 0.96 | 0.92 | 0.00 | 1.00 | 1.00 | 1.00 | 1.00 | 0.33 | **0.00** |
| Gradient Boosting Classifier | **0.92** | 1.00 | 1.00 | 0.95 | 0.98 | 0.01 | 1.00 | 1.00 | 0.98 | 1.00 | 0.22 | **0.00** |

This experiment evaluates the effectiveness of the data enrichment using autoencoder which sets the SANTA model apart. The web attacks data are a new type of attack which was never used for training or validation process. When the web attack data was used for testing the ability of the models to detect an unknown threat, SANTA had a remarkable 0.85 recall whereas other models had a recall value of 0.00 (refer to Table 5). This is because the enriched data used in SANTA model contains the encodings generated by the pruned encoder component of the unsupervised model.

It must be noted that the supervised training process utilises the enriched data, which forces the model to use encodings to detect and identify threats. However, in the case of a new threat (unknown threat) faced by the SANTA model, the unsupervised component containing the encoder produces ineffective encodings which subsequently set this data apart from previously seen (normal) data. These are passed on to the supervised classifier, concatenated with the raw data, to classify the threat. Since the encodings are significantly different, the deviant signature is detected by the supervised classifier which classifies the input data as an anomaly.

### 4.3  Synthetic Carrier Dataset-Based Evaluation

This section discusses the results produced using the synthetic carrier dataset, where a few selections of supervised and semi-supervised models were used for the benchmarking experiment. Figure 5 shows the widely opted machine learning model evaluation metrics precision, recall and F1-score on a range of models. The XGBOD-41 [8] is a semi-supervised extreme gradient boosted outlier detection model comparing of multiple outlier detection algorithms (KNN, HBOS etc.) stacked in various combination of hyper parameters to include 41 outlier models. Similarly, for XGBOD-25 and XGBOD-15, where the number of outlier models are reduced to 25 and 15 respectively using manual selection process. The XGBOD-41 has the highest precision score reaching 88%, followed by SANTA model reaching 87%. The SANTA models top the recall with 83% and F-1 Score of 85%.

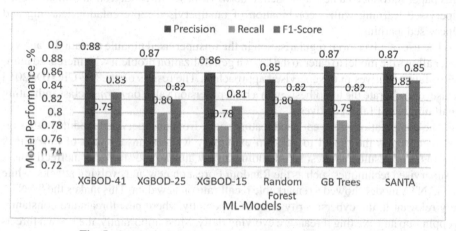

**Fig. 5.** Synthetic Carrier NetFlow data - Classification results

It must be noted that the XGBOD model is computationally expensive for training and inference. For example, the SANTA is 18 times faster compared to XGBOD during the inference and this makes the SANTA an optimal solution for real-time high-volume deployments with minimal computational requirements, even edge deployments.

The initial results also indicate the SANTA's resiliency to increase in quantities of training data. Figure 6 compares the performance of SANTA model and random forest on 30% of training data and 100% of training data. The results indicates that the SANTA models trained on just 30% of total training data outperforms the random forest model trained on 100% of training data. This also indicates the low quantity ground truth training data requirement for SANTA model.

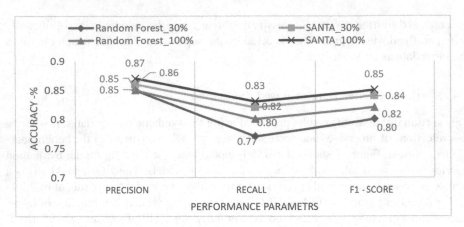

**Fig. 6.** 30% labelled data Vs 100% labelled data model performance

## 5 Conclusion

This paper introduced a new approach to network-based threat detection utilising semi-supervised learning with a combination of unsupervised representation learning and supervised learning.

The use of adversarial regularisation in the unsupervised module to train the autoencoder allows the model to cater to the known generalization problem with increased number of false positives in unsupervised approaches. The results on the NF-CIC-IDS2018 dataset corroborate the hypothesis with a high precision value on *normal* class indicating small number of false positives.

The combination of the enriched feature space from unsupervised module with original data allows the model to perform extremely well on unseen data of new attack patterns. The results on a test set including a new attack type show the ineffectiveness of supervised techniques such as the Random Forest on new and evolving attacks, while the SANTA model showed a remarkable recall rate on new data. This makes the SANTA very relevant in the cybersecurity domain especially where new threats are constantly cropping up and existing threats are evolving daily. Most importantly, the known threats tend to evolve over time (concept drift) to fool the security systems with new patterns of attack, SANTA model's initial analysis indicates it potential to detect such change in behaviours over time.

Future work is needed research into improving the ability of the unsupervised module in enriching the dataset and further development of the supervised algorithm's detection logic to improve accuracy and robustness on new and existing attack patterns. There is also scope for empirical investigation into the threshold value that is set for interpretation of classification results.

## References

1. Statistica Research Department: Internet of things - Number of Connected Devices Worldwide 2015–2025 (2022). https://www.statista.com/statistics/471264/iot-number-of-connected-devices-worldwide

2. Charles, G.: AAG IT: The Latest Cybercrime Statistics (2023). https://aag-it.com/the-latest-cyber-crime-statistics
3. Li, B., Springer, J., Bebis, G., Gunes, M.H.: A survey of network flow applications. J. Netw. Comput. Appl. **36**(2), 567–581 (2013)
4. Lunardi, W.T., Lopez, M.A., Giacalone, J.-P.: Arcade: adversarially regularized convolutional autoencoder for network anomaly detection. IEEE Trans. Netw. Serv. Manag. **20**(2), 1305–1318 (2023). https://doi.org/10.1109/TNSM.2022.3229706
5. Thaseen, S., Kumar, C.A.: An analysis of supervised tree based classifiers for intrusion detection system. In: Proceedings of the 2013 International Conference on Pattern Recognition, Informatics and Mobile Engineering, Salem, India, 21–22 February 2013, pp. 294–299 (2013)
6. Syarif, I., Prugel-Bennett, A., Wills, G.: Unsupervised clustering approach for network anomaly detection. In: Benlamri, R. (ed.) NDT 2012. CCIS, vol. 293, pp. 135–145. Springer, Heidelberg (2012). https://doi.org/10.1007/978-3-642-30507-8_13
7. Ran, J., Ji, Y., Tang, B.: A semi-supervised learning approach to IEEE 802.11 network anomaly detection. In: 2019 IEEE 89th Vehicular Technology Conference (VTC2019-Spring), Kuala Lumpur, Malaysia, pp. 1–5 (2019). https://doi.org/10.1109/VTCSpring.2019.8746576
8. Zhao, Y., Hryniewicki, M.K.: XGBOD: improving supervised outlier detection with unsupervised representation learning. In: IJCNN. IEEE (2018). https://arxiv.org/abs/1912.00290
9. Jerome, H.: Friedman: greedy function approximation: a gradient boosting machine. Ann. Stat. **29**(5), 1189–1232 (2001)
10. A Realistic Cyber Defense Dataset (CSE-CIC-IDS2018). https://registry.opendata.aws/cse-cic-ids2018. Accessed 01 June 2023
11. Gharib, A., Sharafaldin, I., Habibi Lashkari, A., Ghorbani, A.A.: An evaluation framework for intrusion detection dataset. In: International Conference on Information Science and Security (ICISS), pp. 1–6 (2016)
12. Sharafaldin, I., Lashkari, A.H., Ghorbani, A.A.: Toward generating a new intrusion detection dataset and intrusion traffic characterization. ICISSp **1**, 108–116 (2018)

# Hybrid Dual-Resampling and Cost-Sensitive Classification for Credit Risk Prediction

Emmanuel Osei-Brefo$^{(\boxtimes)}$ , Richard Mitchell , and Xia Hong

University of Reading, Reading, UK
e.osei-brefo@pgr.reading.ac.uk

**Abstract.** The class imbalance in financial data sets is prevalent and problematic when evaluating credit risks. This paper proposes a Hybrid dual Resampling and cost-sensitive classification approach by creating heuristically balanced data sets. Given an imbalanced credit data set, a synthetic minority class is generated using a resampling learning technique based on Gaussian mixture modelling from the minority class data. Simultaneously, k-means clustering is applied to the majority class. Then, feature selection is performed using an Extra Tree Ensemble technique. Finally, a cost-sensitive logistic model is estimated and applied to predict the probability of default using the heuristically balanced datasets. The results show that the proposed technique achieves superior performance in comparison with other imbalanced preprocessing approaches.

**Keywords:** Class imbalance · Credit Risk Modelling · Gaussian Mixture Modelling · Logistic Regression · Cost-Sensitive Learning

## 1 Introduction

Financial risk management involves the identification, assessment and mitigation of potential risks that may impact an organisation's financial performance [10]. There exist various risks faced by financial institutions [13], including credit risk, market risk, liquidity risk, operational risk, and many others [2]. In the event of a severe crisis, such as the 2008–2009 financial crisis, these risks can flow from credit risk to liquidity risk and to market risk. Financial institutions actively utilise financial risk management techniques to detect, manage and measure these risks [2], and effective management of credit risks is key to a bank's performance and survival.

Credit risk is defined as the risk of a borrower defaulting on a loan or other related financial obligation, and is the single largest risk faced by financial institutions [21]. Logistic regression is one of the most widely used statistical models for classification and makes it convenient for credit risk modelling [12]. It predicts the probability of a class by explaining a linear combination of a set of input features. Since insignificant/irrelevant features often exist in many data sets, feature selection is often applied as a preprocessing step. An Extra Tree Ensemble technique [3] has been introduced to obtain improved predictive accuracy and controlled over-fitting. The class imbalance problem is known to be a major obstacle to the use of a good classifier in machine learning algorithms [7]. Imbalanced datasets [23] present themselves in financial credit data, where the number of positive class observations is significantly lower than the number of negative class observations. It is essential that a robust estimation technique is investigated and implemented to predict the probability of default (PD), as an inaccurate PD results in a false valuation of risk, a wrong rating, and incorrect pricing of financial instruments.

Three main approaches can be used to mitigate the problem of imbalanced datasets; these are (i) the data-level approaches, (ii) the algorithm-level approaches, and the hybrid approaches [7,15]. Data-level approaches involve the manipulation of data sets to result in balanced data [1], which has the advantages of being external and can be integrated into different algorithms. To address the lack of positive instances in applications, the Synthetic Minority Oversampling Technique (SMOTE) was introduced [6] and applied to several real and simulated imbalanced datasets to illustrate the behaviour of the algorithm. On the other hand, the Centroid-based Under-sampling Technique (CBUT) [16] aims to represent majority class data via clusters to balance the number of positive data samples. Algorithm-level approaches are based on the use of improving existing algorithms with the main aim of shifting the decision hyper-plane from the minority class, such as the cost-sensitive learning method [22]. Rather than artificially creating balanced class distributions via sampling techniques, cost-sensitive learning solves the imbalanced class problem by utilising cost matrices that outline the costs associated with the misclassification of the various classes, since the misclassification costs are imbalanced, e.g. in medical diagnostics. Aimed at medical data sets, Cost-Sensitive Logistic Regression (CSLR) [18] was introduced as a cost-sensitive learning framework and evaluated with several machine learning algorithms, including logistic regression. The third approach is the combination of the data-level and algorithm-level approaches [15] to which the relevant technique proposed in this paper fits in, which resolves the problem that there is still a need to ensure each data-level or algorithm-level component in the hybrid approach contributes adequately to obtain the best performance.

The main aim of this paper is to investigate the concept of class imbalance prevalent in financial datasets and propose a robust solution. This paper proposes a Hybrid dual-resampling cost-sensitive (HDRCS) algorithm that simultaneously applies Gaussian mixture modelling (GMM) on the minority class to generate a synthetic minority class, as well as applies k-means clustering to create a new majority class data set. This results in a recommended heuristic Imbalance Ratio to strike an appropriate balance between the number of the majority class under-sampled and the number of minority class oversampled. The Extra Tree Ensemble technique [3] is then applied, and a cost-sensitive weighting technique, which further addresses the remaining minor imbalance, is then applied to a logistic regression classifier to the final data set based on the most important features.

The rest of the paper is organized as follows; Sect. 2 introduces the proposed HDRCS algorithm. Section 3 presents comparative experiments demonstrating the effectiveness of the proposed using several real credit risk data sets. The conclusions are presented in Sect. 4.

# 2   Proposed Hybrid Dual Resampling and Cost-Sensitive Technique (HDRCS)

## 2.1   Cost-Sensitive Logistic Classifier

For a given imbalanced data set, $X = \{x_i\}$ with binary class $y_i \in \{0, 1\}$, $x$ is $m$-dimensional feature vector. $X$ can be divided as positive/minority class $X^+$ and negative/majority class $X^-$. The imbalance ratio, $\lambda \gg 1$ is calculated as $\lambda = \frac{N^-}{N^+}$, where, $N^-$ is the number of data points for the majority class and $N^+$ is the number of data points for the minority class, $N = N^- + N^+$. Cost-Sensitive Logistic Regression (CSLR) involves the modification of the objective function of a logistic classifier to ensure that it focuses more on accurately predicting the minority class [18]. The coefficients $\beta$ are updated by maximizing the log-likelihood function of a logistic regression, given by Eq. (1).

$$\beta^* = \max_\beta \sum_{i=1}^{N} \left\{ w^- * \left( y_i \log(p_i) \right) + w^+ * \left( (1 - y_i) \log(1 - p_i) \right) \right\} \quad (1)$$

with $p_i = \frac{1}{1+\exp(-[1 \ \ x_i^T]\beta)}$ is the probability of $y(x_i) = 1$, $w^-$ is the weight for the majority class ($y_i = 1$) and $w^+$ is the weight for the minority class, $y_i = 0$. $\beta = [\beta_0, ...., \beta_m]^T$. The class weights is set such that the total number of effective samples is equal to the total number of samples ($N$) as [11]:

$$w^- \times N^- + w^+ \times N^+ = N, \quad \text{subject to} \ \ w^- \times N^- = w^+ \times N^+$$

which yields $w^- = \frac{N}{2 \times N^-}$ and $w^+ = \frac{N}{2 \times N^+}$.

By introducing penalties for each of the classes being considered, the algorithm aims to minimize the total misclassification cost. Through the assignment of a higher penalty on the less represented class (Minority class), its importance is boosted during the training process. However, in the case of a highly imbalanced dataset, it is desired to use a combination of the data-level and algorithm-level approaches [15] to further improve the classifier's performance and robustness.

## 2.2   HDRCS

In this work, the Hybrid Dual-Resampling and Cost-Sensitive (HDRCS) is introduced which aims to balance the data sets, followed by the use of CSLR. A summary of the proposed procedure is shown in Algorithm 1.

**Algorithm 1.** Proposed Hybrid Dual-Resampling and Cost-Sensitive Learning (HDRCS) logistic classifier.

---

1: **Require:** For a given dataset, $\mathbf{X}$ with binary class $y_i \in \{0,1\}$, desired final imbalance ratio $\lambda^*$, desired top $F$ features.

2: **Ensure:** Logistic model is optimized.

3: Split the training dataset $(\mathbf{X}_{tr})$ into majority class $(\mathbf{X}^-)$ and minority class $(\mathbf{X}^+)$.

4: **for** The Majority Class, $\mathbf{X}^-$ : **do**

5:   Determine the optimal number of centroids to be used to produce the number of Clusters, $K$ using the heuristics below:

$$K = N^- - N^+ \times r$$

   where $r = \frac{N^-}{N} - 0.6$.

6:   Use the k-means clustering algorithm to form $K$ clusters.

7: **end for**

8: Synthetic majority data set is composed with $K$ centres, still referred to as $\mathbf{X}^-$, with $N^- = K$.

9: Set the number of components used in GMM using Silhouette analysis [20]

10: Fit GMM model using EM algorithm [5] from $\mathbf{X}^+$,

11: Randomly draw $N_{new}^+ = \frac{K}{\lambda^*} - N^+$ data samples from resultant GMM model.

12: Merge $N_{new}^+$ data samples into minority class, so that $N^+ \leftarrow N^+ + N_{new}^+$, the preprocessed minority data set is still referred to as $\mathbf{X}^+$.

13: Apply Extra Tree Classifier algorithm [3] to select top $F$ features based on the modified two-class datasets $\{\mathbf{X}^-, \mathbf{X}^+\}$ which has an imbalance ratio $\lambda^*$

14: Apply the CSLR algorithm to the modified two-class datasets, $\{\mathbf{X}^-, \mathbf{X}^+\}$ which has an imbalance ratio $\lambda^*$.

15: **Return** Predicted Classes for the test data set.

---

The k-means clustering is applied to the majority class $\mathbf{X}^-$, the number of centroids is used to be the majority data set, with a number of centres $K$ set by using the heuristics below:

$$K = N^- - N^+ \times r \tag{2}$$

where the desired $r$ value was calculated using Eq. (3)

$$r = \frac{N^-}{N} - 0.6 > 0 \tag{3}$$

It is assumed that $\frac{N^-}{N} > 0.6$ for any imbalanced data considered, hence $0 < r < 0.4$, providing a range of reduction option when using (2) to downsampling dependent on the imbalance in the data set. These heuristics to determine how much data samples are reduced by downsampling is to increase according to either the number of minority data samples $(N^+)$ or the degree of imbalance in the data set. From (2), it can be seen that at the down-sampling stage using k-means clustering, the imbalanced ratio is reduced by $r$. Since the higher $r$ is, the more imbalanced the data set is, the heuristic for the downsampling stage is designed that the higher the imbalance ratio in a data set, the more it is reduced.

A Gaussian Mixture Model (GMM) is a parametric probability density function represented as a weighted sum of the densities of Gaussian components, [4] with its parameters estimated using Expectation Maximisation (EM) [5]. It is proposed to fit the GMM model using $\mathbf{X}^+$, then more minority class samples are generated by sampling from the estimated distribution. For a desired imbalanced ratio, $\lambda^*$, $N_{new}^+$ samples are drawn, as

$$N_{new}^+ = \frac{K}{\lambda^*} - N^+,$$

which is added to the minority class, which increases its number as $N^+ \leftarrow N^+ + N_{new}^+$. A series of experiments using trial and error determined that $\lambda^* = 1.67$ can produce the best results. This is because while $\lambda^* = 1$ may help to create a totally balanced data sets, it equally means that more synthetic data samples than true data samples are needed from the GMM model, which may introduce inaccuracies since there is a lack of original minority data samples. For example, the choice $\lambda^* = 1.67$ which was used in the experiments would still have a more balanced data set than the original data set, but with higher in fidelity to the original minority data set.

**Remarks:**

– The motivation of the proposed approach is to introduce a heuristic approach that can realize the dual resampling (downsample majority class and oversample minority class) automatically. From (3) it can be seen the more imbalanced the data is, there is more the reduction in the down samples using the k-means cluster algorithm. This helps to reduce the demand for generating too many synthetic minority class samples. Furthermore, the CSLR algorithm addresses remaining imbalanced by setting higher costs to minority data. In doing so, each data-level or algorithm-level component contributes with the aim of obtaining the best performance.

## 3   Experiments

The proposed HDRCS algorithm is compared with several resampling algorithms, including SMOTE [7], CBUT [16], GMMOT [17] on four real data sets, as shown in Table 1 which lists a summary of dimension and sizes, with more details in Sect. 3.1. The data sets were subjected to the appropriate data preprocessing techniques, where they were divided into training and test data sets. The split had 85% as the training data set and 15% test data set. For fair comparison and completeness, all three imbalanced data resampling techniques SMOTE [7], CBUT [16] and GMMOT [17] were applied to bring the imbalanced ratio to 1:1, then the same Extra Tree Classifier algorithm is applied to select a set of features [3], followed by logistic classifier. The same algorithms of feature selection, and then logistical classifier were also applied to the original imbalanced data sets, referred to as the baseline model.

**Table 1.** Size and dimension of original data sets, their degrees of imbalance, calculated $r$ values which are used in heuristic duel-resampling.

| Data set | $m$, no. of features | $N^+$ | $N^-$ | $N$ | $\%(\frac{N^+}{N})$ | Imbalance Ratio $\lambda$ | r |
|---|---|---|---|---|---|---|---|
| LCU | 24 | 38 | 173 | 211 | 18% | 4.55:1 | 0.2 |
| UCI German | 21 | 300 | 700 | 1000 | 30% | 2.33:1 | 0.1 |
| Give Me Some Credit | 11 | 67 | 933 | 1000 | 6.7% | 13.98:1 | 0.3 |
| Lending Club | 94 | 122 | 1078 | 1200 | 10% | 8.84:1 | 0.3 |

## 3.1   Data Description

For transparency and reproducibility purposes, the description and overview of the datasets used in this study are presented. Three out of the four datasets used are in the public domain and provided by reputable financial institutions. The sources of the dataset their quality, and their characteristics are described.

**Local Credit Union (LCU) Data Set:** The first data set used is a non-public data set from a local credit union, called LCU data [19] in this work. It has 211 observations, of which 173 belonged to the non-defaulters and classified as the good payers. The remaining 38 are bad-payers who defaulted on loan payments. This translates to 82% non-defaulters and 18% defaulters, respectively. This gives an imbalance ratio of 4.55:1, as can be seen in Table 1. 63.2% of the bad payers were females, while 36. 8% were males. It has a total of 20 independent features and a target variable. There are 10 categorical features and 11 numerical features in the datasets. The features in the data are membership length, Gender, Dependents Permanent UK Residence, Age, Employment status, Time with employer, Current Balance, Regular Saver, Previous Loans, past performance, Town, residential status, Time at Address, Loan Applied, Period, Loan Purpose, Top Up, Adverse credit History, Docs, Loan Given, Decision evaluator and Status. The features with some missing values that were treated are Dependents, Time with an employer, past performance, residential status, Time at Address, Period, Loan Purpose, adverse credit History, Docs and Decision evaluator variables.

For this data set, the rate of default varies significantly between year groups, demonstrating that 60% of customers aged 20–25 years defaulted on their loans; while about 5% of those aged 65–70 years defaulted on their loans. For the purpose of these experiments, the LCU datasets were subdivided into LCU (a) and LCU (b). The LCU (b) had an extra feature known as GR Decision Eval, which is the pre-screening results offered by a credit risk expert at the financial institution that scores applicants according to their risk profile. This means that there was no credit risk expert who scored the applicants according to their risk profile.

**German Data Data:** The second set of data used was from the UCI depository called German data [14]. It has 1000 observations with 20 independent features and a target variable. The majority class had 700 observations, whilst the minority class had 300 observations. This represents a class imbalance ratio of 2.33:1, where 70% belonged to the majority class and 30% belonged to the minority class, as can be seen in Table 1. Refer to the link of the datasets [14] for more information on this data set, including a detailed description of the features.

**Give Me Some Credit Data:** The third set of data used was offered by a US-based company called Give Me Some Credit [9]. It has an original data size of 150,000 customers and 10 independent features together with 1 target or dependent variable, making it a total of 11 features. Stratified sampling was used to extract a small sample size of 1000 datasets, which was very representative of the original datasets based on the inherent class imbalances. 933 of this belonged to the majority class and 67 belonged to the minority class that defaulted; representing 93.3% and 6.7% of the datasets, respectively. These are considered to be of an imbalanced nature with an imbalance ratio of 13.93:1, as can be seen in Table 1. These data had 16.4% of customers aged 30–35 years who defaulted on their loans; while 3% of those aged 60 to 65 years who defaulted on their loans.

**Lending Club Data Data:** This publicly available data used in this work were provided by the Lending Club [8] Due to its size, only 1200 observations were used for this study using a stratified sampling approach. The majority class had 1078 observations, which represents 89.83% of the data, whilst the minority class had 122 observations, which represented 10.17% of the observations. This gives a class imbalance ratio of 8.84:1, as can be seen in Table 1. This data had 94 features, with their full description provided in the link to the source provided in [8].

**Table 2.** Sizes and dimensions of the datasets produced, showing the standardized and desired imbalance ratio $\lambda^*$ (1.67) across all the datasets after the heuristic dual-resampling approach and feature selection.

| Data set | $F$, no. selected features | $N^+$ | $N^-$ | $N$ | $\%(\frac{N^+}{N})$ | Imbalance Ratio $\lambda^*$ |
|---|---|---|---|---|---|---|
| LCU | 5 | 99 | 165 | 264 | 37% | 1.67:1 |
| UCI German | 5 | 401 | 670 | 1071 | 37% | 167:1 |
| Give Me Some Credit | 5 | 546 | 912 | 1458 | 37% | 1.67:1 |
| Lending Club | 5 | 624 | 1041 | 1665 | 37% | 1.67:1 |

## 3.2    Results

The proposed HDRCS are applied to each data set. Table 2 contains a summary of the data sets and variables after the application of dual resampling and feature selection. The resulting imbalance ratio of the re-sampled data sets is 1.67, and the top five features are selected. Finally, the cost-sensitive logistic classifier is applied. Tables 3, 4, 5, 6 and 7 show the results of the proposed HDRCS algorithm compared to several algorithms including SMOTE [7], CBUT [16], GMMOT [17] and HDRCS when applied to LCU (a), LCU (a), UCI German, Give Me Some Credit, and Lending Club data, respectively. Tables 3, 4, 5, 6 and 7 capture the respective evaluation metrics used in this study, which are Precision, Recall and f1-score. The rest are True Negatives (TN), False Positives (FP), False Negatives (FN) and True Positives (TP).

**Table 3.** Modeling performance for LCU (a) datasets

| Data Set | Metric | Model | | | | |
|---|---|---|---|---|---|---|
| | | Baseline | SMOTE | CBUT | GMMOT | HDRCS |
| Local Credit Union (a) | TN | 23 | 23 | 20 | 24 | **24** |
| | FP | 3 | 3 | 6 | **2** | **2** |
| | FN | 1 | 3 | 1 | 2 | 2 |
| | TP | 5 | 3 | 5 | 4 | 4 |
| | Precision | 0.63 | 0.50 | 0.45 | **0.67** | **0.67** |
| | Recall | **0.83** | 0.5 | **0.83** | 0.67 | 0.67 |
| | f1-score | **0.71** | 0.30 | 0.59 | 0.67 | 0.67 |

**Table 4.** Modelling performance for LCU(b) dataset.

| Data Set | Metric | Model | | | | |
|---|---|---|---|---|---|---|
| | | Baseline | SMOTE | CBUT | GMMOT | HDRCS |
| Local Credit Union (b) | TN | **26** | 24 | 20 | 21 | 21 |
| | FP | **0** | 2 | 6 | 5 | 5 |
| | FN | 6 | 5 | 2 | 3 | 2 |
| | TP | 0 | 1 | 4 | 3 | 4 |
| | Precision | 0 | 0.33 | 0.40 | 0.38 | **0.44** |
| | Recall | 0 | 0.17 | **0.67** | 0.50 | **0.67** |
| | f1-score | 0 | 0.22 | 0.50 | 0.43 | **0.53** |

Analysis of the results of the imbalanced LCU (a) datasets from Table 3 shows that having a credit risk expert in the assessment and risk profiling of loan applicants leads to an increase in performance metrics compared to the LCU (b) datasets which did not have a credit risk expert evaluation of loan applicants, as shown in Table 4.

It can therefore be seen in Table 3 that the application of the Baseline model on the LCU (a) data set resulted in Precision of 0.63, Recall of 0.83 and f1-score of 0.71 as compared to the application of the same model on the LCU(b) dataset

**Table 5.** Modelling performance for UCI German dataset.

| Data Set | Metric | Model | | | | |
|---|---|---|---|---|---|---|
| | | Baseline | SMOTE | CBUT | GMMOT | HDRCS |
| UCI German | TN | **91** | 71 | 67 | 71 | 70 |
| | FP | **20** | 40 | 38 | 34 | 35 |
| | FN | 20 | **9** | 13 | 10 | 11 |
| | TP | 19 | 30 | 32 | **35** | 34 |
| | Precision | 0.49 | 0.43 | 0.46 | **0.51** | 0.49 |
| | Recall | 0.49 | 0.77 | 0.71 | **0.78** | 0.76 |
| | f1-score | 0.49 | 0.55 | 0.56 | **0.61** | 0.60 |

**Table 6.** Modelling performance for Give Me Some Credit dataset.

| Data Set | Metric | Model | | | | |
|---|---|---|---|---|---|---|
| | | Baseline | SMOTE | CBUT | GMMOT | HDRCS |
| GiveMe Some Credits | TN | 134 | 99 | 98 | 137 | **137** |
| | FP | 0 | 35 | 42 | 3 | 3 |
| | FN | 16 | 6 | **3** | 5 | 5 |
| | TP | 0 | **10** | 8 | 6 | 6 |
| | Precision | 0 | 0.22 | 0.16 | 0.67 | **0.67** |
| | Recall | 0.0 | 0.63 | **0.73** | 0.55 | 0.55 |
| | f1-score | 0 | 0.33 | 0.26 | **0.60** | **0.60** |

**Table 7.** Modelling performance for Lending Club dataset.

| Data Set | Metric | Model | | | | |
|---|---|---|---|---|---|---|
| | | Baseline | SMOTE | CBUT | GMMOT | HDRCS |
| Lending Club | TN | 160 | 137 | 101 | 157 | **162** |
| | FP | 0 | 23 | 61 | 5 | 0 |
| | FN | 9 | 2 | 1 | 6 | 7 |
| | TP | 11 | **18** | **18** | 13 | 12 |
| | Precision | 1 | 0.44 | 0.23 | 0.72 | 1 |
| | Recall | 0.55 | 0.90 | **0.95** | 0.68 | 0.632 |
| | f1-score | 0.71 | 0.59 | 0.37 | 0.70 | **0.77** |

in Table 4 which had relatively lowered precision of 0, recall of 0 and f1-Score of 0. This was equally true when the SMOTE technique was applied to both the LCU (a) and LCU(b) where the f1-score improved to 0.30 in the LCU (a) from 0.22 in the LCU (b) resulting in a 36.7% increase in the f1-score with the introduction of a credit risk expert. This trend was consistent for all the other 6 metrics used under this model. Overall, between these two data, it can be seen that the Baseline model achieved the highest f1-score and recall when there was the involvement of a credit risk expert with figures of 0.71 and 0.83 respectively. This shifted completely when there was no involvement of a credit risk expert in the scoring process, whereby the Baseline model achieved the lowest f1-score and recall values with figures of 0 for each of them. This made the proposed HDRCS the best-performing model between the two datasets with an f1-score and recall of 0.53 and 0.67 respectively. This observation was also true when the CBUT technique was applied to the LCU (a) and LCU (b) data. The f1-score increased from 0.50 to 0.59, representing an increase of 18% as a result of the introduction of a credit risk expert in the process. The GMMOT had similar trends, in which the introduction of a credit risk expert in the decision-making process resulted in an increase of 55.81%. The proposed HDRCS followed a similar trend and exhibited an increase in the f1-score from 0.53 to 0.67 when a credit risk expert was involved. For the LCU (a) dataset, the HDCRS technique had Precision, Recall and f1-score values of 0.67, 0.67 and 0.67 respectively as demonstrated in the Table 3.

From Table 5, it can be observed that the GMMOT model achieved the highest performance metric in 4 of the total available metrics when applied to the UCI German dataset. It had the highest precision of 0.52, the highest Recall of 0.78 and the highest f1 score of 0.61. The proposed HDRCS could not achieve the highest metric in any of the available total metrics used in this study. However, it compared well with the highest-performing GMMOT model, with a very small difference between them. One hypothesis that could be attributed to the fact that the model failed to take any of the highest performing spots on this dataset could be because this dataset happened to be the least imbalanced dataset out of all the four datasets used, with an imbalance ratio of 2.33:1. However, the proposed model was designed for datasets with relatively high imbalanced ratios.

For the Give Me Credit data set shown in Table 6, the proposed model obtained the same performance values with the GMMOT with Precision, Recall and f1-score figures of 0.67, 0.55 and 0.60 respectively for both models. The f1-score and recall of these two models are both 100% in excess of the f1-score and recall figures obtained by the Baseline model, which both had a f1-score and recall values of 0. The baseline model performed poorly on this data set in terms of f1-score and recall due to the highly imbalanced nature of this dataset; with the highest imbalance ratio of 13.98:1, which is the highest among the four data sets used.

Finally, from Table 7, it can be observed that the proposed model achieved the highest performance in the precision metric with an impressive value of 1 and the highest f1-score of 0.77. The CBUT model had the lowest f1-score of 0.37 but achieved the highest recall value of 0.95.

From Tables 3, 4, 5, 6 and 7 it can be observed that of the 7 metrics used in all data sets used, the HDRCS achieved superior performance in 15 of the total of 35 available performance metrics. This represented 54.57% of the total, which is 26.13% higher than the metric achieved by the CBUT model, which was the next best performing model in all data sets and models used. It had a superior performance of 10 out of the total performance metrics. Again, the proposed HDRCS obtained the highest proportion of the 5 f1-scores available across the 5 datasets used. It achieved a superior f1-score in 3 of the 5 datasets used in this work, representing 60% of the total available.

## 4   Conclusion

This paper has highlighted the potential problems caused by the use of insufficient and imbalanced data sets in classification tasks. The Hybrid Dual-Resampling and Cost-Sensitive (HDRCS) algorithm has been proposed as a solution to address the class imbalance problem in credit risk prediction. The HDRCS algorithm combines Gaussian mixture modelling (GMM) for generating synthetic minority classes and k-means clustering for creating a new data set for the majority class, resulting in a dataset with a desired imbalance ratio suitable for cost-sensitive logistic regression prediction operations. The HDRCS algorithm offers a comprehensive hybrid approach that leverages both data-level and algorithm-level techniques to address the class imbalance problem in the credit risk domain. Its effectiveness in achieving balanced datasets and accurate predictions makes it a valuable tool for financial risk management. The performance of the HDRCS algorithm on four real-world credit risk datasets which are; LCU, UCI German, Give Me Some Credit, and Lending Club has been evaluated. The experimental results have demonstrated that the proposed HDRCS algorithm outperformed other algorithms in most of the metrics used. The experimental results have demonstrated the effectiveness of the HDRCS algorithm compared to other resampling approaches, including SMOTE, CBUT, and GMMOT. The recommended heuristic Imbalance Ratio provides a practical means to achieve better balancing.

Future work will explore the effect of the resampling coefficient $r$ on a variety of data sets with varying degrees of class imbalances, and will also investigate the possibility of improving the efficiency of the HDRCS model. As part of future work, it would be interesting to compare different classification models to show the benefit the cost-sensitive logistic regression adds to the HDRCS algorithm in terms of model explainability to users. The HDRCS method will be applied to other machine learning models, where it will be extended to other domains and use large datasets compared to the size of the data used in this work. By scaling up the dataset size, it will allow the algorithm's performance to be assessed in real-world large-scale credit risk prediction scenarios.

## References

1. Akbani, R., Kwek, S., Japkowicz, N.: Applying support vector machines to imbalanced datasets. In: Boulicaut, J.-F., Esposito, F., Giannotti, F., Pedreschi, D. (eds.) ECML 2004. LNCS (LNAI), vol. 3201, pp. 39–50. Springer, Heidelberg (2004). https://doi.org/10.1007/978-3-540-30115-8_7

 2. Apostolik, R., Donohue, C., Went, P., et al.: Foundations of Banking Risk: An Overview of Banking, Banking Risks, and Risk-based Banking Regulation. Wiley, Hoboke (2009)
 3. Arya, M., Sastry, G.H., Motwani, A., Kumar, S., Zaguia, A.: A novel extra tree ensemble optimized DL framework (ETEODL) for early detection of diabetes. Front. Public Health **9**, 797877 (2022)
 4. Biprodip, P., Mahit, K.P.: A Gaussian mixture based boosted classification scheme for imbalanced and oversampled data. In: 2017 International Conference on Electrical, Computer and Communication Engineering (ECCE). IEEE (2017)
 5. Bishop, C.M.: Pattern Recognition and Machine Learning. Springer, New York (2006)
 6. Chawla, N.V., Bowyer, K.W., Hall, L.O., Kegelmeyer, W.P.: SMOTE: synthetic minority over-sampling technique. J. Artif. Intell. Res. **16**, 321–357 (2002)
 7. Chawla, N., Japkowicz, N., Kotcz, A.: Editorial: special issue on learning from imbalanced data sets. SIGKDD Explor. Newsl. **6**(1), 1–6 (2004)
 8. Lending Club: Lending club data set. https://www.openintro.org/data/index.php?data=loans_full_schema
 9. Give Me Some Credit: Give me some credit data set. https://www.kaggle.com/c/GiveMeSomeCredit/data
10. Crouhy, M., Galai, D., Mark, R.: The Essentials of Risk Management, 2nd edn. McGraw-Hill Education, New York (2014)
11. D'Arco, L., Wang, H., Zheng, H.: DeepHAR: a deep feed-forward neural network algorithm for smart insole-based human activity recognition. Neural Comput. Appl. (2023). Funding Information: Luigi D'Arco was funded by Ulster University Beitto Research Collaboration Programme. This research was supported by the European Union's Horizon 2020 research and innovation programme under the Marie Skłodowska-Curie Grant agreement No. 823978. Publisher Copyright: 2023, The Author(s)
12. Ershadi, M.J., Omidzadeh, D.: Customer validation using hybrid logistic regression and credit scoring model. Calitatea **19**, 59–62 (2018)
13. Ghenimi, A., Chaibi, H., Omri, M.A.B.: The effects of liquidity risk and credit risk on bank stability: evidence from the MENA region. Borsa Istanbul Rev. **17**(4), 238–248 (2017)
14. Hofmann, H.: Statlog (German Credit Data). UCI Machine Learning Repository (1994). https://doi.org/10.24432/C5NC77
15. Johnson, J.M., Khoshgoftaar, T.M.: Survey on deep learning with class imbalance. J. Big Data **6**(1), 27 (2019)
16. Lin, W.C., Tsai, C.F., Hu, Y.H., Jhang, J.S.: Clustering-based undersampling in class-imbalanced data. Inf. Sci. **409–410**, 17–26 (2017)
17. Liu, Z., Osei-Brefo, E., Chen, S., Liang, H.: UoR at SemEval-2020 task 8: Gaussian mixture modelling (GMM) based sampling approach for multi-modal memotion analysis. In: Proceedings of the Fourteenth Workshop on Semantic Evaluation, pp. 1201–1207. International Committee for Computational Linguistics, Barcelona (online) (2020)
18. Mienye, I.D., Sun, Y.: Performance analysis of cost-sensitive learning methods with application to imbalanced medical data. Inform. Med. Unlock. **25**, 100690 (2021)
19. Osei-Brefo, E.: Credit risk modelling for small datasets. Master's thesis, University of Southampton (2015)
20. Rousseeuw, P.J.: Silhouettes: a graphical aid to the interpretation and validation of cluster analysis. J. Comput. Appl. Math. **20**, 53–65 (1987)

21. Siddiqi, N.: Intelligent Credit Scoring: Building and Implementing Better Credit Risk Scorecards. Wiley, Hoboken (2017). Illustrated edn
22. Yan, Q., Xia, S., Meng, F.R.: Optimizing cost-sensitive SVM for imbalanced data: connecting cluster to classification. CoRR abs/1702.01504 (2017)
23. Yap, B.W., Rani, K.A., Rahman, H.A.A., Fong, S., Khairudin, Z., Abdullah, N.N.: An application of oversampling, undersampling, bagging and boosting in handling imbalanced datasets. In: Herawan, T., Deris, M.M., Abawajy, J. (eds.) Proceedings of the First International Conference on Advanced Data and Information Engineering (DaEng-2013). LNEE, vol. 285, pp. 13–22. Springer, Singapore (2014). https://doi.org/10.1007/978-981-4585-18-7_2

# Machine Vision Applications

# ReFrogID: Pattern Recognition for Pool Frog Identification Using Deep Learning and Feature Matching

Vetle Nesland Evensen[1], Gabriel Bergman Henriksen[1], Sondre Melhus[1],
Ole Steine Olsen[1], Kristina Haugen[3], Dag Dolmen[4], Arne Wiklund[2],
Per-Arne Andersen[2(✉)], Morten Goodwin[2], Lars Mørch Korslund[3],
and Nadia Saad Noori[2]

[1] Department of Information and Communication Technology, University of Agder,
Kristiansand, Norway
[2] Centre for Artificial Intelligence Research, University of Agder,
Kristiansand, Norway
per.andersen@uia.no
[3] Centre for Coastal Research, Department of Natural Sciences,
University of Agder, Kristiansand, Norway
[4] Norwegian University of Science and Technology (NTNU),
The University Museum, Trondheim, Norway

**Abstract.** The global decline in amphibian populations is a pressing issue, with numerous species facing the threat of extinction. One such species is the pool frog, *Pelophylax lessonae*, whose Norwegian population has experienced a significant long-term decline since monitoring began in 1996. This decline has pushed the species to the verge of local extinction. A substantial knowledge gap in the species' biology hinders the proposal and evaluation of effective management actions. Consequently, there is a pressing need for efficient techniques to gather data on population size and composition.

Recent advancements in Machine Learning (ML) and Deep Learning (DL) have shown promising results in various domains, including ecology and evolution. Current research in these fields primarily focuses on species modeling, behavior detection, and identity recognition. The progress in mobile technology, ML, and DL has equipped researchers across numerous disciplines, including ecology, with innovative data collection methods for building knowledge bases on species and ecosystems. This study addresses the need for systematic field data collection for monitoring endangered species like the pool frog by employing deep learning and image processing techniques.

In this research, a multidisciplinary team developed a technique, termed ReFrogID, to identify individual frogs using their unique abdominal patterns. Utilizing RGB images, the system operates on two main principles: (1) a DL algorithm for automatic segmentation achieving AP@89.147, AP50@99.123, and AP75@98.942, and (2) pattern matching via local feature detection and matching methods. A new dataset, pelophylax_lessonae, addresses the identity recognition problem in pool frogs. The effectiveness of ReFrogIDis validated by its ability to identify frogs even when human experts fail. Source code is available at here.

© The Author(s), under exclusive license to Springer Nature Switzerland AG 2023
M. Bramer and F. Stahl (Eds.): SGAI 2023, LNAI 14381, pp. 365–376, 2023.
https://doi.org/10.1007/978-3-031-47994-6_33

**Keywords:** Deep Learning · Feature Matching · Biology · Segmentation

# 1    Introduction

The rate of species going extinct today is 100 to 1000 times higher than the normal rate throughout geological time [19], and human disturbances are the leading cause of the worldwide decline in biodiversity [6]. Amphibians represent one of the most threatened groups, with 35–51% of all living species being threatened with extinction [12]. Norway harbors six amphibian species, three of which are threatened with extinction [4]. One is the pool frog - *Pelophylax lessonae*. Systematic monitoring of the species was initiated in 1996, and since then, the population has experienced a long-term decline. Today, the national population comprises less than 50 adult individuals confined to three small lakes [7].

The dire situation for the pool frog and other species calls for more research by studying existing data and collecting novel data. Ecological data collection usually involves capturing and permanently marking individuals [26]. Unfortunately, physical tagging is invasive and leads to discomfort, pain, and in some cases, even death [14]. Fortunately, some species have a consistent spot- or stripe pattern that can be used for individual identification, thus eliminating invasive tagging [8]. Manual identification based on photographs of such patterns is thus possible, but it quickly becomes time-consuming.

Attributes for animal or individual identification depend largely on identifying unique species or individual animal characteristics, such as body shape or pattern. Examples of patterns for individual species identification are stripe coats in zebras, or unique ear patterns in rhinoceros, where the accuracy of individual identification ranged between 58%–83.87% using different machine learning methods [18]. The pool frogs have a unique abdominal pattern that distinguishes each individual (see Fig. 1. Thus, in this paper, the abdominal pattern is the key feature in the method designed for identifying individual frogs.

ML and DL fields witnessed tremendous advancements during the last decade, and recent studies have shown promising results in using ML/DL. Examples include Support Vector Machine (SVM), Convolutional Neural Networks (CNN), and Object-based image analysis in the field of ecology [5]. In [18], review key approaches for data collection and processing for individual wildlife identification, animal monitoring capabilities, and tracking species population. Manual data collection or using technology (like cameras) are widely used approaches for data collection using drawings, ground cameras, aerial cameras, or moving cameras. Furthermore, several ML/DL methods applied for automatic species and individual identification with variations of success, such as SVM [11], Scale-Invariant Feature Transform (SIFT) [17], the k-nearest neighbor classifier (kNN), VGG-Face CNN, Deep segmentation CNN and You Only Look Once (YOLO) [20].

The key contributions of this paper are:

1. Development of a novel end-to-end system, ReFrogID, uses deep learning to identify individual pool frogs based on their unique abdominal patterns. This

**Fig. 1.** Abdominal spot pattern in a young (left) and older (right) version of the same individual. Note how spots have enlarged over time, and how the contrast of the spots can vary.

system achieves state-of-the-art performance with near-perfect segmentation of the abdominal regions of the pool frog.

2. Introduction of a novel dataset, pelophylax_lessonae, aimed at comprehensively addressing the identity recognition problem in pool frogs.
3. Demonstration of the efficacy of the proposed approach, ReFrogID, by showing its ability to correctly identify frogs where human experts fail.
4. Utilization of the ORB detector algorithm, a traditional machine learning method, to effectively complement the deep learning algorithm for detecting unique features of individual pool frogs.
5. Development of a mobile app prototype to facilitate data collection, aiding ecologists in their fieldwork and data collection efforts.
6. Expansion of the range of applications where machine learning and deep learning can assist in addressing critical environmental issues, such as preserving fragile and endangered ecological systems.

The paper is further organized as follows. Section 2 outlines the data acquisition and preparation phase, where ecologists capture data for the ReFrogID pipeline. Section 3 represents ReFrogID, an effective method for end-to-end individual identification of pool frogs. Section 4 presents the results of an initial study using Mask R-CNN for image segmentation to identify the abdominal area of frogs and a combination of ORB detector and BF matcher to identify the individual frog's unique abdominal pattern. Results from the proposed method demonstrate the successful identification of frog individuals and assist human experts in the classification process. Finally, Sect. 5 concludes the study and defines a path forward for future studies in the individual identification of amphibian species.

## 2    Data Acquisition and Preparation

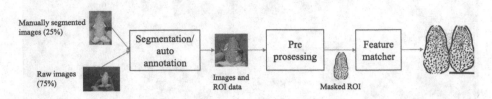

**Fig. 2.** The ReFrogID method is a two-step system where (1) the dataset is auto-annotated using a segmentation model, and (2) the images along with the ROI data are used to match features in the abdominal part of the frog.

The initial version of the dataset pelophylax_lessonae consists of 1012 images of 414 individual pool frogs (1–15 images/individual, captured between 2007 and 2019. All photos are of the ventral side of the individual, taken while the observer immobilizes the frog. The background in the photographs is usually blurred ground vegetation, but the brightness of the background, and thus contrast to the frog, varies with lighting conditions. The quality of images varies because images are taken under field conditions with animals that are often reluctant to cooperate. In some cases, the forelimbs, including the toes, block part of the abdominal area, the region of interest (ROI). In other cases, the moist skin reflects the sunlight, resulting in parts of the ROI being overexposed. Shadow from the observer can make part of the ROI underexposed. All individuals captured have been photographed on every capture occasion, and based on manual identification, it is recognized that all individuals have a unique pattern of dark spots on the belly that is maintained over the individual's lifetime. The belly is otherwise pale white, and the spots are usually clearly visible on individuals older than one year. During the first year of life, however, the spots on the belly are often not established, and identification based on spot pattern is impossible.

Consequently, pictures of individuals younger than one year have been excluded from the dataset. Although the position of the spots on the belly is fixed, the spots tend to enlarge with age (see Fig. 1), and closely located spots can thus merge over time, resulting in more intricate shapes and patterns. The spots are usually clearly contrasted against the white skin, but occasionally the spots on the belly can be quite pale, making the pattern harder to detect.

An initial small dataset was created to introduce the new "frog stomach" class to retrain the DL algorithm, which is later used for the automatic annotation/segmentation. The 255 (25% of total images) images were split 20/80% (204/51) between training and testing. The tool MakeSense.ai was used to annotate ROI, i.e., the frog stomach area as a polygon and not as a bounding box, as seen in Fig. 3.

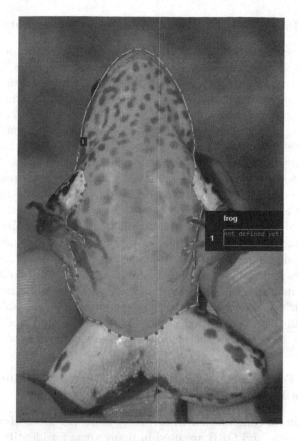

**Fig. 3.** Abdominal pattern: ROI annotation.

# 3   Method

This section introduces ReFrogID, an end-to-end method for identifying individual pool frogs. Two steps are involved; 1) re-train using a small dataset of a pre-trained Mask R-CNN algorithm (transfer learning) [21], to predict the segmentation mask of new frog images to extract the relevant abdominal area, 2) feature detection and matching to identify the individual frog (see Fig. 2).

**Fig. 4.** Instance Segmentation using Mask R-CNN ResNet-101 on 6 unique frogs from the test-set.

### 3.1    Step 1: Image Segmentation and Automatic Annotation

DL methods, such as VGGNet or Fast R-CNN [9,23], are known to be used for species or individual animal recognition [3]. However, further processing was required to perform image segmentation to extract the individual animals [3]. The role of DL in this work was mainly to facilitate automatic image segmentation and labeling for the abdominal ROI in RGB images. Image annotation is a key element that influences the performance of deep learning algorithms. It is a process usually carried out by humans (e.g., domain experts) where the quality depends on individual experience and knowledge. After 2012, automatic annotation or deep feature extraction became a trend in the fields related to image processing and computer vision [2,27]. Hence, in this work, we apply Mask R-CNN [10], which can be used for object instance segmentation, bounding box detection, and object recognition. Mask R-CNN is known for generating high-quality segmentation masks [10]. Thus, a Mask R-CNN was trained with COCO weights using the manually annotated images to process the entire dataset. The resulting images and annotation files to further isolate the pixels within ROI, i.e., the abdominal area of the individual frog, and label/annotate the area as a "frog stomach", as seen in 4). Afterward, the ROI image is isolated from the background, and the identification process passes mask data, i.e., segmentation coordinates (see metadata in the pelophylax_lessonae dataset) to "step 2".

### 3.2    Step 2: Feature Detection and Matching for Abdominal Patterns Identification

Feature detection in combination with feature matching methods such as SIFT, SURF, Brute Force, and ORB are used in many areas for identifying key points in an image and calculating the similarities towards matching these points [25]. In this work, for feature detection and matching, the choice was made to use ORB(Oriented FAST and rotated BRIEF)and Brute Force marcher [1,15]. A set of key points of desired features (i.e., dark spots) is described by its corresponding fixed-length vector (descriptor) in a feature extraction process. ORB is one of the fast and robust feature detectors, that could be used for matching images compared to SIFT and SURF [22]. Next, matching detected and described features depends on determining the correspondence between descriptors in images that show the particular object (dark spots patterns) in different perspectives [13]. To improve the efficiency of the detection and matching process, images are pre-processed as follows: convert from RGB to grayscale to reduce the color space, and apply Gaussian blur to reduce noise (smoothing). If an image has low light and much noise, then Gaussian blurring would be used to mute the noise. And finally, apply a bit-wise AND mask to isolate the ROI.

## 4    Results

This section describes the technical experimental setup and summarizes the initial identification system of individual pool frogs using the ReFrogID method and the novel pelophylax_lessonae dataset.

**Table 1.** Model precision using Mask R-CNN with ResNet-50 and ResNet-101, respectively. The ResNet-101 model performs best, however, at the cost of significantly higher training times.

| Model | AP | AP50 | AP75 | APl | Iterations |
|-------|-----|------|------|-----|-----------|
| R50 | 87.069 | 98.846 | 98.830 | 87.069 | 70000 |
| R101 | **89.147** | **99.123** | **98.942** | **87.122** | 70000 |

**Mask R-CNN Training and Empirical Validation.** 25% (255 images) of the entire dataset is used to train the Mask R-CNN model, where the data is labeled manually. The remaining 75% (757 images) are left for the test set and automatic recognition of the abdominal area. The training set is split further into 80% (204 images) training images and 20% (51 images) validation images. We test the Mask R-CNN using transfer learning with COCO-trained ResNet 50 and ResNet 101 backends. The Mask R-CNN model achieves over 90% accuracy on the comparatively modest number of supplied data samples after 7000 training iterations, as seen in Table 1. The anticipated segmentation mask resembles Fig. 4[1]. We estimate segmentation masks for the abdomen region for every frog image and verify the results empirically. Figure 5 depicts the training and validation loss for the Mask R-CNN model, clearly demonstrating that the model learns to correctly identify the segmentation mask[2].

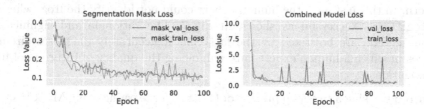

**Fig. 5.** Transfer Learning loss for Mask R-CNN on the frog dataset for 100 epochs. In the first plot, the fluctuating line is the mask_train_loss and in the second plot, the val_loss is the line with spikes.

---

[1] Please consult the source code repository for additional training graphs.
[2] More detailed results can be found in the Tensorboard recording here.

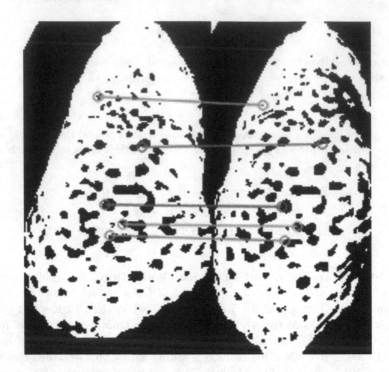

**Fig. 6.** Success in individual recognition

**Identification of Frogs Using ORB Feature Detector and Brute Force Matching.** Figure 6 demonstrates that the system can successfully identify unique frog patterns under optimal lighting and obstacle conditions. However, there are instances in which frog pattern recognition is hard. Such instances include poor lighting, rotation, sun glare, and frog limbs obscuring the abdomen pattern. In this instance, the human expert could not identify the frog, whereas ReFrogID was successful as shown in Fig. 7. The rationale and significance of our method are bolstered by the fact that it accurately diagnoses circumstances in which a human expert fails, enhancing the quality of future pool frog investigations.

**Summary.** Using a two-step process of (1) transfer learning using Mask R-CNN and automatic segmentation of frog species, and (2) identification of individual frogs using a combination of ORB feature detector and Brute Force feature matcher based on the abdominal pattern of frogs, we find ReFrogID to be a very effective tool for identifying the individual animal of the pool frog.

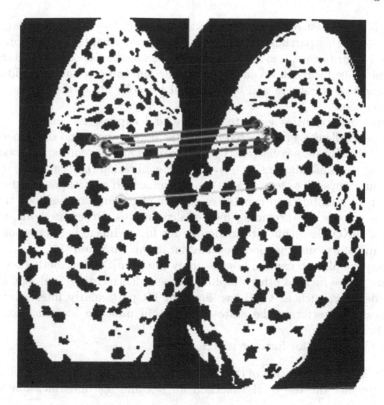

**Fig. 7.** Miss-labelling in individual recognition

# 5   Conclusion and Future Work

This paper presents a comprehensive methodology for data acquisition, preprocessing, and individual frog identification based on abdominal patterns. The
accuracy of the identification results is influenced by several factors, including
lighting conditions, the animal's position or pose, occlusion (partially obscured
stomach patterns), and the contrast of the spots depending on the animal's age.
The primary contribution of this work is to expand the range of applications
where machine learning and deep learning can assist in addressing critical environmental issues, such as the preservation of fragile and endangered ecological
systems.

ReFrogID is a novel end-to-end system that achieves state-of-the-art performance with near-perfect segmentation of the abdominal regions of the pool frog
using DL, opening up a wealth of new research opportunities related to pool
frogs. These opportunities include health, age, and injury classification, but this
paper focuses on individual identification. In the second step of ReFrogID, the
ORB detector algorithm, a traditional ML method, effectively complements the
DL algorithm to detect unique features of individual pool frogs. However, there
are instances where individuals are incorrectly identified due to factors such as

the depth or contrast of the patterns (e.g., young versus old individuals), occlusion (e.g., patterns partially obscured), or inadequate lighting conditions. As a secondary contribution, a mobile app prototype was developed to facilitate data collection[3]. The future development of mobile applications and the addition of more convenience features will be beneficial to ecologists during fieldwork and data collection.

Several opportunities exist to enhance and expand the current work to address the challenges encountered during the development and implementation of the method. For data collection, we plan to develop a systematic approach that includes a) recommendations on device setup/calibration (i.e., cameras) used for data acquisition, such as lens, resolution, recommended animal pose, and lighting condition; b) a mobile app capable of streamlining (auto-annotation) the data collection process and providing high-quality images. Other methods, such as the Mask DINO algorithm, are intriguing for future image segmentation work, and we aim to expand the model evaluation in this direction [16].

Finally, we plan to explore how to apply the identification methods to other problems. These include other amphibians, sex identification, and age. For the feature detector, such as ORB, we find LoFTR particularly interesting, as it significantly outperforms the state-of-the-art in multiple identification problems [24].

Possible avenues for future research include:

1. Exploring the application of the proposed method to other amphibian species.
2. Investigating the use of the method for sex and age identification in pool frogs.
3. Evaluating the performance of other feature detectors, such as LoFTR, in the context of the proposed method.
4. Developing a systematic approach for data collection, including device setup and calibration recommendations.
5. Enhancing the mobile app to streamline the data collection process and provide high-quality images.
6. Exploring other image segmentation methods, such as the Mask DINO algorithm, for potential improvements in model performance.

This paper demonstrates the potential of applying Deep Learning to identify individual pool frogs. We hope that ReFrogID will provide a valuable method for conserving vulnerable amphibians, such as the pool frog, in the future.

# References

1. Awaludin, M., Yasin, V.: Application of oriented fast and rotated brief (ORB) and bruteforce hamming in library opencv for classification of plants. J. Inf. Syst. Appl. Manage. Account. Res. **4**(3), 51–59 (2020)
2. Chen, Y.: The image annotation algorithm using convolutional features from intermediate layer of deep learning. Multimedia Tools Appl. **80**(3), 4237–4261 (2021)

---

[3] The mobile application can be found in the source code repository.

3. de Arruda, M.S., Spadon, G., Rodrigues, J.F., Gonçalves, W.N., Machado, B.B.: Recognition of endangered pantanal animal species using deep learning methods. In: 2018 International Joint Conference on Neural Networks (IJCNN), pp. 1–8. IEEE (2018)

4. Dervo, B., van der Kooij, J., Johansen, B.S.: Artsgruppeomtale amfibier og reptiler (amphibia og reptilia). norsk rødliste for arter 2021. artsdatabanken (2021)

5. Dujon, A.M., Schofield, G.: Importance of machine learning for enhancing ecological studies using information-rich imagery. Endangered Species Res. **39**, 91–104 (2019)

6. Díaz, S., et al.: Pervasive human-driven decline of life on earth points to the need for transformative change. Science, **366**(6471), eaax3100 (2019). ISSN 0036–8075

7. Engemyr, A.K., Reinkind, I.R.: Handlingsplan for damfrosk Pelophylax lessonae 2019–2023. Report, The Norwegian Environment Agency (2019)

8. Ferner, J.W.: Measuring and Marking Post-Metamorphic Amphibians. Amphibian Ecology and Conservation: A Handbook of Techniques, pp. 123–141 (2010)

9. Girshick, R.: Fast R-CNN. In: Proceedings of the IEEE International Conference on Computer Vision, pp. 1440–1448 (2015)

10. He, K., Gkioxari, G., Dollár, P., Girshick, R.: Mask R-CNN. In: Proceedings of the IEEE International Conference on Computer Vision, pp. 2961–2969 (2017)

11. Hearst, M.A., Dumais, S.T., Osuna, E., Platt, J., Scholkopf, B.: Support vector machines. IEEE Intell. Syst. Appl. **13**(4), 18–28 (1998)

12. IUCN. The IUCN red list of threatened species (2022). https://www.iucnredlist.org

13. Jakubović, A., Velagić, J.: Image feature matching and object detection using brute-force matchers. In: 2018 International Symposium ELMAR, pp. 83–86. IEEE (2018). https://doi.org/10.23919/ELMAR.2018.8534641

14. Jewell, Z.: Effect of monitoring technique on quality of conservation science. Conserv. Biol. **27**(3), 501–508 (2013). ISSN 0888–8892

15. Karahan, Ş., Karaöz, A., Özdemir, Ö.F., Gü, A.G., Uludag, U.: On identification from periocular region utilizing sift and surf. In: 2014 22nd European Signal Processing Conference (EUSIPCO), pp. 1392–1396. IEEE (2014)

16. Li, F., et al.: Mask DINO: towards a unified transformer-based framework for object detection and segmentation. arXiv preprint arXiv:2206.02777 (2022)

17. Lindeberg, T.: Scale invariant feature transform (2012). QC 20120524

18. Petso, T., Jamisola, R.S., Mpoeleng, D.: Review on methods used for wildlife species and individual identification. Eur. J. Wildl. Res. **68**(1), 1–18 (2022)

19. Pimm, S.L., et al.: The biodiversity of species and their rates of extinction, distribution, and protection. Science **344**(6187), 1246752 (2014). ISSN 0036–8075

20. Redmon, J., Farhadi, A.: YOLOv3: an incremental improvement. arXiv preprint arXiv:1804.02767 (2018)

21. Rezvy, S., Zebin, T., Braden, B., Pang, W., Taylor, S., Gao, X.: Transfer learning for endoscopy disease detection and segmentation with mask-R-CNN benchmark architecture. In: 2020 IEEE 17th International Symposium on Biomedical Imaging (2020)

22. Rublee, E., Rabaud, V., Konolige, K., Bradski, G.: ORB: an efficient alternative to sift or surf. In: 2011 International Conference on Computer Vision, pp. 2564–2571 (2011). https://doi.org/10.1109/ICCV.2011.6126544

23. Simonyan, K., Zisserman, A.: Very deep convolutional networks for large-scale image recognition. arXiv preprint arXiv:1409.1556 (2014)

24. Sun, J., Shen, Z., Wang, Y., Bao, H., Zhou, X.: LoFTR: detector-free local feature matching with transformers. In: 2021 IEEE/CVF Conference on Computer Vision and Pattern Recognition (CVPR), pp. 8918–8927. IEEE (2021)
25. Szeliski, R.: Feature detection and matching. In: Computer Vision. TCS, pp. 333–399. Springer, Cham (2022). https://doi.org/10.1007/978-3-030-34372-9_7
26. Tourani, M.: A review of spatial capture-recapture: ecological insights, limitations, and prospects. Ecol. Evol. **12**(1), e8468 (2022). https://doi.org/10.1002/ece3.8468. ISSN 2045-7758
27. Wu, J., Yu, Y., Huang, C., Yu, K.: Deep multiple instance learning for image classification and auto-annotation. In: Proceedings of the IEEE Conference on Computer Vision and Pattern Recognition, pp. 3460–3469 (2015)

# Cropline and Weed Detection in Corn Using Weak Supervision

Christoph Manss[1]($\boxtimes$)(iD), Isabel Guenther[2](iD), and Florian Rahe[2]

[1] DFKI GmbH, Marine Perception, Marie-Curie-Strasse 1,
26129 Oldenburg, Germany
christoph.manss@dfki.de
[2] AMAZONEN-WERKE H. Dreyer SE & Co. KG, Am Amazonenwerk 9-13,
49205 Hasbergen, Germany
{isabel.guenther,dr.florian.rahe}@amazone.de

**Abstract.** Intelligent weed management is crucial for sustainable and economical crop production. It optimizes agricultural machinery usage and reduces herbicide dependency. Advances in artificial intelligence and object detection algorithms have allowed for the use of cameras on land machines for real-time crop and weed detection. Robotic systems incorporate intelligent camera systems for weed identification and removal. However, training deep learning algorithms requires labor-intensive data cleaning and labeling. Weak supervision techniques offer a solution by reducing labeling efforts. This study explores inaccurate labeling for weed-crop differentiation in selective hoeing. A sensor-carrier with four cameras captures diverse images which are then labeled with inaccurate supervision. Multiple neural networks, including DeepLabV3, FCN, LRASPP, and U-Net, are trained using inaccurately labeled semantic masks. Results demonstrate reasonable performance while having less labeling time for developing smart weeding applications. For the considered data, the U-Net model exhibits the best mean intersection-over-union (IOU). This research emphasizes the potential of weak supervision and AI-based weed management for sustainable agriculture.

**Keywords:** Plant identification · Image Segmentation · Precision Agriculture · Computer Vision · Edge Intelligence

## 1 Introduction

Intelligent weed management is key for a sustainable and economical agricultural crop production. It can lead to a more efficient use of agricultural devices, e.g. weeding machines, and can also lead to a reduced usage of herbicides [3,15]. With the advance of artificial intelligence and the increased performance of object detectors and semantic segmentation algorithms, cameras are employed in weeding applications directly on farm machines. These cameras then provide images for neural networks, which in turn detect crops and weeds on the agricultural

© The Author(s), under exclusive license to Springer Nature Switzerland AG 2023
M. Bramer and F. Stahl (Eds.): SGAI 2023, LNAI 14381, pp. 377–390, 2023.
https://doi.org/10.1007/978-3-031-47994-6_34

machine in real-time [3]. Especially, robotic systems are utilizing intelligent camera systems for detecting and removing weeds [9,16,17]. The resulting selective weeding offers several benefits: It minimizes soil penetration, helping to retain moisture in the ground [3,11], and it promotes biodiversity by preserving some plants instead of removing them entirely [3].

However, artificial intelligence (AI) – and especially deep learning algorithms – require a lot of data which has to be cleaned and labeled to train AI algorithms. In AI development, this step is labour intensive and takes up a large percentage of the development time. Weak supervision techniques [14,18] can reduce this time for labeling. In [14], Shen et al. provide a taxonomy of different weak supervision techniques. Accordingly, these techniques can be categorized into no supervision, inexact supervision, incomplete supervision, and inaccurate supervision [7]. Inexact supervision comprises image-level [10], box-level, or scribble labels, whereas incomplete supervision includes semi and domain-specific supervision. In this paper, the inaccurate supervision is of particular interest. In the considered scenario, weeds have to be differentiated from crops for selective weeding applications. The camera position, therefore, steers forwards for the plant detection. To label these images accurately, many small weed segments would have to be labeled which is labour-intensive. Moreover, a detailed and accurate labeling of all weeds is unnecessary for the weeding process. Hence, we use inaccurately labeled semantic masks to train neural networks for weed and crop detection. The detected weeds can then be accessed and transferred to a density metric for the specific crop row.

In this paper, we present a time efficient approach to create semantic labels for selective weeding applications. With the labeled data, we train and evaluate multiple neural networks for semantic segmentation. Furthermore, we present how the object detectors can be deployed on the edge for real-time detection and we present preliminary results on the weed detection.

The structure of the paper is as follows. The next section presents related work to the presented approach. Section 3 shows how we acquired the data and how we used weak supervision to label the data. Afterward, in Sec. 4, we present the neural networks that we evaluated for image segmentation along with their training results. In the following section, we demonstrate the workflow on an agricultural machine to get weed density estimates which can then be used for any weed management system. Section 6 concludes this work.

## 2  Related Work

As mentioned above, in [14,18] the authors present surveys on object detection with weak supervision. Although the reviewed literature is large, the authors focused more on applications with more general data sets instead of agricultural data sets. Regarding inaccurate labeling, the authors in [7] looked into the learning dynamics of deep segmentation networks if inaccurate labels are used for training. The authors show that this relates to learning noisy labels and that the networks tend to overfit at later epochs as they memorize the errors in the annotations. However, the authors didn't look into time savings due to inaccurate labels during the labeling process. On the other side, in [3,15], the authors survey multiple approaches to weed management in the agricultural sector. However, they do not mention weak supervision. Thus, the current work can contribute to the agricultural sector and create links between these two research fields. Regarding the application of weed control and cropline detection, Gerhards et al. [4] show a camera guided system that uses a low-pass filter on the Green color channel to distinguish the crops from the soil. The detected crops are then connected to lines and tracked by a Kalman filter. A hoeing device is then controlled such that the hoeing blades cut the inter-row weeds. Techniques for robotic weed control are presented in [2,17]. Here often a top-down view – nadir – is used. This view is reasonable as the robots can move slowly over the field and weed directly. For the considered use-case in this work, we want to use regular hoeing devices attached to a farm machine that moves considerably faster. Thus, we use a different sensor configuration as will be presented in the next section. In [2], Cicco et al. mention the labeling effort for agricultural applications, and propose to use synthetic data generation, data set reduction, and transfer learning. Although transfer learning is a good option for small data sets, the pre-trained models should have been trained on data from similar data domains. As we use a different camera view, we have not been able to find data with a similar view in the agricultural domain.

## 3   Data Acquisition and Labeling

This section describes the data acquisition setup and the labeling process with inaccurate labeling.

### 3.1   Setup for Data Acquisition

To gather a variety of data with persistent camera-parameters, i.e. camera height, angle, and position, we used a sensor-carrier that can easily be attached to the three-point mount at the front of any tractor, as shown in Fig. 1a. On this carrier, we mounted four cameras on equidistant points, where each camera view overlaps with the view of the neighboring camera, see Fig. 1b. To enable all cameras to send their images to a controller node, we used robot operating system (ROS)[1], a meta operating system, which provides a communication infrastructure and standardized data types for inter-component communication. These data types are also referred to as ROS messages and can be customized by a schema. In order to ensure synchronicity, all four cameras are triggered by the same clock: the controller sends a hardware-pulse to each camera as well as a ROS message prompting each camera-interface-component to fetch the new image via Ethernet. The, the camera-interface-component publishes the image as a ROS message which is in turn recorded into a ROS-bag. All ROS messages include a timestamp that is synchronized to the clock of the controller node. To ensure getting

---

[1] https://www.ros.org.

(a)                                    (b)

**Fig. 1.** (a) The sensor-carrier with four cameras for weed and maize detection. Here the carrier is mounted at the front of the tractor. (b) A schematic view of the camera positions and their coverage.

a diverse set of data, we gathered images in different locations, multiple growth stages, and weather conditions. The weather conditions include multiple sun elevations, cloudy weather, and even rain. Once the ROS-bags have been collected, the stored ROS messages can be filtered and the images can be extracted. In this manner, we amassed a data set of over 30,000 images and selected 2,000 of them for labeling, while ensuring the preservation of data diversity. In the following, we discuss the labeling procedure.

### 3.2  Weak Supervision by Inaccurate Labeling

We selected the images for labeling such that they have a variety of different weed densities and environmental conditions. The densities vary from almost no weeds to almost only weeds. For images with a high weed density and many small weed instances, labeling can become cumbersome. However, depending on the weeding application, semantic labels with high accuracy are not necessarily useful, e.g., if larger areas are weeded, it is not necessary to label a dense group of small weeds individually but they can be labeled jointly. Such labeling reduces the effort and time because the labeler does not need to be very accurate while preserving the usability. Moreover, the review of the labeling becomes much easier as errors in the labels are expected.

An example image of the labeling is presented in Fig. 2. The labeling process for the selected images is as follows. Each labeler was instructed to first draw a trapezoid around each row of crops (see Fig. 2 in dark grey). Afterward, the labeler loosely draws polygons around areas of weeds or single weeds; the polygon does not need to be accurately drawn around the leafs. Although this creates an additional error to the semantic labels, the shapes of the polygons become simpler, which in turn can be beneficial to train simpler neural networks, as presented later. The images were labeled using computer vision annotation tool (CVAT) [13], which is available as a self-hosted solution and as open source.

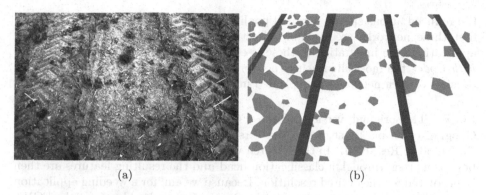

**Fig. 2.** Example image with a weed density of 58% in the second inter-row-area from the left, 26% in the middle and 13% in the second from the right. (a) RGB image in greyscale. (b) Labeled mask. (Color figure online)

As the amount of weeds varies from image to image, so does the labeling-time. Here, if there are little to no weeds present, it is enough to mark the crop rows. This takes a practiced labeler about 30 s. While the labeling time for no weeds in the image is obviously low, it increases along with the amount of weeds. In rare cases the time to label the image increased up to 15 min for a very high number of very small an well distributed weeds. However, if a certain coverage of weeds is exceeded, the labeling time decreases, because weeds are so close that, due to overlap; fewer and larger polygons are necessary to label them. Eventually, the whole area between the crop rows can be labeled as weed. Thus, a single polygon encompasses the area between the crop rows. In this case, the labeling time is only minutely more than it is for a no-weed image.

Determining accurate labeling times, however, is difficult. The labeling time depends on the applications and the amount of classes that have to be labeled. Additionally, in the agricultural use-case, regional and seasonal changes have a large impact on the weed pressure and the growth of plants, and, therefore, also on the labeling effort. Thus, in this work, we focus more on the application results by using inaccurate labeling.

## 4 Image Segmentation

The following section introduces the considered neural networks for image segmentation and briefly describes their features. We selected these networks regarding their accessibility and methodologies for object detection. Afterward, the training results are presented.

### 4.1 Models Used for Image Segmentation

For this paper, we focused on the following neural networks for semantic segmentation: DeepLabV3 [5], fully convolutional network (FCN) [8], lite reduced atrous spatial pyramid pooling (LRASPP) [1], and U-Net [12]. The first three networks are available directly in Pytorch. Hence, for agricultural applications the integration of these is easy. The U-Net is according to *Papers with Code*[2] the most cited neural network on image segmentation. The characteristics of each network are explained in the following.

**FCN.** The original version of the FCN [8] used AlexNet, VGG net, or GoogLeNet as backbone, while the version directly available in Pytorch uses ResNet50 or ResNet101. In the Pytorch version, the last layer of the used backbone runs then through a classification head and the resulting features are then interpolated for the desired resolution. Because we aim for a weeding application on the edge, we decided to use only the ResNet50 as a backbone for the FCN.

**U-Net.** The U-Net consist of an encoder and a decoder. The encoder consists multiple cells with convolutional layers followed by a pooling layer. The decoder is build accordingly but the order in each cell is reversed with a deconvolutional layer followed by convolutional layers. Furthermore, the output of each encoder cell is passed to the corresponding decoder cell by a skip connection. The arrangement of all cells is often pictured in a U-shape, hence the name. The benefits of this network are that it has a simple structure and it can be trained with few images. According to its initial paper [12], it relies heavily on data augmentation techniques. The version used here is implemented by us and additionally uses batch normalization. Here, encoder and decoder consist each of four cells.

**DeeplabV3.** Chen et al. [1] thought of using atrous convolution for image segmentation upsampling instead of deconvolution. In atrous convolution the filter is spatially spread such that the resolution of the image does not need to be changed but only the rate of the atrous convolution. Essentially, the size of the convolutional filter becomes larger and sparser with a higher rate. Pytorch provides two backbones for these networks: MobilenetV3 and ResNet50.

**LRASPP.** In [5], the authors wanted to run an object detection network on a mobile phone CPU. Therefore, they applied a hardware aware network architecture search. They found the MobileNetV3 as potential backbone architecture in two versions – small and large – which have different hardware requirements. For the semantic segmentation task, the authors developed LRASPP, which uses atrous convolution and some tweaks to reduce the computational cost. Pytorch provides the LRASPP with the MobileNetV3 large backbone.

### 4.2   Training Results of the Networks

To train the networks, the data was split into a train and test split with 80% and 20%, respectively. During training the data gets augmented by two operators from

---

[2] https://paperswithcode.com/, accessed at 13th of June 2023.

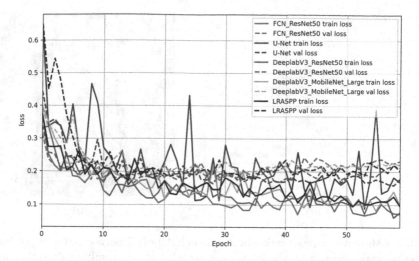

**Fig. 3.** Training and validation loss of all networks.

Albumentations[3]: *ShiftScaleRotate* and *ColorJitter*. The parameters of these operators and were tuned by using sequential model-based algorithm configuration (SMAC) [6]. The parameters define the range of the augmentations and include: shift, scale, rotation, brightness, contrast, saturation, and hue. The training was conducted on a Nvidia Tesla V100 GPU. For all networks the batch size was 32 except for the U-Net where the batch size was set to 12. This was evaluated by cross validation and the learning rate was tuned with the help of sequential model-based algorithm configuration (SMAC). All networks were trained for 60 epochs.

The training and validation loss of all networks is presented in Fig. 3. All networks, except the U-Net, seem to over-fit as training and validation loss diverge at later epochs; the networks learn the data instead of the concepts behind the data. This can usually be solved by using more data during training. In [7], Liu et al. observed that due to the inaccurate labels, the segmentation networks memorize the labeling error of the inaccurate supervision and, thus, tend to over-fit. This could have happened here as well, yet the U-Net seems to generalize well. Liu et al. propose to mitigate over-fitting by using an adaptive early stopping mechanism. The over-fitting can also be an issue due to the higher error in the labels. Then, it could make sense to access the error compared with accurate labels and account for the error as noise. The error can be reflected in the loss function during training. Yet, both approaches are not considered here in this work. As an evaluation metric, we used the mean intersection-over-union (IOU), where the IOU $J$ is defined as the overlap of the predicted semantic label $A$ and the ground truth label $B$ divided by their union as

---

[3] https://www.albumentations.ai/, accessed at 30th of June, 2023.

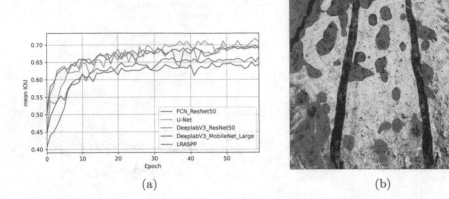

(a)                                                    (b)

**Fig. 4.** (a) Mean Mean intersection-over-union (IOU) of all networks. (b) Input image for the network (here in greyscale) with an overlay of the resulting detection mask made by the DeepLabV3 with MobileNet large. (Color figure online)

$$J(A, B) = \frac{|A \cap B|}{|A \cup B|}. \tag{1}$$

The mean IOU is then the mean over all $N$ labels, meanIOU $= \sum_{n=1}^{N} J(A_n, B_n)$. Figure 4a displays the mean IOU of all trained networks. The networks with a ResNet50 as a backbone tend to have a better mean IOU compared with the networks that use a MobileNet as backbone. For this set of data, the U-Net yields the best mean IOU and did not over-fit. Figure 4b displays the input image in greyscale for a network together with the resulting detection as an overlay. The crop rows are shown in dark grey and the detected weeds in lighter grey.

## 5 Experimental Evaluation

This section describes the used system to deploy the detection algorithms on the farm machines. We further present the process flow from data acquisition to the detection algorithms on the farm machine, and show results from a field trial where weed densities were detected by the proposed system.

### 5.1 Setup at the Farm Machine

To validate the practicality of the trained neural networks, a system as shown in Fig. 5 was set up on a farm machine. The goal was to detect weeds with the neural network and use this detection for later weed removal. In this system, each camera has its own dedicated computation unit to prevent any bottlenecks that might arise due to shared and limited processing power. The dedicated computation unit was an AVerMedia NX215B Box PC[4] which contains a NVIDIA Jetson Xavier NX[5] Module and offers two Ethernet ports.

Using this hardware, the setup for data collection described in Sect. 3 was extended by the segmentation network and a module to process the resulting segmented image on each worker-unit. In addition to this, one module was assigned to be the controller, a task which comprises triggering the cameras and their respective interface modules, collecting and evaluating the results of each processed inference, and controlling the implement according to the logic described in Sect. 5.2.

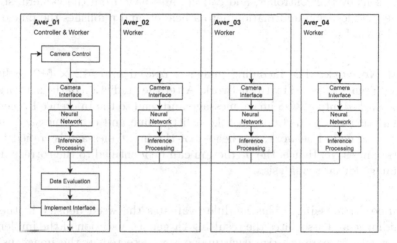

**Fig. 5.** The setup for the field-trial. The setup consisted of four AVerMedia Nx215B boxes, each connected to a camera. The large vertical boxes represent the software stack that runs on each AverMedia box. The first box initiated the image acquisition and provided the clock for all boxes. Additionally, the first box (controller) runs the data evaluation.

## 5.2   Software Structure on the Farm Machine

This section elaborates on the software for data-collection, data-processing, data-evaluation, as well as the resulting control decisions. The data flow in the software is depicted in Fig. 5. If not explicitly mentioned, the described module can be found on each unit.

**Camera Control.** This module is limited to the controller unit. It is responsible for cyclically triggering the image capture, based on a set frequency. The

---

[4] https://www.avermedia.com/professional/product-detail/NX215B, accessed at 28th of June, 2023.

[5] https://nvidia.de, accessed at 28th of June, 2023.

triggering of all cameras is implemented by transmitting a hardware pulse and by sending the ROS message, containing a timestamp and a location-reference, received by the *Implement Interface* (see below). This prevents the need for further synchronisation between time and location which may result in discrepancies between each unit.

**Camera Interface.** This module is responsible for initializing the connected camera using the parameters (i.e. exposure time, white balance, etc.) defined in a configuration file. Once the camera is running, this module reacts to the ROS message sent by the controller, and collects an image from the camera, stamps the time- and location-information onto a header, and publishes the image with its header via ROS.

**Neural Network.** The incoming image is resized into $512 \times 512$ to fit the input requirements posed by the network. After the prediction of the network, the image is packed into a ROS image message and send to the Inference Processing. As calculating the prediction can take a little time and other messages might arrive to the neural network, the header of the input message is copied to the prediction message. Hence, the prediction can be identified to the corresponding input image for later analysis.

**Inference Processing.** This module evaluates the weed density in the segmented image and associates the resulting targets to a section of the implement. The first step is parameterize each maize row detected in the image using a straight line. It is then necessary to check the plausibility of the detected rows as rows can be missing, falsely detected, or incomplete. Once all the maize-rows are identified and parameterized, a buffer-margin around each detected row is added along which the image can be cut into inter-row segments. This step is depicted in Fig. 6a. Then, the weed density is determined for each row of pixels of the cropped image, as shown in Fig. 6b. An adjustable threshold controls the strictness of the weed control measure. Here the threshold was set to 20%, meaning that any area where the density is above this level should be treated. These areas are subsequently called targets. Each of these targets is defined by its start and end pixel coordinates, which are then projected onto a coordinate system with the corresponding camera at the origin. Using the location data from the header of the image, they are converted into coordinates corresponding to the current field, which are then published as a ROS message.

**Data Evaluation.** This module is limited to the controller unit, and collects the detected targets of all modules. Since there is an overlap between the cameras, this module is responsible for the consolidation of targets by different sources in the same area. The cleaned up list of targets is then forwarded to the Implement Interface.

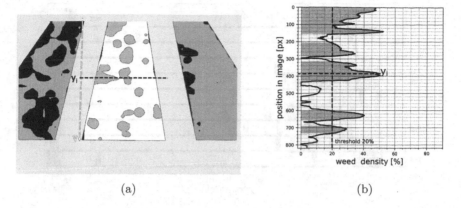

(a)                                                      (b)

**Fig. 6.** Processing of segmentation mask. (a) Splitting of image according to croplines. (b) Density and threshold calculation for areas.

**Implement Interface.** The Implement Interface is also limited to the controller unit and uses a Controller Area Network (CAN) bus to communicate with the implement. From there, among other variables, the current speed and location of the farm machine are read. The current speed, together with the reaction time of the implement, is used to calculate the locations for activation and deactivation. These locations are then compared to the current location of the implement and, if an action is required, the corresponding command is sent to the implement via the CAN bus.

### 5.3 Results from Field Trials

Using the method described in Sect. 5.2, during our field-trials, the data showed that weed-specific actuation has its applications. Depending on the time passed since sowing and since the last weed-regulation measure, the detected weed densities vary greatly. This in turn leads to fluctuations in the required regulatory measures. Even on a single image the necessity for regulation can differ drastically between inter-row-areas. For example, in Fig. 2b (see Sect. 3) the left inter-row-area would be weeded entirely, the center inter-row-area would yield disjointed applications, and the right inter-row-area would barely be weeded.

Figure 7 shows all targets identified for regulatory measures on a 70 m path through a field observed during our field trials. A threshold of 20 % was used and the test was conducted with a speed of 8 km/h, which in this case resulted in a minimal target width of 0.5 m. The first 5 m of the field appear to be without targets. This is due to the distance between the cameras and the implement: The distance in the field is measured according to the frame of reference of the implement and the first instance where the implement can actuate is when it reaches the lower edge of the first images, at about 5 m.

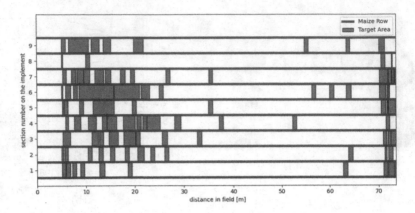

**Fig. 7.** Targets for weed regulation from a field trial.

# 6    Conclusion

In this paper, we presented the acquisition of data for a selective weeding application. To reduce the labeling effort for semantic labels we used inaccurate supervision for labeling. Multiple neural networks for semantic segmentation, specifically FCN, U-Net, DeeplabV3, and LRASPP have been trained on the inaccurately labeled data and evaluated. The U-Net yields the best results and does not seem to over-fit although we used the inaccurately labeled data. The other networks however, still yield reasonable results for the agricultural weeding application. Last, we present a validation setup for the proposed weed detection and the processing of the predicted semantic maps.

This paper indicates that for agricultural applications, less accurate labels can be reasonable, depending on the application. For the application considered in this paper, the inaccuracies for the labels do not corrupt the expected detections significantly. Generally, agricultural applications often see a huge data-drift due to seasonal and climate change and, therefore, often require to label new data. Inaccurate labels can help to reduce the labeling effort. Yet, over-fitting can be problem that either has to be dealt with by labeling more or by using more advanced loss functions during training. Labeling more images to tackle the over-fitting, however, can diminish the time savings due to inaccurate labeling. As future work, we would like to quantify the time savings during the labeling with focus on regional and seasonal changes.

**Acknowledgment.** The DFKI Lower Saxony (DFKI NI) is funded by the Lower Saxony Ministry of Science and Culture and the Volkswagen Foundation. The project Agri-GAIA on which this report is based is funded by the German Federal Ministry for Economics and Climate Action under the funding code 01MK21004A: Responsibility for the content of this publication lies with the author. Many thanks to Hof Langsenkamp, Belm, Germany for providing the fields for data acquisition and testing as well as a tractor and someone to drive it. We would also like to thank our labelers: Saskia Landwehr, Wiebke Bangert and Christoph Schwenne.

# References

1. Chen, L.C., Papandreou, G., Schroff, F., Adam, H.: Rethinking atrous convolution for semantic image segmentation (2017). https://doi.org/10.48550/arXiv.1706.05587

2. Cicco, M.D., Potena, C., Grisetti, G., Pretto, A.: Automatic model based dataset generation for fast and accurate crop and weeds detection. In: 2017 IEEE/RSJ International Conference on Intelligent Robots and Systems (IROS), pp. 5188–5195 (2017). https://doi.org/10.1109/IROS.2017.8206408

3. Gerhards, R., Andújar Sanchez, D., Hamouz, P., Peteinatos, G.G., Christensen, S., Fernandez-Quintanilla, C.: Advances in site-specific weed management in agriculture—a review. Weed Res. **62**(2), 123–133 (2022). https://doi.org/10.1111/wre.12526

4. Gerhards, R., et al.: Camera-guided weed hoeing in winter cereals with narrow row distance. Gesunde Pflanzen **72**(4), 403–411 (2020). https://doi.org/10.1007/s10343-020-00523-5

5. Howard, A., et al.: Searching for MobileNetV3 (2019). https://doi.org/10.48550/arXiv.1905.02244

6. Lindauer, M., Eggensperger, K., Feurer, M., Biedenkapp, A., Deng, D.: SMAC3: a versatile bayesian optimization package for hyperparameter optimization. J. Mach. Learn. Res. (23), 1–9 (2022)

7. Liu, S., Liu, K., Zhu, W., Shen, Y., Fernandez-Granda, C.: Adaptive early-learning correction for segmentation from noisy annotations. In: Proceedings of the IEEE/CVF Conference on Computer Vision and Pattern Recognition, pp. 2606–2616 (2022)

8. Long, J., Shelhamer, E., Darrell, T.: Fully convolutional networks for semantic segmentation. In: Proceedings of the IEEE Conference on Computer Vision and Pattern Recognition, pp. 3431–3440 (2015)

9. Lottes, P., Behley, J., Chebrolu, N., Milioto, A., Stachniss, C.: Joint stem detection and crop-weed classification for plant-specific treatment in precision farming. In: 2018 IEEE/RSJ International Conference on Intelligent Robots and Systems (IROS), pp. 8233–8238. IEEE, Madrid (2018). https://doi.org/10.1109/IROS.2018.8593678

10. Lu, Z., Fu, Z., Xiang, T., Han, P., Wang, L., Gao, X.: Learning from weak and noisy labels for semantic segmentation. IEEE Trans. Pattern Anal. Mach. Intell. **39**(3), 486–500 (2017). https://doi.org/10.1109/TPAMI.2016.2552172

11. Manss, C., et al.: Towards selective hoeing depending on evaporation from the soil. In: 43. GIL-Jahrestagung, Resiliente Agri-Food-Systeme, pp. 149–158. Gesellschaft für Informatik e.V., Osnabrück (2023)

12. Ronneberger, O., Fischer, P., Brox, T.: U-net: convolutional networks for biomedical image segmentation (2015). https://doi.org/10.48550/arXiv.1505.04597

13. Sekachev, B., et al.: OpenCV/CVAT: v1.1.0 (2020). https://doi.org/10.5281/zenodo.4009388

14. Shen, W., et al.: A survey on label-efficient deep image segmentation: bridging the gap between weak supervision and dense prediction. IEEE Trans. Pattern Anal. Mach. Intell. 1–20 (2023). https://doi.org/10.1109/TPAMI.2023.3246102

15. Slaughter, D.C., Giles, D.K., Downey, D.: Autonomous robotic weed control systems: a review. Comput. Electron. Agric. **61**(1), 63–78 (2008). https://doi.org/10.1016/j.compag.2007.05.008

16. Weyler, J., Milioto, A., Falck, T., Behley, J., Stachniss, C.: Joint plant instance detection and leaf count estimation for in-field plant phenotyping. IEEE Robot. Autom. Lett. **6**(2), 3599–3606 (2021). https://doi.org/10.1109/LRA.2021.3060712
17. Wu, X., Aravecchia, S., Lottes, P., Stachniss, C., Pradalier, C.: Robotic weed control using automated weed and crop classification. J. Field Robot. **37**(2), 322–340 (2020). https://doi.org/10.1002/rob.21938
18. Zhang, D., Han, J., Cheng, G., Yang, M.H.: Weakly supervised object localization and detection: a survey. IEEE Trans. Pattern Anal. Mach. Intell. **44**(9), 5866–5885 (2022). https://doi.org/10.1109/TPAMI.2021.3074313

# Interpretable Weighted Siamese Network to Predict the Time to Onset of Alzheimer's Disease from MRI Images

Misgina Tsighe Hagos[1,2](✉)(iD), Niamh Belton[1,3](iD), Ronan P. Killeen[3,4,5](iD),
Kathleen M. Curran[1,3](iD), Brian Mac Namee[1,2](iD),
and for the Alzheimer's Disease Neuroimaging Initiative

[1] Science Foundation Ireland Centre for Research Training in Machine Learning,
Dublin, Ireland
misgina.hagos@ucdconnect.ie
[2] School of Computer Science, Dublin, Ireland
[3] School of Medicine, University College Dublin, Dublin, Ireland
[4] Department of Radiology, Dublin, Ireland
[5] UCD-SVUH PET CT Research Centre, St Vincent's University Hospital,
Dublin 4, Ireland

**Abstract.** Alzheimer's Disease (AD) is a progressive disease preceded by
Mild Cognitive Impairment (MCI). Early detection of AD is crucial for
making treatment decisions. However, most of the literature on computer-
assisted detection of AD focuses on classifying brain images into one
of three major categories: healthy, MCI, and AD; or categorizing MCI
patients into (1) *progressive*: those who progress from MCI to AD at a
future time, and (2) *stable*: those who stay as MCI and never progress to
AD. This misses the opportunity to accurately identify the trajectory of
progressive MCI patients. In this paper, we revisit the AD identification
task and re-frame it as an ordinal classification task to predict *how close
a patient is to the severe AD stage*. To this end, we construct an ordinal
dataset of progressive MCI patients with a prediction target that indicates
the time to progression to AD. We train a Siamese network (SN) model
to predict the time to onset of AD based on MRI brain images. We also
propose a Weighted variety of SN and compare its performance to a baseline model. Our evaluations show that incorporating a weighting factor to
SN brings considerable performance gain. Moreover, we complement our
results with an interpretation of the learned embedding space of the SNs
using a model explainability technique.

**Keywords:** Alzheimer's Disease · Mild Cognitive Impairment ·
Computer Assisted Diagnosis · Siamese Networks

Data used in preparation of this article were obtained from the Alzheimer's Disease
Neuroimaging Initiative (ADNI) database (adni.loni.usc.edu). As such, the investigators within the ADNI contributed to the design and implementation of ADNI and/or
provided data but did not participate in analysis or writing of this report. A complete
listing of ADNI investigators can be found at: https://adni.loni.usc.edu/wp-content/
uploads/how_to_apply/ADNI_Acknowledgement_List.pdf.

M. Bramer and F. Stahl (Eds.): SGAI 2023, LNAI 14381, pp. 391–403, 2023.
https://doi.org/10.1007/978-3-031-47994-6_35

# 1    Introduction

Although it has been more than a century since Alois Alzheimer first described the clinical characteristics of Alzheimer's Disease (AD) [3,4], the disease still eludes early detection. AD is the leading cause of dementia, accounting for 60%-80% of all cases worldwide [20,34], and the number of patients effected is growing. In 2015, Alzheimer's Disease International (ADI) reported that over 46 million people were estimated to have dementia worldwide and that this number was expected to increase to 131.5 million by 2050 [29]. Since AD is a progressive disease, computer assisted early identification of the disease may enable early medical treatment to slow its progression.

Methods that require intensive expert input for feature collection, such as Morphometry [13], and more automated solutions based on deep learning [5,8,24] have been utilized in the computer assisted diagnosis of AD literature. These automated detection methods usually classify patients as belonging to one of three stages: Normal (patients exhibiting no signs of dementia and no memory complaints), Mild Cognitive Impairment (MCI) (an intermediate state in which a patient's cognitive decline is greater than expected for their age, but does not interfere with activities of their daily life), and full AD.

A participant's progression from one of the stages to the next, however, can take more than five years [30]. This can mean that when automated disease classification systems based on these three levels are used, patients at a near severe stage do not receive the required treatment because they are classified as belonging to the pre-severe stage. This is illustrated in Fig. 1(a) for five participants from the Alzheimer's Disease Neuroimaging Initiative (ADNI) study [28]. Using the typical classification approach (See Fig. 1(b)), for example, even though participant five is only a year away from progressing to the severe AD stage, they would be classified as MCI in the year 2009. To address this issue we focus on the clinical question "how far away is a progressive MCI patient on their trajectory to AD?" To do this we propose an ordinal categorization of brain images based on participants' level of progression from MCI to AD as shown in Fig. 1(c). Our approach adds ordinal labels to MRI scans of patients with progressive MCI indicating how many years they are from progressing to AD, and we construct a dataset of 444 MRI scans from 288 participants with these labels and share a replication script.

In addition to constructing the dataset, we also develop a computer assisted approach to identifying a participant's (or more specifically, their MRI image's) progression level. Accurately identifying how far a patient is from progressing to full AD is of paramount importance as this information may enable earlier intervention with medical treatments [2]. Rather than using simple ordinal classification techniques, we use Siamese networks due to their ability to handle the class imbalance in the employed dataset [21,33]. We use a Siamese network architecture, and a novel Weighted Siamese network that uses a new loss function tailored to learning to predict input MRI image's likelihood of progression. Furthermore, we complement results of our Siamese network based method with interpretations of the embedding space using an auxiliary model explanation technique, T-distributed Stochastic Neighbor Embedding (t-SNE) [26]. t-SNE

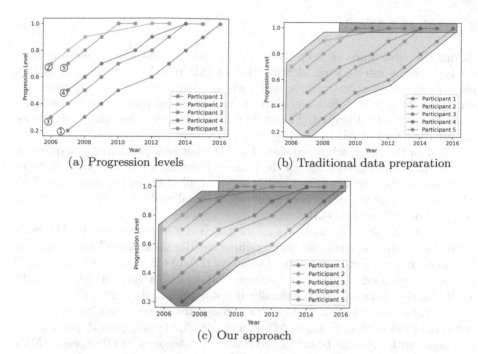

(a) Progression levels

(b) Traditional data preparation

(c) Our approach

**Fig. 1.** (a) Progression levels of five sample MCI participants where each dot represents an MRI image during an examination year. (b) shows the typical approach of organizing images for identification of progressive MCI or classification of MCI and AD. The images in the lower light orange section are categorized as MCI when preparing a training dataset (this includes those images from patients nearing progression to AD — near progression level 1.0). The images in the upper red section are categorized as AD. In (c) our approach to organizing brain images is illustrated using a Viridis map. Images are assigned ordinal progression levels $\in [0.1, 0.9]$ based on their distance in years from progressing to AD stage. (Color figure online)

condenses high dimensional embedding spaces learned by a Siamese network into interpretable two or three dimensional spaces [9].

The main contributions of this paper are:

1. We provide a novel approach that interpolates ordinal categories between existing MCI and AD categories of the ADNI dataset based on participants' progression levels.
2. We apply the first Siamese network approach to predict interpolated progression levels of MCI patients.
3. We propose a simple and novel variety of triplet loss for Siamese networks tailored to identifying progression levels of MCI patients.
4. Our experiments demonstrate that using our version of the triplet loss is better at predicting progression level than the traditional triplet loss. Code is shared online[1].

---

[1] https://github.com/Msgun/WeightedSiamese.

## 2  Related Work

Before the emergence of deep learning, and in the absence of relevant large datasets, computer-assisted identification of AD relied on computations that require expensive expert involvement such as Morphometry [13]. However, the release of longitudinal datasets, such as ADNI [28], inspired research on automated solutions that employed machine learning and deep learning methods for the identification of AD.

Most of the approaches proposed for AD diagnosis perform a classification among three recognized stages of the disease: Normal, MCI, and AD [23]. Some examples in the literature distinguish between all three of the categories [36], while others distinguish between just two: Normal and MCI [19], Normal and AD [32], or MCI and AD [31].

Patients at the MCI stage have an increased risk of progressing to AD, especially for elderly patients [30]. For example, in the Canadian Cohort Study of Cognitive Impairment and Related Dementia [17] 49 out of a cohort of 146 MCI patients progressed to AD in a two-year follow-up. In general, while healthy adult controls progress to AD annually at a maximum rate of 2%, MCI patients progress at a rate of 10%-25% [15]. This necessitates research on identifying MCI subjects at risk of progressing to AD. In a longitudinal study period, participants diagnosed with MCI can be categorized into two categories: (1) Progressive MCI, which represents participants who were diagnosed with MCI at some stage during the study but were later diagnosed with AD, and (2) Stable MCI, patients who stayed as MCI during the whole study period [16]. This excludes MCI participants with chances of reverting back to healthy, since they were also reported to have chances of progressing to AD [30]. There are some examples in the literature of using machine learning techniques such as random forest [27] and CNNs [16] to classify between stable and progressive MCI. While feature extraction is used prior to model training towards building relatively simpler models [23,35], 3D brain images are also deployed with 3D CNNs to reduce false positives [5,25].

The brain image classification task can also be transformed to ordinal classification to build regressor models. For example, four categories of AD: healthy, stable MCI, progressive MCI, and AD were used as ordinal labels to build a multivariate ordinal regressor using MRI images in [14]. However, the output of these models gives no indication of the likelihood of a patient to progress from one stage to another. Furthermore, this does not provide prediction for interpolated intercategory progression levels. Albright et al. (2019) [2] used a longitudinal clinical data including ADAS13, which is a 13-item Alzheimer's Disease Assessment Scale, and Mini-Mental State Examination (MMSE) to train multi-layer perceptron and recurrent networks for AD progression prediction. This work, however, uses no imaging data and it has been shown that brain images play a key role in improving diagnostic accuracy for Alzheimer's disease [18].

Siamese networks, which use a distance-based similarity training approach [10,12], have found applications in areas such as object tracking [7] and anomaly detection [6]. Although it does not focus on AD detection, we found [22] to be the closest approach to our proposed method in the literature. Li et al. [22]

report that a Siamese network's distance output could be translated to predict disease positions on a severity scale. Although this approach takes the output as severity scale without any prior training on disease severity, only deals with existing disease stages, and does not interpolate ordinal categories within, it does suggest Siamese networks as a promising approach for predicting ordinal progression levels.

## 3   Approach

In this section, we describe the datasets (and how they are processed), model architectures, model training and evaluation techniques used in our experiments, as well as our proposed triplet loss for Siamese networks.

### 3.1   Dataset Preparation

The data used in the experiments described here was obtained from the Alzheimer's Disease Neuroimaging Initiative (ADNI) database. ADNI was launched in 2003, led by Principal Investigator Michael W. Weiner, MD (https://adni.loni.usc.edu). For up-to-date information, see https://adni.loni.usc.edu/.

Table 1. Image distribution across progression levels, $\rho$.

| $\rho$ | 0.2 | 0.3 | 0.4 | 0.5 | 0.6 | 0.7 | 0.8 | 0.9 | 1.0 |
|---|---|---|---|---|---|---|---|---|---|
| Number of images | 4 | 4 | 6 | 10 | 24 | 56 | 172 | 273 | 467 |

From the ADNI dataset we identified MRI brain images of 1310 participants who were diagnosed with MCI or AD. 288 participants had progressive MCI, 545 had stable MCI, and the rest had AD. We used MRI images of the 288 progressive MCI participants to train and evaluate our models. We labeled the progressive MCI participants based on their progression levels towards AD, $\rho \in [0.1, 1.0]$ with a step size $= 0.1$, where for a single participant, $P$, $min(\rho) = 0.1$ represents the first time $P$ was diagnosed with MCI and $P$ transitions to stage AD at $max(\rho) = 1.0$. This transforms the binary MCI and AD labels to 10 ordinal labels. An example of the data organization based on progression level is plotted in Fig. 1. The distribution of the constructed ordinal regression levels is shown in Table 1 (where $\rho = 1.0$ represents AD) where the imbalance between the different labels is clear. Within the ADNI dataset, the maximum number of MRI scans that the progressive MCI participants have had until they progressed to AD ($\rho = 1.0$) is 9, which means that the smallest $\rho$ is 0.2. We took advantage of Siamese networks robustness to class imbalance to circumnavigate the imbalance in the ordinal labels. By sub-sampling from the majority classes, we selected 444 3D MRI images (shape $= 160 \times 192 \times 192$) for the negative, anchor, and positive datasets (each holding 148 images) required when training a Siamese network using triplet loss. We used 80% of the images for training and the rest for testing. AD images were randomly separated to the anchor and positive dataset. We ensure that there is no participant overlap between sets when performing the data splitting between training and testing dataset, and between anchor and positive dataset.

## 3.2 Weighted Siamese Network

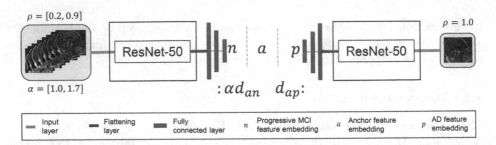

$\rho = [0.2, 0.9]$

$\alpha = [1.0, 1.7]$

$n \quad a \quad p$

$: \alpha d_{an} \quad d_{ap}:$

$\rho = 1.0$

| | | | | | | |
|---|---|---|---|---|---|---|
| — | Input layer | — Flattening layer | — Fully connected layer | $n$ Progressive MCI feature embedding | $a$ Anchor feature embedding | $p$ AD feature embedding |

**Fig. 2.** Weighted Siamese network. The text ResNet-50 here refers to the base layers of the ResNet-50 architecture which are trained from scratch for extracting image embeddings, i.e. excluding the fully connected classifier layers. While we used 3D MRI images for model training and evaluation, sagittal plane is used here only for visualization purposes.

Siamese networks are usually trained using a triplet loss or its variants. While a traditional triplet loss teaches a network that a negative instance is supposed to be at a larger distance from the anchor than a positive instance, we propose a Weighted triplet loss that teaches a network that instances, which can all be considered to be in the negative category, are not at the same distance from the anchor and that their distance depends on their progression level, $\rho$. So that lower progression levels have larger distance from an anchor instance, we transform $\rho$ to a weighting coefficient $\alpha = 1.9 - \rho$, excluding $\rho = 1.0$, as shown in Fig. 3. The architecture of our proposed Weighted Siamese network is shown in Fig. 2.

We used two different loss functions to train our Siamese networks. The first is a traditional triplet loss, which we refer to as Unweighted Siamese:

$$L_u = max(d_{ap} - d_{an} + margin, 0) \tag{1}$$

where $margin = 1.0$, $d_{ap}$ is the Euclidean distance between anchor and positive embeddings, and $d_{an}$ is the distance between the embeddings of anchor and negative instances.

The second loss is a newly proposed Weighted triplet loss—Weighted Siamese which introduces a coefficient $\alpha \in [1.0, 1.8]$ to $d_{an}$ in $L_u$:

$$L_w = max(d_{ap} - \alpha d_{an} + margin, 0) \tag{2}$$

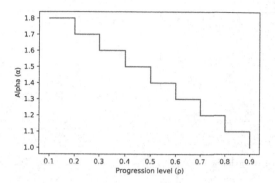

**Fig. 3.** Transforming progression level, $\rho$, to $\alpha$.

## 3.3 Training and Evaluation

We implemented all of our experiments using TensorFlow [1] and Keras [11]. After comparing performance between different architectures and feature embedding size, we chose to train a 3D ResNet-50 model from scratch by adding three fully connected layers of sizes 64, 32, and 8 nodes with ReLu activations, taking the last layer of size 8 as the embedding space. We used an Adam optimizer with a decaying learning rate of 1e-3. We trained the model with five different seeds for 150 epochs, which took an average of 122 min per a training run on an NVIDIA RTX A5000 graphics card.

For model evaluation on training and testing datasets, we use both the Unweighted Siamese and Weighted Siamese losses as well as Mean Absolute Error (MAE) and Root Mean Squared Error (RMSE). MAE and RMSE are presented in Eqs. 3 and 4 respectively, for a test set of size $N$ where $y_i$ and $Y_i$ hold the predicted and ground truth values for instance $i$, respectively. We turn the distance outputs of the Siamese networks into $y$ by discretizing them into equally spaced bins, where the number of bins equals the number of progression levels.

$$MAE = \frac{1}{N} \sum_{i=1}^{N} |y_i - Y_i| \tag{3}$$

$$RMSE = \sqrt{\frac{1}{N} \sum_{i=1}^{N} (y_i - Y_i)^2} \tag{4}$$

We make use of t-SNE to explain the 8 dimension embedding space learned by the Weighted Siamese network by condensing it two dimensions. For presentation purposes and in order to fit the t-SNE well, we drop underrepresented progression levels; while we dropped progression level 0.2 from the training dataset, progression levels 0.2, 0.3, and 0.5 were removed from the testing dataset. The t-SNE was fitted over a 1000 iterations using Euclidean distance metric with a perplexity of 32 and 8 for the training and testing datasets, respectively.

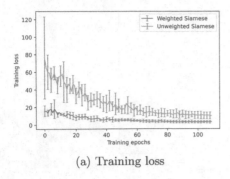
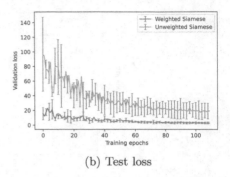

(a) Training loss                    (b) Test loss

**Fig. 4.** Training and testing losses of the Weighted and Unweighted Siamese models. The first 40 epochs are cropped out for easier visualization. Bars represent std. errors over five runs.

## 4    Results and Discussion

In this section, we present training and testing losses, MAE and RMSE metrics of evaluation, a plot showing comparison between predicted and ground-truth progression levels, as well as interpretation of the results.

Training and testing losses over five runs of model training for both the Unweighted and Weighted Siamese networks are shown in Fig. 4. While the average training and testing losses of the Weighted Siamese network are 2.92 and 2.79, the Unweighted Siamese achieves 10.02 and 17.53, respectively. We were able to observe that the Unweighted Siamese network had a hard time learning the progression levels of all the ordinal categories. However, our proposed approach using Weighted loss was better at fitting to all the levels. We accredit this to the effects of adding a weighing factor using $\rho$.

A plot of predicted vs. ground truth MCI to AD progression levels is presented in Fig. 5. Our proposed Weighted Siamese network outperforms the Unweighted Siamese network at predicting progression levels(Fig. 5 and Table 2).

We observed that the simple modification of factoring the distance between an embedding of anchor and negative instances by a function of the progression level brought considerable performance gain in separating between the interpolated categories between MCI and AD.

In Fig. 5, although the Weighted Siamese outperforms the Unweighted Siamese, it also usually classifies the input test images with lower progression levels as if they are on a higher progression levels. This would mean brain images

**Table 2.** Average MAE and RMSE over five runs.

| Method | MAE | RMSE |
| --- | --- | --- |
| Unweighted Siamese | 2.30 | 2.94 |
| Weighted Siamese | 2.00 | 2.40 |

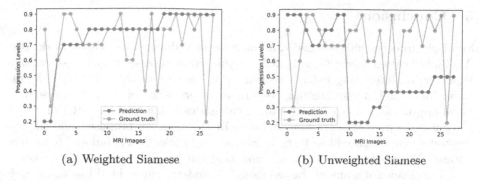

(a) Weighted Siamese                    (b) Unweighted Siamese

**Fig. 5.** Predicted progression levels of test MRI images against ground truth levels.

of patients that are far away from progressing to AD would be identified as if they are close to progressing. While it's important to correctly identify these low risk patients, we believe it's better to report the patients at lower risk as high risk and refer them for expert input than classifying high risk patients as low risk.

An interpretation of the results of the proposed Weighted Siamese method using t-SNE is displayed in Fig. 6. The clustering of the embedding of input instances according to their progression levels, especially between the low-risk and high-risk progression levels assures us that the results represent the ground truth disease levels.

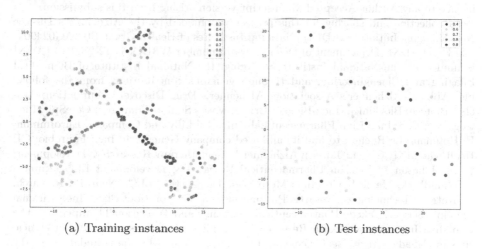

(a) Training instances                  (b) Test instances

**Fig. 6.** Visualization of t-SNE of the embedding spaces of training and test instances.

# 5    Conclusion

Similarly to other image-based computer assisted diagnosis research work, the AD identification literature is heavily populated by disease stage classification. However, an interesting extra step can be taken to identify how far an input brain image is from progressing to a more severe stage of AD. We present a novel approach of interpolating ordinal categories in-between the MCI and AD categories to prepare a training dataset. In addition, we proposed and implemented a new Weighted loss term for Siamese networks that is tailored to such a dataset. With our experiments, we show that our proposed approach surpassed the performance of a model trained using a standard Unweighted loss term; and we show how the predicted levels translate to the ground truth progression levels by applying a model interpretability technique on the embedding space. We believe our approach could easily be transferred to other areas of medical image classification involving progressive diseases.

The diagnosis results taken in our study are bounded by the timeline of the ADNI study—meaning, even though based on extracted information a participant may have MCI during an examination year and they may progress to AD after some year(s), they could have had MCI before joining the ADNI study and their progression to AD might have taken longer than what we have noted. Future work should consider this limitation.

**Acknowledgment.** This publication has emanated from research conducted with the financial support of Science Foundation Ireland under Grant number 18/CRT/6183. For the purpose of Open Access, the author has applied a CC BY public copyright licence to any Author Accepted Manuscript version arising from this submission.

Data collection and sharing for this project was funded by the Alzheimer's Disease Neuroimaging Initiative (ADNI) (National Institutes of Health Grant U01 AG024904) and DOD ADNI (Department of Defense award number W81XWH-12-2-0012) (ADNI is funded by the National Institute on Aging, the National Institute of Biomedical Imaging and Bioengineering, and through generous contributions from the following: AbbVie, Alzheimer's Association; Alzheimer's Drug Discovery Foundation; Araclon Biotech; BioClinica, Inc.; Biogen; Bristol-Myers Squibb Company; CereSpir, Inc.; Cogstate; Eisai Inc.; Elan Pharmaceuticals, Inc.; Eli Lilly and Company; EuroImmun; F. Hoffmann-La Roche Ltd and its affiliated company Genentech, Inc.; Fujirebio; GE Healthcare; IXICO Ltd.; Janssen Alzheimer Immunotherapy Research & Development, LLC.; Johnson & Johnson Pharmaceutical Research & Development LLC.; Lumosity; Lundbeck; Merck & Co., Inc.; Meso Scale Diagnostics, LLC.; NeuroRx Research; Neurotrack Technologies; Novartis Pharmaceuticals Corporation; Pfizer Inc.; Piramal Imaging; Servier; Takeda Pharmaceutical Company; and Transition Therapeutics. The Canadian Institutes of Health Research is providing funds to support ADNI clinical sites in Canada. Private sector contributions are facilitated by the Foundation for the National Institutes of Health (www.fnih.org) The grantee organization is the Northern California Institute for Research and Education, and the study is coordinated by the Alzheimer's Therapeutic Research Institute at the University of Southern California. ADNI data are disseminated by the Laboratory for Neuro Imaging at the University of Southern California).

# References

1. Abadi, M., et al.: TensorFlow: Large-scale machine learning on heterogeneous systems (2015). https://www.tensorflow.org/, software available from tensorflow.org
2. Albright, J., Initiative, A.D.N., et al.: Forecasting the progression of Alzheimer's disease using neural networks and a novel preprocessing algorithm. Alzheimer's Dementia: Transl. Res. Clin. Interventions **5**, 483–491 (2019)
3. Alzheimer, A.: Uber eine eigenartige erkrankung der hirnrinde. Zentralbl. Nervenh. Psych. **18**, 177–179 (1907)
4. Alzheimer, A., Stelzmann, R.A., Schnitzlein, H.N., Murtagh, F.R.: An english translation of alzheimer's 1907 paper," uber cine eigenartige erkankung der hirnrinde". Clin. Anat. (New York, NY) **8**(6), 429–431 (1995)
5. Basaia, S., et al.: Automated classification of alzheimer's disease and mild cognitive impairment using a single MRI and deep neural networks. NeuroImage: Clinical **21**, 101645 (2019)
6. Belton, N., Lawlor, A., Curran, K.M.: Semi-supervised siamese network for identifying bad data in medical imaging datasets. arXiv preprint arXiv:2108.07130 (2021)
7. Bertinetto, L., Valmadre, J., Henriques, J.F., Vedaldi, A., Torr, P.H.S.: Fully-convolutional Siamese networks for object tracking. In: Hua, G., Jégou, H. (eds.) ECCV 2016. LNCS, vol. 9914, pp. 850–865. Springer, Cham (2016). https://doi.org/10.1007/978-3-319-48881-3_56
8. Billones, C.D., Demetria, O.J.L.D., Hostallero, D.E.D., Naval, P.C.: Demnet: a convolutional neural network for the detection of Alzheimer's disease and mild cognitive impairment. In: 2016 IEEE Region 10 Conference (TENCON), pp. 3724–3727. IEEE (2016)
9. Borys, K., et al.: Explainable AI in medical imaging: an overview for clinical practitioners-beyond saliency-based XAI approaches. Eur. J. Radiol. 110786 (2023)
10. Bromley, J., Guyon, I., LeCun, Y., Säckinger, E., Shah, R.: Signature verification using a "Siamese" time delay neural network. In: Advances in Neural Information Processing Systems, vol. 6 (1993)
11. Chollet, F., et al.: Keras (2015). https://keras.io
12. Chopra, S., Hadsell, R., LeCun, Y.: Learning a similarity metric discriminatively, with application to face verification. In: 2005 IEEE Computer Society Conference on Computer Vision and Pattern Recognition (CVPR 2005), vol. 1, pp. 539–546. IEEE (2005)
13. Dashjamts, T., et al.: Alzheimer's disease: diagnosis by different methods of voxel-based morphometry. Fukuoka igaku zasshi= Hukuoka acta medica **103**(3), 59–69 (2012)
14. Doyle, O.M., et al.: Predicting progression of Alzheimer's disease using ordinal regression. PLoS ONE **9**(8), e105542 (2014)
15. Grand, J.H., Caspar, S., MacDonald, S.W.: Clinical features and multidisciplinary approaches to dementia care. J. Multidiscip. Healthc. **4**, 125 (2011)
16. Hagos, M.T., Killeen, R.P., Curran, K.M., Mac Namee, B., Initiative, A.D.N., et al.: Interpretable identification of mild cognitive impairment progression using stereotactic surface projections. In: PAIS 2022, pp. 153–156. IOS Press (2022)
17. Hsiung, G.Y.R., et al.: Outcomes of cognitively impaired not demented at 2 years in the Canadian cohort study of cognitive impairment and related dementias. Dement. Geriatr. Cogn. Disord. **22**(5–6), 413–420 (2006)

18. Johnson, K.A., Fox, N.C., Sperling, R.A., Klunk, W.E.: Brain imaging in Alzheimer disease. Cold Spring Harb. Perspect. Med. **2**(4), a006213 (2012)
19. Ju, R., Hu, C., Zhou, P., Li, Q.: Early diagnosis of Alzheimer's disease based on resting-state brain networks and deep learning. IEEE/ACM Trans. Comput. Biol. Bioinform. (TCBB) **16**(1), 244–257 (2019)
20. Kalaria, R.N., et al.: Alzheimer's disease and vascular dementia in developing countries: prevalence, management, and risk factors. Lancet Neurol. **7**(9), 812–826 (2008)
21. Koch, G., Zemel, R., Salakhutdinov, R., et al.: Siamese neural networks for one-shot image recognition. In: ICML Deep Learning Workshop, vol. 2. Lille (2015)
22. Li, M.D., et al.: Siamese neural networks for continuous disease severity evaluation and change detection in medical imaging. NPJ Digital Med. **3**(1), 48 (2020)
23. Li, Q., Wu, X., Xu, L., Chen, K., Yao, L., Initiative, A.D.N.: Classification of Alzheimer's disease, mild cognitive impairment, and cognitively unimpaired individuals using multi-feature kernel discriminant dictionary learning. Front. Comput. Neurosci. **11**, 117 (2018)
24. Liu, M., Cheng, D., Wang, K., Wang, Y.: Multi-modality cascaded convolutional neural networks for Alzheimer's disease diagnosis. Neuroinformatics **16**(3), 295–308 (2018)
25. Liu, M., Zhang, J., Nie, D., Yap, P.T., Shen, D.: Anatomical landmark based deep feature representation for MR images in brain disease diagnosis. IEEE J. Biomed. Health Inform. **22**(5), 1476–1485 (2018)
26. Van der Maaten, L., Hinton, G.: Visualizing data using t-SNE. J. Mach. Learn. Res. **9**(11) (2008)
27. Moradi, E., Pepe, A., Gaser, C., Huttunen, H., Tohka, J., Initiative, A.D.N., et al.: Machine learning framework for early MRI-based Alzheimer's conversion prediction in MCI subjects. Neuroimage **104**, 398–412 (2015)
28. Mueller, S.G., et al.: Ways toward an early diagnosis in Alzheimer's disease: the Alzheimer's disease neuroimaging initiative (ADNI). Alzheimer's & Dementia **1**(1), 55–66 (2005)
29. Prince, M.J., Wimo, A., Guerchet, M.M., Ali, G.C., Wu, Y.T., Prina, M.: World alzheimer report 2015-the global impact of dementia: An analysis of prevalence, incidence, cost and trends (2015)
30. Roberts, R.O., et al.: Higher risk of progression to dementia in mild cognitive impairment cases who revert to normal. Neurology **82**(4), 317–325 (2014)
31. Wegmayr, V., Aitharaju, S., Buhmann, J.: Classification of brain MRI with big data and deep 3D convolutional neural networks. In: Medical Imaging 2018: Computer-Aided Diagnosis, vol. 10575, p. 105751S. International Society for Optics and Photonics (2018)
32. Xiao, R., et al.: Early diagnosis model of Alzheimer's disease based on sparse logistic regression with the generalized elastic net. Biomed. Signal Process. Control **66**, 102362 (2021)
33. Yang, W., Li, J., Fukumoto, F., Ye, Y.: HSCNN: a hybrid-siamese convolutional neural network for extremely imbalanced multi-label text classification. In: Proceedings of the 2020 Conference on Empirical Methods in Natural Language Processing (EMNLP), pp. 6716–6722 (2020)

34. Zhang, R., Simon, G., Yu, F.: Advancing Alzheimer's research: a review of big data promises. Int. J. Med. Informatics **106**, 48–56 (2017)
35. Zheng, C., Xia, Y., Chen, Y., Yin, X., Zhang, Y.: Early diagnosis of Alzheimer's disease by ensemble deep learning using FDG-PET. In: Peng, Y., Yu, K., Lu, J., Jiang, X. (eds.) IScIDE 2018. LNCS, vol. 11266, pp. 614–622. Springer, Cham (2018). https://doi.org/10.1007/978-3-030-02698-1_53
36. Zhou, T., Thung, K.H., Zhu, X., Shen, D.: Effective feature learning and fusion of multimodality data using stage-wise deep neural network for dementia diagnosis. Hum. Brain Mapp. **40**(3), 1001–1016 (2019)

# Knowledge Discovery and Data Mining Applications

# Heuristic Search of Heuristics

Angelo Pirrone[1,3](✉) [iD], Peter C. R. Lane[2] [iD], Laura Bartlett[1] [iD],
Noman Javed[1] [iD], and Fernand Gobet[1] [iD]

[1] Centre for Philosophy of Natural and Social Science, London School of Economics
and Political Science, London, UK
{a.pirrone,l.bartlett,n.javed3,f.gobet}@lse.ac.uk
[2] Department of Computer Science, University of Hertfordshire, Hatfield, UK
p.c.lane@herts.ac.uk
[3] Department of Psychology, University of Liverpool, Liverpool, UK

**Abstract.** How can we infer the strategies that human participants
adopt to carry out a task? One possibility, which we present and discuss here, is to develop a large number of strategies that participants
could have adopted, given a cognitive architecture and a set of possible operations. Subsequently, the (often many) strategies that best
explain a dataset of interest are highlighted. To generate and select candidate strategies, we use genetic programming, a heuristic search method
inspired by evolutionary principles. Specifically, combinations of cognitive operators are evolved and their performance compared against
human participants' performance on a specific task. We apply this
methodology to a typical decision-making task, in which human participants were asked to select the brighter of two stimuli. We discover several
understandable, psychologically-plausible strategies that offer explanations of participants' performance. The strengths, applications and challenges of this methodology are discussed.

**Keywords:** Decision Making · Heuristic Search · Program Synthesis ·
Genetic programming

## 1 Introduction

One aim of cognitive scientists is to understand the strategies (heuristics) that
human participants adopt in order to solve a problem; whether it is a 'simple'
problem, such as deciding to accept or reject a bet, or a more complex problem,
such as planning the next move during a chess game.

Understanding which strategies participants use is an inferential problem. No
unique procedure exists to infer theories of cognitive capacities, and, in general,
this is a problem that can be addressed in several different ways. For instance,
based on previous data and on principles such as computability or parsimony, a
researcher may hypothesise a specific strategy and design experiments that test
qualitative or quantitative predictions of that strategy.

Another approach is to consider a large number of possible strategies and
select the best ones on the basis of principles such as goodness of fit and/or

M. Bramer and F. Stahl (Eds.): SGAI 2023, LNAI 14381, pp. 407–420, 2023.
https://doi.org/10.1007/978-3-031-47994-6_36

simplicity. This process is known as a heuristic search in the space of possible alternatives [19], a principle that AI pioneers Herbert Simon and Allen Newell proposed as an explanation of how humans and computers solve problems and make scientific discoveries.

Here we present and apply a methodology [2,3,10] that supports researchers in considering a large range of strategies, built from a set of minimal building blocks of cognitive processes. In this paper, strategies are represented as computer programs, running on a virtual machine embodying a cognitive model of human behaviour. First, a set of strategies is created at random; subsequently, these strategies (i.e., computer programs) are modified using evolutionary techniques, in order to minimise a fitness function. In the current case, fitness is assessed using mean reaction time and mean choice. This yields many strategies that quantitatively explain the data. After post-processing, the number of candidate programs is significantly reduced and insights can be gained regarding the processes underlying the observed behaviour.

Automated theory/program/equation discovery based on evolutionary approaches and other algorithms for combinatorial search has a long history in science [2,6,8]; however, applications to cognitive science are rare (but see [12,16,20,21]), especially in the form of symbolic, more easily understandable, cognitive architectures [3,10]. In the following section, we present an application of this methodology to a decision-making task. We are especially interested in discussing the strengths, challenges and limitations of this methodology with regard to aiding inference in cognitive science.

## 2   A Value-Sensitive Decision-Making Task

We consider a typical decision-making task [13,17,22]; participants need to decide which of two gray patches presented on a computer screen is brighter, Fig. 1. Specifically, during each trial, participants are presented with a fixation cross at the centre of the screen, and, equidistant from the fixation cross, two stimuli, in the form of homogeneous, round, grey patches on a black background. The brightness of each patch is sampled from a normal distribution and varies from frame to frame. That is, the patches have momentary, normally distributed, fluctuations in brightness - to make a choice, participants are assumed to integrate evidence over time to decide which patch is brighter. In other words, to decide which is brighter, participants build up an 'average feel' regarding the brightness of each patch. Participants respond in their own time, meaning that the patches remain on screen until they make a response. To select which alternative is brighter, participants press 'left' or 'right' on a keyboard. Shortly after responding, participants are presented with a new trial.

Crucially, in diagnostic conditions, the two stimuli have identical brightness – these conditions are labelled 'equal alternatives'. Across 'equal alternatives' conditions, the experimenter varies the absolute brightness. That is, physical and psychological differences between stimuli are kept constant (i.e., zero, since they are identical) while their absolute value is increased or decreased. Note

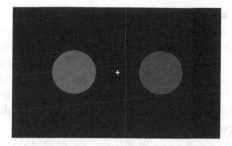

**Fig. 1.** Stimuli example. Participants need to decide, by pressing one of two buttons on a keyboard, which of the two stimuli patches is brighter. In this example, stimulus patch size is exaggerated for visibility.

that, when deciding which of the two stimuli is brighter, their absolute brightness is irrelevant and the only relevant feature should be relative brightness. Nonetheless, results show that decisions are made faster as absolute value is increased, even though participants are required to choose the brighter of the two stimuli and the difference between the two stimuli is null [18]. This result is replicated across very different types of choices (e.g., between consumer items, foraging scenarios, etc.) and species, such as non-human primates [17], and highlights a hard-wired property of our decision architecture – value-sensitivity (for details on value-sensitivity, see [18]). Note that 'value' is not to be confused with 'reward' – here 'value' only refers to the intensity or magnitude of the stimuli. Value-sensitivity, in which decisions are made faster and more random (i.e., less accurate) as absolute input value increases, challenges dominant theories of decision-making, in which it is only the difference between alternatives that drives decision-making [18], while absolute value is deemed irrelevant.

Here, we only model the 'equal alternatives' conditions from the original dataset [17]. The original dataset contained four 'equal alternatives' conditions; for simplicity we median-split these into low-value and high-value conditions. The average reaction time for low-value equal conditions was 784 ms, and 704 ms for high-value conditions. We require that a response is made, but ignore which response is given (i.e., left or right), since for equal alternatives responses should be random, in the absence of a response bias. No bias is reported in the data and analyses.

The two conditions had a mean brightness of .35 (low value) and .55 (high value) on a 0-black to 1-white scale of brightness. We know from psychophysical research [4,22] that the psychological representation of brightness follows that of the physical stimulus value to a power coefficient $\gamma = 0.5$; hence we assume that participants 'experience' stimuli with intensity $.35^{.5} \approx .6$ and $.55^{.5} \approx .75$.

Our goal is to discover a set of candidate computer programs that achieve a similar performance to that of human participants. We model the decision process by assuming that participants extract samples of evidence from the stimuli and combine them in order to trigger a response. A response is initiated when *model-current* reaches the arbitrary threshold value of 1.2 and the *threshold* operator is selected, setting *model-response* to 1. Note that no single sample of evidence can reach a threshold, since samples have values of .6 and .75 (lower than the 1.2 value needed) – in order to reach a threshold, the system would need to perform operations on the samples (for instance, sum multiple samples) so that a response can be initiated. For simplicity, we set the threshold hyperparameter to an arbitrary value that requires more than one sample of evidence to trigger a choice. However, the value of the threshold could also be evolved as part of the model development system.

As in the lab experiment [17], in our simulations, programs (i.e., our artificial participants) are presented with 360 random repetitions of stimuli for both conditions, for a total of 720 trials.

In this study, we are interested in finding and comparing candidate models when sampling is noiseless vs when sampling is noisy, so that we can compare solutions for a noiseless system (i.e., perfect processing of sensory inputs) to solutions for a system with gradual and noisy accumulation of evidence.

## 3   Model Development System

We developed a simple symbolic cognitive architecture able to manipulate inputs (a numeric representation of stimuli) into outputs (a response). The cognitive architecture and other applications of the model development system are described in depth in previous articles [1–3,10] in which this methodology was primarily applied to memory research in cognitive psychology.

There are some task-independent components: a three-slot short-term memory (STM) [5], a clock which records in-task time, a *current* value in working memory, and a *response* value of the system. As explained above, stimuli are represented as numerical values. At the beginning of each trial, all task-independent components are set to zero.

The aim of the system is to make a choice that minimises the discrepancy between reaction time data and the model for the two conditions. A set of *operators* (Table 1) can manipulate the components of the cognitive architecture. For instance, the system can extract samples of evidence from the stimuli, write their values to short-term memory, and perform various other operations that would lead the system to execute a response within the desired time window. These operators, with timings derived from previous research [3,10] or set arbitrarily, are combined in sequence using genetic programming – these sequences de facto represent a cognitive strategy to solve the problem at hand.

At the beginning of the search, a defined number of strategies are generated at random; in later generations, genetic programming allows the combination and modification of the programs via mechanisms such as *mutation* and *crossover* [9]. For in-depth details on genetic programming, readers should refer to the literature on the topic [9].

The aim of the genetic programming system is to generate strategies that minimise the discrepancy between the data and the generated solutions – in our case, this means minimising the difference in mean reaction times (for each of

**Table 1.** The operators used in our model development system. Operator timings are as follows: input operators (100 ms), output operators (140 ms), cognitive operators (70 ms), STM operators (50 ms), syntax operators (0 ms), time operators last as long as declared (e.g., wait-25 lasts 25 ms, while-50 lasts 50 ms). Note that, in two separate runs, participants use either *sample* or *noisy-sample*, but not both in the same run.

| name | function | type |
|---|---|---|
| access-stm-X | reads the value of slot X in STM. Sets model-current to the value of the slot | STM |
| compare-X-Y | compares the values of the slots X and Y in STM. If both are equal, it sets model-current to value in slot X, otherwise it leaves model-current unchanged | cognitive |
| sum-1-2 | sets model-current to the sum of the values of the slots 1 and 2 in STM | cognitive |
| putstm | pushes value in model-current to top of STM | STM |
| sample | extracts a sample (a reading) from the stimuli and sets model-current to that | input |
| noisy-sample | extracts a sample (a reading) from the stimuli and sets model-current to that with probability of .75, otherwise it sets model-current to 1 | input |
| threshold | sets model-response to 1 if model-current >1.2 or to 0 if not | output |
| wait | advances model-clock (in ms): 25 50 100 200 1000 or 15000 | time |
| donothing | does nothing | syntax |
| dotimesX | repeats a program 2, 3 or 5 times | syntax |
| prog-x | a sequence of 2, 3 or 4 programs | syntax |
| if-bigger | if model-current is bigger than 1.2 perform action A otherwise perform action B | syntax |

the two conditions) and choice between the model and the data. The fitness function includes three components: reaction times for the two conditions, and choice. Recall that 'choice' is modelled as executing a response; which alternative is selected is irrelevant given that alternatives are identical. The reaction times component had a weight of .35 for each of the two conditions, while the choice component had a weight of .30. We chose these values to give an approximate equal weight to each of the three components of the fitness function.

We note here that the operators reported in Table 1 could give rise to sophisticated decision regimes. For instance, participants could extract multiple samples of evidence, write them to short-term memory and then compare or sum them to reach a threshold for a decision. Alternatively, since for equal alternatives information about multiple samples is redundant, participants could simply extract

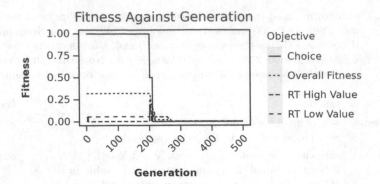

**Fig. 2.** Fitness against generation. The plot shows the evolution of the overall fitness, and of the sub-components of the fitness function (reaction time for the two conditions, and choice).

a single sample of evidence and apply a sequence of if-rules in order to arrive at a decision.

After the search phase, the solutions need to be post-processed. Post-processing removes operators that have no effect on the solution (also known as dead-code) [7,10]. For instance, consider an if-statement such as: 'if 1>2, then action A is performed, otherwise action B is performed'. In this case, action A will never be performed; hence, post-processing would simplify the if-statement into simpler syntax that executes action B only. The amount of dead-code is a function of the number of generations and individuals used during the search phase, and can account for a large percentage of operations included in the solutions generated [7,10]. Removing dead-code significantly improves the ease of interpretation of the best solution(s), which is important when evaluating whether two models are qualitatively similar, as is often the case [7,10].

For the search, we evolved 500 individuals for 500 generations. The search was performed using SBCL – the code used for the heuristic search is available by contacting the authors. For the GP implementation, we used mini-gp (https://github.com/jorgetavares/mini-gp) with default values.

## 4   Results

### 4.1   Simulation 1: Noiseless Sampling

In this simulation we used the *sample* operator, rather the *noisy-sample* operator. Overall, fitness approaches zero (i.e., perfect prediction) after approximately 250 generations, see Fig. 2. That is, models after the 250th generation quantitatively explain the data well; as Fig. 2 shows, each of the components of the fitness function (reaction times, and choice), and the global fitness function itself, reach a perfect prediction. Models (i.e., individuals) in the final generation have low fitness values, approaching zero. Note the drop in fitness at generation 200 -

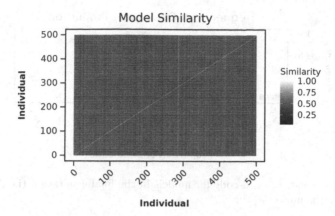

Fig. 3. Model similarity for models in the last generation. Despite all being 'good' enough models (i.e., fitness near zero), the models show low similarity (i.e., they are dissimilar).

models after generation 200 are better than those generated at random at the beginning of the search.

Even though these models have a similar fitness value, they represent different decision-making strategies (see Fig. 3). That is, the data are well explained by models that are dissimilar. The similarity between two models is computed by breaking the program down into components and then measuring their similarity using the Jaccard similarity coefficient.

Models include a high proportion of dead-code, an expected feature of GP – program size increases as a function of the number of generations, Fig. 4. At generation 200 there is a drop in size that coincides with an increase in fitness this means that models become better and simpler. However, as common with GP, the programs 'bloat' after each generation. As shown in Fig. 5, almost half of the models in the final generation consist of about 40–60% of dead-code; few models have a proportion of dead-code higher than 60%.

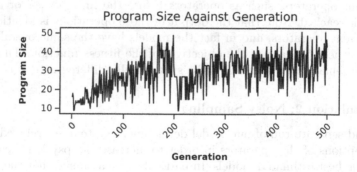

Fig. 4. Increase in program size as a function of generation.

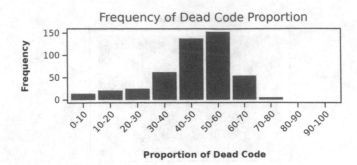

**Fig. 5.** The frequency of dead-code for models in the final generation (i.e., proportion of a model that is unnecessary).

The best models are defined as models within a tolerance of 0.01 in fitness value from the single best model with the lowest fitness. After post-processing, 66 best models were found; note that they all have identical fitness of 0.002. As in Fig. 3, we can show similarity across the best models; Fig. 6 shows that the best models have a very similar structure. Note that the fact that models have an identical fitness of 0.002 is no guarantee that the models are syntactically and/or semantically identical; in fact, very different models could achieve a similar fitness.

A representative model from the best solutions is reported in Fig. 7. Note that some nodes in the tree are irrelevant (e.g., the first sum-1-2). The model can be interpreted as follows: participants extract a single sample from the stimulus (i.e., they extract a reading from the stimuli and set *model-current* to that value), write that value to each of the three slots in STM, and then sum those values until a threshold is reached. If it is a low value stimulus, they perform an additional operation (*put-stm*), as shown in the right side of the if-statement.

We can further perform multi-dimensional scaling to generate a 2D representation of similarity between models and highlight the presence of clusters of models. Figure 8 shows that there are two distinct classes of models that explain the data equally well. The main difference between the two classes is the use of irrelevant operators, such as operators before the first *sample* or after the *threshold* is reached. Note that the output of those operations is identical while using different operators, and in fact the models have the same overall fitness, and same fitness for each of the objectives of the fitness function. That is, the models are semantically identical while syntactically different.

## 4.2   Simulation 2: Noisy Sampling

In a second separate run of our model development system, we relaxed some of the assumptions of the operators in order to increase the psychological plausibility of the best-estimated models. In particular, we assumed that the operator *sample* is noisy (hence the name *noisy-sample*) and it sets the value of *model-current* to the value of the stimuli only 75% of the time – the remaining 25% of

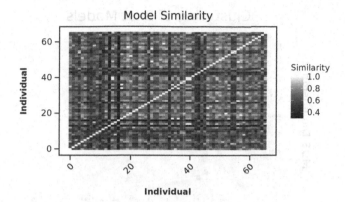

**Fig. 6.** Model similarity for the 'best' models, after post-processing. 'Best' models are those within a difference of 0.01 from the single best model – note however that in our case, the 66 best models have the same identical fitness of 0.002. The figure shows that these models have a high degree of similarity.

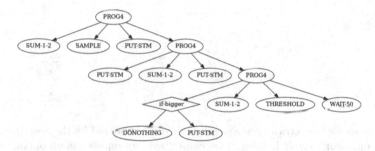

**Fig. 7.** One of the solutions from the best generation. The strategy is represented using a tree structure; this is standard for solutions from genetic programming. This strategy achieves a fitness of 0.002 (0 is perfect fit), RTs of 780 ms and 710 ms for low and high value conditions, and a probability of responding of 1.

the time the value of *model-current* is set to an arbitrary value of 1. The search estimated a single best tree, reported in Fig. 9.

Interestingly, the strategy reported in Fig. 9 extracts multiple, separate samples of evidence, writes them to STM and finally sums the values of STM slots 1 and 2 to trigger a response. This model is qualitatively akin to what would be predicted by an evidence-accumulation architecture [11]. Given the presence of noise, multiple separate samples are extracted and integrated to arrive at a decision – on the other hand, in the fully deterministic, noiseless model, a single sample triggers a decision. Contrary to classical evidence-accumulation models, the strategy reported in Fig. 9 requires fewer iterations - in fact, in evidence-accumulation models sampling lasts 1ms and a multitude of samples are extracted to arrive to a decision. Here we find that such a strict requirement may not be necessary.

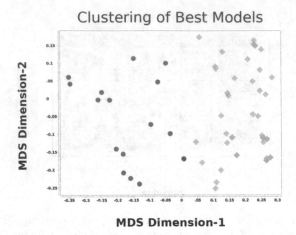

**Fig. 8.** Clusters for the best models in the final generation. MDS is short for multi-dimensional scaling.

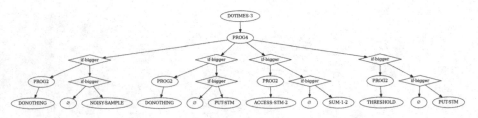

**Fig. 9.** The single best strategy across all strategies considered by the search algorithm when the operator *sample* is noisy. The 'empty' symbol represents an operator that is never executed, because it is dependent on a value of the model that is never met.

The methodology presented here allows a wealth of additional analyses. Analyses could focus on aspects such as varying the precision of the sampling operator across runs, estimating the best solution across different sets of operators, highlighting sub-classes of best solutions for different participants rather than considering averaged data or more. These are all exploratory/confirmatory analyses that depend on the specific goal, focus and interest of the researcher. For the remainder of our article, we decided to focus on the implications of this methodology, rather than performing additional analyses.

## 5    Discussion

We have presented a methodology that allows a researcher, given a dataset and a set of basic building blocks of cognition, to search a wide space of possible strategies that participants may have adopted. To demonstrate the utility of this approach, we applied it to a task in which participants select the brighter of two stimuli. In the experiment, unbeknownst to the participants, conditions of interest are those in which the brightness of the two stimuli are identical.

Our analyses focused on estimating the 'best' strategies in the absence vs presence of noise in the operators. That is, we were interested in evaluating differences in best strategies as a function of the parameterisations in our model development system and underlying assumptions. We found that if we assume a fully noiseless, deterministic strategy, participants extract a single sample of evidence from the stimulus and essentially 'boost' the sample in order to reach a threshold for a response. Intuitively, this is what would be expected in the absence of noise – since a single sample of evidence provides perfect information about the stimuli, it is unnecessary to sample more than once. On the other hand, if sampling is noisy and unreliable, participants extract multiple samples and combine them in order to arrive at a consensus for a response, in an evidence-accumulation fashion. That is, if sampling is noisy, more than one sample is needed to arrive at a decision. In both the noiseless and noisy case, value-sensitivity is implemented via the operator *if-bigger* which, depending on the value of *model-current*, executes one of two operators.

The methodology that we presented here is agnostic concerning applications – while in this case it was applied to a single decision-making task, it has been applied to different domains, such as research on working memory [3, 10]. That is, the same discovery process can be adopted in different domains and applications. Similarly, while for simplicity we applied the methodology to averaged data, this methodology could be adopted to find strategies accounting for individual data. For instance, researchers could use this methodology to infer individual and average strategies during decision-making in order to estimate between-subject similarities in decision strategies, and deviance of individuals from the strategy that explains aggregated results. The same rationale applies to the cognitive architecture and the operators - they can be adjusted by the researcher according to their specific needs.

Even in the case of a typical decision-making task, there are many strategies (virtually an infinite number) that could account for patterns in a dataset; as the complexity of tasks or the number of operators increases, the number of strategies increases exponentially and we believe that this methodology could aid a first exploratory phase in which candidate alternative strategies are discovered. Subsequently, other analyses or ad-hoc experimental work can be devised to compare alternative explanations. For instance, previous work [10] used this methodology for the Delayed Matched to Sample task (an experiment used to study short-term memory) and, over multiple runs, found that three distinct classes of models could explain the data equally well.

The task presented here is arguably a phenomenologically simple task. Despite this, several strategies could explain the simulated data since the decision performance is determined by a large number of underlying factors. The fact that a large number of models can explain any finite set of data is the well known problem of underdetermination of theory from data – especially when both stimulus representations and processes are unknown. However, the general approach in cognitive science is to test predictions of one model/strategy or compare two of them [14]. We believe that in the early phases of theory development, the tool presented here could aid in the search for sensible theories to be considered, beyond those proposed by the researcher's intuition.

This methodology could be useful in multiple cases. Firstly, for researchers who are interested in estimating optimal solutions for a specific problem, given a set of basic cognitive processes. Estimating optimal solutions is hard [21] and often mathematically prohibitive. As a search-based optimization technique, genetic programming could be adopted to estimate optimal strategies for a specific decision problem – this methodology allows researchers to evaluate a large range of solutions and contrast and compare similarities and differences. An interesting avenue for future research is to evaluate how optimal strategies vary when aspects of the system, such as the number or precision of operators, are varied.

A second case in which this methodology could prove useful is to aid researchers in developing hypotheses regarding which strategies could have generated data. For instance, this methodology could support a researchers' hypothesis if it is congruent with the best strategy estimated. On the other hand, if the working hypothesis is not in line with the best strategy estimated, that may lead to a reconsideration of theories.

## 6    Limitations and Future Directions

While researchers' intuition may or may not be directly influenced by data when generating theories, the methodology presented here is data-based. If data are of poor quality, the resulting theory will be a theory that explains poor-quality data. To mitigate this risk, this methodology should be applied to large datasets across different types of tasks; if the best strategy *simultaneously* accounts for datasets across domains, conclusions limited by the specifics of the experimental procedure are less likely.

Crucially, this methodology relies on the operators, the building blocks of cognition, to generate a theory. A current limitation of the methodology is that the timings of operators are fixed, either to values from the literature [3] or, for convenience, to arbitrary values. For instance, here we assume that sampling lasts 100 ms. Similarly, all memory operators have an arbitrarily fixed duration of 50 ms. While setting features of cognitive capacities to fixed values is often standard practice, for instance in unified theories of cognition [15], one risk with this approach is to perform computationally expensive model search between models that are unreasonable to begin with, due to incorrect assumptions regarding the timings of operators. However, assumptions, implicit or explicit, permeate every theory of cognitive capacity – indeed, every theory in the empirical sciences. A benefit of this approach is that it makes a wider number of assumptions explicit (e.g., the timing of operators, the cognitive architecture) and it allows the estimation of how changing specific assumptions changes what can be said about cognitive capacities. Our current work is focusing on minimising the risk of fixing certain features to arbitrary values, by varying parameters that we previously kept fixed in our search. This is done by co-evolving crucial features of our system that were hard-coded, such as the timings of operators or the set of operators used as part of the search. That is, hyper-parameters which we have set to arbitrary values in the current article can be evolved as part of the search process. Some hard-coded parameters require extensive changes to the code and architecture in order to be evolved – for instance, the number of slots in short-term memory. Future work will focus on estimating solutions while these hard-coded parameters are either manually varied across runs, or are varied using grid search.

Recently, the use of machine learning has allowed statistical models to be evaluated against large datasets in cognitive science [16]. The methodology described here differs from statistical approaches – here we develop solutions in terms of symbolic, information-processing architectures, and without a dependence on large datasets needed to train statistical models. Crucially, compared to statistical models based on machine learning approaches, solutions are easier to explain and interpret since they are expressed as a symbolic architecture and clearly defined operations performed by the architecture.

Opinions regarding the impact and role of methodologies that semi-automate aspects of scientific discovery vary in the literature. However, one clear benefit of these approaches is to provide an 'existence proof' – given a set of assumptions, we can demonstrate the existence of candidate models for our experimental data. This can then provide insights for the cognitive scientist to develop broader or more understandable theories. The methodology presented here is a potentially useful tool for cognitive scientists when developing theories of cognitive capacities. By generating a wide range of cognitive strategies/models, this methodology aids the cognitive scientist in considering *candidate models*, as opposed to fixating on predictions of a single model or comparisons between two models [14].

**Acknowledgment.** Funding from the European Research Council (ERC-ADG-835002-GEMS) is gratefully acknowledged.

# References

1. Bartlett, L., Pirrone, A., Javed, N., Lane, P.C., Gobet, F.: Genetic programming for developing simple cognitive models. In: Proceedings of the 45th Annual Meeting of the Cognitive Science Society, pp. 2833–2839 (2023)
2. Bartlett, L.K., Pirrone, A., Javed, N., Gobet, F.: Computational scientific discovery in psychology. Perspect. Psychol. Sci. **18**(1), 178–189 (2022)
3. Frias-Martinez, E., Gobet, F.: Automatic generation of cognitive theories using genetic programming. Mind. Mach. **17**(3), 287–309 (2007)
4. Geisler, W.S.: Sequential ideal-observer analysis of visual discriminations. Psychol. Rev. **96**(2), 267 (1989)
5. Gobet, F., Clarkson, G.: Chunks in expert memory: evidence for the magical number four... or is it two? Memory **12**(6), 732–747 (2004)
6. Holland, J.H.: Genetic algorithms. Sci. Am. **267**(1), 66–73 (1992)
7. Javed, N., Gobet, F.: On-the-fly simplification of genetic programming models. In: Proceedings of the 36th Annual ACM Symposium on Applied Computing, pp. 464–471 (2021)

8. King, R.D., et al.: The automation of science. Science **324**(5923), 85–89 (2009)
9. Koza, J.R.: Genetic Programming II: Automatic Discovery of Reusable Programs. MIT press, Cambridge (1994)
10. Lane, P.C., Bartlett, L., Javed, N., Pirrone, A., Gobet, F.: Evolving understandable cognitive models. In: Proceedings of the 20th International Conference on Cognitive Modelling, pp. 176–182 (2022)
11. Lee, M.D., Cummins, T.D.: Evidence accumulation in decision making: unifying the "take the best" and the "rational" models. Psychonomic Bull. Rev. **11**(2), 343–352 (2004)
12. Lieder, F., Krueger, P.M., Griffiths, T.: An automatic method for discovering rational heuristics for risky choice. In: 39th Annual Meeting of the Cognitive Science Society, pp. 742–747 (2017)
13. Marshall, J.A., Reina, A., Hay, C., Dussutour, A., Pirrone, A.: Magnitude-sensitive reaction times reveal non-linear time costs in multi-alternative decision-making. PLoS Comput. Biol. **18**(10), e1010523 (2022)
14. Meehl, P.E.: Theory-testing in psychology and physics: a methodological paradox. Philos. Sci. **34**(2), 103–115 (1967)
15. Newell, A.: Unified Theories of Cognition. Harvard University Press (1994)
16. Peterson, J.C., Bourgin, D.D., Agrawal, M., Reichman, D., Griffiths, T.L.: Using large-scale experiments and machine learning to discover theories of human decision-making. Science **372**(6547), 1209–1214 (2021)
17. Pirrone, A., Azab, H., Hayden, B.Y., Stafford, T., Marshall, J.A.: Evidence for the speed-value trade-off: human and monkey decision making is magnitude sensitive. Decision **5**(2), 129 (2018)
18. Pirrone, A., Reina, A., Stafford, T., Marshall, J.A., Gobet, F.: Magnitude-sensitivity: rethinking decision-making. Trends Cogn. Sci. **26**(1), 66–80 (2022)
19. Simon, H.A.: Models of Discovery, and Other Topics in the Methods of Science. Reidel, Dordrecht, Holland (1977)
20. Skirzyński, J., Becker, F., Lieder, F.: Automatic discovery of interpretable planning strategies. Mach. Learn. **110**, 2641–2683 (2021)
21. Tajima, S., Drugowitsch, J., Pouget, A.: Optimal policy for value-based decision-making. Nat. Commun. **7**(1), 1–12 (2016)
22. Teodorescu, A.R., Moran, R., Usher, M.: Absolutely relative or relatively absolute: violations of value invariance in human decision making. Psychonomic Bull. Rev,. **23**, 22–38 (2016)

# Bias in Recommender Systems: Item Price Perspective

Ramazan Esmeli[1]([✉]) [iD], Hassana Abdullahi[2], Mohamed Bader-El-Den[1], and Ansam Al-Gburi[1]

[1] School of Computing, University of Portsmouth, Portsmouth, UK
{ramazan.esmeli,mohamed.bader,ansam.al-gburi}@port.ac.uk
[2] Cardiff School of Management, Cardiff Metropolitan University, Cardiff, UK
HAbdullahi@cardiffmet.ac.uk

**Abstract.** Recommender systems are a widely studied application area of machine learning for businesses, particularly in the e-commerce domain. These systems play a critical role in identifying relevant products for customers based on their interests, but they are not without their challenges. One such challenge is the presence of bias in recommender systems, which can significantly impact the quality of the recommendations received by users. Algorithmic bias and popularity-based bias are two types of bias that have been extensively studied in the literature, and various debiasing methods have been proposed to mitigate their effects. However, there is still a need to investigate the mitigation of item popularity bias using product-related attributes. Specifically, this research aims to explore whether the utilization of price popularity can help reduce the popularity bias in recommender systems. To accomplish this goal, we propose mitigation approaches that adjust the implicit feedback rating in the dataset. We then conduct an extensive analysis on the modified implicit ratings using a real-world e-commerce dataset to evaluate the effectiveness of our debiasing approaches. Our experiments show that our methods are able to reduce the average popularity and average price popularity of recommended items while only slightly affecting the performance of the recommender model.

**Keywords:** Bias in recommender systems · Price bias · Popularity bias · Fairness in recommendation

## 1 Introduction

Recommender Systems (RS) are critical components of e-commerce platforms because they boost sales by providing personalised product recommendations that encourage shoppers to visit the product page and, as a result, make a purchase [28]. RS has applications outside of e-commerce, such as music [22], news [26], and movies [24]. Collaborative Filtering (CF) [15] is a well-known traditional recommendation model that has been utilised in almost all of these application

© The Author(s), under exclusive license to Springer Nature Switzerland AG 2023
M. Bramer and F. Stahl (Eds.): SGAI 2023, LNAI 14381, pp. 421–433, 2023.
https://doi.org/10.1007/978-3-031-47994-6_37

domains. The other methods, like content-based RS [21] and session-based RS (SBRS) [25], also have applications in these domains. The use of different recommendation models depends on the domain-specific characteristics and the available data.

Aside from these benefits, RS may face a number of challenges. For example, the bias problem in RS is investigated in some works [9,12], where the RS algorithm can favour certain items over others. This is because some products appear more frequently than others in a training dataset. As a result, the model tends to make recommendations based on popular items [4]. Another type of bias in recommendations could be regarding demographic distributions in the dataset. For example, uneven representation of a gender or age group in the dataset could be a reason for bias recommendations in favour of this group [11,16,19]. The bias toward popular items is well investigated in the literature. For instance, [1] developed algorithms to address the popularity bias in RS. [2] proposed a method to control popularity bias using a learning to rank algorithm in another paper. The main idea behind such methods was to include items that were less popular in the recommendation list as well as items that were more popular. These studies also emphasised the importance of retaining items that are of interest to the users. In other words, these methods are not intended to recommend an item that is outside the scope of the user's interests.

Building unbiased methods and re-ranking approaches are two current approaches to dealing with bias in recommender systems [29]. These methods are categorised under three main methods: Inverse Propensity Scoring (IPS) [9,23], which helps to rebalance the distribution of the dataset for model training, Causal Embedding [30] uses unbiased data for the model training to learn unbiased embedding, while Ranking Adjustment [9,29] applies re-ranking on the recommendation list after the model is built.

While previous studies in the literature have examined biases in recommender systems related to popularity and demographics, our understanding of biases towards item attributes such as pricing remains limited. The aim of this research is to investigate whether recommendations have a bias towards the pricing of items and to propose methods to mitigate popularity bias using price popularity. This study employs a real-world e-commerce dataset that includes item pricing information and session-item interactions to investigate price and product popularity biases in recommendation algorithms. We conduct experiments with various recommendation models using two versions of the datasets: the original and one with adjusted implicit ratings. A thorough analysis of the recommendation models' performance is performed to compare the average item popularity, average price popularity, and item price group diversity. Also, a comparison of the models in terms of recall, precision, and NDCG metrics is conducted to evaluate the impacts of the proposed solution on the performance of recommendation models.

## 2    Related Works

Discrimination and bias in user interaction, data, and algorithms have been extensively studied [17]. In general, recommendation output bias can be rooted in pre-existing biases in the input data. Moreover, as machine learning (ML) algorithms rely on data, they are highly susceptible to bias if the data used to train them contains biases. The algorithm can then amplify such bias, perpetuating the existing bias from the input data through the knock-on effect on user behavior. A recent study by [12] investigated the impact of continuous user interaction from various groups and how it contributes to bias in recommender systems. They found that repeated user interactions intensified existing bias, especially for users belonging to a minority group.

One prevalent type of bias is the popularity-based bias problem, where a few popular items tend to dominate the recommendations given to all users. This phenomenon leads to the neglect of the majority of other, less popular items, known as "long-tail" item bias. This bias is commonly observed in datasets with a small number of popular items (short head) and a large number of items with low popularity (long tail) [12]. As a result, this type of recommendation bias favors more popular items, while the least popular items are recommended the least, even if some users might prefer those less favored items [4,10,13].

Studies have shown that bias in recommender systems can limit their potential benefits, particularly in e-commerce, where long-tail items that are less recommended may actually be preferred by some users [6]. If recommender systems always recommend popular items, the user experience may suffer, especially for those who prefer niche items [9]. Other types of bias, such as bias towards certain subgroups or populations, have also been studied [23,27]. To address these biases, researchers have proposed various debiasing methods, including re-ranking, post-processing, and regularisation approaches [2,4,18]. For instance, [2] proposed a factorisation model that encodes long-tail item preferences to mitigate long-tail item bias. However, this approach does not consider the level of acceptability or preference of the user towards long-tail items. To overcome this limitation, [3] extended the model by allowing for penalisation of long-tail item promotion. In another approach, [27] used a value-aware ranking method, which employs a weighting strategy and enhanced group re-ranking, to address bias towards certain subgroups.

## 3    The Proposed Price-Debiassing Methods for Top-N Recommendations

### 3.1    Problem Definition

Given a dataset of session-item interactions $\mathcal{D} = (\mathbf{s}_i, \mathbf{v}_j, r_{ij})$, where $\mathbf{s}_i \in \mathcal{S}$ is a session, $\mathbf{v}_j \in \mathcal{V}$ is an item assigned to an item group $g(\mathbf{v}_j)$, and $r_{ij}$ is the implicit rating that indicates item $\mathbf{v}_j$ is interacted by user $\mathbf{u}_i$. The goal is to develop a recommendation algorithm $\mathcal{R}(\mathbf{s}_i, \mathcal{V})$ that recommends next items based on user preferences and identify if the recommendation algorithm $\mathcal{R}$ is exhibiting price category popularity bias and item popularity bias, which can be defined as the tendency of the algorithm to disproportionately recommend items from popular items and certain price categories over others. Then, we proposed an adjusted implicit rating method that we updated implicit rating $r_{ij}$ based on item's price popularity as well as item's popularity.

## 3.2    Introducing Implicit Rating Adjusting

To adjust the implicit rating in the dataset, we utilise popularity of the item's attribute as well. For example, $i$ is item, $i_{pop}$ is item's popularity and $i_{price}$ is item's price. We calculate the popularity of $i_{price}$ in the dataset and is represented as $i_{pricepop}$. Based on $i_{pop}$ and $i_{pricepop}$ information, an item group $\epsilon\{0,1\}$ is found and assigned to the item using clustering, we call this as item label $i_l$. $i_l$ is used to adjust implicit feedback. In order to penalise popular item group, 0 is assigned for label of items which are in larger group size. The original implicit feedback is shown as in Eq. 1 and updated implicit ratings are shown in Eq. 2 and Eq. 3.

$$rating(s,i) = \begin{cases} 1 & \text{if item } i \text{ is interacted in session} s \\ 0 & \text{otherwise} \end{cases} \tag{1}$$

In Eq. 2, $L_i\epsilon\{0,1\}$ shows the group label assigned for item $i$. In this method, we use direct group labels assigned to the items as implicit ratings. As a result, we call this method $Direct_i$.

$$r_1(s,i) = \begin{cases} i_l & \text{if item } i \text{ is interacted in session } s \\ 0 & \text{otherwise} \end{cases} \tag{2}$$

In Eq. 3, the implicit rating is updated with the opposite of the assigned group label. Therefore, we call this method $Adjusted_i$.

$$r_2(s,i) = \begin{cases} 1 - i_l & \text{if item } i \text{ is interacted in session } s \\ 0 & \text{otherwise} \end{cases} \tag{3}$$

Overall, after updating the implicit ratings, we build the models for each case and examine model outcomes using the metrics below to see the effect of our method on handling item and price popularity bias in the recommendations.

The debiasing procedure 1 works by incorporating the popularity value of items and items' price into the recommendation models and can be used to adjust the ranking of the items. This ranking method could sacrifice some level of accuracy but could help to mitigate the bias in recommendation systems and increase the diversity of the recommendations.

---

**Algorithm 1.** Debiasing Procedure

---

1: **procedure** RATING SCORE$(S, I)$

> $\triangleright$ $S$: Sessions
> $\triangleright$ $I$: Items
> $\triangleright$ $i_{price}$: Item price

2:    $i_{pricepop} \leftarrow$ Find price popularity scores of each item based on $i_{price}$    $\triangleright$ using unique price of items in the dataset

3:    $i_{pop} \leftarrow$ Find item popularity scores of each item $\triangleright$ using user-item interactions in the dataset

4:    $Cluster(i_{pricepop}, i_{pop}) \leftarrow$ Run clustering    $\triangleright$ using $i_{pricepop}$ and $i_{pop}$, assign group labels for each item

5:    $r_1(S, I) \leftarrow$ Adjust ratings using Eq. 2

6:    $r_2(S, I) \leftarrow$ Adjust ratings using Eq. 3

7:    **return** $r1, r2$

8: **end procedure**

---

## 4    Dataset Analysis

We use anonymised real-world dataset collected from an e-commerce business by a content personalisation company[1]. The dataset includes 1436099 interactions from 557976 unique sessions and 17936 unique items. In this context, unique sessions refers to each individual session for a user while unique items refers to distinct products available in the dataset. We analyse the number of items interacted in the sessions and distribution of sizes among the sessions with the highest 10,000 number of item interactions to eliminate the sessions with less interacted items. The analysis of the dataset reveals that 54% (5456) of the sessions from this group exhibit between 14–20 interactions. In contrast, when the analysis is applied to all sessions, it is found that approximately 56% of the sessions have only one item interaction.

The Figs. 1a and 1b aim to compare and identify any price variations between the prices of highly popular products and those of unique products by analysing their price distributions. The analysis found that the most common price among unique products was £ 9.99, while the most prevalent price among highly popular products was £ 99.99. The findings reveal that despite the majority of products in e-commerce being priced at £ 9.99, users tend to show more interest in products priced at £ 99.99.

---

[1] freshrelevance.com.

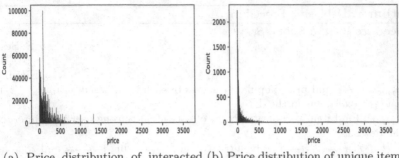

(a) Price distribution of interacted items

(b) Price distribution of unique items in the dataset

**Fig. 1.** Price distribution in the dataset

# 5    Experiments, Results and Discussion

## 5.1    Aim of Experiments

The proposed experiments have two key aims. Firstly, we aim to investigate whether there is a correlation between a product's price and its popularity in recommender systems (RS). Secondly, we will investigate the effect of using price popularity as a penalty score to mitigate bias towards popular items and popular prices on the performance of RS. Through this study, we aim to provide a deeper understanding of how popular items and prices can impact recommendation algorithms and to propose a framework for mitigating such biases.

## 5.2    Experimental Design

**Clustering.** To achieve our goals, we compute a popularity score for each item ($i_{pop}$) and its price ($i_{pricepop}$) in the dataset. Based on this data about the items, we run clustering to have two groups of items to separate items with interrelated connection between item and price popularity. For clustering method, we used Kmeans [5] clustering method due to its simplicity and well known applicability, which is implemented in scikit-learn [20] library The parameters used are: Number of clusters (k): 2, maximum number of iterations ($max_{iter}$): 300, tolerance for stopping criteria ($tol$): 0.0001, method for initialisation of centroids ($init$): "k-means++", distance metric ($metric$): "Euclidean".

**Recommendation Models.** For the recommendation model, we use RankALS to learn the ranking of items based on pair-wise comparisons. The algorithm works by iteratively comparing and adjusting the scores of pairs of items, with the aim of achieving an optimal ranking. It uses an alternating least squares (ALS) optimisation technique to iteratively improve the ranking. We used the RankALS model implemented by [8] using Python. The model settings are kept as in the default setting. We modify these models by adding a rating adjusting method, which is explained in the methodology section. For evaluation, the dataset is split into a training and a testing dataset. The test dataset consists of 20% of the interactions randomly selected for each session. The remaining parts are used for training. To keep consistency throughout the experiments, we saved the train and test splits to be used in model training and testing stages with different settings. Considered models in this study are:

*Base*: This model is trained using the original implicit rating on the dataset.
*Direct$_i$*: This model is trained adjusted implicit rating which is assigned as item label ($i_l$).
*Adjusted$_i$*: This model is trained replaced implicit rating which is opposite of assigned item label ($i_l$).

**Metrics.** We used the following metrics to assess item and price popularity:
*Average Item Popularity (AIP):* This metric calculates average popularity of recommended items for a given recommendation list [3,14].

$$AIP = \frac{1}{S_t} \sum_{s \in S_t} \frac{\sum_{i \in I_s} i_{pop}}{|I_s|} \tag{4}$$

where $I_s$ is items in session $s$ where $s$ is a session in selected test sessions $S_t$, $i_{pop}$ is number of times item $i$ has been interacted in the training set (popularity score).

*Average Price Popularity (APP):* We propose this metric to measure the average price popularity of recommended items for a given recommendation list.

$$APP = \frac{1}{S_t} \sum_{s \in S_t} \frac{\sum_{i \in I_s} i_{pricepop}}{|I_s|} \tag{5}$$

where $I_s$ is items in session $s$, $i_{pricepop}$ is number of times item's price ($i_{price}$) has been appeared in the training set (popularity scores). It is important to note that $i_{pricepop}$ is determined based solely by the unique item price data in the dataset and not by any interaction information.

*Item Coverage:* Item coverage in a RS refers to the percentage of items in the item set that are recommended by the model. It measures the percentage of items in the test set that are recommended by the model. A high item coverage indicates that the model makes recommendations for a large number of items, while a low item coverage shows that the model makes recommendations for a small portion of the test set items.

$$Average\ Coverage = \frac{\sum_{s \in S_t} Coverage_s}{|S_t|} \tag{6}$$

where $Coverage_s$ shows the coverage of session $s$, defined as the number of unique items recommended in at least one in the top-k recommendation lists for

$s$ divided to all number of unique items in the dataset, $S_t$ is the test session, and $|S_t|$ is the number of test sessions. Ranking accuracy is evaluated using Normalised Discounted Cumulative Gain (NDCG), Precision, and Recall metrics. Higher scores for these metrics are generally regarded as indicating improved ranking [14]. *Precision:* measures the ratio of recommended items that are relevant. *Recall:* measures the proportion of relevant items that have been recommended. *NDCG:* assesses the effectiveness of the recommended item order.

## 5.3   Results

Our aim in this study was to investigate price popularity bias in recommender systems, and the correlation between recommendation bias in popular items and popular prices. Moreover, we aimed to propose approaches to mitigate price popularity with minimum sacrificing from the model effectiveness. In order to satisfy these aims, first we showed the price popularity and item popularity distribution in the clusters. Figure 2a shows the cluster labelled with 0 is dominant in the dataset, while in terms of average price popularity, the products in cluster 1 has higher price popularity. We also examine the connections between item price and popularity for the clusters. Figure 2b shows the item price and its popularity in the dataset. It can be observed that items which have higher price popularity are labelled as 1, despite the fact that the number of items in this group is less than the size of cluster 0.

We further investigated the distribution of item prices and popularity in the clusters. Figures 2c and 2d illustrate a kernel density estimate (KDE) of price popularity and item popularity for clusters, which can be useful for understanding the distribution of values. The figures suggest that in cluster 0, the density of price popularity is concentrated mostly below 5000, while in cluster 1, the majority of the price popularity is above 5000.

After cluster label identification, we run the models with different rating settings by following the procedure in Algorithm 1. We reported the average item and price popularity scores and item coverage for each model in the Table 1. To check impact of the proposed methods on the model effectiveness scores, we also reported recall, precision, and NDCG scores.

It can be seen from the experimental results that both $Direct_i$ and $Adjusted_i$ significantly reduced the average item popularity (AIP) in comparison to the base model. AIP scores in @10 and @20 is better in $Adjusted_i$ model than $Direct_i$. In this category, a lower score means a higher chance of finding less popular items in recommendations. As expected, Mostpop RS recommends the most popular items; accordingly, the highest AIP scores are observed in this model.

In terms of Item coverage, $Direct_i$ produces significantly highest percentages in comparision to $Adjusted_i$ and $Base$ models. As high item coverage is desired, we can conclude from the results that $Direct_i$ is the best one for this metric. A new metric we introduced in this study is average price popularity (APP), which indicates the recommended items' price popularity score. The $Direct_i$ model provided items recommendations that had lower $APP$ in comparison to other models. The highest score in this group was observed for $Base$ model.

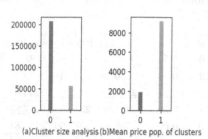
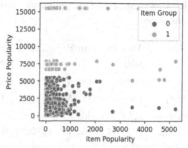

(a) Cluster size and average price popularity in the clusters

(b) Item price and price popularity based on the clusters

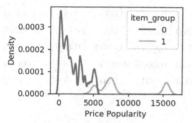
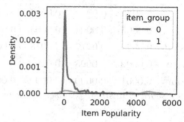

(c) Price popularity density analysis for clusters

(d) Item popularity density analysis for clusters

**Fig. 2.** Item and price analysis in clusters

However, even $Adjusted_i$ model was providing less popular item recommendations comparing to $Direct_i$ model for cutoff @10, @20, the $APP$ was not in the same line. This suggests that decreasing the recommendation of popular items may not have the same impact on the $APP$ of the recommended items. Thus, it is possible for an item to have a price that is popular within the dataset, but for the item itself to have low popularity.

We also examined the performance sacrifice after implementing our methods. In Table 1, the models evaluated in terms of Precision, Recall and NDCG. Higher values of these metrics are better for model performance. As expected, attempts to mitigate popularity bias can cause reducing on the models' effectiveness [1,7]. The results show that $Direct_i$ has more effect on reducing model's performance comparing to $Adjusted_i$. As a result of the rating adjustment in $Direct_i$, more ratings are updated (Fig. 2a), and this may constrain the model ability to learn the latent factors underlying user-item interactions. Meanwhile, the $Adjusted_i$ model has almost comparable effectiveness to the $Base$ model. In $Adjusted_i$, items with the cluster label 1 were penalised due to the fact that they had the highest popularity in this cluster group. Additionally, the number of impacted user-item ratings was significantly smaller in the $Adjusted_i$ model compared to our previous approach, as shown in Fig. 2a.

**Table 1.** Comparison of proposed models' performance for mitigating bias towards popular price

| Model | Average Item Popularity↓ | | | Item coverage↑ | | | Average Price Popularity↓ | | |
|---|---|---|---|---|---|---|---|---|---|
| | @10 | @20 | @50 | @10 | @20 | @50 | @10 | @20 | @50 |
| Base | 676.16 | 514.14 | 351.26 | 0.07 | 0.12 | 0.23 | 2610.30 | 2530.31 | 2379.78 |
| $Direct_i$ | 448.59 | 341.35 | <u>223.24</u> | <u>0.51</u> | <u>0.60</u> | <u>0.71</u> | <u>2369.58</u> | <u>2332.64</u> | 2246.58 |
| $Adjusted_i$ | <u>401.01</u> | <u>333.79</u> | 251.49 | 0.12 | 0.18 | 0.29 | 2484.88 | 2357.64 | <u>2237.86</u> |
| Mostpop | 2920.34 | 2031.77 | 1170.00 | 0.00 | 0.00 | 0.00 | 2558.84 | 2377.96 | 2109.81 |
| Random | 10.00 | 20.00 | 50.00 | 0.96 | 0.96 | 0.96 | 1993.55 | 2005.29 | 2005.62 |
| Model | Precision↑ | | | Recall↑ | | | NDCG ↑ | | |
| | @10 | @20 | @50 | @10 | @20 | @50 | @10 | @20 | @50 |
| Base | <u>0.0023</u> | <u>0.0019</u> | <u>0.0014</u> | <u>0.0091</u> | <u>0.0150</u> | <u>0.0277</u> | <u>0.0058</u> | <u>0.0077</u> | <u>0.0110</u> |
| $Direct_i$ | 0.0005 | 0.0004 | 0.0003 | 0.0046 | 0.0070 | 0.0122 | 0.0024 | 0.0030 | 0.0041 |
| $Adjusted_i$ | 0.0020 | 0.0017 | 0.0013 | 0.0089 | 0.0146 | <u>0.0277</u> | 0.0054 | 0.0072 | 0.0105 |
| Mostpop | 0.0002 | 0.0003 | 0.0004 | 0.0008 | 0.0026 | 0.0086 | 0.0004 | 0.0010 | 0.0024 |
| Random | 0.0001 | 0.0000 | 0.0000 | 0.0003 | 0.0004 | 0.0011 | 0.0001 | 0.0002 | 0.0003 |

↑: *higher score is desired,* ↓: *lower score is desired.*

It is also observed that *AIP* score of *Random* RS model is the lowest compared to the other models. However, in terms of the effectiveness metrics (precision, recall and NDCG), the *Random* RS model performs poorly. Therefore, this model is unsuitable for application in this dataset. Overall experimental results from $Adjusted_i$ model indicate that by incorporating a penalisation term considering both item and price popularity in the adjustment of the implicit rating and by using this adjusted implicit rating as the input for the recommendation algorithm, we were able to effectively reduce both price popularity bias and item popularity bias while maintaining a comparable level of recommendation efficiency as compared to the base model. This suggests that our proposed method effectively mitigates the aforementioned biases with minimal sacrifice to recommendation performance.

# 6   Conclusion and Future Works

The popularity bias in recommendation systems (RS) presents a significant challenge as it can result in an unequal distribution of attention among items. This occurs when an RS frequently recommends popular items, leading to an increase in their interactions and resulting in them being recommended even more frequently. This creates a self-reinforcing cycle where less popular items are less likely to be recommended and, therefore, less likely to receive interactions. As a result, users may only be exposed to a limited number of products, reducing the diversity of the recommendation.

In this work to mitigate the popularity bias for item and price, we designed rating adjustment methods. This method depends on item popularity and item's price popularity in the dataset. In this work, we utilised a K-means clustering method to have two item groups by considering item popularity and price popularity of items as factors. After thorough analysis of the item popularity and price popularity of items distributions in the clusters, we assigned item groups for each item as a factor for adjusting implicit ratings. We use RankALS recommendation model as base model. We employed an e-commerce dataset to assess the success of our approach. Our results showed that the $Adjusted_i$ model was able to reduce the item and price popularity bias in recommendations while only slightly sacrificing model effectiveness. One of the limitations of our approach is that it was only tested on a single dataset, and further validation using additional datasets is needed to establish the robustness of the method. Further research could explore the interplay of other factors that may contribute to popularity bias. Additionally, different numbers of clusters and diverse rating strategies could be generated based on the combination of items within each cluster.

# References

1. Abdollahpouri, H.: Popularity bias in ranking and recommendation. In: Proceedings of the 2019 AAAI/ACM Conference on AI, Ethics, and Society, pp. 529–530 (2019)
2. Abdollahpouri, H., Burke, R., Mobasher, B.: Controlling popularity bias in learning-to-rank recommendation. In: Proceedings of the Eleventh ACM Conference on Recommender Systems, pp. 42–46 (2017)
3. Abdollahpouri, H., Burke, R., Mobasher, D.: Managing popularity bias in recommender systems with personalized re-ranking. In: The Thirty-Second International Flairs Conference (2019)
4. Abdollahpouri, H., Mansoury, M., Burke, R., Mobasher, B., Malthouse, E.: User-centered evaluation of popularity bias in recommender systems. In: Proceedings of the 29th ACM Conference on User Modeling, Adaptation and Personalization, pp. 119–129 (2021)
5. Ahmed, M., Seraj, R., Islam, S.M.S.: The k-means algorithm: a comprehensive survey and performance evaluation. Electronics 9(8), 1295 (2020)
6. Baeza-Yates, R.: Bias in search and recommender systems. In: Proceedings of the 14th ACM Conference on Recommender Systems, p. 2 (2020)
7. Boratto, L., Fenu, G., Marras, M.: Connecting user and item perspectives in popularity debiasing for collaborative recommendation. Inf. Process. Manag. 58(1), 102387 (2021)
8. Boratto, L., Fenu, G., Marras, M.: Interplay between upsampling and regularization for provider fairness in recommender systems. User Model. User-Adap. Inter. 31(3), 421–455 (2021)
9. Chen, J., Dong, H., Wang, X., Feng, F., Wang, M., He, X.: Bias and debias in recommender system: a survey and future directions. arXiv preprint arXiv:2010.03240 (2020)
10. Ciampaglia, G.L., Nematzadeh, A., Menczer, F., Flammini, A.: How algorithmic popularity bias hinders or promotes quality. Sci. Rep. 8(1), 15951 (2018)
11. Ekstrand, M.D., et al.: All the cool kids, how do they fit in?: popularity and demographic biases in recommender evaluation and effectiveness. In: Conference on Fairness, Accountability and Transparency, pp. 172–186. PMLR (2018)

12. Elahi, M., Kholgh, D.K., Kiarostami, M.S., Saghari, S., Rad, S.P., Tkalčič, M.: Investigating the impact of recommender systems on user-based and item-based popularity bias. Inf. Process. Manag. **58**(5), 102655 (2021)
13. Introna, L., Nissenbaum, H.: Defining the web: the politics of search engines. Computer **33**(1), 54–62 (2000)
14. Klimashevskaia, A., Elahi, M., Jannach, D., Trattner, C., Skjærven, L.: Mitigating popularity bias in recommendation: potential and limits of calibration approaches. In: Boratto, L., Faralli, S., Marras, M., Stilo, G. (eds.) BIAS 2022. CCIS, vol. 1610, pp. 82–90. Springer, Cham (2022)
15. Koren, Y., Rendle, S., Bell, R.: Advances in collaborative filtering. In: Ricci, F., Rokach, L., Shapira, B. (eds.) Recommender Systems Handbook, pp. 91–142. Springer, New York (2022). https://doi.org/10.1007/978-1-0716-2197-4_3
16. Lesota, O., et al.: Analyzing item popularity bias of music recommender systems: are different genders equally affected? In: Proceedings of the 15th ACM Conference on Recommender Systems, pp. 601–606 (2021)
17. Mehrabi, N., Morstatter, F., Saxena, N., Lerman, K., Galstyan, A.: A survey on bias and fairness in machine learning. ACM Comput. Surv. (CSUR) **54**(6), 1–35 (2021)
18. Naghiaei, M., Rahmani, H.A., Deldjoo, Y.: CPFair: personalized consumer and producer fairness re-ranking for recommender systems. In: Proceedings of the 45th International ACM SIGIR Conference on Research and Development in Information Retrieval, pp. 770–779 (2022)
19. Neophytou, N., Mitra, B., Stinson, C.: Revisiting popularity and demographic biases in recommender evaluation and effectiveness. In: Hagen, M., et al. (eds.) ECIR 2022. LNCS, vol. 13185, pp. 641–654. Springer, Cham (2022). https://doi.org/10.1007/978-3-030-99736-6_43
20. Pedregosa, F., et al.: Scikit-learn: machine learning in Python. J. Mach. Learn. Res. **12**, 2825–2830 (2011)
21. Raj, N.S., Renumol, V.: A systematic literature review on adaptive content recommenders in personalized learning environments from 2015 to 2020. J. Comput. Educ. **9**(1), 113–148 (2022)
22. Schedl, M., Zamani, H., Chen, C.W., Deldjoo, Y., Elahi, M.: Current challenges and visions in music recommender systems research. Int. J. Multimed. Inf. Retrieval **7**, 95–116 (2018)
23. Schnabel, T., Swaminathan, A., Singh, A., Chandak, N., Joachims, T.: Recommendations as treatments: debiasing learning and evaluation. In: International Conference on Machine Learning, pp. 1670–1679. PMLR (2016)
24. Tang, M.C., Liao, I.H.: Preference diversity and openness to novelty: scales construction from the perspective of movie recommendation. J. Am. Soc. Inf. Sci. **73**(9), 1222–1235 (2022)
25. Wang, S., Zhang, Q., Hu, L., Zhang, X., Wang, Y., Aggarwal, C.: Sequential/session-based recommendations: challenges, approaches, applications and opportunities. In: Proceedings of the 45th International ACM SIGIR Conference on Research and Development in Information Retrieval, pp. 3425–3428 (2022)
26. Wu, C., Wu, F., Huang, Y., Xie, X.: Personalized news recommendation: methods and challenges. ACM Trans. Inf. Syst. **41**(1), 1–50 (2023)
27. Yalcin, E., Bilge, A.: Investigating and counteracting popularity bias in group recommendations. Inf. Process. Manag. **58**(5), 102608 (2021)
28. Yang, X.: Influence of informational factors on purchase intention in social recommender systems. Online Inf. Rev. **44**(2), 417–431 (2020)

29. Zhang, Y., et al.: Causal intervention for leveraging popularity bias in recommendation. In: Proceedings of the 44th International ACM SIGIR Conference on Research and Development in Information Retrieval, pp. 11–20 (2021)
30. Zheng, Y., Gao, C., Li, X., He, X., Li, Y., Jin, D.: Disentangling user interest and popularity bias for recommendation with causal embedding. arXiv preprint arXiv:2006.11011, p. 64 (2020)

# Other AI Applications

# Automating Question Generation From Educational Text

Ayan Kumar Bhowmick(✉), Ashish Jagmohan, Aditya Vempaty,
Prasenjit Dey, Leigh Hall, Jeremy Hartman, Ravi Kokku,
and Hema Maheshwari

Merlyn Mind Inc., New York City, NY 10174, USA
{ayan,ashish,aditya,prasenjit,leigh,jeremy,ravi,hema}@merlyn.org

**Abstract.** The use of question-based activities (QBAs) is wide-spread in education, traditionally forming an integral part of the learning and assessment process. In this paper, we design and evaluate an automated question generation tool for formative and summative assessment in schools. We present an expert survey of one hundred and four teachers, demonstrating the need for automated generation of QBAs, as a tool that can significantly reduce the workload of teachers and facilitate personalized learning experiences. Leveraging the recent advancements in generative AI, we then present a modular framework employing transformer based language models for automatic generation of multiple-choice questions (MCQs) from textual content. The presented solution, with distinct modules for question generation, correct answer prediction, and distractor formulation, enables us to evaluate different language models and generation techniques. Finally, we perform an extensive quantitative and qualitative evaluation, demonstrating trade-offs in the use of different techniques and models.

**Keywords:** Automatic question generation · Large language models · Generative AI · Distractors · Question-based activities · Multiple-choice questions

## 1 Introduction

Recent advancements in generative artificial intelligence (AI) techniques [18], propelled by the development of large language models (LLMs) [9,19], have demonstrated remarkable capabilities in a wide array of natural-language processing tasks. State-of-the-art models such as ChatGPT and GPT-4 [24] have shown promising results in tasks like text summarization, translation, and question answering, setting a new benchmark for natural language understanding. These breakthroughs have sparked a growing interest in leveraging the potential of generative AI to address challenges and automate tasks in several domains. In particular, education is expected to be one of the sectors most impacted by generative AI[1].

---

[1] https://tinyurl.com/97e7bwv3.

M. Bramer and F. Stahl (Eds.): SGAI 2023, LNAI 14381, pp. 437–450, 2023.
https://doi.org/10.1007/978-3-031-47994-6_38

Generative AI has several applications in education, such as developing conversational agents to analyze student data and interactions for personalized feedback and guiding students through learning materials. It can also help automate time-consuming administrative tasks for teachers and analyze individual student performance for providing personalized feedback on necessary improvements, thereby saving teachers a significant amount of time and allowing them to maximize their focus on in-classroom teaching. While generative AI should not replace teachers, it can assist them in augmenting their abilities to enhance the learning experience for students.

Automated question generation for assessments in the form of question-based activities (QBAs) [1,2] holds significant importance in modern classrooms as it alleviates teachers' burden, allowing for more focus on student-centered endeavors. AI-driven techniques for automated question generation can greatly simplify the process of generating meaningful and relevant questions from textual educational material. This would facilitate personalized and engaging learning experiences, efficient evaluation of students' understanding, targeted feedback, and improved educational outcomes for students.

In this paper, we first conduct a survey of teachers to understand the importance of QBAs and the challenges faced in preparing them. Based on the survey insights, we leverage recent generative AI advancements, we develop a system for automatically generating multiple-choice questions (MCQs) from educational text. We follow a modular approach for automatic generation of MCQs with separate modules for question generation, correct answer pre- diction and distractor formulation, implemented using transformer based language models such as T5 and GPT-3. Our goal is to create a scalable, reliable, and privacy-preserving question generation framework, prioritizing these aspects over high accuracy for the educational domain. The modular approach enhances the proposed system's adaptability and efficiency, catering to various educational requirements. Compared to state-of-the-art LLMs such as GPT-4 which could generate MCQs of superior quality, smaller models such as T5 and GPT-3 may trade off MCQ quality. Nevertheless, teachers can always refine the generated MCQs to better suit their needs but concerns related to latency, privacy and reliability (GPT-4 suffers from these) remain vital and non-negotiable in the field of education.

The proposed modular framework for MCQ generation offers various benefits, including independent development and optimization of each module and integration of diverse language models. This helps to accommodate the strengths and minimize the limitations of individual models in generating various MCQ components, while making the framework adaptable and future-proof. This flexibility also enhances the overall MCQ quality and achieves a wide range of educational objectives. Thus, the proposed framework successfully combines the advantages of T5, GPT-3, and other transformer based language models, resulting in a robust, scalable, and highly customizable MCQ generation system.

Our quantitative evaluation shows that the proposed modular MCQ generation framework generates high quality question text with decent grammar and well-formedness. It also has reasonably good accuracy in predicting correct answers. Qualitative evaluation conducted by human annotators further substantiates the quality of questions, answers, and effectiveness of the generated distractors. The annotators found that distractors were indistinguishable from correct answers, making it challenging to guess the correct option based on MCQ structure.

In short, major contributions of this paper include: (a) conducting a survey of teachers to understand the need for an AI-assisted question generation system for QBAs to help teachers, (b) proposing an end-to-end AI Question Generation ($QGen$) system for generating relevant and content grounded MCQs from educational text, (c) creating a flexible framework with individual modules accommodating different generative models for generating questions, answers and distractors, and (d) evaluating the $QGen$ system both quantitatively and qualitatively, demonstrating its effectiveness in creating high quality MCQs.

## 2    Question-Based Activities in Education

There is a wealth of literature that explores how formative and summative assessments can improve learning outcomes by measuring learner progress along various objectives and identifying gaps [3,23]. While assessments can take a variety of forms (essays, discussions, surveys etc.), question-based activities (QBAs) have traditionally been an integral part of assessment and the learning process. QBA's are all activities that invite students to answer questions, which can include unit tests, quizzes, games, exit tickets, study or practice sessions, small group discussions and worksheets. These activities may be used to help students learn concepts and skills, as well as to assess their knowledge and abilities.

In order to better understand the role of QBAs in the modern classroom, we conducted a survey on Survey Monkey that examined how teachers use QBAs in their instruction. One hundred and four teachers in grades three through eight participated. All teachers taught English language arts, science, and/or social studies. The survey included a range of queries examining: (i) How frequently do teachers use QBAs, (b) what outcomes are teachers trying to achieve by using QBAs, (iii) What sources, materials and tools do they use to create their QBAs? (iv) How much time do teachers spend creating QBAs, and (v) what challenges do teachers experience with QBAs?

Respondents answered 33 questions that were a mix of multiple-choice and written responses. The written responses were analyzed following the recommendations in [12,20]. We first analyzed each question individually. Responses were read repeatedly in order to identify patterns within them. We looked across pattern codes to determine what assertions could be made about each of the areas we were investigating. Once assertions had been identified, we reread the pattern codes and determined which assertion, if any, they served as evidence for. Pattern codes were then grouped under the appropriate assertion. The survey resulted in several interesting findings, that are summarized below.

**Frequency of Usage and Outcomes**: Fig. 1 confirms the ubiquity of QBAs in instruction. 28% teachers reported using QBAs two-three times a week, and

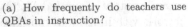

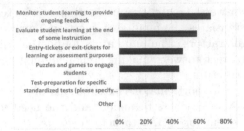

(a) How frequently do teachers use QBAs in instruction?

(b) What outcomes are teachers trying to achieve?

**Fig. 1.** Frequency of QBA usage in classroom instruction, and desired outcomes

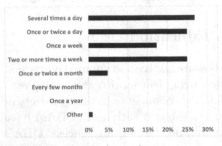

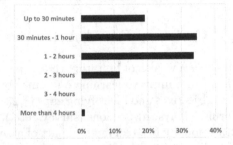

(a) How frequently do teachers prepare QBAs?

(b) How much time is spent on each prep session?

**Fig. 2.** Frequency and time spent on QBA preparation.

37% reported using them daily. While teachers' purposes for using QBAs varied, 70% were using them to monitor student learning and provide ongoing feedback while 59% were using them as a way to evaluate student learning after a set period of instruction. Other uses of QBAs included: (a) entry and/or exit tickets (used by 48% of teachers), (b) creating puzzles and games to engage students (45% of teachers) and (c)standardized test preparation (43%). In summary, our data suggests that QBA usage is widespread in the classroom and that teachers use them to achieve a variety of objectives.

**Creation Time**: Fig. 2 shows how, despite (or perhaps because of) the diversity of available sources, teachers still spend considerable amount of time on preparing QBAs. First, 52% reported spending time on preparing QBAs at least daily. Out of that, 27% reported working on QBAs multiple times daily. Additionally, 25% reported working on QBAs multiple times a week. Further, 69% of teachers reported spending 30 min to two hours per session of QBA preparation. This suggests that most teachers allocate multiple days a week, at a minimum of 30 min per session, to creating QBAs. This can result in teachers spending a minimum of 2.5 h per week on creating QBAs.

**Challenges**: As Fig. 3 shows, teachers still experienced challenges in preparing QBAs despite the amount of time they spent on them. 63% noted they did not have enough time to prepare questions for class, making preparation time the single most significant reported challenge. 38% noted that they did not have access to quality question preparing resources, and 31% said there was a lack of personalized and adaptive question-asking resources that would work for each class.

In short, we can summarize the main findings of the survey as follows: (i) QBA usage remains ubiquitous for instruction, (ii) Teachers spend significant amounts of time on preparing QBAs, and (iii) time, sources and question adaptivity remain challenging. Given that AI can potentially help with mitigating all of these, the survey included several queries on AI use, which yielded another important set of insights.

**AI Use**: Most surveyed teachers (82%) had not used an AI tool to generate QBAs in the past. Of those who had, most had used tools that retrieved questions from question-banks (rather than create questions from content) while more than 50% of such teachers reported that such tools saved time. Interestingly, almost 60% of teachers had, currently or in the past, had human assistants, and 70% of such teachers used their human assistants to create QBAs.

**Requirements and Concerns**: Most teachers (> 70%) reported interest in using AI tools to generate questions for QBAs, believing that such tools could save time, generate real-time questions that would seamlessly blend with their instruction, and improve question diversity and personalization. Teachers expressed strong preferences in having such tools integrated with lesson content and existing digital tools.

Based on the above, we believe that AI generated QBAs can fill an important gap for teachers, freeing them up for other instructional tasks, and teachers are open to such AI assistance. In the remainder of this paper, we will describe the AI question-generation system we have built, based on the insights above.

## 3 Solution Architecture

In this section, we describe the proposed Question Generation system. The architecture of our proposed AI **Q**uestion **Gen**eration system (henceforth, we will refer to it as *QGen*) is shown in Fig. 4. As shown in the figure, *QGen* takes either a topic (eg. "American Civil War", "Mahatma Gandhi" etc.) or a content (we use the terms 'context' and 'content' interchangeably throughout the paper), which is usually a body of text extracted from a given source, (eg. a summary paragraph from Wikipedia page of "Mahatma Gandhi" or a text snippet from the corresponding page of "Mahatma Gandhi" in https://www.history.com/) as input modalities. *QGen* generates a set of multiple-choice questions, grounded in the input context, and returns them as output. Each generated multiple-choice question (MCQ) has three components - the question text, the correct answer text (that forms one of the $n$ options of the MCQ) and a set of $n-1$ distractors

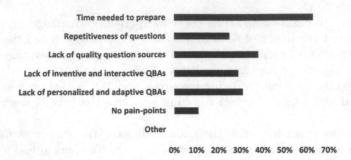

**Fig. 3.** Key challenges faced by teachers in creating QBAs.

that forms the remaining options of the MCQ. The correct answer and the set of distractors might appear in any random order in the generated MCQ. *QGen* comprises of five modules to generate MCQs, described in subsequent sections.

### 3.1  Module 0: Content Extraction from Topic

This module takes a topic as input and extracts a piece of text which may range from a few sentences to a paragraph or a sequence of multiple paragraphs retrieved from a given source (eg. school repository, Wikipedia, https://www. history.com/ etc.). This extracted text is then returned as the context to be used as input for question generation. Note that this step is ignored if topic is not provided as input by the end user.

### 3.2  Module 1: Question Generation from Content

This module takes the context (either provided by the end user or generated from some topic in Module 0) as input and generates a set of natural-language questions relevant and grounded to the context. We perform both quantitative and qualitative evaluation (based on human judgement) of the quality of generated questions. We use the following metrics to quantitatively evaluate the quality of generated questions:

a. **Perplexity:** Perplexity (PPL) is a standard metric used for evaluating the quality of text generated using language models [4]. We compute the perplexity of each question text generated in Module 1 of *QGen* to evaluate their quality. In general, lower the perplexity value of a question, better is its quality.

b. **Query well-formedness:** This metric evaluates the well-formedness score of a generated question [8] i.e. if the question is incomplete or grammatically correct. The value of query well-formedness varies in the range of [0, 1]. Higher the value of well-formedness, better is the question quality.

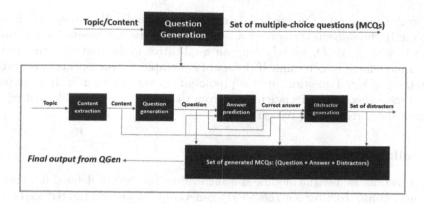

**Fig. 4.** Architectural flow of the proposed Question Generation system (QGen)

### 3.3 Module 2: Correct Answer Prediction from Content for a Generated Question

For each question generated in Module 1, we predict the correct answer in Module 2 by identifying the answer span within the content from which the question was generated. This task is similar to a closed domain factual question answering system [14]. We perform both quantitative and qualitative evaluation (based on human judgement) to determine the correctness of the predicted answer to a generated question. We rely on the following metrics to quantitatively evaluate the correctness of the predicted answer given the reference answer string:

a. **Exact Match:** Exact Match (EM) [5] is a binary metric whose value is equal to 1 if the predicted correct answer string is exactly the same as the reference correct answer string, otherwise its value is equal to 0.
b. **F1-score:** This metric denotes the extent of word overlap [5] between predicted and reference correct answer strings with value in the range of $[0, 1]$.
c. **ROUGE:** This is a suite of metrics to evaluate the quality of the predicted correct answer string by measuring its correspondence with a reference correct answer string [21] in terms of unigram, bigram and n-gram overlaps. The metric values range between $[0, 1]$.

### 3.4 Module 3: Distractor Generation

This is the last module of *QGen* that corresponds to the generation of the set of distractors for a given question generated in Module 1. Distractors are options in a MCQ [16] other then the correct answer option (obtained in Module 2). Ideally, distractors should be as conceptually close to the correct answer as possible so that it becomes difficult to guess the correct answer from among the set of options in the MCQ. Thus, Module 3 takes the generated question, the corresponding predicted answer as well as the content from which the question-answer pair has been generated as input. It generates a set of distractors that are similar in type to the predicted (correct) answer for the question, though not exactly the same as the correct answer. To evaluate the quality of generated distractors for a MCQ, we rely only on qualitative evaluation wherein we use human judgement to determine if the set of generated distractors are acceptable, given the generated question and the predicted correct answer or if they are poor (one or more distractors deviate in type from the correct answer, making it trivial to guess the correct MCQ option).

## 3.5  Filtering Module

In this section, we use the module specific evaluation metrics defined in previous sections in order to filter out the poorly generated MCQs and the reduced set of MCQs after filtering is the final output of *QGen* provided to the end user. We consider a generated MCQ as a poorly generated candidate and filter it out if one or more of the following conditions are satisfied:

a. **Generated question is of bad quality:** Question is either grammatically incorrect, not naturally sounding, not well-structured or it is an incomplete question (reflected by high perplexity and/or low query-wellformedness value).
b. **Generated question is not grounded in the content:** The question cannot be answered correctly using the input content (Module 2 predicts correct answer to the question with a pretty low confidence score).
c. **Predicted answer is incorrect:** Answer predicted by Module 2 for a generated question is incorrect (reflected by low confidence score).
d. **Predicted answer is same as topic:** For a generated MCQ, the correct answer predicted is same as the topic input by user from which the content was extracted in Module 0.
e. **Predicted answer is a span within the corresponding generated question:** The correct answer predicted is contained within the question text itself for a generated MCQ.
f. **Generated distractors are poor:** The set of distractors conceptually belong to a different type of entity than the correct answer entity.
g. **Repetitiveness of MCQs:** If the same MCQ is generated multiple times from given content, we prefer to keep only one occurrence of that MCQ and delete all other occurrences to ensure good diversity in the final generated set.
h. **MCQ has more than one correct answer:** Multiple options correspond to correct answers for the generated MCQ.

## 4  Evaluation and Results

In this section, we evaluate the performance of *QGen* in terms of generating high quality MCQs for a given textual content. Firstly, we introduce the datasets we use for analyzing the performance of individual *QGen* modules. Next, for each individual module, we specify the model choices we have employed for performing the corresponding modular tasks. We then present the results corresponding to both quantitative and qualitative evaluation. Finally, we summarize the different variants of *QGen* we have experimented with using combinations of various model choices for individual modules and compare their performance.

### 4.1 Datasets

For evaluation of *QGen* modules, we rely on three datasets. One of them is the reading comprehension dataset *SQuAD2.0*, consisting of questions posed by crowdworkers on a set of Wikipedia articles[2]. Another dataset consists of 869 human generated MCQs (with 4 options) limited to science, ELA and social sciences domain, extracted from a learning platform [22]. Thirdly, we rely on a set of 100 topics from Wikipedia [13] and the data consists of corresponding reading passages extracted from Wikipedia pages.

### 4.2 Model Details

We rely on the following model choices for individual modules of *QGen*:

**1. Question Generation in Module 1:** We generate the set of questions from a given piece of content using T5-based transformer models [11] as well as the recently released InstructGPT model by OpenAI. We use one of two different sized T5 models, namely a fined-tuned version of T5-base model and a fine-tuned version of T5-large model, both of which are trained on the *SQuAD* dataset[3] for generating questions based on some content.

On the other hand, *Instruct GPT* is a large language model (LLM) that has been developed by aligning the GPT-3 LLM [9] from OpenAI, with user intent on a wide range of tasks by supervised fine-tuning followed by reinforcement learning from human feedback (RLHF) [10]. In case of InstructGPT, we use few-shot prompts consisting of three to five passages (content) with a set of example questions for each passage, for generating questions following a similar style and type for the input content.

**2. Answer Prediction in Module 2:** For each question, given the content, we use two different models to predict the (correct) answer (usually a span within the content) to the generated question, depending on the type of model used in Module 1. For instance, if T5 is used for question generation in Module 1, we use the *RoBERTa* model [17] trained on *SQuAD2.0* dataset (described in previous section)[4], which is an improvement over the *BERT* model [6] leading to better downstream task performance.

On the other hand, we use *InstructGPT* model for answer prediction if *InstructGPT* has been used to generate questions in Module 1. Similar to Module 1, we use few-shot prompts for *InstructGPT* consisting of three to five passages

---

[2] https://rajpurkar.github.io/SQuAD-explorer/explore/v2.0/dev/.

[3] https://tinyurl.com/yntc6thk, https://tinyurl.com/mrymx4b8.

[4] https://github.com/facebookresearch/fairseq/tree/main/examples/roberta.

**Table 1.** Model configuration of individual modules for different *QGen* variants

| Type of QGen model used | Module 1 | Module 2 | Module 3 |
|---|---|---|---|
| T5-base | *T5-base* | *RoBERTa-large* | *Ensemble* |
| T5-large | *T5-large* | *RoBERTa-large* | *Ensemble* |
| Fixed prompt GPT | *Instruct GPT* | *Instruct GPT* | *Instruct GPT* |
| Variable prompt GPT | *Instruct GPT* | *Instruct GPT* | *Instruct GPT* |
| Hybrid | *T5-large* | *RoBERTa-large* | *Instruct GPT* |

with a set of example questions and also the corresponding answers for each passage. Then we predict the correct answer based on this prompt for the input content and a generated question from the content.

**3. Distractor Generation in Module 3:** For each pair of generated question and predicted answer, given the content, we rely on one of two methods depending on the variant of *QGen* model (determined by model choices taken in previous modules) to generate distractors. For instance, we use *InstructGPT* to generate distractors if it is used as the model in Modules 1 and 2 as well. In that case, similar to Module 2, we use few-shot prompts but additionally, we also provide a set of three distractors along with the correct answer for each of the example questions corresponding to a passage. Then for the input triplet of content, a generated question from the content and the corresponding answer, we obtain the generated distractors as output.

Alternatively, if T5 and *RoBERTa* are chosen as the models in Modules 1 and 2, we use an ensemble approach which is a combination of methods based on sense2vec, wordnet, conceptnet, densephrases[5] as well as human curated MCQ datasets to generate relevant distractors. For *sense2vec*, we generate candidate distractors that are similar to correct answer entity in terms of sense2vec embeddings. In case of both *wordnet* and *conceptnet*[6], we return co-hyponyms of the hypernym of correct answer entity as the set of relevant distractors.

In case of *Densephrases* [15], we retrieve the top-$k$ most relevant passages useful for answering the generated question provided as input. Then we retrieve a list of entities from each top-$k$ passage and rank the combined list in decreasing order of semantic similarity with correct answer. Top-$n$ entities from this final ranked list are chosen as distractors for corresponding MCQ. Finally, we rely on community driven free MCQ datasets such as the open source Trivia API and the SciQ dataset[7] for generating distractors for each unique answer option across the  26K MCQs in these two datasets.[8]

Based on these model choices, we obtain different *QGen* variants depending on the model type used in each individual module, as summarized in Table 1.

---

[5] https://tinyurl.com/fevvjuzw, https://tinyurl.com/y4p9n4wc.
[6] https://wordnet.princeton.edu/, https://conceptnet.io/.
[7] https://the-trivia-api.com/, https://allenai.org/data/sciq.
[8] We use these datasets only to evaluate our research for non-commercial purposes.

## 4.3   Evaluation Results

**Quantitative Evaluation.** Here we quantify the performance of the Modules 1, 2 and 3 for the QGen system in terms of the evaluation metrics defined in Sect. 3 as follows:

**Module 1:** We evaluate Module 1 by considering the set of reading passages (or content) available in *SQuAD2.0* dataset. We provide each such content as input to Module 1 of *QGen* in order to generate a set of grounded and relevant questions. We repeat this exercise across each content and obtain a combined set of generated questions across all the reading passages. Finally, we compute the value of perplexity (using the causal language model GPT-2 [7]) and well-formedness score for each generated question. We obtain a mean value of perplexity equal to 37.3 and a mean value of query well-formedness score equal to 0.864 over all the generated questions. This verifies the high quality of generated questions obtained from Module 1 of *QGen* in terms of natural soundedness, completeness and grammatical correctness.

**Module 2:** Next, we evaluate Module 2 by providing each question available in *SQuAD2.0* dataset and its corresponding reading passage as input to Module 2 of *QGen*. We then obtain a predicted answer for each such question as the output of Module 2. We now compare the predicted answer string with the reference answer to the question available in *SQuAD2.0* dataset. We compute the values of *EM*, *F1-score* and *ROUGE* for each predicted answer and compute their mean values over all question-answer pairs. We obtain a mean *EM* score of 0.64 which means that the predicted answer string exactly matches the reference *SQuAD2.0* answers for 64% of cases. Similarly, the mean *F1-score* obtained is 0.84 which is consistent with the *EM* values as *F1-score* considers the word overlap and is less stricter than *EM* score. Further, mean *ROUGE* scores are also pretty high with *ROUGE-1 = 0.84*, *ROUGE-2 = 0.54* and *ROUGE-L = 0.84*. This denotes a high overlap of word units (n-grams) between the predicted and reference *SQuAD2.0* answers. Overall, we can say that Module 2 of *QGen* performs reasonably in terms of predicting the correct answer to questions.

**Module 3:** We use the dataset from the learning platform (see Sect. 4.1) to evaluate the quality of generated distractors in Module 3. Precisely, we consider the question text as well as the correct answer option for each MCQ in this dataset as input to Module 3 and generate a set of distractors as output. We then determine if the set of distractors are acceptable or not to humans. If the distractors are topically unrelated to the correct answer or if multiple distractors are different to the correct answer in terms of entity type or semantic similarity, we consider the generated distractor set for the MCQ to be unacceptable or poor. Following this criteria, we observe that 58% of the MCQs in the data from learning platform have acceptable set of generated distractors. Given the difficulty of generating good and relevant distractors for MCQs, we consider the performance of Module 3 of *QGen* to be pretty decent.

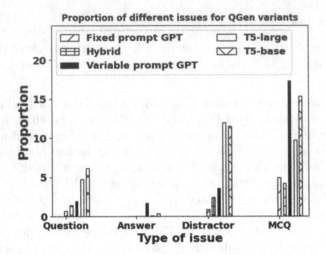

**Fig. 5.** Different issues identified by annotators for variants of *QGen*

**Qualitative Evaluation.** In this section, we compare the quality of the MCQs generated by the different variants of *QGen* shown in Table 1 through human judgement. For this purpose, we generated a set of 500 MCQs from each *QGen* variant from the set of 100 reading passages in the *Wikipedia* dataset (see Sect. 4.1). We then hired a group of three annotators to evaluate each generated MCQ and label them with one or more of the following types of issues (see Sect. 3.5) if they exist with the MCQ:

**1. Question:** The corresponding question in the MCQ is of bad quality.

**2. Answer:** The predicted correct answer for the MCQ is incorrect.

**3. Distractor:** The corresponding set of distractors for the MCQ are of poor quality or there are multiple correct answers for the MCQ.

**4. MCQ:** The MCQ as a whole has an issue. This include issues such as repetitiveness, question is not grounded, the answer is trivial or same as topic, incorrect extrapolation etc.

If the end-to-end MCQ is of good quality with none of the above four issues as a whole or in any of its individual components, we consider it to be a MCQ of desirable quality (human likeness). From the annotations of generated MCQs, we observe that among the different *QGen* variants, the *Hybrid* variant where Module 1 is based on *T5-large*, Module 2 is based on *RoBERTa-large* and Module 3 is based on *Instruct GPT* and the *Fixed prompt GPT* variant where all modules are based on *Instruct GPT* shows the best performance as 92% and 93.53% of the generated MCQs respectively are of desirable quality as agreed upon by all three annotators. On the other hand, proportion of generated MCQs that are of desirable quality (consensus reached among annotators) for the other three *QGen* variants varies between 67 − 76% of all MCQs. This shows that a combination of *T5-based* (for question generation) and *Instruct GPT* based (for all modules) *QGen* model variants are best suited for generating high quality MCQs.

We plot the frequency distribution of the above four issue types for the different *QGen* variants (see Table 1) in Fig. 5 as labeled by the annotators. We observe that the most frequent issues for poorly generated MCQs in case of the *Variable prompt GPT* model are the non-groundedness of questions in the content passage ( 12% of cases) and there is incorrect extrapolation (or hallucination) wherein the four answer options are wrongly misinterpreted ( 10% of cases). On the other hand, one of the most frequent issues for *QGen* variants that relies on T5 for question generation step is poorly generated distractors ( 12% of cases) and repetitiveness of MCQs ( 5% of cases). In addition, 6.5% of cases have an issue of answer being same as topic for such variants.

The main challenge that we faced while qualitatively evaluating a generated MCQ in this manner involves a rigorous iterative process that we underwent to calibrate researcher-annotator agreement. This helped us to reach a consensus on the quality of a generated MCQ between annotators and the research team as well as agree on the type of issue, if any, that may be present for a MCQ. In future, we aim to evaluate the time it takes for a teacher to use *QGen* to generate questions for content provided by them and the effort needed to refine these questions through suitable experiments and surveying teachers.

## 5   Conclusion

In conclusion, this paper highlights the potential of generative AI in addressing educational challenges, particularly in automating question-based activities (QBAs) for assessments. Leveraging transformer-based language models like T5 and GPT-3, we have designed a scalable, reliable, and privacy-preserving modular framework for multiple-choice question generation. Quantitative and qualitative evaluations verified the effectiveness of the proposed framework in generating high quality questions and answers as well as challenging and indistinguishable distractors, with GPT-3 based modules demonstrating better performance compared to their T5 counterparts. This work not only demonstrates the successful integration of various language models but also paves the way for further exploration of generative AI tools in educational applications, ultimately augmenting teachers' abilities and enhancing students' learning experiences.

## References

1. Ahmad, S.F., Rahmat, M.K., Mubarik, M.S., Alam, M.M., Hyder, S.I.: Artificial intelligence and its role in education. Sustainability **13**(22), 12902 (2021)
2. Bethencourt-Aguilar, A., Castellanos-Nieves, D., Sosa-Alonso, J.J., Area-Moreira, M.: Use of generative adversarial networks (GANS) in educational technology research (2023)
3. Bhat, B., Bhat, G.: Formative and summative evaluation techniques for improvement of learning process. Eur. J. Bus. Soc. Sci. **7**(5), 776–785 (2019)
4. Chen, S.F., Beeferman, D., Rosenfeld, R.: Evaluation metrics for language models (1998)

5. Choi, E., et al.: QUAC: question answering in context. arXiv preprint arXiv:1808.07036 (2018)
6. Devlin, J., Chang, M.W., Lee, K., Toutanova, K.: BERT: pre-training of deep bidirectional transformers for language understanding. arXiv preprint arXiv:1810.04805 (2018)
7. Ethayarajh, K.: How contextual are contextualized word representations? Comparing the geometry of BERT, ELMO, and GPT-2 embeddings. arXiv preprint arXiv:1909.00512 (2019)
8. Faruqui, M., Das, D.: Identifying well-formed natural language questions. arXiv preprint arXiv:1808.09419 (2018)
9. Floridi, L., Chiriatti, M.: GPT-3: its nature, scope, limits, and consequences. Mind. Mach. **30**, 681–694 (2020)
10. Griffith, S., Subramanian, K., Scholz, J., Isbell, C.L., Thomaz, A.L.: Policy shaping: integrating human feedback with reinforcement learning. In: Advances in Neural Information Processing Systems, vol. 26 (2013)
11. Grover, K., Kaur, K., Tiwari, K., Kumar, P.: Deep learning based question generation using t5 transformer. In: Garg, D., Wong, K., Sarangapani, J., Gupta, S.K. (eds.) IACC 2020. Communications in Computer and Information Science, vol. 1367, pp. 243–255. Springer, Singapore (2021). https://doi.org/10.1007/978-981-16-0401-0_18
12. Huberman, A., et al.: Qualitative data analysis a methods sourcebook (2014)
13. Kriangchaivech, K., Wangperawong, A.: Question generation by transformers. arXiv preprint arXiv:1909.05017 (2019)
14. Kwiatkowski, T., et al.: Natural questions: a benchmark for question answering research. Trans. Assoc. Comput. Linguist. **7**, 453–466 (2019)
15. Lee, J., Wettig, A., Chen, D.: Phrase retrieval learns passage retrieval, too. arXiv preprint arXiv:2109.08133 (2021)
16. Liang, C., Yang, X., Dave, N., Wham, D., Pursel, B., Giles, C.L.: Distractor generation for multiple choice questions using learning to rank. In: Proceedings of the Thirteenth Workshop on Innovative Use of NLP for Building Educational Applications, pp. 284–290 (2018)
17. Liu, Y., et al.: RoBERTa: a robustly optimized BERT pretraining approach. arXiv preprint arXiv:1907.11692 (2019)
18. Radford, A., Metz, L., Chintala, S.: Unsupervised representation learning with deep convolutional generative adversarial networks. arXiv preprint arXiv:1511.06434 (2015)
19. Radford, A., Narasimhan, K., Salimans, T., Sutskever, I.: Improving language understanding by generative pre-training (2018)
20. Saldaña, J.: The Coding Manual for Qualitative Researchers. Kindle e-reader Version (2016)
21. Schluter, N.: The limits of automatic summarisation according to rouge. In: Proceedings of the 15th Conference of the European Chapter of the Association for Computational Linguistics, pp. 41–45. Association for Computational Linguistics (2017)
22. Solas, E., Sutton, F.: Incorporating digital technology in the general education classroom. Res. Soc. Sci. Technol. **3**(1), 1–15 (2018)
23. Stanja, J., Gritz, W., Krugel, J., Hoppe, A., Dannemann, S.: Formative assessment strategies for students' conceptions–the potential of learning analytics. Br. J. Edu. Technol. **54**(1), 58–75 (2023)
24. Zhang, C., et al.: A complete survey on generative AI (AIGC): Is chatGPT from GPT-4 to GPT-5 all you need? arXiv preprint arXiv:2303.11717 (2023)

# Comparison of Simulated Annealing and Evolution Strategies for Optimising Cyclical Rosters with Uneven Demand and Flexible Trainee Placement

Joseph Collins[1,2,3]($\boxtimes$) (iD), Alexandru-Ciprian Zăvoianu[1,2] (iD),
and John A. W. McCall[1,2] (iD)

[1] School of Computing, Robert Gordon University, Aberdeen, Scotland, UK
{j.collins1,c.zavoianu,j.mccall}@rgu.ac.uk
[2] National Subsea Centre, Aberdeen, Scotland, UK
[3] Port of Aberdeen, Aberdeen, Scotland, UK

**Abstract.** Rosters are often used for real-world staff scheduling requirements. Multiple design factors such as demand variability, shift type
placement, annual leave requirements, staff well-being and the placement of trainees need to be considered when constructing good rosters.
In the present work we propose a metaheuristic-based strategy for designing optimal cyclical rosters that can accommodate uneven demand patterns. A key part of our approach relies on integrating an efficient optimal trainee placement module within the metaheuristic-driven search.
Results obtained on a real-life problem proposed by the Port of Aberdeen
indicate that by incorporating a demand-informed random rota initialisation procedure, our strategy can generally achieve high-quality end-
of-run solutions when using relatively simple base solvers like simulated
annealing (SA) and evolution strategies (ES). While ES converge faster,
SA outperforms quality-wise, with both approaches being able to improve
the man-made baseline.

**Keywords:** Simulated annealing · Evolution strategies · Staff
rostering · Staff training · Combinatorial optimisation · Uncertainty

## 1 Introduction and Motivation

Staff rosters are an essential tool in scheduling personnel, as the usage of well-
established rota patterns allows personnel to plan their activities, both in and
out of work. In general, a successful roster considers the needs of the personnel,
while aiming to satisfy work commitments. Highly advanced staff rosters involve
hundreds or thousands of employees and can incorporate multiple rota patterns
as well as dedicated training time for staff members [1].

In recent decades, specialised metaheuristic solvers have become an increasingly popular option for automatically generating timetables [2], complex rosters

© The Author(s), under exclusive license to Springer Nature Switzerland AG 2023
M. Bramer and F. Stahl (Eds.): SGAI 2023, LNAI 14381, pp. 451–464, 2023.
https://doi.org/10.1007/978-3-031-47994-6_39

and rota patterns [3]. While having strong interactions with timetabling problems from sectors like education [4,5], transport [6] and sports [7], efficient personnel scheduling is important in scenarios where a limited but skilled workforce must ensure adequate service availability even when confronted with dynamic demand patterns. This is often the case with emergency response staff [8,9], airline crew [10], healthcare workers [11] and even call centre staff [12].

Popular solvers used include tabu search (TS) [13], hybrid scatter search [14], noising methods combined with simulated annealing (SA) [15], ant colony optimisation (ACO) [16] and evolutionary algorithms (EAs) [17].

The present work is motivated by a pilot roster modelling scenario proposed by the Port of Aberdeen (PoA). As pilots provide a critical service for vessels, full daily coverage must be ensured. However, PoA receives most pilotage requests during early and late shifts, and least on night shifts. Furthermore, pilotage needs also vary per weekday. For example, Tuesdays have the highest demand and Saturdays the lowest. These demand trends are consistent over multiple years. The historical PoA pilot roster, shown in Fig. 1, is cyclical and based on a weekly rota pattern. Designed for twelve staff members, the rota pattern is twelve weeks long with a single shift type – Early ($d$), Late ($l$), Night ($n$), Flexible ($a$) or TimeOff ($o$) – assigned to each day in the rota. The ratios of each shift type within the rota are based on consultation with staff. There is a mandated three week block of time off at the end of the rota. The PoA currently used the man-made pilot rota shown in Fig. 1. The inauguration of a new harbour within the PoA is expected to increase pilot demand and challenge the existing roster. A critical feature when designing a new rota is a bespoke requirement to consider placement of a variable number of trainee pilots. A rota should factor in the need to train pilots without impacting high levels of service or overall schedule quality in terms of work-life balance. Automation of rota generation will allow the PoA the flexibility of easily testing and adapting to staffing scenarios that can rapidly adjust to unknown demand dynamics introduced by the Port's extension.

The remainder of this paper is organised as follows: Sect. 2 describes our formalisation of the PoA pilot rostering problem. Section 3 describes our approach

| Monday | Tuesday | Wednesday | Thursday | Friday | Saturday | Sunday |
|---|---|---|---|---|---|---|
| Flexi | Early | Early | Early | Night | Night | Night |
| Night | TimeOff | TimeOff | TimeOff | Late | Late | Late |
| Late | Night | Night | Night | TimeOff | TimeOff | TimeOff |
| Early | Early | Early | Early | Early | Early | Early |
| TimeOff | TimeOff | TimeOff | TimeOff | TimeOff | TimeOff | TimeOff |
| Flexi | Late | Late | Late | Night | Night | Night |
| Night | TimeOff | TimeOff | TimeOff | Early | Early | Early |
| Late | Night | Night | Night | TimeOff | TimeOff | TimeOff |
| Early | Late | Late | Late | Late | Late | Late |
| TimeOff | TimeOff | TimeOff | TimeOff | TimeOff | TimeOff | TimeOff |
| TimeOff | TimeOff | TimeOff | TimeOff | TimeOff | TimeOff | TimeOff |
| TimeOff | TimeOff | TimeOff | TimeOff | TimeOff | TimeOff | TimeOff |

**Fig. 1.** Historical / baseline pilot rota pattern ($x_h$) at PoA

to optimising the pilot rota and the placement of trainees. In Sect. 4 we present the setup and results of our numerical experiments alongside their interpretation. Finally, Sect. 5 contains conclusions and gives an outlook on future work.

## 2    Problem Formalisation

Using previous notations for shift types, a rota pattern to the PoA rostering problem can be encoded by an $n$-tuple (i.e., array $x$ of size $N$) where $N$ is the total number of days in the roster – i.e., $x \in \{d, l, n, a, o\}^N$. As the rotas we aim to generate are cyclical, $N$ is equal to the number of staff multiplied by seven. However, given that the number of time off weeks at the end of the rota is predefined based on user input, this part of the roster can be decoupled to reduce problem size (e.g., $N = 63$ instead of $N = 84$ for the 12 person rota in Fig. 1) and complexity (i.e., enforcing extended time off periods via constraints).

Discussions with the PoA have revealed the best way to model the quality of a given rota $x$ is by penalising undesirable shift sub-patterns and understaffing.

Penalties were allocated on a scale from zero to one hundred, based on relative severity of constraint violations elicited from end users. These penalties were observed empirically to generate an appropriate response from the tested solvers.

**Isolated Shift Penalty:** $p_I(x)$ A shift $x_i \neq f, 1 \leq i \leq N$ is considered isolated if $x_i \neq x_{i-1}$ and $x_i \neq x_{i+1}$[1]. When marking with $\omega_I$ the number of isolated shift occurrences: $p_I(x) = 50 \cdot \omega_I$.

**Late Shift Before Early Shift Penalty:** $p_{LE}(x)$ If $x_i = l$ and $x_{i+1} = d$ a medium base penalty is incurred. If $\omega_{LE}$ marks the number of late→early infringements: $p_{LE}(x) = 50 \cdot \omega_{LE}$.

**Insufficient Rest Penalty:** $p_R(x)$ If the set $R$ contains all the disjoint rota sub-patterns $r_i = x_{s+1} \ldots x_{s+k}$ with the property that $|r_i| = k \geq 7$ and $x_{s+i} \neq o, \forall 0 \leq i \leq k$ then $p_R(x) = 25 \cdot \sum_{r_i \in R}(2^{|r_i|-6} - 1)$ as the aim is to generally discourage working more than 6 days in a row without rest. This penalty is designed to increase exponentially based on the seriousness of its violation(s).

**Too Many Successive Night Shifts Penalty:** $p_{SN}(x)$ If the set $SN$ contains all the disjoint rota sub-patterns $n_i = x_{s+1} \ldots x_{s+k}$ with the property that $|n_i| = k \geq 4$ and $x_{s+i} = n, \forall 0 \leq i \leq k$ then $p_{SN}(x) = 10 \cdot \sum_{n_i \in SN}(2^{|n_i|-3} - 1)$ as the aim is to discourage working more than 3 night shifts in a row.

**Insufficient Time Off After Night Shift Penalty:** $p_O(x)$ If $\omega_O$ denotes total number of occurrences when $x_i = n$ and $x_{i+1} \neq n$, and for the $j^{th}$ such occurrence $o_j$ denotes number of consecutive time off shifts after the night shift (with the count starting at $x_{i+1}$), the partial time off penalty score is defined as:

$$p(o_j) = \begin{cases} 7 & \text{if } o_j = 0 \\ 3 & \text{if } o_j = 1 \\ 1 & \text{if } o_j = 2 \\ 0 & \text{if } o_j \geq 3 \end{cases}$$

---

[1] As we are operating on cyclical rotas, $x_0 = x_N$ and $x_{N+1} = x_1$.

and the total penalty is $p_O(x) = 100 \cdot \sum_{1 \leq j \leq \omega_O} p(o_j)$. The idea behind this penalty is to encourage adequate rest periods after night shifts.

**Unmatched Shift Demand Penalty:** $p_U(x)$ Let $dd_i, dl_i, dn_i \in \mathbb{N}$ with $1 \leq i \leq 7$ denote the historical/expected demand for early, late and night shift pilots on the $i^{th}$ day of the week. The supply of pilots for each (day, shift) pair is marked by $sd_i, sl_i, sn_i$ and computed via a column-wise summation of the relevant shifts in the rota pattern (e.g., for the rota in Fig. 1, $sd_i = sl_i = sn_i = 2, \forall i$). The unmatched shift demand penalty is computed as:

$$p_D(x) = 100 \cdot \sum_{1 \leq i \leq 7} [max(dd_i - sd_i, 0) + max(dl_i - sl_i, 0) + max(dn_i - sn_i, 0)]$$

**Insufficient Trainee Supervision Penalty:** $p_T(x)$ Given that both trainee and experienced pilots can be placed on the rota, the previously defined supply of pilots can be broken down into $sd_i = sd_i^T + sd_i^E$, $sl_i = sl_i^T + sl_i^E$, $sn_i = sn_i^T + sn_i^E$ with $sd_i^E, sl_i^E$ and $sn_i^E$ denoting the number of experienced pilots for each (day, shift) pair. Given that it is highly preferable for trainees to always be supervised by at least one experienced member of staff, rota occurrences when this is not the case are penalised using:

$$p_T(x) = 80 \cdot \sum_{1 \leq i \leq 7} [max(1 - sd_i^e, 0) + max(1 - sl_i^e, 0) + max(1 - sn_i^e, 0)].$$

It is important to note that the particular placement of trainees on the rota heavily impacts the value of $p_T$. For example: when placing two trainees on start weeks 1 and 2 (as trainee placement combination $C1$) on the rota in Fig. 1 we obtain $p_T(x, C1) = 0$, but when the trainees are assigned start weeks 2 and 7 (as placement combination $C2$) we obtain $p_T(x, C2) = 80$ as $sn_1^e = 0$. This aspect is discussed at length in Sect. 3.2. The total penalty associated with a rota $x$ is obtained by summing the seven penalty types and the search for a high-quality rota can be formalised as:

$$\min f(x) = p_I(x) + p_{LE}(x) + p_R(x) + p_{SN}(x) + p_O(x) + p_U(x, D) + p_T(x, C_b), \quad (1)$$

where $D$ is a set that aggregates predefined pilot demand values for all (day, shift) pairs and $C_b$ denotes the best possible start week placement for a predefined number of trainees that must be placed on the rota.

The global optimum for Eq. 1 is $f(x^*) = 0$ and indicates a rota pattern $x^*$ that does not incur any penalties. When considering the pilotage demand vectors obtained from historical PoA data:

$$\begin{cases} dd &= [1, 2, 2, 2, 2, 2, 1] \\ dl &= [2, 3, 2, 2, 2, 2, 2] \\ dn &= [2, 1, 2, 2, 1, 1, 1] \end{cases} \quad (2)$$

and no trainee placement, the total penalty associated with the rota $x_h$ shown in Fig. 1 is $f(x_h) = 470$ as: $p_I(x_h) = 100$, $p_{LE}(x_h) = 0$, $p_R(x_h) = 250$, $p_N(x_h) = 20$, $p_O(x_h) = 0$, $p_U(x_h, D) = 100$ and $p_T(x_h, C_b) = 0$. One trainee can also be placed on $x_h$ without penalty (irrelevant of start week). If two trainees are to be placed on $x_h$, starting them in weeks 1 and 4 would not impact $p_T(x_h)$.

# 3   Proposed Approach

## 3.1   Rota Initialisation

After fixing $N$ – the size of the rota – and subtracting the total number of flexible ($a$) and time off ($o$) days, the main focus of the initialisation stage is to compute how many Early ($d$), Late ($l$) and Night ($n$) shifts are to be allocated.

This allocation is based on historical or expected total relative demand across the three types of work shifts. Assuming that Eq. (2) reflects expected demand trends for each weekday, the total relative demand for late shifts is: $\mathbb{F}_l = \frac{\sum dl_i}{\sum dd_i + \sum dl_i + \sum dn_i}, 1 \leq i \leq 7 \Rightarrow \mathbb{F}_l = \frac{15}{12+15+10} = 0.4054$. Similarly $\mathbb{F}_d = 0.3243$ and $\mathbb{F}_n = 0.2702$. For example, given that after removing 40 time off and 2 flexible shifts from the rota in Fig. 1, 42 days remain to be allocated among the three types of work shifts, we would obtain an allocation of $\mathbb{F}_d \cdot 42 = 13.62$ early shifts, $\mathbb{F}_l \cdot 42 = 17.02$ late shifts and $\mathbb{F}_n \cdot 42 = 11.34$ night shifts for $x_h$ based on the previously computed relative work shift demand. Settling on the initialisation of (i) 17 Late shifts, 14 Early shifts and 11 Night shifts or (ii) 17 Late shifts, 13 Early shifts and 12 Night shifts is a somewhat subjective modelling decision. In the experiments we report on in Sect. 4, we opted for (ii) in light of the heavy penalties related to Night shift placements (i.e., $p_N$ and $p_O$).

Once all the individual shift type counts have been determined based on historical/expected demand for the analysed use case, our rota patterns are initialised randomly to reflect the desired distribution of shift types.

## 3.2   Trainee Placement

A key part of our automated rostering strategy revolves around the optimal placement of a variable number of trainees. This feature allows the Port of Aberdeen flexibility to balance conflicting objectives under uncertain pilotage demand trends. Rosters with an overconcentration of trainees will be unsatisfactory should there be a surge in demand for highly skilled pilotage. Rosters with insufficient trainee slots will fail to provide sufficient pilotage experience.

For determining trainee placement, we first compute all combinations of locations where a predefined number of trainees $nt$ can be assigned a start week on a rota pattern that covers $nw$ work weeks. The total number of distinct trainee placement locations is $\binom{nw}{nt}$. As the roster is cyclical, initial trainee placements will iterate in a round robin fashion that induces an equivalence relation between different placements. For example, in the case of a four week roster, with two trainees (T) and two experienced staff members (E), as we have $nt = 2$ and $nw = 4$, there are $\binom{4}{2} = 6$ individual trainee placements and they are grouped into two equivalence classes: $\{TETE, ETET\}$ and $\{TTEE, ETTE, EETT, TEET\}$.

Our strategy for efficiently evaluating trainee placements applies a min-max approach on top of the resulting trainee placement equivalence classes and is described in Algorithm 1. As our goal is to discover a placement that results in a minimal insufficient trainee supervision penalty for a given rota $x$, our approach:

1 computes the class penalty score associated with each equivalence class of placements as the maximum $p_T(x)$ among the distinct trainee placements (i.e., members) of that class;

2 selects the minimum class penalty score among all equivalence classes as $p_T(x, C_b))$ and a class representative (e.g., the first member) as $C_b$ – the best trainee placement option.

3 preemptively stops evaluating an equivalence class once a member displays a $p_T(x)$ value that is higher than a previously computed class penalty score.

---

**Algorithm 1.** Trainee Placement Approach

---

**Require:** Rota $x$, number of trainees $nt$
**Ensure:** Best trainee placement $C_b$, insufficient trainee supervision penalty $p_t(x, C_b)$
1: Extract the number of weeks in $x$: $nw$
2: Compute the trainee placement combinations: $C_1, C_2, \ldots, C_{\binom{nw}{nt}}$
3: Divide $C_1, C_2, \ldots, C_{\binom{nw}{nt}}$ into equivalence classes: $E_1, E_2, \ldots E_k$
4: Initialise: $C_b = C_1$, $p_T(x, C_b) = \infty$
5: **for** $i = 1$ to $k$ **do**
6:    Initialise: $cps = 0$
7:    **for** $C \in E_k$ **do**
8:        Compute penalty score for trainee placement $C$: $p_T(x, C)$
9:        **if** $p_T(x, C) \geq cps$ **then**
10:            $cps = p_T(x, C)$
11:        **end if**
12:        **if** $p_T(x, C) \geq p_T(x, C_b)$ **then**
13:            Break the loop
14:        **end if**
15:    **end for**
16:    **if** $cps < p_T(x, C_b)$ **then**
17:        Extract class representative from $E_k$: $C_r$
18:        $C_b = C_r$
19:        $p_T(x, C_b) = cps$
20:    **end if**
21: **end for**
22: **return** $C_b$, $p_T(x, C_b)$

---

## 3.3   Metaheuristic Solvers

Given that the initialisation method described in Sect. 3.1 ensures that the distribution of work shifts required for obtaining a reasonable solution is present in any randomly generated rota, our optimisation strategy is centred on the deployment of a simple *shift swap (variation) operator* within several metaheuristic approaches that (re)-position shifts whilst aiming to solve Eq. 1. When applied on a given rota $x$, the shift swap operator randomly selects two (day) indices $i$ and $j$, with $1 \leq i, j \leq N$, and switches their shift types:

$$\begin{cases} aux & = x_i \\ x_i & = x_j \\ x_j & = aux \end{cases}$$

The first strategy experimented with was local search (LS) [18], but a majority of LS runs fell into local minima. Therefore, we continued with a slightly more advanced trajectory-based solver: Simulated Annealing (SA) [19]. Similarly to LS, at each iteration of SA a new candidate solution $x'$ is generated by applying the swap operator on the current solution of the algorithm: $x^c$. Unlike in LS, $x'$ can be accepted, with a certain probability, as the new current solution in SA even when $f(x^c) < f(x')$, thus enabling the avoidance of local minima. The acceptance probability of a non-improving candidate solution is inversely proportional to the difference in quality with respect to $f(x^c)$ and directly proportional to a temperature parameter that is gradually reduced to 0 during the search (i.e., annealed). Preliminary parameter tuning tests with SA indicated that the solver is able to produce high-quality solutions for our use cases.

In order to contextualise SA performance in terms of convergence speed and final solution quality, we integrated the swap operator in a population-based solver, namely a $(1+\lambda)$ Evolution Strategy (ES) [20], as a mutation operator. At each iteration (i.e., generation) of the ES, $\lambda$ offspring (i.e., candidate solutions) are created by applying the mutation operator to a single parent $x^p$ (i.e., current solution). $x'$ – the best among the $\lambda$ offspring – becomes the parent of the next generation provided that $f(x') < f(x^p)$. Otherwise, $x^p$ remains the parent.

We used standard versions for both solvers as they discovered high-quality solutions for the tested use case with zero trainees.

As the ability to optimally place trainees on the rosters is a PoA requirement, an aim of our numerical optimisation runs with SA and ES is studying differences in final rota qualities when opting between two trainee integration strategies:

- *SwapCheck (SC)*: computes the trainee placement penalty using the strategy outlined in Algorithm 1 in order to accurately evaluate $f(x')$ whenever the solver generates a new candidate solution $x'$;
- *FinalCheck (FC)*: disregards the $p_l(x', C_b)$ component from the computation of $f(x')$ during the run and applies Algorithm 1 only on the best rota to estimate its final quality and associated best possible trainee placement.

The *SwapCheck* strategy provides the solvers with an accurate view of the fitness landscape at all stages of the optimisation run whilst the *FinalCheck* strategy has the advantage of proposing a simplified (but hopefully similar) fitness formulation during the search. The main disadvantage of *SwapCheck* is that it is computationally expensive. The main disadvantage of the *FinalCheck* strategy is that the best possible trainee placement on a high-quality solution for a problem formulation lacking trainees might still yield very large penalties.

## 4 Numerical Experiments and Results

### 4.1 Experimental Setup

While a limited test series indicates that our proposed approach can scale well across problem instances of up to 26 weeks (i.e., $N = 175$) and 7 trainees (especially with the *FinalCheck* strategy), the single use case focused on in this work is optimising the 12 week pilot rota used by the PoA when considering the historical pilotage demand of previous years (see Eq. 2) and a wish to place one, two or no trainees on the rota. As previously mentioned, the historic rota $x_h$ in Fig. 1 has a baseline quality of 470 regardless of the number of trainees.

Across all SA and ES optimisation runs, we used a computational budget of 20,000 shift swap operations (each generating a new candidate solution). We performed 1000 independent repeats for each solver run on the no trainees scenario and 100 independent repeats for each solver run on the one and two trainees scenarios. The reduced runs on the latter scenarios were due to significantly increased computational cost of checking trainee constraints. Sufficient experiments were conducted to support statistical testing. When testing the statistical significance of differences between central tendency estimators, we applied a one-sided Mann-Whitney U Test [21] with a preset significance level of 0.025.

Given the simplistic nature of our two solvers, the options for parameterising them are fairly limited and are mainly intended to discover their best search space exploration-intensification trade-off for the analysed use case.

In the case of SA, we experimented with different parameterisations of the annealing schedule in order to force LS runs of various lengths at the end of the optimisation. Thus, we tested variants that dedicated the last 10000, 7500, 5000, 2500 shift swaps to LS and also tested an SA variant with 0 dedicated LS swaps.

For the $(1 + \lambda)$ ES, we used population sizes of $\lambda = 100$, $\lambda = 50$, $\lambda = 40$ and $\lambda = 25$ which resulted in optimisation runs of 200, 400, 500 and 800 generations.

### 4.2   Results and Interpretation

**No Trainees Scenario.** In Fig. 2 we plot the average convergence behavior of SA and ES across the tested parameterisation options when there is no need to place trainees on the optimised rotas.

Results indicate that ES has a faster convergence speed as all 4 variants are, on average, able to discover rotas with a lower penalty (i.e., higher quality) than the baseline after only 4000 shift swap operations. Conversely, all 4 SA variants that have dedicated LS shift swaps after their hot working (HW) phase discover end-of-run solutions that are better than ES results. Across both solvers, it is noteworthy that the two variants that prioritise exploitation of the search space by integrating a long LS component (i.e., SA 10HW, 10K LS) or by evolving a smaller population over a longer period (i.e., ES 800gen $\lambda = 25$) outperform their peers both in terms of convergence speed and end-of-run solution quality.

Penalty-wise distributions of end-of-run solutions discovered by SA and ES are plotted in Fig. 3. Details regarding the central tendency indicators of these distributions alongside information regarding the quality of the best solutions can be found in Table 1. Statistical significance testing confirms three observations:

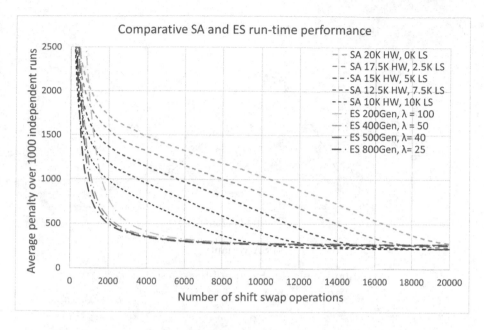

**Fig. 2.** Comparative convergence behavior of 5 SA and 4 ES variants.

1. Each of the SA variants that includes a meaningful LS phase (i.e., 10K, 7.5K, 5K, 2.5K) delivers better results than any ES variant.
2. The SA variant without a dedicated LS phase at the end of the run (i.e., 0K LS) underperforms the other 4 SA variants.
3. There is no meaningful difference between the end-of-run solution qualities obtained by the 4 ES variants.

Despite their average underperformance when compared with SA, three ES variants were able to find near-perfect solutions (i.e., $f(x) \leq 25$).

**1 Trainee Scenario.** Table 2 contains information regarding the differences between end-of-run solution penalties when wishing to place one trainee on the 12 week rota compared with complementary end-of-run results for the no trainee scenario. All solver variants used the computationally expensive *SwapCheck (SC)* strategy for determining the optimal placement of the trainee on the rota.

As expected, the lowest (i.e., best), average and median penalties achieved when placing one trainee on generated rotas are higher than equivalents for the no trainee scenario. Across all variants[2] differences are slightly higher than 80 – the minimal non-zero value of the insufficient trainee supervision penalty $p_T(x)$. As standard deviations are similar between scenarios, magnitude and

---

[2] Apart from the best penalties for ES 200gen, $\lambda = 100$.

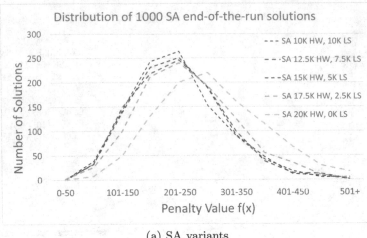

(a) SA variants

(b) ES variants

**Fig. 3.** Histograms of end-of-run solution penalty.

**Table 1.** End-of-run solution quality for the no trainees scenario

| Solver: variant | Best | Average ($\mu$) | Median | Std. deviation ($\sigma$) |
|---|---|---|---|---|
| SA: 10K HW, 10K LS$^+$ | 30 | 222 | 215 | 81.1 |
| SA: 12.5K HW, 7.5K LS$^+$ | 40 | 224.7 | 215 | 79.6 |
| SA: 15K HW, 5K LS$^+$ | 55 | 224.8 | 215 | 78.9 |
| SA: 17.5K HW, 2.5K LS$^+$ | 40 | 239.8 | 230 | 84 |
| SA: 20K HW, 0K LS$^-$ | 60 | 283.2 | 280 | 92.8 |
| ES: 200gen, $\lambda = 100$ | 105 | 271.9 | 257.5 | 115.8 |
| ES: 400gen, $\lambda = 50$ | 25 | 256.6 | 265 | 115.9 |
| ES: 500gen, $\lambda = 40$ | 25 | 275.2 | 260 | 115.9 |
| ES: 800gen, $\lambda = 25$ | 10 | 263.4 | 250 | 117.3 |

consistency of the best, average and median penalty increases indicate that any form of trainee placement (i.e., including $P_T(x, C_b)$ in Eq. 1) over-constrains the PoA rostering.

**Table 2.** End-of-run differences in solution quality for the 1 trainee scenario when compared with results from Table 1. Positive values indicate the 1 trainee result is worse.

| Solver: variant | $\Delta$Best | $\Delta\mu$ | $\Delta$Median | $\Delta\sigma$ |
|---|---|---|---|---|
| SA: 10K HW, 10K LS | 125 | 127 | 125 | 10.4 |
| SA: 12.5K HW, 7.5K LS | 100 | 100.4 | 110 | 4.7 |
| SA: 15K HW, 5K LS | 135 | 92.3 | 97.5 | 0.5 |
| SA: 17.5K HW, 2.5K LS | 115 | 98.4 | 95 | 3 |
| SA: 20K HW, 0K LS | 105 | 96.9 | 95 | 0.4 |
| ES: 200gen, $\lambda = 100$ | 5 | 100.5 | 107.5 | 0.5 |
| ES: 400gen, $\lambda = 50$ | 150 | 128.5 | 117.5 | -3.5 |
| ES: 500gen, $\lambda = 40$ | 120 | 87.6 | 90 | -1.2 |
| ES: 800gen, $\lambda = 25$ | 175 | 123.0 | 137.5 | -8.6 |

**2 Trainees Scenario.** Results in Table 3 indicate that when compared with the 1 trainee scenario – solved using *SwapCheck (SC)* –, the best end-of-run rotas for the 2 trainees scenario have a generally increased average and median penalty only when using the faster *FinalCheck (FC)* trainee placement strategy. When applying solvers on the 2 trainees scenarios using the *SC* trainee placement strategy, the impact of the extra trainee placement on $P_T(r, C_b)$ is minimal for SA variants and reduced in comparison with *FC* in the case of ES.

**Table 3.** End-of-run differences in quality for 2 trainee scenario compared with 1 trainee *SwapCheck (SC)* results. Positive values mean 2 trainees result is worse.

| Solver: variant | $\Delta$Best | | $\Delta\mu$ | | $\Delta$Median | | $\Delta\sigma$ | |
|---|---|---|---|---|---|---|---|---|
| | SC | FC | SC | FC | SC | FC | SC | FC |
| SA: 10K HW, 10K LS | 20 | 30 | -12.3 | 39.3 | -20 | 40 | -1.6 | -6.5 |
| SA: 12.5K HW, 7.5K LS | -20 | 60 | 3.1 | 50 | 0 | 45 | 4.2 | -4.7 |
| SA: 15K HW, 5K LS | -25 | -25 | 30 | 62.3 | 37.5 | 55 | 21.8 | 8.7 |
| SA: 17.5K HW, 2.5K LS | 10 | -15 | -3 | 54.8 | 15 | 57.5 | 3.4 | 17.4 |
| SA: 20K HW, 0K LS | 0 | -25 | 0.5 | 42 | 5 | 55 | 18 | 15.7 |
| ES: 200gen, $\lambda = 100$ | 15 | -30 | 26 | 31.25 | 40 | 37 | 11 | -13.1 |
| ES: 400gen, $\lambda = 50$ | -10 | -35 | -9.7 | 22 | -15 | 22 | -8.6 | 10.2 |
| ES: 500gen, $\lambda = 40$ | 30 | 10 | 29.4 | 79.65 | 32.5 | 87.5 | 6.2 | 16 |
| ES: 800gen, $\lambda = 25$ | -50 | 5 | 13.7 | 36.7 | 0 | 30 | 31.5 | 22.8 |

Figure 4 shows the penalty-wise distributions of the end-of-run solutions discovered by the best performing SA and ES variants when using *SwapCheck* and *FinalCheck*. Statistical significance testing confirms the observation that the best performing SA variant obtains better results than the best performing ES variant regardless of which trainee placement strategy is used.

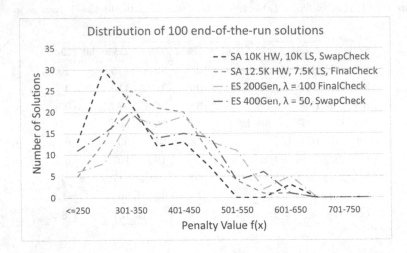

**Fig. 4.** Histograms of end-of-run solution penalty distribution for best performing SA and ES variants using *SwapCheck* and *FinalCheck* placement strategies.

The best solution obtained by the ES: 200gen, $\lambda = 100$ variant on the 2 trainee scenario achieved a total penalty of $f(x) = 80$ that was entirely due to a trainee supervision penalty (i.e., $p_T(x) = 80$). This means that the discovered rota (shown in Fig. 5) is a perfect solution (i.e., global optimum) for the no trainee scenario (see Table 1).

| Monday | Tuesday | Wednesday | Thursday | Friday | Saturday | Sunday |
|---|---|---|---|---|---|---|
| Late | Late | Night | Night | Night | TimeOff | TimeOff |
| TimeOff | Late | Late | Late | Flexi | Early | Early |
| TimeOff | TimeOff | Early | Early | Early | Night | Night |
| Night | TimeOff | TimeOff | TimeOff | Late | Late | Flexi |
| Early | Early | TimeOff | TimeOff | Late | Late | Night |
| Night | Night | TimeOff | TimeOff | TimeOff | Late | Late |
| Late | Late | Late | Late | TimeOff | TimeOff | Late |
| Late | Night | Night | Night | TimeOff | TimeOff | TimeOff |
| TimeOff | Early | Early | Early | Early | Early | Early |
| TimeOff | TimeOff | TimeOff | TimeOff | TimeOff | TimeOff | TimeOff |
| TimeOff | TimeOff | TimeOff | TimeOff | TimeOff | TimeOff | TimeOff |
| TimeOff | TimeOff | TimeOff | TimeOff | TimeOff | TimeOff | TimeOff |

**Fig. 5.** Perfect solution for the no trainee scenario discovered using ES.

# 5 Conclusions and Future Work

The presented work shows how a bespoke trainee placement method based on an efficient min-max search that speculates equivalent placements in cyclical rosters can be combined with basic metaheuristic solvers like simulated annealing (SA) and evolution strategies (ES) to produce high-quality rotas that can successfully accommodate uneven shift demand patterns while also satisfying multiple staff preferences related to their work-life balance.

Our numerical experiments indicate that SA variants that allow for a significant LS phase at the end of the optimisation run outperform their faster-converging ES counterparts with regard to final solution quality. Furthermore, whilst solver performance is improved by evaluating trainee placement suitability during all stages of the optimisation, a much faster approach of simply placing the required number of trainees on the best solution for the simplified no trainee scenario also produced high quality rotas (for a limited number of trainees).

Future work will address larger problem instances (increased length and number of trainees) likely to pose difficulties to both our optimal trainee placement approach and the two base solvers we considered in our experiments so far.

**Acknowledgment.** The authors would like to acknowledge the support of staff members at the Port of Aberdeen that have kindly contributed to this research by providing the historical pilot roster pattern, demand data and feedback that informed the problem formalisation.

This work was supported by the Port of Aberdeen and InnovateUK through a Knowledge Transfer Partnership project (KTP reference number 12046).

# References

1. Fyvie, M., McCall, J.A.W., Christie, L.A., Brown-lee, A.E.: Explaining a staff rostering genetic algorithm using sensitivity analysis and trajectory analysis. In: Genetic and Evolutionary Computation Conference Companion (GECCO 2023 Companion), 15–19 July 2023, Lisbon, Portugal (2023)
2. Burke, E.K., Petrovic, S.: Recent research directions in automated timetabling. Eur. J. Oper. Res. **140**(2), 266–280 (2002)
3. Ernst, A.T., Jiang, H., Krishnamoorthy, M., Sier, D.: Staff scheduling and rostering: a review of applications, methods and models. Eur. J. Oper. Res. **153**(1), 3–27 (2004)
4. Petrovic, S., Burke, E.K.: University timetabling. (2004)
5. Qu, R., Burke, E.K., McCollum, B., Merlot, L.T., Lee, S.Y.: A survey of search methodologies and automated system development for examination timetabling. J. Sched. **12**, 55–89 (2009)
6. Kwan, R.S., Wren, A., Kwan, A.S.: Hybrid genetic algorithms for scheduling bus and train drivers. In: Proceedings of the 2000 Congress on Evolutionary Computation. CEC00 (Cat. No. 00TH8512), vol. 1, pp. 285–292. IEEE (2000)
7. Ribeiro, C.C.: Sports scheduling: problems and applications. Int. Trans. Oper. Res. **19**(1–2), 201–226 (2012)

8. Li, Y., Kozan, E.: Rostering ambulance services. In: Industrial engineering and management society, pp. 795–801 (2009)
9. Taylor, P.E., Huxley, S.J.: A break from tradition for the San Francisco police: patrol officer scheduling using an optimization-based decision support system. Interfaces **19**(1), 4–24 (1989)
10. Arabeyre, J., Fearnley, J., Steiger, F., Teather, W.: The airline crew scheduling problem: a survey. Transp. Sci. **3**(2), 140–163 (1969)
11. Maenhout, B., Vanhoucke, M.: The impact of incorporating nurse-specific characteristics in a cyclical scheduling approach. J. Oper. Res. Soc. **60**, 1683–1698 (2009)
12. Gans, N., Koole, G., Mandelbaum, A.: Telephone call centers: tutorial, review, and research prospects. Manuf. Serv. Oper. Manage. **5**(2), 79–141 (2003)
13. Burke, E., De Causmaecker, P., Vanden Berghe, G.: A hybrid Tabu search algorithm for the nurse rostering problem. In: McKay, B., Yao, X., Newton, C.S., Kim, J.-H., Furuhashi, T. (eds.) SEAL 1998. LNCS (LNAI), vol. 1585, pp. 187–194. Springer, Heidelberg (1999). https://doi.org/10.1007/3-540-48873-1_25
14. Maenhout, B., Vanhoucke, M.: A hybrid scatter search heuristic for personalized crew rostering in the airline industry. Eur. J. Oper. Res. **206**(1), 155–167 (2010)
15. Parr, D., Thompson, J.M.: Solving the multi-objective nurse scheduling problem with a weighted cost function. Ann. Oper. Res. **155**(1), 279 (2007)
16. Gutjahr, W.J., Rauner, M.S.: An ACO algorithm for a dynamic regional nurse-scheduling problem in Austria. Comput. Oper. Res. **34**(3), 642–666 (2007)
17. Ainslie, R., McCall, J., Shakya, S., Owusu, G.: Tactical plan optimisation for large multi-skilled workforces using a bi-level model. In: 2018 IEEE Congress on Evolutionary Computation (CEC), pp. 1–8. IEEE (2018)
18. Russell, S., Norvig, P.: Artificial Intelligence: A Modern Approach (2003)
19. Kirkpatrick, S., Gelatt, C.D., Jr., Vecchi, M.P.: Optimization by simulated annealing. Science **220**(4598), 671–680 (1983)
20. Beyer, H.G., Schwefel, H.P.: Evolution strategies-a comprehensive introduction. Nat. Comput. **1**, 3–52 (2002)
21. Mann, H.B., Whitney, D.R.: On a test of whether one of two random variables is stochastically larger than the other. Ann. Math. Stat. **18**, 50–60 (1947)

# Interpreting NMR Spectra by Constraint Solving

Haneen A. Alharbi[1,2](✉) , Igor Barsukov[1] , Rudi Grosman[1] ,
and Alexei Lisitsa[1]

[1] University of Liverpool, Liverpool, UK
{haneen.alharbi,igb2,r.grosman,a.lisitsa}@liverpool.ac.uk
[2] King Abdulaziz University, Rabigh, Kingdom of Saudi Arabia

**Abstract.** Nuclear Magnetic Resonance (NMR) spectroscopy is a widely used analytical technique for identifying the molecular structure of complex organic compounds. However, NMR data interpretation can be complex and challenging to decipher. This paper presents a practical approach utilising a generic constraint satisfaction (CS) to interpret NMR spectra and determine molecular structures. It is based on the translation of NMR signals into the sets of constraints on molecular structure. When solved by a constraint solver, these constraints generate a set of all possible molecular structures consistent with the observed NMR spectra data. Based on our previous work accompanied by a prototype implementation, we report here further developments and improvements. These include more precise modelling of NMR constraints and new implementation using the constraint modelling language MiniZinc. We enhance the user experience by adding more functionalities to the system and providing a graphical user interface. Spectroscopists can select from a list of complementary constraints obtained/known outside the scope of NMR. We integrate the PubChem database to find matches for molecular structures. In addition, we use the Cheminfo website's prediction services to provide users with convenient and on-demand access to NMR predictions. To evaluate the effectiveness of our approach, we conducted extensive experiments on diverse NMR spectra from a range of 20 problems. By applying all the constraints, we were found to provide accurate and efficient solutions in all cases.

**Keywords:** Constraint satisfaction problem · Constraint programming · NMR data interpretation · Molecular structure generation

## 1 Introduction

Nuclear Magnetic Resonance (NMR) is an analytical method that provides atomic-level structural information on molecules. NMR measures the resonance frequency of atoms, which is affected by neighbouring atoms, thereby providing structural information. Combining information from multiple nuclei, NMR can be used for elucidating molecular structures. This process of structural elucidation through NMR is typically time-consuming and requires the expertise of specialists. The interpretation of NMR spectral data currently involves human experts as the elucidation process is complex, laborious, and the outcomes may be ambiguous. Since the 1960s, research has been conducted on automating the NMR spectra interpretation and developing Computer-Assisted Structure Elucidation (CASE) systems [12]. Several such systems are available as research prototypes or commercial propositions [2]. Computer-assisted NMR analysis faces various ongoing challenges, including achieving higher levels of automation, effectively managing spectrum uncertainty, handling the ambiguity inherent in the analysis, and addressing the complexities introduced by mixtures rather than pure substances. NMR analysis's main aim lends itself naturally to the constraint satisfaction (CS) area. The structural information obtained from NMR data can be seen as a set of constraints, and an elucidated molecular structure is a solution to this set of constraints. This observation was the foundation of our investigation. We found it quite surprising that only a few recent attempts have been made to apply generic CS techniques to NMR analysis.

There are some automated implementations, but their applications are for specific cases and/or require additional information on top of what NMR provides. In [17] and [18], the authors have validated that the problem of structure elucidation can be solved by reformulation of the structural information obtained from NMR spectra as constraints and employing generic constraint solvers. The open-source system [18] allows applying basic types of NMR constraints and user-specified allowed/forbidden molecular structures. While this research has proven the feasibility of the CS-based NMR analysis, important theoretical and practical questions have been left open. First, the assessment of the proposed method has been illustrated by case studies but was not systematically assessed. Second, the investigation of NMR constraints was conducted from an idealised standpoint without considering the practical limitations of the NMR technique. For example, in the practice of NMR analysis, it is expected that certain NMR constraints that are theoretically possible may not be extractable from the spectra. These types of questions and concerns have been addressed in a more recent paper [1], where a more systemic approach addressing both theoretical principles and practical limitations of NMR analysis was followed, and a prototype implementation has been presented.

NMR can record information based on the connectivity of multiple nuclei, and using such information alone provides a great deal of structural information [6]. The current automated systems do not utilise this fact to the fullest. Such information, coupled with basic physiochemical rules, can be used to generate constraints on which molecular structures are possible. Consequently, applying a constraint satisfaction-based approach to provide a generalised method to aid structural elucidation is favourable.

This paper reports on further developments and improvements of the approach from [1] as outlined below:

– On the conceptual side, we present more precise modelling of NMR constraints, including:

- Handling of negative constraints, meaning that not only the presence but also an absence of NMR signal in the spectrum implies structural constraints on a molecule (a form of closed world assumption)
- More precise modelling of NMR constraints concerning non-carbon atoms in so-called HMBC spectra
- Improved design of the system, including novel workflows:
  - Supporting work with mixtures as opposed to only pure chemical substances
  - Generation of synthetic NMR data for testing and evaluation using publicly available *Cheminfo* web service
  - Testing of obtained solutions, that is, molecular structures/fragments, by querying the publicly available chemical databases to match the solutions
  - Unified interfaces and data formats for experimental and synthetic data
- Novel implementation, including:
  - Using more common and popular high-level modelling language MiniZinc [16] to improve modelling transparency and efficiency of constraint solving
  - Advanced graphical user interface to support flexible user interaction with a system

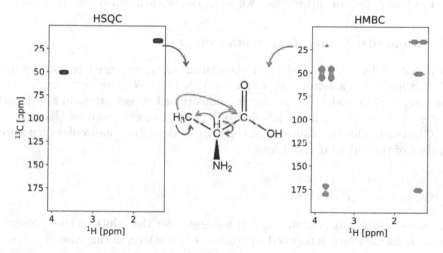

**Fig. 1.** The connectivity information is derived from HSQC (left panel) and HMBC (right panel) for alanine (middle panel). Each small spot located at the intersection of the chemical shifts of the atoms involved represents a peak [1].

## 2   Constraint-Based NMR Analysis

This paper focuses on two primary types of 2D NMR spectra commonly employed in molecular structure elucidation: Heteronuclear Single Quantum Coherence (HSQC) and Heteronuclear Multiple Bond Correlation (HMBC) experiments. These experiments aim to correlate the signals of $^{13}C$ and $^1H$

atoms. They are typically represented as contour plots, where the axes represent so-called chemical shifts. In Fig. 1, the NMR spectra are presented, with the left panel showing the HSQC spectrum and the right panel displaying the HMBC spectrum. The units of these chemical shifts are Hertz or the widely used normalised scale of parts per million (ppm) by convention[1].

The structural information of a molecule is represented in NMR spectra through peaks, which are illustrated as small spots located at the intersection of the chemical shifts of the atoms involved. The peaks observed in the HSQC spectrum correspond to pairs of directly bonded $C$ and $H$ atoms, indicating a graph distance of 1 between their corresponding vertices in the multigraph representation. In contrast, the peaks in the HMBC spectrum represent pairs of $C$ and $H$ atoms separated by two or three bonds, denoting a graph distance of 2 or 3 between their respective vertices in the multigraph.

Notice that peak selection/picking from the spectra is a separate processing stage in the NMR spectra interpretation and we assume that it is already done before our system is applied, so information about peaks is supplied to the input of constraint-based framework.

The high-level design of the NMR constraint satisfaction framework from the discussed principles is presented in Fig. 2. There are different types of constraints used in this paper. In this section, we will present each constraint in detail.

## 2.1   Molecular Graph Representation

As proposed by [1], the molecular structures are represented as multigraphs $(V, e)$, where $V$ is a set of nodes and $e : V \times V \rightarrow N$ is an edge multiplicity function, used to model *multiple bonds* connections between atoms in a molecule. Nodes of the multigraph are labelled by types of atoms (such as (H)ydrogen, or (C)arbon). The first category of constraints describing molecular structures consists of the following conditions.

- $e(x, y) = e(y, x)$   (**U**)ndirected
- $e(x, x) = 0$      (**N**)osLoops

When analysing pure substances, it is necessary for the solutions to represent a single molecule which is opposed to mixtures. Therefore, in this case, a *connectedness* constraint should be imposed to ensure that the molecular multigraph represents a single molecule.

- Multigraph $(V, e)$ is connected (**C**)onnectedness

Notice that to analyse mixtures with unknown numbers of components, it is sufficient to omit **C** constraint. The connected components of disconnected multigraph solutions will then represent the molecular structures of the components.

---

[1] Detailed introduction to all relevant chemical concepts is out of the scope of this paper. An interested reader with a Computer Science background may find an appropriate introduction in [6].

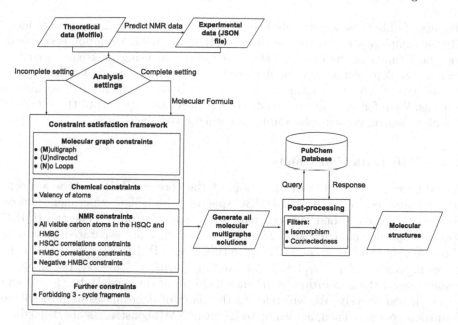

**Fig. 2.** The system's workflow. Demonstrating the different data inputs, constraints satisfaction framework and the post-processing stage. PubChem Database query is optional.

Thus, constraint-based NMR analysis provides a simple and elegant approach to the analysis of mixtures, which is out of the scope of many alternative computer-assisted methods for NMR spectra interpretation. Connectedness constraints, when applied to the search of large molecular structures, may impose high computational costs. After experimentation with a prototype implementation, we have found that it is more efficient to handle it at the post-processing stage, generating all solutions and filtering them on connectedness conditions. This solution was adopted in the implementation.

Valency is the fundamental chemical property of the constituting atoms, so all molecular structures should satisfy valency constraints. Depending on whether we are looking for solutions representing complete molecular structures or just molecular fragments, one of the following constraints is used [1]:

- $\forall x \in V \; d(x) = v(l(x))$ (complete setting)     **(VC)**
- $\forall x \in V \; d(x) \leq v(l(x))$ (incomplete setting)     **(VI)**

Here $d(x)$ is a degree of a vertex $x$ in a multigraph, that is $\Sigma_{y \in V} e(x, y)$, $v$ is a (predefined) valency function, and $l$ is an atom type labelling function.

Notice that for HMBC and HSQC spectra analysis *incomplete setting* is the most fundamental, for these types of spectra bear structural information about bonds only between carbon ($C$), hydrogen ($H$) and possibly other unidentified types ($X$) of atoms required for the satisfaction of $dist^3$ conditions in HMBC constraints. If only these spectra are known, then it is generally impossible to identify the complete structure of the molecule. If additional information is supplied, e.g. the formula of the chemical substance obtained using mass spectrometry, then a complete setting may be deployed. We have implemented both settings in our system, but in this paper, we discuss only developments for incomplete settings. We refer an interested reader to our previous paper [1] to the details of complete setting implementation, largely unchanged since then.

## 2.2  NMR Data Constraints

As we have noticed in the Introduction, at the core of NMR analysis are constraints imposed by HSQC and HMBC spectra. The HSQC experiment is used to identify a direct bond between pairs of $H$ and $C$ atoms, while the HMBC spectroscopy detects correlated $H$ and $C$ atoms that are separated by two or three bonds in the multigraphs. Let the HSQC and HMBC spectra contain the peaks $p_{i,j}$ with $1 \leq i \leq t_1; 1 \leq j \leq t_2$ and $q_{k,m}$ with $1 \leq k \leq s_1; 1 \leq m \leq s_2$, respectively. Let the coordinates (chemical shifts) of these peaks be $(h_i, c_j)$ and $(h_k, c_m)$, respectively. We will refer to the pairs of coordinates as peaks if no confusion appears. Then, according to [1] basic NMR constraints are defined as:

$$\exists \bar{x} \exists \bar{y} \, (HSQC(\bar{x}, \bar{y}) \wedge HMBC(\bar{x}, \bar{y}) \wedge ID(\bar{x}, \bar{y})) \tag{1}$$

where $\bar{x} = x_1, \ldots x_m$ and $\bar{y} = y_1, \ldots y_n$ are sequences of variables,

$$HSQC(\bar{x}, \bar{y}) :=$$

$$\bigwedge_{i,j} (dist^{(1)}(x_{h_i}, y_{c_j}) \wedge l(x_{h_i}) = H \wedge l(y_{c_j}) = C); \tag{2}$$

$$HMBC(\bar{x}, \bar{y}) :=$$

$$\bigwedge_{k,m} ((dist^{(2)}(x_{h_k}, y_{c_m}) \vee dist^{(3)}(x_{h_k}, y_{c_m})) \wedge l(x_{h_k}) = H \wedge l(y_{c_m}) = C); \tag{3}$$

$$ID(\bar{x}, \bar{y}) :=$$

$$\bigwedge_{c_i \neq c_j} (x_{c_i} \neq x_{c_j}) \wedge \bigwedge_{h_i \neq h_j} (y_{h_i} \neq y_{h_j}) \tag{4}$$

Here $d^{(n)}(x, y)$ denotes the constraint asserting that the distance between vertices $x$ and $y$ in a multigraph, defined in the usual way, is $n$. In fact, the representation of HMBC constraints above is somewhat simplified and additionally, one needs to require some conditions on the types of atoms lying on paths connecting $x$ and $y$ which witness $dist^2(x, y)$ and $dist^3(x, y)$ conditions. We discuss these in the next section.

Therefore, the fundamental NMR constraints assert the existence of pairs of $C$ and $H$ atoms satisfying necessary graph distance conditions provided by HSQC and HMBC spectra.

## 2.3   Modifications of NMR Data Constraints

**Negative Constraints.** Basic NMR data constraints as introduced in [1] and discussed above, assume *permissive* interpretations of spectra. That means the constraints state only the existence of pairs of atoms satisfying some distance conditions, – these are indicated by peaks in the spectra, – but do not say anything about the non-existence of any other pairs of atoms, permitting arbitrary fragments to occur elsewhere. This approach can be justified in some practical NMR interpretation scenarios, where one assumes that some peaks expected in the spectra may be missing due to experimental errors and uncertainty. However, in many other scenarios, one may wish to apply a kind of *closed world assumption*, meaning if there is no peak/signal in HMBC spectra, the configurations described by HMBC constraints should not occur. To express such an assumption, we define **(N)**egative constraint as follows:

$$\bigwedge_{i,j} \neg[((dist^{(2)}(x_{h_i}, y_{c_j}) \vee dist^{(3)}(x_{h_i}, y_{c_j})) \wedge l(x_{h_i}) = H \wedge l(y_{c_j}) = C)] \quad (5)$$

for all $(h_i, c_j)$ *not peaks* in HMBC spectrum. We have implemented negative constraints in our framework and the user has a choice to include or exclude them during analysis. These constraints not only allow more precise modelling of assumptions under which the interpretation of NMR spectra is conducted but also allow to reduce the number of solutions.

**More Precise HMBC Constraints.** As we mentioned in the previous section, a peak in HMBC spectra imposes the existence of a path of the form $H\text{-}X\text{-}C$ (length two) or $H\text{-}X\text{-}Y\text{-}C$ (length three) formed by atoms in the molecule and bonds between them. In fact, more information is available from the spectra and the type of $X$ atoms in the shown paths is known to be $C$. That means the precise condition is the existence of either $H\text{-}C\text{-}C$ or $H\text{-}C\text{-}X\text{-}C$ paths, where the type of $X$ atom is generally unknown. In the implementation reported in [1], a simplifying assumption was made, where the unknown atom $X$ in possible paths $H\text{-}C\text{-}X\text{-}C$ is assumed to be carbon ($C$). While it can be justified in many practical applications, where indeed $X$ is most commonly $C$ there are cases when $X$ should be interpreted by non $C$ atoms. In such cases, the solutions representing true structures may be missed, which is not fully satisfactory from the principle viewpoint. If we require our system to be *complete*, that is among potentially many possible solutions, it always generates a true (sub)structure, then one needs more precise modelling of HMBC constraints allowing unknown atoms $X$ to appear in possible solutions. This modified type of HMBC constraint is implemented in our new system and a user has a choice either to leave atoms of unknown type $X$ in the solutions or to resolve all of them by $C$. The latter choice is a kind of optimisation that makes finding solutions more efficient but at the expense of potentially missing true solutions.

## 2.4   Further Constraints

In the structure elucidation process, any additional information is valuable for reducing the solution space due to the inherent ambiguity of NMR-derived structural information through bond correlations only. In this process, it is often possible to have prior information regarding expected or impossible fragments within a molecule. This information can be derived from various sources, including existing knowledge in the field, NMR data or functional groups - specific groups of atoms within a molecule - present in the molecule. In this paper, we present a particular type of further constraint, forbidding a 3-cycle constraint, newly implemented in our system.

**Forbidding 3-Cycle Constraint.** This constraint can be expressed by forbidding specific fragments that are unlikely in organic chemistry to appear in the set of candidate molecular structures. Multigraphs with a cycle of 3 are one of the forbidden fragments in our work. A cycle fragment occurs when three vertices are connected in a closed chain. To ensure generating 3-cycle-free multigraphs, we define the following constraint:

$$\forall x, y, z((e(x, y) > 0 \land e(y, z) > 0) \rightarrow e(x, z) = 0 \tag{6}$$

# 3   Post-processing Stage

We realise that certain constraints can be challenging to handle computationally using a general constraint-solving approach. Expressing these constraints within the solver's input language may also be demanding, depending on the solver used. As a result, we employ these constraints as filters during the post-processing stage to filter the generated solutions. In our implementation, there were two options at this stage. Firstly, we used the connectedness filter at the post-processing stage. Another option was to decrease the solution count further by eliminating equivalent multigraphs. In this regard, we experimented with partial or full isomorphism checks and filtering of the obtained multigraphs. Thus, we explored alternative approaches by the post-processing stage to speed up the analysis and to handle computationally expensive or infeasible constraints.

# 4   Implementation

This paper aims to develop a practical approach to generating molecular structures based on satisfying a set of constraints utilising a generic constraint satisfaction framework. We have different settings in our framework to achieve this goal. The incomplete setting will generate structures using NMR data, producing either carbon skeleton or carbon-hydrogen bond structures. In comparison, the complete setting will include the molecular formula (MF) and NMR data to produce all possible structures. In our implementation, users can explore a database of chemical molecules to identify comparable matches. In addition, our method can apply filters on the generated solutions, specifically in terms of connectedness and isomorphism verification. The system has been developed in Python 3.9.10, and constraint modelling language MiniZinc 0.5.0 [16]. All models have been implemented in Gecode solver 6.3.0 [20]. We utilise the NMR prediction services offered by the ChemInfo website [4] to provide users with convenient and readily available predictions for HSQC and HMBC spectra data. To visualise the molecular structures and to handle the connection between atoms, the RDKit software 2021.09.4 [13] is used. To check the isomorphism of labelled graphs, we integrate the Nauty tool version 2_8_6 in the system, which applies canonical labelling algorithms [14] to identify isomorphic structures and to enumerate all nonisomorphic ones. To query the generated solutions against molecular structural databases, we utilise the PubChem database [10] via the Python package PubChemPy version 1.0.4. PubChemPy is accessible at the following URL: https://github.com/mcs07/PubChemPy. It enables us to interact with the PubChem database using Python.

There are two different sources of input data that the system supports, as can be seen in Fig. 2. The first is pre-processed experimental spectra in the form of lists of peaks/chemical shifts. The peak lists can be obtained as ready JSON files or predicted from the ChemInfo platform at nmr.cheminfo.org. The prediction process was performed by submitting theoretical files to the platform to obtain lists of chemical shifts. Another input type is theoretical data as molecular structures (MDL molfile). A user can select either incomplete or complete settings. Then, the user can choose the required constraints from a list of all the framework constraints. Our method also allows to set timeout limit for the process and limits the number of generated solutions. Based on the input data, a generic constraint solver is applied once all selected constraints are formulated. As a result, the system generates a set of all possible molecular structures/ labelled multigraphs that satisfy the selected constraints. At the post-processing stage, there are two choices for further filtering: connectedness and isomorphism can be applied. After that, the set of constraints can be updated, and the processing can be repeated. In our work, we use known structures of chemical compounds to test the system's performance. Thus, the NMR spectra data of amino acids are chosen from the Biological Magnetic Resonance Data Bank (BMRB) website as the data set for the system [22].

## 5   Results and Evaluation

All the experiments were implemented on an Intel Core processor with a frequency of 1.60 GHz running Microsoft Windows version 10.0.19045 and using 16.0 GB of RAM. Our approach utilises experimental and theoretical data to ensure a more comprehensive evaluation, guides improvements in the method, and provides a better understanding of the studied cases.

**Table 1.** Carbon skeleton results for amino acids under the incomplete setting, along with the respective number of solutions achieved by applying specific constraints in an accumulative manner. These constraints include HSQC & HMBC, negative HMBC, and forbidden 3-cycle, identified as $C_1$, $C_2$, and $C_3$, respectively. In the post-processing stage, the table presents the list of nonisomorphic structures.

| Amino acid | MF | $C_1$ | $C_1 + C_2$ | $C_1 + C_2 + C_3$ | Time | Nonisomorphic |
|---|---|---|---|---|---|---|
| Alanine | $C_3H_7NO_2$ | 227 | 227 | 118 | 00.012 | 32 |
| Arginine | $C_6H_{14}N_4O_2$ | 55400 | 33 | 25 | 00.001 | 13 |
| Asparagine | $C_4H_8N_2O_3$ | 2486 | 2486 | 795 | 00.063 | 97 |
| Aspartic acid | $C_4H_7NO_4$ | 2486 | 2486 | 795 | 00.063 | 97 |
| Cysteine | $C_3H_7NO_2S$ | 227 | 227 | 118 | 00.016 | 32 |
| Glutamine | $C_5H_{10}N_2O_3$ | 12846 | 264 | 180 | 00.018 | 41 |
| Glutamic acid | $C_5H_9NO_4$ | 12846 | 264 | 180 | 00.018 | 41 |
| Glycine | $C_2H_5NO_2$ | 5 | 5 | 4 | 00.001 | 3 |
| Histidine | $C_6H_9N_3O_2$ | 96578 | 655 | 332 | 00.038 | 129 |
| Isoleucine | $C_6H_{13}NO_2$ | 25593 | 132 | 99 | 00.011 | 47 |
| Leucine | $C_6H_{13}NO_2$ | 29275 | 321 | 148 | 00.017 | 49 |
| Lysine | $C_6H_{14}N_2O_2$ | 30217 | 228 | 144 | 00.015 | 66 |
| Methionine | $C_5H_{11}NO_2S$ | 6820 | 54 | 40 | 00.004 | 11 |
| Phenylalanine | $C_9H_{11}NO_2$ | - | 1761 | 804 | 00.259 | 243 |
| Proline | $C_5H_9NO_2$ | 8484 | 418 | 218 | 00.045 | 33 |
| Serine | $C_3H_7NO_3$ | 227 | 227 | 118 | 00.012 | 32 |
| Threonine | $C_4H_9NO_3$ | 1545 | 200 | 136 | 00.018 | 30 |
| Tryptophan | $C_{11}H_{12}N_2O_2$ | - | 209 | 106 | 00.066 | 52 |
| Tyrosine | $C_9H_{11}NO_3$ | - | 2042 | 942 | 00.427 | 275 |
| Valine | $C_5H_{11}NO_2$ | 8484 | 418 | 218 | 00.040 | 33 |

In order to obtain experimental data more efficiently, the nmr.cheminfo.org platform was used to predict and simulate NMR data [19].

To evaluate our chosen methodology, we produced complete sets of HSQC and HMBC constraints for all 20 amino acids based on their structures. After that, we computed carbon skeleton solutions as a part of our testing process. In each case, the solutions were subsequently filtered at the post-processing stage to find all nonisomorphic multigraphs.

Table 1 demonstrates the numbers of the carbon skeleton structures obtained during the experiment conducted under the incomplete setting with different sets of constraints $C_1$, $C_2$, and $C_3$ and their combinations.

Applying these constraints in an accumulative manner ($C_1$, $C_2$, and $C_3$) has proven to progressively eliminate improbable structures. This approach is efficient when the number of possible structures is extremely large and needs to be significantly reduced for practical analysis. For all 20 amino acids, we reported the number of all possible solutions with time in seconds and the number of nonisomorphic structures. While running the system, we discovered an out-of-memory case denoted by (-) for several amino acids. These cases are caused when a solver generates an excessive number of solutions, leading to performance or termination issues.

To tackle this issue, we improved our implementation to generate a limited number of solutions instead of all possible structures. In all mentioned cases, limiting the number of solutions to 100 we can obtain them in less than 00.080 s.

HMBC correlations

| Atom | Correlated atoms | | | |
|------|------|------|------|------|
| C1 | C2 | C4 | C5 | C6 |
| C2 | C1 | C3 | C4 | - |
| C3 | C2 | C4 | - | - |
| C5 | C1 | C4 | C6 | - |

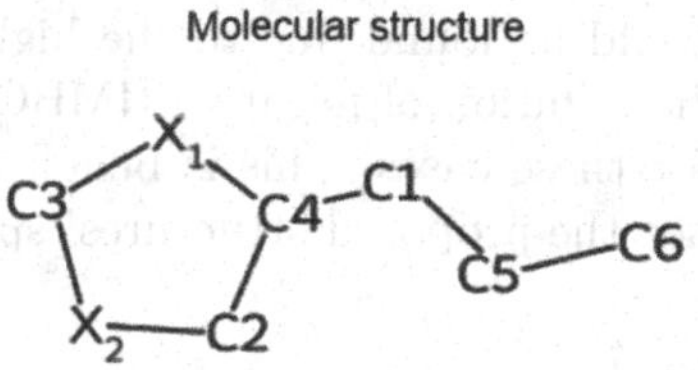

Molecular structure

**Fig. 3.** Correlated carbon atoms with the corresponding carbon skeleton generated from all constraints derived from histidine. Demonstrating more precise modelling of HMBC constraints when it is for non-carbon atoms.

As we seek incomplete molecular structures or fragments, we employ carbons and hydrogen atoms to generate structures. Therefore, in our incomplete setting approach, we incorporated additional $X$ atoms to represent the case when two carbons are connected via a non-carbon atom such as nitrogen $N$, oxygen $O$ and sulfur $S$. Figure 3 demonstrates the result of the HMBC correlations and the precise molecular structure for histidine. In this case, two carbons are either connected directly or via another carbon, except for $C3$, which is connected to $C2$ and $C4$ indirectly through intermediate atoms labelled as $X1$ and $X2$. This connectivity pattern accurately represents the structural arrangement of histidine. The absence of $X$ atoms would limit our ability to represent certain chemical structures accurately. These structures frequently involve intermediate non-carbon atoms, where including these atoms is crucial for a comprehensive depiction. Including $X$ atoms as placeholders between two carbons may expand the number of solutions available in the solution space. However, this inclusion also leads to more precise and accurate solutions.

Most current CASE systems require MF constraints to elucidate structures. Without defining these parameters, the software would often be unable to execute or run as intended. On the other hand, one drawback is that obtaining the exact MF of a compound can be challenging as it could be influenced by various experimental factors, especially for complex or impure samples. Inaccurate or incomplete MF data can lead to incorrect structural assignments [11]. In contrast, our system explicitly defines all constraints used in the solution-finding process and enables systematic exploration of these constraints. It can be utilised with any set of constraints, even incomplete ones, making it applicable throughout the various stages of NMR analysis. By inspecting the results, as described earlier, further experiments can be suggested to resolve ambiguities until a definitive solution is obtained.

In this work, we look deeper into the underlying principles and characteristics of the constraints that allow us to understand better utilising the constraint satisfaction (CS) framework to analyse NMR data. We improve our approach's accuracy, reliability, and overall performance by fine-tuning the implementation process. By incorporating negative HMBC constraints into our implementation, we made significant progress. Previously, there were three cases where no solutions could be found due to the higher number of atoms in the MF. However, with the addition of negative HMBC constraints, we were able to identify solutions for these cases. This is beneficial as it narrows the potential options and increases the proposed structures' specificity.

## 6   Related Work

This study has enhanced our understanding of determining the structure of compounds. It tackles various challenges associated with elucidating molecular structure. In contrast to similar constrained-based structure-generating systems, this paper proposes a realistic and feasible analytical method. Thus, our software generates all plausible structures while considering real-life constraints and utilising the minimal information available.

A set of limitations may affect the molecular structure elucidation results. One potential drawback that might be encountered is the uncertainty of NMR data caused by the different environments, especially during the acquisition of NMR data for solvent or temperature, which can create significant noise in the spectra data. Further improvements should be taken into account to tackle these problems.

Several studies have developed different CASE systems. The Dendral project [21], and their pioneering work in structure elucidation systems using NMR spectra. Since the development of NMR experiment techniques, the number of CASE systems' approaches has remarkably increased, such as [5,7–9] and [15].

Most approaches employ specialised algorithms and complex rules defined by experts, which limits their effectiveness and adaptation to deal with complicated systems, such as molecular mixtures. Our constraint-based system separates rules (constraints) formulation and constraint solving, which allows for much more flexibility and adaptability.

A recent study by [3] applied constraint programming to computational chemistry. Their aim is to generate benzenoids with specific structural properties, such as a prescribed number of hexagons or specific graph-based structures. This focus differs significantly from our own work. In contrast, the framework of CS in [17,18], provides an effective solution to structure elucidation problems. A new open-source system called CP-MolGen was developed to generate molecular structures based on satisfying several predefined constraints. The first constraint is the MF. In practical terms, obtaining the minimum required information to utilise the framework from [17,18] can be challenging and, in some cases, even unfeasible. The availability of MFs is not always readily accessible. Determining the number of bonds often necessitates extensive analytical data from various instruments. Creating a detailed map of specific distances between atoms is a complex and intricate process; the available data is often incomplete.

# 7  Conclusion and Future Work

This paper presents a practical approach to interpreting NMR data to elucidate molecular structures using a constraint satisfaction framework. Our approach uses a set of constraints that define the relationships between NMR signals and structural features to generate a set of all possible candidate structures that are compatible with the observed NMR spectra. We have demonstrated that our approach effectively solves challenging NMR problems, producing accurate and efficient solutions in most cases.

For future work, we plan to extend our approach by incorporating additional types of spectroscopic data, such as infrared spectroscopy. Including different spectroscopic techniques aims to provide further constraints on the candidate structures. We also plan to develop more advanced algorithms to optimise candidate structure filtering, improving our approach's accuracy and efficiency. Furthermore, we will explore the application of our approach to larger and more complex molecules, which will require the development of more sophisticated rules and algorithms.

# References

1. Alharbi, H.A., Barsukov, I., Grosman, R., Lisitsa, A.: Molecular fragments from incomplete, real-life NMR data: framework for spectra analysis with constraint solvers. In: Proceedings of the 14th International Conference on Agents and Artificial Intelligence - Volume 3: ICAART, pp. 834–841. INSTICC, SciTePress (2022). https://doi.org/10.5220/0010915800003116
2. Burns, D.C., Mazzola, E.P., Reynolds, W.F.: The role of computer-assisted structure elucidation (case) programs in the structure elucidation of complex natural products. Nat. Prod. Rep. **36**(6), 919–933 (2019)
3. Carissan, Y., Hagebaum-Reignier, D., Prcovic, N., Terrioux, C., Varet, A.: Using constraint programming to generate benzenoid structures in theoretical chemistry. In: Simonis, H. (ed.) CP 2020. LNCS, vol. 12333, pp. 690–706. Springer, Cham (2020). https://doi.org/10.1007/978-3-030-58475-7_40
4. Cheminfo website. http://www.cheminfo.org/. Accessed 22 Jan 2023
5. Elyashberg, M., Williams, A.: ACD/structure elucidator: 20 years in the history of development. Molecules **26**(21), 6623 (2021)
6. Elyashberg, M.E., Williams, A.J.: Computer-Based Structure Elucidation from Spectral Data. LNC, vol. 89. Springer, Heidelberg (2015). https://doi.org/10.1007/978-3-662-46402-1
7. Elyashberg, M.E., Blinov, K.A., Williams, A.J., Martirosian, E.R., Molodtsov, S.G.: Application of a new expert system for the structure elucidation of natural products from their 1D and 2D NMR data. J. Nat. Prod. **65**(5), 693–703 (2002)

8. Gugisch, R., et al.: MOLGEN 5.0, a molecular structure generator. In: Advances in Mathematical Chemistry and Applications, pp. 113–138. Elsevier (2015)
9. Kessler, P., Godejohann, M.: Identification of tentative marker in Corvina and Primitivo wines with CMC-se. Magn. Reson. Chem. **56**(6), 480–492 (2018)
10. Kim, S., et al.: PubChem substance and compound databases. Nucleic Acids Res. **44**(D1), D1202–D1213 (2016)
11. Kind, T., Fiehn, O.: Metabolomic database annotations via query of elemental compositions: mass accuracy is insufficient even at less than 1 ppm. BMC Bioinf. **7**(1), 1–10 (2006)
12. Koichi, S., et al.: Chemical structure elucidation from 13C NMR chemical shifts: Efficient data processing using bipartite matching and maximal clique algorithms. J. Chem. Inf. Model. **54**(4), 1027–1035 (2014)
13. Landrum, G.: RDKit: open-source cheminformatics software. GitHub SourceForge **10**, 3592822 (2016)
14. McKay, B.D., Piperno, A.: Practical graph isomorphism, II. J. Symb. Comput. **60**, 94–112 (2014)
15. Mnova structure elucidation. http://mestrelab.com/software/mnova/. Accessed 21 Feb 2023
16. Nethercote, N., Stuckey, P.J., Becket, R., Brand, S., Duck, G.J., Tack, G.: MiniZinc: towards a standard CP modelling language. In: Bessière, C. (ed.) CP 2007. LNCS, vol. 4741, pp. 529–543. Springer, Heidelberg (2007). https://doi.org/10.1007/978-3-540-74970-7_38
17. Omrani, M.A., Naanaa, W.: A constrained molecular graph generation with imposed and forbidden fragments. In: Proceedings of the 9th Hellenic Conference on Artificial Intelligence, pp. 1–5 (2016)
18. Omrani, M.A., Naanaa, W.: Constraints for generating graphs with imposed and forbidden patterns: an application to molecular graphs. Constraints **25**, 1–22 (2019)
19. Patiny, L., Bolaños, A., Castillo, A.M., Bernal, A., Wist, J.: Teaching NMR spectra analysis with NMR. cheminfo.org. Magn. Reson. Chem. **56**(6), 529–534 (2018)
20. Schulte, C., Tack, G., Lagerkvist, M.Z.: Modeling and programming with GECODE. In: Schulte, Christian and Tack, Guido and Lagerkvist, Mikael, vol. 1 (2010)
21. Smith, D.H., Gray, N.A., Nourse, J.G., Crandell, C.W.: The DENDRAL project: recent advances in computer-assisted structure elucidation. Anal. Chim. Acta **133**(4), 471–497 (1981)
22. Ulrich, E.L., et al.: BioMagResBank. Nucleic Acids Res. **36**(suppl_1), D402–D408 (2007)

# Short Application Papers

# On the Application of Feed-Forward Artificial Neural Networks to the Maritime Target Motion Analysis Problem

Till Schlüsselburg[1], Christoph Tholen[2(✉)], and Lars Nolle[1,2]

[1] Department of Engineering Sciences, Jade University of Applied Sciences, Wilhelmshaven, Germany
lars.nolle@jade-hs.de
[2] German Research Center for Artificial Intelligence GmbH, RG Marine Perception, Oldenburg, Germany
christoph.tholen@dfki.de

**Abstract.** This work presents a novel approach for the fast prediction of future positions of marine vessels utilizing a simple feed-forward artificial neural network. It is shown that this simple network architecture with a single hidden layer, containing three hidden neurons is capable of predicting the future position of a maritime vessel with an accuracy of 99.26% . For this research a simulation was developed, in order to generate enough track data needed to train the network. The input data had to be converted from common polar coordinate system used by navigators into Cartesian coordinates in order to increase the accuracy of the predictions. The predictions are based on three previous observed positions and their corresponding observation times. It was shown that the accuracy decreased linearly with an increasing noise level of the observations. If the noise level exceeded a maximum noise level c of 20 m, the performance of the network degraded beyond its practical use.

**Keywords:** Feed-Forward Neural Network · Target Motion Analysis

## 1 Introduction

Target Motion Analysis (TMA) in the maritime context aims to make predictions about the state of a signal-emitting object, known as the target, by considering its location, bearing, and velocity based on past observations [1]. However, in practical applications, the accuracy of time delay measurements is affected by noise. This noise might be caused by various factors, such as the cross-correlation function used to find a common signal in a pair of sensors or environmental influences [2]. Another source of errors is false readings or clutter. This clutter is usually assumed to be uniformly distributed over an area $A$.

Figure 1 shows a typical scenario for the TMA problem, where Fig. 1a depicts the ideal scenario, while Fig. 1b shows a real-world scenario with clutter and noise.

M. Bramer and F. Stahl (Eds.): SGAI 2023, LNAI 14381, pp. 481–486, 2023.
https://doi.org/10.1007/978-3-031-47994-6_41

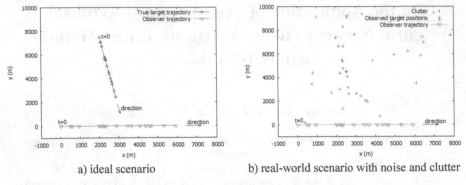

a) ideal scenario                b) real-world scenario with noise and clutter

**Fig. 1.** Scenario for the Target Motion Analysis problem

An observer and a target are moving with constant speed and the target is detected at unequally spaced time instances by the observer.

In the ideal scenario (Fig. 1a), Newtonian physics can be used to calculate the future position, based on the current bearing, speed and location of an object. However, due to the noise and clutter affected measurements, in a real-world scenario (Fig. 1b), the prediction of the future position, more robust methods, such as Kalman filters [3, 4] or Particle filters [5] are employed. More recently, artificial intelligence methods, like LSTM [6] or Ant Colony Optimisation [7] were successfully applied to the TMA problem achieving better accuracy than classical methods used for TMA [6]. Since it was proven by Hornik *et al.* [8, 9] that feed forward neural networks are capable of approximating any given function with any required level of accuracy, this study tries to answer the question, are simple feed-forward neural networks, in principle, capable of solving the TMA problem? Training a feed-forward neuronal network usually requires a large amount of linearly independent training examples. It is very difficult to acquire these amount of real-world training data. Therefore, a simulation was developed, that generates target tracks in a marine environment for training and evaluation.

## 2  Simulations

A simulation tool was developed, which generates target tracks in relation to the ownships position. The parameters of the simulated targets are based on the limitations of real-world targets like ships and boats.

The main parameter used for track generation is the speed of the target. The maximum speed is based on generally known speeds of ships, boats, and other water vehicles. These reach up to 90 km/h or 25 m/s. For each target a constant speed $v$ was chosen randomly from the interval:

$$\left\{ v \in \mathbb{R} | 0\frac{m}{s} \leq v \leq 25\frac{m}{s} \right\}. \tag{1}$$

Due to the problem at hand, it cannot be guaranteed that observations are equidistant in the time domain. Therefore, the time between two observations $t$ was selected randomly from the interval:

$$\{t \in \mathbb{R} \mid 1\,\text{s} \le t \le 10\,\text{s}\}. \tag{2}$$

In principal targets in different distances are of interest. However, due to physical limitations of passive sonar systems measurements up to 6 km are assumed to be sufficiently accurate under most conditions [10]. The initial distance $r$ of the targets is chosen randomly from the interval:

$$\{r \in \mathbb{R} \mid 0\,\text{m} \le r \le 6000\,\text{m}\}. \tag{3}$$

The initial position of the targets are determined by the radius $r$ and the bearing $\varphi$. The bearing was also chosen randomly from the interval:

$$\{\varphi \in \mathbb{R} \mid -180° \le \varphi \le 180°\}. \tag{4}$$

In order to test the reliability of the network, the simulation offers the possibility of adding noise to the track data generated. In order to generate realistic error curves, the added noise is randomly chosen from a Gaussian distribution with mean of zero and a distance depending standard deviation. The track data generated by the simulation was validated by human experts. Figure 2 shows a plot of 1,000 simulated target tracks. For training the artificial feed-forward network, sets of 10,000 were used, as discussed in the next section.

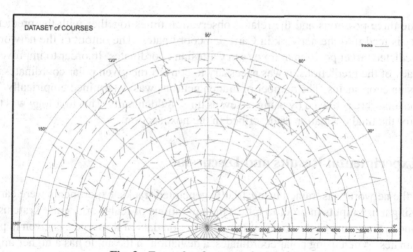

**Fig. 2.** Example of generated track data

# 3   Network Type and Architecture

It has been proved by Hornik, Stinchcombe and White that standard multilayer feedforward networks with one hidden layer using arbitrary squashing functions are capable of approximating any measurable function from one finite dimensional space to another to any desired degree of accuracy [8, 9]. Here, a multilayer perceptron network with one hidden layer, utilizing Sigmoid and ReLU activation functions were used and the topology was determined empirically (Fig. 3). The training of the network was undertaken with 70% of the data is for training while 30% of the data were used for testing.

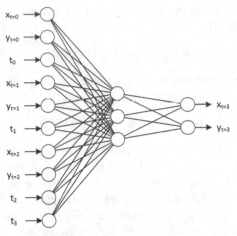

**Fig. 3.** Network topology

The three positions and the related observation times together with the prediction time $t_3$ is feed into the network in Cartesian coordinates. The output of the network is the predicted target position at time $t_3$ in Cartesian coordinates. In order to improve the accuracy of the predictions, it was necessary to convert the given polar coordinates into Cartesian coordinates. The number of hidden neurons was determined empirically. The best results were achieved by using as few as three hidden units. This topology was then used for the final evaluation as described in the next section.

## 4   Experimental Results and Discussion

Once the network was trained using 10,000 generated tracks, experiments were carried out using noisy inputs in order to reflect the limitations of real-world sonar systems.

Due to the nature of the sonar system, the motion data of the targets is given in polar coordinates. When using polar coordinates, a deviation in the angle has a higher impact on the error than a similar deviation in the radius. Therefore, an accuracy metric, based on the absolute distance $d$ between two points given in polar coordinates is used in this research:

$$d = \sqrt{\left(r_t^2 + r_p^2 - \left(2 \cdot r_t \cdot r_p \cdot \cos(\varphi_t - \varphi_p)\right)\right)}. \tag{5}$$

where $d$ represents the absolute distance between the true position and the predicted position represented in polar coordinates. Here $r_i$ represents the radius while $\varphi_i$ represents the angle of the polar coordinate $i$. The index $t$ represents the true position, while the index $p$ represents the predicted position.

The accuracy $acc$ is calculated using the maximum distance of 6,000 m as follows:

$$acc = 1 - \frac{d}{6,000\,m}. \tag{6}$$

A distance $d$ above 30 m, reflecting in an accuracy smaller than 0.995, is deemed insufficient for practical applications.

The noisy inputs $\hat{x}$ were calculated according to:

$$\hat{x} = x + \min(r(\sigma(d)), c). \tag{7}$$

where $\hat{x}$ represents the noise affected positon, $x$ denotes the real position, $r(c)$ represents the Gaussian random number with a standard deviation of $r(\sigma(d))$ depending on the distance $d$. The constant $c$ is used to limit the maximum noise level and is chosen from the interval:

$$\{c \in \mathbb{N}|0, 20, \ldots, 120\}. \tag{8}$$

- Experiments for all seven values of $c$, were carried out using 10,000 new generated tracks each. The mean accuracy following Eq. (6) for the different noise levels $c$ are depicted in Fig. 4.

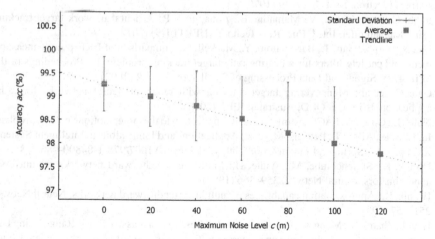

**Fig. 4.** Experimental results

It can be seen from the figure that the average accuracy of the predictions without noise was 99.26%. This is slightly worse than the target accuracy of 99.5% given for practical applications. In addition, it can be seen that the accuracy decreases linearly with increasing noise with an $R^2$ value of 0.9979, whereas the standard deviation increases following an exponential equation with an $R^2$ value of 0.9888.

## 5 Conclusions and Future Work

It was shown that a simple feed-forward network with a single hidden layer, containing three hidden neurons is capable of predicting the future position of a maritime vessel. The prediction for a variable chosen point in the future is based on three previous observed positions and their corresponding observation times. The accuracy achieved in these early experiments was near the accuracy required for real-world applications. It was shown that the accuracy decreased linearly with an increasing noise level of the observations. If the noise level exceeded a maximum noise level $c$ of 20 m, the performance of the network degraded beyond its practical use.

Also, the experiments did not include clutter, i.e. observations that do not originate from the target. In future work the influence of clutter on the predictions will be examined. In addition, the network will be fine-tuned using real-world data based on Automatic Identification System (AIS) tracks of seagoing vessels. This will potentially increase the accuracy of the network.

## References

1. Hassab, J.C., Guimond, B.W., Nardone, S.C.: Estimation of location and motion parameters of moving source observed from a linear array. J. Acoust. Soc. Am. **70**(4), 1054–1061 (1981)
2. Carevic, D.: Robust estimation techniques for target motion analysis using passively sensed transient signals. IEEE J. Oceanic Eng. **28**(2), 262–270 (2003)
3. Aidala, V.J.: Kalman filter behavior in bearings-only tracking applications. IEEE Trans. Aerosp. Electron. Syst. **1**, 29–39 (1979)
4. Babu, G., Jayaprakash, V., Mamatha, B., Annapurna, P.: A neural network target tracking using Kalman filter. Int. J. Eng. Res. Technol. (IJERT) **1**(9) (2012)
5. Lin, X., Kirubarajan, T., Bar-Shalom, Y., Maskell, S.: Comparison of EKF, pseudo measurement, and particle filters for a bearing-only target tracking problem. In: Proceedings of the SPIE 4728, Signal and Data Processing of Small Targets 2002 (2002)
6. Gao, C., et al.: Maneuvering target tracking with recurrent neural networks for radar application, Brisbane, QLD, Australia: IEEE (2018)
7. Nolle, L.: On a novel ACO-estimator and its application to the target motion analysis problem. In: Ellis, R., Allen, T., Petridis, M. (eds.) Applications and Innovations in Intelligent Systems XV, pp. 3–16. Springer, London (2008). https://doi.org/10.1007/978-1-84800-086-5_1
8. Hornik, K., Stinchcombe, M., White, H.: Multilayer Feedforward networks are universal approximators. Neural Netw. **2**, 359–366 (1989)
9. Hornik, K.: Approximation capabilities of multilayer feedforward networks. Neural Netw. **4**, 251–257 (1991)
10. Han, J., Zhang, X., Meng, C., Cao, F.: Simulated Research on Passive Sonar Range Using Different, Science and Technology on Underwater Test and Control Laboratory, Dalian, China: EDP Sciences (2015)

# Detecting Bias in University News Articles: A Comparative Study Using BERT, GPT-3.5 and Google Bard Annotations

Rawan Bin Shiha[1,2](✉) [iD], Eric Atwell[1] [iD], and Noorhan Abbas[1] [iD]

[1] School of Computing, University of Leeds, Leeds, UK
{e.s.atwell,n.h.abbas}@leeds.ac.uk
[2] Imam Mohammad Ibn Saud Islamic University, Riyadh, Saudi Arabia
rmbinshiha@imamu.edu.sa

**Abstract.** This study focuses on the detection of bias in news articles from a British research-intensive university, given the substantial significance of higher education institutions as information sources and their considerable influence in shaping public opinion. While prior research has underscored the existence of bias in news content, there has been limited exploration of bias detection in the specific realm of higher education news articles. To address this gap, we adopt a similar approach to Raza et al. [9] by utilising DistilBert to classify news articles published on a university website. Our primary objective is to evaluate the performance of the model in detecting bias within this domain. Furthermore, we utilise the capabilities of GPT-3.5-turbo for annotation tasks, supported by recent studies showcasing its effectiveness. In addition, we conduct performance comparisons by testing Google's Bard for annotation tasks alongside GPT-3.5-turbo. To assess the quality of DistilBert, GPT-3.5-turbo, and Google's Bard annotations, we acquired ground truth labels through Amazon Mturk to annotate a subset of our data. The experimental findings demonstrate that the DistilBert model, trained on the MBIC dataset, shows moderate performance in detecting biased language in university news articles. Moreover, the assessment of GPT-3.5-turbo and Google Bard annotations against human-annotated data reveals a low level of accuracy, highlighting their unreliable annotations in this domain.

**Keywords:** University news · Bias · GPT · BERT · Google Bard · Neural Networks

## 1 Introduction

Bias detection in news articles has been a subject of significant interest among researchers due to the pervasive presence of bias in media content [2, 8, 10]. Several methodologies have been proposed to detect and identify bias in news articles. Notably, Raza et al. [9] investigated bias detection using DistilBert, a condensed variant of BERT, which they fine-tuned on the MBIC dataset. Their model classified news articles as either biased or non-biased. However, there is a research gap concerning bias detection specifically

© The Author(s), under exclusive license to Springer Nature Switzerland AG 2023
M. Bramer and F. Stahl (Eds.): SGAI 2023, LNAI 14381, pp. 487–492, 2023.
https://doi.org/10.1007/978-3-031-47994-6_42

in higher education news articles. Higher education institutions hold substantial significance as information sources and wield considerable influence in shaping public opinion. Therefore, understanding and identifying bias in news articles related to higher education is crucial for promoting accurate and balanced reporting. News articles covering topics such as university policies, research breakthroughs, student experiences, and educational initiatives can often be subject to various forms of bias. On the other hand, recent studies have demonstrated the effectiveness of GPT [4–6] for annotation tasks, surpassing crowd-workers in areas such as relevance, stance, topics, and frame detection. These studies indicate the potential of GPT for annotation tasks. Given the insights from these GPT studies, it is reasonable to consider Google AI Bard as a potential annotation tool, given its status as a large language model trained on a substantial corpus consisting of 1.56 trillion words [1]. In this study, we aim to address the research gap by adopting a similar methodology to Raza et al. [9] to classify news articles published on a university website. Additionally, we explore the application of GPT-3.5 and Google Bard for annotation purposes in our dataset.

## 2 Related Work

### 2.1 Bias in the News Articles

Based on the literature, it has been established that news articles often exhibit significant bias [2, 8, 10]. Consequently, many researchers have designed methodologies to detect and identify bias within news articles. As mentioned previously, a notable investigation into bias detection in news was conducted by Raza et al. [9] This study employs DistilBert, a condensed variant of BERT, which they fine-tune using the MBIC dataset, for binary classification. As a result, their bias detection model generates classifications of news articles as either biased or non-biased. Adopting a similar methodology to Raza et al.'s [9] study, we aim to classify news articles published on a university website. To the best of our knowledge, there is currently no existing research that specifically examines news articles within the domain of higher education news.

### 2.2 GPT and Google Bard Annotation

Several recent studies [4–6] have employed GPT, showcasing its efficacy. These studies go as far as demonstrating that GPT surpasses crowd-workers in various annotation tasks, such as determining relevance, stance, topics, and detecting frames. Huang et al. [5] investigate the effectiveness of GPT in detecting implicit hateful tweets and its implications for generating accurate and high-quality natural language explanations (NLEs). Using the LatentHatred dataset [3], which comprises 795 instances, they assess GPT's performance in identifying implicit hateful tweets. The analysis reveals that GPT labels 80% of the instances as 'Implicitly Hateful', but also misclassifies 20% as 'Not Implicitly Hateful', conflicting with the original dataset labels. However, the results indicate that in the cases where there was a 20% disagreement between GPT's classifications and the original dataset labels, the workers tended to align more with GPT's classification outcomes. In this research study, we perform a comparable task by employing

GPT to annotate a subset of data from our dataset. This approach allows us to assess the performance of our model.

Although no specific studies utilising Google Bard for annotation purposes were found, a study conducted by Raimondi et al. [7] tried to employ Google Bard in question-answer tasks. This research demonstrated the impressive performance of Large Language Models (LLMs) in providing highly accurate responses to postgraduate Ophthalmology specialty exams in the UK. The study's evaluation argues that Google Bard demonstrated competitive accuracy rates, achieving 62.6% accuracy for part 1 questions and 51.9% accuracy for part 2 questions. While Google Bard's accuracy was not the highest among the other LLM chatbots, it showcased its potential as a valuable tool.

## 3 Datasets

### 3.1 MBIC – a Media Bias Annotation Dataset [10]

The MBIC (i.e., A Media Bias Annotation Dataset Including Annotator Characteristics) dataset [10] was employed in the training of DistilBert, as observed in Raza et al.'s study [9]. The dataset consists of records of both biased and non-biased sentences of news articles. Raza et al. [9] extended the dataset by identifying and including biases related to gender, race, ethnicity, education, religion, and language, as gleaned from pertinent literature [11, 12].

### 3.2 University's News Dataset

To compile the dataset, we used a web scraping approach to extract news articles from a research-intensive British university. The extracted articles spanned from April 2009 to mid-March 2023, resulting in a total of 5,782 news articles. The dataset encompasses various features, including topics, the content of the news articles themselves, and corresponding URLs.

## 4 Methodology

We employed a pre-trained model for the classification of our dataset. Specifically, we selected DistilBert, a model introduced by Raza et al. [9] which had been trained on the MBIC dataset [10]. We then utilised GPT-3.5-turbo and Google Bard for annotation purposes. Out of the original dataset comprising 7259 records, we randomly selected 110 records for annotation using GPT-3.5-turbo and Google Bard. Since our dataset lacked labels in its raw form, we annotate the same random subset of 110 records using Amazon Mechanical Turk (MTurk). To create a ground-truth sample data, three MTurk workers were tasked to annotate the sample data for bias and subjectivity. The annotations generated by MTurk workers were then compared to the labels produced by DistilBert, GPT-3.5-turbo and Google Bard to assess their reliability and accuracy.

# 5 Experiments and Results

## 5.1 Experimental Setup

The experiments were conducted on a Jupyter Notebook running on a MacBook Pro with 32 GB of RAM and an Apple M2 Pro chip. The parameters used for the DistilBert model (the bias detection model) were consistent with those chosen by Raza et al. [9] including a batch size of 16, 10 epochs, a sequence length of 512, and 2 labels (biased and non-biased) for news classification. The specific DistilBert model variant employed was "distilbert-base-uncased" which has 6 layers, 768 hidden units, 12 attention heads, and a total of 66 million parameters. The bias detection model was employed to classify a dataset consisting of 7,259 records from the University's news articles. Each news article was assigned a state (biased or not biased) by the bias detection module, along with the corresponding probability of the assigned class. GPT-3.5-turbo was employed for annotating a sample data of 110 records within the University's news dataset at a rate of $0.002 per 1,000 tokens. In contrast, Google Bard provided annotations for the same sample data without any cost. Ground truth for the sample data was constructed by employing three human annotators from MTurk. To assess the models performance, a comparison was made between the annotations generated by the models and those provided by MTurk annotators. This evaluation employed metrics including accuracy (ACC), precision (PREC), recall (Rec), and F1-score (F1). Furthermore, by leveraging the predicted probabilities of the model for both classes, log loss and the area under the receiver operating characteristic curve (AUC-ROC) were computed as additional evaluation measures.

## 5.2 Results and Analysis

**Comparative Evaluation of DistilBert and MTurk Worker Annotations.** The performance of the DistilBert model on our dataset was evaluated using several evaluation metrics. The model classification was compared with the MTurk worker annotations to compute these metrics as shown in Table 1. Additionally, DistilBert's accuracy score of 68.8% implies that it accurately classified a majority of the instances. This suggests that the model demonstrates moderate proficiency in identifying biased language within our dataset. The precision score stands at 89.9%. This indicates that the DistilBert model exhibits high precision in detecting biased language, as a substantial portion of its predicted positive instances are indeed true positives. In terms of recall, the model achieved a score of 73.2%. This suggests that the model has a good ability to identify a significant portion of the biased language present in the dataset. Furthermore, the F1 score is calculated at 80.7%, which indicates that the model strikes a good trade-off between precision and recall, making it a promising for identifying biased language. The assessment of the model, characterised by a Log Loss value of 0.457 and an AUC-ROC score of 0.539, reveals that the model exhibits a degree of confidence in its predictive capabilities as indicated by the Log Loss metric. However, the AUC-ROC score intimates that the model's capacity to discern between biased and unbiased text is only marginally superior to random chance. These metrics collectively highlight the DistilBert model's moderate proficiency in detecting biased language. Nevertheless, it is evident that the language used in news articles varies depending on the specific domain. Online-published news articles employ a distinct language compared to the content found on universities' websites. Consequently, to achieve optimal performance, it is imperative to train the model on data within the same domain.

**Table 1.** Performance of DistilBert in bias annotation task.

| Model | ACC | PREC | REC | F1 |
|-------|------|------|------|------|
| DistilBert [9] | 68.8% | 89.9% | 73.2% | 80.7% |

**GPT-3.5 and Google Bard Annotations against MTurk Worker Annotations.** To assess the quality of GPT-3.5 and Google Bard annotations, we used the same sample records annotated by MTurk workers. The evaluation aimed to determine the reliability and accuracy of GPT-3.5 and Google Bard in generating annotations. The results of the evaluation are shown in Table 2.

**Table 2.** Performance of GPT-3.5-turbo and Google Bard in bias annotation task.

| Model | ACC | PREC | REC | F1 |
|-------|------|------|------|------|
| GPT-3.5-turbo | 30.2% | 95.2% | 20.6% | 33.9% |
| Google Bard | 40.4% | 94.4% | 35.1% | 51.1% |

Based on these results, it can be observed that Google Bard outperforms GPT-3.5-turbo in terms of accuracy. However, GPT-3.5-turbo has a higher precision of 95.2%, indicating that when it predicts a positive class, it is more likely to be correct compared to Google Bard. However, the difference in precision is relatively small. Google Bard has a higher recall compared to GPT-3.5-turbo. This suggests that Google Bard is better at identifying positive instances in the dataset. Moreover, Google Bard achieved a higher F1 score compared to GPT-3.5-turbo. Overall, when comparing the two models Google Bard emerges as the superior performer, boasting higher accuracy, recall, and F1 score, whereas GPT-3.5-turbo exhibits a slightly superior precision. However, both models did not achieve high accuracy for bias annotation tasks in the domain of education. This could be attributed to the fact that both models are trained on information found online, which might not be directly applicable to the specificities of educational content.

## 6  Conclusion

Our evaluation of the DistilBert model's performance on our dataset reveals a notably high accuracy of 68.8%. This surprising result indicates the model's proficiency in correctly classifying instances within our study, despite the disparity between our data and the data it was originally pre-trained on, which belong to different domains. This underscores DistilBert's capacity to effectively capture language patterns and contextual information within the specific domain of university news articles. Nevertheless, it remains imperative to tailor language models to specific domains to achieve even higher accuracy, recognising the inherent variations in language usage between different domains, such as online news articles and university news articles. Furthermore, the evaluation of GPT-3.5 and Google Bard annotations in comparison to human annotations revealed subpar performance, achieving respective accuracy rates of 30.2% and 40.4% for correct identifications. These evaluation outcomes underscore the less-than-optimal reliability of GPT-3.5 and Google Bard in producing annotations when contrasted with human-annotated data. While Google Bard exhibits a superior accuracy level compared to GPT-3.5, there is still room for improvement in the overall performance to generate high-quality annotations. In our analysis, we found that training machine learning models on domain-specific data is essential for optimal performance. Our future work will involve using annotated data focused on higher education news articles to train our models. By incorporating domain-specific data and exploring alternative techniques, we aim to improve bias detection accuracy in this context.

# References

1. Ahmed, I., Kajol, M., Hasan, U., Datta, P.P., Roy, A., Reza, M.R.: ChatGPT vs. Bard: a comparative study. UMBC Student Collection. (2023)
2. Baly, R., Karadzhov, G., Alexandrov, D., Glass, J., Nakov, P.: Predicting factuality of reporting and bias of news media sources (2018)
3. ElSherief, M., et al.: Latent hatred: A benchmark for understanding implicit hate speech (2021)
4. Gilardi, F., Alizadeh, M., Kubli, M.: ChatGPT outperforms crowd-workers for text-annotation tasks (2023)
5. Huang, F., Kwak, H., An, J.: Is chatGPT better than human annotators? Potential and limitations of chatGPT in explaining implicit hate speech (2023)
6. Kuzman, T., Ljubešić, N., Mozetič, I.: ChatGPT: beginning of an end of manual annotation? Use case of automatic genre identification (2023)
7. Raimondi, R., Tzoumas, N., Salisbury, T., Di Simplicio, S., Romano, M.R.: Comparative analysis of large language models in the Royal College of Ophthalmologists fellowship exams (2023)
8. Raza, S.: A news recommender system considering temporal dynamics and diversity (2021)
9. Raza, S., Reji, D.J., Liu, D.D., Bashir, S.R., Naseem, U.: An approach to ensure fairness in news articles (2022)
10. Spinde, T., Rudnitckaia, L., Sinha, K., Hamborg, F., Gipp, B., Donnay, K.: MBIC--a media bias annotation dataset including annotator characteristics (2021)
11. Gaucher, D., Friesen, J., Kay, A.C.: Evidence that gendered wording in job advertisements exists and sustains gender inequality. J. Pers. Soc. Psychol. **101**(1), 109 (2011)
12. Matfield, K.: Gender decoder: find subtle bias in job ads. http://gender-decoder.katmatfield.com/. Accessed 09 June 2023

# Hybrid System for Prostate MR Image Segmentation Using Expert Knowledge and Machine Learning

Lars E. O. Jacobson[1,2,3($\boxtimes$)], Adrian A. Hopgood[1,2,3],
Mohamed Bader-El-Den[1,2,3], Vincenzo Tamma[1], David Prendergast[2],
and Peter Osborn[3]

[1] University of Portsmouth, Portsmouth, UK
{adrian.hopgood,mohamed.bader,vincenzo.tamma}@port.ac.uk
[2] Innovative Physics Ltd, Portsmouth, UK
lars.jacobson@port.ac.uk, david.prendergast@inphys.com
[3] Portsmouth Hospitals, University NHS Trust, Portsmouth, UK
peter.osborn@porthosp.nhs.uk

**Abstract.** In 2020 1,414,259 new cases and 375,304 deaths were estimated for prostate cancer worldwide. Diagnosis of prostate cancer is primarily based on prostate-specific antigen (PSA) screening and transrectal ultrasound (TRUS)-guided prostate biopsy. PSA has a low specificity of 36% since benign conditions can elevate the PSA levels. The data set used for prostate cancer consists of t2-weighted MR images for 1,151 patients and 61,119 images. This paper presents an approach to applying knowledge-based artificial intelligence together with image segmentation to improve the diagnosis of prostate cancer using publicly available data. Complete and reliable segmentation into the transition zone (TZ) and peripheral zone (PZ) is required in order to automate and enhance the process of prostate cancer diagnosis.

**Keywords:** Image segmentation · Prostate · Magnetic resonance imaging · Hybrid system

## 1 Introduction

In 2020 1,414,259 new cases and 375,304 deaths were estimated for prostate cancer worldwide [1]. Prostate cancer is more prevalent in men older than 65 years. Clinicians and patients would benefit from noninvasive tools that differentiate prostate cancer's severity other than active surveillance [2]. Diagnosis of prostate cancer is primarily based on prostate-specific antigen (PSA) screening and transrectal ultrasound (TRUS)-guided prostate biopsy. PSA has a low specificity of 36% since benign conditions can elevate the PSA levels. Thus, high PSA does not guarantee a tumour and normal PSA does not exclude a tumour [3]. Additionally, TRUS is based on a systematic approach that targets the peripheral aspects

© The Author(s), under exclusive license to Springer Nature Switzerland AG 2023
M. Bramer and F. Stahl (Eds.): SGAI 2023, LNAI 14381, pp. 493–498, 2023.
https://doi.org/10.1007/978-3-031-47994-6_43

of the gland. Significant tumours can be missed because 30–40% of prostate cancer is anterior in the midline transition zone (TZ). The peripheral zone (PZ) is sampled randomly since ultrasound is poor at differentiating cancer from benign tissue [4]. Therefore, there is a need for alternative tests. Magnetic resonance (MR) imaging can assist in identifying tumours both before and after biopsy, leading to the possibility of increased accuracy [5–8].

The process description and the semantics of the prostate cancer use case have been detailed in Fig. 1.

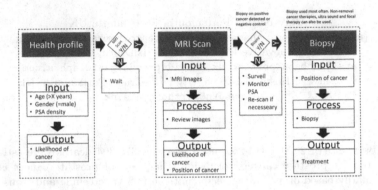

**Fig. 1.** Process description of prostate cancer procedure and diagnosis.

The Prostate Imaging Reporting and Data System (PI-RADS) was developed as a tool to measure criticality and improve cancer characterisation from MRI Images. PI-RADS consists of a score from 1–5. The score is determined based on a clinician's location and characterisation of MR images. The clinician identifies the two prostate zones of a prostate from the MR images, transition and peripheral, denoted TZ and PZ.

There is potential for knowledge-based artificial intelligence (AI) within the field of medicine to improve early diagnosis of many diseases e.g. cancer [9]. One branch of AI that has proven to be useful in diagnosis is computer vision, where properties can be extracted and processed from medical images. Convolutional neural networks (CNNs) can be applied. The algorithm learns which features are indicative of disease but with an accuracy that potentially can exceed any human physician because CNNs can read properties not visible to the human eye [10].

Litjens et al. [11] leverage MR image segmentation combined with PI-RADS classification to investigate automated prostate cancer diagnosis. The results from the system were compared with the radiologists' opinions and were validated for 347 patients. The system did not show any significant difference in performance from the radiologists at high specificity but at lower specificity the radiologists performed significantly better. Masoudi et al. [12] further support the potential of deep learning applications in prostate cancer research.

Bardis et al. confirm deep learning methods can segment the prostate into TZ and PZ. Furthermore, they show that using three U-Nets can produce a "near radiologist" level of performance. To improve the highlighted zones' detection, pre-processing the MR images can enhance the system's specificity. Luo et al. [7] show that a weighted low-rank matrix restoration algorithm (RLRE) can improve MRI images' display effect and resolution.

## 2   Methods

The proposed method consists of three steps illustrated in Fig. 2, i.e. i) pre-processing of MR images to normalise quality, ii) segment the prostate into TZ and PZ, and iii) apply knowledge-based rules as a multiagent system. The t2-weighted MR images from the dataset are annotated and pre-processed for use as a training dataset.

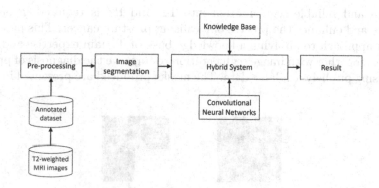

**Fig. 2.** Proposed model.

### 2.1   U-Net Architecture

This research leverages a base U-net model depicted in Fig. 3. The U-net architecture has 10 stages in the encoding & decoding part. A skip connection between the encoding and decoding parts is included in each stage to speed up convergence and to compensate for information loss across the stages.

### 2.2   Data Description

The data relate to prostate cancer medical applications and have been sourced from The Cancer Imaging Archive (TCIA), which is publicly available [13]. The data set used for prostate cancer consists of 61,119 t2-weighted MR images for 1,151 patients.

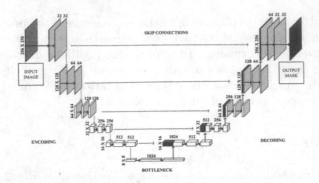

**Fig. 3.** Proposed U-net architecture.

## 3   Conclusion

Complete and reliable segmentation into TZ and PZ is required in order to automate and enhance the process of localising prostate cancer. This paper proposes an approach to applying a knowledge base of domain expertise and visual properties together with image segmentation to improve the diagnosis of prostate cancer using publicly available data. The masks produced are presented in Fig. 4.

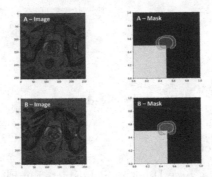

**Fig. 4.** Original MR Image together with mask of TZ, PZ and visualisation of image where prostate is not present.

This paper uses an MR image dataset obtained from patients with biopsy-confirmed prostate cancer. The annotations are stored in an annotation format with a link to the original DICOM file. The training dataset's handling and preparations are visualised in Fig. 5. The pre-processing of the MR images is presented in Fig. 6.

The contribution of this paper is to provide a system to analyse and classify prostate cancer using MR images. The trained model is based on domain expert knowledge and a developed set of rules. It brings together existing work

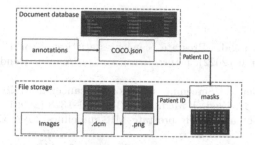

**Fig. 5.** Training dataset preparations.

on image segmentation and industry knowledge. By combining the complementary advantages of the approaches, this research aims to overcome the limitations of single-sided segmentation methods and achieve increased performance in prostate MR image segmentation. The hybrid system approach leverages complementary capabilities from traditional image processing, expert knowledge, and deep learning methods. This approach can achieve enhanced segmentation accuracy and improve overall diagnostic confidence. Furthermore, this research uses explainable artificial intelligence in order to identify suspicious cases based on PI-RADS score on a data set of 1151 patients.

Experimental results demonstrate that the proposed model has the potential to produce satisfactory results and, together with expert knowledge, achieve additional useful understanding of the field. Future work includes combining the image segmentation with an applied knowledge base using a hybrid-system approach. This approach can be further extended and refined to address other similar challenges in medical imaging research.

**Fig. 6.** Pre-processing of one MR image.

# References

1. WCRF International. Prostate cancer statistics: World Cancer Research Fund International (2022). https://www.wcrf.org/cancer-trends/prostate-cancer-statistics/
2. Schröder, F.H., et al.: Screening and prostate-cancer mortality in a randomized European study. N. Engl. J. Med. **360**(13), 1320–1328 (2009)
3. Barentsz, J.O., et al.: ESUR prostate MR guidelines 2012. Eur. Radiol. **22**(4), 746–757 (2012)
4. Ahmed, H.U., et al.: Is it time to consider a role for MRI before prostate biopsy? Nat. Rev. Clin. Oncol. **6**(4), 197–206 (2009)
5. Huang, S., Yang, J., Fong, S., Zhao, Q.: Artificial intelligence in cancer diagnosis and prognosis: opportunities and challenges. Cancer Lett. **471**, 61–71 (2020)
6. Murphy, G., Haider, M., Ghai, S., Sreeharsha, B.: The expanding role of MRI in prostate cancer. AJR Am. J. Roentgenol. **201**(6), 1229–38 (2013)
7. Luo, R., Zeng, Q., Chen, H.: Artificial intelligence algorithm-based MRI for differentiation diagnosis of prostate cancer. Comput. Math. Meth. Med. (2022)
8. Lawrentschuk, N., et al.: Prostatic evasive anterior tumours: the role of magnetic resonance imaging. BJU Int. **105**(9), 1231–1236 (2010)
9. Ardila, D., et al.: End-to-end lung cancer screening with three-dimensional deep learning on low-dose chest computed tomography. Nat. Med. **25**(6), 954–961 (2019)
10. Anwar, S.M., Majid, M., Qayyum, A., Awais, M., Alnowami, M., Khan, M.K.: Medical image analysis using convolutional neural networks: a review. J. Med. Syst. **42**(11), 1–13 (2018)
11. Litjens, G., Debats, O., Barentsz, J., Karssemeijer, N., Huisman, H.: Computer-aided detection of prostate cancer in MRI. IEEE Trans. Med. Imaging **33**(5), 1083–1092 (2014)
12. Masoudi, S., et al.: Quick guide on radiology image pre-processing for deep learning applications in prostate cancer research. J. Med. Imaging **8**(1), 010901 (2021)
13. The Cancer Imaging Archive (TCIA). Prostate-MRI-US-Biopsy [Data file] (2022). https://wiki.cancerimagingarchive.net/pages/viewpage.action?pageId=68550661

# COVID-19 Liquor Sales Forecasting Model

Uttam Paul[✉]

University of Leeds, Leeds, UK
uttpaul@gmail.com

**Abstract.** The COVID-19 pandemic brought significant shifts in consumer behavior, impacting the Consumer-Packaged Goods (CPG) sector, including a 22% sales drop for Coca-Cola in concentrate sales for soda fountains [8]. This study aims to devise a demand forecasting framework to assist CPG firms in navigating similar crises, ensuring precise demand predictions, preventing stock-outs, and optimizing supply chains for profit gains, using five years of Iowa Class "E" liquor sales data employs various statistical, machine learning, ensemble, and deep learning methods across different product categories and durations. Different techniques have been applied to deal with missing data and outliers, adding new features like lag and simple moving averages (SMA) to the dataset for seasonality and trend and implementing feature engineering. The statistical method is a good starting point to get some benchmark results. The support vector regressor (SVR) model yields the best result (near 99% accuracy) out of all the models, and the outcome of the SVR model was consistent across datasets and products. Ensemble methods also produce consistent performance across products (average accuracy between 93% and 95%). Long short-term memory (LSTM) network performance was below expectation (average accuracy between 79% and 87%).

**Keywords:** COVID-19 · Volatile Demand · CPG · Demand Forecasting · Supply chain · Time series · Machine learning · Ensemble · Deep learning

## 1 Introduction and Background

The COVID-19 pandemic severely disrupted food supply chains, exposing vulnerabilities and causing food security concerns. Lockdowns, panic buying, and shifting consumer demand disrupted the flow of materials and finished goods, leading to manufacturing stoppages and staff shortages. This imbalance between supply and demand posed significant challenges for organizations. In 2021, NielsenIQ reported a shift in alcohol consumption habits from on-premises to off-premises due to bar and restaurant closures. To recover, the US alcohol market needed substantial volume growth. Traditional forecasting models struggled with such sporadic market conditions, highlighting the need for more robust and resilient demand forecasting systems to anticipate unforeseen events and minimize revenue losses.

In 2022, researchers developed a classification-based model using historical demand data in categories like fruits, vegetables, and bake-offs across five regional fulfillment centers. They utilised the Euclidean distance metric for feature selection and trained a decision tree model to optimize future demand forecasting. This research aims to enhance profitability through improved inventory planning, considering various forecasting models like linear regression, Generalized Additive Model for Location, Scale, and Shape (GAMLSS), quantile regression, and Autoregressive Integrated Moving Average with Explanatory Variable (ARIMAX), but further investigation is needed for model optimization and benchmarking, especially regarding market volatility and changing purchase behavior [7].

In 2021, Wolters & Huchzermeier researched retail promotional demand forecasting, focusing on seasonal and frequently promoted items. Using German supermarket data, various models were tested, with Promotional Harmonic Regression (PHR) excelling in demand prediction. Future research may involve additional variables for improved forecasting [9].

Abbasimehr et al. (2020) developed an optimised demand forecasting model using a multilayer LSTM deep learning network [1]. They applied the model to a furniture company's sales data from 2007 to 2017. The study compared the LSTM model to various statistical and machine learning algorithms, with the LSTM network showing significant improvement after hyperparameter tuning. However, further evaluation is needed on different industry data, like food and beverage sales, and considering external factors such as the COVID-19 disruption, which the dataset did not cover.

Peipei Liu (2020) addressed the challenge of intermittent demand for short-life medical consumables during COVID-19 using dynamic neural networks. The study used a point-of-sale dataset spanning 2.5 years, applying techniques like outlier removal and seasonal demand adjustment. The proposed model outperformed six other methods. However, the dataset didn't cover COVID-19's erratic demand, suggesting the need for further research integrating supply chain and pricing forecasts [4].

Doszyń (2019) researched forecasting intermittent demand in enterprises, addressing the challenge of limited non-zero observations for items, such as seasonal sales. Six statistical methods were employed, with TSB and SESAP proving the most effective. The study did not explore machine learning algorithms and suggested further research for mixed forecasting models [3].

A study was conducted to investigate predictive big data analytics (BDA) for supply chain demand forecasting, highlighting gaps for future research. A literature review from 2005 to 2019 identified increasing research in demand forecasting for supply chains. The most effective techniques included Neural Networks, Regression, Time-series forecasting (ARIMA), Support Vector Machines, and Decision Trees. The study emphasizes the need for research in closed-loop supply chains and reverse logistics due to growing environmental awareness and government incentives but lacks specific demand forecasting techniques [6].

In 2015, research focused on improving a food company's demand forecasting and production planning. The study analyzed food industry products aimed at the food service market. Various exponential smoothing methods were applied, with the Holt-Winters method proving superior for time series analysis, especially for products with trends and seasonality. The optimization led to a 5% improvement in demand forecasting [2].

In 2013, a study addressed demand challenges in the fashion industry: short selling seasons, uncertainty, and limited historical data. Using Average inter-demand Interval (ADI) and Coefficient of Variation (CV), they created four product demand attributes and selected specific forecasting techniques. Artificial Neural Networks (ANN) outperformed traditional methods due to data nonlinearity. However, this approach was case-specific and not a comprehensive forecasting system framework [5].

## 1.1 Research Hypothesis and Objectives

This study aims to build a forecasting framework to address the volatility in sales for the spirits purchase information of Iowa Class "E" liquor products.

Here are the objectives that have been formulated in alignment with the research:

1. Perform exploratory data analysis to understand different factors that can help address the volatility in demand.
2. Apply different Statistical methods: Exponential Smoothing, Holt-Winters, and ARIMA, machine learning classical processes: linear regression, logistic regression, SVR, etc. Advanced deep learning (LSTM) network to predict demand.
3. Ensemble of various machine learning to address the demand volatility.
4. Finally, propose a demand forecasting solution framework that helps address or accurately forecast the demand.

## 1.2 Dataset Description

The website data.iowa.gov serves as a public data platform, offering access to Iowa and state government data for exploration and sharing research findings with others. Specifically, the website provides access to Iowa Liquor Sales data dating from January 1, 2012, to the present day, encompassing the purchase details of Iowa Class "E" liquor [10]. Below are some critical attribute descriptions.

| Attribute Name | Description |
| --- | --- |
| Date | sales date |
| Category | Product category |
| Category Name | Product category name |
| Item Description | Sales Product Description |
| Pack | Pack size of the product |
| Bottle Volume (ml) | The volume of each bottle in ml |
| State Bottle Cost | Purchase Cost per bottle |
| State Bottle Retail | Retail sale cost per bottle |
| Bottles Sold | The number of bottles ordered by the store |
| Sale (Dollars) | Number of bottles ordered * Retail sale cost per bottle in USD |
| Volume Sold (Liters) | Volume sold in liters |

# 2 Methodology

## 2.1 Exploratory Data Analysis

The following represent noteworthy findings derived from exploratory analysis:

1) Amidst the COVID-19, a discernible surge in liquor sales was evident.
2) A seasonal pattern was discernible in the sales data.
3) Notable instances of negative sales and missing values were identified within crucial attributes of the dataset.
4) Column "Volume Sold (Liters)" exhibited 12,496 outliers, while column "Retail cost per Liter" featured 83,685 outliers in the dataset.

## 2.2 Data Pre-processing and Data Transformation

This section outlines several pre-processing procedures that have been executed.

a) Ensure the date column type is datetime and add year_month and year_week columns for month and week-wise data analysis. Create an index on the date column, essential for time series analysis.
b) Eliminate redundancies like Invoice/Item Number, Store Name, Address, City, Zip Code, Store Location, Vendor Name, Item Description, etc.
c) Group data on index column and use the mean function for summarisation.
d) Split data for training and testing. As this is time series data to preserve temporal order, I have used the "Time Series Split" technique which sequentially splits the time series data into training and testing sets.
e) Min-max scaler has been used to normalize data.
f) Features like LAG (Lagged) to capture trends and SMA (Simple Moving Average) have been added to deal with the seasonality effect.
g) A derived price feature "Retail cost per Liter" = ("State Bottle Retail"/Bottle Volume (ml)) *1000 has been created to rationalize the price.
h) The correlation matrix (Fig. 1) helps us understand the features' importance.

## 2.3 Outlier Detection

a) There were negative values (232 records) in the column "Volume Sold (Liters)." As the sale volume cannot be negative, the transaction has been treated as an outlier, removing the rows from the data set.
b) It is crucial to detect outliers in columns "Volume Sold (Liters)" and "Retail cost per Liter." Scipy's stats library has been used to calculate the Z-score where the Z-score value exceeds three, treated as an outlier. There were 12496 outliers in column "Volume Sold (Liters)" and 83685 outliers in column "Retail cost per Liter."

## 2.4   Feature Selection

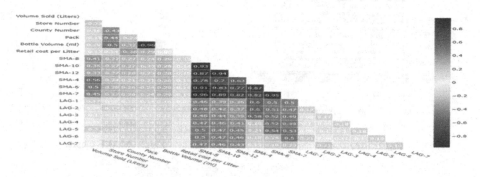

**Fig. 1.** Correlation Matrix to select important features.

## 2.5   Hyperparameter Tuning

Hyperparameter tuning must be done to achieve better accuracy and avoid under and overfitting. To tune the hyperparameters of machine learning methods, cross-validation using GridSearchCV has been implemented. For the LSTM network, a combination of hyperparameters (Batch size, learning rate, epoch size, hidden layers, dropout rate, etc.) has been used to select the best model.

# 3   Experimental Results, Conclusion, and Future Work

The evaluation metric considered in the experiment is MAPE (Mean Absolute Percentage Error) $(1/n) * \Sigma$ (|Actual - Forecast|/Actual) * 100 (n is the sample size), and accuracy is the complementary value (100-MAPE) of MAPE.

This research has been conducted on sales data of the top three products on two datasets. Dataset 1 contains five years of data starting from 2018 and Dataset 2 contains two years of data beginning in 2020.

As shown in Fig. 2 and Fig. 3, below are the key findings and conclusion of the study:

The study employs various forecasting methods to address the challenge of demand volatility in the context of the COVID-19 pandemic. Traditional time series methods, including additive and multiplicative Holt-Winter techniques, were employed, with multiplicative methods proving to be more effective. The selection of the best ARIMA model was based on the lowest AIC value, considering both accuracy and model simplicity. This traditional time series approach demonstrated favorable performance for the second dataset, exhibiting an average accuracy between 86% and 92%.

In contrast, machine-learning models were applied with derived variables to capture data temporal characteristics. Among the three machine learning models (XGBRegressor, RandomForestRegressor, SVR), SVR consistently outperformed, achieving an

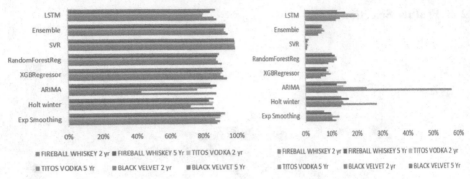

**Fig.2.** Accuracy Chart          **Fig.3.** MAPE Chart

accuracy of approximately 98% to 99% for all products. However, the machine learning approach exhibited degraded performance on dataset 2.

The ensemble method combined the outputs of all three machine learning models, yielding consistent accuracy ranging from 93% to 95% across all datasets and products. Deep learning was also explored, utilising a five-layer LSTM sequential network. While this approach showed promise, it required more time and had variable accuracy, ranging from 79% to 88% across different datasets and products.

The study's forecasting framework effectively addresses demand volatility, particularly during events like the COVID-19 pandemic. Traditional time series methods provide quick and reliable benchmarks, while the SVR model stands out as the top performer. The ensemble method offers a reliable alternative, consistently delivering above-average accuracy. However, the LSTM approach, while innovative, requires more time and falls short of expectations in terms of accuracy.

Future research could expand this framework to different product categories and incorporate macroeconomic factors for optimisation, exploring additional methods such as Temporal Convolutional Networks and Facebook Prophet. The framework's potential extends to various industries beyond alcoholic beverages, facilitating informed decision-making during volatile demand situations.

# References

1. Abbasimehr, H., Shabani, M., Yousefi, M.: An optimized model using the LSTM network for demand forecasting. Comput. Ind. Eng. **143**, 106435 (2020)
2. Barbosa, N.D.P., Christo, E.D.S., Costa, K.A.: Demand forecasting for production planning in a food company. ARPN J. Eng. Appl. Sci. **10**(16), 7137–7141 (2015)
3. Doszyń, M.: Intermittent demand forecasting in the enterprise: empirical verification. J. Forecast. **38**(5), 459–469 (2019)
4. Liu, P.: Intermittent demand forecasting for medical consumables with short life cycle using a dynamic neural network during the COVID-19 epidemic. Health Inf. J. **26**(4), 3106–3122 (2020)
5. Nenni, M.E., Giustiniano, L., Pirolo, L.: Demand forecasting in the fashion industry: a review. Int. J. Eng. Bus. Manage. **5**(Godište 2013), 5–36 (2013)

6. Seyedan, M., Mafakheri, F.: Predictive big data analytics for supply chain demand forecasting: methods, applications, and research opportunities. J. Big Data **7**(1), 1–22 (2020)

7. Ulrich, M., Jahnke, H., Langrock, R., Pesch, R., Senge, R.: Classification-based model selection in retail demand forecasting. Int. J. Forecast. **38**(1), 209–223 (2022)

8. Why some food and drink companies lost sales during the COVID-19 pandemic. https://www.fooddive.com/news/food-drink-sales-lost-Covid-19-pandemic/598428/

9. Wolters, J., Huchzermeier, A.: Joint in-season and out-of-season promotion demand forecasting in a retail environment. J. Retail. **97**(4), 726–745 (2021)

10. https://data.iowa.gov/Sales-Distribution/Iowa-Liquor-Sales/m3tr-qhgy/data

# On the Development of a Candidate Selection System for Automated Plastic Waste Detection Using Airborne Based Remote Sensing

Christoph Tholen[✉] and Mattis Wolf

German Research Center for Artificial Intelligence, Oldenburg, Germany
{christoph.tholen,mattis.wolf}@dfki.de

**Abstract.** This paper presents the initial steps of the development of a candidate selection system (CSS) for the PlasticObs + project. The aim of the PlasticObs + system is the monitoring of plastic waste in waterways and onshore utilizing airborne based remote sensing and Artificial Intelligence. The intended use of the CSS is to use the output of an upstream AI-system used for waste assessment utilizing low resolution imagery to choose promising regions for further investigation by a downstream AI system depending on images with a higher resolution. The CSS is modelled as a cost constrained travelling salesman (CCTSP). For solving the CCTSP a greedy algorithm based on weighted distances is utilized. In this research two different methods of calculating the weighted distances are used and their impact strategies on the performance of the greedy algorithm is investigated. It is shown by the experiments conducted within this research that the ratio combination of the value of the next node and the distance outperforms the linear combination of value and distance within all the experiments conducted.

**Keywords:** Cost Constrained Travelling Salesman · CCTSP · PlasticObs + · Plastic Pollution

## 1 Introduction

Plastic pollution is a 'hazardous environmental problem' with annual estimations indicating global rivers discharging several million metric tons of plastic waste into the oceans [1]. It is critical to implement cost-effective and innovative monitoring strategies to improve waste and plastic management in the marine environment. These strategies must allow the identification of sources and amounts of litter in different towns, states, and countries. Additionally, information about the types of plastic litter, for instance polymer types, are needed to develop targeted policies and legislation for the collection and recycling of priority plastic items. These actions are consistent with major political initiatives, such as the EU Marine Strategy Framework Directive's descriptor 10 [2], the Single-use Plastics Directive 2019 [3], UN Sustainable Development Goal 14 target 14.1, and the UN Decade of Ocean Science for Sustainable Development (2021–2030), which all aim to reduce marine pollution and improve ocean health [4].

M. Bramer and F. Stahl (Eds.): SGAI 2023, LNAI 14381, pp. 506–512, 2023.
https://doi.org/10.1007/978-3-031-47994-6_45

The detection of pollution on the ocean surface is of crucial interest for the protection of the marine ecosystem and the safety of human activities [5]. In the past, several studies on the detection of plastic using remote sensing techniques were conducted [6, 7]. However continuous monitoring of larger, contiguous marine areas has not been established yet. Current models and estimations about plastic waste to date are therefore essentially based on temporally and spatially punctual measurements. The highly inhomogeneous distribution of plastic allows only inadequate generalizations about the sources, distribution routes, and accumulation sites as well as their development over time.

This is where the PlasticObs + project comes in. The long-term goal of the project is to develop an airborne method for monitoring plastic waste on the water surface. The PlasticObs + system is based on an overview sensor, a fast VIS-AI for anomaly detection, an AI based system for candidate selection and a detail sensor to further investigate candidates selected (Fig. 1). This work will focus on the development of the Candidate Selection System (CSS). The overview sensor provides line-images consisting of 1 × 4096 pixels. During operation, different lines are combined, to produce an image consisting of $k$ × 4096 pixels, where $k$ is the number of lines used. In this research 480 lines are combined to produce an image. The images are used as input to the VIS-AI system for anomaly detection. The output of this AI-system is than used as input to select candidates which should be further investigated using the high-resolution imagery system (EOIR).

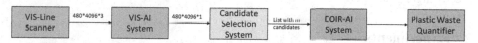

**Fig. 1.** System overview as block diagram

The optimisation problem described can be understood as cost-constrained traveling salesman problem (CCTSP) [8]. The CCTSP is an adaptation of the well-known traveling salesman problem (TSP) [9]. In CCTSP each city or node is given a certain value $v$ and a fixed cost-constrained $B$ is defined [8]. The aim is to find a subtour including $m$ nodes with $m \leq n$ that maximises the total value and where the total costs does not exceed the given cost constrain $B$.

$$\sum_{i=1}^{m-1} C_{\pi(i),\pi(i+1)} + C_{\pi(m),\pi(1)} \leq B. \tag{1}$$

where $C_{\pi(i),\pi(i+1)}$ denotes the cost from node $\pi(i)$ to node $\pi(i+1)$ and $C_{\pi(m),\pi(1)}$ denote the cost to return from the last node back to the start node. A side condition in CCTSP is to maximise the fitness $F$, i.e. the sum of the values, of the chosen subset:

$$F = \max\left(\sum_{i=1}^{m} v_{\pi(i)}\right). \tag{2}$$

where $v_{\pi(i)}$ represents the value of the node $\pi(i)$. Dynamic programming or branch and bound methods can be used to generate an exact solution for the given CCTSP problem [10]. However, these approaches are time consuming, and it cannot be guaranteed that a solution is available within the given time constraint. Instead, a heuristic approach is used in this research. Here a greedy algorithm, based on a nearest neighbour approach will be used to generate an initial solution. However, in cost constrained applications not only the distance between the nodes should be used to choose the next neighbour, rather the values of the different nodes should be considered. This can be achieved in different ways, for instance by using the linear combination of the distance between the nodes and the value of the new node [11] as follows:

$$d_i = C_{\pi(n),\pi(i)} \cdot v_{\pi(i)}. \tag{3}$$

where $C_{\pi(n),\pi(i)}$ denotes the cost from the last node in the subset to the current node and $v_{\pi(i)}$ denotes the value of the current node. Another option is to take ratio of the value of the next node and the distance between the last node and the next node [12] as follows:

$$d_i = \frac{v_{\pi(i)}}{C_{\pi(n),\pi(i)}}. \tag{4}$$

In both cases the weighted distance $d_i$ is calculated for all open nodes, i.e., nodes which are not included in the subset so far, and the best option is chosen as next node and inserted into the subset. It is assumed that the way on calculation has an impact on the performance of the greedy algorithm. Therefore, a set of experiments was carried out to investigate the influence of the two different methods on the performance of the greedy algorithm.

## 2 Experiments

Currently no real-world data from the VIS-Line scanner is available. Therefore, the proposed CSS is evaluated using simulated output data of the edge-AI system utilizing two different functions, i.e. power law and Gaussian hills.

When using the power law function a random number between 0 and 100 representing the probability that the pixel contains plastic is chosen for each pixel as follows:

$$O = \frac{1}{m^\alpha} + \left(m + \frac{1}{m^\alpha}\right) \cdot r^{\frac{-1}{\alpha}}. \tag{5}$$

where $O$ represent the output value of the edge-AI system, $m$ represent the maximum output value, $r$ represent a random number uniformly chosen from 0 to 1 and $\alpha$ represents a tuning factor usually chosen from the interval:

$$\{\alpha \in \mathbb{R} | 1 \le \alpha \le 2\}. \tag{6}$$

The power law distribution represents a scenario, without plastic waste hotspots. In this case the output of the edge-AI system does not indicate regions of interest. On the other hand, when plastic waste accumulations are visible the output of the edge-AI potentially can be modelled using Gaussian hills. In this case a certain number of hills $h$ are added to the output of the edge-AI. Both position and shape of the Gaussian hills are chosen randomly.

The simulated output of the edge-AI system is used to generate a list of candidates for further investigation by the EOIR. Referring to Fig. 1, the edge-AI output contains approx. 1.97 million pixels, while each pixel is a single node in the CCTSP problem. Therefore, the number of nodes needs to be reduced in the first step of the processing. First neighbor pixels are summarized using a kernel size of $8 \times 8$ pixels resulting in a resolution of approx. 2 m per super pixel. Each super pixel can be seen as a single node in the CCTSP. This resolution corresponds to the footprint of the EOIR system used. Afterwards the 100 nodes with the highest values are chosen as initial subset for the candidate selection system. The generation of the subset is summarized in Algorithm 1.

---

**Algorithm 1** Subset selection

---

```
Generate output of edge-AI
Summarize pixels to super-pixels
choose n super-pixels
calculate Euclidean distances between super-pixels
```
**while** $\sum_{i=1}^{m-1} C_{\pi(i),\pi(i+1)} \leq B$
**do**
```
    calculate weighted distance d_i for all pixels n\m
    using equation (3) or (4)
    add best node to m
```
**end while**
**return** $m$

---

Due to the unknown specifications of the EOIR sensor the real value of the cost constrained $B$ is currently unknown. The cost constrained is expressed as maximum distance in the different nodes to be visit in meter. Experiments are carried out using different values of $B$, chosen from the interval $\{B \in \mathbb{N}|100m, 10m, \ldots, 1000m\}$. Experiments are carried out using both power law distribution and Gaussian hills as simulated output of the edge-AI When using the power law distribution, experiments are carried out using different values for the parameter $\alpha$ from the interval $\{\alpha \in \mathbb{R}|1, 0.1, \ldots, 2\}$. When using the Gaussian hills, experiments are carried out for a different number of hills $h$ chosen from the interval: $\{h \in \mathbb{N}|1, 1, \ldots, 20\}$. . For all different combinations the experiments were repeated 1,000 times. For each run the achieved fitness (Eq. (2)) is stored.

## 3  Results and Discussion

Figure 2 shows the simulation results for the edge-AI output for both power law distribution and Gaussian hills. Due to limited space the figure only contains a graph for a smaller subset of the results. The plots show the average fitness for 1,000 experiments dependent on the maximal budget $B$. It can be observed that in all cases the weighted distance based on the ratio of value and distance outperforms the method based on the liner combination. For the power law distribution, it can be observed that the difference between both methods is smaller for smaller values of $\alpha$. For the Gaussian hills the difference between both methods is higher for a smaller number of hills.

In all the experiments conducted, the ratio combination of value and distance outperformed the linear combination. Therefore, it can be concluded that for this particular

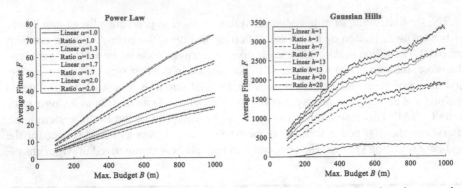

**Fig. 2.** Average fitness $F$ over different maximal budgets $B$ for the input based on the power law distribution using different values of $\alpha$ (left) and the Gaussian hills with different numbers of hills $h$ (right)

application the ratio weighted distance should be used for the calculation of the initial solution.

Furthermore, if only one hill is included in the edge-AI output, it can be observed from Fig. 2 that the fitness does not improve for increasing budget $B$. In addition, it can be observed that for higher budgets $B$ both strategies give similar results. Due to the limitation of numbers of hills, the distance between the 100 nodes chosen for including is small and all nodes could be inserted into the subset.

In addition, it can be noted that the difference between the two strategies, i.e. linear combination and ratio, is dependent either on the chosen value of $\alpha$ or the number of hills h.

For the Gaussian hills it can be obtained from Fig. 2 that the difference between both methods is small for edge-AI outputs containing only a single hill. In this case, all 100 chosen nodes belong to the same hill. Then the performance of the weighting method is not crucial. In the case that some hills are included in the output of the edge-AI, the nodes chosen may belong to different nodes distributed over the search space. In this case the performance of the weighting method can have a significant impact on the performance. With an increasing number of hills, the 100 nodes chosen are more distributed over the search space and thus also weighting strategies with a worse performance can achieve a rather good performance.

To discuss the results of the power law distribution it is important to keep the influence of different values of $\alpha$ on the appearance of the VIS-AI output in mind, a small value of $\alpha$ results in a fitness function with many high peaks, while higher values of $\alpha$ result in a smaller number of smaller peaks.

For small values of $\alpha$ the output of the edge-AI contains many high peaks well distributed all over the search space. Hence, the performance of the weighting strategy is less important because almost all parts of the search space contain nodes with high values. For medium high values of $\alpha$ the performance of the weighting strategy has the highest impact on the results, because the distances between the good nodes increase and it is important to choose the right nodes to achieve a good fitness. For higher values of $\alpha$ the number of nodes with a high value rapidly decrease. Thus, the overall performance decreases and more nodes with a smaller value needs to be chosen by both weighting strategies. Hence, the impact of the strategy on the performance decreases.

## 4 Conclusion and Future Work

This research is describing the initial steps of the development of a candidate selection system for the PlasticObs + project. The intended use of such a system is to use the output of a previous AI-system to choose the optimal regions of interest for further investigation by a second AI system. The candidate selection system (CSS) is modelled as a cost constrained travelling salesman problem (CCTSP). The problem of selecting the right nodes is solved by a greedy algorithm utilizing weighted distances. It is shown by the experiments conducted within this research that a ratio combination of the value of the next node and the distance outperforms the linear combination of value and distance within all the experiments.

In this research the initial solution of the CCTSP using a greedy algorithm is evaluated. However, in future work it is planned to improve this initial solution by utilizing different optimization algorithms like simulated annealing or hill climbing. The techniques described in this work is based on the output of one second of operation. In the real-world application the CSS needs to run in real time delivering a list of candidates every second. Therefore, the integration of parallel optimisation algorithms like asynchronous population based hill climbing [13] will also be evaluated to speed up the candidate selection process.

In the final phase of this research the performance of the candidate selection system developed will be evaluated using real world data, gathered during test flights. Afterwards the CSS will be integrated into the PlasticObs + system for operational use.

**Acknowledgements.** Funded by the German Federal Ministry for the Environment, Nature Conservation, Nuclear Safety and Consumer Protection (BMUV) based on a resolution of the German Bundestag (Grant No. 67KI21014A).

## References

1. Lebreton, L.C.M., van der Zwet, J., Damsteeg, J.-W., Slat, B., Andrady, A., Reisser, J.: River plastic emissions to the world's oceans. Nat. Commun. **8**, 15611 (2017). https://doi.org/10.1038/ncomms15611
2. Galgani, F., Hanke, G., Werner, S., De Vrees, L.: Marine litter within the European marine strategy framework directive. ICES J. Mar. Sci. **70**, 1055–1064 (2013). https://doi.org/10.1093/icesjms/fst122
3. Directive (EU) 2019/ of the European Parliament and of the Council of 5 June 2019 on the reduction of the impact of certain plastic products on the environment
4. Recuero Virto, L.: A preliminary assessment of the indicators for sustainable development goal (SDG) 14 "conserve and sustainably use the oceans, seas and marine resources for sustainable development." Mar. Policy **98**, 47–57 (2018). https://doi.org/10.1016/j.marpol.2018.08.036
5. Environment, U.N.: Global Environment Outlook 6. http://www.unep.org/resources/global-environment-outlook-6. Accessed 09 Jan 2023

6. Topouzelis, K., Papageorgiou, D., Karagaitanakis, A., Papakonstantinou, A., Arias, M.: Remote sensing of sea surface artificial floating plastic targets with sentinel-2 and unmanned aerial systems (plastic litter project 2019). Remote Sens. **12**, 2013 (2020). https://doi.org/10.3390/rs12122013

7. Garaba, S.P., et al.: Sensing ocean plastics with an airborne hyperspectral shortwave infrared imager. Environ. Sci. Technol. **52**, 11699–11707 (2018). https://doi.org/10.1021/acs.est.8b02855

8. Sokkappa, P.R.: The cost-constrained traveling salesman problem (1990).https://doi.org/10.2172/6223080

9. Flood, M.M.: The traveling-salesman problem. Oper. Res. (1956). https://doi.org/10.1287/opre.4.1.61

10. Radharamanan, R., Choi, L.I.: A branch and bound algorithm for the travelling salesman and the transportation routing problems. Comput. Ind. Eng. **11**, 236–240 (1986). https://doi.org/10.1016/0360-8352(86)90085-9

11. Golden, B., Levy, L., Dahl, R.: Two generalizations of the traveling salesman problem. Omega **9**, 439–441 (1981). https://doi.org/10.1016/0305-0483(81)90087-6

12. Tsiligirides, T.: Heuristic methods applied to orienteering. J. Oper. Res. Soc. **35**, 797–809 (1984). https://doi.org/10.1057/jors.1984.162

13. Nolle, L., Werner, J.: Asynchronous population-based hill climbing applied to SPICE model generation from EM simulation data. In: Bramer, M., Petridis, M. (eds.) SGAI 2017. LNCS (LNAI), vol. 10630, pp. 423–428. Springer, Cham (2017). https://doi.org/10.1007/978-3-319-71078-5_37

# Estimations of Professional Experience with Panel Data to Improve Salary Predictions

Frank Eichinger[1]([⊠])([iD]), Jannik Kiesel[2], Matthias Dorner[1], and Stefan Arnold[2]

[1] DATEV eG, Nuremberg, Germany
{frank.eichinger,matthias.dorner}@datev.de
[2] Friedrich-Alexander-Universität Erlangen-Nürnberg, Nuremberg, Germany
{jannik.kiesel,stefan.st.arnold}@fau.de

**Abstract.** Predicting salaries is crucial in business. While prediction models can be trained on large and real salary datasets, they typically lack information regarding professional experience, an essential factor for salary. We investigate various regression techniques for the estimation of professional experience based on data from the Socio-Economic Panel (SOEP) to augment data sets. We further show how to integrate such models into applications and evaluate the usefulness for salary prediction on a large real payroll dataset.

**Keywords:** Salary prediction · Regression · Socio-economic panel

## 1 Introduction

Salary predictions are important for employers and (prospective) employees alike. When it comes to salary negotiations, both sides need to know the market value of an employee. Many tools on the Internet offer free salary predictions. However, many of them build on data obtained by questioning their users. Such data is notoriously poor in quality, as self-reports are often biased or wrong by purpose. Other approaches are built on objective data from official notifications to state authorities or on data from payroll software. Examples of such tools include the "Gehaltsvergleich BETA" [5] of the German Federal Office of Statistics which makes salary predictions with a linear-regression approach [6] or the application "Personal-Benchmark online" [3] (see Fig. 1) from the German company DATEV eG making predictions based on a neural network [4][1].

While salary predictions based on large amounts of real salary data certainly result in better predictions than other approaches based on less data of questionable quality, such datasets rarely come with all the information needed. While the profession and regional information is typically available as well as the age and education of an employee, the professional experience is frequently missing as in the two applications mentioned (but can be obtained by questioning users directly). However, professional experience is widely considered being a crucial

---

[1] [4] builds on random forests, the current application is based on a neural network.

M. Bramer and F. Stahl (Eds.): SGAI 2023, LNAI 14381, pp. 513–518, 2023.
https://doi.org/10.1007/978-3-031-47994-6_46

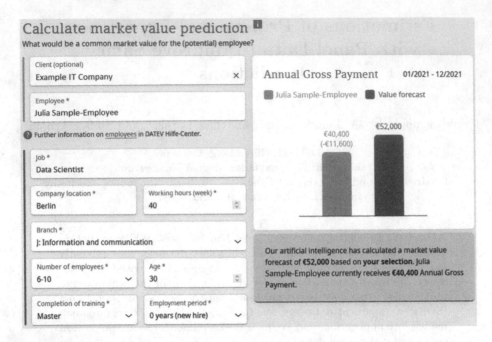

**Fig. 1.** Screenshot of "Personal-Benchmark online" from DATEV eG [3].

factor for productivity, which – besides further factors – determines salaries [10]. Further, the customers of DATEV eG request possibilities to enter this information. To improve predictions, it is desirable to augment and additionally consider the professional experience in datasets where it is missing.

Augmentation of information regarding professional experience to a dataset is not trivial, as this information is typically not available in large salary datasets, and crafting basic deterministic rules like "age minus default education time for reported degree minus 6" [10] would be too simple. Further, we are not aware of any research investigating the relationship between professional experience and other factors available in payroll data.

We present our approach for estimating professional experience based on external panel data. We use the dataset of the German Socio-Economic Panel (SOEP) [7] where a representative sample of employees has been questioned systematically. This dataset includes, among others, the age, the education and the professional biography. It is one of Europe's most important research datasets in the social and economic sciences. Our work contributes as follows:

1. We train and evaluate several machine-learning models for the estimation of professional experience on the SOEP panel dataset using variables available in payroll data and publish them to the public [8].
2. We present how a regression model for the augmentation of the professional experience can be integrated into an application for salary prediction.
3. We show in a large-scale evaluation with real payslip data from more than 4.3 million employees that salary prediction benefits from augmentation.

## 2    The Socio-economic Panel and the Relevant Variables

The German Socio-Economic Panel (SOEP) [7] is an annual survey that has interviewed persons since 1984 systematically. It contains a representative sample of persons living in Germany and serves as a valuable resource for studying various socio-economic phenomena, particularly regarding social and labour-market policy, as well as income and career trajectories. We use the dataset published in 2022 [9] encompassing information from 13,616 individuals being employed at the time of interview (after omitting some data records in our preprocessing, e.g., where no education is captured or employees are older than the usual retirement age). Within this dataset, two specific subsets are of particular relevance:

- `bkpbrutto` – *Individual-specific data*: This subset contributes the essential variable *age* to our study, which we derive from `bkgeburt` (year of birth).
- `pgen` – *Occupation-specific data*: From this subset we derive the variable *professional_experience* in years, which serves as our target variable. We derive it from `pgexpft` (working experience in full-time employment) and `pgexppt` (working experience in part-time employment) with equal weight. Further, we determine *highest_education* based on `pgpbbil01` (vocational degree received), `pgpbbil02` (college degree), `pgpbbil03` (no vocational degree) and `pgisced11` (international standard classification of education). We adjust the values of *highest_education* to match the ones used in payroll software and official statistics in Germany as listed in Table 1.

**Table 1.** The variable *highest_education* as used in official statistics in Germany. The description enumerates the typical representative but includes all equivalent degrees.

| Value | Description | | Value | Description |
|-------|-------------|---|-------|-------------|
| 1 | no professional qualification | | 4 | bachelor degree |
| 2 | vocational education | | 5 | master degree |
| 3 | master craftsperson/tradesperson | | 6 | doctoral degree |

Overall, the SOEP dataset provides a robust foundation for investigating the interrelationships of the variables mentioned. By considering the *age* and the *highest_education*, we can estimate the variable *professional_experience*. Note that we explicitly do not investigate the variable *gender*, even if it would be available in the SOEP dataset and payroll data alike and would positively influence the quality of estimations of *professional_experience* as our preliminary experiments have shown. The reason is that this would contribute to the gender pay gap in the salary predictions we make in the next step.

## 3    Estimation of Professional Experience

In this section, we describe and evaluate different approaches to estimate the *professional_experience* using the variables *age* and *highest_education*. We encode the *highest_education* using one-hot encoding and apply and evaluate several regression algorithms [1] using standard parameters: Linear regression, polynomial regression (degree 2–4), regression trees, random forests and neuronal networks with two hidden layers. Figure 2 displays two regression functions.

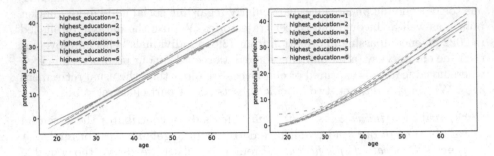

**Fig. 2.** A linear and a polynomial (degree 3) regression function (see Table 1 ).

We now present our experimental results with the different regression models in a 10-fold cross-validation setup measured by the standard mean absolute error (*MAE*). This measure is intuitive and makes sense from an application perspective.

**Table 2.** Experimental results in estimating the *professional_experience*.

| Experiment | Technique | MAE |
|---|---|---|
| R1 | Linear regression | 3.90 years |
| R2 | Polynomial regression (degree 2) | 3.75 years |
| R3 | Polynomial regression (degree 3) | 3.74 years |
| R4 | Polynomial regression (degree 4) | 3.75 years |
| R5 | Regression tree | 3.78 years |
| R6 | Random forest | 3.78 years |
| R7 | Neuronal network | 3.72 years |

Table 2 contains the results. The linear regression provides good results with an absolute error of 3.9 years. This seems to be acceptable, as biographies of employees are diverse, and estimations cannot be made without error (considering that they are built on two variables only). The polynomial regression techniques are more complex and lead to better results on all three metrics, with degree 3 as a winner. Surprisingly, the more advanced tree-based techniques perform a little worse. An explanation could be that these techniques have their strengths in settings with more variables. The neural network is the overall winner.

One advantage of linear and polynomial regression models – besides the prediction quality – is their simplicity [2]. Such a model is a simple mathematical formula that can be easily integrated into any software application, regardless of the programming language. As the neural network performs only marginally better, we consider the polynomial regression with degree 3 as the best model for applications. We publish some of our models to the public [8].

# 4    Applicability for Salary Predictions

As motivated in the introduction, we aim at improving salary predictions such as [4] and [6] by augmenting salary datasets with an estimated variable describing the professional experience. This does not mean that we expect more accurate predictions (on a dataset where no *professional_experience* is available), but that users can obtain predictions – as requested – based on variation introduced by the new variable *professional_experience*.

In this section, we prototypically integrate the published regression models [8] into the neural network for salary predictions of the application "Personal-Benchmark online" [3] as described in [4] (See footnote 1). We perform augmentation of the new variable in a dataset of 4.3 million employees from the payroll software from DATEV eG from 2023 by applying the winning regression function of degree 3 from the previous section. To deal with missing *highest_education* information, we first impute this variable by using the most frequent value from employees having the same profession. We then train the existing neural network of the application with the additional variable.

We are particularly interested in the question if the *professional_experience* performs as well as a similar actual variable already present in the payroll data and used in the application, namely *employment_period* (see Fig. 1). The *employment_period* is the time with the current employer in years, i.e., after changing the employer, it is 0. It has a Pearson correlation of 0,48 with the augmented *professional_experience* in our dataset. To ablate the benefits of the two variables, we conduct four experiments: with/without both variables and with both variables separately (see Table 3). We use a random 10% sample of the dataset for testing which we do not use for training. Table 3 contains the results with the mean absolute percentage error (*MAPE*) as evaluation metric as in [4].

**Table 3.** Experimental results in salary prediction.

| Experiment | employment_period | professional_experience | MAPE |
|---|---|---|---|
| S1 | – | – | 15.17% |
| S2 | – | ✓ | 15.15% |
| S3 | ✓ | – | 14.94% |
| S4 | ✓ | ✓ | 14.90% |

While Experiment S1 has a *MAPE* of 15.17%, S2 with the added estimated *professional_experience* performs almost equally. Adding the *employment_period* in S3, however, improves the performance considerably. The reason is probably that a real variable describing the relationship of an employee with their employer better explains the salary than an estimated experience (which certainly is not correct in some cases). Adding *employment_period* additionally in S4 leads to an almost unchanged but slightly better result. We conclude that using both variables seems to be the best solution in terms of quality. The *professional_experience* however does not improve the results considerably in our test setup, where only estimated values are available, but allows the user to make better salary predictions based on this variable entered additionally as requested.

## 5   Conclusion

We have presented an approach for the estimation of the professional experience based on regression on data from the German Socio-Economic Panel (SOEP). We have shown how the variable can be integrated into software for salary prediction that is originally unavailable, and we have successfully evaluated the approach on a large real payroll dataset. Our plan is to integrate the solution into the application "Personal-Benchmark online". Our future research includes the investigation of regression models with more variables that are available in the SOEP and payroll data alike, such as school education, region and profession.

## References

1. Aggarwal, C.C.: Data Mining: The Textbook. Springer, Cham (2015). https://doi.org/10.1007/978-3-319-14142-8
2. Cheng, X., Khomtchouk, B., Matloff, N., Mohanty, P.: Polynomial Regression As an Alternative to Neural Nets. CoRR in arXiv abs/1806.06850 (2019). https://doi.org/10.48550/arXiv.1806.06850
3. DATEV eG: Personal-Benchmark online. https://datev.de/web/de/mydatev/online-anwendungen/datev-personal-benchmark-online/. Accessed 10 July 2023
4. Eichinger, F., Mayer, M.: Predicting salaries with random-forest regression. In: Alyoubi, B., N'Cir, C.B., Alharbi, I., Jarboui, A. (eds.) Machine Learning and Data Analytics for Solving Business Problems. Unsupervised and Semi-Supervised Learning, pp. 1–21. Springer, Cham (2022). https://doi.org/10.1007/978-3-031-18483-3_1
5. German Federal Office of Statistics: Gehaltsvergleich BETA. https://service.destatis.de/DE/gehaltsvergleich/. Accessed 10 July 2023
6. German Federal Office of Statistics: Interaktiver Gehaltsvergleich. https://www.destatis.de/DE/Service/Statistik-Visualisiert/Gehaltsvergleich/Methoden/Methodenbericht.pdf. Accessed 10 July 2023
7. Goebel, J., et al.: The German socio-economic panel (SOEP). Jahrbücher für Nationalökonomie und Statistik **239**(2), 345–360 (2018). https://doi.org/10.1515/jbnst-2018-0022
8. Kiesel, J.: Prediction Models for Professional Experience. https://www.it-management.rw.fau.de/sgai/. Accessed 12 Sep 2023
9. Liebig, S. et al.: Socio-Economic Panel, data from 1984–2020 (SOEP-Core, v37, Onsite Edition) (2022). https://doi.org/10.5684/SOEP.CORE.V37O
10. Mincer, J.: Schooling, Experience, and Earnings. National Bureau of Economic Research (1974)

# Goals and Stakeholder Involvement in XAI for Remote Sensing: A Structured Literature Review

Carolin Leluschko[✉] and Christoph Tholen

German Research Center for Artificial Intelligence RG Marine Perception,
Oldenburg, Germany
{carolin.leluschko,christoph.tholen}@dfki.de

**Abstract.** A currently upcoming direction in the research of explainable artificial intelligence (XAI) is focusing on the involvement of stakeholders to achieve human-centered explanations. This work conducts a structured literature review to asses the current state of stakeholder involvement when applying XAI methods to remotely sensed image data. Additionally it is assessed, which goals are pursued for integrating explainability. The results show that there is no intentional stakeholder involvement. The majority of work is focused on improving the models performance and gaining insights into the models internal properties, which mostly benefits developers. Closing, future research directions, that emerged from the results of this work, are highlighted.

**Keywords:** Explainable AI · Remote Sensing · Aerial Imagery

## 1 Introduction

The use of artificial intelligence is getting more prominent in a variety of domains which is why the need for interpreting and understanding model predictions is of utmost importance. A potential future application of artificial intelligence (AI) methods is the assessment of marine litter using airborne based remote sensing. This is the goal, the PlasticObs+ project is aiming for. In this project, different AI systems are developed utilizing aerial images with varying resolutions from different sensors [30]. The assessment of plastic litter is of importance for different stakeholders, for instance local governments, NGO's or members of the society. In this project, the resulting information is provided using a geographic information system (GIS) which builds the interface to the stakeholder. The AI systems are developed using neural network which makes the overall system a black box, not providing any information about the decision making process to the stakeholders. However, explanations are needed to aid the stakeholders' informed decision making. Here, explainable AI (XAI) [9] could be a valuable asset to the application.

The field of XAI has emerged in recent years with intense research being conducted to open the "black-box" nature of the state-of-the-art machine learning

© The Author(s), under exclusive license to Springer Nature Switzerland AG 2023
M. Bramer and F. Stahl (Eds.): SGAI 2023, LNAI 14381, pp. 519–525, 2023.
https://doi.org/10.1007/978-3-031-47994-6_47

systems. While early research focused on the development of methods for delivering explanations of a models behaviour and its output, the focus is now shifting towards human-centered XAI [19]. Not all kinds of explanations are relevant and useful for all stakeholders of an AI system, therefore the need for individual explanations is arising across domains. In this work, a structured literature review is conducted to assess the current state of integrating XAI methods into the domain of remotely sensed aerial images with a focus on goals and stakeholder involvement. In particular the following two research questions will be investigated: (1) are stakeholders involved in applying XAI to remote sensing data, and (2) what goals are pursued when applying XAI to aerial imagery?

Different tools and algorithms that make the machine learning models more interpretable and explainable resulted from the intense research in the area of XAI. Many authors have categorized such algorithms and tools [2,7,34] for instance into model agnostic or model specific methods, their output formats or whether they provide global or local explanations.

Arrieta et al. [3] categorize and describe different general goals that are targeted with XAI methods. In addition to those goals, the authors gave an overview of stakeholders involved in AI systems which are *domain experts/users of the model, regulatory entities, managers, developers, and people affected by model decisions*. Considering different stakeholders during the development of XAI methods and when integrating explainability frameworks into deployed AI systems is a topic which is focused on in the research area of human-centered XAI [19]. The different stakeholders of an AI system have different backgrounds and agendas, which is why one single explanation may not be beneficial or effective for every person interacting with the system. In addition to that, the evaluation of XAI methods is still an ongoing open research question. Hoffmann et al. [11] discussed different user-centered evaluation measurements that can be applied to get a quality measure of XAI methods.

This work is focusing on XAI methods in the application domain of remote sensing. In order to gain more information and insights about the earth's surface, remotely sensed data from different platforms, e.g. ground, aerial, or satellites, is used [28]. In addition to different platforms, different sensors are used to receive diverse characteristics about the regarded area. These sensors include, amongst others, hyperspectral sensors, visual imaging sensors and LiDAR sensors [31]. Remote sensing applications have been used in various fields, including marine pollution monitoring [38], plastic waste assessment [35], or the mapping of earthquake-induced building damage [23]. With the vast progress and intense research on artificial intelligence, applying machine learning to remote sensing applications became more and more common [21].

## 2   Methodology

To answer the research questions posed, databases relevant to computer science were searched using specific keyphrases applied to the content of the full paper. The literature search was conducted in the databases Association for Computing Machinery Digital Library (ACM) (31 results), Science Direct (133 results),

IEEE Xplore (30 results) and Web of Science (55 results). In addition to the simple keyphrase search in the databases mentioned above, a forward and backward search was performed. The keyword search was conducted using a combination of *("Explainable AI" OR XAI) AND ("remote sensing" OR "aerial image")*. Literature published and indexed before 12th of July 2023 was considered.

The resulting papers from the database search were examined for relevance by reviewing the content of the paper. Papers that covered the topics of Explainable AI in combination with remote sensing data were shortlisted. The remaining literature was critically assessed to determine whether or not they are relevant to answer the research questions. In order to do that, two main criteria regarding the content are applied. The potentially included literature has to be an actual application of one or multiple methods of XAI to remote sensing data. In addition, the data that the methods are applied to, need to be aerial image data in the domain of remote sensing. In this study, there are no restrictions regarding the origin, for instance satellite or UAV images, of the data.

The final selection of literature was investigated under certain criteria targeting the posed research question of this literature review. It was investigated if stakeholders were considered when applying XAI methods to the application. Building on that, it was assessed which groups of stakeholder were addressed or even intentionally targeted. Derived from a subset of the goals of applying explainability methods in [3], the intentions the authors in the reviewed literature had, when using XAI methods in their work, were assessed, categorized into *informativeness, trustworthiness, model performance and causality*. Abbreviated from [3], informativeness regards acquiring information about the internal operations of the system, trustworthiness targets the confidence in the models output and causality refers to finding relations among the dataset. Model performance is an additional considered goal which means that the authors intend to improve the models performance by applying XAI methods. Apart from the intentions regarding the benefit of adding explainability methods, the selected literature was searched regarding the evaluation of the applied XAI methods. The analysis was conducted by one reviewer.

## 3  Results and Discussion

The first selection of literature lead to 52 shortlisted publications which covered the fields of remote sensing and XAI. From this first selection, all papers which are not based on imagery as well as papers which did not apply XAI methods to the imagery data were excluded. The remaining literature which was further analyzed consisted of 25 publications. It can be observed that 72% of the publications address the goal of informativeness, while 44% fall into the category of trustworthiness. The goals of model performance and causality were equally present with 24% and 20% respectively.

The results show that the majority of reviewed literature fit into the category of *informativeness* as the pursued goal for utilizing explainability methods. This consisted, in many cases, in analyzing which data attributes contributed the most to a models output [36], finding a feature importance metric [12] and gaining information about individual model layers [10]. In the case of informativeness, there was no specific stakeholder standing out to be the one benefiting from the findings the most. The evaluation of whether or not the integration of XAI methods helped achieving the goal of informativeness happened in a more qualitative way where the assessed information were presented as additional findings.

In case of *trustworthiness*, the literature in this category tried to achieve a (mostly visual) explanation on what the model is focusing on in the input data to assess if this is in line with the authors expectations of what is important [5]. Another finding in the category of trustworthiness is, that there was no evaluation of whether or not the shown explanations actually helped improving the trust in the model for the various stakeholders.

Another prominent goal for applying explainable AI was found to be the improvement of *model performance*. This goal is closely related to the goal of informativeness in terms of finding the most relevant features or those parts of a model, that are less important for a models decision [1]. In the case of model performance, however, this information was then used to improve the models performance by, for instance, training a scarcer model [4]. The evaluation, if utilizing explainability tools helped to improve model performance, was performed using common metrics for model performance such as accuracy or inference and training time. This category, in most cases, took the developers into account as they are usually the ones evaluating the models performance.

The literature categorized into the goal of *causality* applied XAI to gain more insight into relations among the input features, the model was trained with. In case of remotely sensed images, that information consisted, for instance, in finding different combinations of spectral bands to understand which information is the most influential for certain decisions [25].

During the reviewing process of the selected literature, there was neither any mentioning of specifically targeted stakeholders nor involvement of external stakeholders. The shown results can therefore not be split into the categories of stakeholders introduced in Sect. 2 but rather into the categories of no stakeholders or exclusively developers which were, to some extend, involved when applying the XAI methods. This lead to 32 % of the publications being categorized into involving the developer as stakeholder. This was the first important finding, that there is no active involvement of different stakeholders when applying XAI methods to remotely sensed images. The applications can therefore not be considered human-centered. The results of both, stakeholders and goal analysis are summarized in Table 1.

After reviewing and categorizing the selected literature, there are a few things that are worth mentioning. First, there are some similarities between the different goals, which, in combination with the fact that the authors, in most cases, did not specifically state an intended goal, made the process of categorizing the literature into pursued goals less straight forward. In addition, none of the reviewed literature involved any external stakeholders which is why the question of stakeholder involvement can only indirectly be answered. As it is usually the

**Table 1.** Resulting literature categorized into stakeholders and goals.

|  | Category | References |
|---|---|---|
| Stakeholder | Developer | [1,6,8,10,12,23,26,37] |
|  | None | [4,5,15,17,18,20,24,25,29,33,36] [13,14,16,22,27,32] |
| Goal | Informativeness | [1,4,6,12,15,17,24,33,36,37] [8,10,14,16,18,20,23,29] |
|  | Trustworthiness | [5,6,8,13,14,16,17,22,23,27,29] |
|  | Model Performance | [1,4,10,12,26,37] |
|  | Causality | [18,25,29,32,36] |

model developers that are participating in the scientific publications, this category of stakeholders was the only one that was, to some extend, involved in applying the XAI methods. This category was, however, only considered if the developers did actually benefit from applying XAI e.g. by improving the model performance, or if they contributed to an evaluation of the methods.

## 4    Conclusion and Future Work

The conducted literature review on goals and stakeholder involvement in XAI for remote sensing imagery revealed that stakeholders are not yet an actively considered part when applying and evaluating XAI methods. The only stakeholders that are indirectly involved to this state are the model developers. Another finding was, that the goals, the authors had in applying XAI methods were mostly not clearly stated or evaluated, especially when the general goal of improving trust in the model was among the motivations of their work. Future research should take up on that in involving stakeholders to 1) define goals that are pursued when providing model explanations and to 2) evaluate the goals and the XAI methods from the different stakeholders perspectives. In doing this, the application domain of remote sensing could benefit even more from the opportunities that come with machine learning by providing user-centric explanations.

**Acknowledgements.** Funded by the German Federal Ministry for the Environment, Nature Conservation, Nuclear Safety and Consumer Protection (BMUV) based on a resolution of the German Bundestag (Grant No. 67KI21014A).

## References

1. Abdollahi, A., Pradhan, B.: Urban vegetation mapping from aerial imagery using explainable AI (XAI). Sensors **21**(14), 4738 (2021)
2. Angelov, P.P., et al.: Explainable artificial intelligence: an analytical review. WIREs Data Min. Knowl. Discov. **11**(5), e1424 (2021)

3. Arrieta, A.B., et al.: Explainable artificial intelligence (XAI): concepts, taxonomies, opportunities and challenges toward responsible AI. Inf. Fusion **58**, 82–115 (2019)

4. Burgueño, A.M., et al.: Scalable approach for high-resolution land cover: a case study in the Mediterranean Basin. J. Big Data **10**(1), 91 (2023)

5. Carneiro, G.A., et al.: Segmentation as a preprocessing tool for automatic grapevine classification. In: IGARSS 2022–2022 IEEE International Geoscience and Remote Sensing Symposium, pp. 6053–6056 (2022). ISSN: 2153–7003

6. Chen, L., et al.: Towards transparent deep learning for surface water detection from SAR imagery. Int. J. Appl. Earth Obs. Geoinf. **118**, 103287 (2023)

7. Das, A., Rad, P.: Opportunities and challenges in explainable artificial intelligence (XAI): a survey (2020)

8. Feng, J., et al.: Bidirectional flow decision tree for reliable remote sensing image scene classification. Remote Sens. **14**(16), 3943 (2022)

9. Gohel, P., et al.: Explainable AI: current status and future directions (2021)

10. Guo, X., et al.: Network pruning for remote sensing images classification based on interpretable CNNs. IEEE Trans. Geosci. Remote Sens. **60**, 1–15 (2022)

11. Hoffman, R.R., et al.: Metrics for explainable AI: challenges and prospects (2019)

12. Hosseiny, B., et al.: Urban land use and land cover classification with interpretable machine learning - A case study using Sentinel-2 and auxiliary data. Remote Sens. Appl.: Soc. Environ. **28**, 100843 (2022)

13. Huang, X., et al.: Better visual interpretation for remote sensing scene classification. IEEE Geosci. Remote Sens. Lett. **19**, 1–5 (2022)

14. Ishikawa, S.N., et al.: Example-based explainable AI and its application for remote sensing image classification. Int. J. Appl. Earth Obs. Geoinf. **118**, 103215 (2023)

15. Jeon, M., et al.: Recursive visual explanations mediation scheme based on dropattention model with multiple episodes pool. IEEE Access **11**, 4306–4321 (2023)

16. Kakogeorgiou, I., Karantzalos, K.: Evaluating explainable artificial intelligence methods for multi-label deep learning classification tasks in remote sensing. Int. J. Appl. Earth Obs. Geoinf. **103**, 102520 (2021)

17. Kawauchi, H., Fuse, T.: SHAP-based interpretable object detection method for satellite imagery. Remote Sens. **14**(9), 1970 (2022)

18. Levering, A., et al.: Liveability from above: understanding quality of life with overhead imagery and deep neural networks. In: 2021 IEEE International Geoscience and Remote Sensing Symposium IGARSS, pp. 2094–2097 (2021). ISSN: 2153–7003

19. Liao, Q.V., Varshney, K.R.: Human-centered explainable AI (XAI): from algorithms to user experiences (2022). arXiv:2110.10790

20. Luo, R., et al.: Glassboxing deep learning to enhance aircraft detection from SAR imagery. Remote Sens. **13**(18), 3650 (2021)

21. Ma, L., et al.: Deep learning in remote sensing applications: a meta-analysis and review. ISPRS J. Photogramm. Remote. Sens. **152**, 166–177 (2019)

22. Marvasti-Zadeh, S.M., et al.: Crown-CAM: interpretable visual explanations for tree crown detection in aerial images. IEEE Geosci. Remote Sens. Lett. **20**, 1–5 (2023)

23. Matin, S.S., Pradhan, B.: Earthquake-induced building-damage mapping using explainable AI (XAI). Sensors **21**(13), 4489 (2021)

24. Moradi, L., et al.: On the use of XAI for CNN model interpretation: a remote sensing case study. In: 2022 IEEE Asia-Pacific Conference on Computer Science and Data Engineering (CSDE), pp. 1–5 (2022)

25. Saeidi, V., et al.: Water depth estimation from Sentinel-2 imagery using advanced machine learning methods and explainable artificial intelligence. Geomat. Nat. Haz. Risk **14**(1), 2225691 (2023)

26. Seydi, S.T., et al.: BDD-Net+: a building damage detection framework based on modified coat-net. IEEE J. Sel. Top. Appl. Earth Obs. Remote Sens. **16**, 4232–4247 (2023)
27. Su, S., et al.: Explainable analysis of deep learning methods for sar image classification. In: IGARSS 2022–2022 IEEE International Geoscience and Remote Sensing Symposium, pp. 2570–2573 (2022). ISSN: 2153–7003
28. Sugumaran, R., et al.: Processing remote-sensing data in cloud computing environments (2015)
29. Temenos, A., et al.: Interpretable deep learning framework for land use and land cover classification in remote sensing using SHAP. IEEE Geosci. Remote Sens. Lett. **20**, 1–5 (2023)
30. Tholen, C., et al.: Machine learning on multisensor data from airborne remote sensing to monitor plastic litter in oceans and rivers (plasticobs+). In: OCEANS 2023 Limerick. OCEANS MTS/IEEE Conference (OCEANS-2023), 5–8 June, Limerick, Ireland, pp. 1–7. IEEE (2023)
31. Toth, C., Jóźków, G.: Remote sensing platforms and sensors: a survey. ISPRS J. Photogramm. Remote. Sens. **115**, 22–36 (2016)
32. Valdés, J.J., Pou, A.: A machine learning - explainable AI approach to tropospheric dynamics analysis using Water Vapor meteosat images. In: 2021 IEEE Symposium Series on Computational Intelligence (SSCI), pp. 1–8 (2021)
33. Vasu, B., Savakis, A.: Resilience and plasticity of deep network interpretations for aerial imagery. IEEE Access **8**, 127491–127506 (2020)
34. Vilone, G., Longo, L.: Classification of explainable artificial intelligence methods through their output formats. Mach. Learn. Knowl. Extr. **3**(3), 615–661 (2021)
35. Wolf, M., et al.: Machine learning for aquatic plastic litter detection, classification and quantification (aplastic-q). Environ. Res. Lett. (ERL) **15**(11), 1–14 (2020)
36. Woo Kim, Y., et al.: Validity evaluation of a machine-learning model for chlorophyll a retrieval using Sentinel-2 from inland and coastal waters. Ecol. Ind. **137**, 108737 (2022)
37. Zaryabi, H., et al.: Unboxing the black box of attention mechanisms in remote sensing big data using XAI. Remote Sens. **14**(24), 6254 (2022)
38. Zielinska, U., et al.: Detecting marine hazardous substances and organisms: sensors for pollutants, toxins, and pathogens. Ocean Sci. **5**(3), 329–349 (2009)

# Author Index

Printed in the United States
by Baker & Taylor Publisher Services